Renaissance Portraits

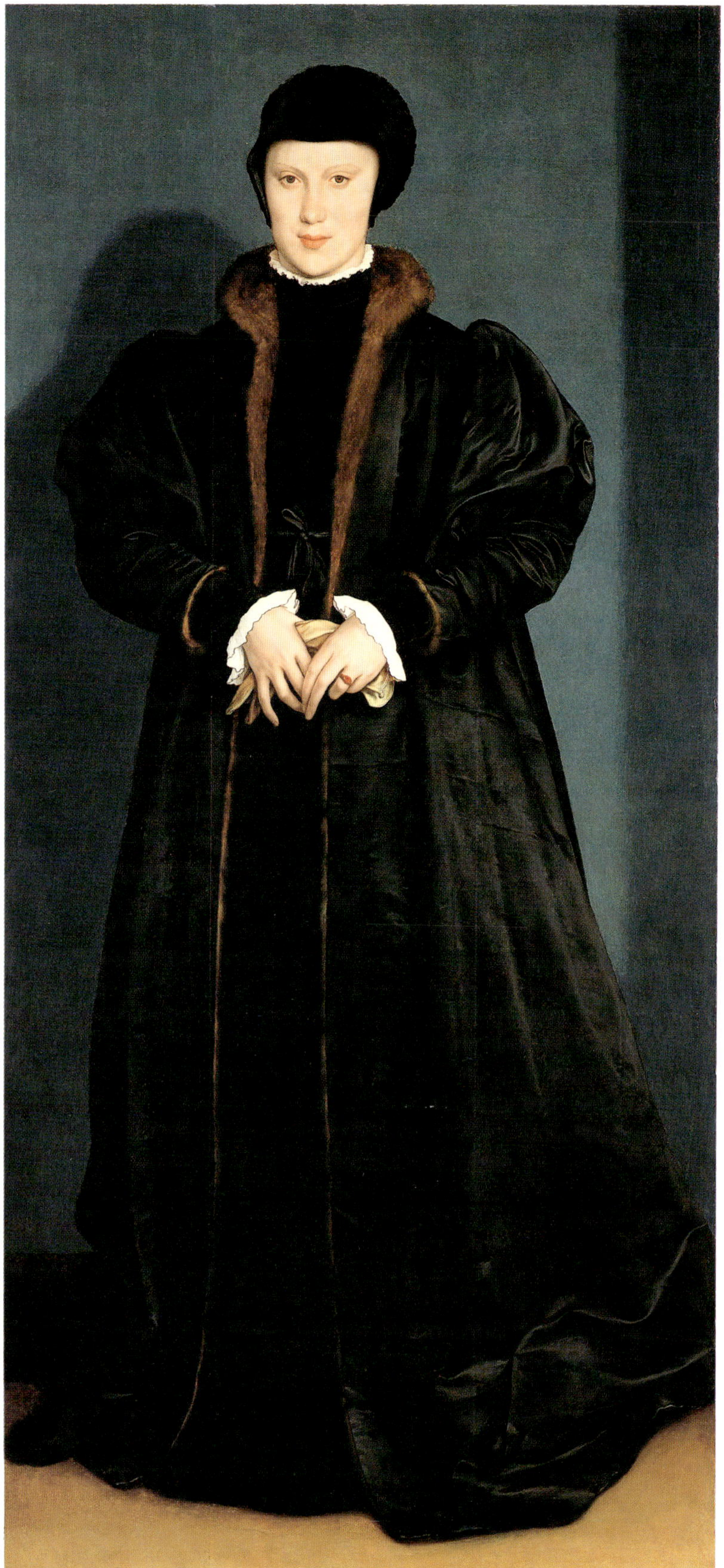

Lorne Campbell

Renaissance Portraits

European Portrait-Painting in the 14th, 15th and 16th Centuries

Yale University Press · New Haven and London · 1990

Designed by Gillian Malpass
Set in Linotron Bembo by Best-set Typesetter Ltd, Hong Kong
Printed in Hong Kong by
Kwong Fat Offset Printing Co., Ltd

Library of Congress Cataloging-in-Publication Data

Campbell, Lorne,
Renaissance portraits: European portrait painting in the 14th, 15th, and 16th centuries/Lorne Campbell,
p. cm.
Includes bibliographical references.
ISBN 0-300-04675-8
1. Portrait painting, Renaissance – Europe. 2. Portrait painting, European. I. Title.
ND1313,2C36 1990 89-22686
757'.094'09024–dc20 CIP

This book is dedicated to the memory of my parents
IAN CAMPBELL (1902–84), portrait-painter
NOREEN K. CAMPBELL (1904–85)

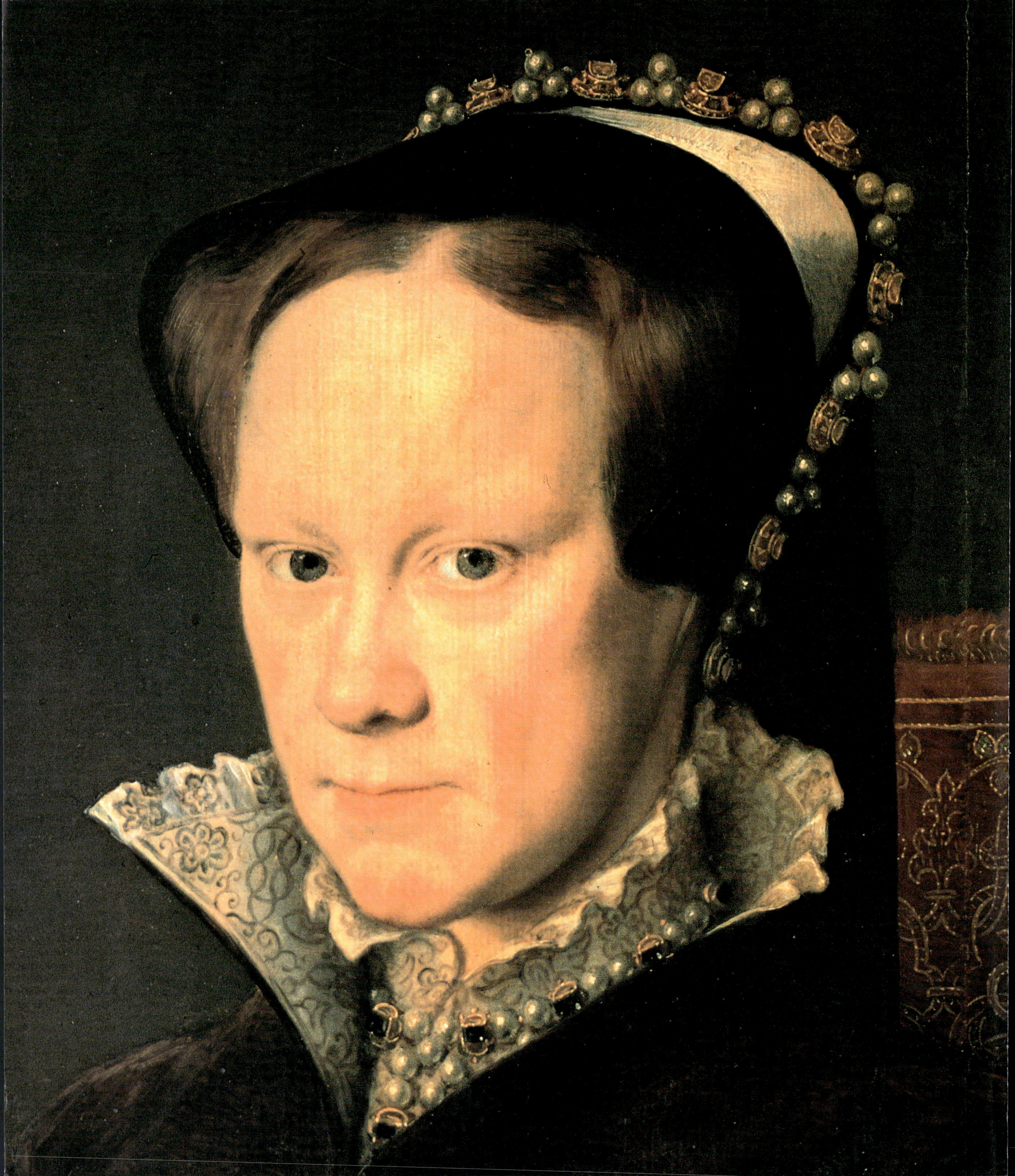

Contents

2 Antonis Mor, *Mary I, Queen of England*, detail (see plate 216).

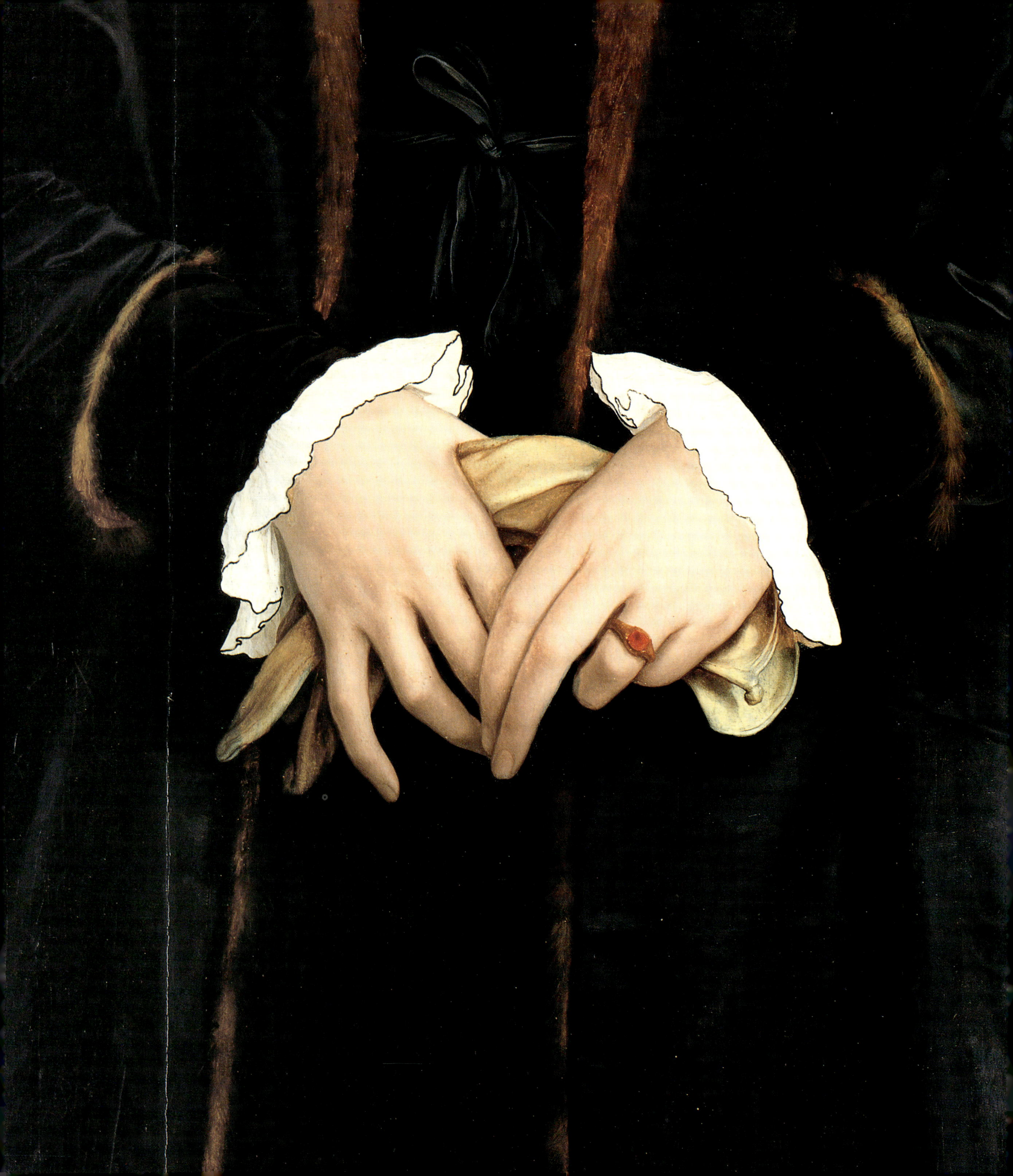

Preface

1 (frontispiece) and 3 (left) Hans Holbein the Younger, *Christina of Denmark, Duchess of Milan*, oak panel, painted surface 179 × 82.5 cm, National Gallery, London (2475).

The sitter (1522–90), identified by a late sixteenth-century inscription removed during cleaning in 1967–8, was the younger daughter of Christian II, King of Denmark (see also plate 128). In 1533, she married Francesco Maria Sforza, Duke of Milan, but on his death in 1535 she returned to the Netherlands, where she had been brought up and where she lived at the court of her aunt, Mary of Hungary. In 1538–9, Henry VIII of England attempted unsuccessfully to take her as his fourth wife. Early in March 1538, the English ambassador in Brussels managed to obtain for Henry a portrait of Christina by a Netherlandish artist. On 10 March, Holbein arrived in Brussels and was permitted to take her portrait: on 12 March at 1 p.m., Christina sat to Holbein 'who havyng but thre owers space hathe shoid hym self to be master of that siens, for it is very perffight; the other is but sloberid in comparison . . .'. He left Brussels that night and arrived back in London on 18 March 'with the duchess's likeness, which . . . has singularly pleased the king, so much so that, since he saw it, he has been in a much better humour than he ever was, making musicians play on their instruments all day long'. Holbein had presumably executed a drawing or drawings of Christina; the 'likeness' that delighted Henry can hardly have been the painting, which he must have worked up later from drawings made in Brussels. The painting was listed in the 1542 inventory of Henry's collection as 'oone great table with the picture of the Duches of Mylayne being her whole stature' but by 1551 had left the royal collection.

See Chamberlain, 1913, II, pp. 114–25; Levey, 1959, pp. 54–7; here, pp. 84, 94, 109, 112, 164, 197, 236.

The term Renaissance is here used in its widest sense to cover the fourteenth, fifteenth and sixteenth centuries: from the time of Giotto and Simone Martini to that of Titian and El Greco. It is neither possible nor desirable to attempt too precise a definition of the word portrait. My concern is with independent painted portraits and not with donor portraits or images of saints which, like Bartolomeo Vivarini's *St John of Capistrano* of 1459 (Louvre), are probably accurate renderings of individuals but which were painted for devotional purposes. I have treated painted and drawn portraits and portraits in tapestry, since they were woven from painted cartoons; I have not dealt with portraits in illuminated manuscripts.

At certain points in the text I have found it legitimate, as well as convenient, to set aside some of these limitations and to include portraits painted in the early years of the seventeenth century, to refer to seventeenth-century texts, to discuss in some detail donor portraits of Nicolas Rolin and Maria Portinari, to mention Bourdichon's posthumous portrait of St Francis of Paola and to consider certain portraits in sculpture. In every case, the justification for my departure from my definition of my subject should be apparent and it seems unnecessary to explain my reasons at length.

Many portraits of the period have been destroyed. It is not possible to deduce, or even to estimate, the extent of destruction, but the surviving portraits, scattered across the world, are only a small fraction, and not necessarily a very representative fraction, of the portraitists' production. It is therefore essential to consider copies as well as originals and three collections of copies are of particular importance: the 'Recueil d'Arras', probably put together in the 1560s by a herald of Valenciennes (plates 81, 108); the 'Mémoriaux' of the painter and antiquarian Antoine de Succa, most of which date from 1601–2 (plates 204–205); and the numerous copies assembled for the French antiquarian Roger de Gaignières (1642–1715). The visual evidence must also be assessed in conjunction with documentary evidence. Inventories of pictures, like those of the collections of Margaret of Austria, Governess of the Netherlands (1480–1530), and lists of pictures, for example in the *Notizia* of Marcantonio Michiel, often contain quite full descriptions of lost portraits.

Vast quantities of documentary and literary evidence exist concerning painted and drawn portraits of the period. The writings of artists, notably Leonardo and Dürer, are of exceptional interest; Vasari's and Van Mander's biographies of painters are full of informative details. Only the Portuguese court painter Francisco de Holanda (1516/17–84) wrote a treatise on portraiture, the dialogue *Do tirar polo natural*, composed in 1549 and translated into Spanish in 1563 by another painter, Manuel Denis. Nicholas Hilliard's *The Arte of Limning*, written between 1598 and 1603, is concerned largely with portraiture. Both these texts give much practical information and advice on the processes of portrait-painting. Other sources of great importance are notes made by painters on their drawings (plates 25, 185), the memorandum books kept by Lorenzo Lotto and by Alessandro Allori, the letters of artists, for example Mantegna and Titian, to their patrons and bills sent to their employers by such painters as Van Orley and Seisenegger.

The writings of theorists who were not themselves artists are less helpful, for many of them became so entangled in metaphysics that they forgot the practicalities of artistic creation. An exception was Gabriele Paleotti, writing in 1582, who had a great deal to say about the making and uses of portraits.

Much can be deduced from official records, from ambassadors' dispatches and from the private correspondence of the patrons, their families and their friends. Letters provide perhaps the most important source of information on the subject of portraiture but memoirs (notably those of Brantôme), autobiographies (for example that of the English musician Thomas Whythorne) and contemporary poems and plays can contain valuable and enlightening references to portraits.

It is clearly impossible for one person to exploit all these sources in a systematic way. Most of my sources are published; a glance at the notes and the list of references will show that I have drawn on a wide variety of historical publications. Some of them I have discovered by happy accident and it would obviously be possible to spend a lifetime searching out and collecting such material. I have, however, had to be rigorously selective in my use of the documentary and literary sources that I have consulted.

The available evidence, visual and written, is heavily biassed towards portraits of princes, which are more likely to have been preserved or copied or to have been mentioned in the accessible documents. It should also be stressed that many more portraits and documents survive from the sixteenth century than from the fourteenth and fifteenth; and that, for various reasons, more documentation exists in some areas of Europe, notably in parts of Italy and in England, than in others, notably in France and the Low Countries. It is arguable that sixteenth-century Italian portraits were more assiduously collected and more carefully kept by succeeding generations than earlier Italian portraits and than portraits painted in other regions of Europe. Variations, according to social, chronological and geographical divisions, in the quality and quantity of the available evidence must be constantly borne in mind.

This book is not a straightforward history of portrait-painting in Renaissance Europe, though the second, third and fourth chapters give accounts of some major chronological developments. It is rather an attempt to raise and, so far as is feasible, to answer, some very basic questions: what kinds of portrait were produced during the period, who produced them and for whom, how were they painted, why were they wanted and how were they used? It has been my aim to set the study of portraiture on a more rational basis, for many writers on the subject have been content to make subjective and unsupported statements about portraits which relate to their personal reactions to and apprehensions of the sitters and have little to do with analyses of the paintings themselves. I have tried, especially in the first and ninth chapters, to show that it is possible, by examining the portraits very carefully and by paying close attention to the practicalities of portraiture, to make reasoned deductions about the painters' intentions and to describe and explain those small distortions by which, instinctively or consciously, they individualised, idealised and characterised their sitters. I have worked on the assumption, which I see no need to justify, that great artists do not make mistakes in drawing.

It has also been my intention to counter the assertions of those who, since the time of Michelangelo and Vasari, have been saying or implying that portraiture is not a serious intellectual pursuit and that, as mere representation, it is scarcely worthy of being called an art form. I have furthermore sought to demonstrate

4 Bronzino, *Eleonora da Toledo, Grand Duchess of Tuscany, with her Son Giovanni*, detail (see plate 37).

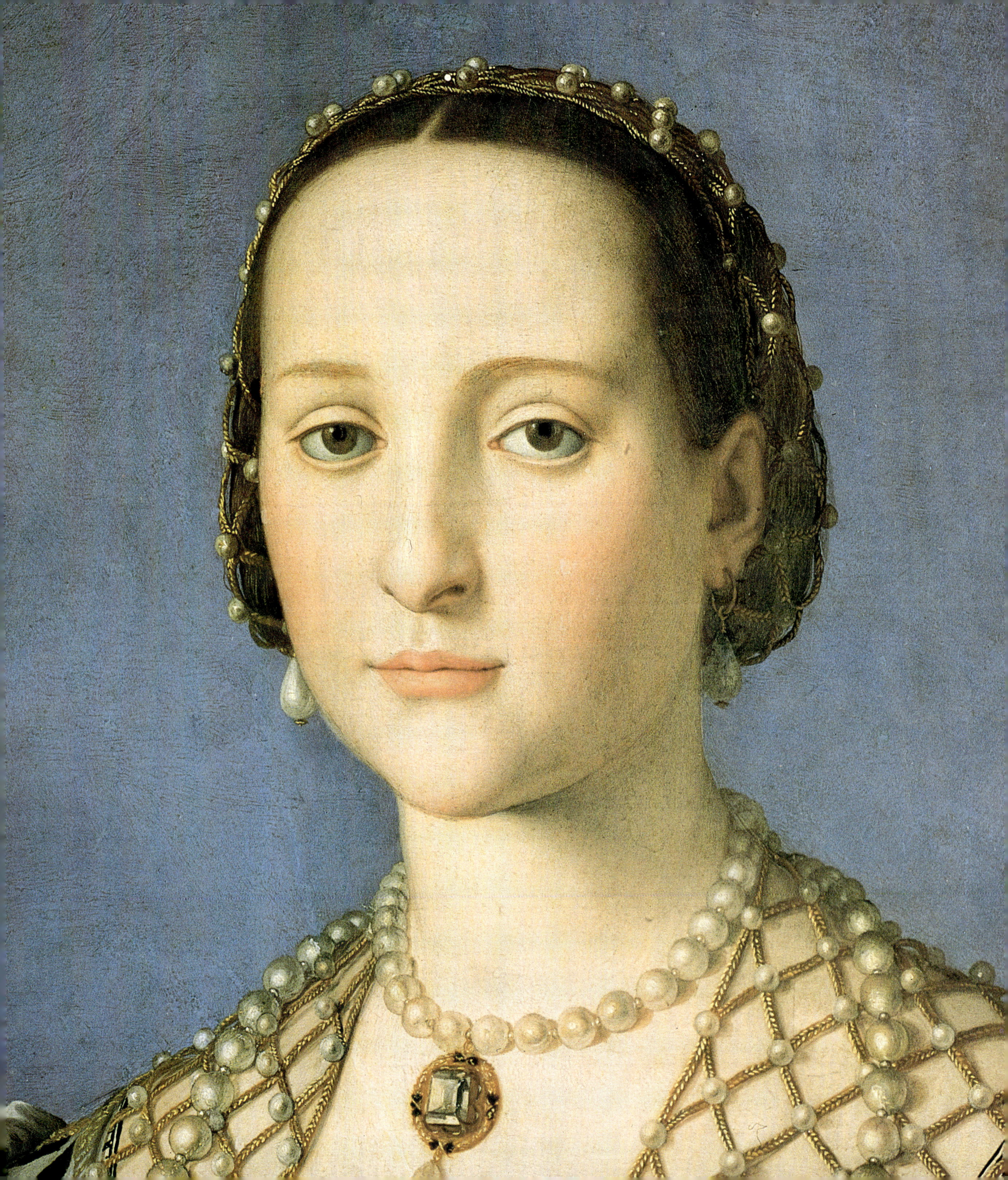

how concepts of imitation and idealisation developed by classical and Renaissance theorists have had a fatal effect on efforts to give discerning consideration to portraiture and to assess objectively the work of certain German and Netherlandish portraitists. It seems to me a mistake to follow the example and aesthetic principles of Vasari, to measure any achievement according to Florentine standards and to think in terms of Florentine notions of artistic 'progress'. Some previous writers on the subject have done exactly that, while Vasarian prejudices perhaps explain the paucity of literature on the subject of portraiture. Vasari's followers will no doubt accuse me of prejudice against Florence, perhaps even against Italy, and in favour of the Netherlands and Germany: that would be to misinterpret my admiration for the work of Van der Weyden, Holbein and Mor. Finally, I hope that I have managed to convey in my text something of the enthusiasm that most contemporaries felt for portraits and of the enjoyment that they had from them.

As I have explained in my first chapter, many of the terms used in discussions of portraiture have not been, or cannot be, defined with complete precision. 'Half length' and 'three-quarter length' are used in different ways by different authors. While an average human figure may be divided in half in the region of the hips and in three-quarters in the region of the knees, these divisions do not always reflect what is meant in descriptions of portraits. It has seemed advisable to use 'half length' in a very loose way to mean merely less than full length and to abandon altogether the term 'three-quarter length'. Though acknowledging that many of the sitters, and some of the portrait-painters, were women, I have found it convenient to treat the words artist, painter, sitter and subject as masculine nouns; my use in those connections of the words he and his should not be taken as an expression of sexist prejudice. Proper names have, or have not, been anglicised, according to current conventions. The names of towns in the Flemish-speaking areas of Belgium have been given in their French forms if these are more familiar to the English-speaking reader; but I intend no disrespect to the Dutch- or Flemish-speaking reader.

In the notes on the plates, I have generally provided basic relevant information on the work of art reproduced and references to the pages in the text where it is mentioned. When possible, I have cited a catalogue, monograph or article in which it is discussed in greater detail and in which a full bibliography is given. The references here and for publications frequently cited in the notes are by author and date; the full titles will be found in the list of references, which is no more than that and which is certainly not intended to be an exhaustive bibliography on the subject of Renaissance portraiture.

During the preparation of this book, I have received much help from many persons. Though considerations of space prevent me from acknowledging every obligation incurred, I am not unmindful of the varied kinds of assistance that have been given and for all of which I am sincerely grateful. I would like to thank the British Academy for awarding a Research Grant which enabled me to travel in Austria and Italy in the summer of 1986; the staffs of the many museums that I have visited and where I have often been allowed privileged access to pictures and drawings; and the librarians who have assisted me in my research, particularly those at the Bibliothèque Royale in Brussels, the British Library, the Courtauld Institute, the Institute of Historical Research, the Victoria and Albert Museum and the Warburg Institute in London and the Bibliothèque Nationale in Paris. Among the many students, colleagues and friends who have helped me in different ways, I am especially grateful to: Rocío Arnáez; Katharine Baetjer; John Bury; Marco Chiarini; Micheline Comblen-Sonkes; Klaus Demus; Jennifer Fletcher; Jacques Foucart; Giovanna Galante Garrone; John Hand; Constance Hill; Diane Hirst; Michael Hirst; Charles Hope; Amelia Jackson; Pierluigi Leone de Castris; Kristen Lippincott; Rhona MacBeth; Neil MacGregor; Jane Martineau; Silvia Meloni-Trkulja; Sir Oliver Millar; Henri Pauwels; Viola Pemberton-Pigott; Alan Phenix; Jane Roberts; Patricia Rubin; Margaret Scott; Alistair Smith; Carlenrica Spantigati; Caroline Villers; Alison Wright. Nicola Stanley undertook the onerous task of typing the text. Over many years, Susan Foister and Joanna Woodall have discussed with me their researches respectively on Holbein and on Mor and it has not been possible to acknowledge fully all the information and ideas that they have contributed. During the writing of the text, Marion and Iain MacCallum helped me in more ways than they perhaps realise, with much practical advice and assistance, great patience and constant moral support.

My late father Ian Campbell, to whose memory I dedicate this book, trained me as a draughtsman and gave invaluable advice on the practical problems of portraiture. My upbringing in a portrait-painter's household allowed me opportunities to observe closely his working methods as well as to undergo frequently, sometimes unwillingly, the experience of sitting for my portrait. It has left me with a profound respect for good portrait-painters and with an apprehensive distrust of difficult sitters and their foolish friends. My sisters the illustrator Jennifer Campbell and the portrait-painter Catriona Campbell have read and discussed with me much of the text and their interest and their opinions on questions visual and practical have been much appreciated. Catherine Reynolds has read the entire text, has contributed many extremely valuable observations and points of fact and has been a most constructive and tactful critic as well as a constant source of encouragement.

I am further indebted to Sally Salvesen, who has compiled the index, and to the staff of Yale University Press, particularly John Nicoll and Gillian Malpass, for the care and trouble they have taken over the production of this book.

Tayness and London, December 1988

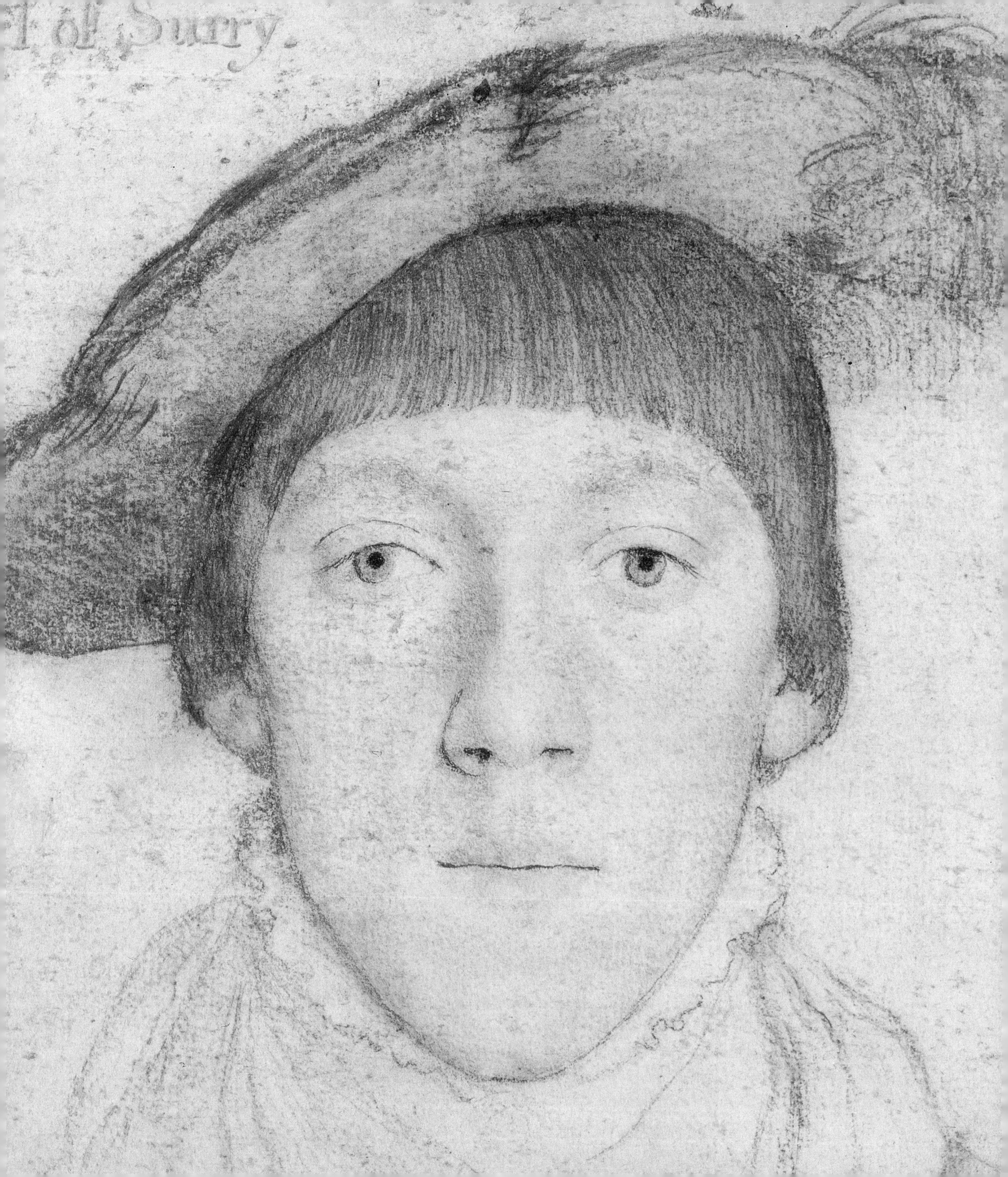
l of Surry

1 Introduction

The terms used in western European languages for portraits and the processes of portraiture were and are unsatisfactory in the looseness of their application. In Latin, the words for portrait – *imago*, *effigies* and *simulacrum* – could carry various other meanings: 'image' was, and continues to be, a term so widely applied that its significance has become hopelessly vague. The Italians of the fifteenth and sixteenth centuries commonly employed the noun *ritratto* and the verb *ritrarre* for 'portrait' and 'to portray' and these are the words currently used; yet *ritrarre* meant 'to render' or 'to reproduce'. Vasari stated that, at Bologna in 1529–30, Parmigianino 'fece senza ritrarlo l'imagine di esso Cesare': Parmigianino had painted a portrait of Charles V without sittings and from memory, after seeing him dine in public (plate 177).[1] *Ritrarre* here means 'to reproduce' and Vasari's passage may be literally translated 'he made without copying him an image of this emperor'. The noun *ritratto* was applied to works of art that would not now be classified as portraits. In 1493, for example, a Mantuan envoy wrote of a '*retrato* of San Marco, with the piazza and palace of Venice'[2] and in 1579 another Mantuan courtier wrote that 'if the *ritratto* of Parma, Milan and Pavia, which will be represented in these pictures, cannot be found in Venice, they will be sent from here'.[3] Titian, in a letter of 1552 to Philip II of Spain, described as 'il retratto di S.ta Margarita' a painting of St Margaret that, though doubtless based on studies from life, was clearly a religious picture and could not now be categorised as a portrait.[4] In Spanish, the noun *retrato* was used in a similar way.[5] In French, the terms *portrait* and *portraiture* might describe, besides portraits, pictures of religious subjects or heraldic designs.[6]

In German, Dutch and English, portraits were often called 'counterfeits', and the word carried its modern meaning also. Occasionally it was applied to paintings or drawings that were not portraits.[7] The verb 'counterfeit' was sometimes used in French and Italian to mean 'portray': for example, in 1493, Isabella d'Este complained of the difficulty in finding 'painters who can perfectly counterfeit the natural face'.[8] Despite the imprecision with which such terms appear to have been used, references to portraits in contemporary documents are normally obvious. Contemporary writers were perhaps more aware than we are of the inadequacies of their vocabulary and generally expressed what they meant with care and exactness, if not with brevity and elegance.

In the *Concise Oxford Dictionary*, 'portrait' is defined as a 'Likeness of person or animal made by drawing, painting, photography, etc.'. This equation of portrait with likeness is not altogether satisfactory, for some portraits are not likenesses and not all likenesses are portraits. Some painters flattered their sitters to the extent that their portraits could not be recognised. Van Dyck's portraits of Queen Henrietta Maria were apparently so deceptive that her husband's niece, on meeting her for the first time in 1642, was surprised to find her 'so beautiful in her picture, a little woman . . . with long, lean arms, crooked shoulders and teeth like defence works projecting from her mouth'.[9] A few artists have taken the rather overbearing view that likeness is of no account. Michelangelo, disregarding completely the appearance of the Medici dukes whom he represented on their tombs in

5 Hans Holbein the Younger, *Henry Howard, Earl of Surrey*, detail (larger than actual size; see plate 24).

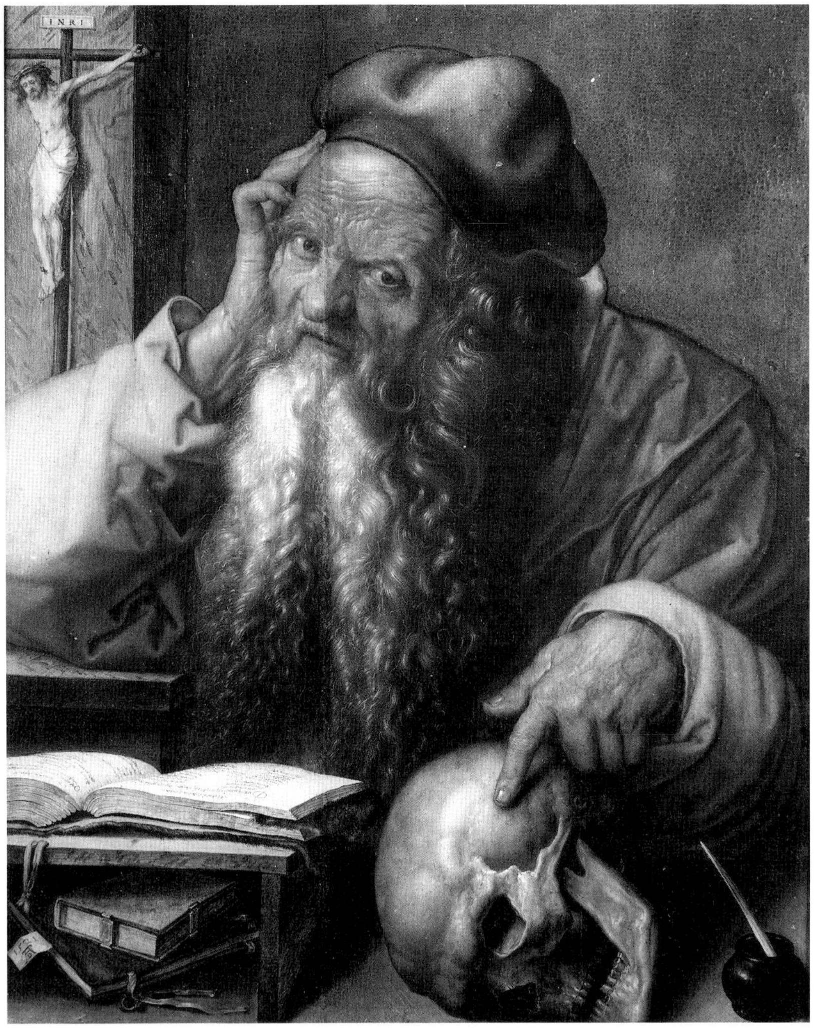

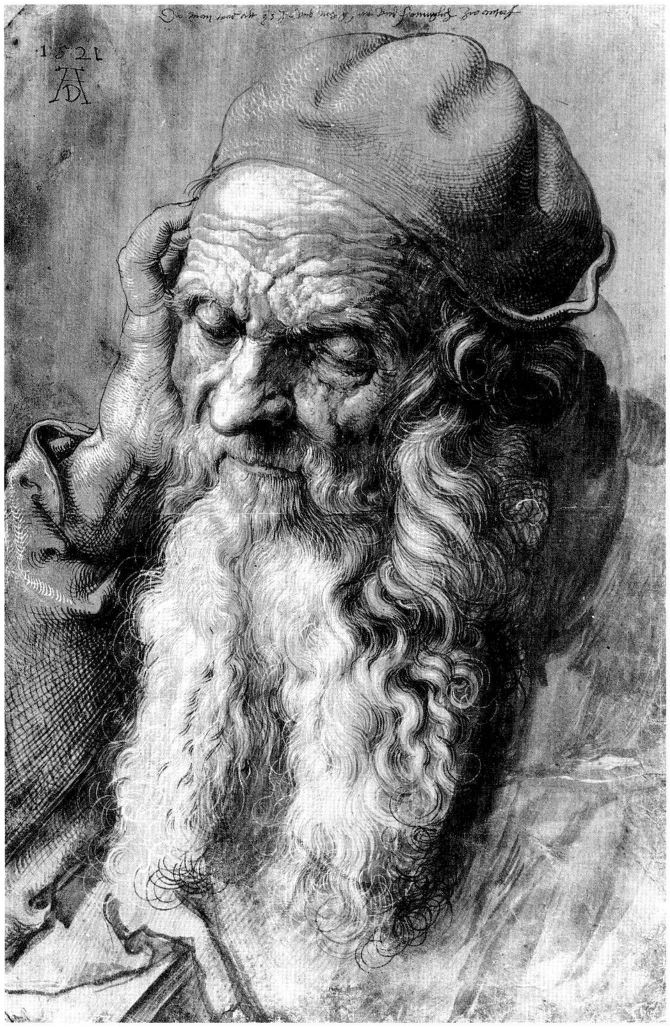

6 (above left) Albrecht Dürer, *St Jerome*, oak panel, 59.5 × 48.5 cm., Museu Nacional de Arte Antiga, Lisbon (828).

In the course of his stays at Antwerp in 1520–1, Dürer made the acquaintance of the Portuguese Rodrigo Fernandes, who gave him and his wife several expensive and exotic presents. In return, Dürer gave many of his prints to Rodrigo and drew his portrait. In March 1521, he recorded in his journal: 'I painted a *Jerome* carefully in oils and gave it to Rodrigo of Portugal'. The picture, signed with Dürer's monogram and dated 1521, was acquired by the museum in 1882 from a descendant of Rodrigo. Several of Dürer's preliminary drawings have been preserved (see plate 7).

the New Sacristy of San Lorenzo in Florence, was reported to have said that, in a thousand years' time, no one would be in a position to know that they looked otherwise.[10] Picasso remarked about his portrait of Gertrude Stein: 'everybody says that she does not look like it but that does not make any difference, she will'.[11] In posthumous depictions, for dynastic series or for sets of famous men and women, it was often impossible to achieve likenesses; but such paintings are in some sense portraits, as they are immediately recognisable as secular subjects and as representations of distinct individuals (plates 47, 49).

Conversely, many likenesses are not portraits. Dürer's *St Jerome* is a good example (plate 6). It is based on drawings of a ninety-three-year-old man whom Dürer met at Antwerp in 1521 and whom he almost certainly paid to sit for him (plate 7).[12] Yet the *St Jerome* cannot be called a portrait, though it is undoubtedly a likeness of the unnamed ninety-three-year-old. Vasari believed that he could identify many of the models used by Florentine painters in their religious paintings. He stated, for instance, that Fra Filippo Lippi painted the nun Lucrezia Buti, who was to become his mistress, as the Virgin, and that Antonio Pollaiuolo's model for the figure of St Sebastian in his *Martyrdom of St Sebastian* was Gino di Ludovico Capponi.[13] Savonarola in 1496 criticised, and the Counter Reformation theorists censured, the practice of using recognisable models for the figures

7 (left) Albrecht Dürer, *A Man aged Ninety Three*, brush drawing in black ink, heightened with white, on purple prepared paper, 41.5 × 28.2 cm., Graphische Sammlung Albertina, Vienna (3167).

Dürer monogrammed the drawing, dated it 1521 and wrote on it: 'The man was 93 years old and still healthy and active at Antwerp'. He made at least one other drawing of the man's head and evidently paid him to sit. Early in 1521 he recorded in his journal: 'I gave 3 *stuivers* to the man whose portrait I drew'. The drawings were used for his painting of *St Jerome* (plate 6).

See White, 1971, pp. 186–91; here p. 2.

8 Bronzino, *Andrea Doria as Neptune*, canvas, 115 × 53 cm., Pinacoteca di Brera, Milan (565).

The sitter is identified by the inscription 'A. DORIA' on the mast behind him; the portrait is attributed to Bronzino on stylistic grounds. As it was in the museum of portraits established at Como by Paolo Giovio, it may be equated with the painting of Doria that, according to Vasari, Bronzino painted for Giovio shortly after he returned to Florence in 1532 (Vasari-Milanesi, 1878–85, VII, p. 595). The nobleman Andrea Doria (1466–1560) commanded the Genoese fleet and was admiral of the naval forces of the Emperor Charles V during his conquest of Tunis in 1535. It was therefore appropriate that Bronzino should depict him as Neptune. He originally held an oar, transformed by a later painter into a trident.

See Baccheschi, 1973, p. 99; here pp. 3, 7.

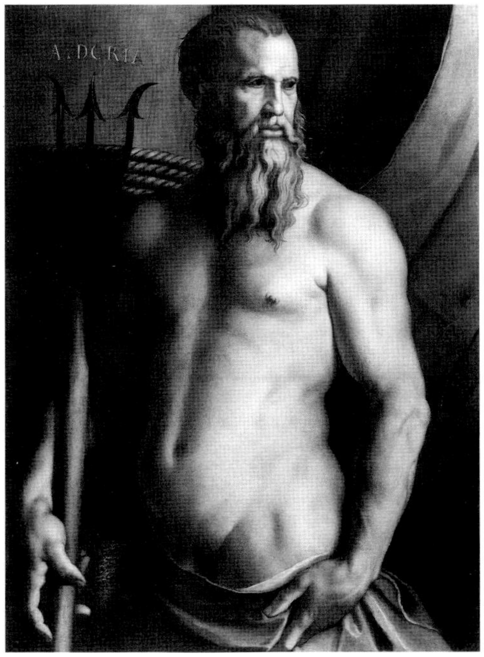

of saints. In 1582, Gabriele Paleotti enjoined that saints should never on any account be represented with the faces of worldly persons recognisable by others.[14] El Greco, in his *Virgin of Charity* commissioned in 1603 for the Hospital of Charity at Illescas, was blamed for having included representations of recognisable individuals 'wearing ruffs'. It was perhaps the contemporary dress of the subsidiary figures which allowed the hospital authorities to recognise them as portraits, but that, evidently, had not been El Greco's intention.[15]

Inevitably, artists continued to use models and to depict their features as well as their limbs in religious as in profane subjects. It can on occasion be difficult to distinguish between such heads and portraits. A portrait that remained with the artist, usually because it had not been paid for, could easily be converted into a genre or religious image to make it saleable. Torbido painted a gentleman of the Badovaro family who neglected to pay for his portrait; Torbido later sold it to another of his patrons, who had it turned into a picture of a shepherd.[16] In 1538, Lorenzo Lotto was commissioned to paint Gian Maria Pizzoni, protonotary in Ancona, but the portrait remained with Lotto because of a 'difference' between him and the sitter. He later converted it into an image of St Bartholomew which eventually, in 1542, he sold or gave to his landlord in Venice, whose patron saint was Bartholomew.[17]

Lotto, however, also painted portraits of sitters in the guise of saints: for example, in 1551 at Ancona, he depicted Alessandro Robaza as St Alexander.[18] Many sitters of the period had themselves painted as biblical, saintly, mythological or allegorical figures, and in such circumstances the problem of telling true portraits from studies based on models becomes still more difficult. Fouquet's *Virgin* of about 1450 is almost certainly a disguised portrait of Agnès Sorel, the mistress of Charles VII of France (plate 10); Margaret of Austria was represented as St Elizabeth in a miniature of the *Visitation* of about 1520 (plate 9); Bronzino represented the admiral Andrea Doria in the guise of Neptune (plate 8).

Portraits were similarly introduced into narrative compositions. Figures from the past could be given the features of contemporaries, who enacted the roles of their predecessors. In the frescoes of the Vatican *Stanze*, Raphael and his pupils depicted some of the early popes, who have assumed the likenesses of their successors, Raphael's patrons, Julius II and Leo X.[19] In the fourth of the tapestry series of the *Legend of Our Lady of the Sablon*, designed by Van Orley and dated 1518, living members of the Habsburg family participate in a narrative set in 1348.[20] If the subject was not strictly historical, it was easier unobtrusively to include portraits, as in Rogier van der Weyden's triptych of the *Seven Sacraments*, where the donor, Jean Chevrot, Bishop of Tournai, appears as the bishop administering the sacrament of Confirmation.[21] Whether or not the subject was historical, figures of bystanders might be included who were portraits of contemporaries. Van der Weyden painted himself among the bystanders in his four great panels of the *Justice of Trajan and Herkinbald* which he executed in the 1430s and 1440s for the town hall of Brussels.[22] Some Italian artists, notably Ghirlandaio, filled their religious subjects with portraits of contemporaries who intrude upon, rather than participate in, the scenes represented.[23]

Later writers have been, and are, fond of finding portraits of the famous in narrative compositions, but it is impossible to know for certain whether the sixteenth-century tradition is reliable which claims that two of the Just Judges in the Ghent altarpiece are portraits of Hubert and Jan van Eyck,[24] or whether all Vasari's identifications of portrait heads in fourteenth- and fifteenth-century nar-

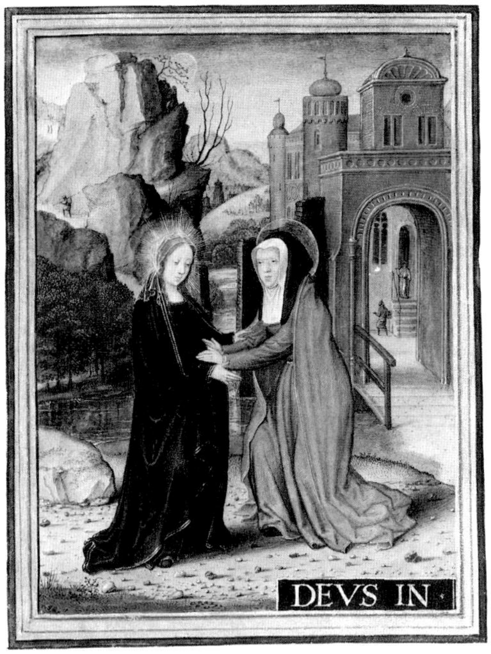

9 (above) Gerard Horenbout, *The Visitation* from the 'Sforza Hours', parchment, 13.1 × 9.3 cm., British Library, London, MS Add. 34294, f. 61.

The manuscript known as the 'Sforza Hours' was made for Bonne of Savoy, widow of Galeazzo Maria Sforza, Duke of Milan. She gave or bequeathed it, in an unbound and unfinished state, to her nephew's wife Margaret of Austria. In 1517, Margaret paid a scribe for completing the text and in 1521, the Ghent painter and illuminator Gerard Horenbout sent Margaret a bill for sixteen miniatures which he had added to the book. The *Visitation* was one of the sixteen. The head of St Elizabeth, which connects uneasily with her body, is a portrait of Margaret (compare plate 86). In Van Orley's *Crucifixion*, now at Rotterdam (1629), the head of the allegorical figure of Charity is similarly a portrait of Margaret (Friedländer, 1967–76, VIII, pl. 105).

See the exhibition catalogue Malibu, 1983–4, pp. 113–22 (15); here p. 3.

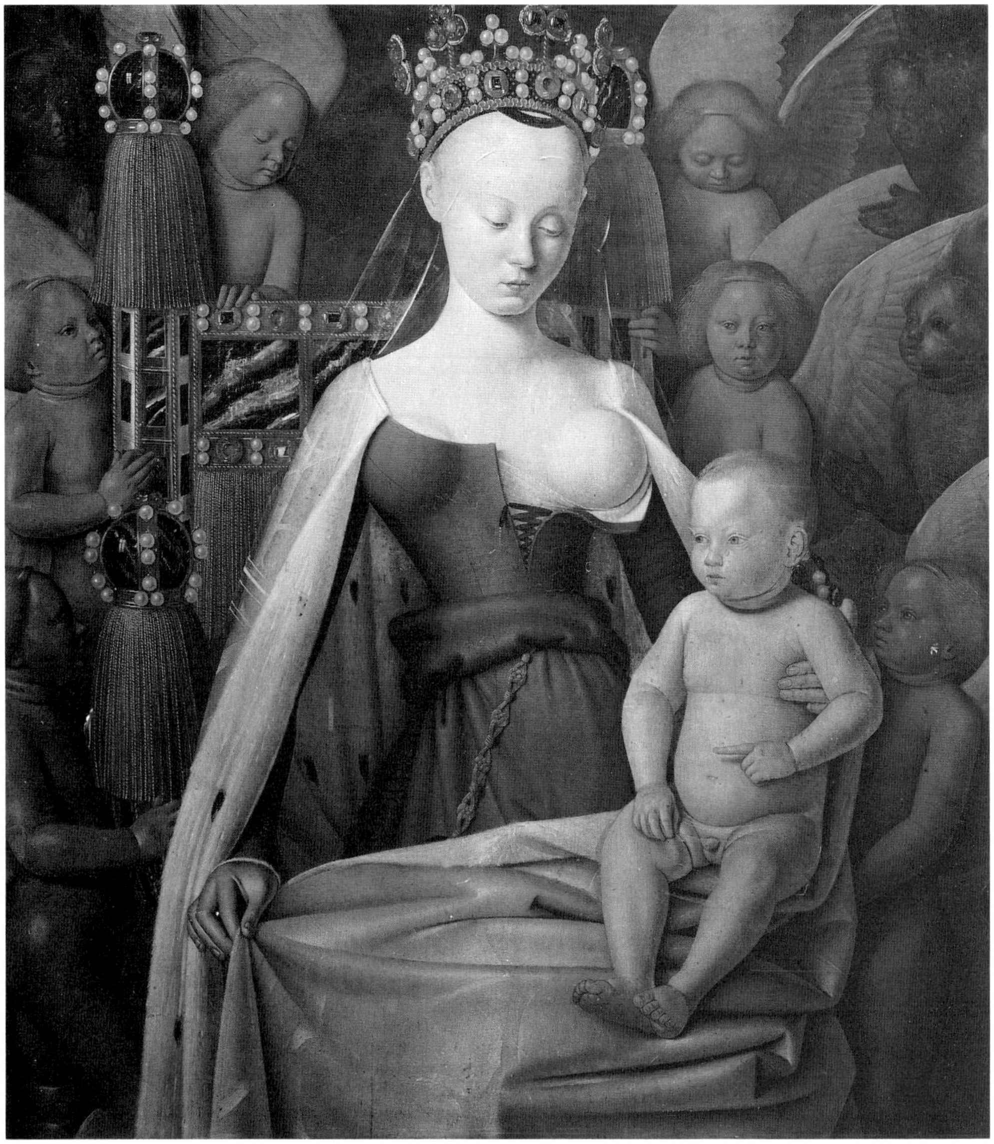

10 Jean Fouquet, *Virgin and Child with Angels*, panel, 94.5 × 85.5 cm., Koninklijk Museum voor Schone Kunsten, Antwerp (132).

This is the right wing of the 'Melun Diptych' of which the left wing, *Etienne Chevalier presented by St Stephen*, is at Berlin (1617). The diptych was placed in the Collegiate Church of Our Lady at Melun, south east of Paris, and in 1608, was shown to the future Louis XIII. The panels were then described as 'the pictures of *la belle Agnès* and of Etienne Chevalier' (Héroard, 1868 ed., I, p. 323): perhaps the earliest-known reference to the tradition that the Virgin is here represented with the features of *la belle Agnès*, Agnès Sorel, mistress of Charles VII of France. The tradition is borne out by early copies of a portrait of Agnès in which the sitter, though seen from a different angle, is clearly the same woman depicted by Fouquet as the Virgin. She is, moreover, entirely unlike Fouquet's other, idealised representations of the Virgin. The diptych was commissioned by Etienne Chevalier, a court official who knew Agnès well and whom she made her executor; it is believed to have been painted shortly after her death in 1450. The lost original frames of the panels were described as ornamented with medallions, one of which was almost certainly the enamel roundel of a man's head now in the Louvre (Objets d'art, OA 56). It is inscribed 'JOHES FOVQVET' and is generally considered to be a signed self-portrait by Fouquet. The attribution of the diptych to Fouquet is in any case fully established by stylistic evidence. It has recently been discovered that an unfinished version of the Antwerp *Virgin*, taken from the same cartoon, lies beneath the paint of Fouquet's portrait of Charles VII (plate 66).

See Reynaud, 1981, pp. 18–27; Reynaud, 1983; Vandenbroeck, 1985, pp. 75–7; Sterling, 1988, pp. 27–8; here p. 3.

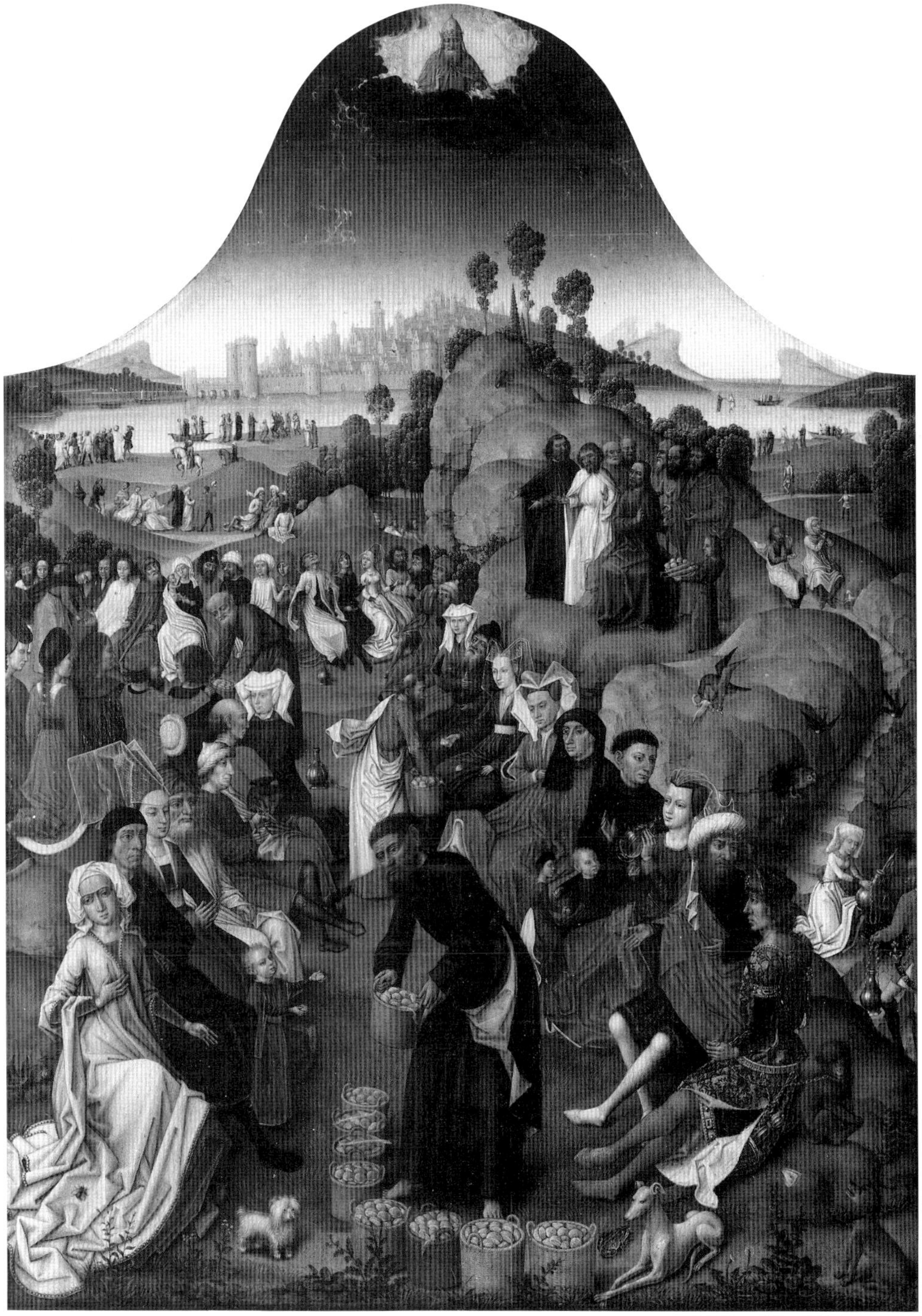

11 Master of the Legend of St Catherine, *The Feeding of the Five Thousand*, centre panel of the triptych of *The Miracles of Christ*, oak panel, painted surface 113 × 82.4 cm., National Gallery of Victoria, Melbourne (1247/3, Felton Bequest 1922).

The triptych was painted in about 1500, probably in Brussels, by several artists working in collaboration. In the left wing and the centre panel, several heads may be recognised as likenesses of various princes: in the centre panel, for example, the lady seventh from the front on our left is Michelle of France, Duchess of Burgundy (1395–1422), while the men fourth and fifth from the front on our right are Philip of St Pol (1404–30) and John IV (1403–27), Dukes of Brabant (compare their portraits copied in 1601 by Antoine de Succa, plate 205). The lady two back from John is Isabella of Portugal, Duchess of Burgundy (1397–1472): she has been adapted from a portrait by Van der Weyden, known from a copy now in the Getty Museum at Malibu (78.PA.3: exhibition catalogue Brussels, 1979, pp. 151–2 (14)). The lady in the foreground on our left corresponds to the seated Mary in the *Lamentation*, attributed to Van der Weyden and his workshop, at The Hague (264: Davies, 1972, pl. 119), while the dog beside her and the greyhound opposite recur in Van der Weyden's *Seven Sacraments* at Antwerp (393–395) and in his 'Columba Triptych' at Munich (WAF 1189–1191: Davies, 1972, pls 56, 57, 61, 63). The artist has here taken figures and animals from earlier religious paintings and portraits and it is most improbable that he wished his sources to be recognised or his 'portrait' heads to be identified.

See Hoff and Davies, 1971, pp. 1–28; here pp. 5–6.

rative paintings are accurate.[25] It should, however, be pointed out that certain artists seem to have included 'portrait' heads indiscriminately in their narrative pictures for no cogent historical reason. The Master of the Legend of St Catherine, for example, in his *Feeding of the Five Thousand*, painted in about 1500, copied old portraits of John IV and Philip of St Pol, Dukes of Brabant, and of Michelle of France and Isabella of Portugal, Duchesses of Burgundy (plates 11, 205). He appears to have had no cause to include them, except to increase his range of figures wearing old-fashioned, and therefore exotic, dress. In the same spirit, he

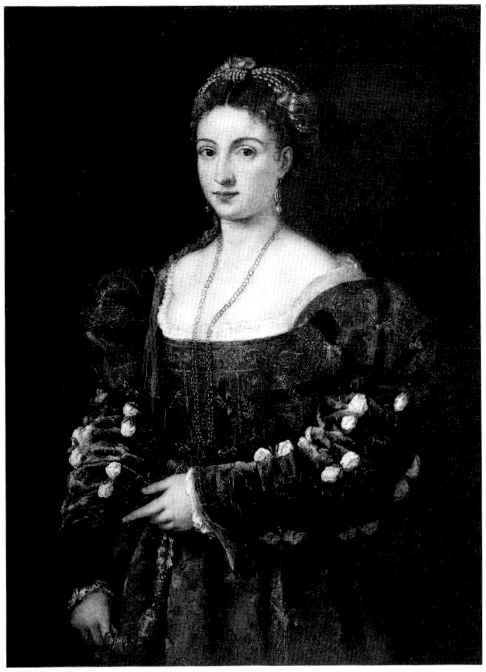

12 Titian, '*La Bella*', canvas, 89 × 75.5 cm., Galleria Palatina, Palazzo Pitti, Florence (18).

Not a true portrait but a painting of a professional model, it was commissioned by Francesco Maria della Rovere, Duke of Urbino, who in May 1536 was anxious for Titian to finish it. His interest lay not in the lady's identity but evidently in her beauty and in the beauty of the picture. It was among the Urbino pictures inherited by Vittoria della Rovere and taken to Florence in 1631, prior to her marriage to Ferdinando II de' Medici, Grand Duke of Tuscany.

See the exhibition catalogue Florence, 1978–9, pp. 110–15 (27); here p. 6.

took the figure of the lady in the lower left corner and the two dogs in the centre of the foreground from Van der Weyden workshop designs. Presumably he was making use of a stock of old workshop drawings; he need not have been aware of the identities of the dukes and duchesses whose portraits he was copying. The sitters have ceased to have any real significance and their 'portraits', if such they may be called, have become meaningless.[26]

Various pictures of beautiful women form another particularly difficult category for those who want to distinguish between paintings that are portraits and those that are not. Titian's *La Bella* (plate 12) shows a model who posed nude for Titian on other occasions;[27] and it was described by its first owner in 1536 as a portrayal of 'that lady wearing the blue garment'.[28] The fact that he had no interest in her identity supports the idea that *La Bella* is not really a portrait but a fancy picture based on studies from life. When no documentary evidence is available, such questions are less tractable. A painting in London, and several similar pictures, all in the style of Botticelli and all representing fancifully attired young women, resemble in feature and costume the Venus in his *Mars and Venus* so closely that they may with some confidence be described not as portraits but as idealised images of beautiful women (plates 13, 14).[29] It would be dangerous, however, to rely too heavily on what is known about the conventions of dress and decency in order to differentiate between such images and portraits. It was acceptable to show ladies of high rank – though not, perhaps, of high moral standards – nude or nearly nude. François Clouet's *Lady in her Bath*, probably of about 1570, represents a sitter who has not yet been identified (plate 15); a picture in the Louvre apparently represents Gabrielle d'Estrées, the mistress of Henry IV of France, who died in 1599 (plate 16). The lady beside her is believed to be one of her sisters, and the painting is thought to refer to the birth of one of Henry IV's illegitimate children. In the case of Giorgione's *Laura*, opinion is still divided: it has been taken to be a portrait of a poetess, part of a marriage or betrothal diptych or an idealised representation of Petrarch's Laura (plate 17). Since a comparison

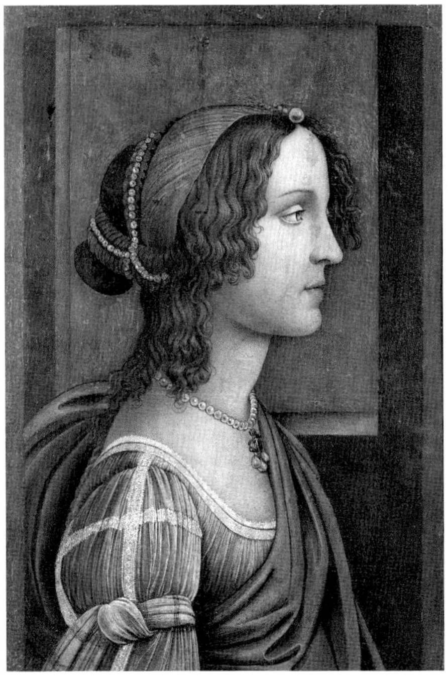

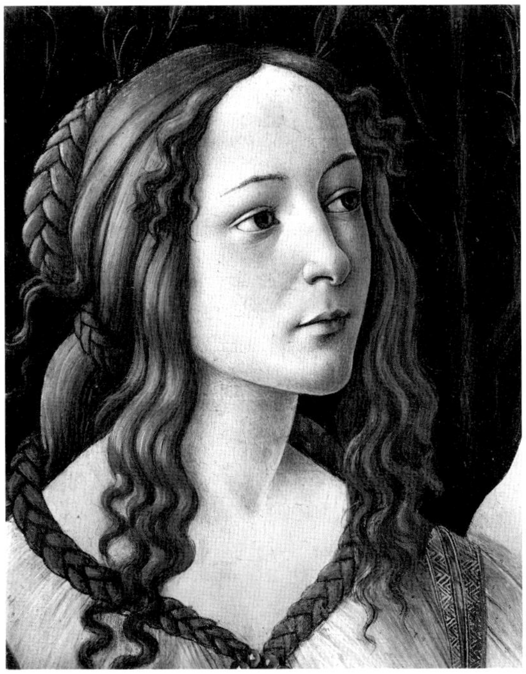

13 (right) Follower of Botticelli, *A Lady*, panel, painted surface 59 × 40 cm., National Gallery, London (2082).

Evidently not a true portrait but a picture of an ideally beautiful young woman, the London panel is one of several similar paintings in the style of Botticelli. It is particularly interesting because of its painted reverse, where there is depicted a winged figure holding an armillary sphere and standing on a rock that resembles certain representations of Purgatory. The significance of the allegory has not been explained, but there are possible connections with Dante's *Divine Comedy*, and it is conceivable that the lady may be intended to be Beatrice.

See Davies, 1961, p. 117; Lightbown, 1978, II, pp. 118–19; here p. 6.

15 François Clouet, *Lady in her Bath*, panel, 92.1 × 81.3 cm., National Gallery of Art, Washington (1961.9.13, Samuel H. Kress Collection, 1961).

Signed below the lady's left hand 'FR IANETII OPVS', the painting has been much discussed. The lady's nude torso is so inaccurate in its anatomy and so generalised in its modelling that it must be the artist's invention, intended to be recognised as such, but her head is clearly based on studies from life and may be seen as a portrait. There have been unconvincing attempts to identify the sitter, for example as Diane de Poitiers, mistress of Henry II of France, or as Mary, Queen of Scots. The lady's hair is dressed in the fashion of about 1570. Clouet has based her pose on that of the nude versions of Leonardo's *Mona Lisa* while he has taken elements of the composition from Raphael's *Joanna of Aragon* (plate 71).

On the iconography and on the several derivative paintings, see the exhibition catalogue Dijon, 1988, pp. 6–14, 20–39 and references; here pp. 6, 109.

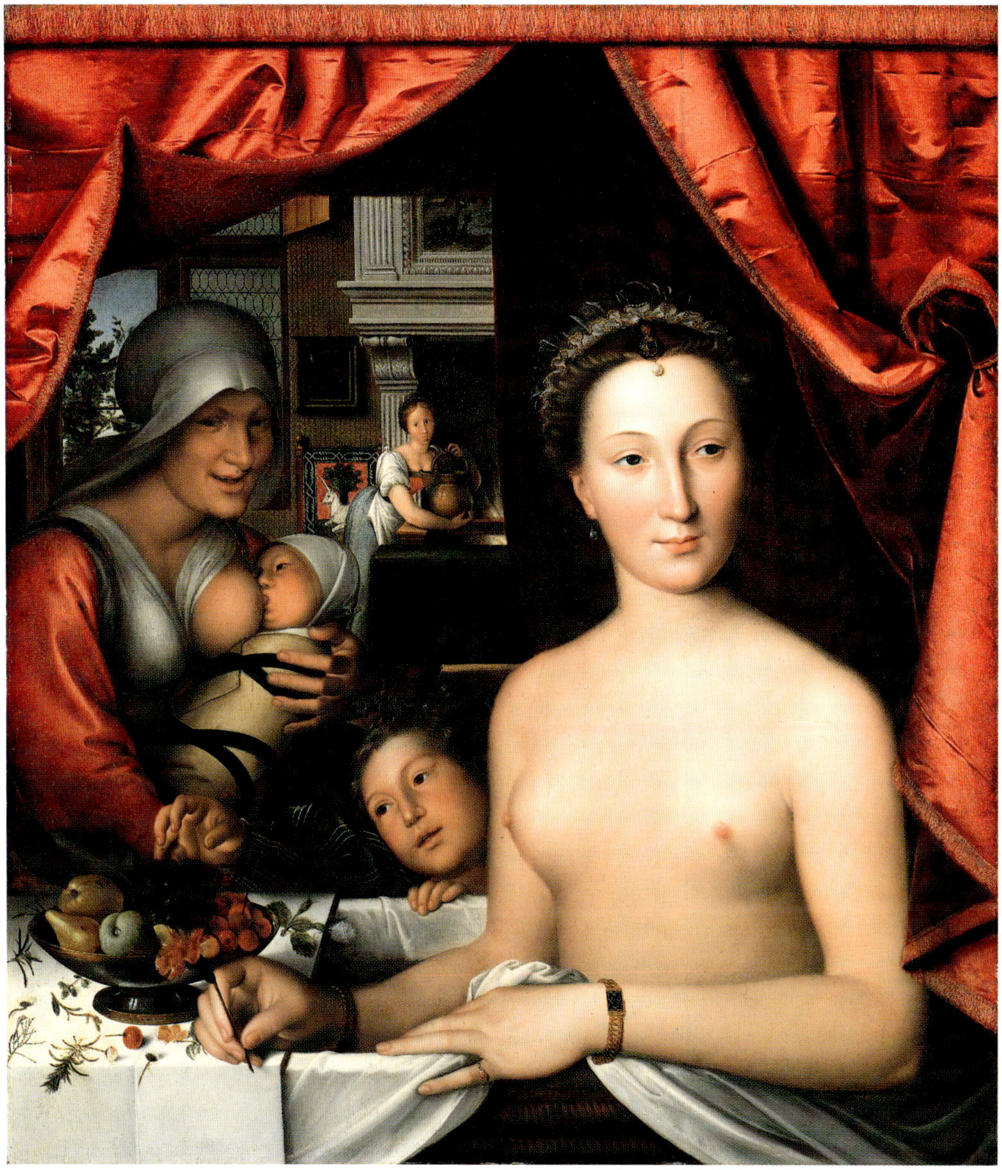

with idealised women in subject pictures by Giorgione seems inconclusive, this question is perhaps insoluble.[30]

If paintings of beautiful, and often half-dressed or nude, women are to be placed in a category apart, is it necessary to look for similar pictures of handsome men? Some of the same difficulties arise, for it became acceptable to produce portraits of nude or nearly nude males, without, in these cases, casting any doubt on their moral standards. Some of them, like Bronzino's *Andrea Doria* (plate 8), masquerade heroically as gods; Alfonso di Tommaso Cambi, 'a very beautiful youth, learned and virtuous and of most agreeable manners', had himself drawn by Vasari nude and in full length as Endymion.[31] Some artists, notably Dürer and Pontormo, drew themselves nude;[32] in 1526, the Augsburg businessman Matthäus Schwarz had himself represented naked in front and back views and recorded that the likenesses were accurate (plate 18). Ironically, the paintings are from the sitter's 'Costume Book' and the reasons for their inclusion are totally

14 (left) Botticelli, *Mars and Venus*, detail showing the head of Venus, panel, painted surface 69 × 173.5 cm., National Gallery, London (915).

See Davies, 1961, pp. 99–101.

16 (right) French, 1590s, *Gabrielle d'Estrées and her (?)Sister*, oak panel, 96 × 125 cm., Louvre, Paris (R.F. 1937–1).

The lady on our right is identified by comparison with other, inscribed portraits as Gabrielle d'Estrées, mistress of Henry IV of France. It is assumed that the other lady is one of her six sisters and that her gesture indicates that Gabrielle is pregnant. Gabrielle's elder son by Henry, César, Duke of Vendôme, was born in June 1594; a daughter and a second son were born in 1596 and 1598; Gabrielle died in 1599. This and another painting of two nude women in the Palazzo Vecchio in Florence (Opere d'arte recuperate, 72) derive from François Clouet's *Lady in her Bath* (plate 15).

See Sterling and Adhémar, 1965, pp. 34–5; here p. 6.

18 (facing page, right) German (Augsburg), 1526, *Matthäus Schwarz Naked* from the '*Trachtenbuch* of Matthäus Schwarz', parchment, each page 16 × 10 cm., Herzog Anton Ulrich-Museum, Brunswick, H. 27, Nr. 67a, pp. 79–80.

The back view is inscribed: 'This was my true form seen from behind on 1 July 1526 when I had grown fat and fleshy/ 29⅓ years 8 days'. The front view is inscribed: 'As opposite, this was my true form seen from the front on 1 July 1526/ This face is truly counterfeited/ 29⅓ years 8 days'. Matthäus Schwarz (1497–1574), an Augsburg merchant, entered the service of the Fuggers in 1516, wrote treatises on double-column book-keeping, was ennobled in 1541 by the Emperor Charles V and was intensely interested in his own appearance. He sat to various portraitists (see plates 33, 152); his *Trachtenbuch* is a pictorial biography as well as a record of his clothes (see plate 230). Why, when he was worried about being overweight, he should have decided to include representations of his naked body, is mysterious.

See Fink, 1963, *passim*; here pp. 7–9.

17 Giorgione, *Laura*, canvas laid down on a spruce panel, cut to an oval and made up again to a rectangle, 41 × 33.6 cm., Kunsthistorisches Museum, Vienna, Gemäldegalerie (31).

On the reverse of the panel is the inscription. 'On 1 June 1506 this was done by the hand of master Giorgio of Castelfranco, colleague of master Vincenzo Catena, for messer Giacomo . . .'. It may be a portrait of a lady in the guise of Laura, Petrarch's mistress; it is perhaps more likely to be a representation of Laura as Giorgione imagined her. He may well have used studies made from a professional model.

See Klauner and Heinz, 1965, pp. 61–2; here pp. 6–7.

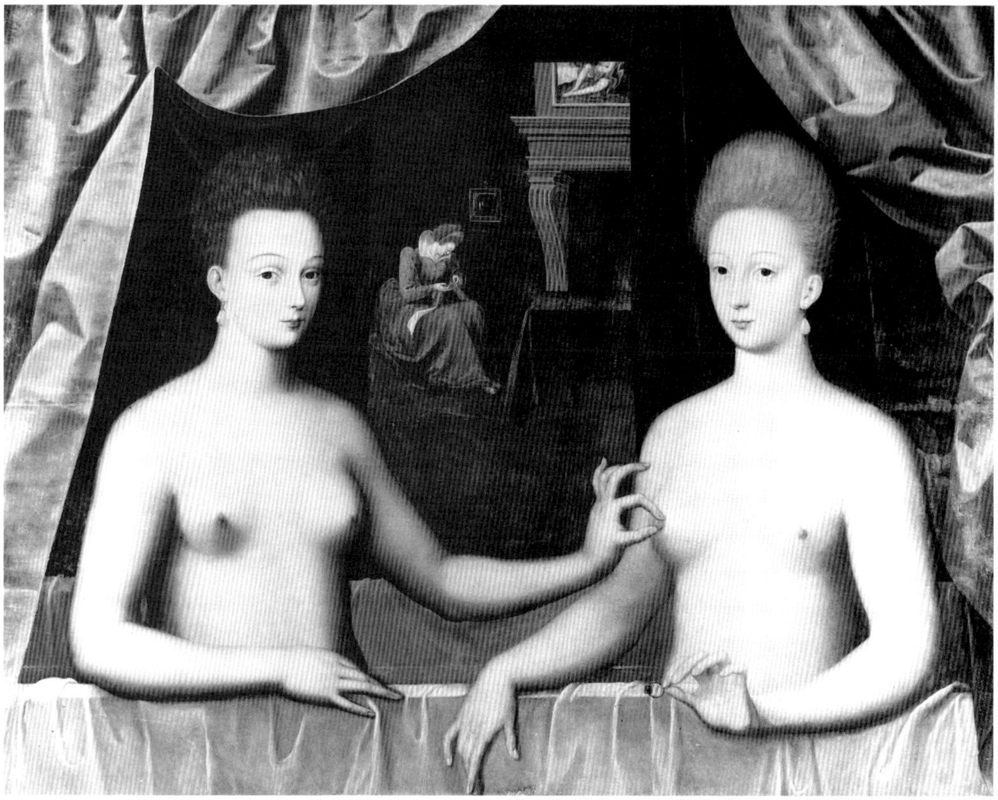

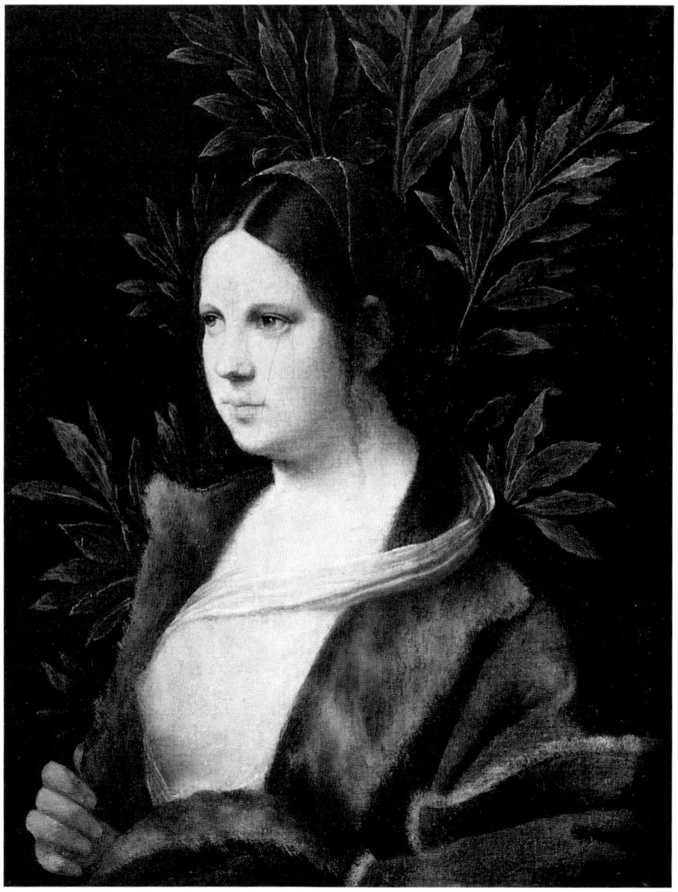

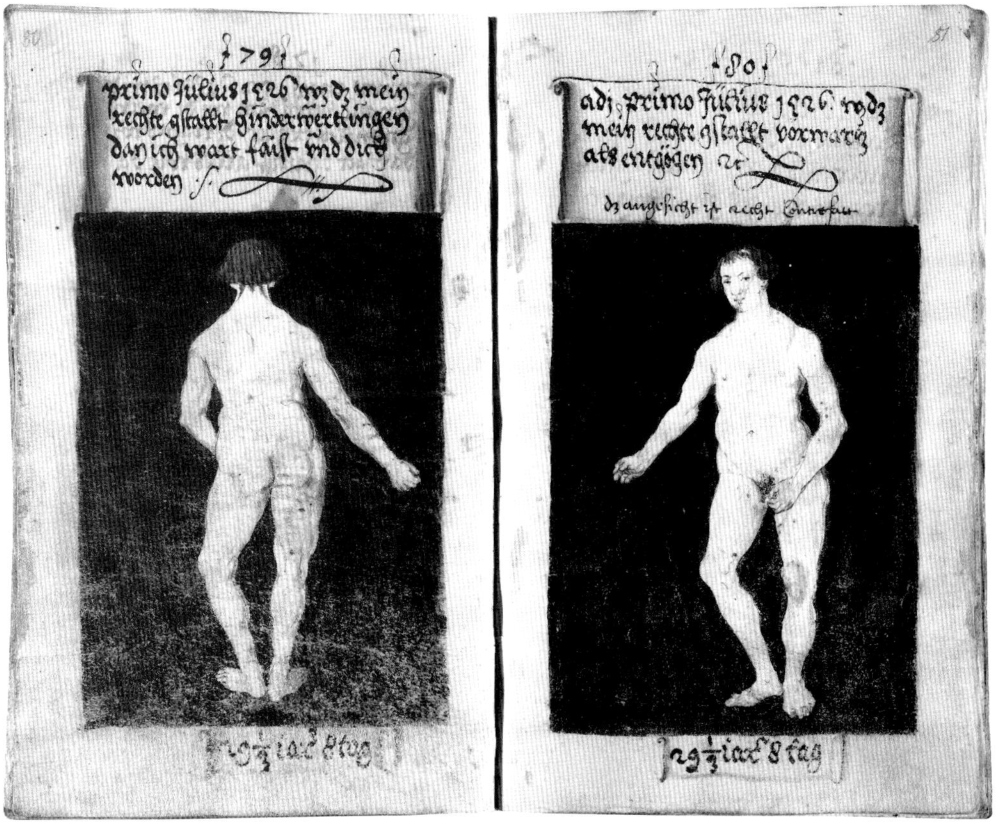

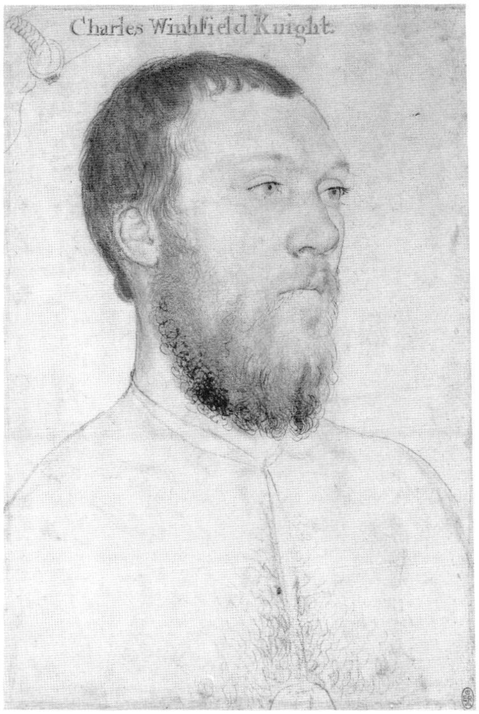

19 Hans Holbein the Younger, *Charles Wingfield*, black and coloured chalks, partly stumped, with some strengthening in pen and ink, on pink prepared paper, 28.2 × 19.7 cm., Royal Library, Windsor Castle, Print Room (RL 12249).

The sitter (1513–40) owned the manor and castle of Kimbolton (Huntingdonshire) where the divorced queen Catherine of Aragon was imprisoned and where she died in 1536.

See Foister, 1983, p. 42 (36); here p. 9.

20 (foll. page) Pontormo, '*A Halberdier*', panel transferred to canvas, 92 × 72 cm., J. Paul Getty Museum, Malibu (California).

Painted in about 1530, the picture was described in 1612 as a portrait of Cosimo I de' Medici, Grand Duke of Tuscany (1519–74). It is arguable, however, that it is not a true portrait but rather an idealised image of a handsome guardsman.

See Langedijk, 1981–3, I, pp. 431–3; here p. 9.

obscure. Holbein's drawing of Charles Wingfield shows the sitter in a surprising and unexplained state of undress (plate 19).

Pictures of ideally handsome and stalwart young warriors, especially those accompanied by pages, like the Giorgionesque '*Gattamelata*' in the Uffizi,[33] could have been used to encourage hero-worship in boys; pictures of ideally pretty youths, like the Giorgionesque *Shepherd* at Hampton Court,[34] would have appealed to the various tastes of many. Pontormo's '*Halberdier*', painted in about 1530, is first traceable in 1612, when it was described as a portrait of Cosimo I de' Medici (plate 20).[35] Though the identification is still accepted by some,[36] the features are not highly particularised but resemble closely those of idealised young men and angels in Pontormo's religious paintings.[37] The youth, with his narrow, slanting shoulders, ridiculously small waist, relatively wide hips, jutting codpiece and rather phallic pike, is sexually ambiguous. His breeches, opening to reveal his shirt, seem insecurely suspended; his pouting, parted lips and expression of almost orgasmic vacancy are peculiar; and his hat badge shows Hercules and Antaeus – two naked men grappling in an embrace to the death. The picture is perhaps not a portrait, but rather an idealised image of a handsome guardsman.

Idealisation, characterisation and individualisation are words frequently used in discussions of portraits, and it is worth examining how the three terms are to be defined and applied and the means by which these qualities may be analysed.

Individualisation is the process by which the artist stresses those particular aspects of his sitter that distinguish him from the rest of humanity. Many portrait-painters, even the most objective, have used the techniques of the modern caricaturist to enhance likenesses. The face, and especially the principal features, the eyes, eyebrows, nose and mouth, are of paramount importance in recognition;

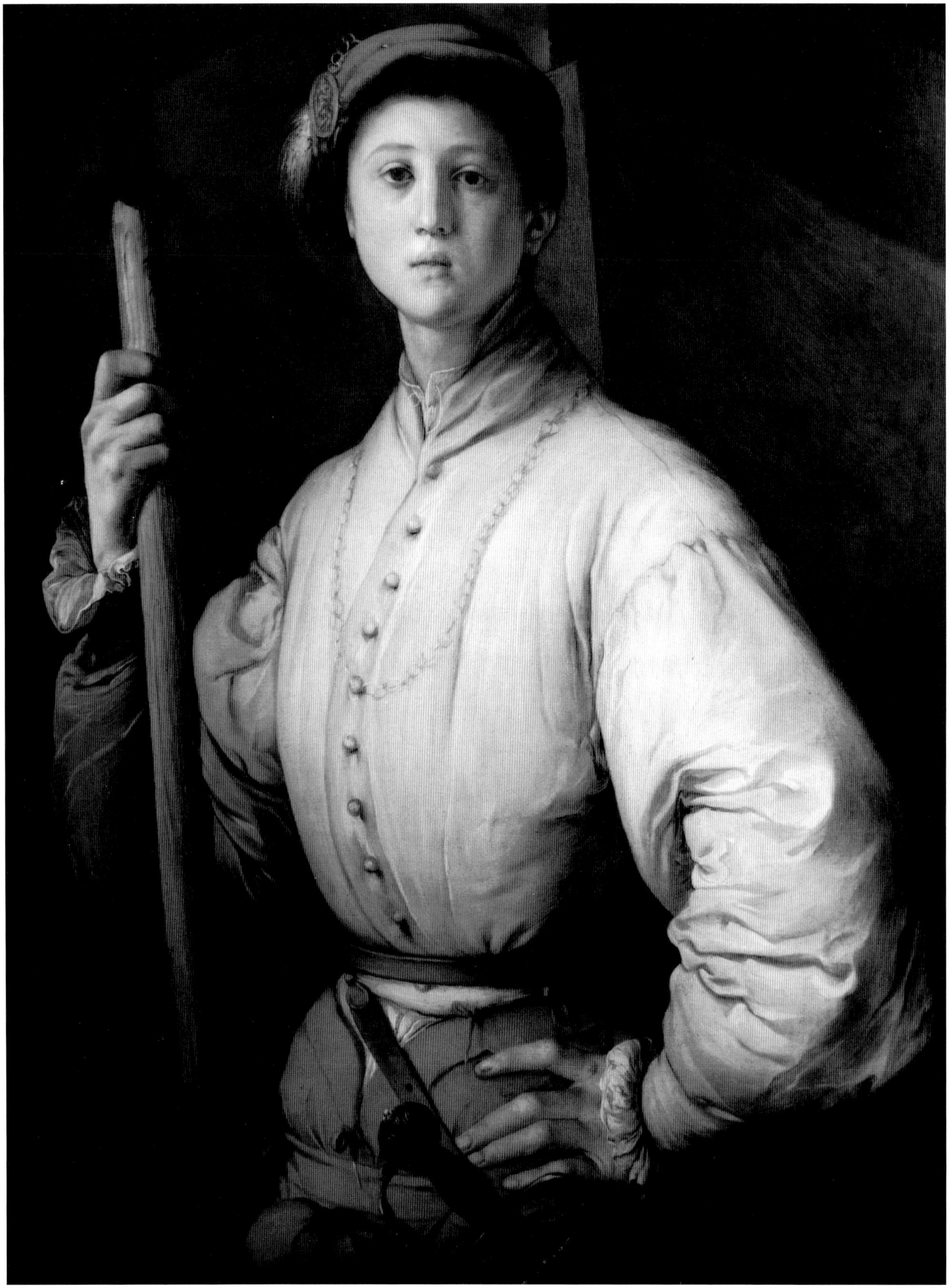

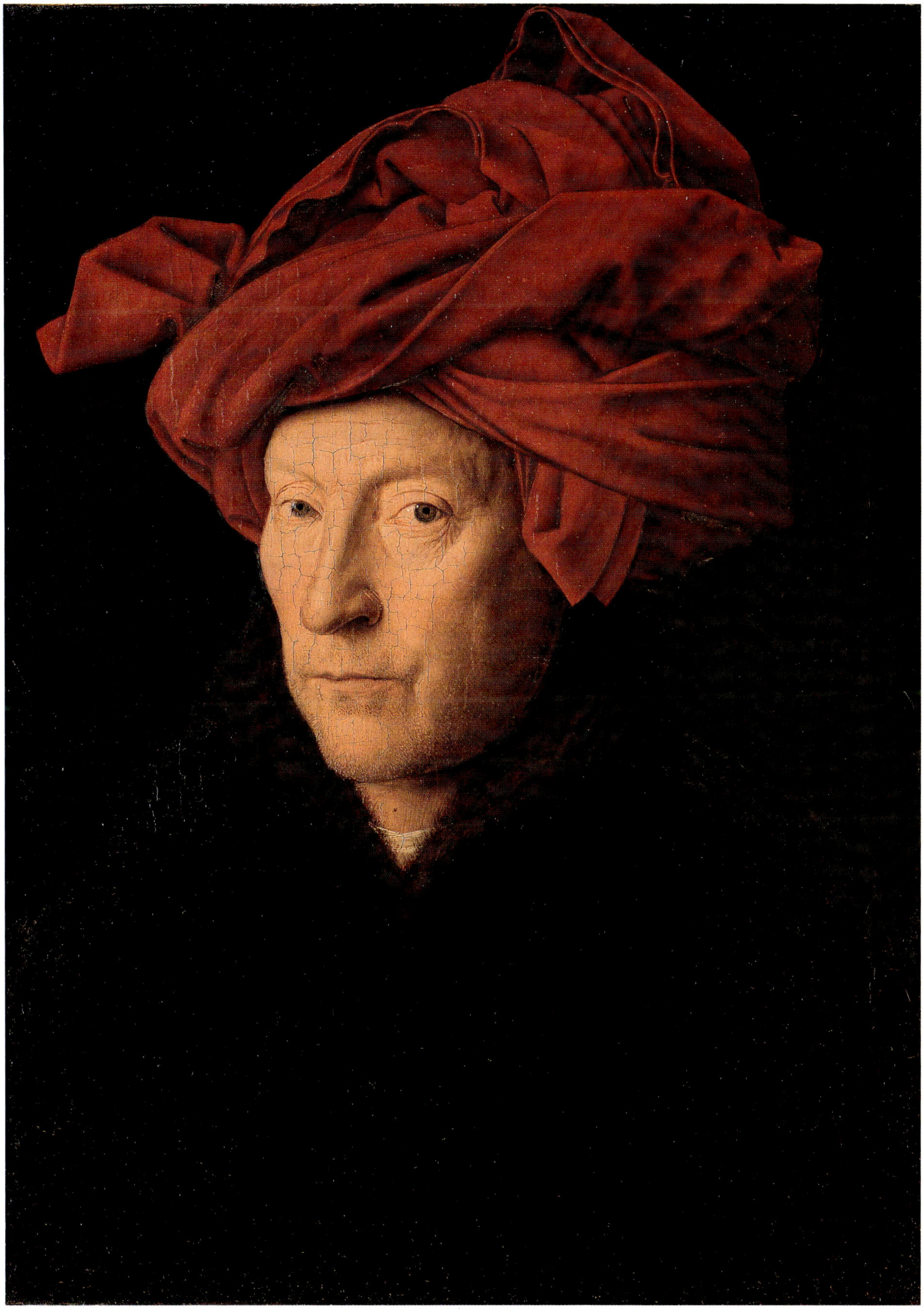

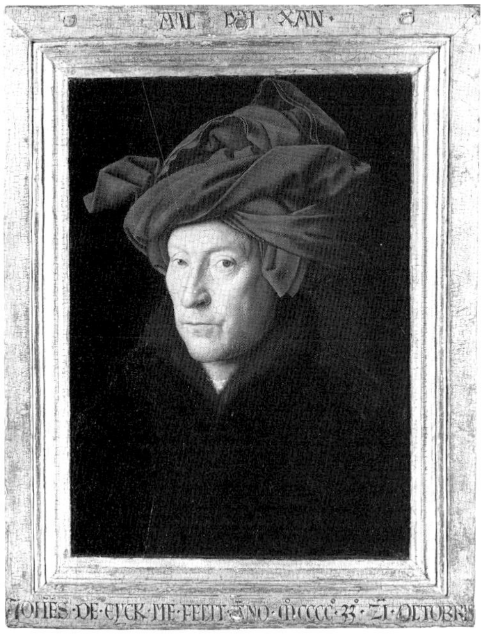

22 Jan van Eyck, *Man in a Red Turban*, oak panel in its original frame: the frame measures 33.3 × 25.8 cm., the painted surface, 25.7 × 19 cm., National Gallery, London (222).

The frame is inscribed 'Jan van Eyck made me on 21 October 1433' and 'As I can', partly written in Greek letters – the personal motto of the artist. Listed in the Arundel inventory of c. 1655 as Jan van Eyck's self-portrait, the painting very probably represents Jan himself: this would explain the prominence accorded to his personal motto. The hat is not, in fact, a turban but a head-dress similar to that seen in plate 104. The hanging scarfs have been wound and knotted round the hat to keep them out of the sitter's way (Scott, 1980, p. 118), which may indicate that he is informally dressed.

See Davies, 1968, pp. 53–4; Dhanens, 1980, pp. 188–92; here pp. 12, 65, 69, 112, plates 21, 169.

unlike the skin and the hair, they cannot be drastically changed by artifice or by age. Emphasis is therefore given to the head, which is frequently rather too large in relation to the body; the face may be enlarged in proportion to the head; the features may be enlarged in proportion to the face. The features may be observed from slightly different angles: in a three-quarters-view portrait, for example, the nose is often turned unnaturally far into profile to give it a more easily perceived and recognised contour. Asymmetries between the eyes and between the corners of the mouth may be exaggerated in order to stress the sitter's unique irregularity of countenance. Such enlargements and exaggerations are generally so small and so subtle as to be barely perceptible. They need not always have been made consciously, but may have resulted from the artist's instinctive search to express his sitter's individuality.

In Jan van Eyck's *Man in a Red Turban*, dated 1433 and very possibly a self-portrait, the darkening of the blue background has obscured the contours of the sitter's shoulders (plates 21, 22). They were perhaps never well defined in tonal terms, so that they would not draw undue attention to the facts that the sitter's body is shrunken, that his head is disproportionately large and that his neck does not provide a totally convincing link between head and torso. Here the lighting and the arrangement of the hat and clothes concentrate attention on the face and features, which are not noticeably too large for the head; but the nose is turned further into profile than the rest of the face, the arches of the eyebrows are contrasted and it is not merely perspective that accounts for the differences in the contours of the eyelids as the upper lids curve towards the tear ducts and the lower lids narrow towards the irises. The centre line of the sitter's mouth rises slightly to his right and drops to his left and the lighting seems to have been contrived to accent the fractional twist.

A greater degree of distortion is to be observed in Botticelli's *Young Man*, probably painted in the 1480s (plate 23). Though the face, turned very slightly towards the sitter's right, is in reasonable proportion to his torso, the cranium has been reduced in size while the eyes have been enlarged. Different areas of the face are seen from different angles, for the artist has looked straight into the eyes and at the eyelids and lower lip but has chosen to view from below the chin, upper lip and nose, the areas between the eyelids and the eyebrows and the forehead. The eyes are so different in shape and the mouth is so completely asymmetrical that it can be stated with every confidence that Botticelli has exaggerated the irregularities of his sitter's features. By using these devices of distortion, he has achieved what must surely have been a striking likeness and one that compels attention partly because it defies in a disturbingly flagrant way the laws of faithful imitation and 'good' draughtsmanship. It was presumably portraits like this one which were produced by the minor Florentine painter Antonio del Ceraiuolo, of whom Vasari wrote: 'he did portraits with the greatest facility, though he had not much design. I have seen some of his heads, for example, with crooked noses, one lip small and the other large, and other deformities, yet they are good likenesses . . .'[38]

Holbein has often been described as an artist of the highest objectivity: some, indeed, have claimed that he may have made his portrait drawings with the aid of a mechanical tracing device.[39] His drawings, however, prove on close examination to be far from photographically accurate renderings of his sitters' heads. With his unsurpassed control of line, he had a capacity that has never been equalled to record, in a slightly exaggerated form and with superb economy, those imperfections in symmetry that distinguished his sitters. In his drawing of the poet

21 (prev. page) Jan van Eyck, *Man in a Red Turban* (see plate 22).

23 Botticelli, *Young Man*, panel, 37.5 × 28.2 cm., National Gallery, London (626).

Attributed to Botticelli on stylistic grounds, the portrait is generally dated in the 1480s.

See Davies, 1961, pp. 98–9; Lightbown, 1978, II, p. 65; here p. 12.

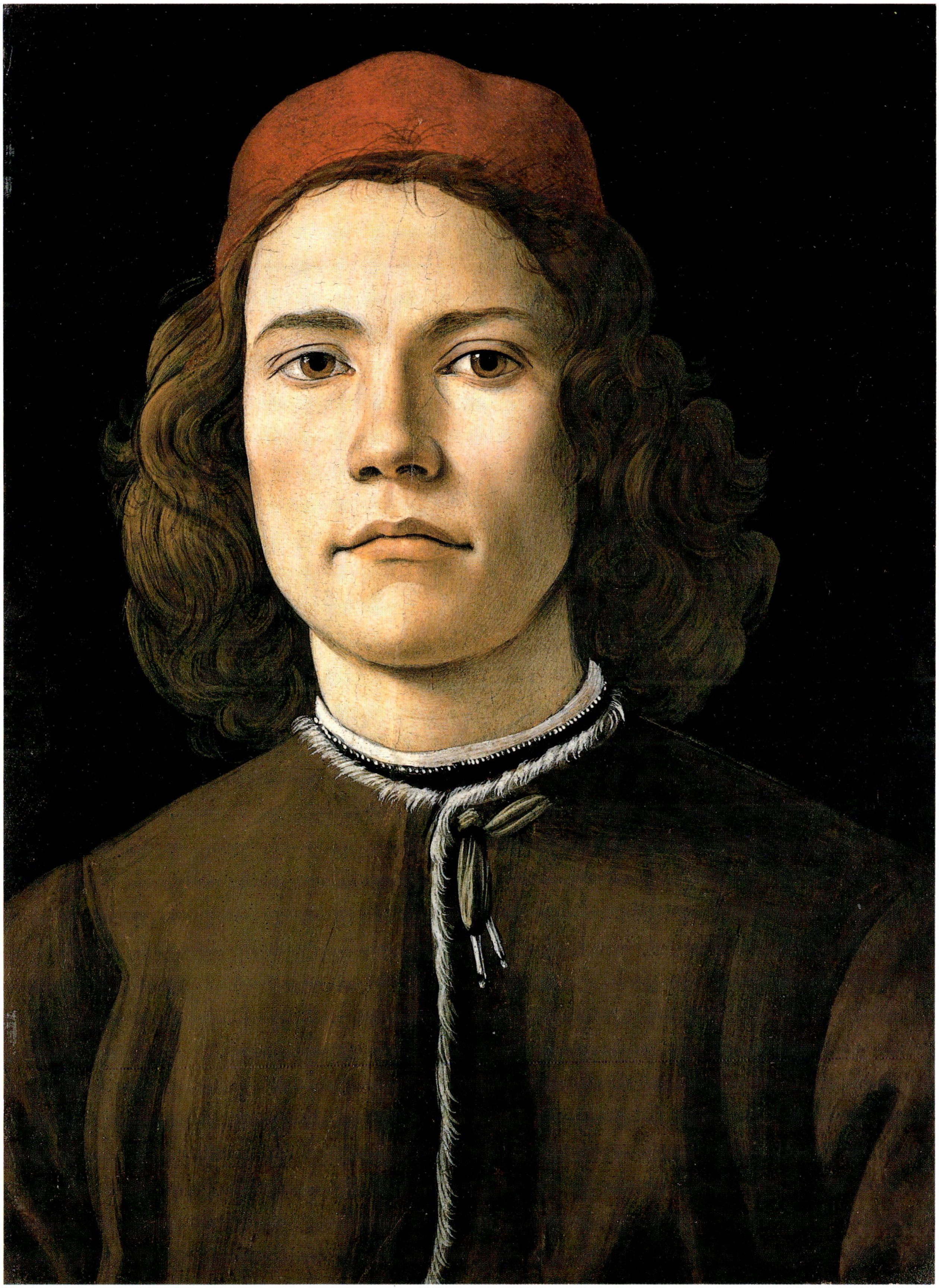

Earl of Surrey, made during the 1530s, the hat conceals to some degree the extent to which the sitter's cranium has been diminished and the sleeves disguise the shrunkenness of the torso (plate 24). The face and eyes are enlarged and the discrepancies in shape between the eyes, eyelids, eyebrows and ears, and even between the nostrils and the pupils of the eyes, suggest that Holbein has exaggerated quite considerably the idiosyncracies of his sitter's facial anatomy. The most striking part of the drawing is perhaps the centre line of the mouth, rendered with infinite care and extraordinary and inimitable subtlety. It is completely asymmetrical.

Francisco de Holanda presumably realised the importance of some of these techniques of individualisation when, in his dialogue 'Of the eyes', he caused his questioner to express the opinion that, if the sitter's eyes were large, they should be made slightly larger; if they were small, they should be made smaller.[40] He did not, however, dwell on the asymmetries of the human head.

Just as the processes of individualisation are akin to those of caricature, idealisation and flattery are often difficult to distinguish. Any artist will have ideals of beauty, which may be absolute, fashionable or purely personal. In making a portrait he will, consciously or unconsciously, impose some of those ideals upon his sitter. As the face most familiar to anyone is likely to be his own, the artist's physical appearance may well affect his personal ideal of beauty. Leonardo observed that 'often a master's shapes resemble himself'; while Dürer stated that 'many painters paint figures resembling themselves'.[41] Dürer had evidently studied his own features so thoroughly that when, at Augsburg in 1518, he drew a portrait of the Emperor Maximilian I, he overlaid upon the emperor's countenance something of the memory of his own face (plate 25). In the drawing, the relative scale of Maximilian's features and even the shapes of his nose, mouth and chin are closer to Dürer's own, as rendered in his self-portrait of 1498 (plate 26), than to those of the emperor, as they were recorded by another artist in 1519 from his corpse (plate 211).

The tendency to idealise must explain why portraits by the same artist share a sort of family likeness. It is partly or mainly because of this process of idealisation that unsigned and undocumented portraits can be attributed to specific painters. Certain artists found it almost impossible to abandon their idealised facial types, and were consequently rather unsatisfactory portraitists.[42] Fashions in beauty also played a part but, interesting as it may be to compare written descriptions of ideally beautiful people with painted images, it seems clear that such fashions were ultimately created and directed by artists.

The degree of idealisation is measurable when there exist two approximately contemporary portraits of the same sitter by different artists. They may be compared with other portraits and with idealised heads by the same artists. Nicolas Rolin, Chancellor of Burgundy, was represented by Jan van Eyck in the *Virgin of Autun*, probably of the late 1430s (plate 27), and, about ten years later, by Rogier van der Weyden on the reverse of the altarpiece of the *Last Judgement* at Beaune (plate 28). That Van Eyck chose to pose Rolin in near profile may have been due to the demands of composition or else to a desire to hide the ugliness of his mouth. Rogier, again, perhaps, as composition dictated, but certainly according to his usual practice, painted his head in full three-quarters view. It is this pose, rather than the sitter's advancing age, that makes him appear more grotesque in Rogier's portrait. The features in both portraits correspond fairly exactly but, if the Van Eyck is taken as a model of accuracy, it becomes evident

24 Hans Holbein the Younger, *Henry Howard, Earl of Surrey*, black and coloured chalks, the outlines strengthened with pen and ink, on pink prepared paper, 24.8 × 20.4 cm., Royal Library, Windsor Castle, Print Room (RL 12215).

The poet Earl of Surrey, in the inscription mistakenly named Thomas, was beheaded in 1547. He sat to Holbein on several occasions. This drawing was probably executed in the mid-1530s, when Surrey was in his late teens; no painting based upon it is known.

See Foister, 1983, p. 40 (17); exhibition catalogue Houston, 1987, p. 76 (21); here pp. 12–14, 65, 81, plate 5.

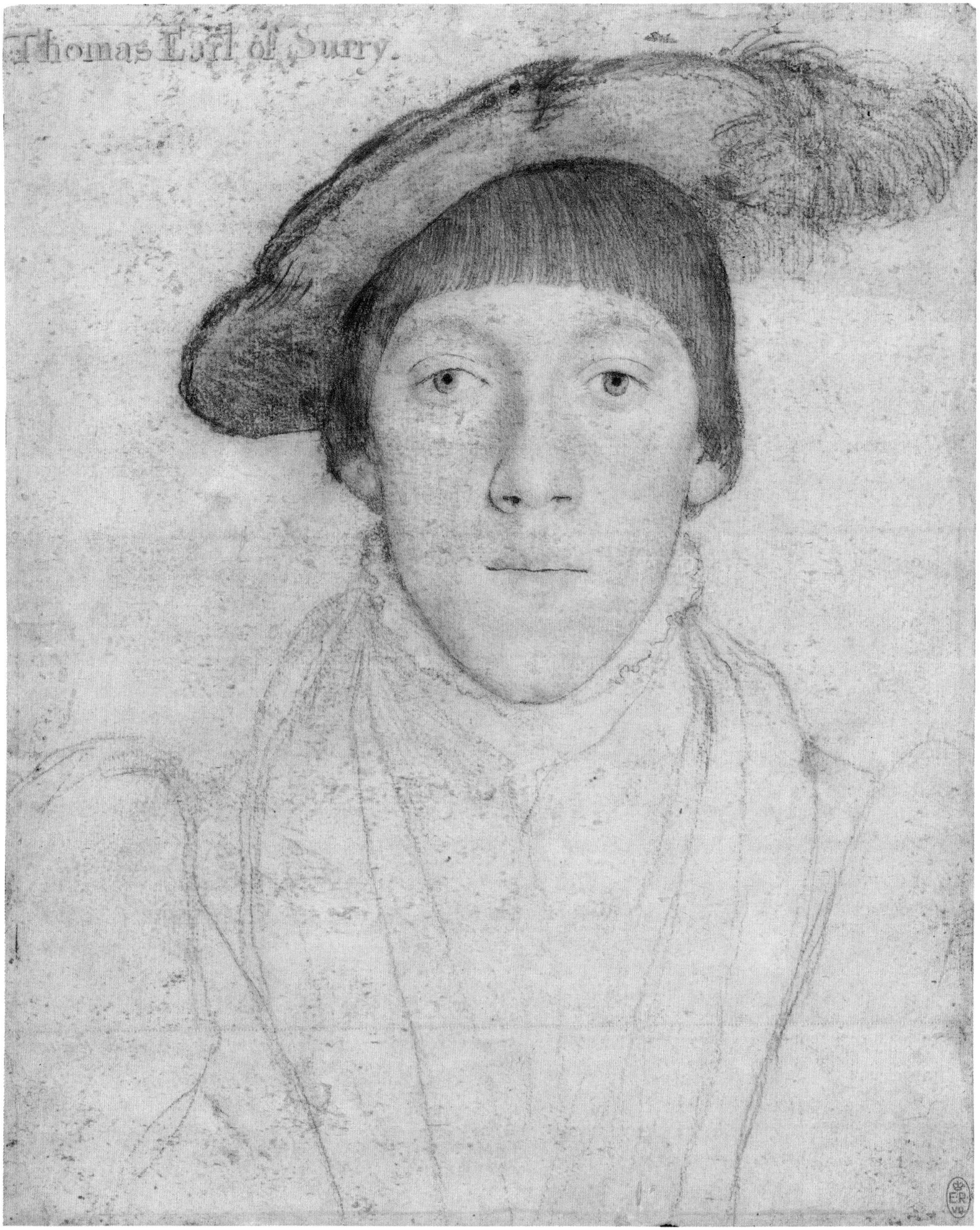
Thomas Earl of Surry.

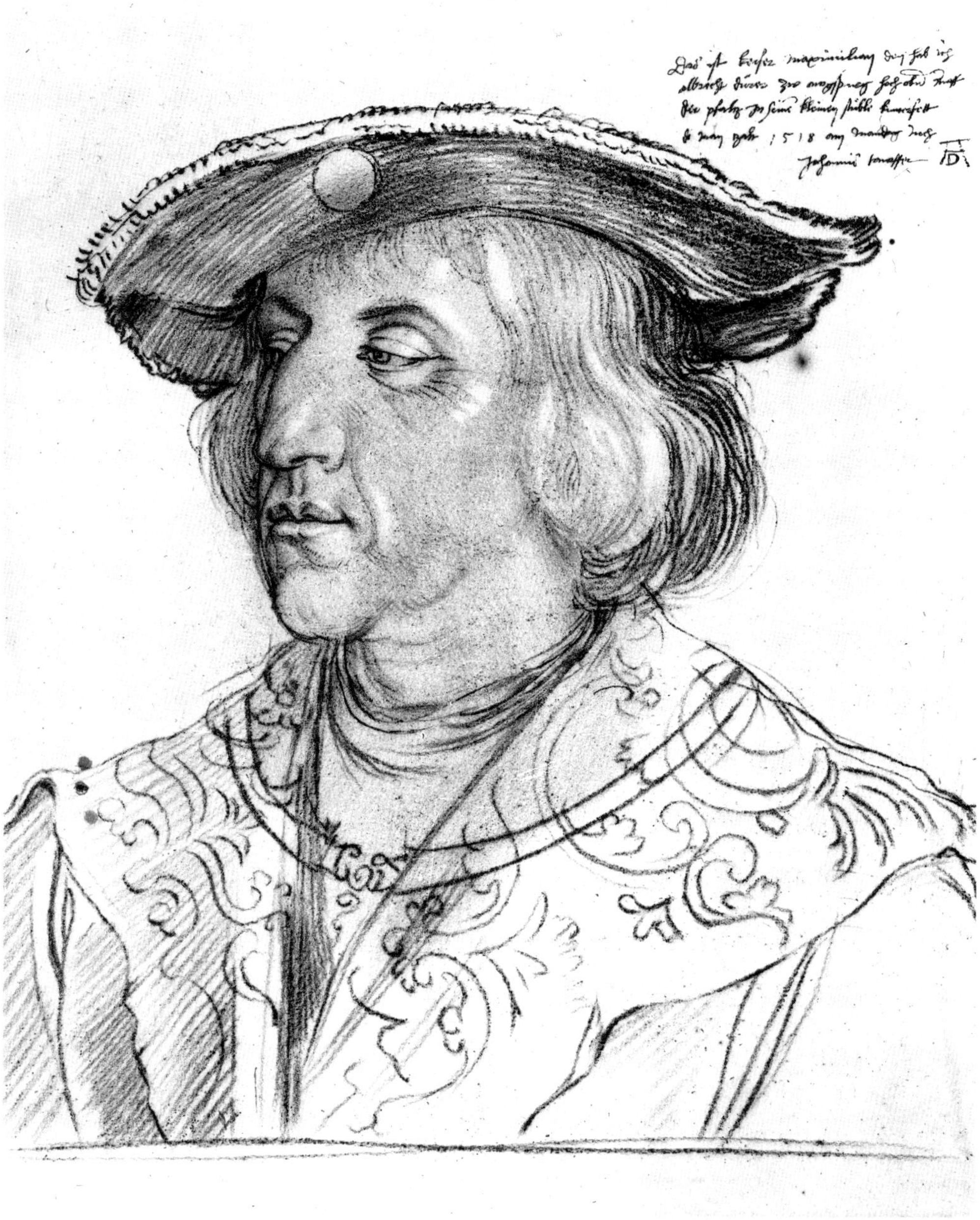

25 Albrecht Dürer, *Emperor Maximilian I*, charcoal with red and yellow wash, heightened with white body colour, on white paper, 38.1 × 31.9 cm., Graphische Sammlung Albertina, Vienna (4852).

The inscription may be translated 'This is the Emperor Maximilian, whom I, Albrecht Dürer, counterfeited at Augsburg in his little cabinet, high up in the palace, in the year reckoned 1518 on the Monday after John the Baptist's day'. Maximilian was at Augsburg for the meeting of the Imperial Diet. Dürer later made two paintings and one woodcut based on the drawing: the paintings are at Nuremberg (Gm 169) and Vienna (825) and all three seem to have been executed after Maximilian's death in January 1519.

See White, 1971, pp. 168–9; here pp. 14, 65.

26 (facing page) Albrecht Dürer, *Self-Portrait*, panel, 52 × 41 cm., Museo del Prado, Madrid (2179).

The inscription may be translated 'In 1498 I painted that from my own form. I was twenty-six years old. Albrecht Dürer.'

See Anzelewsky, 1980, pp. 88–9; here pp. 14, 65.

27 (p. 18) Jan van Eyck, *Virgin of Autun*, detail showing the donor, Nicolas Rolin, oak panel, 66 × 62 cm., Louvre, Paris (INV. 1271).

The picture, which comes from the chapel of St Sebastian in the church of Our Lady at Autun, represents Nicolas Rolin, Chancellor of Burgundy (1376–1462), kneeling before the Virgin and Child. It is generally believed to have been painted in the mid-1430s.

See Dhanens, 1980, pp. 266–81; here pp. 14–16, 115.

28 (p. 19) Rogier van der Weyden, *The Donor Nicolas Rolin*, detail, from the polyptych of the *Last Judgement*, oak panel, 129.5 × 73.1 cm., Hôtel-Dieu, Beaune.

The panel is from the left wing of the exterior of the altarpiece. Opposite Rolin kneels his third wife Guigone de Salins; between them are grisailles of St Sebastian and St Anthony; above the saints is a representation of the Annunciation, again in grisaille. The altarpiece, commissioned by Rolin for the hospital of the Hôtel-Dieu which he had founded, is considered to have been begun in or after 1443 and to have been finished by 1451. The cloth behind Rolin has been damaged but originally bore a rich pattern of scarlet and gold.

See Veronée-Verhaegen, 1973, *passim*; here pp. 14–16, 37.

that Rogier has lengthened Rolin's nose, enlarged his eyes and raised his eyebrows. His expression is similar to those of the sitters in Rogier's other portraits (plates 154, 250), whereas Van Eyck's may be a more objective, impassive likeness. Though both artists noticed the conspicuous smallness of Rolin's hands, Rogier drew them according to his own conventions, with long, tapering and curving fingers and exaggeratedly bent thumbs. Van Eyck faithfully recorded; Van der Weyden imposed a stylised and highly personal vision upon his subject.[43]

Memlinc's portrait of Maria Portinari (plate 29) may be compared with another likeness produced at about the same time, the 1470s, by Hugo van der Goes (plate 30). The Memlinc portrait, from a half-length triptych probably painted for her and her husband's private use, was done in about 1470, when she was fourteen or fifteen. The Van der Goes portrait, from the wing of a very large altarpiece painted for the high altar of a Florentine church, can be dated around 1477–78, when

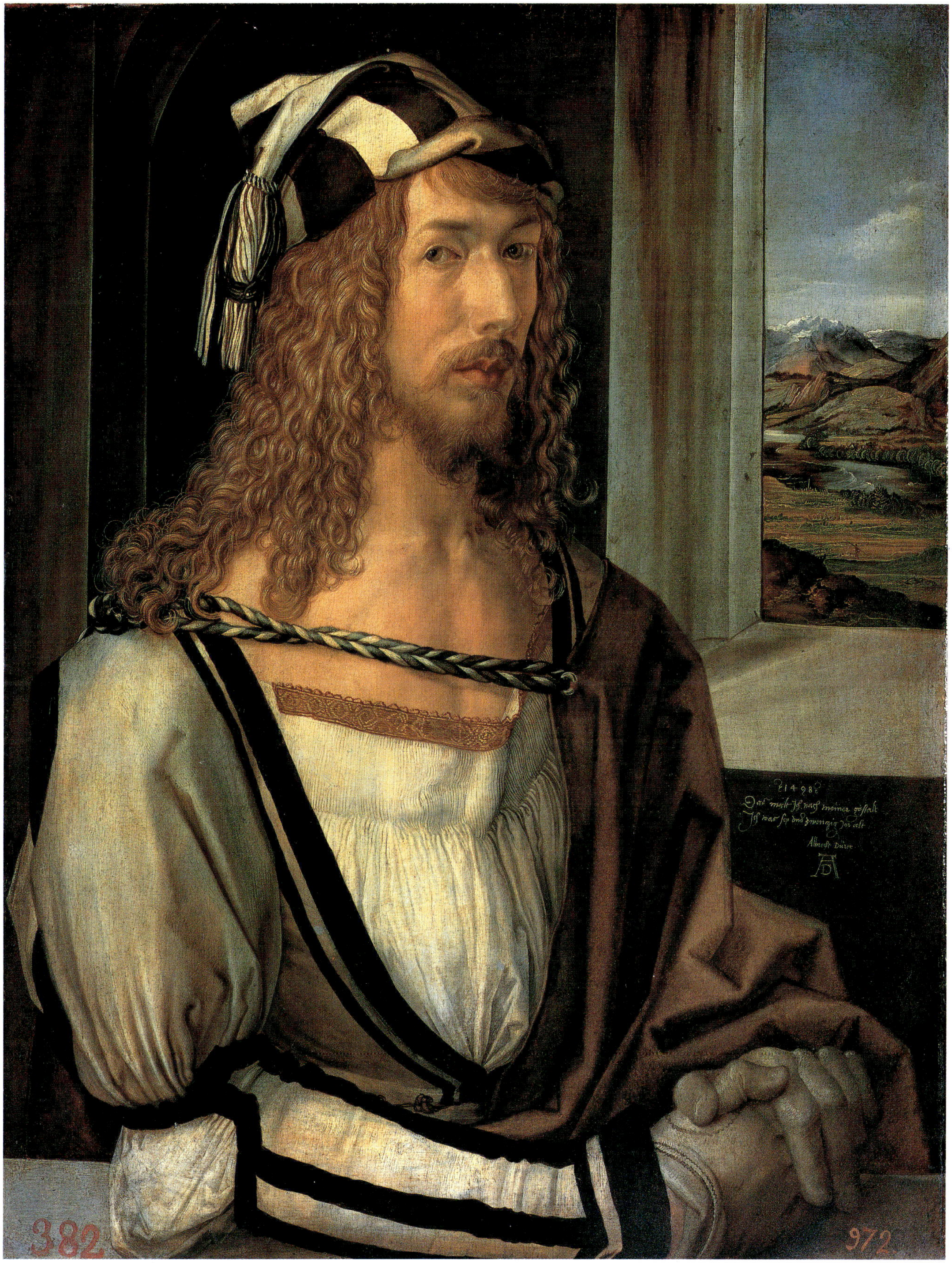
1498
Das malt Ich nach meiner gestalt
Ich was sex und zwenzig Jor alt
Albrecht Dürer
382
972

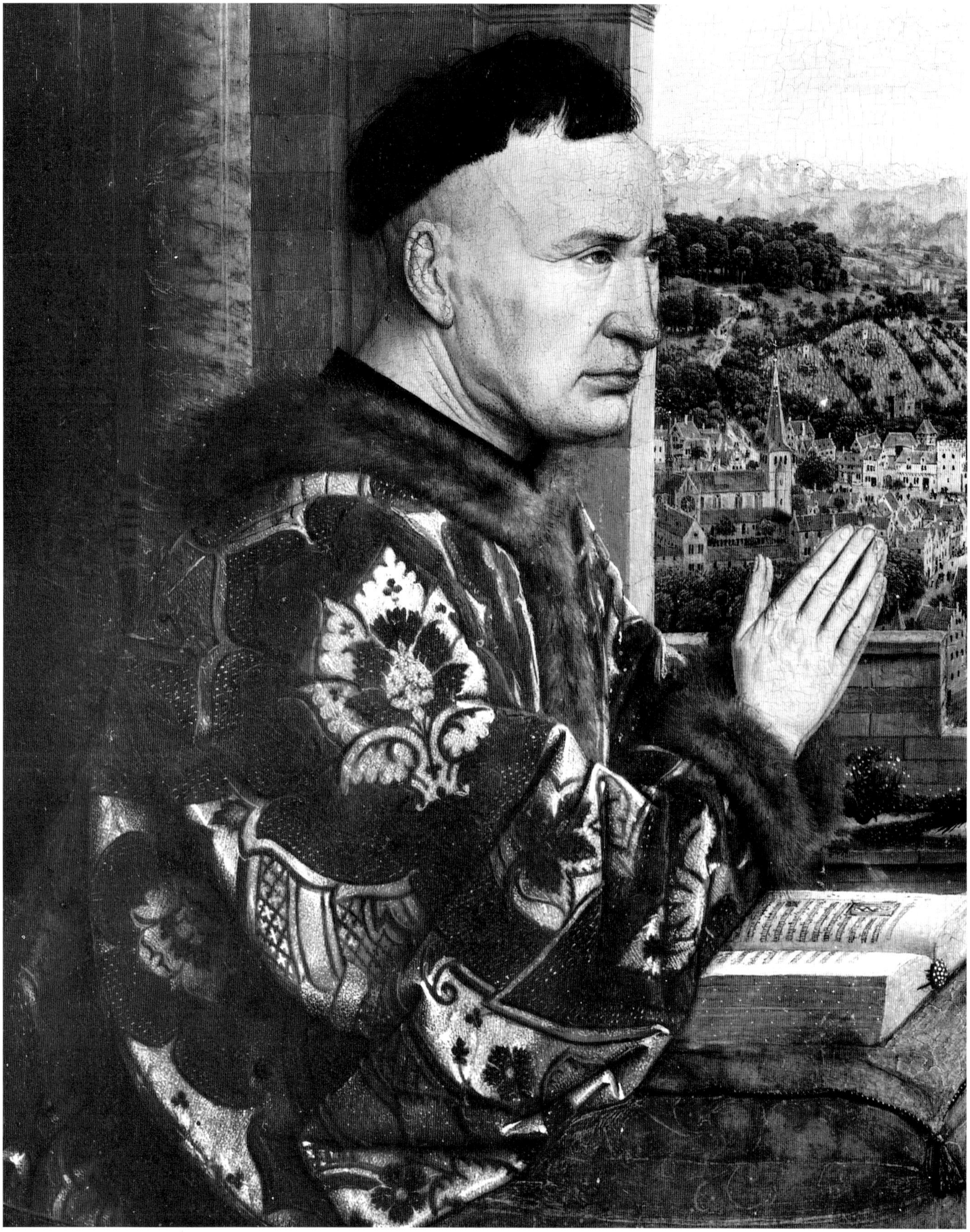

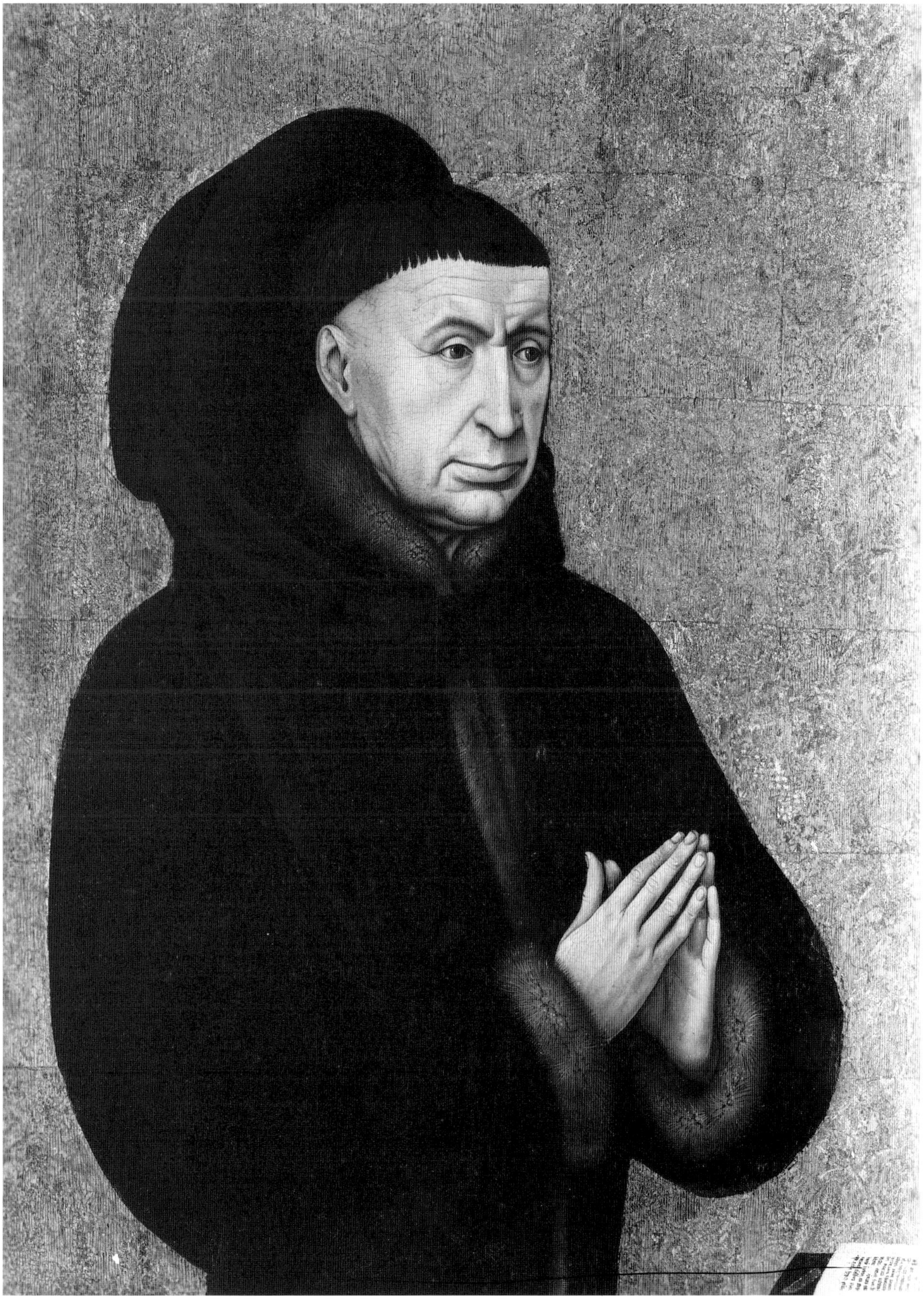

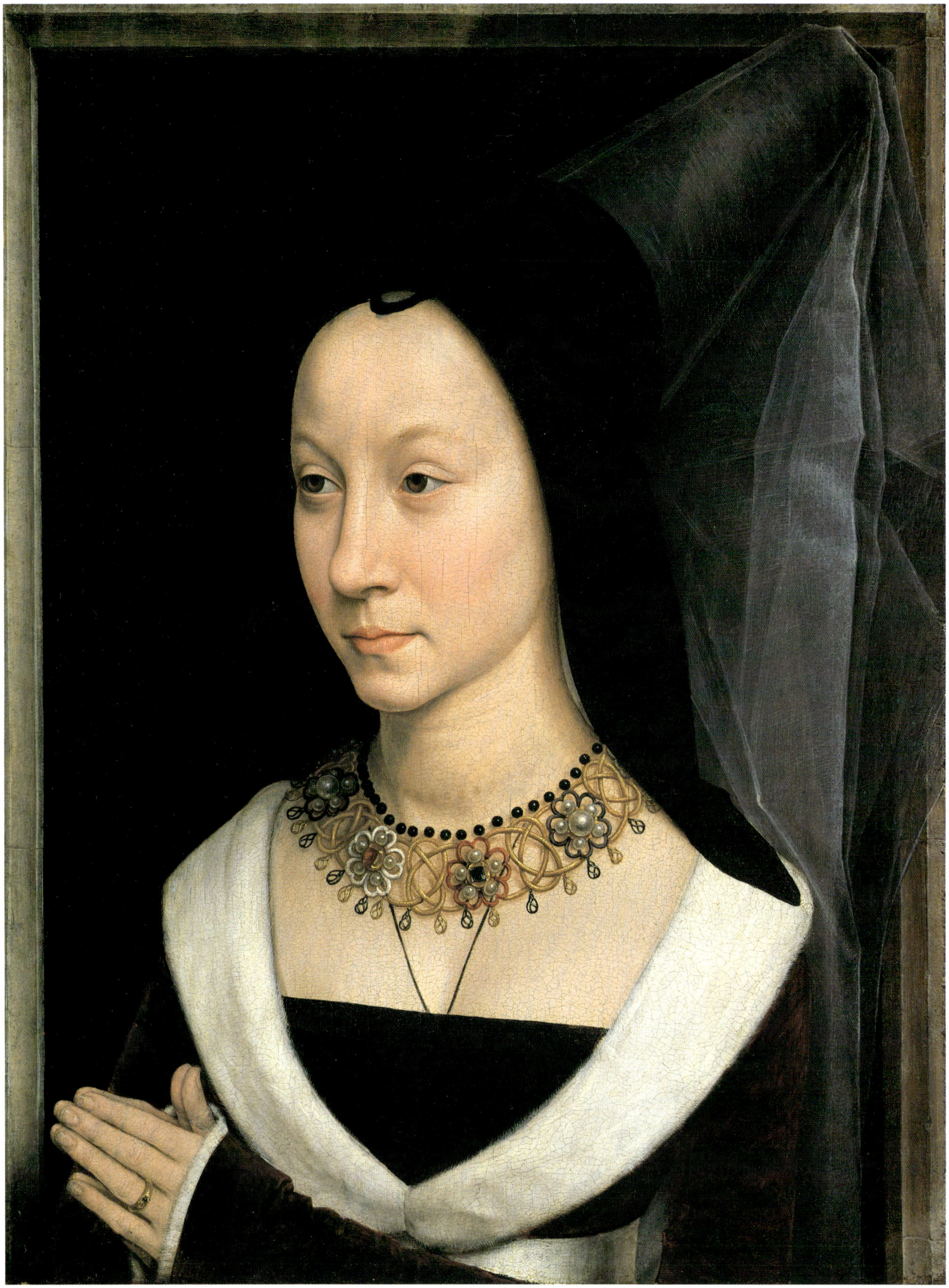

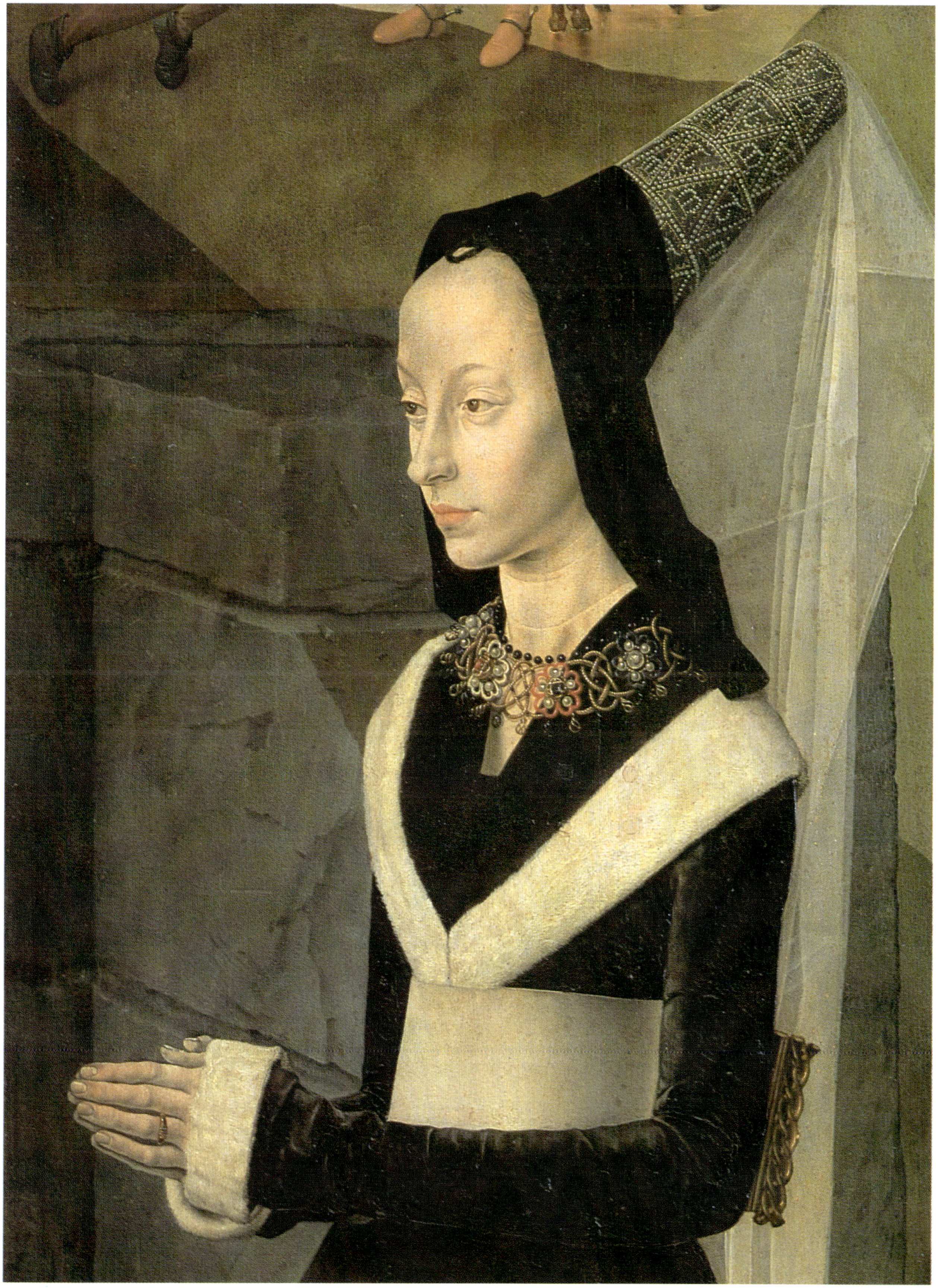

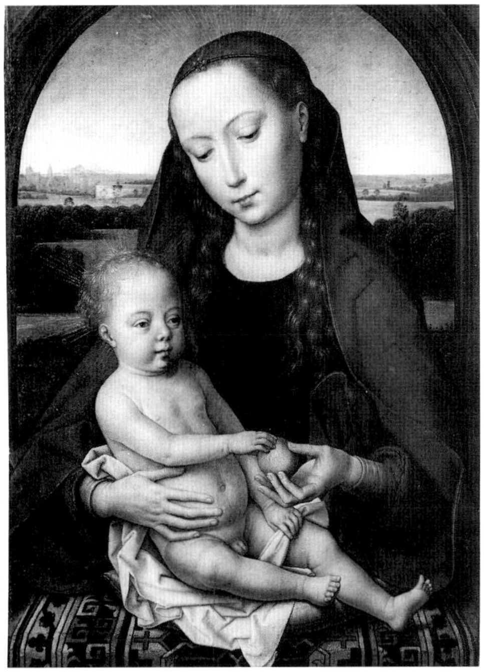

29 (p. 20) Hans Memlinc, *Maria Portinari*, oak panel, painted surface 42 × 31.8 cm., Metropolitan Museum of Art, New York (14.40.627).

The pendant portrait of Maria's husband Tommaso Portinari is also in the Metropolitan Museum (14.40.626). The two portraits were clearly the wings of a small triptych but the centre panel, possibly a *Virgin and Child*, has been lost. The sitters are identified by comparison with the donor portraits in Memlinc's *Passion of Christ* at Turin (Galleria Sabauda, 8: Friedländer, 1967–76, VIa, pl. 86) and in the 'Portinari Triptych' by Van der Goes (plates 30, 32, 192); the attribution to Memlinc is made on stylistic grounds; the portraits are generally dated around 1470, shortly after the sitters' marriage. The Florentine Tommaso Portinari (1428/9–1501) went to the Low Countries at an early age to work in the Bruges branch of the Medici bank. In 1469, he returned to Florence to marry another Florentine, Maria Bandini Baroncelli, who joined him at Bruges in 1470. She was then about fourteen. Memlinc at first set her steeple hat at an angle nearer the vertical; this hat, underpainted in red, was to have carried a zig-zag pattern similar to that appearing on the hat that Maria wears in the 'Portinari Triptych' (plate 30).

See Wehle and Salinger, 1947, pp. 65–8; here pp. 16–22.

30 (prev. page) Hugo van der Goes, 'Portinari Triptych', detail (see plate 32).

the sitter was in her early twenties. She looks older, but presumably she was prematurely aged by constant childbearing. In both portraits she is similarly dressed and wears the same intricate and magnificent necklace.

Memlinc presents his sitter in pure three-quarters view, whereas in the Van der Goes portrait she is more in profile, so that the bulbous end of her nose breaks the contour of her far cheek. This partly explains why she looks thinner, as well as older, in the Van der Goes painting. The stronger shadows there contribute to that effect, for Memlinc lights his sitter with an even, diffused and flattering illumination. Van der Goes's stronger and more dramatic lighting, which is of course in keeping with the lighting of the rest of the altarpiece, is symptomatic of his concern for the structure of the head. Though Memlinc takes extraordinary care over the details of the vital parts of the face, particularly the eyes and mouth, which are revealed under the microscope to be miracles of detail and delicacy, he is less interested in the underlying bones and the recession of the planes of the head is rather ill-defined. Van der Goes is more conscious of the bones beneath the flesh, of the bulge formed by the shaven forehead and of the protuberances of the nose and cheekbones. He also records more sensitively the reflected lights in the shadowed areas of the skin. It may be that both artists have exaggerated the length of Maria's nose, elongated her face and enlarged her rather small eyes. Van der Goes has certainly overstressed the slant of her right eye and both painters have lengthened the eyes to give them a fashionable, almost oriental effect. The plucked eyebrows are raised to heighten the impression of devout and elevated piety. In such respects, both artists are referring to fashionable ideals of feminine beauty that they could interpret more directly in their images of female saints.

Memlinc's portrait may be compared with the idealised head of his *Virgin* at Lisbon, a panel of the same size and approximately the same date (plate 31). The resemblances, which are striking, are far from coincidental. Here are the same raised eyebrows, the same elongated nose, a similar lack of attention to bone structure. Maria Portinari is distinguished from the Virgin mainly by the peculiarities of her nose and chin, which are understressed, and by the particular details of her eyes. There is a less close correspondence between Van der Goes's head of Maria and his idealised representations of saints, for example the two saints standing behind Maria in the altarpiece (plate 32).

Both painters to some extent transformed Maria's features by subjecting them to certain personal or fashionable ideals of beauty, but Memlinc flattered, disguising as far as possible the strange shape of Maria's nose and smoothing out, under an even light, the contours and relief of her face. In the Van der Goes portrait, the nose breaks the contour of the face while the hat meets the head at an angle and the continuity of the contour lines is again interrupted; whereas Memlinc preserves a gentle, curving and continuous contour for both hat and face. Van der Goes does not hesitate to stress the ugly nose and records tendons and bones which Memlinc ignores. From such observations, it may be concluded that Van der Goes's portrait of Maria must be a considerably more truthful and less idealised likeness than Memlinc's.

In sixteenth-century Italy, the enchantment of theorists and artists with the Platonic *idea* and with concepts of absolute beauty led to some confusion over the desirability of idealisation in portraiture. Michelangelo, since he 'abhorred drawing anything from life unless it was of the utmost beauty', was said to have executed only one portrait, a drawing of his handsome friend and patron Tommaso de' Cavalieri.[44] In 1587, the theorist Armenini arrived at a ridiculously

31 (facing page) Hans Memlinc, *Virgin and Child*, oak panel, 44.5 × 32 cm., Museu Nacional de Arte Antiga, Lisbon (1065).

The panel is so similar to Memlinc's authenticated pictures that there can be no doubt about its attribution; its dating is problematic but the style of the landscape indicates that it may have been painted in about 1470.

See Friedländer, 1967–76, VIa, p. 52 (49); here p. 22.

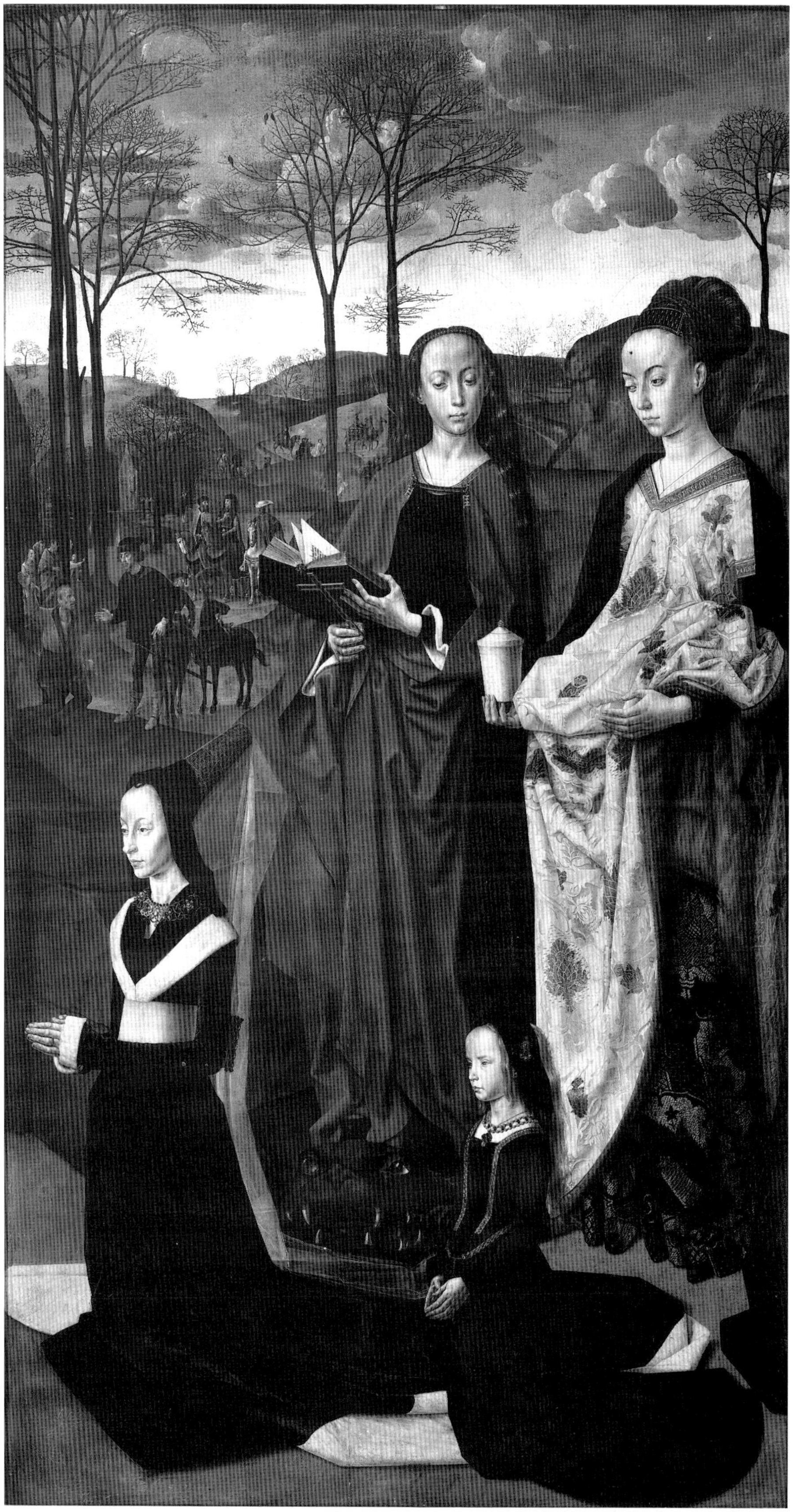

32 Hugo van der Goes, *Maria Portinari and her Daughter Margherita presented by St Margaret and St Mary Magdalen*, right wing of the 'Portinari Triptych', oak panel, 253 × 141 cm., Uffizi, Florence (3193).

Tommaso Portinari, his two eldest sons and two saints appear on the left wing (plate 192); in the centre panel is represented the *Adoration of the Shepherds*. The vast triptych, commissioned by Tommaso for the high altar of the church of Sant'Egidio in Florence, arrived in Florence in 1483. Van der Goes had died during the previous year. He appears to have begun work on the altarpiece in the mid-1470s and to have painted his portrait of Tommaso shortly before Tommaso left the Netherlands for Italy in 1477 (see the note to plate 192). The portraits of Maria and their children were probably executed in 1477–8, for they remained in the Low Countries for some time before rejoining Tommaso in Italy in 1478.

See Berti, 1979, p. 560; here pp. 16–22, 232.

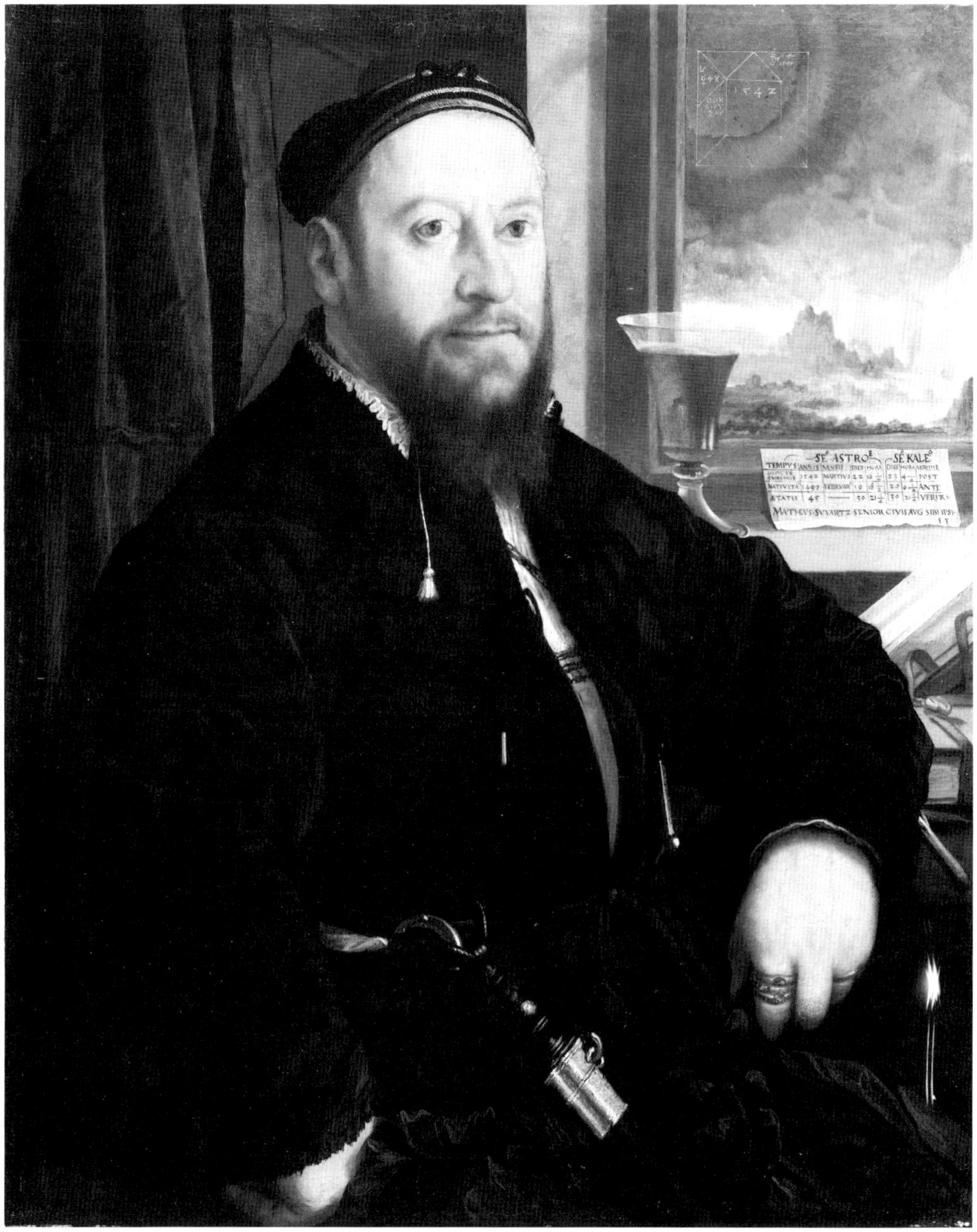

33 Christoph Amberger, *Matthäus Schwarz*, pine panel, 74 × 61.5 cm., Fondazione Thyssen-Bornemisza, Lugano (2).

On the paper are inscriptions stating that 'Matthäus Schwarz the elder, citizen of Augsburg, caused this to be made of himself' and giving the exact time of his birth, his age and the day and hour of painting – 4.15 p.m. on 22 March 1542. On the window pane is his horoscope, again dated 1542. The pendant portrait of his wife Barbara Mangolt, painted in August 1542, is in a private collection. On Matthäus, see the note to plate 18; for other portraits of him, see plates 18, 152, 230. This portrait and its pair were copied, adapted as full lengths, by Jeremias Schemel in the *Trachtenbuch* of Veit Konrad Schwarz, son of Matthäus (Herzog Anton Ulrich-Museum, Brunswick, H. 27, Nr. 51). In the inscriptions above the copies, it is noted that the originals are by Amberger.

See Fink, 1963, pp. 186–9; here pp. 25, 99, 128.

extreme conclusion: 'portraits by excellent artists are considered to be painted with better style [*maniera*] and greater perfection than others, but more often than not they are less good likenesses'.[45]

The penetrating portrait-painter does not merely reproduce what he sees before him; he may exaggerate or distort certain of his sitter's features so as to enhance the likeness; he will almost inevitably idealise; but he must also give some knowledge of the personality and likely behaviour of the sitter. This process, generally known as characterisation, has two principal facets: an expression of the sitter's public identity and status, which is almost always desired; and an analysis of his private self, which may not always be strictly desirable but which came to be expected.

It was obviously important that the sitter could be readily identified and this

34 English, 1390s, *Richard II, King of England*, panel, 213.5 × 110 cm., Westminster Abbey, London.

Much damaged and overpainted, most recently during a campaign of restoration in 1866, when the raised patterns of the gilded background were almost entirely removed, the portrait is difficult to assess. A photograph taken before the restoration is not of very high quality but shows that the picture was in a much damaged state. For a sixteenth-century version, see Strong, 1969^2, p. 46. The head, particularly in its repainted state, closely resembles the effigy on Richard's tomb, made during his lifetime in 1394–9. Attempts to associate the picture with a payment made in 1395 are not altogether convincing. It was possibly painted on the back of a choir stall.

See Hepburn, 1986, pp. 13–26; here pp. 25, 56, 81, 112.

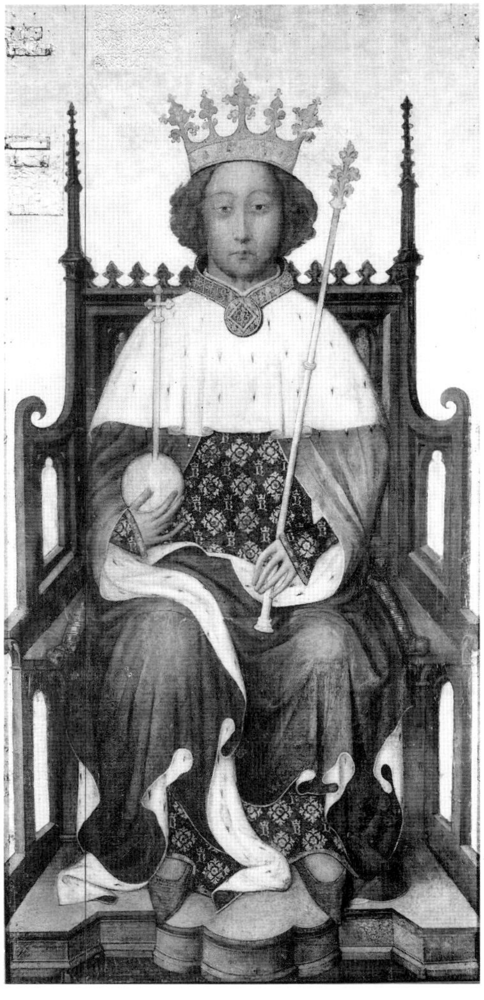

might be simply managed by introducing an inscription recording his name and title or designation, a coat of arms or other heraldic device or a merchant's mark. They could be included, obviously or discreetly, within the painting, on the frame or on the reverse (plates 8, 63–6, 133, 154, 213, 235). The sitter's age and the date of the portrait were very frequently given. In Amberger's portrait of Matthäus Schwarz (plate 33), inscriptions on the paper propped on the window-sill identify the sitter as 'Matthäus Schwarz the elder, citizen of Augsburg', who 'caused this to be made of himself', and state the exact hours and dates of his birth (6.30 p.m. on 19 February 1497) and of the picture (4.15 p.m. on 22 March 1542), as well as his exact age (45 years 30 days and 21¾ hours). Above, as if drawn or engraved on the window-pane, is a diagram of his horoscope. The sitter's clothes and his surroundings will normally give some indication of his wealth and status, and perhaps also of his profession and interests. References to astrology and the physiological and psychological theory of the temperaments may be included, as in Cranach's portraits of Johannes Cuspinian and his wife (plates 143–4), while emblems held by the sitters or worn in the form of jewellery or embroidered ornament may refer to their names, families, occupations, interests or pretensions.

In certain portraits, the sitters are cast in the roles of gods, saints or heroes; in others, visual parallels, which would have been readily understood by a contemporary spectator, are made between the portraits and other works of art. Paintings of enthroned monarchs, for example that of Richard II of England (plate 34), often resemble images of the Deity: the ancient association between kings and gods, and the close relationships between the ways in which gods were represented and in which the persons and images of kings were shown to their peoples, endured for centuries. In 1592 or shortly afterwards, Elizabeth I of England was shown standing on a globe, on which a map of her kingdom was prominently displayed (plate 35). Christ was often depicted with the globe of the world at his feet. Elizabeth is described in the sonnet inserted in the cartouche on her left as 'The prince of light'; darkness is left behind her, banished from her sphere. The verbal and visual parallels between monarch and Christ are fairly explicit. In Bronzino's portrait of Eleonora da Toledo, Grand Duchess of Tuscany, the strangely dark sky pales to an area of almost pure blue pigment around her head, as though she were emitting light like a haloed saint in a religious image (plate 37). Bronzino in a letter of 1551 described her as 'full of goodness' and her husband as 'the most perfect lord who ever has been'; when he saw her children, he seemed to perceive 'so many angels' and, when he heard them, to be listening to 'spirits from Heaven'.[46] In a portrait by Bronzino of an unidentified lady, the draperies behind her appear to spring from her shoulders like angels' wings (plate 38).[47] Here the visual parallel made between sitter and angel need not be taken too seriously, for the painting contains another pictorial jest in the shape of the two grotesque heads carved on the arm of the sitter's chair. Their indecorous expressions contrast entertainingly with the lady's prim countenance, but only her right eye and the right corner of her mouth show a serious concern for propriety, while her left eye and the left corner of her mouth have an expression of amusement not unlike that of the grotesque head beneath her left hand. Even on her serious right side, her hair is in some disarray; perhaps her primness and her angelic qualities were kept up only with much effort. The extremely small book that she holds might be a reference to the extent of her intellectual interests.

Visual parallels might also be made between portraits and antique works of art: portraits, or images of classical deities. Less specific, and less immediately obvious

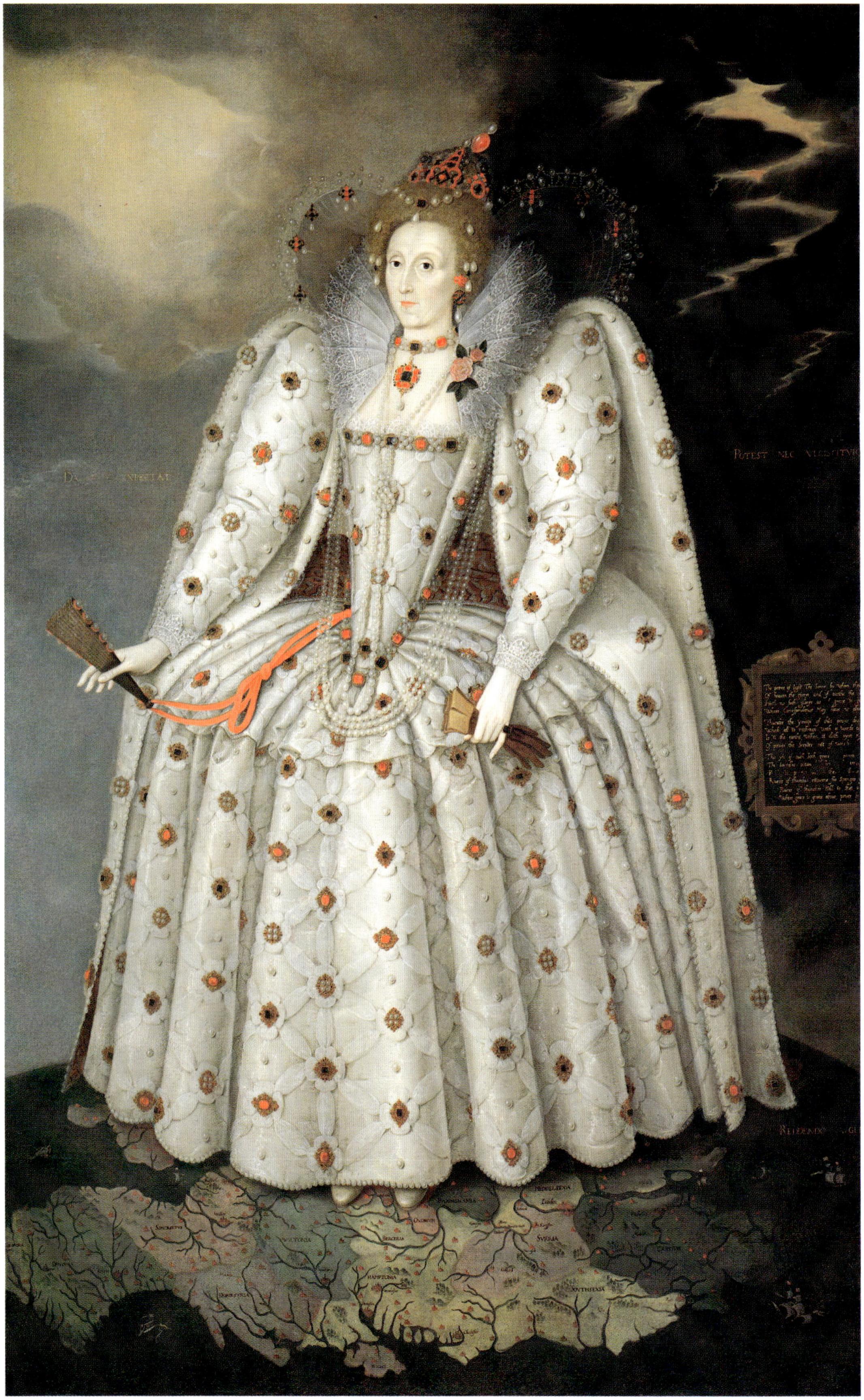

35 English, 1592(?), *Elizabeth I of England: The Ditchley Portrait*, canvas, 241.3 × 152.4 cm., National Portrait Gallery, London (2561).

The picture comes from Ditchley in Oxfordshire, the seat of Sir Henry Lee, who entertained Elizabeth there in September 1592. She stands on a map of England, based on one published in 1583 by John Saxton, and her feet are close to the site of Ditchley. It is assumed that the portrait was commissioned to commemorate the visit; it has been attributed to Marcus Gheeraerts the Younger.

For the inscriptions, and for further comment, see Strong, 1969[1], pp. 104–7; here p. 25.

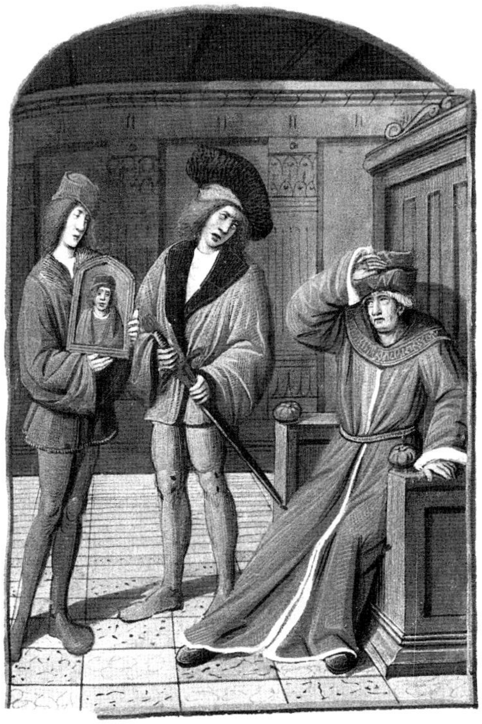

36 French, c. 1490, *Physonomyas and the Disciples of Hippocrates*, parchment, 19 × 13 cm., from the 'Gouvernement des princes' sold at Sotheby's, London, 22 June 1982 (52), f. 85.

See the sale catalogue, pp. 54–60; here p. 27.

37 (foll. page) Bronzino, *Eleonora da Toledo, Grand Duchess of Tuscany, with her Son Giovanni*, panel, 115 × 96 cm., Uffizi, Florence (748).

Eleonora married Cosimo I de' Medici in 1539; their eldest son Francesco was born in 1541, their second son Giovanni in 1543. Bronzino painted a portrait of Eleonora accompanied by Francesco and another of her with Giovanni: both are listed in an inventory of 1560 (Beck, 1974, p. 66) but only the second is mentioned by Vasari (Vasari-Milanesi, 1878–85, vii, p. 598). Comparisons with other portraits indicate that the child here is Giovanni. The picture would therefore have been painted in the mid-1540s.

See Langedijk, 1981–3, i, pp. 98–9, 695–6; Plazzotta, 1988, pp. 16–32; here pp. 25, 65, 121, 124, plates 4, 126.

references to other works of art might occur. In his portrait of Eleonora da Toledo, Bronzino has falsified the tonal relations in the head and the colours in the flesh so that the sitter's face appears unnaturally pale, smooth, shiny and hard, and her eyes are less luminous than the pearls of her necklaces. The sheen of the skin is unexpected and the dullness of the eyes is unnatural, for the whites are far from white, and the small vertical brushstrokes of the catchlights are confined to the irises and do not contrast strongly enough in tone to suggest a glistening translucency. The eyes are merely lustrous. Eleonora is made to resemble a highly finished carving of ivory with eyes of semi-opaque gems (plate 4).

Many contemporaries, seeing the sitters' faces or their portraits, would have recalled the precepts of physiognomy, defined by Pomponius Gauricus in 1504 as 'a way of observing by which we deduce the qualities of souls from the features of bodies'.[48] It was a subject that interested many artists[49] and that was expounded in widely circulated books, the *Physiognomica* and the *Secretum Secretorum*, then believed to have been written by Aristotle. A miniature from a manuscript of the *Secretum*, thought to have been executed in France in about 1490, illustrates a passage in which it is narrated how pupils of Hippocrates brought his portrait to Physonomyas, the supposed founder of the discipline of physiognomy (plate 36). Asked for his opinion of the picture, Physonomyas replied, 'This man is a wrangeler lecherous and rude'. The young men angrily rebutted his claims and returned to Hippocrates, who explained that the diagnosis was indeed correct but that 'reason that is in me ouercometh and ruleth the vyces of my complexyon'.[50] Physiognomy has always been a controversial subject and in England, by an Act of Parliament passed in 1597–8, 'all idle persons . . . fayning themselves to have knowledge in Phisiognomye Palmestry or other like crafty Scyence, or pretending that they can tell Destenyes Fortunes or such other like fantasticall Ymagynacions' were to 'be stripped naked from the middle upwards' and 'openly whipped untill his or her body be bloudye'.[51] In *Macbeth*, Shakespeare wrote for Duncan the lines:

> There's no art
> To find the mind's construction in the face[52]

and indeed the principles of physiognomy seem to be of limited relevance to the study of portraiture.

Further indications of the sitter's personality were given by his pose and facial expression. Influenced by classical texts, Leonardo wrote that 'painting considers the working of the mind as reflected in the movements of the body'.[53] Those who wish to interpret poses and expressions should rely on a combination of empathy and common sense. Contemporary tracts on etiquette are unhelpful, for they are concerned mainly with the rules of precedence; while those on rhetoric and rhetorical gesture tend to follow classical sources rather closely. A cursory look at classical and Renaissance books on rhetoric will demonstrate what should, perhaps, be obvious: that, in European civilisations, the same gestures and expressons have always made the same emotional signals and produced the same reactions. Though Quintilian's advice to the orators of ancient Rome may be useful in explaining the special significance of certain complex gestures of the hands, its value is limited. Gestures and expressions in portraits are open to objective, if empathetic, analysis, which can, if necessary, be backed up by citing contemporary texts.[54] Yet much writing on this aspect of portraiture is wildly subjective and vague and fails to distinguish between the writer's and the artist's apprehensions of the sitter.

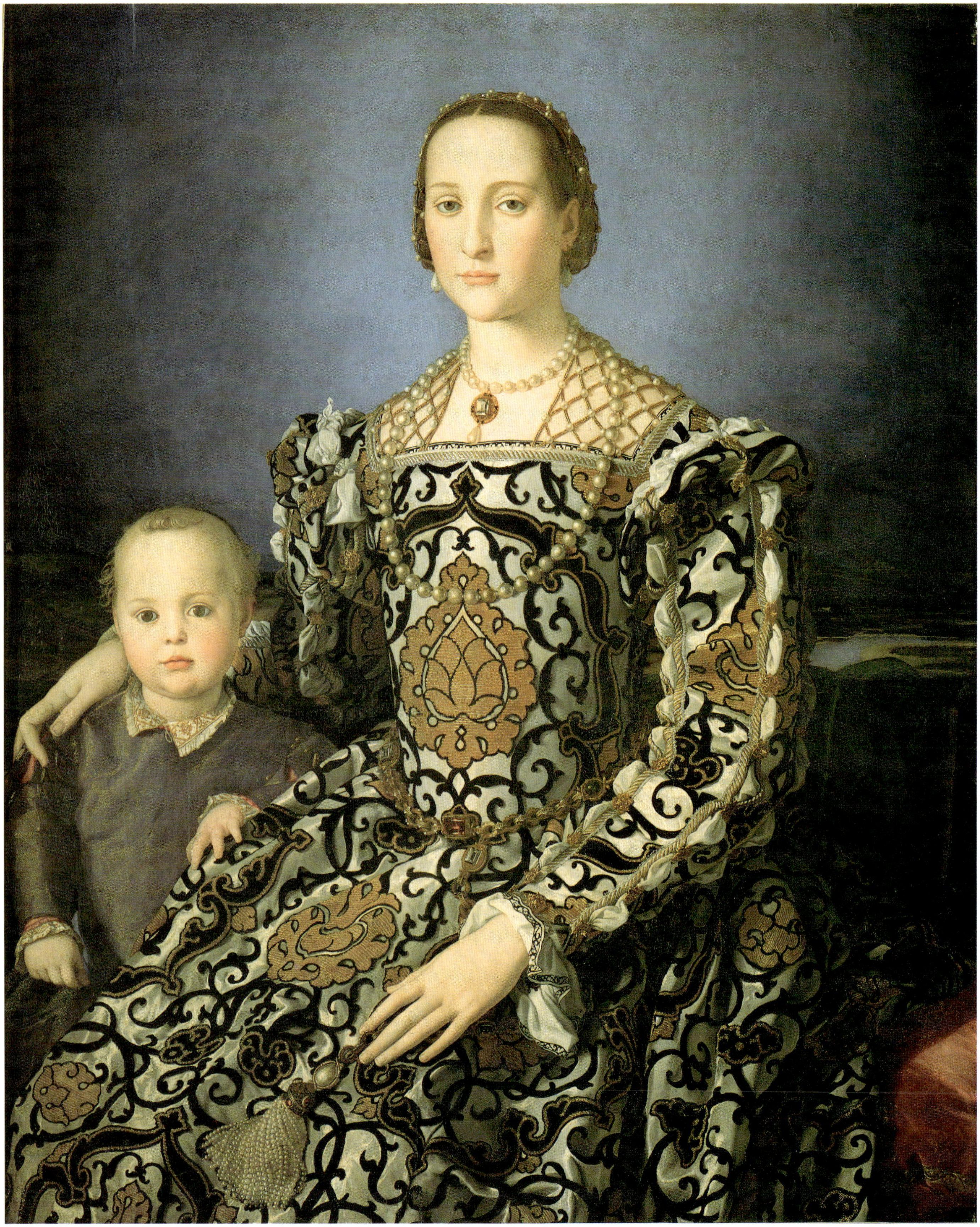

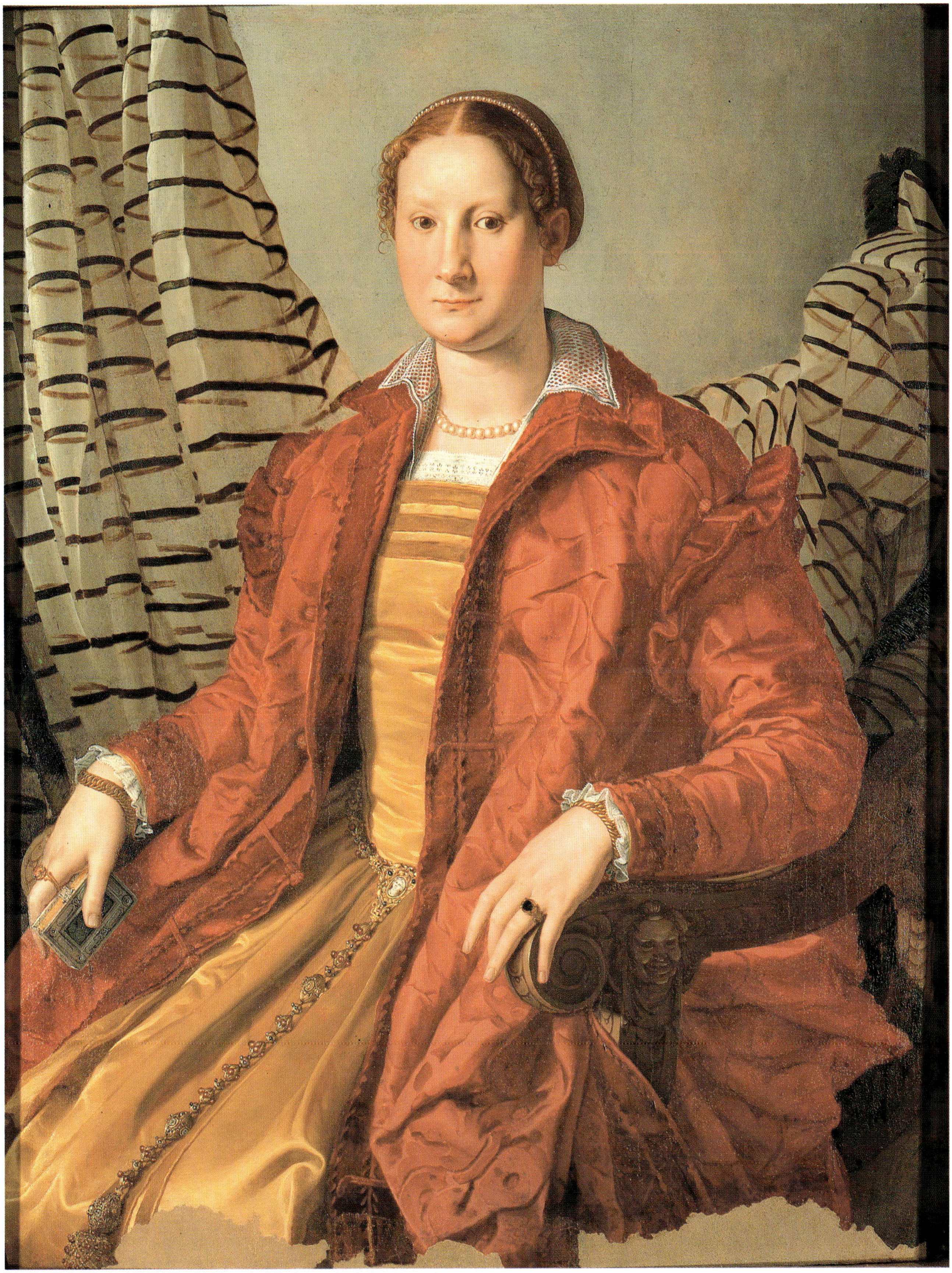

38 (prev. page) Bronzino, *Lady*, panel, 109 × 85 cm., Galleria Sabauda, Turin (262).

There are no indications of the sitter's identity. The portrait is attributed to Bronzino on stylistic grounds and may be dated, from the costume, around 1550.

See Baccheschi, 1973, p. 100; here pp. 25, 61, 65, 99, 115, 124, plate 41.

39 Giovanni Bellini, *Leonardo Loredan, Doge of Venice*, poplar panel, 61.5 × 45 cm., National Gallery, London (189).

The sitter (1436–1521) became doge in 1501. Bellini's portrait, signed but not dated, was probably painted in or shortly after 1501.

See Davies, 1961, pp. 55–6; here pp. 30, 69, 120, plate 46.

Most facial expressions are fleeting, and portrait-painters have rarely chosen to give their sitters fixed and well-defined expressions. Many have either avoided marked facial expressions altogether or rendered expressions of a subtlety difficult to define. Some portrait heads appear to change expression as they are examined: here the artists have made an effort, conscious or instinctive, to achieve a certain mobility in static images by varying slightly the expressions of eyes and mouths so that, when attention is concentrated on one feature, one expression is caught, and when attention is focussed elsewhere, another expression takes its place. Giovanni Bellini's portrait of Leonardo Loredan, probably painted shortly after the sitter became Doge of Venice in 1501, is a static official image with the armless rigidity of a Roman bust (plate 39). Yet the expression seems to change, for the lit side of the sitter's face is more severe, the shadowed side more benign (plate 46). This is to be explained partly in terms of the painter's manipulation of the sitter's features and partly in terms of his use of light. The doge's right eyebrow contracts and weighs heavily on the eye to give a frowning aspect; the catchlight in his right eye is intense and the upper lid is raised well clear of the pupil, to suggest a glare. The eyes are very widely spaced. Above the sitter's left eye, the eyebrow lies more easily in its natural place, the catchlight in this eye is weaker, the upper lid is closer to the pupil and the corner of the eye is raised. The lines running from the cheeks towards the corners of the mouth differ: on the sitter's right the line is straight and suggests a set, stern expression; while on the sitter's left, the line curves, giving a more relaxed impression and appearing to attract into the arc of its curve the centre line of the mouth, which as a result seems to rise upwards. An incipient smile may be suggested by this small area of the face. The strings of the hat, hanging untidily when all else is immaculately ordered, are brought forward in impossible perspective. The string on the sitter's right is assertively straight and vertical and is strongly lit; on the sitter's left, the string is in shadow and falls away from the vertical in a more broken, gentler line. The strings consequently play a secondary part in echoing the contrasts between the two sides of the face.

In his portrait of Baldassare Castiglione, Raphael has achieved a mobility of expression by contrasting the sizes and shapes of the eyebrows and eyes and the differing placings of the catchlights and pupils within the irises (plate 243). The sitter was conscious of the variability of expression in the portrait, if not of the means by which it was effected, for in a poem he imagined his wife, in his absence, contemplating the picture and thinking that it seemed to move and to wish to speak.[55]

Holbein's skill in individualising his sitters by exaggerating the asymmetries of their features has already been commented upon. It inevitably entailed the creation of small contradictions in expression which he exploited with the greatest subtlety in portraits such as the *Man aged Thirty Nine*, dated 1533 (plate 40). The coat of arms in the sitter's ring identifies him as a member of the Wedigh family of Cologne and he is assumed to have been one of the merchants of the Hanseatic community in London. In the portrait there is no allusion to his mercantile interests, but his gloves, ring and clothes give some indication of his prosperity, while the pose of his right hand echoes that used by ancient Roman sculptors in their portraits of orators, seen resting one hand in their togas. Attention is concentrated on the face, for cranium and body are greatly diminished in scale, and the features, which occupy an unnaturally large area of the face, are unusually irregular even in Holbein's work. The sitter's much larger and more open right eye lies beneath an eyebrow quizzically raised; it is separated by a very wide

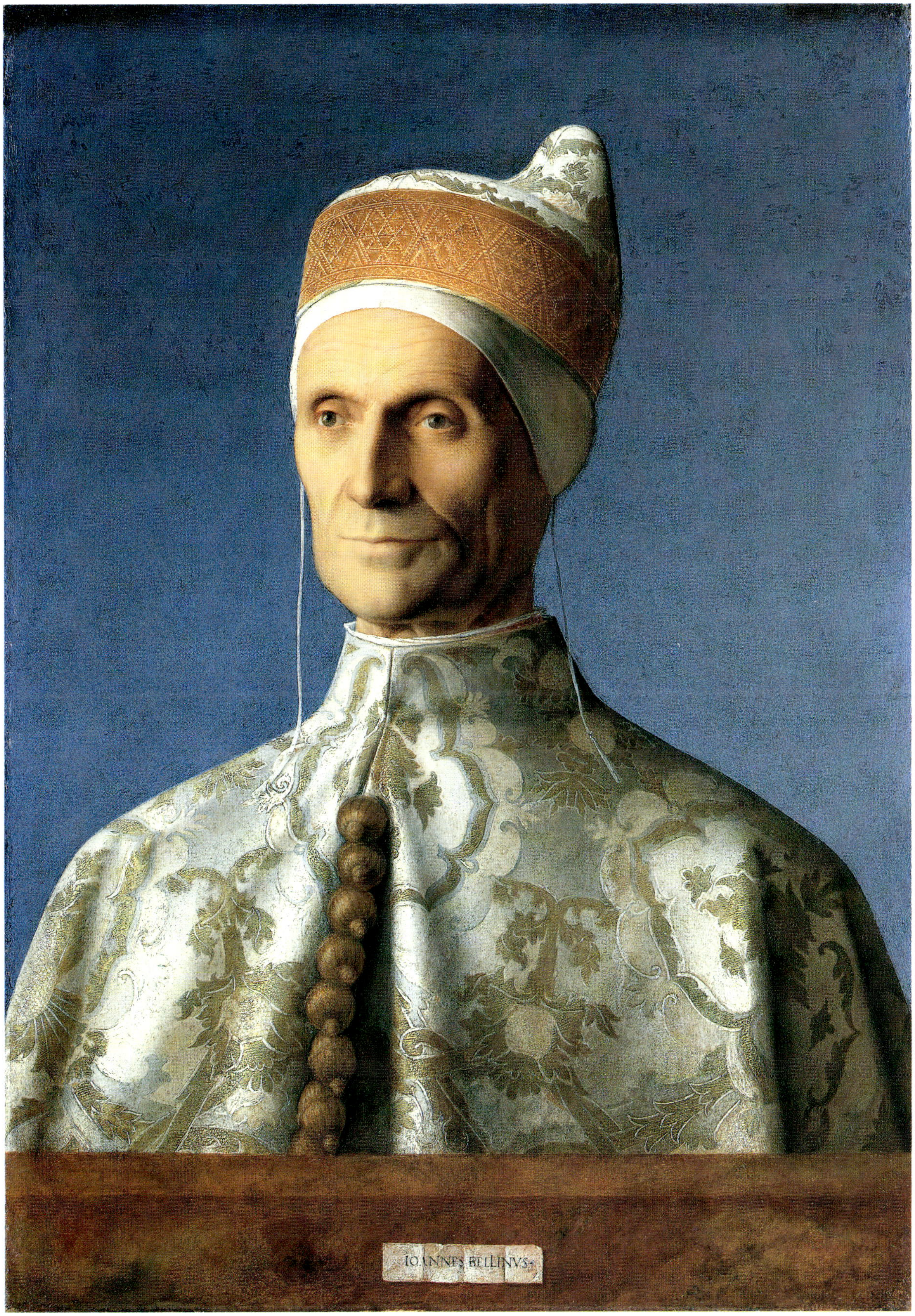
IOANNES BELLINVS

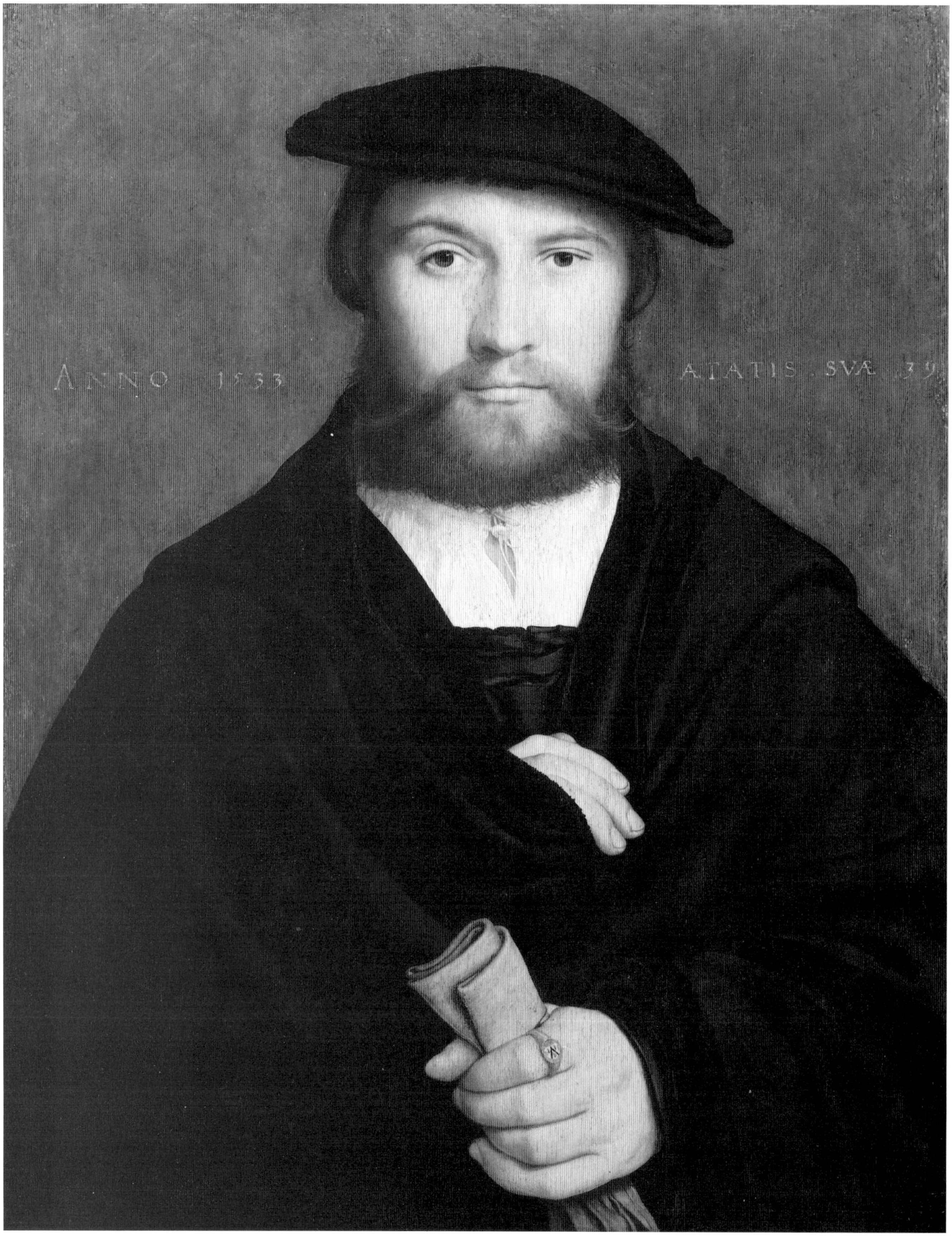
ANNO 1533
ATATIS SVÆ 39

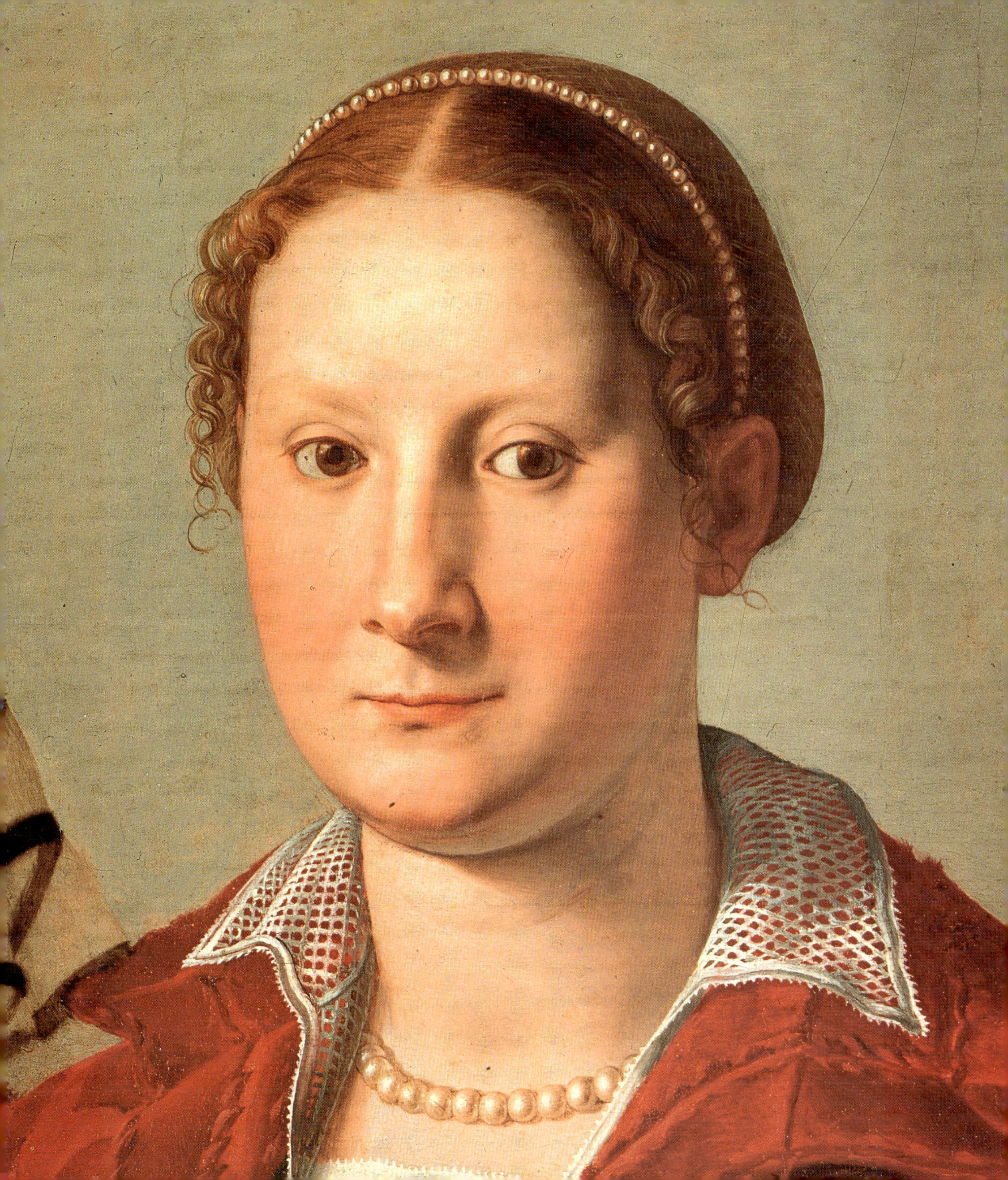

40 (p. 32) Hans Holbein the Younger, *Man aged Thirty Nine*, oak panel, 39 × 30cm., Staatliche Museen Preussischer Kulturbesitz, Berlin (West), Gemäldegalerie (586 B).

Inscribed 'ANNO 1533/ AETATIS. SVAE 39', the portrait would have been painted in London. The coat of arms in the sitter's ring is that of the Cologne family of Wedigh. A companion portrait of Hermann(?) Wedigh, signed with Holbein's monogram and dated 1532, shows a younger sitter wearing a similar ring and is now at New York (50.135.4).

See Rowlands, 1985, pp. 138–9; here pp. 30–4, 81, 127, 128.

41 (prev. page) Bronzino, *Lady*, detail (see plate 38).

42 Hans Holbein the Younger, *Georg Gisze*, oak panel, 96.3 × 85.7 cm., Staatliche Museen Preussischer Kulturbesitz, Berlin (West), Gemäldegalerie (586).

The sitter is identified by the inscriptions on the paper above his head, on the wall on our left and on the letters in his hands and in the rack beside him. Born in 1497 into a merchant family at Gdańsk, he was residing in 1532 in the Hanseatic community in London. He died in 1562.

See Rowlands, 1985, pp. 82–3, 137; here pp. 34, 74, 86, 127, plate 156.

space from his left eye, which looks between narrowed lids from under a nearly horizontal eyebrow. The point of the nose and the centre line of the mouth slant downwards to the sitter's right, so that the counterpoint of expression works on diagonal axes rather than according to the vertical divisions of the faces in the *Loredan* and the *Castiglione*. If concentration is fixed on Wedigh's right eye or the left side of his mouth, his aspect is quite friendly; but his left eye and the right side of his mouth are sadder and more forbidding.

In a larger and much more elaborate portrait of another Hanseatic merchant, Georg Gisze, painted by Holbein in 1532, the process of characterisation is taken further (plate 42). The sitter's name appears on the letter that he is opening, on the letters in the rack beside him and in the inscriptions on the wall behind him and the paper above his head. This paper appears to be stuck with sealing wax either to the panelling or, because it overlaps the ledger on the upper shelf, to the surface of the painting itself. The space in which Gisze is situated, though totally convincing, is seen in completely false perspective. Holbein has flattened out the corner of the panelled room, where the table in the foreground and the shelf in the upper right corner meet the walls in impossible conjunctions, in order to display more effectively around the sitter the many objects that suggest his wealth, his efficiency as a businessman, his piety, his intellectual interests and his love of beautiful things. The design and the distribution of colour are contrived so that the sitter's head dominates the composition and the spectator's attention is not unnecessarily distracted by the subsidiary details. The inscription, in Greek and Latin, on the paper above the head certifies that 'the countenance which you see' is an accurate image of Gisze.[56] Richly dressed, he nevertheless appears uneasy amid all the outward signs of his success. Holbein has made many of his customary adjustments and the head, though doubtless a faithful likeness, is far from a mechanically accurate record of the sitter's features. As usual, the face is enlarged and the cranium diminished; the nose is set further into profile than the rest of the face and its contour is altered at the bridge so that the far eye, brought forward out of perspective, is seen in its entirety. The eyes and eyebrows and the corners of the mouth are not matched in shape. The sitter's right eye and the right side of his mouth turn downwards; the lines of his right eyebrow and above his right eye suggest a slight frown; whereas the left side of his face is relatively more relaxed and serene. The strained glance from the corners of his eyes puts further stress on the unease of the sitter, and it is tempting to associate these signs of evident discomfort with the Latin motto lettered on the wall, 'No joy without sorrow/G. Gisze'.[57] It is almost as if he has written and signed it there, and it can be no accident that the balance which hangs alongside is not securely suspended from its hook and is about to fall to the floor. Holbein must here be making a concealed comment on the mental state of his sitter.

Characterisation is taken to an unusual degree of penetration in two portraits of an unidentified man and woman painted, probably in the 1510s, by Quinten Metsys (plates 43, 44). Though originally they may have formed one picture on a single panel, they are now separated.[58] The sitters, simply enough dressed, are nevertheless sufficiently affluent to own an expensive prayer-book, decorated in a fashionable style. The strange architecture in which they appear, though it does not suggest any specific setting, is luxurious in its materials and modish in its forms. The man looks up at his wife as he nervously fingers his prayer beads: the shy intrusion of his right thumb, just appearing above the lower edge of the panel, gives his gesture a very tentative air. His lips are parted, as if he may be about to

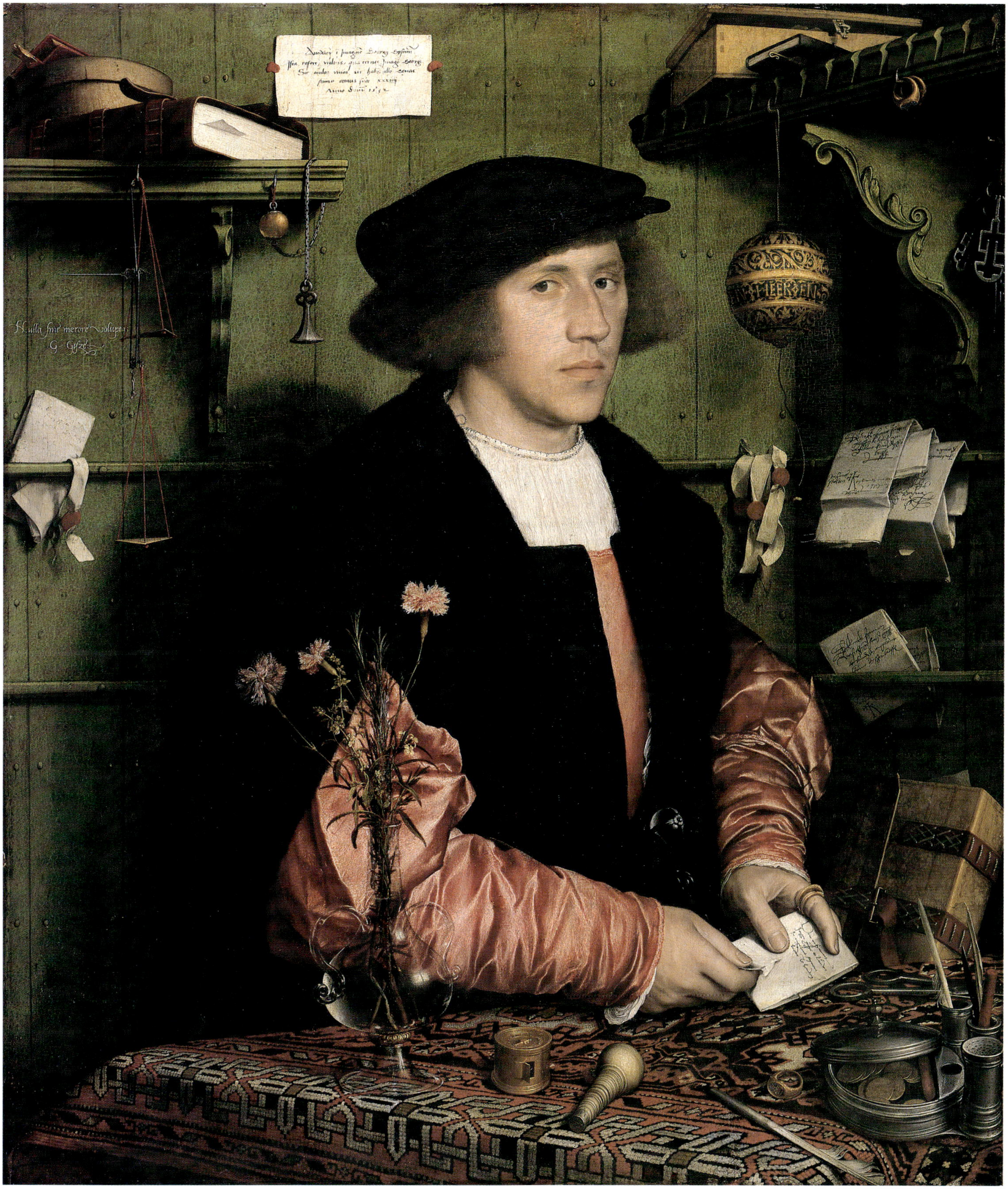

43 Quinten Metsys, *Man*, panel, 47.6 × 41.5 cm., Private Collection, Switzerland.

The pair to the portrait reproduced as plate 44.

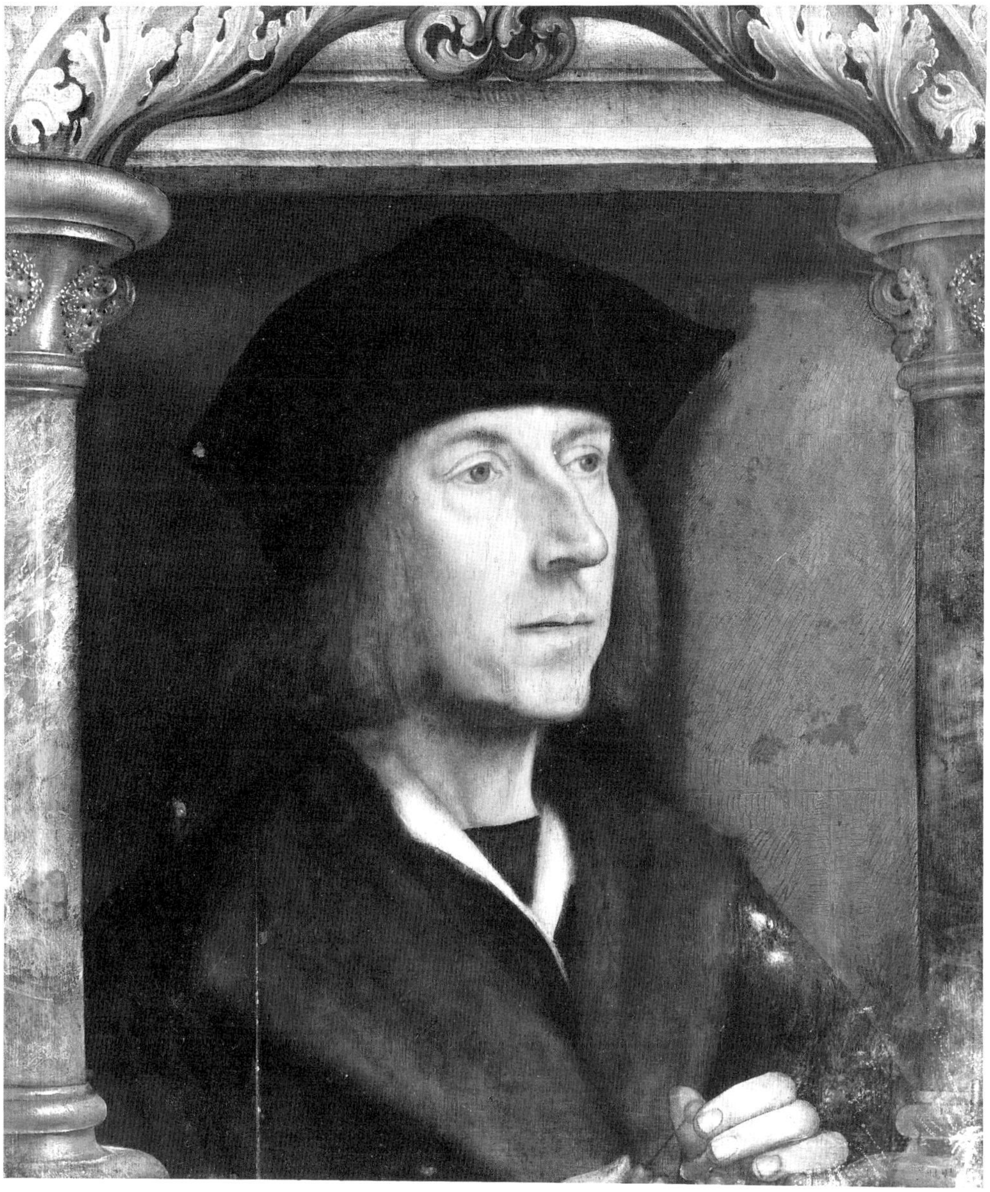

speak; but the lady turns away, determined to ignore not only him but also her prayer-book, and indeed ourselves. Her unassilable solidity is stressed by the lighting and by the rectangles and pyramids of the composition, whereas the composition of her husband's portrait is based on the less stable geometric form of the lozenge. Metsys has given every reason to suspect the lady of uncharitable and uncompromising strength of character. This is perhaps as far as painted criticism can be taken in portraits that were presumably commissioned; the lady herself may have been impervious to Metsys's visual comments.

Metsys's portraits, it may be deduced, are honest expressions of his respectively sympathetic and critical reactions to his two sitters. But for many sitters, the great attraction of portraiture is its power to falsify: if portrait-painters wish, or if they are compelled, they can not only flatter their sitters, dress them in expensive clothes, place them in grand settings and give misleading indications of their ranks, tastes and interests, but also invent for them psychological traits that they

44 Quinten Metsys, *Lady*, panel, painted surface 47.4 × 41.4 cm., Metropolitan Museum of Art, New York (32.100.47).

The pair to the portrait reproduced as plate 43. It is possible that the two paintings were originally a double portrait on one panel, now sawn in two. There are no indications of the sitters' identities. The attribution to Metsys, made on stylistic grounds, is convincing; the sitters' clothes are in the fashion of about 1510–20.

See Wehle and Salinger, 1947, pp. 107–8; here pp. 34–6, 109.

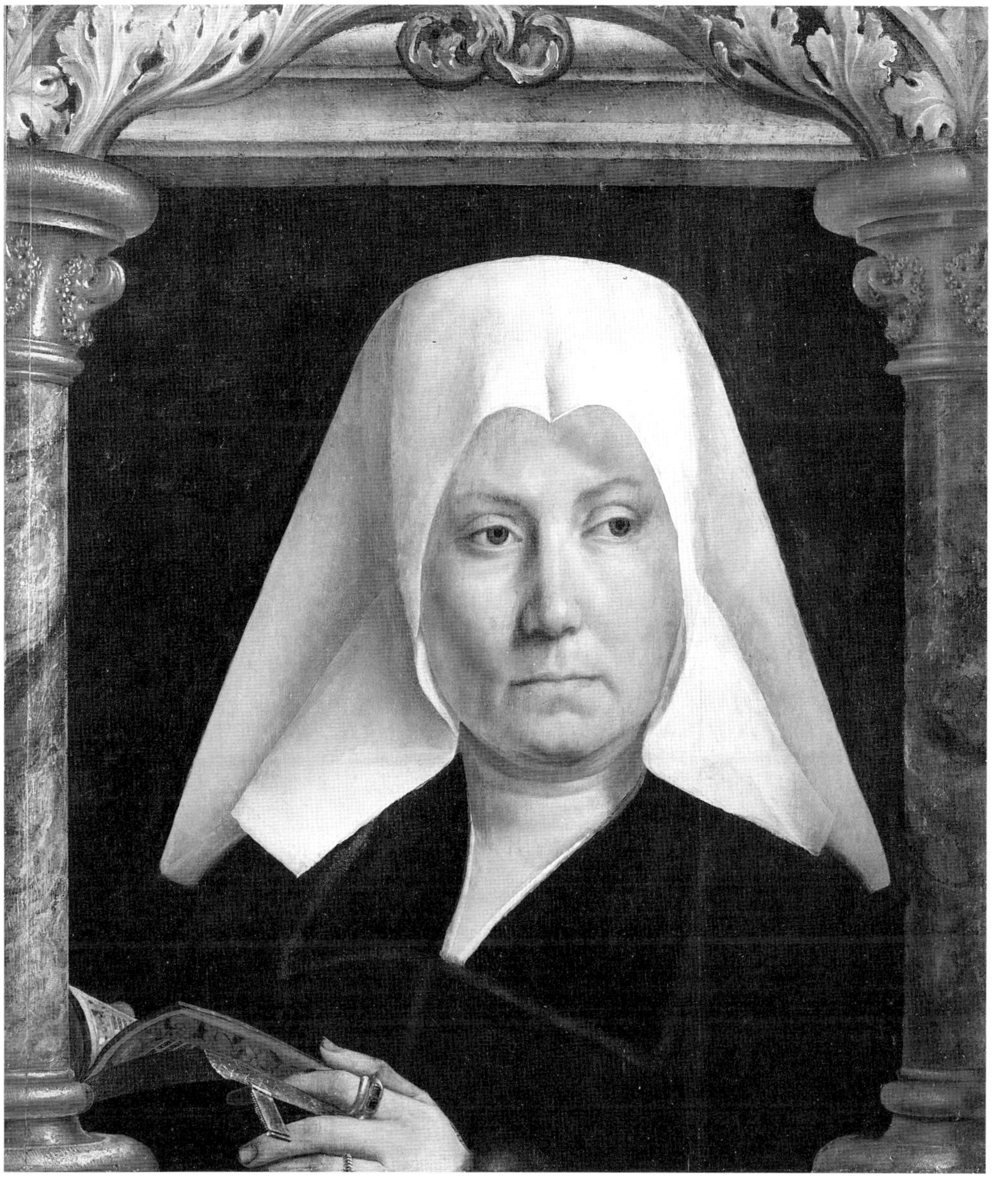

do not in nature possess. It is not always easy to distinguish the honest from the falsified portrait, the more objectively observed from the more subjectively created image, but, if many portraits of different sitters by the same artist are seen, the objectivity of the painter can be assessed. Van der Weyden, for example, was not an objective portraitist. All his sitters are idealised in the same way, are similarly posed and have similar expressions of noble piety (plates 28, 154, 250). Though his portraits present highly subjective, contrived and falsified images of his sitters, they are nonetheless as beautiful and as interesting as his religious subjects, which are treated in much the same manner.[59] A portrait is usually the most intimate record available of a sitter's personality. Written sources are as biassed and as difficult to interpret as visual ones and demand a similar application of critical empathy and sound common sense.

Not surprisingly, contemporaries disagreed about the value of portraits, their reliability and the extent to which deductions could be made from them about the

45 Titian, *Eleonora Gonzaga, Duchess of Urbino*, canvas, 114 × 103 cm., Uffizi, Florence (919).

The pair to the portrait reproduced as plate 198. The sitter (1493–1550) was the daughter of Gianfrancesco Gonzaga, Marquis of Manuta, and Isabella d'Este; she married in 1509 Francesco Maria della Rovere, Duke of Urbino. Titian's portraits of the duke and duchess were painted in 1536–8.

See the exhibition catalogue Florence, 1978–9, pp. 121–4 (29); here pp. 39, 61, 107, 124, 220–2.

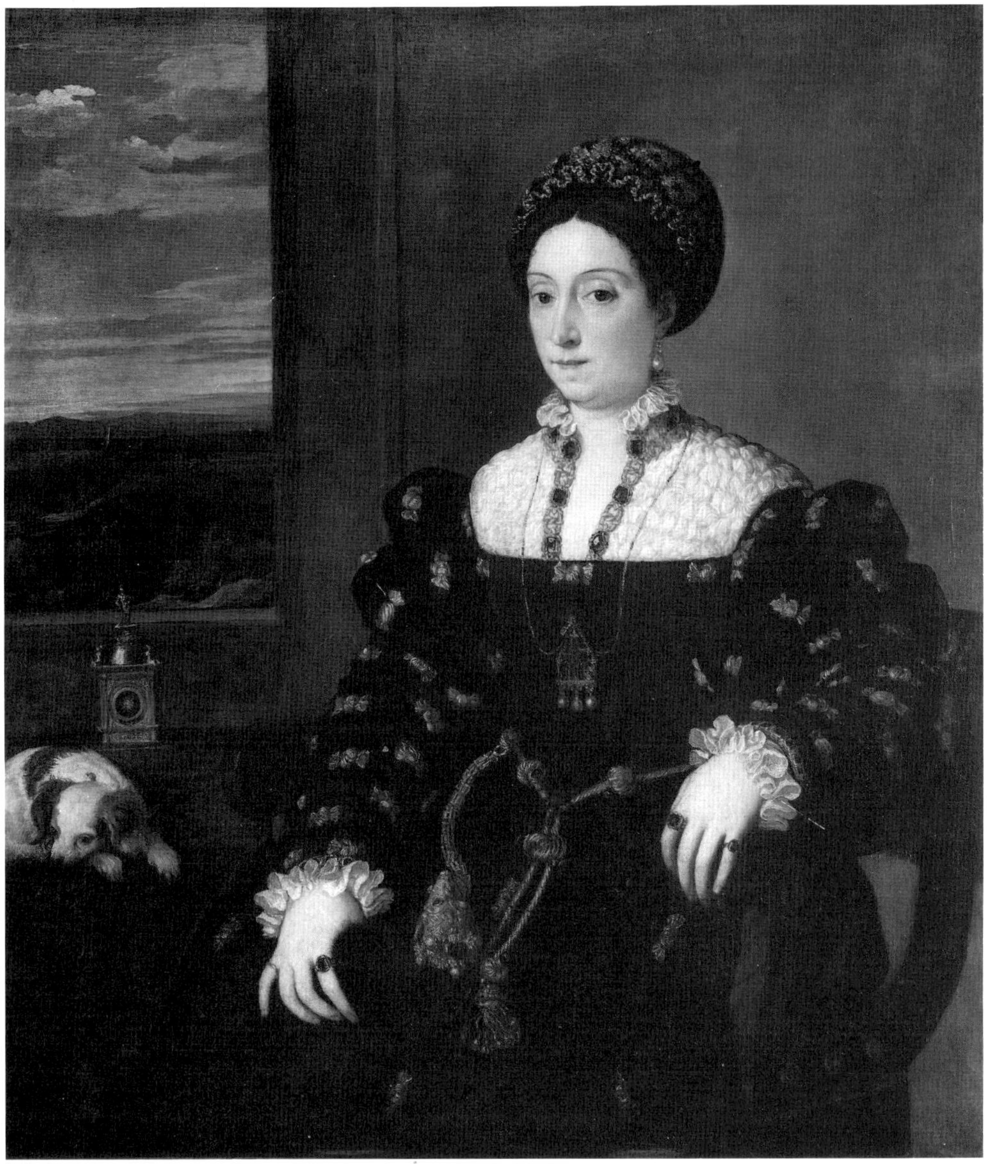

sitters. Sir Thomas Smith, discussing portraits of Queen Elizabeth I's suitors, remarked: 'if ye see two, not one shall be like the other: and if they be, what is the picture to the man?'[60] In 1570, Catherine de' Medici said of her son, Charles IX of France, that 'no painter is good enough to represent him to our satisfaction',[61] and in about 1572, it was apparently reported that her younger son, the future Henry III,

> suffers under the belief that all paintings do him injustice and that even Clouet himself has never captured that admirable *je ne sais quoi* with which nature has endowed him. His eyes, the charming animation of his mouth when he speaks, that gentleness with which he surprises those who have the honour to see him in private, cannot be effectively represented either by the brush or by the pen.[62]

When Henry believed himself in love with Madame de Châteauneuf, Philippe Desportes wrote a sonnet in which he reproved the court painter Jean Decourt for attempting the hopeless task of depicting her beauty: 'You are mistaken, Decourt, in thinking to represent Châteauneuf, the immortal goddess of love. Heaven, like an accomplished painter, has made her so beautiful that the divine portrait cannot be imitated.'[63] Martial's lines on a portrait of Marcus Antonius Primus were known to Renaissance artists, for they are inscribed upon Ghirlandaio's portrait of Giovanna Tornabuoni, which is dated 1488:

> Would that art could portray his/her character and mind!
> No painting in the world would be more beautiful![64]

The sentiments were echoed by Sofonisba Anguissola in a letter of 1561 to Pope Pius IV, to whom she was sending a portrait of Elisabeth of Valois, Queen of Spain: 'if the brush could represent the beauties of the queen's soul, to your eyes they would be marvellous. I have, however, used the utmost diligence to present what art can show . . .'.[65]

The opposite point of view was put, for example, in a letter written by Annibale Caro for the miniaturist Giulio Clovio in which Clovio thanked an unnamed female painter for a self-portrait that she had given to him. He perceived in it 'the grace of your countenance, the liveliness of your spirit and your excellence in that art which I profess'.[66] In a less rational vein, Aretino wrote a sonnet on Titian's portrait of Eleonora Gonzaga, Duchess of Urbino (plate 45):

> The union of colours laid in by Titian's brush expresses, besides the concord that reigns in Eleonora, her gentle spirit. Modesty [*modestia*] is seated with her in an attitude of humility, purity resides in her dress, modesty [*vergogna*] veils and honours her breast and hair. Love fixes on her his lordly glance. Chastity and beauty, eternal enemies, are in her likeness and between her eyelashes the throne of the Graces is seen.[67]

In the first scene of *Timon of Athens*, Shakespeare magnificently burlesqued such over-interpretation. A poet, meeting a painter who is bringing a portrait to Timon's house, praises the picture in extravagant terms:

> Admirable! How this grace
> Speaks his own standing! what a mental power
> This eye shoots forth! how big imagination
> Moves on this lip! to the dumbness of the gesture
> One might interpret . . .
> It tutors nature: artificial strife
> Lives in these touches, livelier than life.[68]

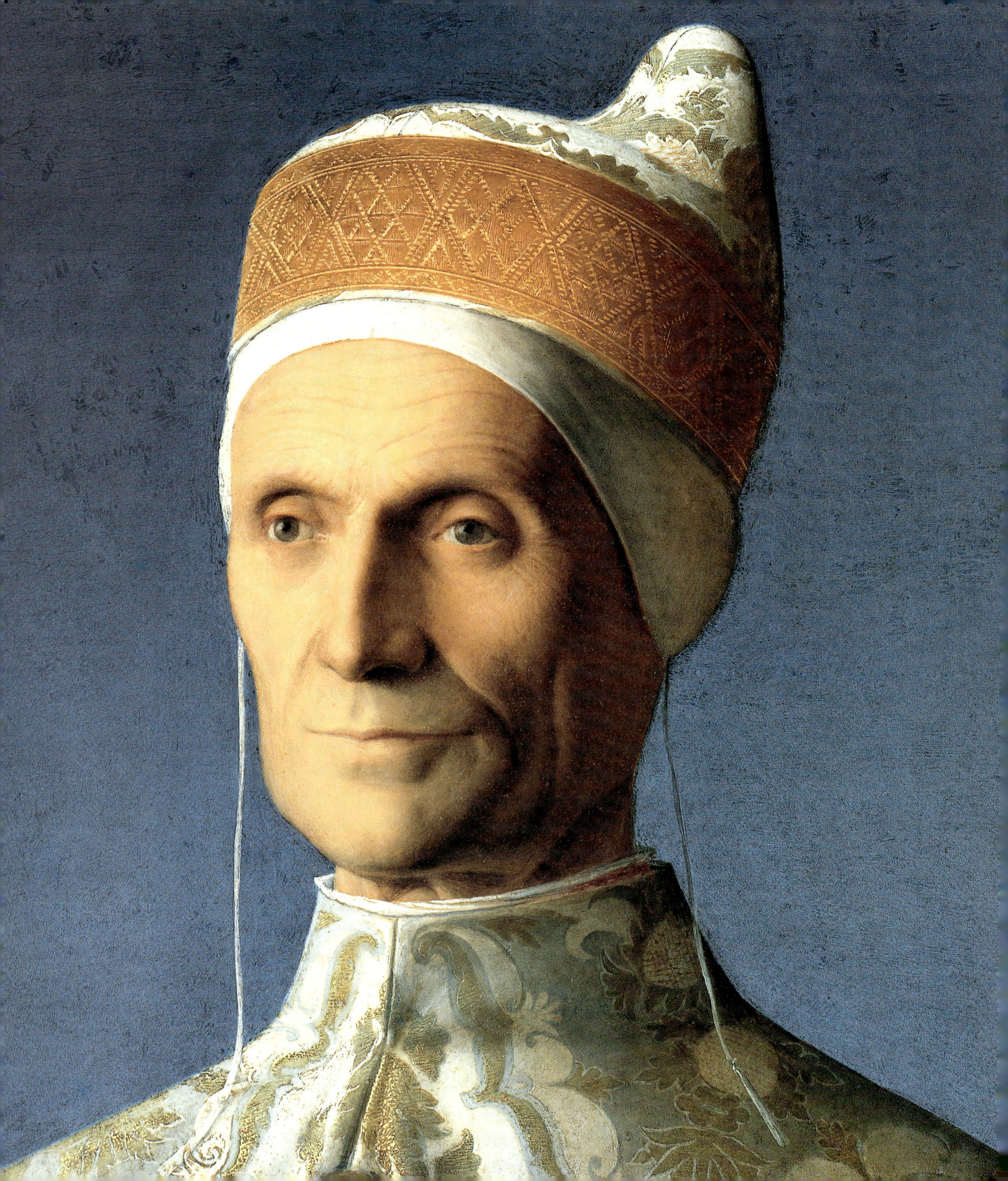

2 Portrait Types

Because vast numbers of portraits have been destroyed and because certain types of portrait and portraits of certain periods have been more vulnerable than others to changes in taste, it is essential to draw on documentary as well as visual evidence in order to establish when and where group portraits, double portraits, full-length and equestrian portraits, half-length portraits, portrait drawings and portrait miniatures were in fashion. Because Vasari and many later historians have tended to think in terms of of artistic 'progress' and have become obsessed with a desire to discover who was the first to employ this or that compositional formula, many rash assertions have been made and some have come to be widely accepted. Here, emphasis is put on fourteenth- and fifteenth-century portraits and documents in order to demonstrate that almost all the types of portrait produced during the sixteenth century were already being painted during the fifteenth century, if not earlier. In a book of this length, however, it is impossible to treat in detail all the ways in which sixteenth-century painters varied and developed the basic types.

1 Portrait Series

Series of portraits, of ruling princes or of famous men, were to be found in most parts of Europe. In 1323, for example, Hanyn Soyer was paid to provide portraits of Louis of Nevers, Count of Flanders (who ruled between 1322 and 1346), and his young wife Margaret of France for the magistrates' chamber at Ypres.[1] A series of murals of the Counts and Countesses of Flanders, preserved there until the building was destroyed during the First World War, showed the counts and their consorts standing in pairs, identified by their coats of arms and by inscriptions.[2] Another series of Counts of Flanders was at Courtrai, in the Chapel of the Counts at the Collegiate Church of Our Lady; the portraits, which were being worked on in 1372 by Jan van Hasselt, painter to the Count Louis of Male, decorated the walls of the chapel where Louis intended to be buried. Fragments of the murals, discovered in the mid-nineteenth century, were then considered too damaged to restore, but copies were made before the originals were covered over with new portraits. The counts were represented in full length, standing within niches, and were identified by their coats of arms and by inscriptions recording their names, dates, and burial places. Only countesses in their own right were included, such as Joanna of Constantinople (1182–1244): she and her husband were depicted standing within the same niche.[3] As at Ypres, the series was kept up to date; portraits of Philip the Bold, Duke of Burgundy, and his wife Margaret of Flanders were added to the Ypres series apparently between 1390 and 1404[4] and to the Courtrai series by Broederlam in 1406.[5]

In the Low Countries, such genealogical series became a common form of decoration. The Ghent painters Willem van Axpoele and Jan Martins contracted in 1419 to restore and complete a series of Counts of Flanders in the Hall of the Magistrates of the *Keure*, which was demolished in 1519. The contract of 1419, however, shows that the Ghent series was to some extent modelled upon that at Courtrai, that the counts' consorts were included and that, behind at least some of

46 Giovanni Bellini, *Leonardo Loredan, Doge of Venice*, detail (see plate 39).

47 Flemish, 1480, *Baldwin II, Arnulf I, Baldwin III and Arnulf II, Counts of Flanders, with their Wives*, panel, approx. 135 × 67 cm., Groot Seminarie, Bruges.

This is the third in a series of ten panels of the Counts and Countesses of Flanders and was painted for the Cistercian abbey of Ter Duinen at Koksijde between Dunkirk and Ostend. All ten panels, damaged by fire and by inexpert restorers, are painted in grisaille; they are designed to hang in pairs. An inscription on the first panel states that, at the pious exhortation of Mary of Burgundy and with the consent of Jan Crabbe, abbot of Ter Duinen, 'brother Pieter Vaillant, cellarer, caused this picture or genealogy to be renewed in the year of Our Lord 1480' ('frater petrus vailliant Cell's hanc picturam seu genealogiam fecit renovari Anno dñi 1480'). The word 'renewed' may indicate that the panels replaced an earlier series and it seems clear that they were executed in 1480. The donor Vaillant succeeded Crabbe as abbot in 1488 and died in 1492. In the panel reproduced, the counts and countesses represented are: in the upper-left section, Baldwin II (d. 918) and his wife Aelfthryth, daughter of Alfred the Great, King of the West Saxons; below them, their son Arnulf I (d. 965) and his wife Adela of Vermandois; in the upper-right section, their son Baldwin III and his wife Matilda of Saxony; below them, their son Arnulf II (d. 987) and his wife Susanna of Lombardy. In the centre are the third, fourth and fifth abbots of Ter Duinen: Albero (resigned 1155); Idesbald (resigned 1167); and Walter de Dikkebus (resigned 1179). Several of the countesses in the series are closely similar to 'weepers' on the tomb of Louis of Male, Count of Flanders, which was set up in 1455 in the Collegiate Church of St Peter at Lille. The painter has based his figures either on the weepers themselves or on the designs from which they were made. Here the countesses Adela, Matilda and Susanna all correspond to weepers on the Lille tomb (see plate 204 for the weeper corresponding to the figure of Adela).

See Dubois and Huyghebaert, 1966, p. 406; here pp. 2, 42–3, 56, 65, 101, 109, 191.

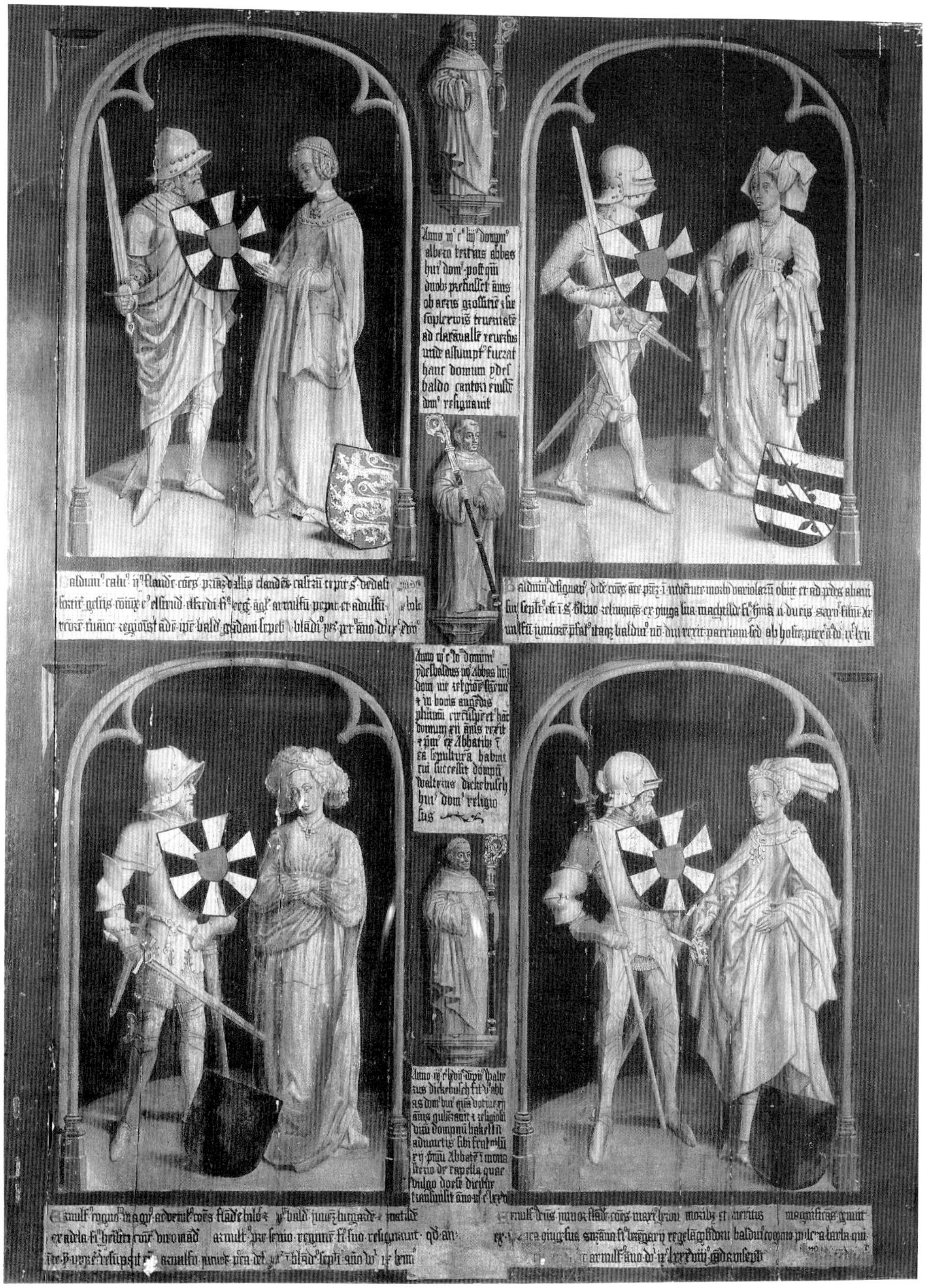

the counts, scenes from their lives were represented.[6] A late fifteenth-century series of Counts of Holland is preserved at the town hall in Haarlem;[7] another, painted in 1462–5 by Jacob Clementsz. and Symon Jansz., was at the town hall in Leyden.[8] Similar series were to be seen in monasteries. A set of panels of Counts and Countesses of Flanders was in the Abbey of St Peter at Ghent: one panel survives.[9] Another set, from the Abbey of Ter Duinen at Koksijde, is preserved in the Episcopal Seminary at Bruges (plate 47). An inscription on one panel states that the series was 'renewed' in 1480.[10] In the Ghent and Bruges panels, the counts and countesses stand in pairs, with their coats of arms and identifying inscriptions. Clearly, in such series, portraits of remote Burgundian ancestors like Liederik de Buc, the first, seventh-century, *forestier* of Flanders, were fanciful creations. When portraits of the ruling or recently deceased princes were added, however, some effort was at least occasionally made to procure acceptable likenesses. When the figures of John the Fearless and Philip the Good were to be included in the Courtrai series in 1467, the church authorities sent to Brussels to obtain cartoons.[11]

One of the most ambitious of these genealogical series was painted in the mid-fourteenth century for the Emperor Charles IV in the great hall of his castle at Karlštejn outside Prague. The murals, known only from sixteenth-century copies, represented over sixty of Charles's real or putative ancestors and relatives: personages of the Old Testament; gods, heroes and rulers of classical antiquity; pagan and Christian princes. They were depicted in full length, standing, or seated upon thrones.[12] There were also equestrian series. In Van Orley's designs for a dynastic series in tapestry of the Counts and Countesses of Nassau made in the 1530s, all the figures were shown mounted on horses or mules (plate 48).

The nobility and gentry followed the example of their superiors by commissioning series of ancestor portraits, usually more modest in scale and conception. Various fifteenth-century Italian sets of heads, for example, appear to be from such family series.[13] The church authorities commissioned series of ecclesiastics: the frescoes of illustrious Dominicans by Tomaso da Modena, dated 1352,[14] and those of the popes in the Sistine Chapel provide the most obvious instances;[15] while beside the Counts and Countesses of Flanders at Bruges appear the Abbots of Ter Duinen (plate 47). Sodoma painted, beneath his frescoes of the life of St Benedict in the monastery of Monte Oliveto at Chiusuri, medallions of all the

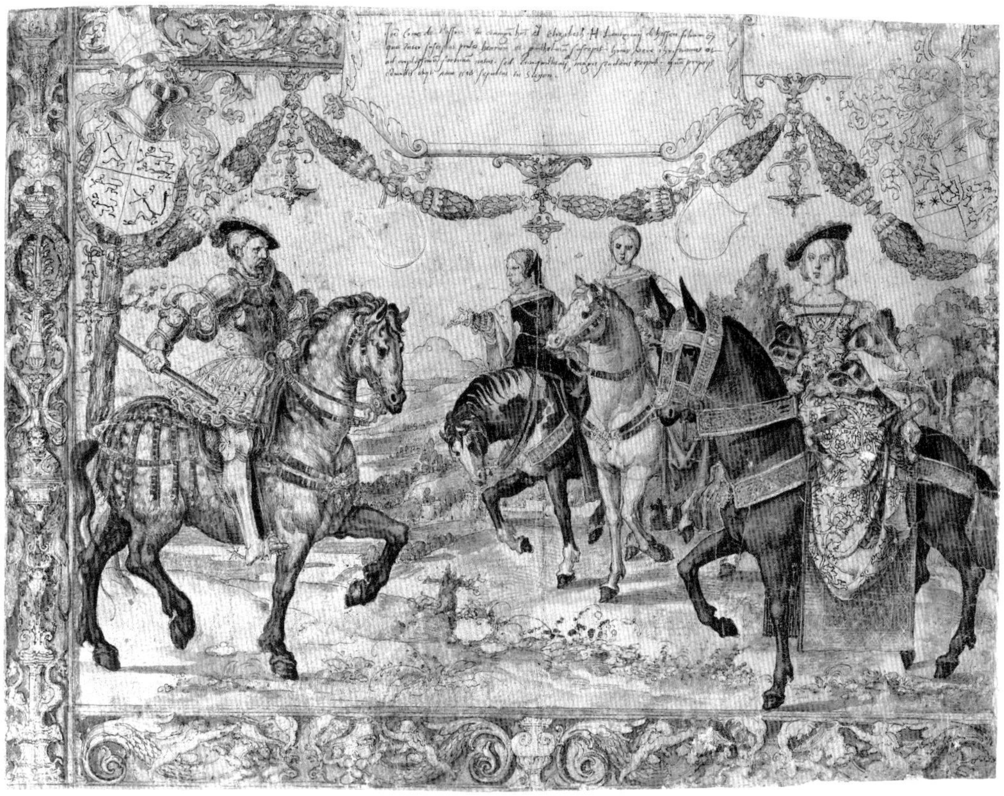

48 Bernard van Orley, *Henry III, Count of Nassau, and his Three Wives*, pen and brown ink with coloured washes on paper, 29.9 × 52.9 cm., Staatliche Graphische Sammlung, Munich (20).

This is one of the five surviving drawings for a series of tapestries of the Counts and Countesses of Nassau. The tapestries, designed by Van Orley for Henry III of Nassau, were apparently being woven in 1531 and were destroyed by fire in 1760. In the drawing reproduced, the inscription and coats of arms, added later in the sixteenth century, identify the man as John V of Nassau (1455–1516) and the foremost lady as his wife Elisabeth of Hesse. This is incorrect: the lady in the foreground is clearly identifiable from other portraits as Mencía de Mendoza, third wife of Henry III of Nassau, and the persons represented are Henry himself (1483–1538) and his three wives: Françoise of Savoy (d. 1511), Claude of Chalon (d. 1521) and Mencía, whom he married in 1524. Both Henry and Mencía were noted collectors and patrons of the arts.

See the exhibition catalogue Washington and New York, 1986–7, pp. 237–9 (91); here pp. 43, 124.

generals of the Olivetan Order.[16] A visitor to the Abbey of Clairvaux in 1517 noted that portraits of all the abbots, from St Bernard onwards, decorated the hall of abbots.[17] In the cathedral of St Stephen at Vienna were portraits of professors of the University of Vienna.[18]

In series of famous men – military heroes, philosophers, poets and politicians – persons of the remote past were often placed alongside recently dead or even living celebrities. The loose category of *uomini famosi* evolved in Italy, where, perhaps not by coincidence, there was a shortage of long-established princely dynastics to provide subject matter for grand portrait series. The category may be related to international interest in the 'Nine Heroes' and 'Nine Heroines', represented, for instance, in murals at the castle of La Manta in Piedmont;[19] but series of famous men were arranged and added to in a much less systematic way. Giotto evidently painted such a series in Naples,[20] while the best-known surviving sets are the nine frescoes by Castagno, painted in about 1450 at the Villa Carducci at Legnaia outside Florence (plate 49), and the twenty-eight panels by Justus of Ghent and his workshop, painted in about 1475 for the *studiolo* of the ducal palace at Urbino (plate 68). In Castagno's frescoes, three warriors and three poets of the recent past and three heroes of the remote past are represented in full length, standing in niches, and resemble closely the portraits of princes in some of the dynastic series. The Urbino pictures are of scholars of the remote and recent past and of Pope Sixtus IV, who was alive at the time of painting (plate 68). All are shown in half length.

The museum of portraits of illustrious men established at Como in 1537–8 by Paolo Giovio was to a large extent a development of the concepts behind the series of famous men and princes.[21] Indeed, it is impossible always to make neat divisions among the categories of dynastic series, series of famous men and portrait galleries. At his castle of Bicêtre, destroyed during riots in 1411, the Duke of Berry had assembled images of the 'faces and bodies' of the Avignon Pope Clement VII and his cardinals, the kings and princes of France and the Roman and Byzantine emperors. As they were considered 'in the judgement of the most erudite painters' to be the most lavish and finest 'work' in France, the 'images' were probably paintings, which may well have formed a series of full-length portraits.[22] If they did form such a series, it cannot easily be categorised.

2 Group Portraits

The survival rate for group portraits is not good, partly because they were often large and cumbersome paintings, more liable than smaller, less obtrusive pictures to be disliked and discarded, and partly because those who inherited them would have been likely to take an interest in only one or two of the sitters and so would have been less inclined to keep them than they would independent portraits of ancestors and relatives.

Group portraits occurred in some of the dynastic series, for example in the Leyden series of Counts of Holland where one painting showed Count Albert, his children and his brother and predecessor, Count William. The panel for this picture was paid for in 1464.[23] Tapestry groups of the *Twelve Peers of France*, which had something in common with the dynastic series, were being manufactured during the fourteenth century and included recognisable portraits. In 1399, Philip the Bold, Duke of Burgundy, authorised a payment to a weaver who had 'removed from one of the large tapestries of the *Twelve Peers of France* the

49 Andrea del Castagno, *Pippo Spano*, detached fresco, transferred to canvas, 250 × 154 cm., Uffizi, Florence (S. Marco e Cenacoli 173).

One of a series of nine famous men and women painted by Castagno in about 1450 at the Villa Carducci at Legnaia outside Florence, the fresco represents Filippo Scolari (1369–1426), a Florentine statesman and soldier who campaigned in Hungary and the Balkans.

See Berti, 1979, p. 128; here pp. 2, 44, 56, 86, 109.

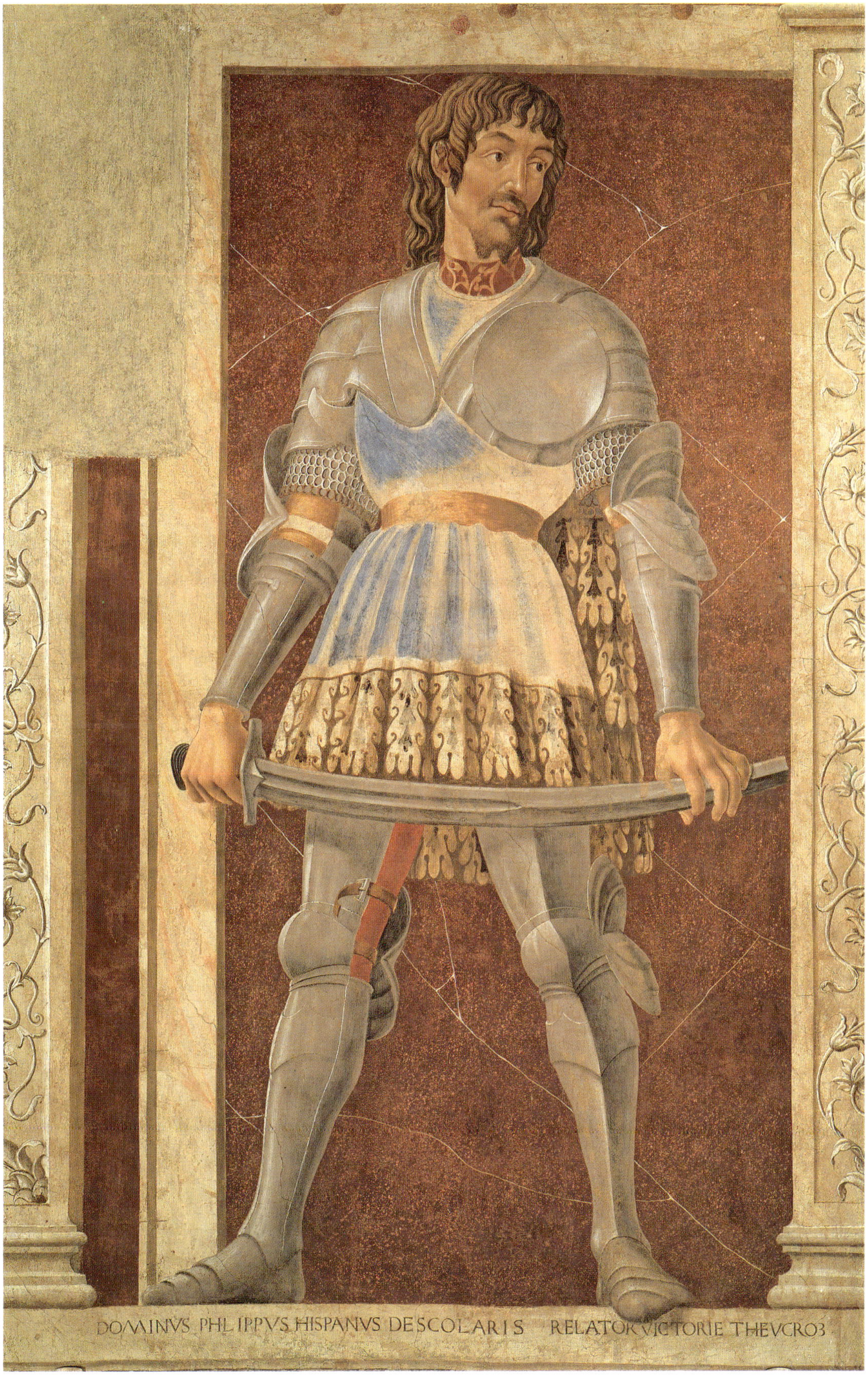
DOMINVS PHILIPPVS HISPANVS DESCOLARIS RELATOR VICTORIE THEVCROR

50 After a Netherlandish painter of c. 1430, *Hunting Festival at the Court of Philip the Good, Duke of Burgundy*, panel, 161 × 117 cm., Musée du Château, Versailles (MV 5423).

This is a mid-sixteenth-century copy after a lost original, probably the picture that in 1582 was prominently displayed at the palace of El Pardo outside Madrid and that was described as representing 'the great duke Charles of Burgundy who goes hunting with the duchess and his ladies and knights, all dressed in white, wearing strange clothes and hats, in the fashion of those lands' (Roblot-Delondre, 1910, p. 56). The duke is in fact not Charles but his father Philip the Good and the heraldic evidence of the copy suggests that the original was painted late in 1430 or in 1431. The setting may be the park of Hesdin, in Artois. Philip, leaning against a table, has evidently just eaten and his servants are washing the gold plate in the fountain on the right. A musician sings to entertain him and the courtiers near him, while other minstrels on the left provide the music to which four couples, in the lower-left corner, are dancing. The duchess, Isabella of Portugal, standing on the left of the table, seems to persuade another couple to join the dance. In the lower-right corner, other courtiers, watched by Philip's jester, prepare to join the falconers who are hunting by the river. In the landscape in the upper-left corner and in the far distance, the copyist has clearly departed from the original and followed his own invention. The original, related to depictions of the 'Garden of Love' and to calendar landscapes, was probably by one of the painters employed at the Burgundian court.

See Van Buren-Hagopian, 1985, *passim*; here pp. 47, 120.

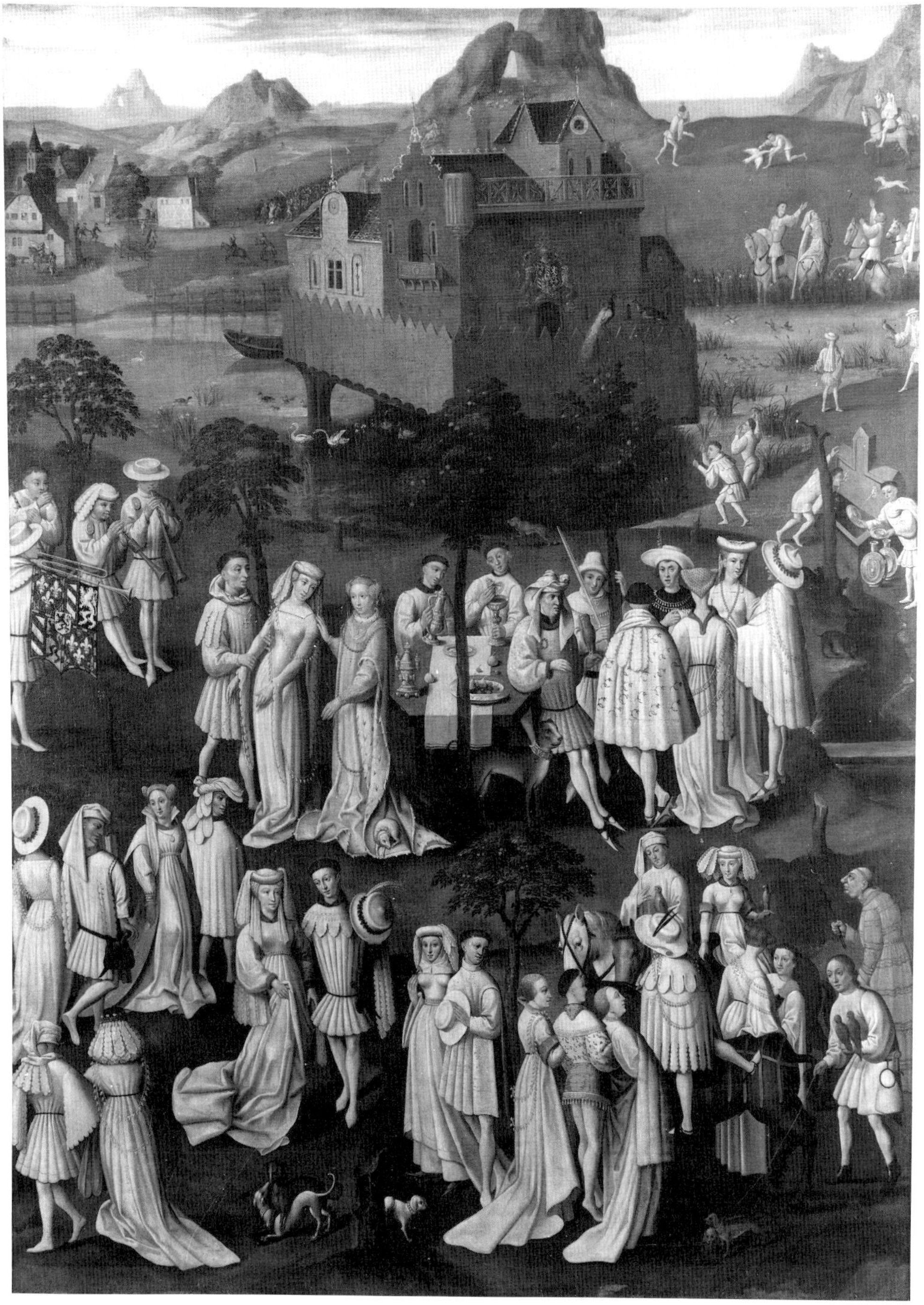

portrait of my lord the late Count of Flanders and inserted in its place another more richly worked'.[24] The late count, Louis of Male, had died in 1384.

Portraits of princes were incorporated into tapestries representing activities of court life. In the 1420 inventory of the Burgundian tapestries were listed nine large and two smaller pieces, worked with gold thread, of scenes of falconry 'in which there are the personages of the late duke John and my lady the duchess his wife, on foot and on horseback'.[25] The late duke was John the Fearless, murdered in 1419, and the tapestries had evidently been made for him and his wife Margaret of Bavaria, whom he had married in 1385. Assuredly they were shown surrounded by courtiers and in many respects the tapestries would have been similar to paintings in which John's son, Philip the Good, appeared with his courtiers and which are known from copies: the '*Hunting Festival*' (plate 50) and the *Dance by Torchlight*.[26]

In Italy, mural paintings often served as substitutes for tapestries. Though cheaper, murals were less useful since they did not control draughts or humidity and since they could not be moved from room to room or from palace to palace. In many, perhaps most, of the palaces of Italy were to be found wall paintings of scenes of court life which included portraits of princes, prominent courtiers and favourite horses and dogs. Unlike the tapestries, which they must have resembled rather closely, they were constantly on view. As the princes grew bored by them and as topical references to favourite courtiers and animals became dated, there was a danger that they might be destroyed and replaced.

At Belfiore outside Ferrara was a loggia decorated with paintings of Alberto d'Este, who died in 1393 and who was shown hunting 'with many lords and ladies on horseback' and presiding over a repast after the hunt in a flowery meadow where youths and ladies danced and made garlands of flowers. It is believed that these paintings were executed during Alberto's lifetime.[27] In or about 1469, Galeazzo Maria Sforza, Duke of Milan, ordered that certain paintings should be created and restored in the castle of Pavia: among them were to be hunting scenes, in which the duke was to be represented standing and on horseback, attended by named courtiers, and a scene in which the duke, seated and accompanied by his brothers, received ambassadors while his chancellor, standing, was consulted and transacted business. In another room, the duke was to be represented at table, eating off gold plate and served by his gentlemen; in another were to be depicted the duchess's marriage by proxy at the French court, her journey to the French coast and her voyage to Genoa, her arrival at Milan, her marriage in the cathedral, her reception of the Milanese vassals and her entry into Pavia. Elsewhere the duke's sister Elisabetta was to be shown with her ladies playing ball games.[28] In 1472 the same duke approved a scheme for the decoration of various rooms in the castle of Milan: in the upper great hall were to be hunting scenes; the duke, mounted on his horse Gallesse, was to be seen raising his sword to wound a stag; more than twenty named courtiers were to accompany him, including Alexio, who was to be depicted being thrown from his horse by a stag, with both his legs in the air 'in the finest possible pose'.[29] In 1474, a very elaborate programme was devised for the decoration of another hall in the same castle. In the first scene the duke, again mounted on Gallesse, was to be represented leaving the castle for the cathedral. He was to be accompanied by a large retinue including various named courtiers and the Marquises of Montferrat and Mantua; all were to be portrayed 'to the life' and their names and their horses' names were to be inscribed in golden letters 'in the most convenient places'.[30] At Belfiore were paintings of the festivities that took place at the time of the marriage in 1473 of Ercole d'Este, Duke of Ferrara, to Eleonora of Naples; Ercole's departure from Ferrara in 1487 on a pilgrimage to Spain (though he got no further than Milan); various hunts; and tournaments.[31] At Belriguardo, also outside Ferrara, were paintings of Ercole surrounded by his courtiers: in one room they were represented on horseback; in another Ercole was shown wearing the Order of the Garter, which he received in 1481, and he and his attendants were magnificently dressed in gold.[32]

A few group portraits of this type survive. In the lowest tier of the frescoes in the Hall of the Months at the Palazzo Schifanoia in Ferrara, Ercole's elder brother

51 Francesco del Cossa, *Borso d'Este, Duke of Ferrara, and his Courtiers*, part of the *Month of March*, fresco, approximately 500 × 320 cm., Palazzo Schifanoia, Ferrara.

The frescoes in the Hall of the Months in the Palazzo Schifanoia occupied all four walls of a large room but those on the west and south walls have been almost totally destroyed. Each fresco is divided into three horizontal bands: in the uppermost is represented the triumph of the classical deity with whom the month is associated; in the middle band are the relevant sign of the Zodiac and attendant astrological spirits; in the lowest register are Borso himself and his subjects, engaged in seasonal activities. In *March*, the triumphant deity is Minerva and the sign of the Zodiac is Aries; in the lowest register, here reproduced, men are pruning and training vines and Borso (1413–71) is portrayed four times. In the background, he leads a group of horsemen towards the edge of a cliff; in the foreground on the left, he is mounted on a white horse in the midst of a group of horsemen, to whom he gestures with his right hand; on the right, he stands to receive a petition and administers justice. On the doorway behind him are the inscription 'IVSTICIA' and a relief carving of his own head. *March*, *April* and *May*, which occupy the east wall, were painted by Francesco del Cossa, who on 25 March 1470 wrote to Borso to complain that he had not been adequately paid. Borso refused to allow his request for more money (Campori, 1885, pp. 259–3). Evidently dissatisfied with the portraits included in the frescoes, he commissioned Baldassare d'Este to 'improve' thirty-six of the heads: those of himself and certain others who were not named (Venturi, 1885[2], p. 721 n. 1).

See Molajoli, 1974, pp. 100–2; here pp. 47–9, 160.

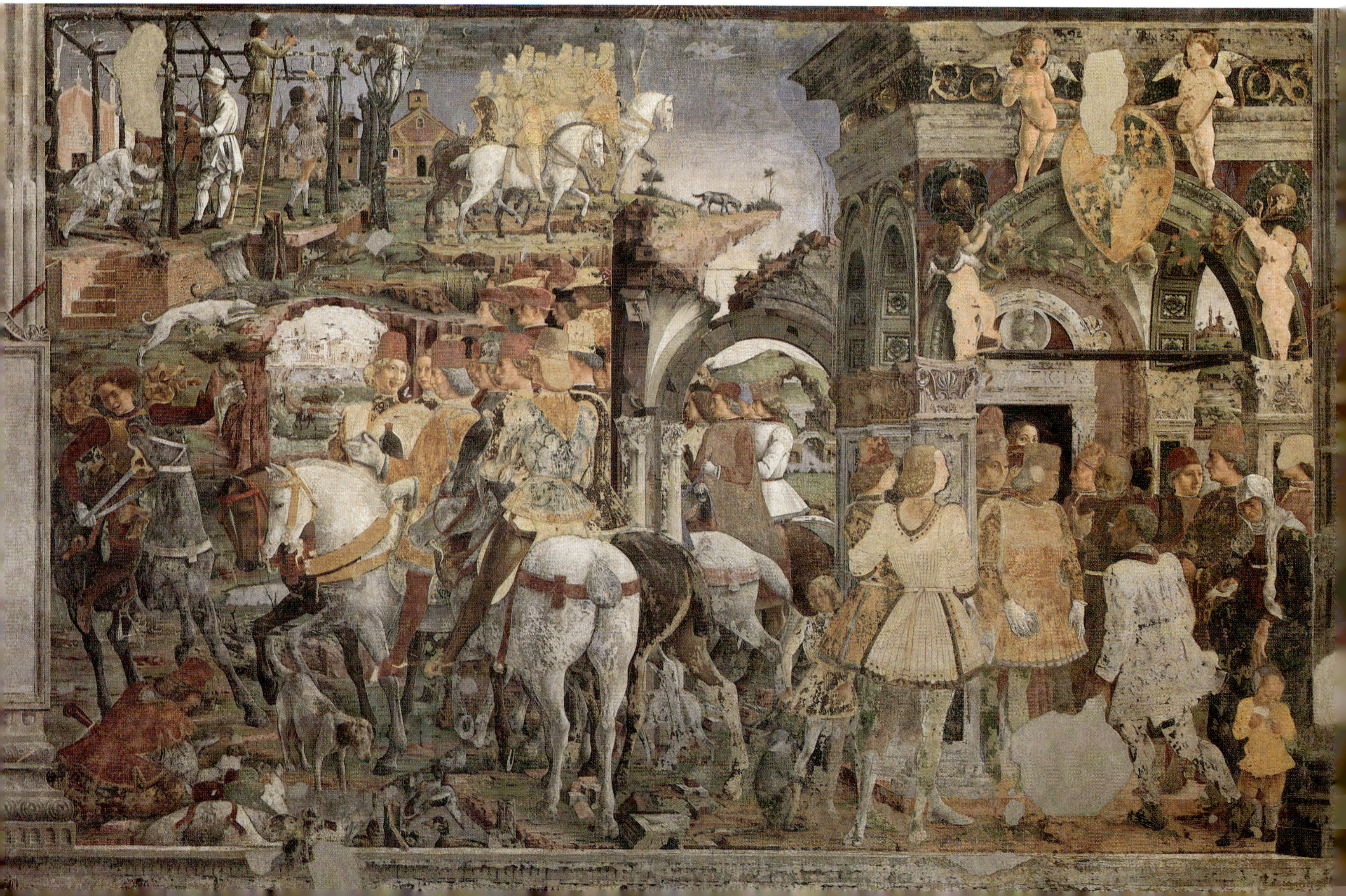

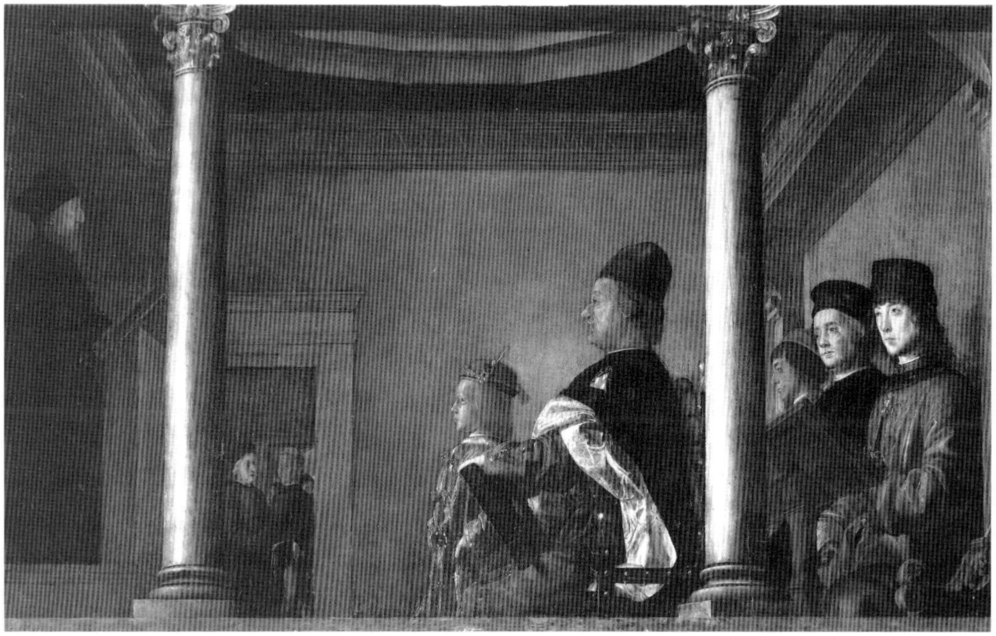

52 Justus of Ghent, *Federico da Montefeltro, Duke of Urbino, his Son Guidobaldo and Others listening to a Discourse*, poplar panel, 130 × 212 cm., Royal Collection, Hampton Court (1418).

A strip about 10 cm. wide has been cut from the left side of the picture, which is sadly damaged and much repainted. The inscription identifies the principal figure as Federico da Montefeltro (1422–82), easily recognised from other portraits. Having lost his right eye and much of his nose during a tournament in 1450, he had to be represented in profile facing left. The child is his son Guidobaldo (1472–1508), whose head is painted on a separate support and has been glued into place on the panel. The other figures cannot be identified with confidence. The architectural setting appears to be the invention of the painter rather than a factual record of a particular space and it is unlikely that a specific event is depicted. The panel, painted in about 1480, is attributed to Justus of Ghent because it is similar in style and technique to his series of famous men (see plate 68).

See Campbell, 1985, pp. 59–65 (37); here pp. 49, 62, 232.

Borso d'Este is represented with his attendants in scenes of courtly activity. The frescoes were painted by Francesco del Cossa and others in about 1470 (plate 51). Mantegna's frescoes in the 'Camera Picta' of the palace at Mantua, finished in 1474–5, show Ludovico Gonzaga, Marquis of Mantua, with members of his family, courtiers and distinguished guests, the Emperor Frederick III and Christian I, King of Denmark. Though the frescoes have narrative interest, they are not representations of actual events.[33]

Similar group portraits were executed in other media. Borso d'Este commissioned from Baldassare d'Este a large and very expensive canvas representing Borso and three of his courtiers on horseback. It had not been finished when Borso died in 1471 and at the end of 1473 had still to be completed.[34] The panel of Federico da Montefeltro, Duke of Urbino, his son Guidobaldo and three courtiers attending a reading was painted in about 1480 in the workshop of Justus of Ghent (plate 52). It is unlikely that a specific event is depicted; the portrait records the intellectual pleasures of life at the court of Urbino.

In the mural cycles, depictions of court activities were intermingled with representations of actual events. Elsewhere, paintings of historical subjects were also executed and of course included portraits. Giotto's fresco of *Pope Boniface VIII proclaiming the Jubilee of 1300*, of which only a battered fragment survives, is an example;[35] another was the remarkable picture of *John II of France receiving a Diptych from Pope Clement VI*, which once hung in the Sainte Chapelle in Paris and is known only from a copy and a written description. The event depicted would have taken place during John's visit to Avignon in 1342.[36] According to Vasari, the fresco by Bicci di Lorenzo showing the consecration in 1420 by Pope Martin V of the church of Sant' Egidio in Florence was 'much admired as something new and beautiful'.[37] It was novel only in the local context of Florentine art. Masaccio's lost fresco of the consecration of Santa Maria del Carmine in Florence, which took place in 1422, included many portraits, some of persons not actually present at the ceremony.[38] Like the scenes of court life, the narrative paintings were easily falsified in historical terms so that portraits of people whom the patrons thought should have been present might be added.

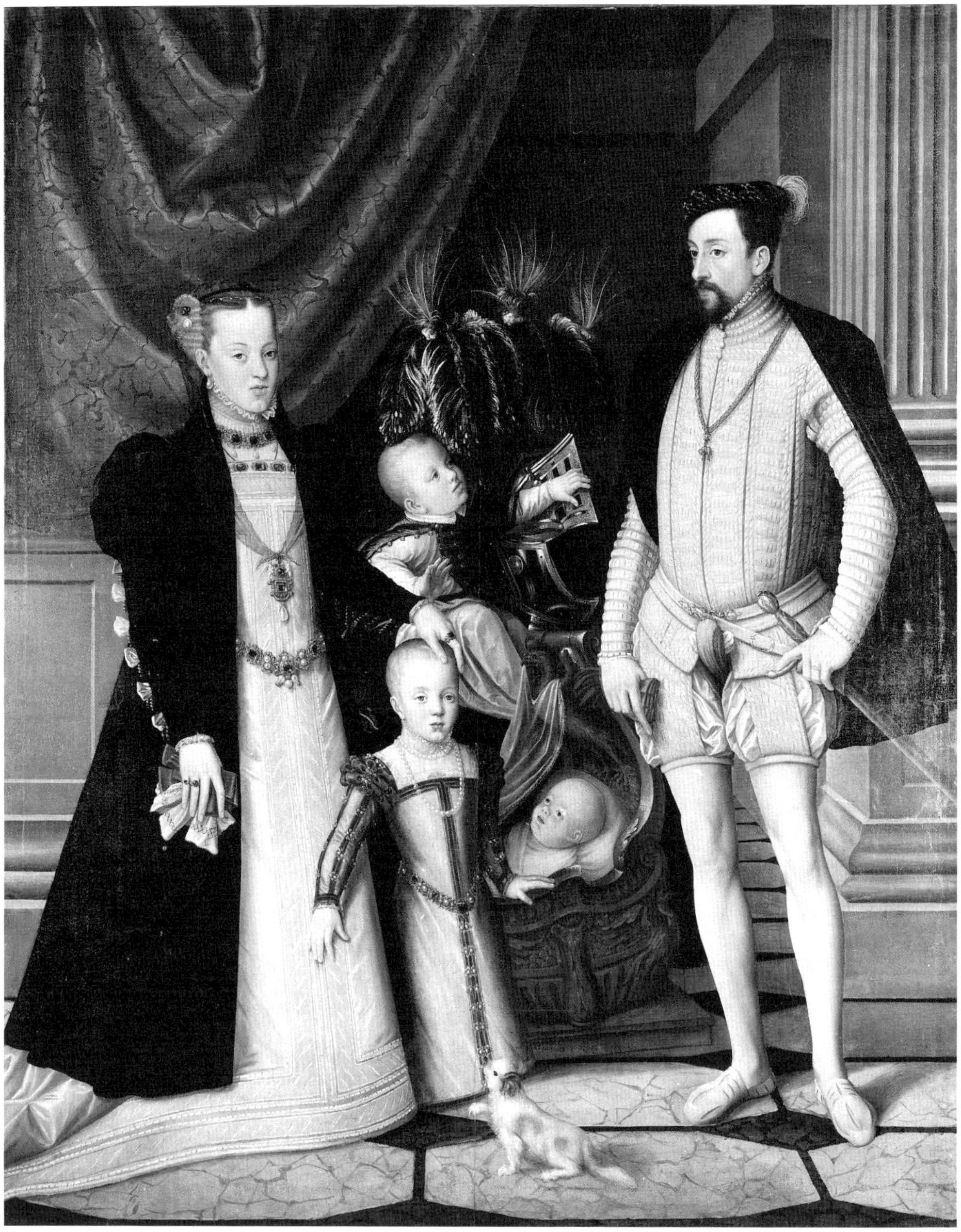

53 Austrian, 1553–4, *The Emperor Maximilian II with his Wife and their Three Eldest Children*, canvas, 240 × 188 cm., Kunsthistorisches Museum, Vienna, Gemäldegalerie (3448: exhibited at Schloss Ambras, Innsbruck).

Maximilian II (1527–76) married in 1548 his cousin Maria (1528–1603), daughter of the Emperor Charles V. They had sixteen children: the eldest, Anne (1549–80), married her uncle Philip II of Spain; the second, Ferdinand (1551–2), died young; the third, Rudolf (1552–1612), succeeded as Emperor; the fourth, Ernest (1553–95), became Regent of the Netherlands. It is thought that the children represented here are Anne, Rudolf and Ernest and that the portrait was painted shortly after the birth of Ernest in June 1553 and before the birth of the next child in June 1554. The current attribution is to the Italian painter Arcimboldo, who worked at Maximilian's court.

See Heinz and Schütz, 1976, pp. 88–9; here p. 53.

It becomes increasingly difficult to make a neat separation between historical narrative paintings and group portraits. Pintoricchio's frescoes of the life of Pope Pius II, painted in the 1500s, many years after the pope's death in 1464, are in some sense group portraits.[39] Such historical narrative cycles were executed throughout Europe: the most celebrated was perhaps the series of tapestries of the Emperor Charles V's conquest of Tunis, designed by Vermeyen, whom Charles had taken to Tunis specifically to make a visual record of the campaign.[40]

Paintings of the festivities organised by confraternities might also be classified as group portraits. In a Tournai will of 1410 is mentioned 'a painted cloth of the *trairie* of Tournai'. The *trairie* was a festival of the longbowmen and crossbowmen, and the picture presumably included portraits of members of the Tournai confraternities of archers.[41] The earliest surviving painting of a comparable sub-

54 Frans Pourbus the Elder, *The Hoefnagel Family*, canvas, 157 × 215 cm., Musées Royaux des Beaux-Arts de Belgique, Brussels (4435).

The picture, which is signed, was painted at Antwerp for Balthazar Hoefnagel (c. 1550–1608), a brother of the painter Joris Hoefnagel. When Pourbus died in September 1581, the portrait had not been paid for. As it had to be valued by the Deans of the Guild of St Luke, no formal contract or agreement about its price can have been entered into; indeed Pourbus seems to have been a family friend, for he has included himself in the picture: he is the man playing the lute, third from the left. The couple on the right, dancing to the music of lutes and virginals, are evidently Balthazar and his wife Anna van Lieffelt. The girl holding the parrot is Balthazar's sister Suzanna, born in 1566; most of the other sitters must be members of Balthazar's family but none has been identified with complete certainity. The portrait presumably represents the wedding festivities of Balthazar and Anna.

See Van de Velde, 1979–80, pp. 135–44, 152; here p. 53.

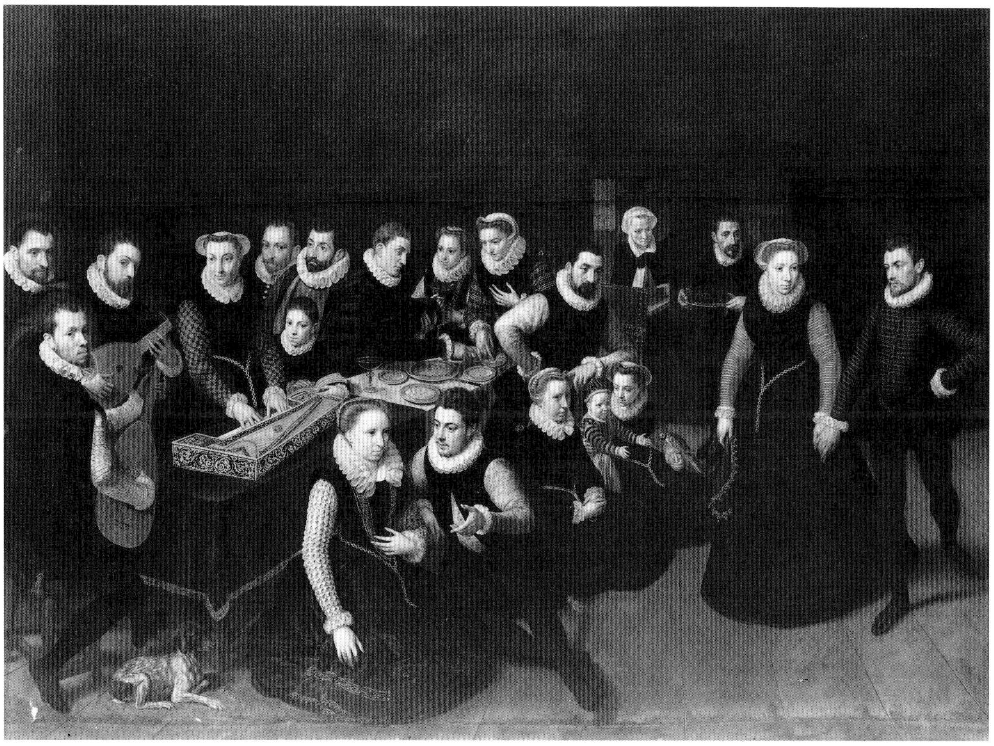

55 Netherlandish, c. 1535, *Thomas de Thiennes and his Family outside the Castle of Rumbeke*, oak panel, 50 × 75 cm., Private Collection, Belgium.

The picture was discovered in about 1830 in the castle of Rumbeke near Roeselare (Roulers) in West Flanders. In the background are views of the castle itself, the mill of Rumbeke on the left and the towers of Roeselare on the right. The principal figures are evidently the owner of the castle and members of his family and, since the costume is of the 1530s, the man in the centre is identified as Thomas de Thiennes (c. 1505–58), who succeeded his father as lord of Rumbeke in 1534. The child in the foreground is his eldest son Jacques (died 1566) and the lady behind him is his mother Marguerite de Hamericourt (died 1572), whom Thomas married in 1529. The older lady on Thomas's left is his stepmother Catherine d'Oignies (died 1545) and behind her are her daughters, Thomas's half-sisters Marie (died 1571) and Anne (1515–96). The other figures in the foreground are presumably relations and members of the household, some of whom are apparently wearing the Thiennes livery and four of whom are singing a madrigal. In the middle ground, gentlemen and ladies on horseback and in a carriage arrive outside the castle. The significance of the stork-like bird in front of Anne de Thiennes has not been explained.

See Goethals, 1849–52, IV, pp. 592–4; Hulin de Loo, 1902, pp. 72–3; here p. 53.

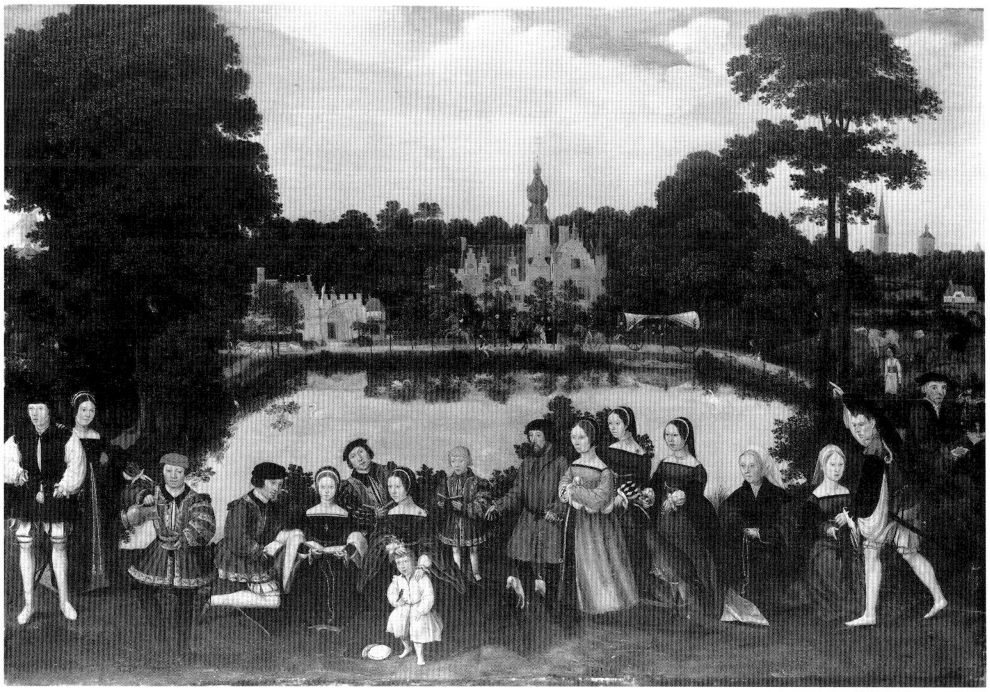

ject seems to be the *Festival of the Antwerp Archers*, painted in the 1490s by the Master of Frankfurt.[42]

Group portraits in which little or no narrative interest was present were apparently being produced by the end of the fourteenth century. The Duke of Berry owned a picture of the Avignon Pope Clement VII, who died in 1394 and who was evidently shown surrounded by his cardinals.[43] What seems to have

56 Dirk Jacobsz., *The Amsterdam Harquebusiers*, panel, 122 × 184 cm., Rijksmuseum, Amsterdam (c 402, lent by the City of Amsterdam).

Signed with the painter's monogram and dated 1529, the portrait came from the *Kloveniersdoelen*, the headquarters of the civic militia company of harquebusiers. Jacobsz. later added wing panels on which further members of the company are represented. This is an early example of the *doelenstuk* or 'militia company piece'.

See Friedländer, 1967–76, XIII, pp. 70, 106; here pp. 53, 69.

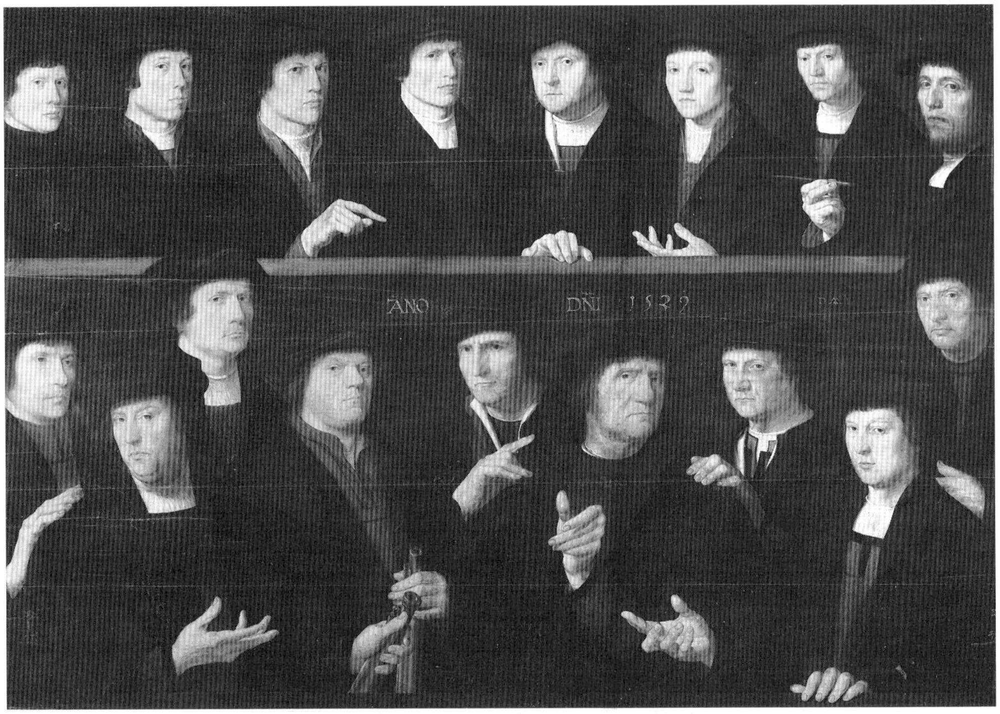

57 Lorenzo Lotto, *A Goldsmith in Three Positions*, canvas, 52 × 79 cm., Kunsthistorisches Museum, Vienna, Gemäldegalerie (92).

As the object in the centre is a case of rings, the sitter is identified as a goldsmith. On grounds of style and costume, the picture is attributed to Lotto and dated towards 1530. No one has explained why it was executed. It later belonged to Charles I, of whom Van Dyck painted a similar portrait in three positions from which Bernini carved a bust of Charles.

See Canova, 1974, p. 112; here p. 53.

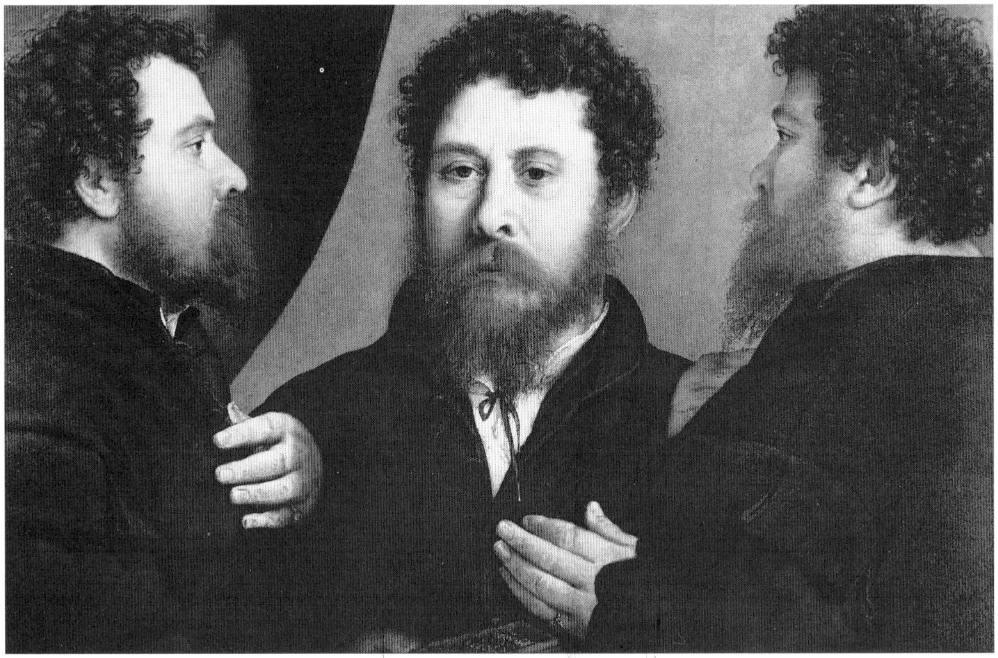

been a similar composition of Pope Martin V and ten cardinals was painted in the Lateran basilica by Gentile da Fabriano: Martin V died in 1431.[44] Fouquet's portrait of Pope Eugenius IV with two of his familiars, painted in Rome in the 1440s, probably showed the sitters in full length but is known only from descriptions and from copies of the head of Eugenius (plate 208). Fouquet was perhaps developing traditions in papal portraiture established in the paintings of Clement VII and Martin V, and seems certainly to have influenced the papal portraits of Melozzo, Raphael and Titian.

In the sixteenth century, family groups were painted for princes and for other patrons. The sitters might be represented in interiors, as in Holbein's portrait of the family of Sir Thomas More, executed in London in 1527–8 (see plate 164), the *Emperor Maximilian II with his Wife and Children*, painted in 1553 (plate 53), or the *Hoefnagel Family* by Frans Pourbus the Elder, which had not been paid for at the time of his death in 1581 (plate 54). In 1584, Otto van Veen executed a group portrait of members of his own family, with himself seated at his easel.[45]

If a family were depicted outdoors in a park or garden, a view of their residence might be included in the background (plate 55). Portraits of groups of friends were also produced. Niccolò Soggi was commissioned during the 1530s by a Portuguese ambassador in Rome to execute a large canvas of the ambassador conversing with some twenty of his acquaintances.[46]

Half-length group portraits evidently became popular throughout Europe towards 1500, but it is possible that such pictures were also produced earlier.[47] The half-length group portrait of pilgrims and the *doelenstuk*, the group portrait of members of a militia company, are best known from North-Netherlandish examples (plate 56);[48] while in an English half-length portrait of about 1550, four gentlemen are depicted playing the card-game of primero.[49]

In certain group portraits, one sitter is represented several times. The English portrait of Sir Henry Unton, painted for his widow shortly after his death in 1596, shows the sitter in half length, surrounded by scenes of his birth, life, death and burial.[50] This kind of biographical picture, related in a general way to the narrative cycles of the deeds and lives of princes, existed much earlier. In Froissart's romance *Méliador*, composed in the 1380s, one of the heroes, Agamanor, paints and presents to his lady, Phénonée, a large picture in grisaille on canvas of his own exploits at the tournament of Tarbonne.[51] In ex-voto paintings, accidents that had befallen the patrons and their miraculous recoveries were often represented in association with the images of the saints whose help had been invoked; some such pictures necessarily included representations of other people and so might be counted as group portraits.[52]

It is convenient to treat under the heading of group portraits Lotto's half-length triple portrait of a goldsmith, in which the same sitter is shown from three different angles (plate 57). This appears to be a unique instance in the period, and the reasons for its painting remain totally obscure.

58 Upper Rhenish, c. 1470, *A Young Couple*, fir panel, painted surface 62.3 × 36.5 cm., Cleveland Museum of Art, Cleveland (32.179, Delia E. Holden and L. E. Holden Funds).

The flowers that the youth presents to the young woman and that he wears in his hair are probably wild chicory and apparently refer to love. The plants in the background are thought to allude both to love and to death. The detached reverse, now at Strasbourg (10), represents in a barren setting the decaying corpses of an elderly man and woman, presumably intended to be recognised as the same couple who appear on the obverse. The picture was evidently painted at the time of the sitters' marriage; it is localised and dated on grounds of style and costume.

See Stechow et al., 1974, pp. 34–6; here pp. 54, 120.

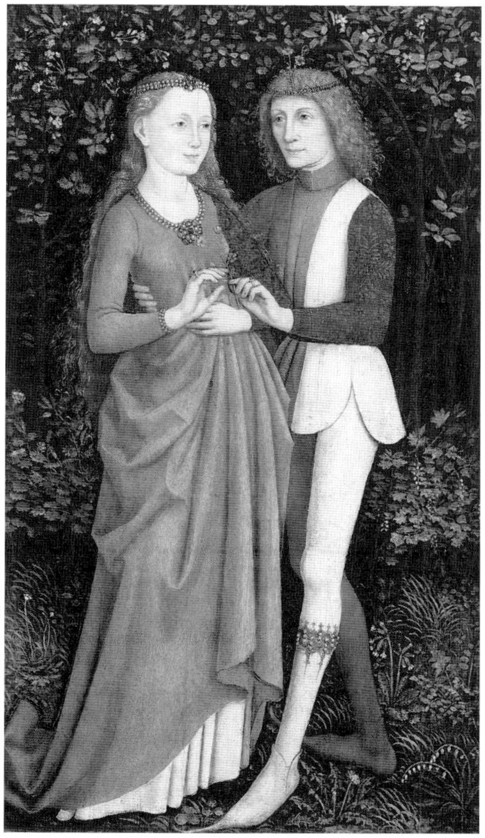

3 Double Portraits

Full-length double portraits occurred more frequently than is often believed, in the dynastic series and elsewhere. 'A large high-warp tapestry, with sheep, where there are portrayed My Lady of Artois and My Lord of Flanders' was listed in the 1404 inventory of the Burgundian tapestries, but was presumably woven much earlier, for the persons represented, Margaret of France, Countess of Artois, and her son Louis of Male, Count of Flanders, died in 1382 and 1384 respectively.[53] Again in Froissart's *Méliador*, Agamanor paints for Phénonée a small canvas showing himself, a falcon on his fist, offering to her a scroll bearing an amorous rondeau.[54] Joan of Arc stated at her trial in 1431 that she knew of only one portrait of herself, a painting which she had seen at Arras and which showed her in full armour kneeling on one knee and presenting a letter to Charles VII of France.[55] However unusual Jan van Eyck's *Giovanni Arnolfini and his Wife*, painted in 1434, may have been in other respects, it was not exceptional as a full-length double

59 Hans Memlinc, *An Old Man and an Old Lady* (reconstruction), oak panels, 34 × 29 cm. and 35 × 29 cm., Staatliche Museen Preussischer Kulturbesitz, Berlin (West), Gemäldegalerie (529 C) and Louvre, Paris (R.F. 1723).

The double portrait has been sawn in two, doubtless by a dealer. There are no indications of the sitters' identities; on grounds of style and costume, the picture may be attributed to Memlinc and dated around 1480.

See Campbell, 1977², *passim*; here pp. 54, 120, 121.

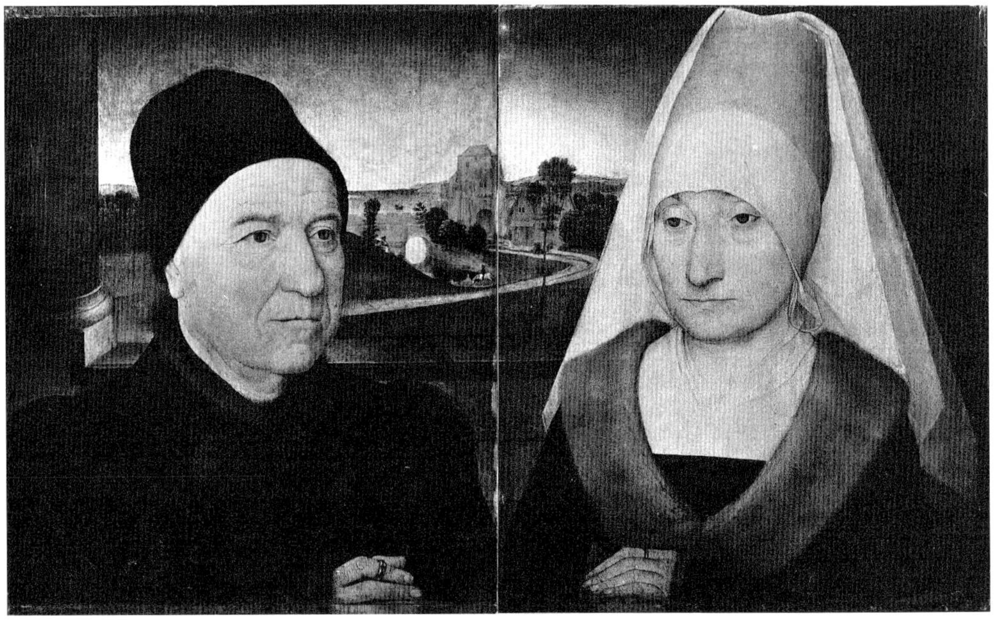

portrait (plate 135). A Netherlandish illuminator of about 1470 painted, in a text of Valerius Maximus' *Facta et dicta memorabilia*, a miniature showing two men, probably the author and the painter, contemplating a full-length double portrait of themselves.[56] In 1486–7 there was set up in the magistrates' chamber of the Palace of the Franc of Bruges a large panel on which were painted portraits of the Emperor Maximilian I and his young son Philip the Handsome.[57]

At Ferrara, Borso d'Este, who died in 1471, commissioned from Baldassare d'Este 'a canvas on which are portrayed to the life duke Galeazzo and his lady' – Galeazzo Maria Sforza, Duke of Milan, and his wife: this was placed in the Palazzo Schifanoia.[58] Justus of Ghent's panel of Federico da Montefeltro, Duke of Urbino, with his son Guidobaldo, was painted in the mid 1470s: the duke, who wears armour but who is reading a large book, is seated while Guidobaldo stands at his knee.[59] Certain German painters of the second half of the fifteenth century executed double-sided pictures showing, on the obverses, full-length portraits of young couples, and, on the reverses, images of their decaying corpses (plate 58). A small painting of this kind, perhaps of about 1490 and now belonging to the church of Lauenburg an der Elbe, is particularly interesting because of the moralising inscriptions on both sides: 'We will give ourselves up to wordly joy . . . We have lost eternal life'.[60]

Half-length double portraits were being produced in Germany, Italy and the Low Countries by the mid-fifteenth century and possibly earlier (plates 59, 61).[61] Portraits in which one sitter is accompanied by an attendant – a servant, a slave or a dwarf – became popular during the sixteenth century, but are not truly double portraits since the attendants' roles are completely subsidiary. Their faces may even be turned away and hidden from the spectator (plates 60, 119, 159).

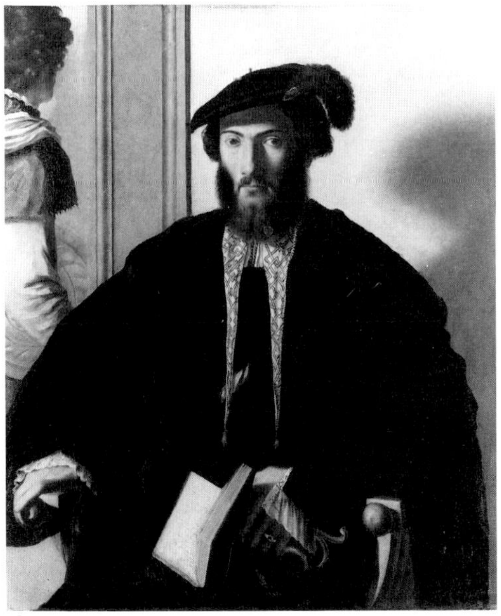

60 Imitator of Parmigianino, *Man holding a Book*, panel, 98 × 84 cm., Museo di Capodimonte, Naples, Pinacoteca (Q 109).

The sitter is dressed in black; the text of his book is no longer legible. The young man behind him, evidently a servant, is dressed in blue and pink and carries a silver dish. The portrait was probably painted in the 1530s.

See Bertini, 1987, p. 90; here p. 54.

4 Single Portraits

Full-length portraits of persons standing, seated or lying, or mounted on horses occur throughout the period. The recumbent pose was usually reserved for the dead: painted effigies were sometimes used to form the lids of wooden sarcophagi,

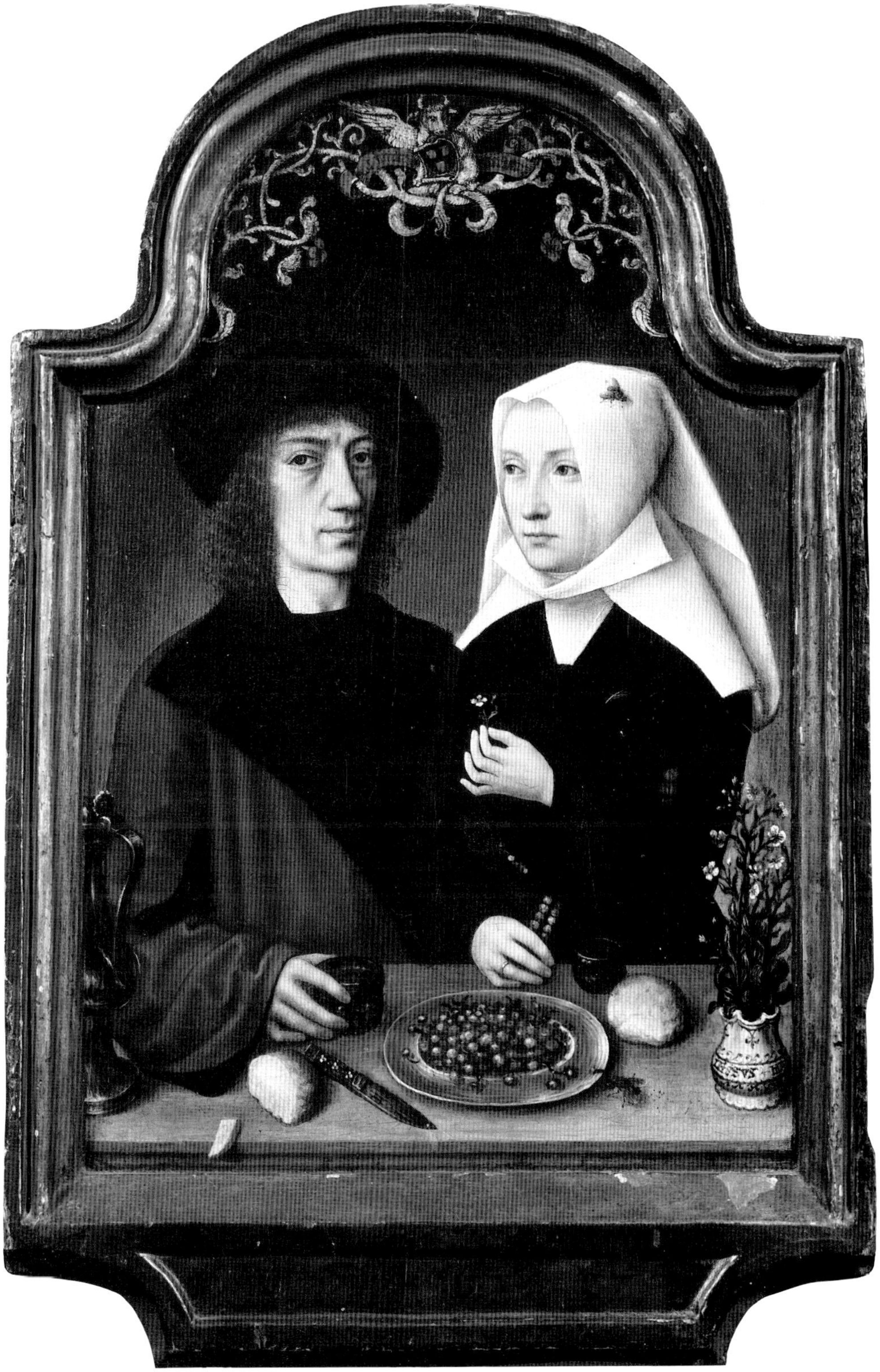

61 Master of Frankfurt, *The Artist and his Wife*, panel, 38 × 26 cm., Koninklijk Museum voor Schone Kunsten, Antwerp (5096).

The original frame bears the date 1496 and the ages of the sitters, 37 and 27. The picture was protected by shutters and one of the hinges to which they were attached is still fixed to the frame. The coat of arms, supported by a winged bull, and the motto *Wt Jonsten versamt* ('gathered from joy') are those of the Antwerp Guild of St Luke; the stock-gillyflowers in the lady's left hand and in the vase also refer to the guild, which in 1480 had amalgamated with the Chamber of Rhetoric known as 'De Violieren' ('The Stock-Gillyflowers'). The flies and other objects on the table are open to various interpretations. The Master of Frankfurt, an Antwerp artist so named after two triptychs now at Frankfurt, included self-portraits in several of his other paintings. The Antwerp double portrait seems to have been by 1516 in the collection of Margaret of Austria.

See Vandenbroeck, 1985, pp. 105–9; here pp. 54, 64–6, 74, 134, 217.

and some fifteenth-century Spanish examples survive;[62] occasionally, pictures of the corpses of celebrated people showed the whole figure in the coffin (plate 180). Both Hilliard and Oliver painted miniatures of young men reclining in landscapes.[63]

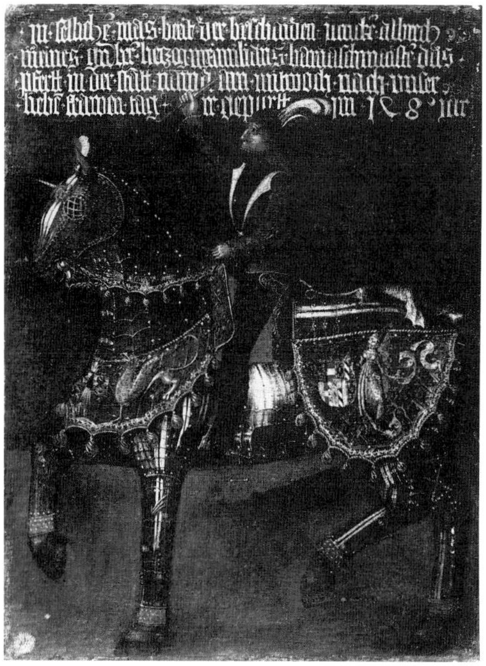

62 After a Netherlandish painter of c. 1480, *Albrecht May*, canvas, 60 × 44 cm., Kunsthistorisches Museum, Vienna, Gemäldegalerie (2375: exhibited in the Waffensammlung).

The inscription states that this is a representation of the 'humble nobleman Albrecht, master of the armoury of my gracious lord duke Maximilian' as he rode 'the horse into the town of Namur on the Wednesday after the Nativity of Our Lady, 1480' (13 September 1480). A companion picture in the same collection (2374) shows Maximilian himself – who was afterwards the Emperor Maximilian I – riding into Luxemburg on 29 September 1480. Albrecht, simply dressed in brown and black, rides a horse magnificently arrayed in an armour acquired by Maximilian early in 1480 from an Augsburg smith and in trappings decorated with Maximilian's coat of arms and devices. During the Luxemburg war of 1480, Maximilian evidently sent his horse to make a formal entry into Namur. Equestrian portraits of Albrecht and Maximilian were presumably painted in the Netherlands to commemorate the campaign; the Vienna pictures are no doubt early copies executed in Austria.

See Anzelewsky, 1963, pp. 77–80; here p. 56.

Most full-length portraits showed the subjects standing. The dynastic series and series of famous men provide numerous examples (plates 47, 49); in Florence, Domenico di Michelino's posthumous portrait of Dante, painted in 1465,[64] and Botticelli's frescoes representing Lorenzo Tornabuoni and his wife with various allegorical figures are further instances (plate 160). Baldassare d'Este painted for Borso d'Este, Duke of Ferrara, shortly before his death in 1471 a full-length, life-size portrait of Borso, which was requested by and presented to Galeazzo Maria Sforza.[65] At the palace of Pesaro in 1500 was a full-length portrait of Alessandro Sforza of Pesaro, who died in 1473.[66] Vasari was therefore quite wrong when he stated that Titian introduced full-length portraits into Italy.[67] Titian may well have popularised the full-length form which, as far as can be judged from surviving pictures and documents, was used before Titian's time more frequently in northern Europe than in Italy (plates 145, 146, 255).

Full-length portraits of seated figures were often of enthroned princes: the portrait of Richard II of England, probably of the 1390s, is one example (plate 34) and others occurred in the mid-fourteenth-century series at Karlštejn of the Emperor Charles IV and his ancestors.[68]

Images of princes and great lords dressed in armour and mounted on horses would have been familiar throughout Europe from their seals, to which many of the earliest surviving painted equestrian portraits are rather similar. The date and authorship of the equestrian portrait of Guidoriccio da Fogliano, formerly believed to have been painted by Simone Martini in 1328, have been called into question;[69] the frescoes of Sir John Hawkwood, painted by Uccello in 1436, and of Niccolò da Tolentino, painted by Castagno in 1455–6, are effectively cheap substitutes for equestrian statues.[70] During the 1440s, an equestrian portrait of Alfonso V of Aragon, surrounded by four virtues, was painted on the Castel Capuano at Naples.[71] A large equestrian portrait on canvas of Francesco Sforza, Duke of Milan, who died in 1466, was in 1469 in the library of the castle at Pavia, from where it was to be transported to Milan. It was perhaps the same equestrian portrait of Francesco that was displayed in 1491 in the castle at Milan and in 1493 in Milan cathedral.[72] In Italy and in northern Europe, group portraits of figures on horseback were being produced in around 1400; by the end of the fifteenth century at the latest, independent painted and tapestry equestrian portraits were being executed in France, the Low Countries and Austria (plate 62).[73] A particularly interesting series of tapestries, known only from copies, illustrated the military career of Pierre de Rohan-Gié: five tapestries showed him on horseback as man-at-arms, ensign, *guidon*, general and marshal of France, which he became in 1475.[74] Equestrian portraits of Mary of Burgundy were produced during her lifetime and probably also after her death in 1482, for she was killed when she was thrown from a horse.[75] In the sixteenth century, printed images of monarchs and princes on horseback began to circulate (plate 257) and painted equestrian portraits were less constrained by the sitters' armours and by heraldic display. Equestrian portraiture in Italy came to be strongly influenced by classical prototypes. In Titian's *Charles V on Horseback*, painted at Augsburg in 1548, the classicising and the northern traditions were combined, and this painting set a standard for subsequent developments in equestrian portraiture (plate 258).

If account is taken solely of surviving portraits and copies, a neat pattern of development of the half-length image may be discerned: it evidently became fashionable for portraitists to depict increasingly large areas of their sitters' bodies. The *John II of France* (plate 63) and the *Rudolf IV of Austria* (plate 64) were both

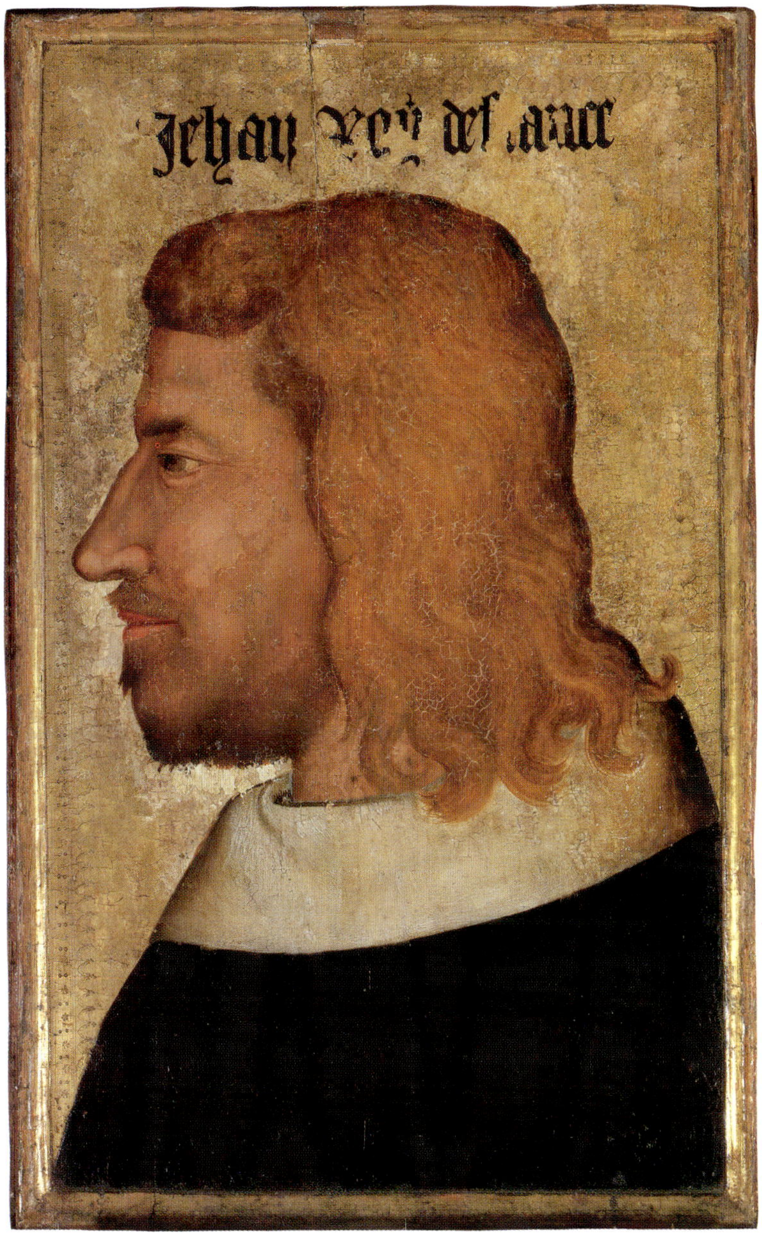

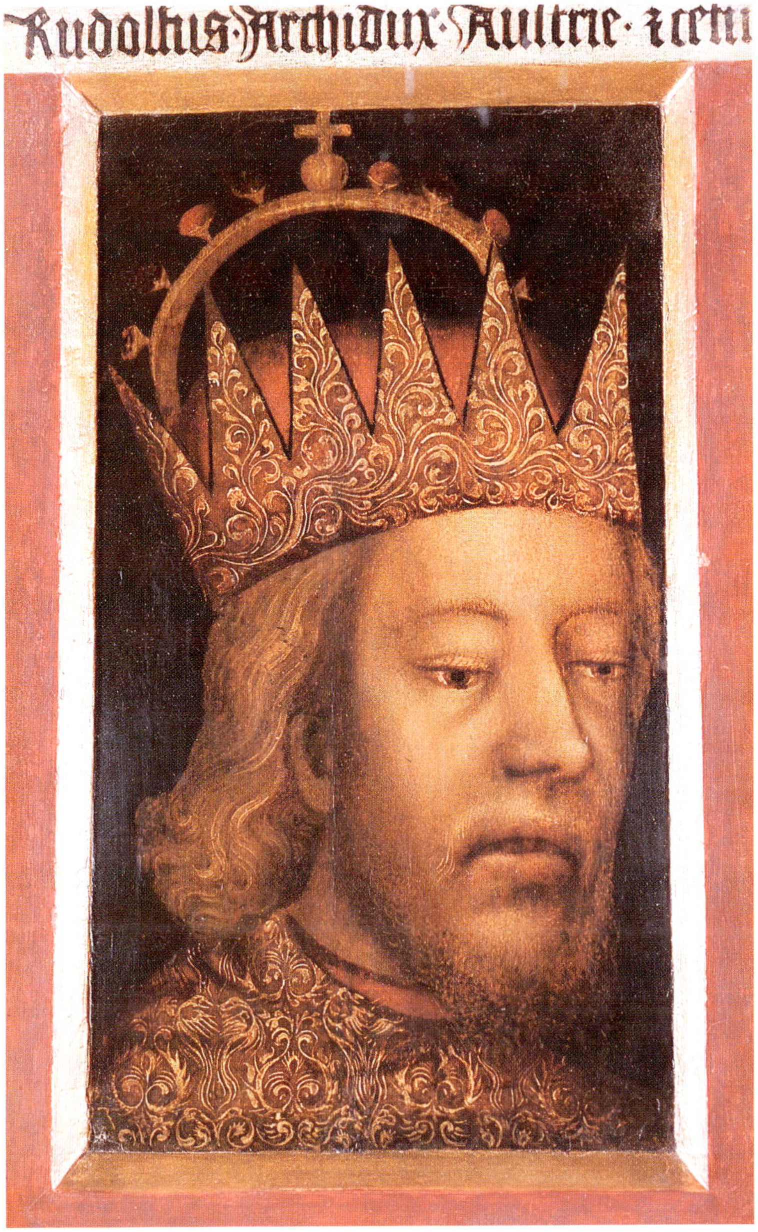

63 French, c. 1360, *John II, King of France*, oak panel, painted surface 55.6 × 34 cm., Louvre, Paris (R.F. 2490).

The paint surface is much damaged and restored. John was born in 1319, succeeded to the throne in 1350 and died in 1364.

See Sterling, 1987, pp. 146–9; here pp. 56–61, 65, 81, 112.

64 Austrian, c. 1365, *Rudolf IV of Austria*, parchment mounted on a fir panel, painted surface 38.7 × 22.2 cm., Dom- und Diözesanmuseum, Vienna (1).

The frame (45 × 30 cm.) is original. Rudolf died in 1365 aged twenty six. The portrait, which was placed in the cathedral of St Stephen in Vienna immediately above the vault in which Rudolf was buried, is thought to have been painted shortly after his death.

See Künstler, 1972, *passim*; here pp. 56–61, 65, 69.

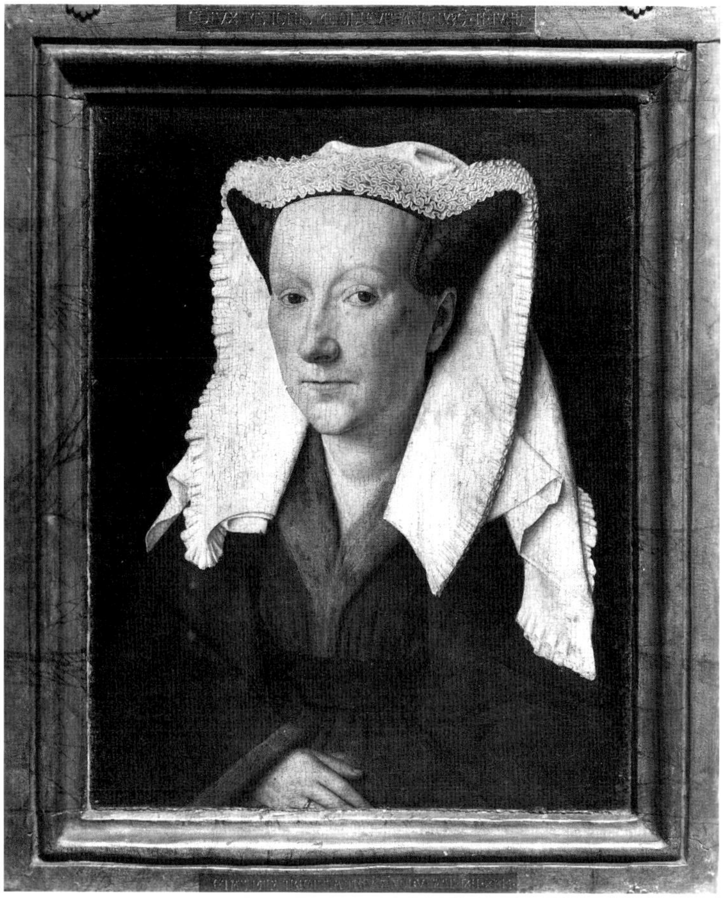

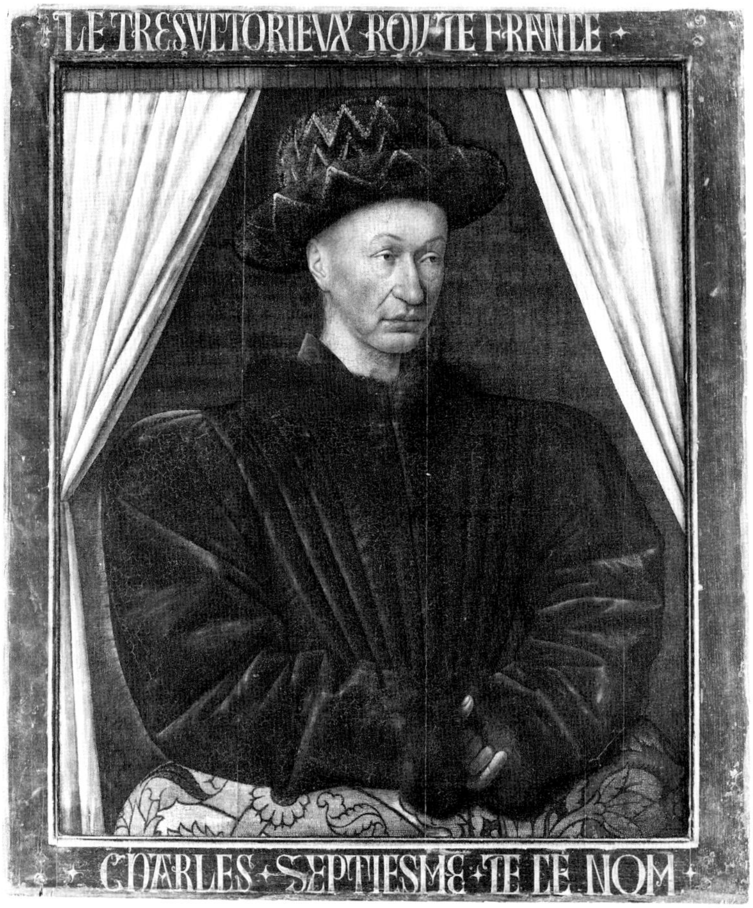

65 Jan van Eyck, *Margaret, the Artist's Wife*, oak panel, painted surface 32.6 × 25.8 cm., Groeningemuseum, Bruges (0.162.1).

The original frame (41.3 × 34.5 cm.) carries Latin inscriptions: 'My spouse Jan finished me on 17 June 1439' and 'My age was thirty three years' and the artist's personal motto 'As I can' (compare plate 22).

See Dhanens, 1980, pp. 302–6; Janssens de Bisthoven, 1981, pp. 175–93; here pp. 61, 65, 127.

66 Jean Fouquet, *Charles VII, King of France*, oak panel, painted surface 85.7 × 70.6 cm., Louvre, Paris (INV. 9106).

The frame is original. Charles was born in 1403, succeeded to the throne in 1422 and died in 1461. During his reign the English were driven from France and there has has been much inconclusive speculation as to the point in the struggle at which he might have been called 'TRESVICTORIEVX', the epithet applied to him in the inscription on the frame. This may well have been painted at the same time as the portrait. It has recently been discovered that beneath the paint surface lies an unfinished version of Fouquet's *Virgin and Child with Angels* (plate 10). The portrait was probably executed early in the 1450s.

See Reynaud, 1981, pp. 12–18; Reynaud, 1983, *passim*; here pp. 61, 65, 109.

67 (right) Leonardo da Vinci, *Lady with a Ferret*, walnut panel, 54.9 × 40.5 cm., Muzeum Narodowe, Cracow (XII–209).

The inscriptions in the upper-left corner are not original; an arch behind the sitter's left shoulder, visible only in ultra-violet light, is claimed to have been included and then painted out by Leonardo. The animal, usually described as an ermine, is too large to be a stoat. Even if Leonardo has adjusted its scale – just as he greatly enlarged the sitter's right hand – it seems more likely that the creature is a ferret. On grounds of style and costume, the portrait is believed to have been painted by Leonardo at Milan in about 1485–90. Leonardo is known to have executed in around 1485 a portrait of Cecilia Gallerani, who in 1481, when she was about sixteen, became the mistress of Ludovico il Moro, Duke of Milan (see pp. 193, 204). The sitter here is often identified as Cecilia because the animal is claimed to allude to Ludovico, who took the ermine as one of his emblems, and to Cecilia herself, whose surname Gallerani sounds like γαλεη, the Greek word for any weasel-like creature.

See Kwiatkowski, 1955, *passim*; here pp. 61, 193.

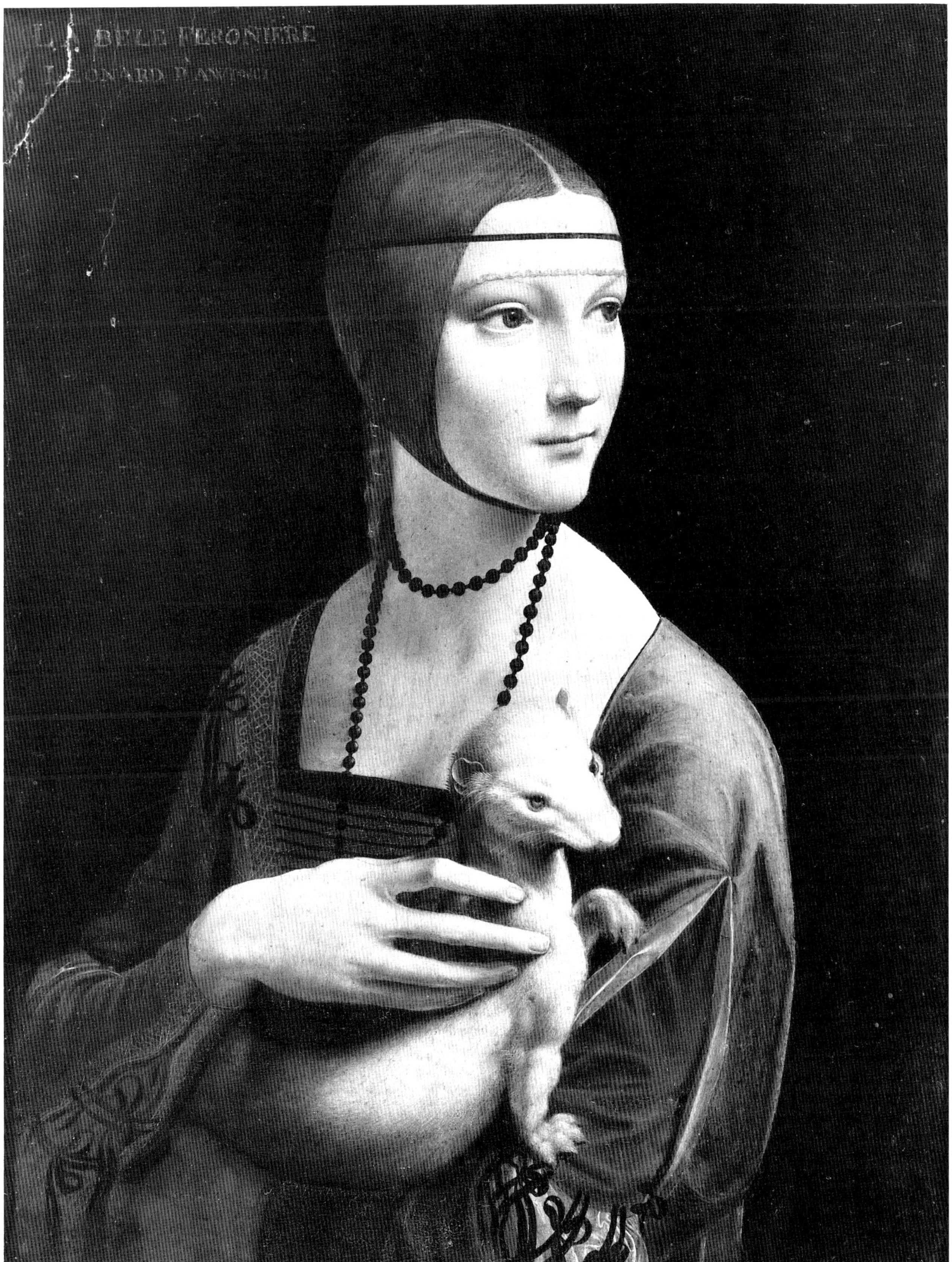
BELE FERONIERE

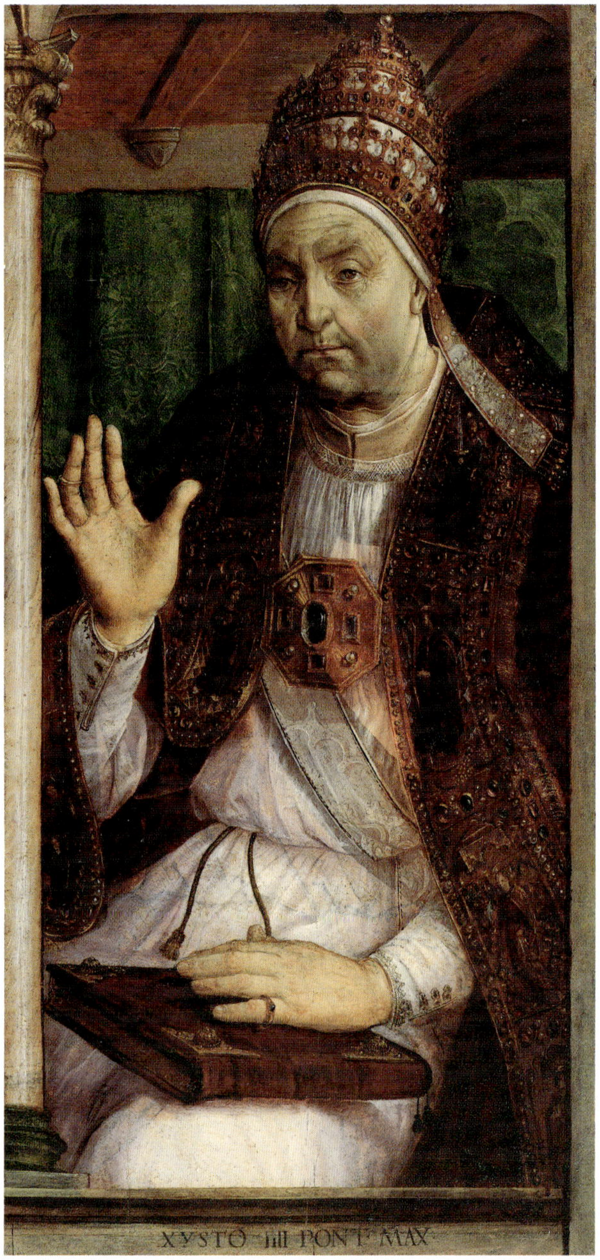

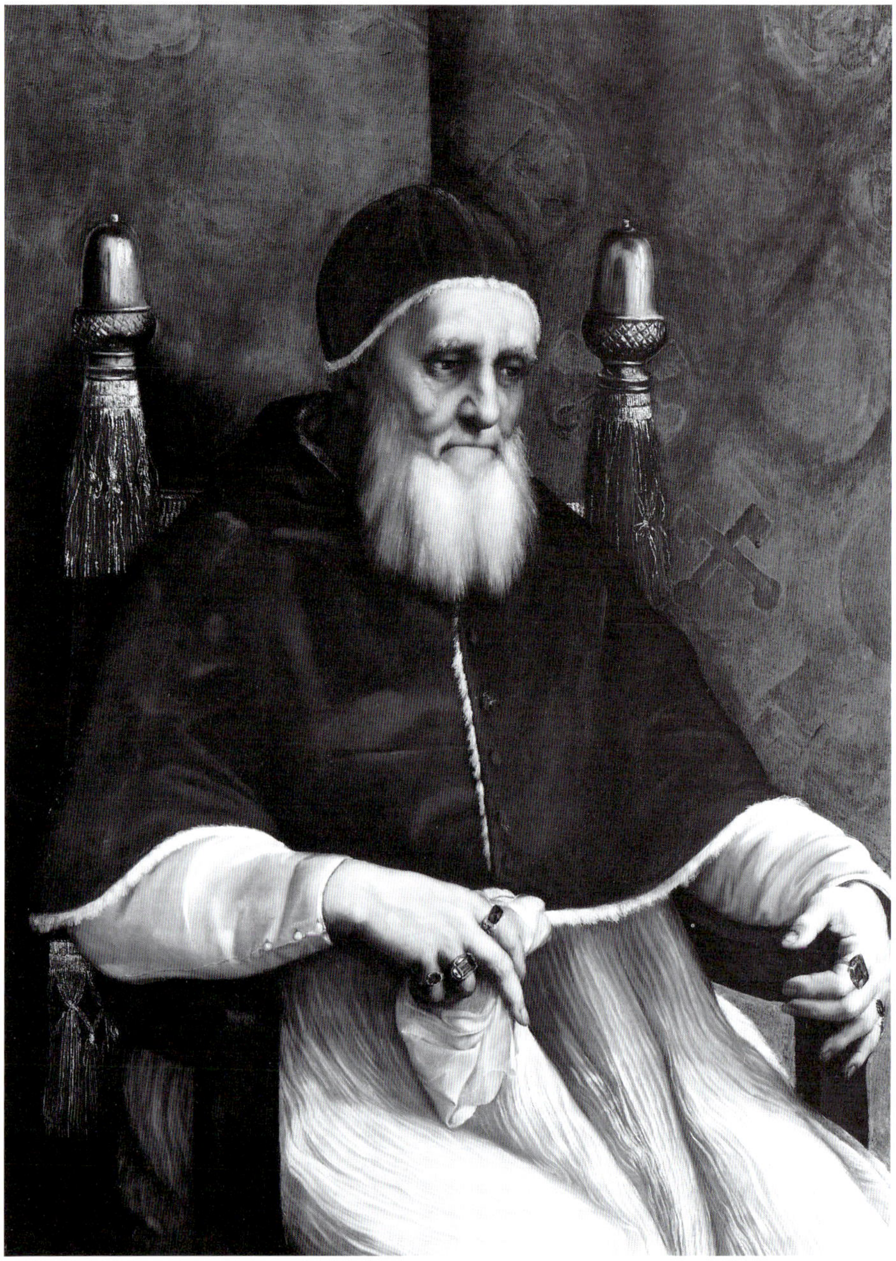

68 Justus of Ghent, *Pope Sixtus IV*, poplar panel, 116 × 56.4 cm., Louvre, Paris (M.I. 644).

Twenty eight representations of 'Famous Men', painted in seven groups of four for the *studiolo* of the palace at Urbino, were subsequently cut into their component parts and have been divided between the Louvre and the Galleria Nazionale at Urbino. The *Sixtus IV*, which formed the lower-right part of one panel, was the only one of the series in which a living person was depicted: Francesco della Rovere was elected Pope in 1471, took the name Sixtus IV and died in 1484. According to Vespasiano da Bisticci (1421–98), the 'Famous Men' were painted for Federico da Montefeltro, Duke of Urbino, who died in 1482, by a '*maestro solenne*' whom he had summoned from Flanders. The 'maestro' was clearly Justus of Ghent, who executed an altarpiece at Urbino in 1473–4. The 'Famous Men' were painted in the mid-1470s. It may be demonstrated, by comparing other portraits of the pope, that Justus's picture is an accurate likeness of Sixtus.

See Lavalleye, 1964, pp. 49, 51; here pp. 44, 61, 69, 109, 232, 233.

69 Raphael, *Pope Julius II*, poplar panel, 108 × 87 cm., National Gallery, London (27).

Giulio della Rovere, born in 1443, was elected pope in 1503, took the name Julius II and died in February 1513. Raphael's portrait, apparently painted in 1511–12, was presented to the church of Santa Maria del Popolo in Rome, where it was exhibited on an altar for eight days. According to Vasari, it was 'so wonderfully life-like and true that it inspired fear as it if were alive'.

See Gould, 1975, pp. 208–10; here pp. 61, 233.

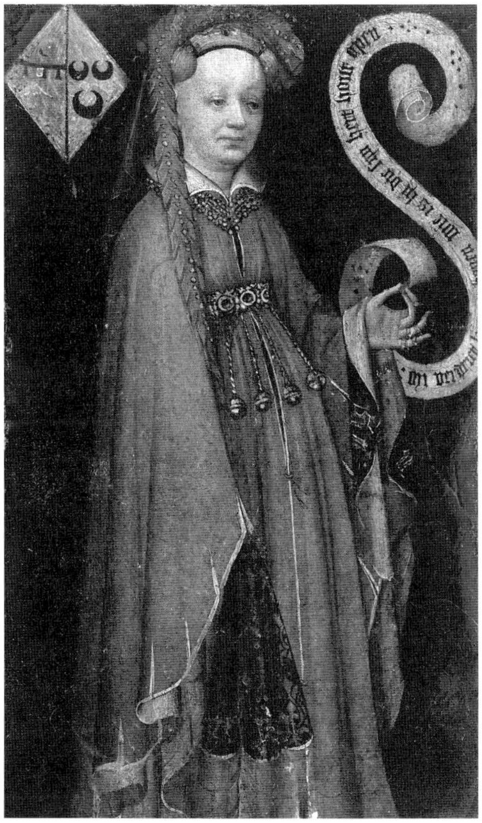

70 Netherlandish, c. 1430, *Lysbeth van Duvenvoorde*, parchment mounted on panel, 32.5 × 20.5 cm., Rijksmuseum, Amsterdam (c 1454, lent from the Mauritshuis, The Hague).

The inscription on the scroll that she holds reads: 'I have long yearned with hope; who is he who will open his heart?' The lost pendant of her husband is known to have borne the inscription 'I am greatly troubled; who is she who will honour me with her love?' An old inscription on the reverse identifies the sitter as Lysbeth van Duvenvoorde, who married Simon van Adrichem on 19 March 1430, died in 1472 and was buried at Beverwijck. The portrait was evidently painted at the time of her marriage.

See the exhibition catalogue Amsterdam, 1958, p. 40 (3); here p. 61.

painted in the mid-fourteenth century: in the former, John's head and shoulder are seen; in the latter, only Rudolf's head, neck and a very restricted area of his torso are represented. By about 1400 in France and the Low Countries, and rather later in Germany and Italy, one or both hands were often included and the figure was seen to the waist (plates 81, 138).[76] Fifteenth-century artists tended to leave little space around their sitters, who generally seem somewhat constricted within their frames. This is particularly apparent in the work of Van der Weyden, whose compositional formula was widely imitated over a long period in the Netherlands and elsewhere (plates 65, 80, 111, 154, 250).[77] In France, however, Fouquet from about 1450 began to allow his sitters more space (plate 66) and to cut their bodies below their waists; while at Urbino in the 1470s the Netherlandish artist Justus of Ghent, in his series of famous men, showed the seated Pope Sixtus IV to the knees (plate 68). Once the subject was represented to below the waist, it became obvious whether he was seated or standing. In Leonardo's portraits of the standing *Lady with a Ferret*, of about 1490 (plate 67), and of the seated *Mona Lisa*, of about 1503–6,[78] the sitters are seen to below their waists; while Cranach, in his portraits of Johannes Cuspinian and his wife, painted in 1502–3, represented them seated and to the knees (plates 143, 144). Raphael, in his portrait of Pope Julius II, painted in about 1512, used in reverse the composition of Justus of Ghent's *Sixtus IV* (plates 68, 69). In his *Joanna of Aragon*, of 1518, he further extended the area of the seated subject's body by showing her to below her knees (plate 71) and the composition of this portrait was much imitated, notably by Titian (plate 45), Bronzino (plate 38) and Mor (plate 216). Portraits of standing people developed in a similar manner, and by the mid-sixteenth century standing subjects were usually cut at mid-thigh level. This was partly so that they could balance portraits of seated subjects of the *Joanna of Aragon* type but perhaps mainly because it was convenient to close the composition just below the hands; and the hands of a relaxed standing figure will fall at thigh level (plates 87, 159, 194).

Head-and-shoulders portraits continued, of course, to be produced throughout the period (plates 162, 181, 199, 233) and would always have been cheaper, but the fashionable trend seems to have been towards including an increasingly large area of the sitter's body. There are, however, exceptions to the pattern: the portrait of Lysbeth van Duvenvoorde, executed in the North Netherlands apparently at the time of the sitter's marriage in 1430, depicts her nearly to the ankles (plate 70); a portrait painted in about 1450 by an artist from the circle of Van der Weyden shows the subject to the hips (plate 212). Since descriptions of lost portraits are rarely precise as to length, it is not possible to check against documentary evidence the impressions formed from a study of originals and copies. As in the demonstrable cases of the group portraits and full-length portraits, accidents of survival may give a falsified idea of the development of the half-length portrait.

5 Portrait Drawings

By the 1470s and perhaps earlier, portrait drawings were being commissioned, given as presents, collected and used in much the same ways as painted portraits, for which they were evidently cheaper and more easily portable substitutes. François Villon in his *Testament* made an ironic reference to an ink drawing that was to serve as a cheap effigy for the author's tomb.[79] In the inventory taken in 1471–2 of René of Anjou's possessions at the castle of Angers were listed eight small panels with portraits in leadpoint of René, his wife, his deceased son and other lords.[80] In a letter of 1475, it was stated that Galeazzo Maria Sforza had been portrayed by Mantegna but that he had 'had the sheets of paper burned because he felt that he had not done him well'.[81] The portraits were presumably drawings. In 1477, Mantegna himself complained to Ludovico Gonzaga, Marquis of Mantua, that he had not specified whether portraits which he had ordered were to be 'in drawing only or in colour';[82] and in 1489, Mantegna promised to send from Rome to Francesco Gonzaga, Marquis of Mantua, a drawing of the Turkish prince Djem, then a prisoner in the Vatican.[83] Frederick the Wise, Elector of Saxony, sent to Milan in 1492 an envoy charged to obtain a portrait of Bianca Maria Sforza. He procured from Giovanni Ambrogio Preda a charcoal drawing of the lady, which evidently interested Frederick, for he then dispatched the same envoy to Milan again to secure a 'coloured portrait'.[84] In 1493, Beatrice d'Este, Duchess of Milan, sent to her mother in Ferrara a drawing of her infant son, which was then forwarded to Beatrice's sister Isabella in Mantua.[85] At Innsbruck in 1493, the Duchess of Tyrol showed two drawn portraits, sent from Flanders, to Bianca Maria Sforza, who had recently married the Emperor Maximilian I. One was of Bianca Maria herself, 'copied from another portrait', while the other was of Maximilian's son Philip the Handsome. The painter Giovanni Ambrogio Preda, who happened to be present, remarked that he had with him a drawing of Bianca Maria's uncle Ludovico il Moro, Duke of Milan. It was brought and shown to the duchess, who afterwards sent for it again so that her husband could see it.[86] In 1495, Isabella d'Este received a portrait of her brother Cardinal Ippolito that was evidently a drawing: she wrote that the portrait pleased her but that it would be much more agreeable if she could have 'the other coloured portrait'.[87]

Leonardo apparently made two versions of his drawn portrait of Isabella d'Este, one of which he kept and the other of which her husband gave away (plate 93). In 1501, she wrote to a Florentine correspondent to ask if Leonardo would supply her with another version of his drawing;[88] in 1504, she wrote to Leonardo himself to remind him that he had promised to work up his drawing of her into a 'coloured face' – a painted portrait.[89] Leonardo had clearly made a presentation portrait drawing and kept a drawn version with the intention of using it as the basis for a painted portrait. This shows how difficult it can be to distinguish between a preparatory and a presentation drawing: in the cases of surviving portrait drawings, it is often impossible to tell preparatory drawings from drawings that were finished works of art and from drawn copies of paintings. Copies were made sometimes by other artists and sometimes by the painters themselves, in order to preserve records of them in case the sitters wished to order further versions (plate 201).[90] Drawn copies of portraits of well-known people were collected and made up into albums;[91] preparatory drawings, too, seem occasionally to have been acquired by the sitters together with their painted portraits,[92] or by collectors when the contents of artists' workshops were dispersed.[93] Copy drawings and preparatory drawings might easily and confusingly come together in the same collections or even albums.[94]

71 Raphael, *Joanna of Aragon*, panel transferred to canvas, 120 × 95 cm., Louvre, Paris (INV. 612).

The sitter (c. 1500–77) was a grand-daughter of Ferdinand I, King of Naples, was betrothed in 1518 to Ascanio Colonna, Constable of Naples, and was celebrated for her supreme beauty and her intellectual accomplishments. The portrait was commissioned by Cardinal Bibbiena as a gift for Francis I, King of France, apparently so that Francis might admire her perfections. Raphael did not himself go to Naples to paint Joanna but sent one of his pupils, who prepared a 'cartoon'. According to Vasari, the portrait was painted by Giulio Romano but Raphael executed the face, where important changes have been revealed by X-ray and infra-red photography. There is, however, no evidence that Raphael saw Joanna. The picture arrived in France before 29 December 1518, when Alfonso I d'Este, Duke of Ferrara, wrote from Paris to express his wish to have the 'cartoon'. It was sent to Ferrara from Rome on 1 February 1519 and Raphael offered to paint a replica in oil on panel. The 'cartoon' has been lost, but clearly impressed artists who saw it, including Titian (see plate 45).

See the exhibition catalogue Paris, 1983–4, pp. 98–101 (12), 421–3; Béguin, 1984, pp. 54–7; here pp. 61, 118, 234, plate 172.

6 Portrait Miniatures

The early history of the portrait miniature is very obscure. In 1405, on the death of Margaret of Flanders, Duchess of Burgundy, there was found among her effects at Dijon 'a panel of wood with an image of my lady, hanging from a little silver

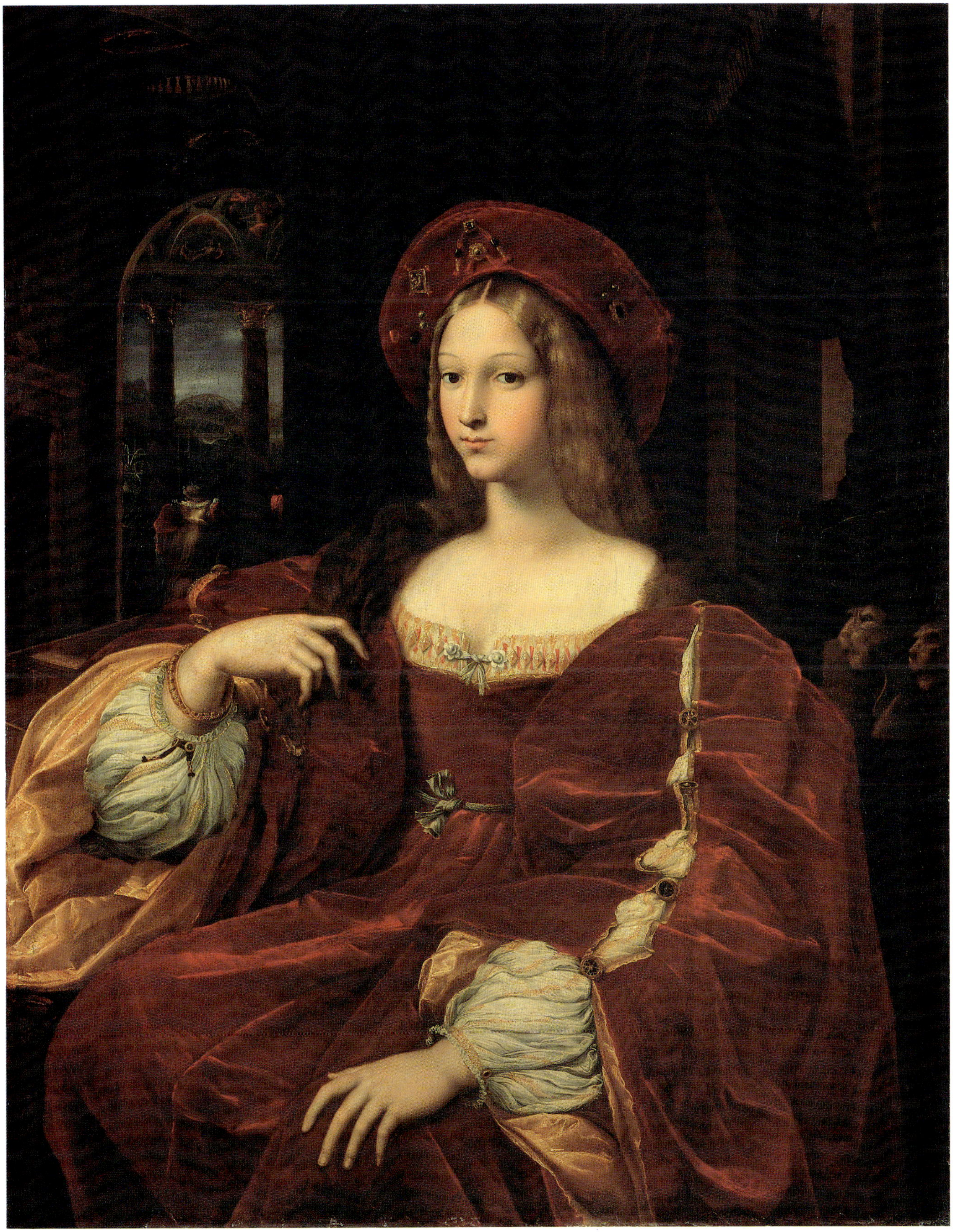

chain'. The little chain, and the fact that the picture turned up in a chest that also contained chemises and kerchiefs, might indicate that it was considered to be an article of apparel, a miniature portrait that was intended to be worn.[95] What seems to have been a fifteenth-century portrait miniature on ivory was given to Margaret of Austria by Guillaume de Croy, Lord of Chièvres, and was described in three sixteenth-century inventories. The most detailed description, in a 1560 inventory of objects that had belonged to Mary of Hungary, is as follows:

> A small picture of ivory of an old personage wearing the Golden Fleece at his neck, the four corners of the said picture being of silver gilt, and at each corner there is a steel; the said picture hangs from a little chain and is said to be a portrait of Philip the Good, Duke of Burgundy.[96]

In 1516, Margaret of Austria owned miniature portraits of herself and the Countess of Hoorn: 'another picture, of limning, with the head of my lady, which is a little spoiled; another of my lady of Hoorn, also of limning'.[97] If not being worn, these small and vulnerable objects were stored with great care. At the castle of Enghien in 1528 were 'eleven small pictures in which are portrayed on parchment several princes, princesses and great lords, framed in gold, in a little silver gilt coffer'.[98] Elizabeth I of England kept in her bedchamber 'a litle lettroun wherin wer dyuers litle pictures wrapped within paiper, and wreten vpon the paiper, thir names with hir awen hand'.[99]

Portraits cut from illuminated manuscripts cannot always be distinguished from independent portrait miniatures. Though traditions in portraiture established in manuscript illumination cannot be treated here, it should be stressed that all the portrait types that exist in large-scale paintings may also be found in manuscripts (plate 206). On occasion, panel painters were employed to paint miniature portraits in manuscripts;[100] one of them was Jean Clouet, whose roundel portraits of the heroes of the Battle of Marignano, painted in 1519 in the second volume of François du Moulin's *Commentaire de la Guerre Gallique*, are virtually indistinguishable from his independent portrait miniatures.[101]

The earliest surviving independent portrait miniatures were produced in the 1520s (plate 183). Though only English examples have been studied with enthusiasm, such miniatures enjoyed a great vogue throughout Europe. While most showed only the sitters' heads and shoulders (plates 163, 183), it is possible to cite examples of miniature group portraits, double portraits, full-length portraits and half-length portraits.[102]

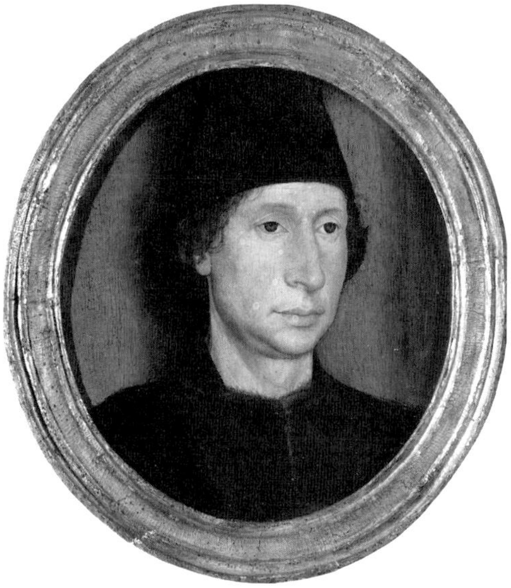

72 Hans Memlinc, *Man*, panel (oval), 21.5 × 19 cm., Private Collection, United Kingdom.

There are no indications of the sitter's identity. On grounds of style and costume, the portrait may be attributed to Memlinc and dated around 1470.

See Friedländer, 1967–76, vib, p. 112 (Add. 258); here p. 64.

7 Shapes, Supports, Pigments, Media

Most portraits are rectangular, but circular or oval portraits survive from the fifteenth century[103] and the majority of portrait miniatures are round or oval (plates 72, 73, 163, 183). In the Netherlands and elsewhere in northern Europe during the later fifteenth and earlier sixteenth centuries, arch-topped supports were in vogue for portraits as for religious and mythological subjects (plates 61, 236). A series of triangular portraits, made for the Archduke Ferdinand of Tyrol in the latter part of the sixteenth century, was a curious experiment and, as far as is known, an isolated case.[104]

The supports most commonly used were panels, and some portrait painters evidently took great care to supervise the construction of their panels. Bronzino, for example, executed several of his large portraits on panels extravagantly formed

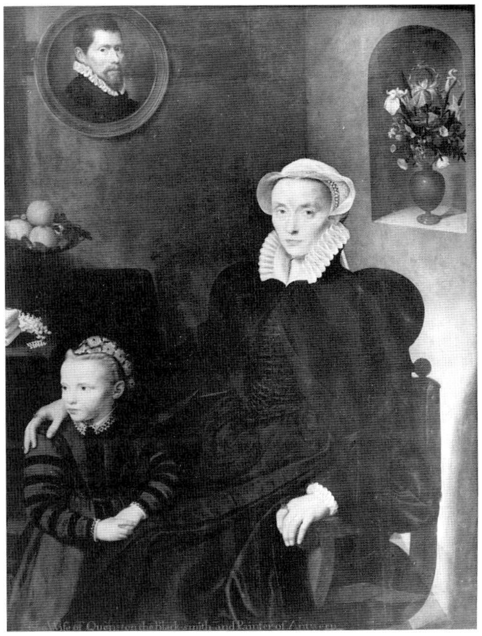

73 Monogrammist CV, *A Lady and her Daughter*, panel, 137 × 107 cm., Louvre, Paris (R.F. 1950–42).

The portrait carries the monogram CV and the date 1576; the inscription identifying the sitter as the wife of Quinten Metsys is a late addition and of no account, though the unidentified artist probably worked in Antwerp. The round painting fixed to the wall behind the sitter may be assumed to be a portrait of the lady's deceased husband, the father of the child.

See Michel, 1953, pp. 99–100; here p. 64.

of one wide central board flanked by two narrow planks: his sitter's head, painted entirely on the central plank, would then not be endangered if the joints of the panel sprang apart (plates 37, 38).[105] Other portraitists, for instance Mor, employed panels of standard sizes, presumably supplied in quantities by the same panel-makers.[106] Panels had the advantage that their reverses might also be decorated; it was more troublesome to frame two canvases back to back (plates 74, 113, 167–8).[107] Canvas was coming increasingly into use, particularly for portraits that were to be transported over long distances: as Mantegna remarked in 1477, these 'should be done on fine canvas so that they can be wound around a small roller'.[108] A portrait of a duke, 'steyned upon cloth of silver' and presented by the Florentine Serjeant Painter Anthony Toto to Edward VI of England in the New Year of 1552, was presumably an expensive curiosity, painted in a technique that cannot have been often or easily employed.[109] Some Italian painters executed portraits in fresco on tiles.[110] Sebastiano del Piombo 'introduced a new method of colouring in oils upon stone, which greatly pleased people, as it seemed that such works ought to last for ever and that neither fire nor worm could harm them'; as a result, he was able to paint several portraits on slate supports.[111] Parchment, ivory and metal were used by miniature painters, and occasionally painters 'in large' used parchment or paper supports laid down on panels or canvases (plates 64, 96).[112]

Paper, often coloured, was the support commonly employed for portrait drawings, but Dürer in 1520 executed a portrait drawing in charcoal on a panel.[113] Drawn or painted portraits could be translated into other media such as mosaic or tapestry, and certain tapestry portraits have been retouched in paint to achieve greater subtlety of detail.[114]

The pigments and media used for portraits were the same as those for other paintings, illuminations and drawings: tempera, oil and fresco for large-scale portraits; gum for miniatures on parchment; oil for miniatures on metal. Portrait drawings were executed with a variety of instruments in a variety of media: metalpoint (plate 185), charcoal (plate 25), chalk (plates 24, 93, 187), ink (plate 164), water-colour, body-colour and oil (plate 193).

Painted monochrome portraits were occasionally produced. Masaccio's fresco of the consecration of Santa Maria del Carmine was painted in *terra verde*;[115] a portrait by Jacometto Veneziano of Francesco Zancho was executed 'in grisaille in black water-colour';[116] the Bruges series of Counts and Countesses of Flanders was painted in monochrome (plate 47); Margaret of Austria owned 'a portrait of the Emperor, made in black and white' and a 'small picture of the head of a Portuguese made without colour by master Jacopo de' Barbari'.[117] The last might conceivably have been a drawing rather than a painting.

8 Frames and Covers

Few portraits of the period have retained their original frames, and even those few frames that have survived have not been adequately studied (plates 22, 61, 63, 64, 65, 66, 74, 83, 102, 113). In the fifteenth and early sixteenth centuries, panels were generally framed before they were painted (plates 182, 191) and occasionally frame and panel were carved from the same piece of wood.

Though not all portraits were designed to be hung on walls,[118] the metal fixtures that would have enabled them to be hung, or to be moved into and out of protective cases, seem normally to have been inserted into the top edges rather

74 Follower of the Master of Flémalle, *Branch of Holly*, reverse of the portrait reproduced as plate 113, panel, painted surface 33.7 × 23.5 cm., Courtauld Institute Galleries, London.

The frame is original and is inscribed 'Je he ce que mord'. The inscription, which appears again on the obverse of the frame, may mean 'I have that which bites' and must be the sitter's motto, just as the holly must be his emblem. Into the top edge of the frame, at the centre of its thickness, is fixed an iron attachment which is possibly original. It would be difficult to hang the picture on a nail from this attachment, but it may have been used either to suspend it from a long chain, on which it could have been turned to show the reverse, or to enable it to be inserted into and removed from a protective case.

See Davies, 1972, p. 227; here pp. 65–6.

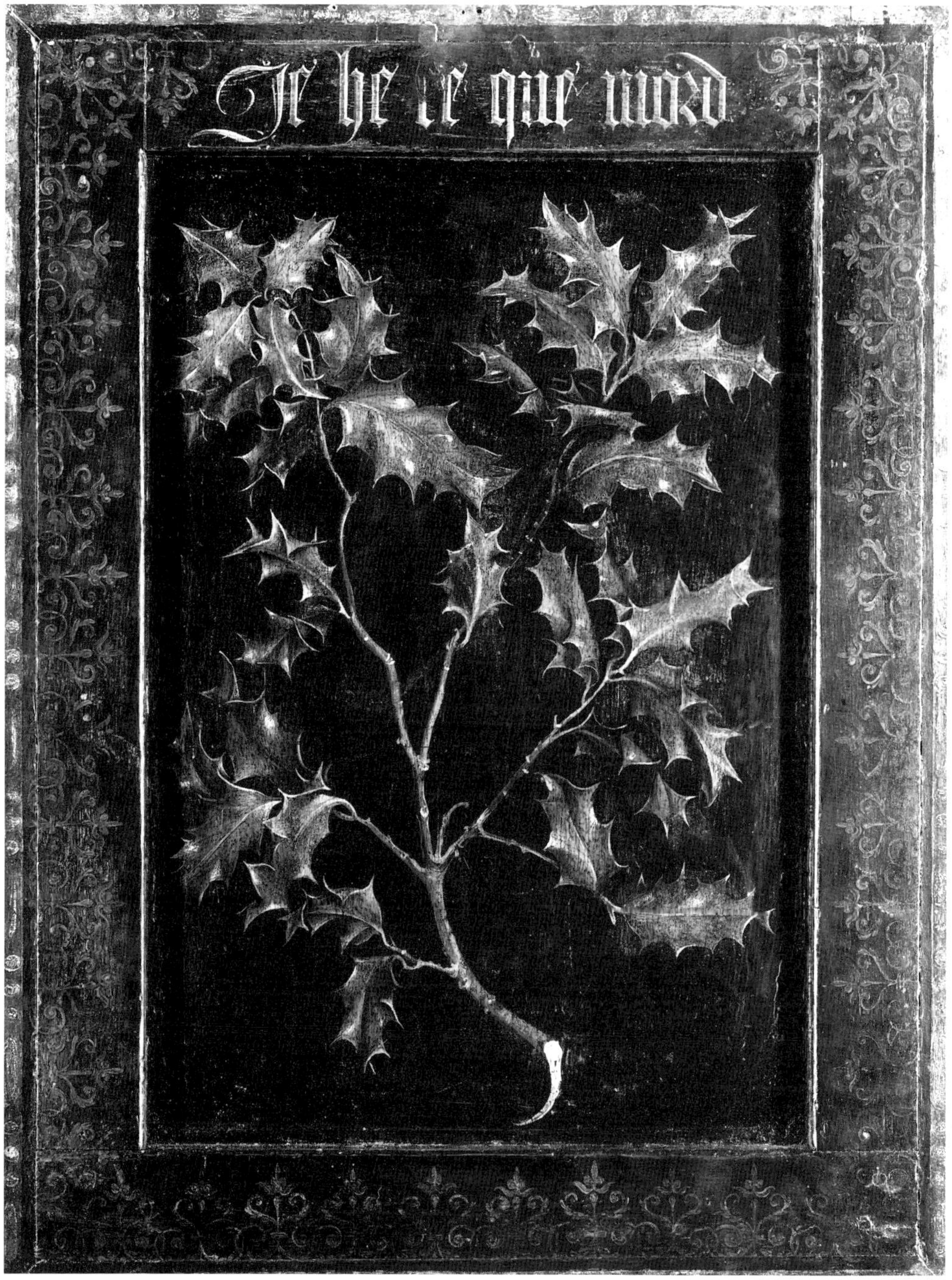

than into the reverses of the frames.[119] It is possible that some portraits with painted reverses were suspended from long chains so that they might be turned (plates 74, 113). Pictures were certainly hung in this way, for in 1404 a chain, hook and reel were supplied to Antoine of Burgundy, Duke of Brabant, 'pour pendre les tableaulx de la portraiture dudit seigneur'.[120] Some portrait frames bear marks left by the hinges to which shutters or covers were attached (plates 61), for most portraits, like other pictures, seem to have been protected by covers, shutters, curtains, cases or bags.[121] Covers were not always hinged: some, like that of Dürer's portrait of Hieronymus Holzschuher, painted in 1526, slid across the paintings in channels carved out of the frames.[122]

Some covers and shutters would certainly have been left undecorated, but others were painted with coats of arms, inscriptions or even maps.[123] Portraits themselves were occasionally used as covers for other portraits or for paintings of different subjects.[124] The most interesting of the few surviving portrait covers, by Lotto and by Bronzino (plate 246), are of an allegorical and a mythological subject.[125] Lotto in 1552 appears to have employed a mirror as a cover for a small portrait;[126] and Brantôme's anecdote of a 'great prince', possibly Louis, Prince of Condé, who gave to his mistress a mirror 'in which was his picture', provides another possible reference to the use of a mirror as a portrait cover.[127]

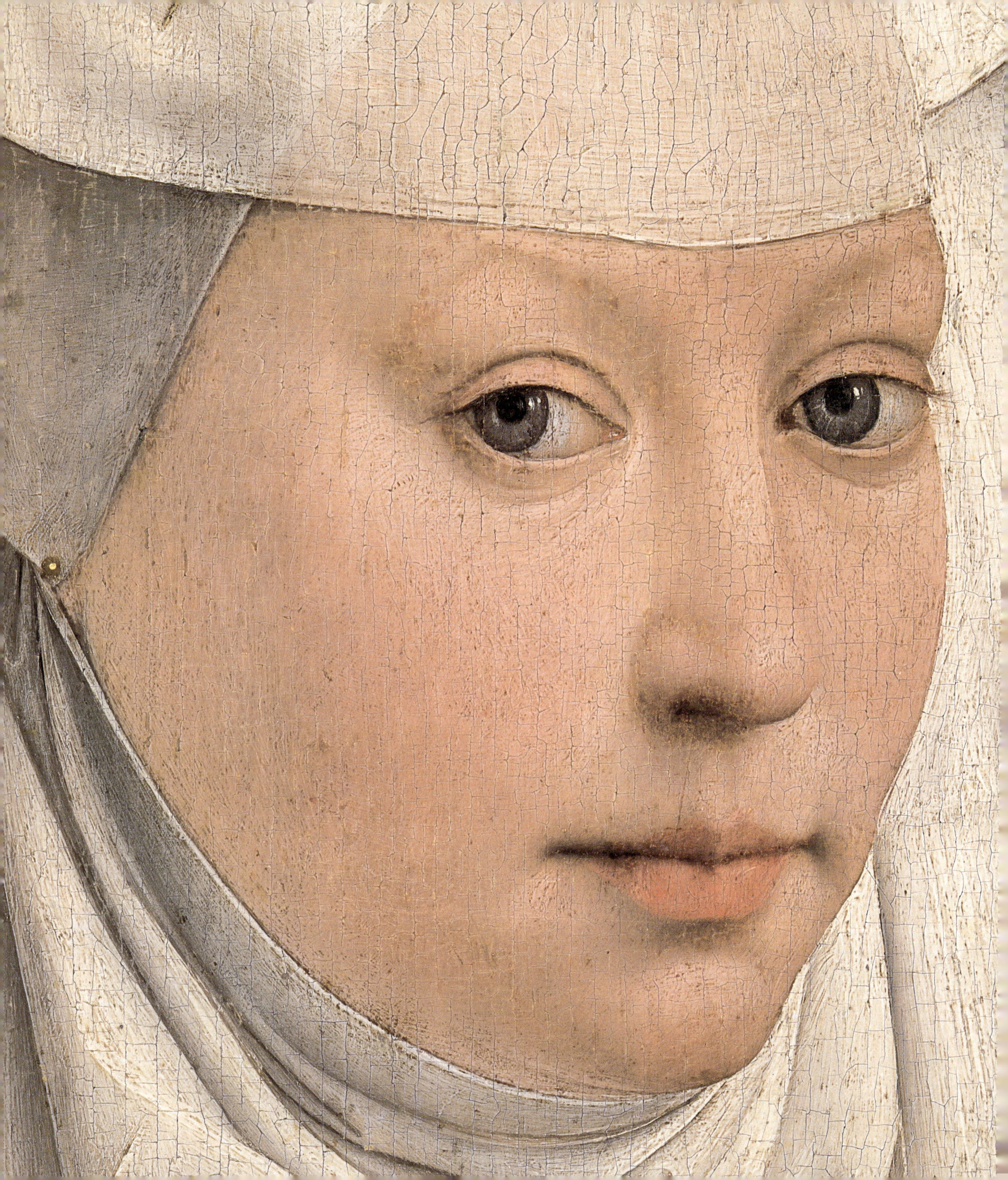

3 Poses

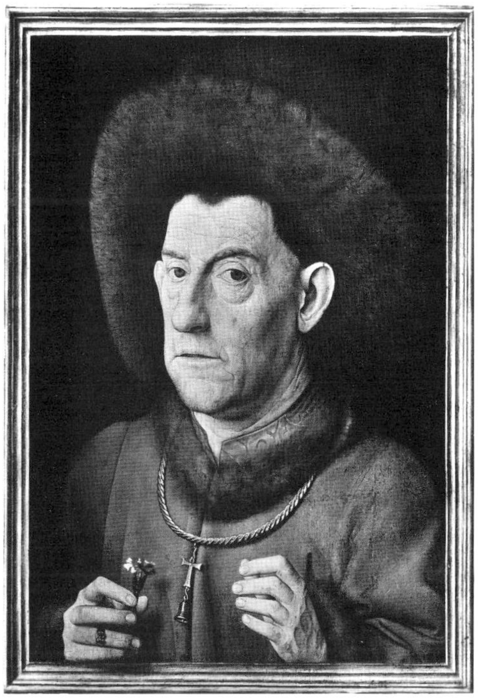

76 Follower of Jan van Eyck, '*The Man with the Pinks*', oak panel, 41.5 × 31.5 cm., Staatliche Museen Preussischer Kulturbestiz, Berlin (West), Gemäldegalerie (525 A).

The old attribution to Jan van Eyck having been unanimously rejected, the interesting portrait has been unjustly neglected. The unidentified sitter wears the collar of the Order of St Anthony, founded in 1382 at Barbefosse in Hainault by Albert of Bavaria, Count of Hainault and Holland. The costume is in the fashion of the 1430s. The picture would appear to be the work of one of Jan's associates or imitators and is remarkable in that the sitter's mouth is open, as if he is speaking or about to speak, in that he gestures with both hands and in that he is surrounded by a fictive framing structure painted to imitate a carved and gilded moulding. His head was copied by a German artist to serve as the face of the eldest king in an *Adoration of the Kings*.

See Friedländer, 1967–76, I, pp. 58–9, pl. 49; here pp. 69, 98, 109.

75 Rogier van der Weyden, *Lady*, detail (larger than actual size; see plate 80).

When composing a full-length portrait, the painter and the patron can freely exercise their inventive talents. In a portrait in which the sitter is seen at less than full length, as in other half-length images, the principal compositional problem is to justify the cutting of the figure. This problem has worried many portrait-painters, who have devised various solutions. Their public, too, seems to have been troubled by the impression that, in half-length portraits, large sections of the sitters' bodies appear to have been amputated. Domenico Mancini, reporting on events in London in 1483, prefaced his narrative with the remark: 'you should not expect from me the names of individual men and places, nor that this account should be complete in all its details: rather it shall resemble the image [*simulacrum*] of a man, which lacks some of the limbs, yet a beholder delineates for himself a man's form.'[1] The way in which the problem of cutting the figure is solved and the manner in which the sitter is posed are very often interdependent.

One simple way in which the termination of the composition might be explained was to make the frame very assertive and to stress its presence by bright colouring, striking patterning or inscriptions in bold, decorative letters (plates 22, 64). The frame would then function like a window frame, and the sitter would appear as at a window opening. Alternatively, the sitter might be surrounded by a painted framing structure, which served much the same purpose (plates 76, 106, 136) and which might also be elaborately patterned,[2] or he might be enclosed by the columns and balustrade of a balcony (plates 52, 68). More commonly, the device of the parapet was used: this might be merely a stripe along the lower edge of the painting, which could carry an inscription (plate 102), but more effective was a solid ledge, seen in three dimensions, which could also carry inscriptions (plates 39, 100, 200), support accessory details or be draped with rich cloths or carpets (plate 122). If the sitter's arms were included, one or both hands, or an elbow, might rest on the ledge (plate 77). Though parapets were used by northern artists (plates 78, 162), even to organise into tiers the many figures of a *doelenstuk* (plate 56), they were evidently more popular in Italy, where they occurred throughout the fifteenth and sixteenth centuries, usually in portraits where only the sitter's head and shoulders were seen but also, on occasion, in those where the sitter was depicted to thigh level.[3] Some North-Italian painters of the early sixteenth century preferred to use a stepped parapet (plate 79)[4] or a parapet that extended across only part of the picture and therefore lost much of its usefulness in closing the composition (plate 158).

In the Netherlands, the devices of the painted fictive frame and the parapet were rarely employed, perhaps because they were considered too obvious and obtrusive. Instead, the real frame was made to act as a parapet to support the sitter's hands. What is possibly an early instance of this practice is found in the portrait of Marie de Molembaix, perhaps of about 1400 and known from a copy in the 'Recueil d'Arras': here the sitter seems to have rested the index finger of her left hand on the frame of her portrait (plate 81). It was, however, the system perfected by Rogier van der Weyden that came to be very widely imitated. His predecessor the Master of Flémalle had decided that it was convenient to cut his half-length

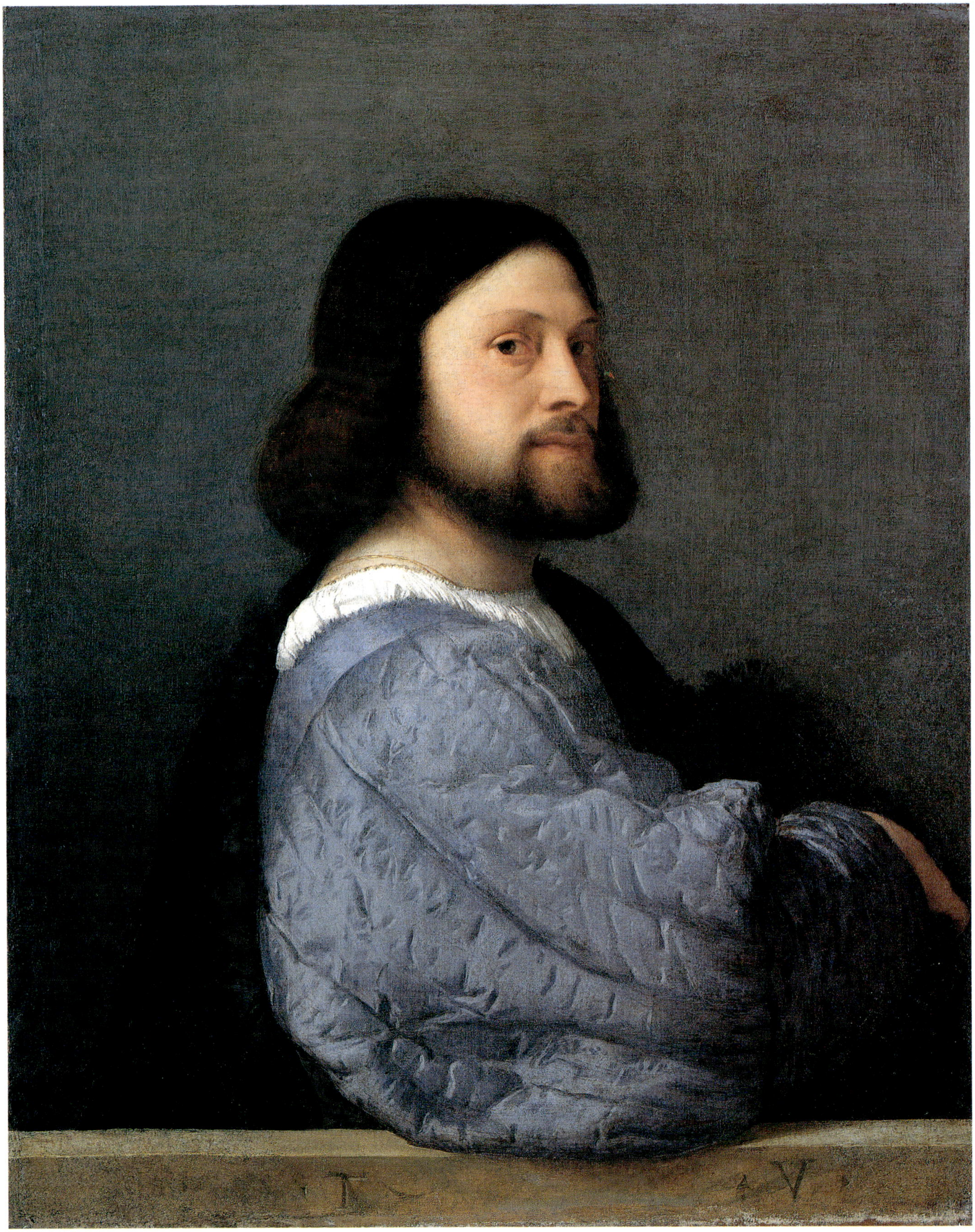

77 (left) Titian, '*The Man with the Blue Sleeve*', canvas, 81.2 × 66.3 cm., National Gallery, London (1944).

Signed with Titian's initials TV (Tiziano Vecellio), the portrait is generally dated around 1511–12; according to Hope, the sitter may be Titian himself.

See Gould, 1975, pp. 280–3; Hope, 1980, p. 30; here pp. 69, 86, 95.

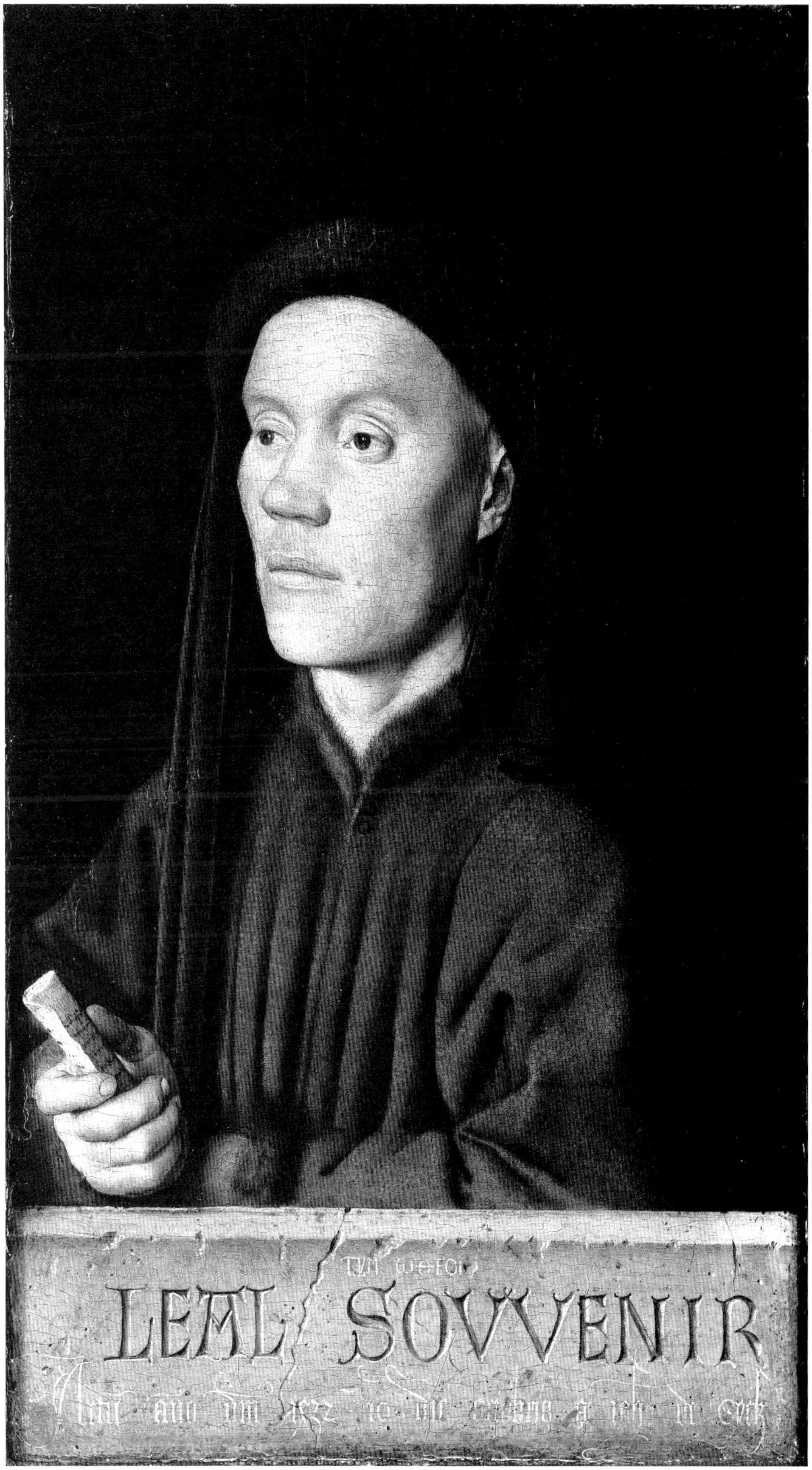

78 Jan van Eyck, '*Léal Souvenir*', oak panel, painted surface 33.4 × 19 cm., National Gallery, London (290).

As if carved into the cracked stone parapet are the words 'LEAL SOVVENIR', 'loyal remembrance'; above, as if lettered onto the stone, is the inscription 'TYM.WθEC.', for which various unsatisfactory explanations have been suggested and which may be the sitter's motto; below, as if chalked onto the stone, are the signature and date (in Latin): 'Done on 10 October 1432 by Jan van Eyck'. The writing on the scroll of paper has not been deciphered. It is not certain whether Van Eyck intended his portrait to look like those ancient Roman tombstones which it resembles in general composition; why the parapet should be damaged and cracked; whether the inscription 'LEAL SOVVENIR' should be taken as an indication that the portrait is posthumous; or why the three inscriptions should differ in style of lettering and means of application. It should also be pointed out that the sitter appears to be bald and that the point of his nose and his nostrils are malformed.

See Davies, 1968, pp. 54–5; Dhanens, 1980, pp. 182–7; here p. 69.

79 Titian, '*La Schiavona*', canvas, 118 × 97 cm., National Gallery, London (5385).

Signed with Titian's initials TV (Tiziano Vecellio), the portrait is generally dated around 1511. The relief on the parapet gives a profile view of the sitter's head; there are no indications of her identity.

See Gould, 1975, pp. 287–90; Hope, 1980, pp. 30–2; here p. 69.

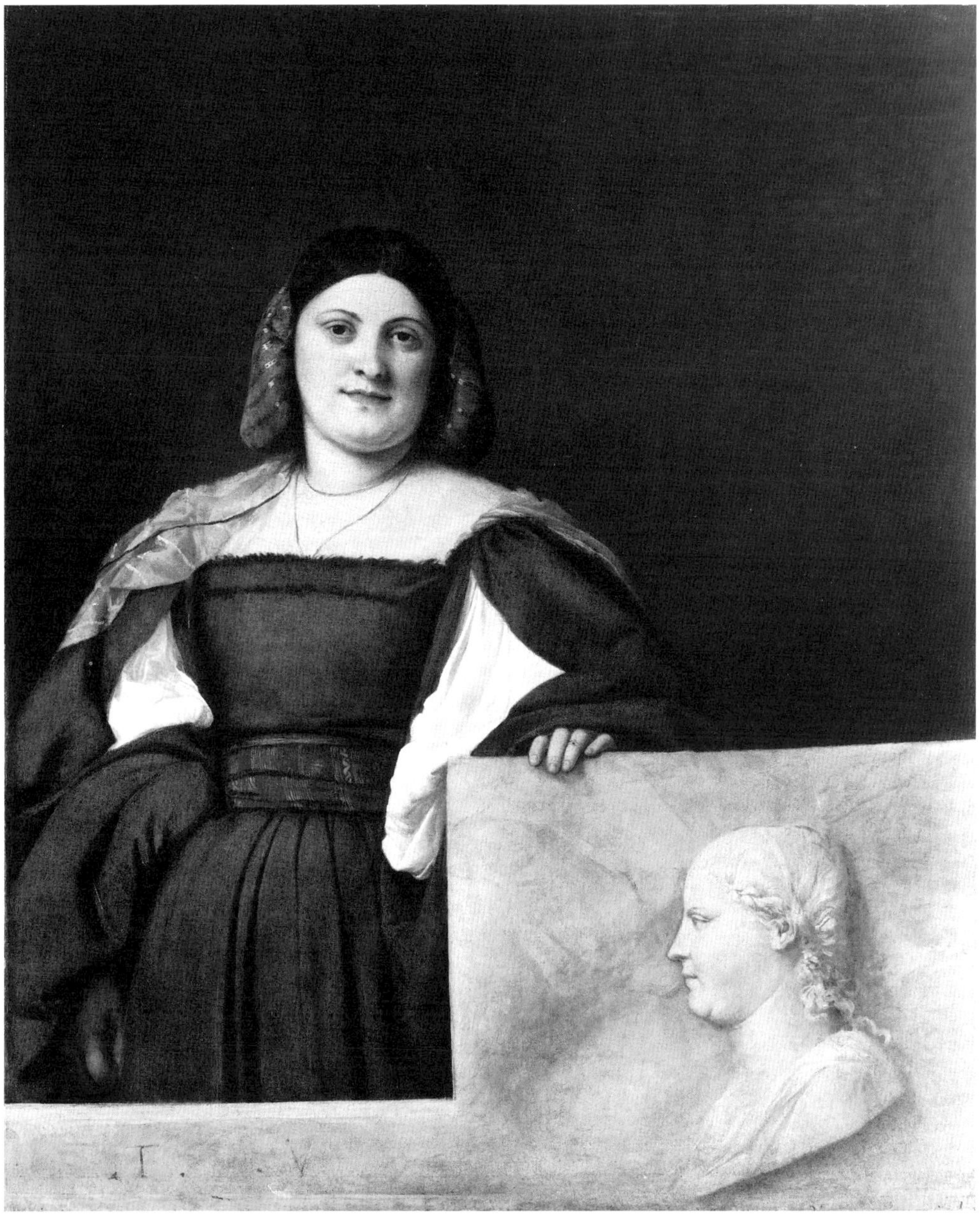

portraits through or just below his sitters' hands (plates 104–5, 231–2). Rogier's sitters rest their folded hands upon the lower edges of their frames, or rather on unseen horizontal surfaces which appear to run for short distances into the picture spaces at that level. The frames therefore act unobtrusively, if artificially, as window frames: the closure of the composition at the lower edge is fully justified and entirely acceptable (plates 80, 111, 154).

The idea of using the frame as a parapet on which the sitter's hands rested was taken up all over Europe, for example in Raphael's '*La Muta*' (plate 82).[5] It was perhaps being mocked by Bronzino in his *Bartolomeo Panciatichi*, where it is not the sitter but his dog that places its right paw on the frame (plate 137). Some of Rogier's followers, notably Memlinc, often reinstated a narrow strip of parapet above the frame, and Memlinc was inclined to disturb the unity of the picture surface, which Rogier had always respected, by making some of his sitters appear

80 (facing page, far right) Rogier van der Weyden, *Lady*, oak panel, 47 × 32 cm., Staatliche Museen Preussischer Kulturbesitz, Berlin (West), Gemäldegalerie (545 D).

On grounds of style and costume, the portrait is attributed to Van der Weyden and dated around 1435–40. Less expensively dressed than Rogier's other sitters, the lady was perhaps the wife of a prosperous burgess of Brussels.

See Davies, 1972, pp. 200–1; here pp. 61, 72, 86, 96, plate 75.

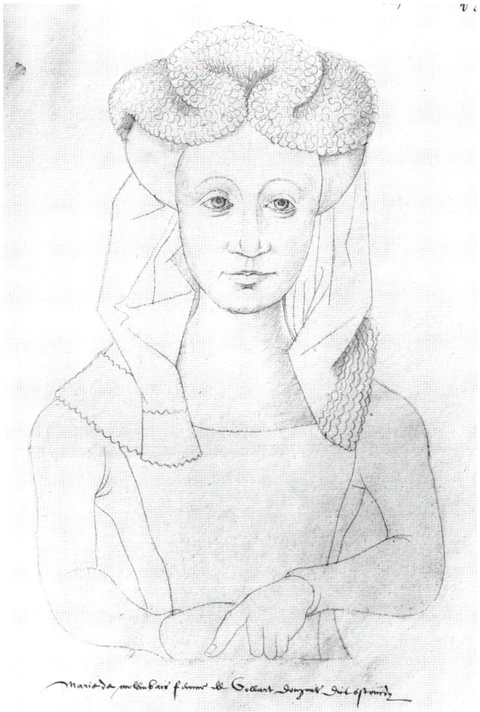

81 (above) Attributed to Jacques Le Boucq, *Marie de Molembaix, Lady of Oignies*, from the 'Recueil d'Arras', Bibliothèque municipale, Arras, MS 266, f. 224.

The 'Recueil d'Arras' is a volume of drawn copies after fourteenth-, fifteenth- and sixteenth-century portraits. The drawings are probably by the herald Jacques Le Boucq, who lived at Valenciennes, and the collection seems to have been put together during the 1560s for Alexandre Le Blancq, a gentleman of Lille (see Campbell, 1977[1], *passim*). It is not always possible to deduce whether the copies are taken from paintings, statues, stained glass or works of art in other media but the drawing of Marie de Molembaix, like that of her husband Colart, Lord of Oignies (f. 223), appears to have been made from a painted portrait. As Marie, who died in 1443, was widowed in 1414 (see the epitaphs copied in Bibliothèque Nationale. Paris, MS Duchesne 59, p. 52), the original portrait may have been painted in about 1400. Oignies is between Douai and Lille, in the French-speaking part of the County of Flanders.

See pp. 61, 69, 81.

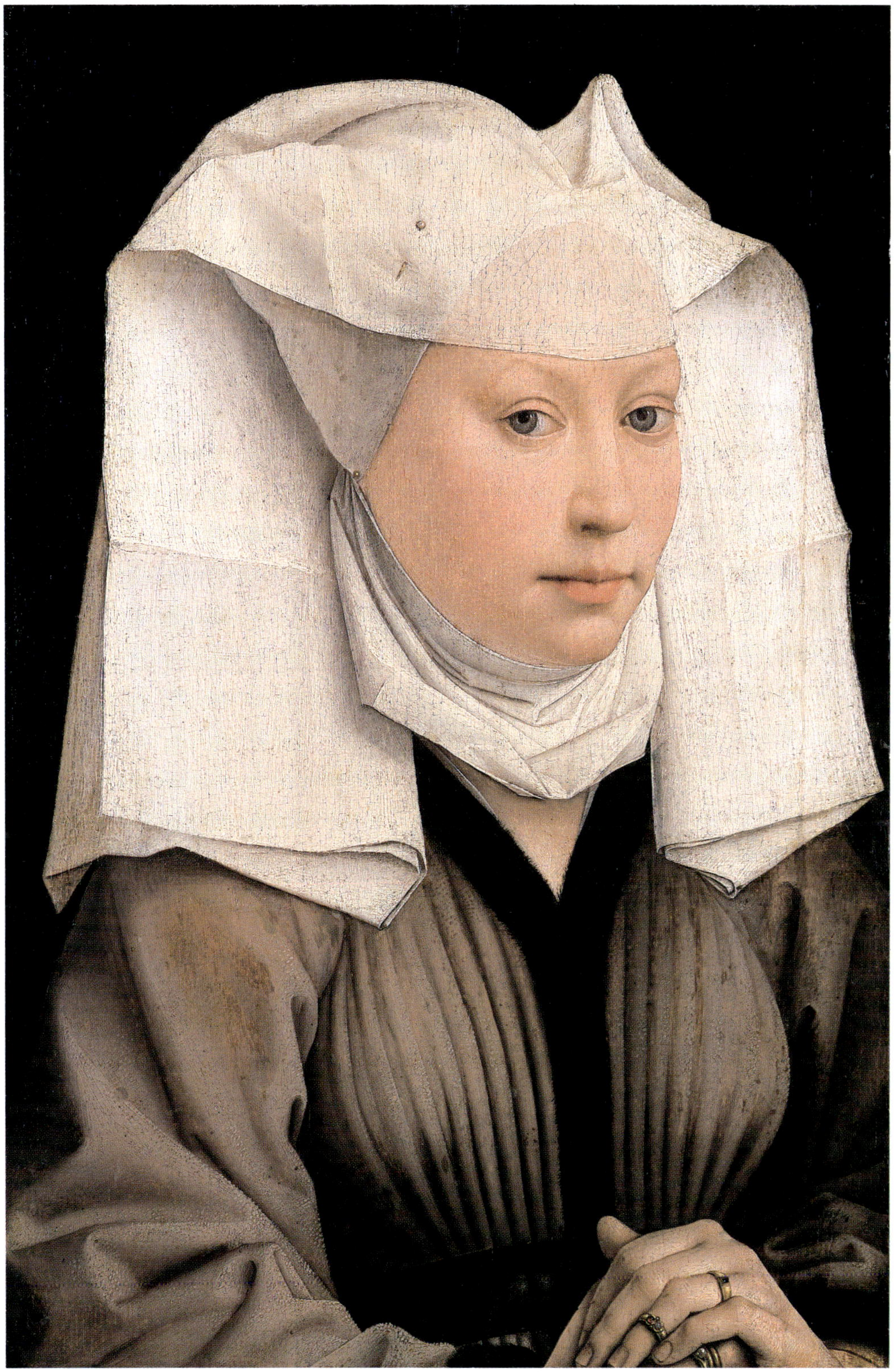

to clutch at their parapets and frames. In his *Portrait of a Lady*, dated 1480, the sitter's hands even protrude from the panel, for the ends of two of her fingers are painted upon the frame (plate 83).[6] Alternatively, the narrow vertical edge of parapet might be replaced by a narrow horizontal strip which may be construed as

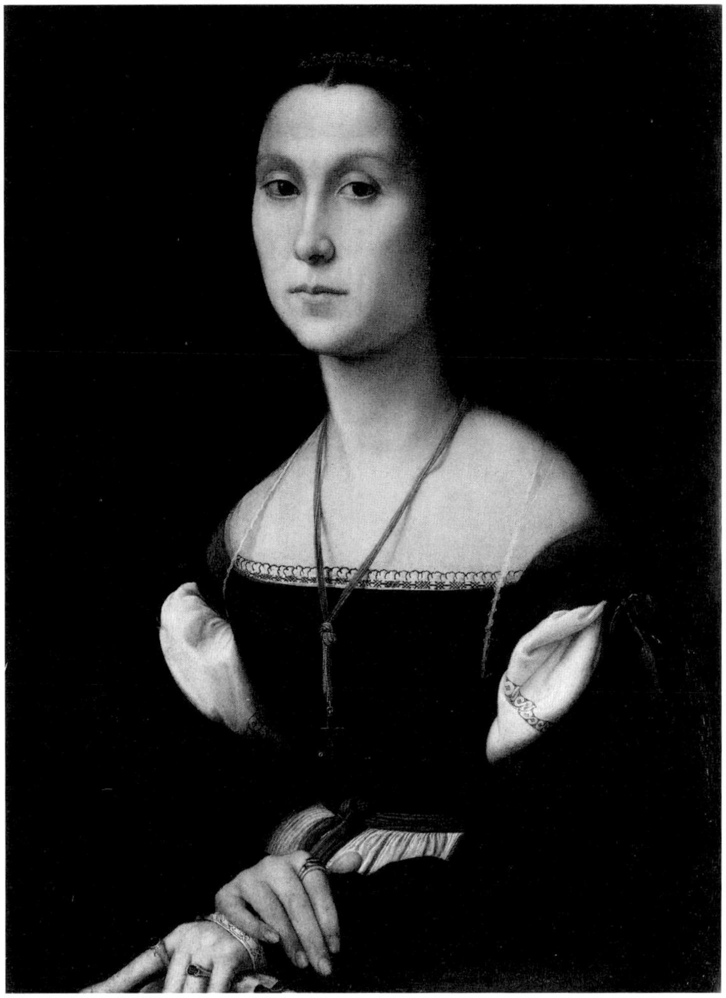

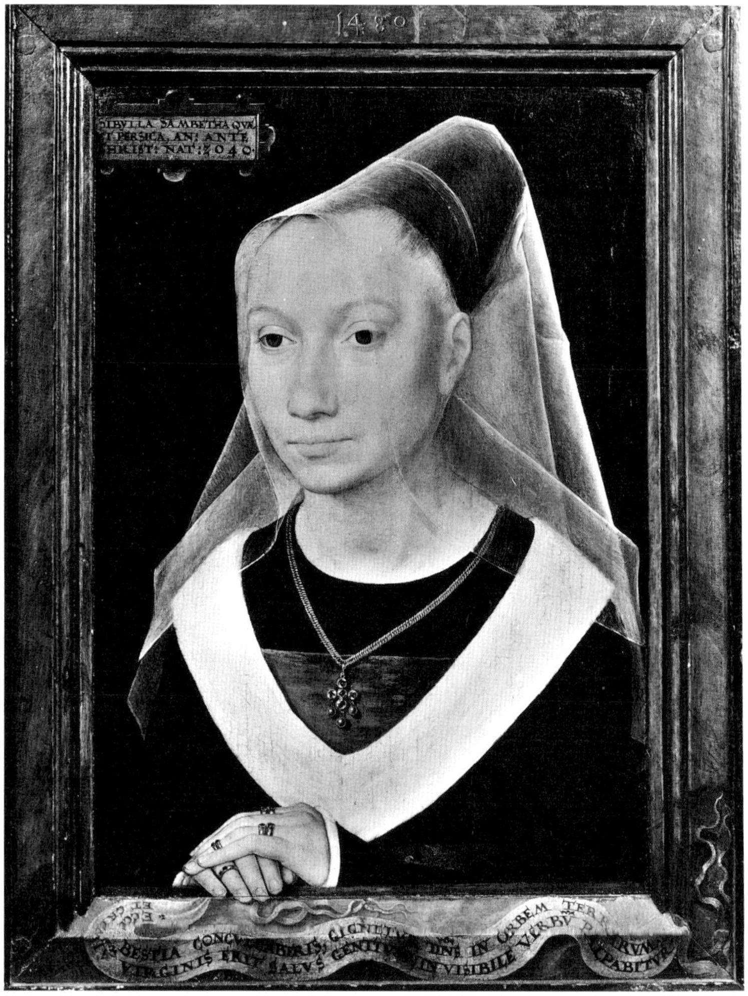

82 Raphael, '*La Muta*', panel, 64 × 48 cm., Galleria Nazionale delle Marche, Urbino (deposited from the Uffizi, 1440).

The sitter has not been identified but the portrait is generally believed to have been painted by Raphael in about 1507.

See Berti, 1979, p. 441; here p. 72.

83 Hans Memlinc, *Lady*, oak panel, 38 × 26.5 cm., Memlingmuseum, St Janshospitaal, Bruges (O.SJ 174 I).

The frame is original but the inscriptions in the upper left corner of the portrait and on the lower section of the frame, identifying the lady as the Persian Sibyl, are much later additions. The date 1480, however, which appears on the top part of the frame, is contemporary with the portrait. The sitter has not been identified; the attribution to Memlinc, made on stylistic grounds, has never been questioned.

See Lobelle-Caluwe, 1985, pp. 80–1; here pp. 65, 73.

part of a tabletop. This could extend across the portrait (plate 252) or could be angled and confined to the area immediately below the sitter's hands (plate 84).

A larger expanse of table surface might be included in front of the sitter on which his hands and other objects might be arranged (plates 61, 85, 97). This compositional scheme had disadvantages, in that the table created a barrier between sitter and spectator and an insistent horizontal accent in the design, and in that it made necessary some degree of foreshortening in the arms and hands. The table edge, however, could be broken or concealed by the sitter's arms and muted by tonal means so that the horizontal of its contour would not be too assertive (plates 86, 128, 179). If the table did not extend across the whole surface of the picture (plates 87, 178) or if it were angled so that its edge did not run parallel to the frame, it became less obtrusive a barrier (plates 42, 101, 234).

In the sixteenth century, perhaps because the half-length convention was becoming better known and more widely accepted, less attention came to be paid to artificial methods of closing such compositions. When they were employed, it may be that patrons were continuing to request, and that painters therefore were continuing to use, fictive frames, parapets and table-tops, but there was a gradual shift towards half-length images in which compositions were brought to satisfactory terminations by the artists' skills in design. If the chair of a seated subject were visible, the lines of the arms or seat of the chair might be effectively used to

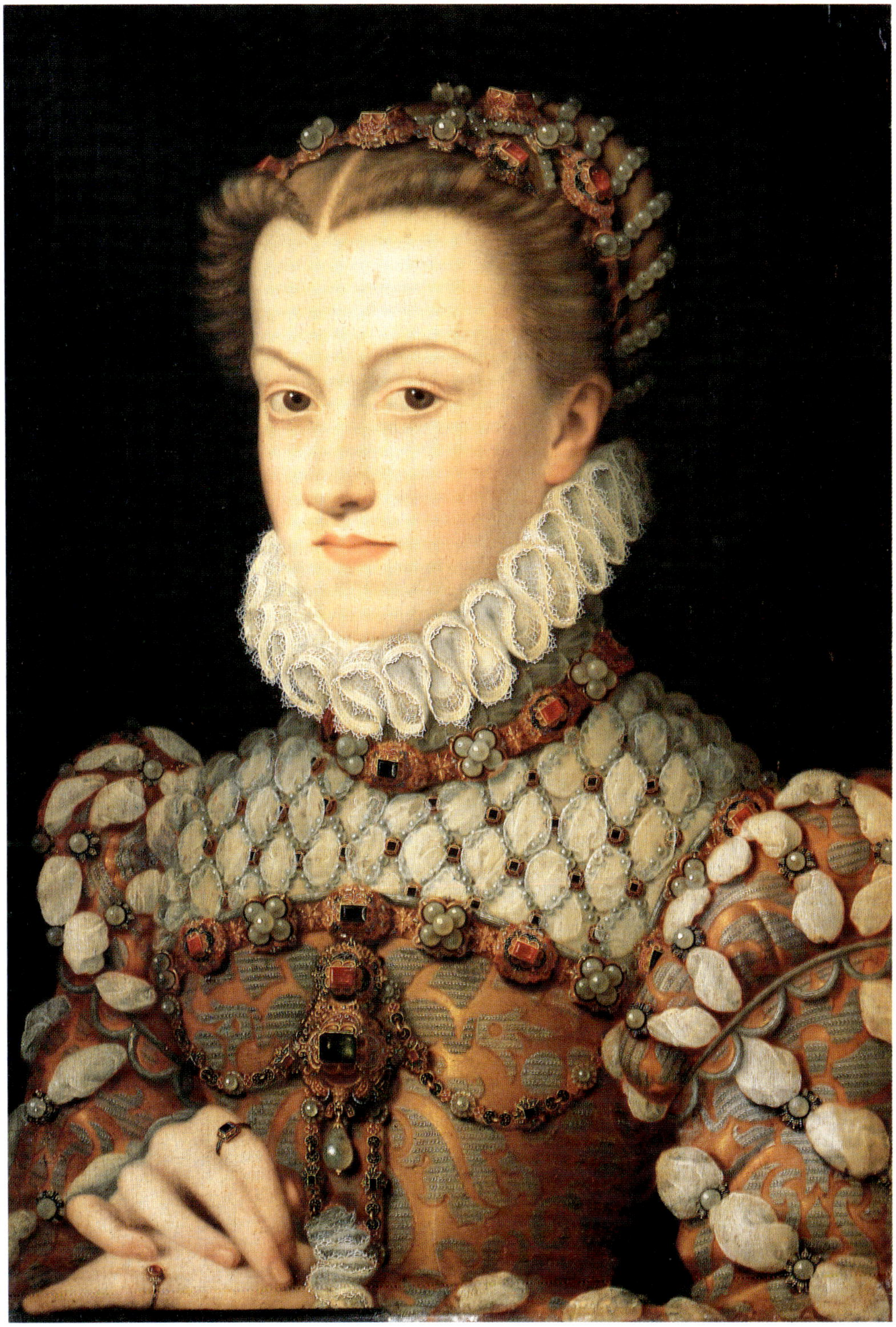

84 François Clouet, *Elisabeth of Austria, Queen of France*, oak panel, 35.9 × 26.2 cm., Louvre, Paris (INV. 3254).

Elisabeth (1554–92) was the daughter of the Emperor Maximilian II and married in 1570 Charles IX of France, who died in 1574. The highly finished preparatory drawing, dated 1571, is in the Bibliothèque Nationale (Estampes, Na 22) but the hands are based on those in a drawing executed by François Clouet about ten years earlier of Elisabeth's sister-in-law Marguerite (Chantilly, MN 42).

See Sterling and Adhémar, 1965, p. 25; here p. 74.

cut the figure (plates 88, 89). The hands provide a convenient point at which the design may be closed, and a careful arrangement of the arms and hands will give an appropriately balanced and convincingly complete composition in which the shapes formed by the sitter and his draperies will meet in quiet accord the lower edge of the support.

The portrait painter may represent his sitter frontally, in three-quarters view or

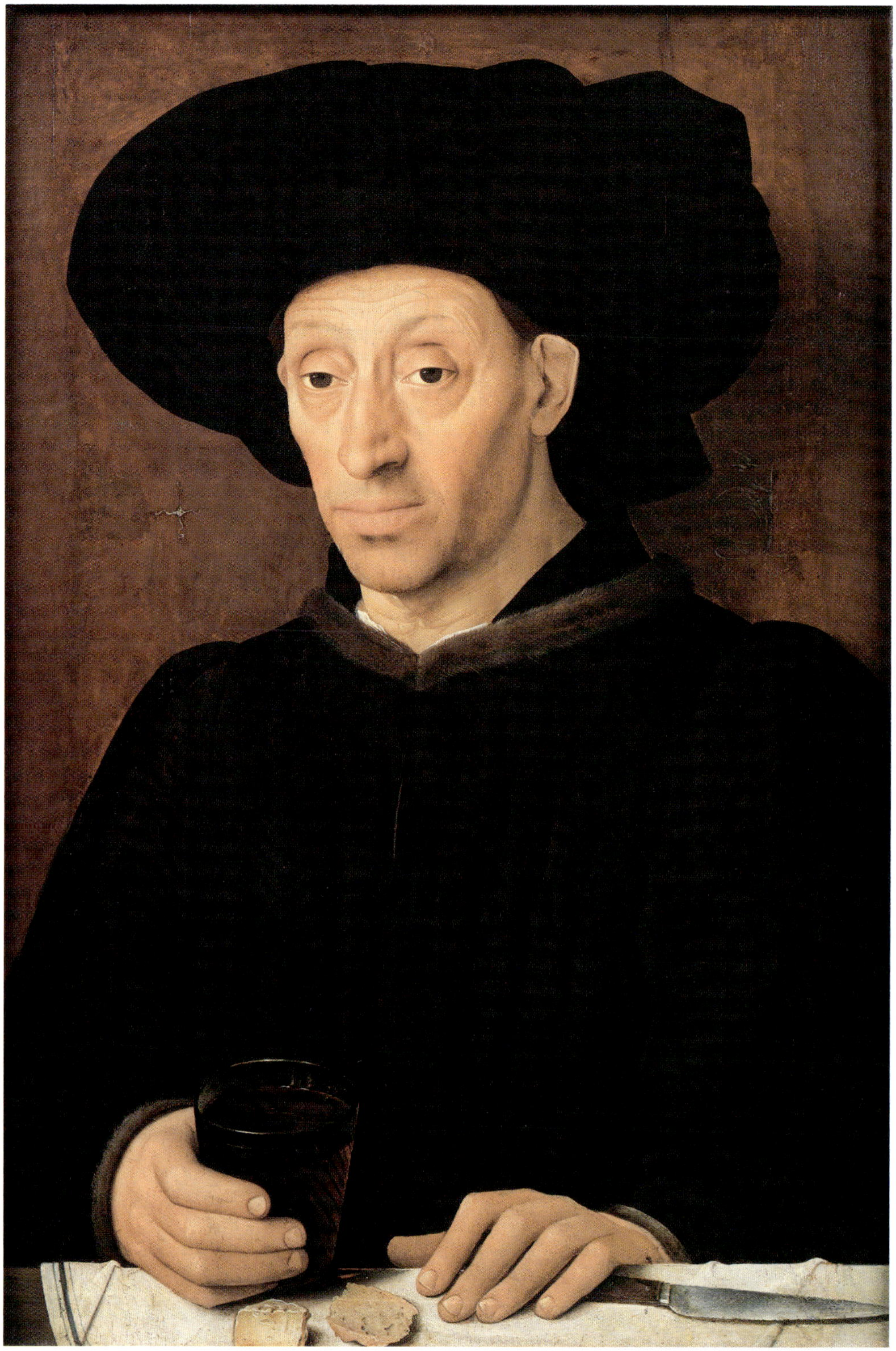

85 (right) French(?), c. 1450, *Man with a Glass of Wine*, walnut panel, 63.6 × 43.6 cm., Louvre, Paris (R.F. 1585).

There are broad vertical additions at both sides. The calligraphic patterns that appear on either side of the sitter's head and which have been damaged by abrasion may provide clues to his identity but they, and the significance of the red wine, bread and cheese, await satisfactory explanations. Currently attributed to a Portuguese artist, the portrait is perhaps more plausibly seen as the work of a French painter influenced by Fouquet. It is dated around 1450 on the basis of the sitter's costume.

See Sterling and Adhémar, 1965, p. 21; here pp. 74, 97.

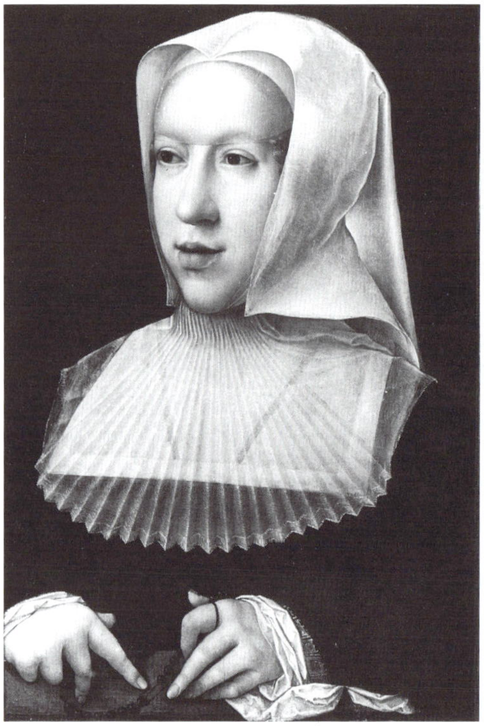

86 (above) Bernard van Orley, *Margaret of Austria*, panel, 37 × 27 cm., Musée de Brou, Bourg-en-Bresse (975.16.AB).

Van Orley, employed by the Habsburg court from 1515, was appointed painter to Margaret of Austria in 1518 and continued in her service until her death in 1530. He was regularly paid for portraits of Margaret, which may all have been taken from one basic 'pattern'. The picture now at Bourg-en-Bresse, where the sitter fingers a string of prayer beads, is so similar to signed and documented pictures by Van Orley that it may be attributed to him with every confidence. There are many versions, where her hands are differently posed; some or all of them may have been produced by him or in his workshop.

See Campbell, 1985, pp. 106–7; here p. 74.

87 (right) Titian, *Federico Gonzaga, Duke of Mantua*, panel, 125 × 99 cm., Museo del Prado, Madrid (408).

Federico (1500–40), the son of Isabella d'Este, was one of Titian's most important patrons. His portrait, signed 'TICIANVS F', was probably painted in 1529.

See Wethey, 1971, pp. 107–8; Hope, 1980, p. 68; here pp. 61, 74, 99, 112, plate 209.

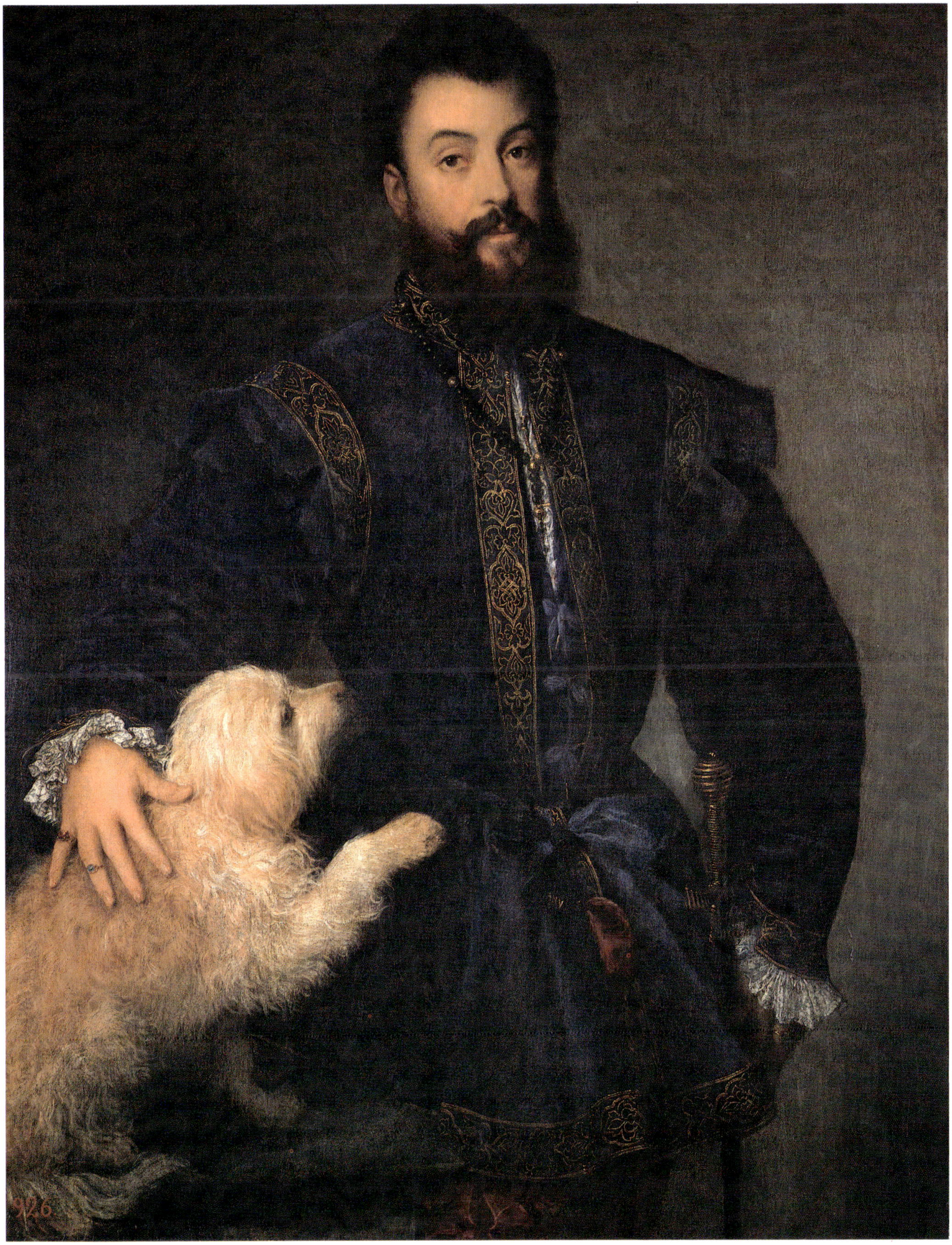
926

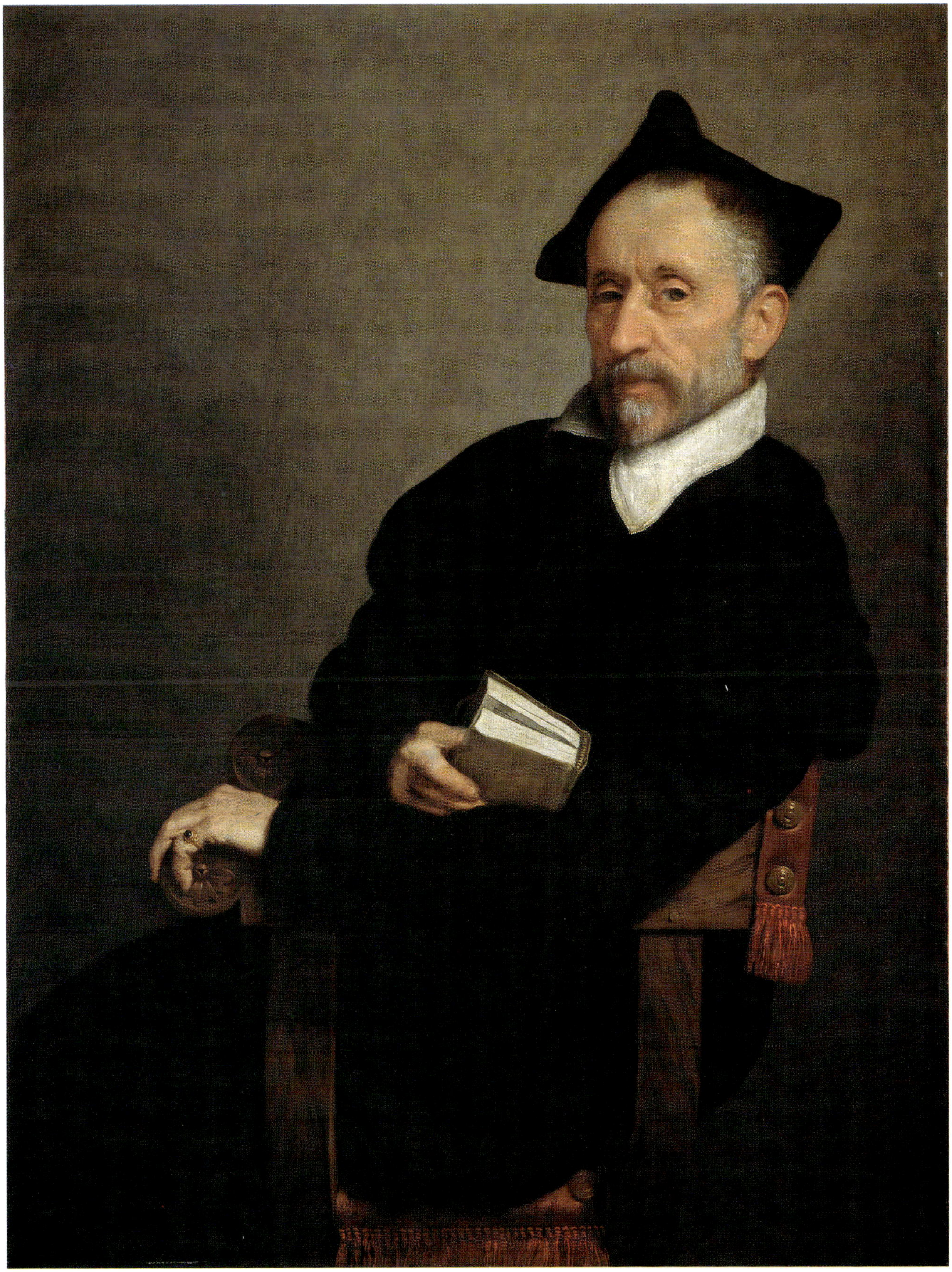

88 (p. 78) Andrea del Sarto, *Young Man*, canvas, 72 × 57 cm., National Gallery, London (690).

Signed with the artist's monogram, the portrait is thought to have been painted in the late 1510s. The sitter has not been identified; the object that he holds and that has been described as a block of stone is obviously a book.

See Gould, 1975, pp. 234–5; here pp. 75, 86, 95, 106.

89 (prev. page) Giovanni Battista Moroni, '*Titian's Schoolmaster*', canvas, 96.8 × 74.3 cm., National Gallery of Art, Washington (1942.9.45, Widener Collection).

The traditional title is entirely fanciful and there are no indications of the sitter's identity. A particularly fine example of Moroni's work, the portrait is generally dated towards 1570 on grounds of style and costume. Moroni was fond of such compositions, which he re-used many times in his half-length portraits. The diagonal formed by the sitter is highly decorative and echoes one of the principal diagonals of the canvas, while the turning pose suggests a degree of intimacy between sitter and spectator.

See Shapley, 1979, pp. 339–40; here pp. 76, 95, 99, 124.

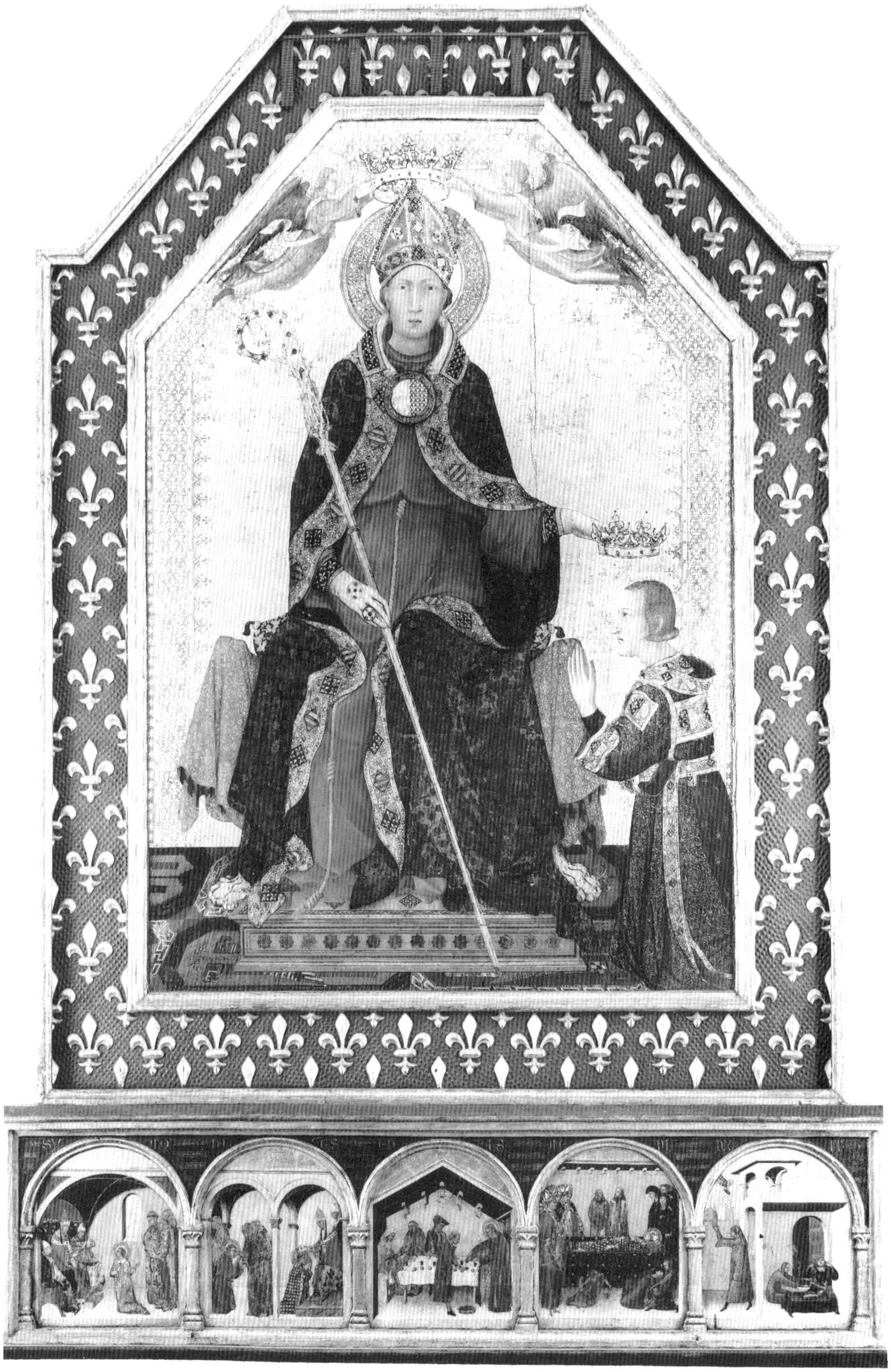

90 (right) Simone Martini, *Altarpiece: St Louis of Toulouse*, poplar panel, 250 × 188 cm.; predella 56 × 205 cm., Museo di Capodimonte, Naples, Pinacoteca (Q 34).

The frame, decorated with the coat of arms of the Angevin Kings of Naples, is original but two pilasters have been removed from its sides and a panel once attached to the horizontal edge at the top to form a pinnacle has been lost. The reverse bears a painted decoration of fleurs-de-lys. St Louis of Toulouse, second son of Charles II, King of Naples, was born in 1274 and in 1296 renounced his rights to the throne, became a Franciscan and was created Bishop of Toulouse. He died in 1297 and was canonised in 1317. He is here depicted dressed in the robe of a Franciscan and the cope and mitre of a bishop. The silver of the cope has oxidised and discoloured and the vestments have lost most of the imitation jewels once fixed upon them. Crowned by two angels, Louis himself crowns his younger brother Robert, who succeeded their father as King of Naples in 1308. In the predella are scenes from the life of Louis, his death and a posthumous miracle; in the spandrels above is the signature 'SYMON DE SENIS ME PINXIT'. The altarpiece is believed to have been painted for Robert shortly after the canonisation of Louis on 7 April 1317; a large payment made in 1317 to a 'Simone Martini, knight' may or may not refer to the painter and relate to the altarpiece. Its original destination is not known but it was later in the church of San Lorenzo in Naples. Though the head of Louis is idealised and is virtually indistinguishable from representations by Simone of saints who had died centuries earlier, the head of Robert is sharply individualised and is similar to other portraits of the king.

See Gardner, 1976, *passim*; Martindale, 1988, pp. 192–4; here p. 81.

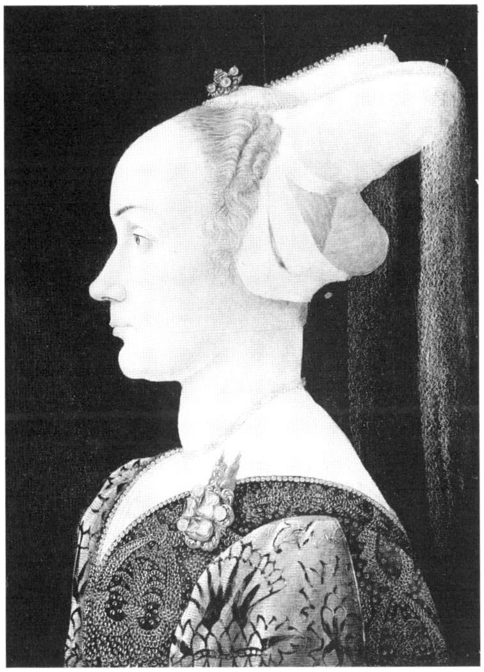

91 Florentine(?), mid-fifteenth century, *Lady*, panel, 42.6 × 20.5 cm., National Gallery of Victoria, Melbourne (1541/4, Felton Bequest 1946).

There is a vertical addition on the left and the original painting terminates at a point just to the left of the junction between the sitter's contour and the lower edge. Though dressed very richly, the sitter has not been identified.

See Hoff, 1973, p. 87; here p. 81.

92 (foll. page) Pisanello, *Ginevra d'Este*, poplar panel, 41.7 × 29.8 cm., Louvre, Paris (R.F. 766).

On the sitter's hanging sleeve is an embroidered(?) vase to which chains are attached and from which roots protrude: this was a device used by Lionello d'Este (1407–50), Marquis of Ferrara, and appeared on the reverses of some of his medals and on an embroidered garment for which he paid in 1441. The sitter is therefore a lady of Lionello's family and, if the sprig of juniper (*ginepro*) pinned to her shoulder is a punning allusion to her name – as in Leonardo's *Ginevra de' Benci*, she would be Lionello's sister Ginevra (1419–40), who married in 1433 Sigismondo Malatesta of Rimini. The butterflies are red admirals, a clouded yellow and a scarce swallowtail; the flowers are carnations, columbines and roses. On grounds of style, the portrait is believed to have been painted by Pisanello in the 1430s.

See Hill, 1905, pp. 70–4; here pp. 81, 120, 128.

in profile. The profile portrait enjoyed such widespread and exclusive success in Italy in the fourteenth and fifteenth centuries that the compiler of an inventory at Pesaro in 1500 was evidently surprised to come upon Italian and Netherlandish portraits that showed the sitters 'with two eyes'.[7] The popularity of profile portraits demands some explanation, for we rarely talk to or look at anyone in profile and may not immediately recognise someone seen in profile. Though it avoids the problem of foreshortening the nose, a profile is by no means easy to draw or paint and, since it shows only half the face, it severely restricts the painter's opportunities to individualise, idealise or characterise the sitter. Why the profile should have found favour with fourteenth-century Italian artists and patrons is not exactly self-evident, but it was clearly considered suitable for donor portraits (plate 90). Since the saintly figures whom the donors worshipped were normally seen in full-face or three-quarters views, donors in profile might be easily distinguished from them in pose as well as in scale. The technique of the shadow profile was possibly used;[8] and perhaps parallels were already being made with antique coins, where the profile view of the head was the simplest to reproduce in relief and had therefore become conventional. In the fifteenth century, parallels with antique coin portraits, and contemporary portrait medals, themselves strongly influenced by antique coins, were of obvious importance (plate 92). The profile view was used even if it prevented the display of the sitter's costume to its best advantage: for example, in a Tuscan portrait of the mid-fifteenth century, the sitter's horned head-dress, the decorative qualities of which could be fully appreciated only from the front, is puzzling in structure and even ugly when viewed in perspective from the side (plate 91).

The profile portrait maintained its popularity in Italy until about 1500 (plate 93) but afterwards fell rapidly out of favour, except in donor portraiture.[9] When in the sixteenth century an Italian painter chose to depict his sitter in profile, particular reasons should be looked for, and can usually be found, for the selection of this outmoded pose (plate 155).[10]

In northern Europe, the situation is less clear. Some, but by no means all, of the portraits known to have been executed in France and the Low Countries in the fourteenth and early fifteenth centuries were profiles (plate 63); but they were perhaps fairly isolated instances of Italian influence.[11] It seems clear that most fourteenth-century northern portraits were not profiles and that, after about 1420, profile portraits became altogether exceptional in northern Europe. They did occasionally occur, but, when they did, reference was often being made to antique coins and Italianate medals.[12] Yet even in portrait medals and other small portraits in relief sculpture, northern artists tended to abandon the profile for a three-quarters view of the sitter's head.

Francisco de Holanda thought the full-face portrait 'graceless'[13] and indeed the full-face view can give the impression of so direct a confrontation with the sitter that the spectator may feel uneasy. This was put to good effect in portraits of monarchs, for example that of Richard II of England, where the hieratic balance possible only with this pose was no doubt calculated to overawe or unnerve (plate 34). Full-face portraits recur infrequently throughout the period (plate 81), but in such instances as Beham's '*Umpire*' and Floris's *Falconer's Wife* (plates 97, 95), the impression of confrontation is less startling when they are considered in conjunction with their pendants, where the sitters are not frontally posed. Holbein seems to have been particularly fond of the full-face view, which was ideally suited to his techniques of individualisation and characterisation (plates 24, 40, 122), and the

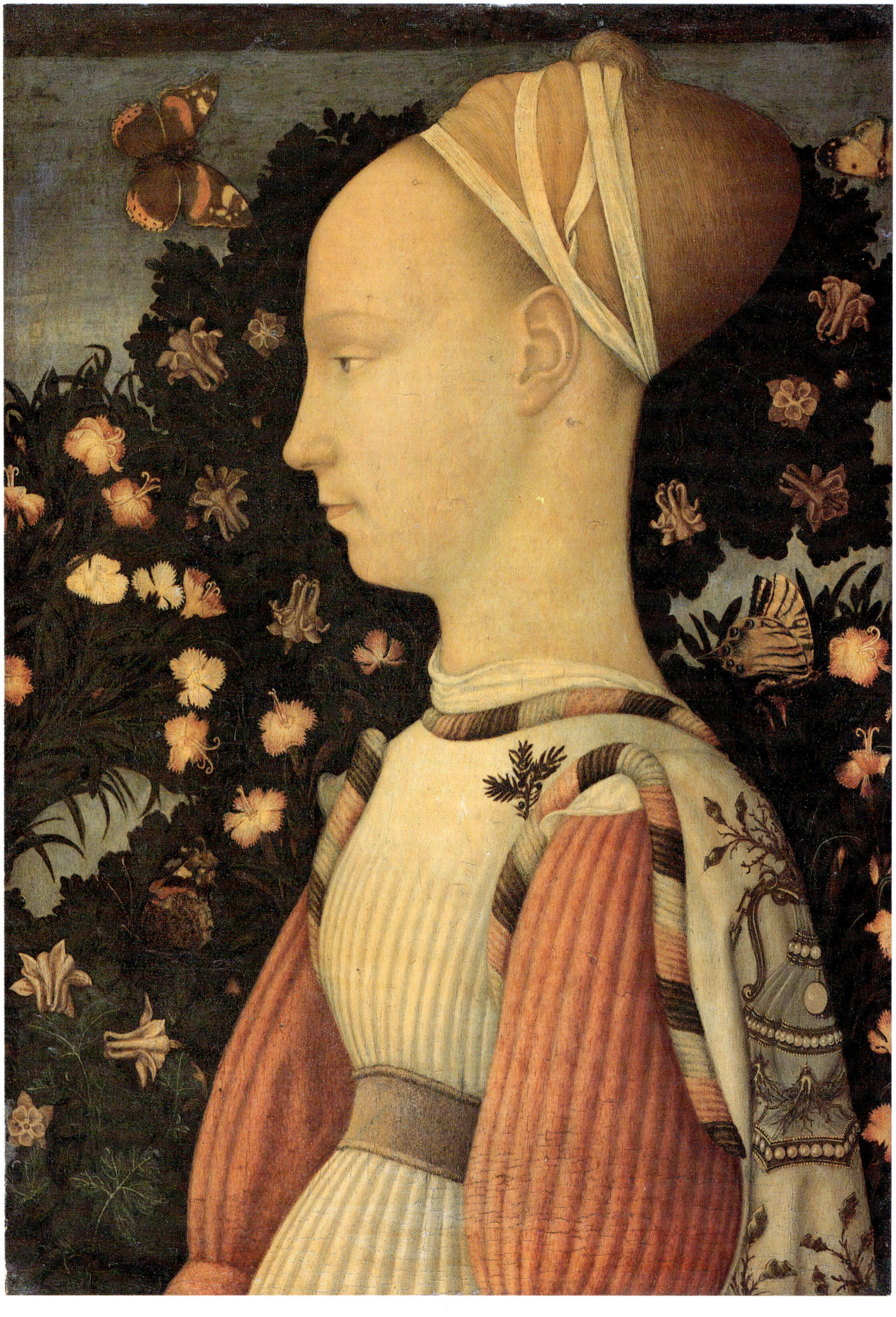

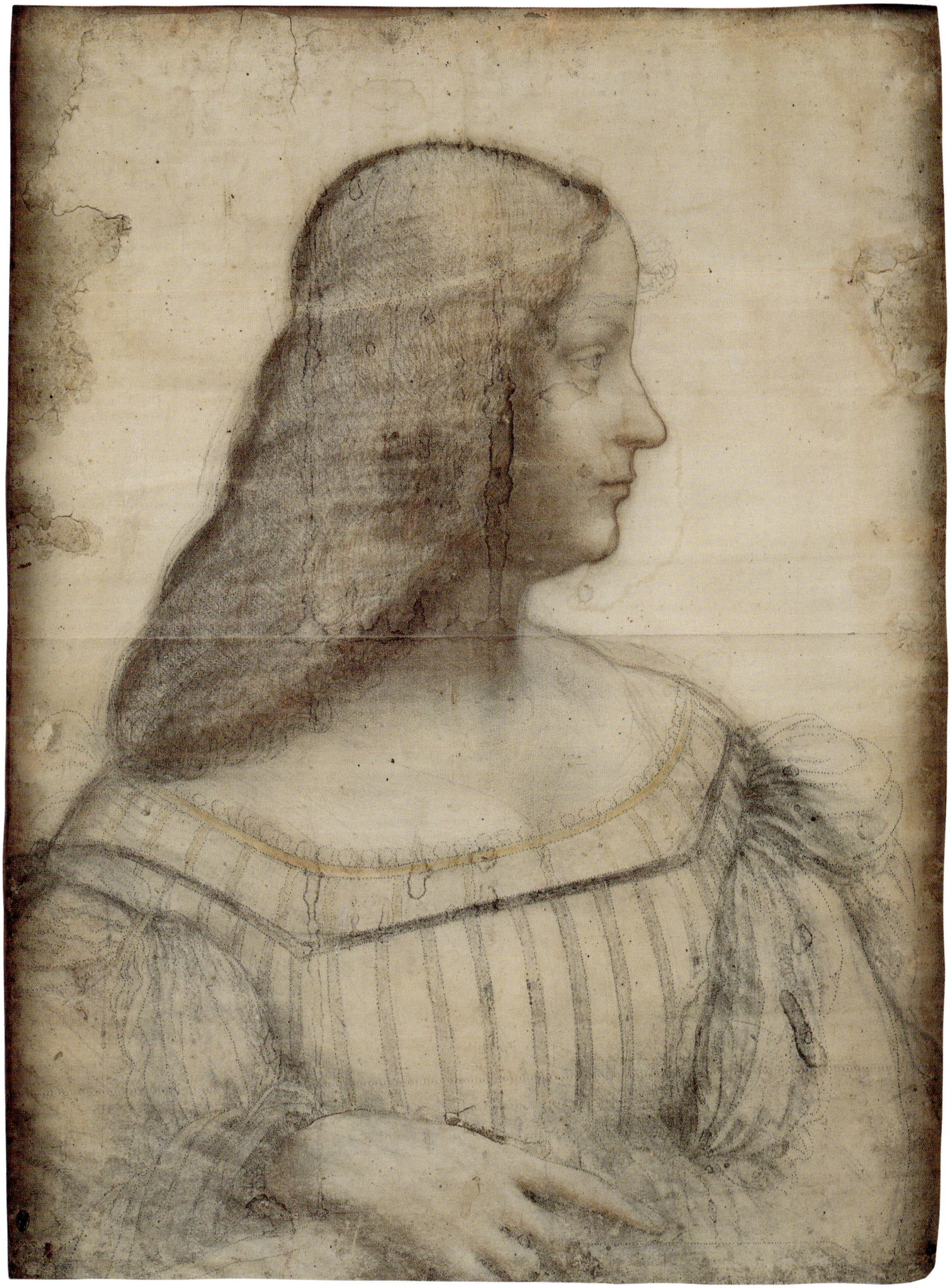

94 Titian, '*The Young Englishman*', canvas, 111.3 × 96.2 cm., Galleria Palatina, Palazzo Pitti, Florence (92).

The traditional title is entirely fanciful; there are no indications of the sitter's identity. On grounds of style and costume, the portrait is attributed to Titian and dated around 1540–5.

See the exhibition catalogue Florence, 1978–9, pp. 285–9 (80); here pp. 86, 99.

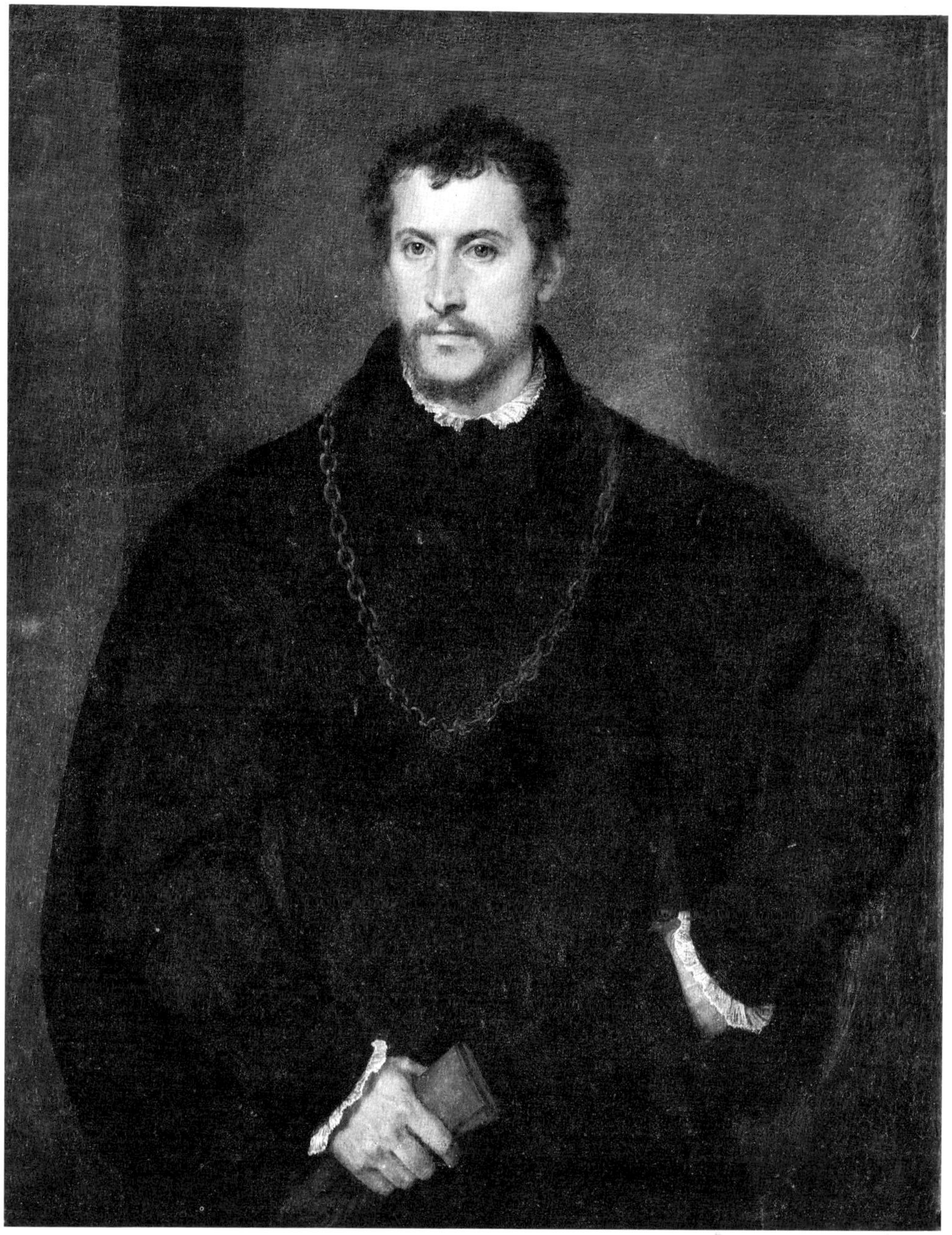

93 (prev. page) Leonardo da Vinci, *Isabella d'Este*, black and red chalk with pastel on paper, 63 × 46 cm., Louvre, Paris (M.I. 753).

As the sitter is identified, by comparison with portrait medals, as Isabella d'Este, and as the drawing is clearly by Leonardo, the portrait must be one of the two drawings of Isabella that Leonardo executed at Mantua in 1500. One of them she kept, until her husband gave it away in 1501. The other, presumably the Louvre drawing, remained with Leonardo, who made a promise, never fulfilled, to make from it a 'coloured face' (see pp. 62, 140). The Louvre drawing, which is life size, has been damaged by folding, by water, by tearing and by abrasion with the result that reproductions are not easily legible. The sitter's crossed hands rest on a table: her left hand is barely discernible; the middle finger of her right hand, seen in its entirety, is foreshortened, while the ring and little fingers are bent so that only the lowest joints are visible and so that their contours are just clear of the lower edge of the paper. The line of the profile has first been established in black chalk and has then been reinforced and corrected with a red chalk line that brings out to our right the lines of Isabella's upper lip and chin and which terminates at her chin. The drawing has been pricked for transfer but the pricking, not particularly neatly done, does not always follow exactly the contours of the drawing. It marks the inner, black line of the upper lip and the outer, red line of the chin and then departs altogether from the chalk lines to run well inside the drawn contour of the junction between chin and neck. The pricked lines give a more elegant profile and are the work of someone who wished to make from the drawing a rather more flattering image of Isabella.

See pp. 62, 65, 81, 140.

disturbing effects of which he appears to have exploited magnificently in his lost portrait of Henry VIII of England in the mural formerly in the Privy Chamber at Whitehall (plate 110). This image was said to have stricken with terror all who saw it.[14] In using the frontal pose for his portraits of the Duchess of Milan and Anne of Cleves, however, Holbein may have been acting on instructions. Henry VIII, commissioning him to paint his prospective wives, perhaps felt that any other view might allow some hideous blemish to be concealed from him (plates 1, 96).

The three-quarters view was commended by Francisco de Holanda for combining the advantages of the full-face and profile views while avoiding most of their drawbacks. He thought that it was the 'surest but most difficult' pose.[15] The main difficulty lies in placing the near eye, for its relation to the nose cannot be conveniently mapped by following well-defined contour lines and even a practised

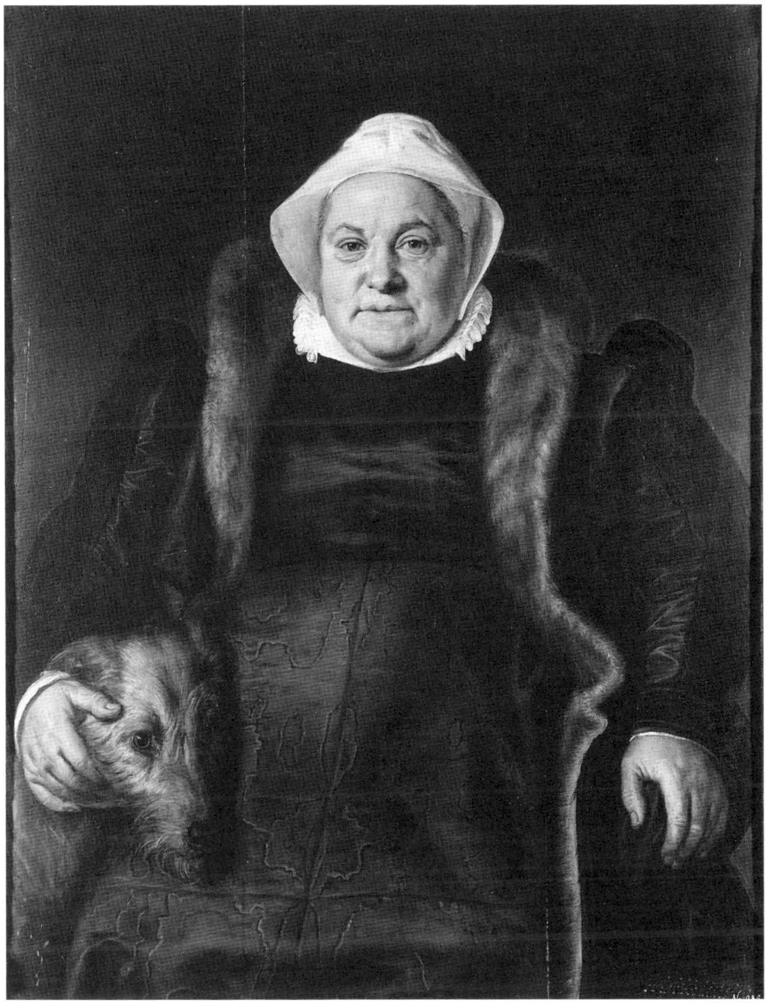

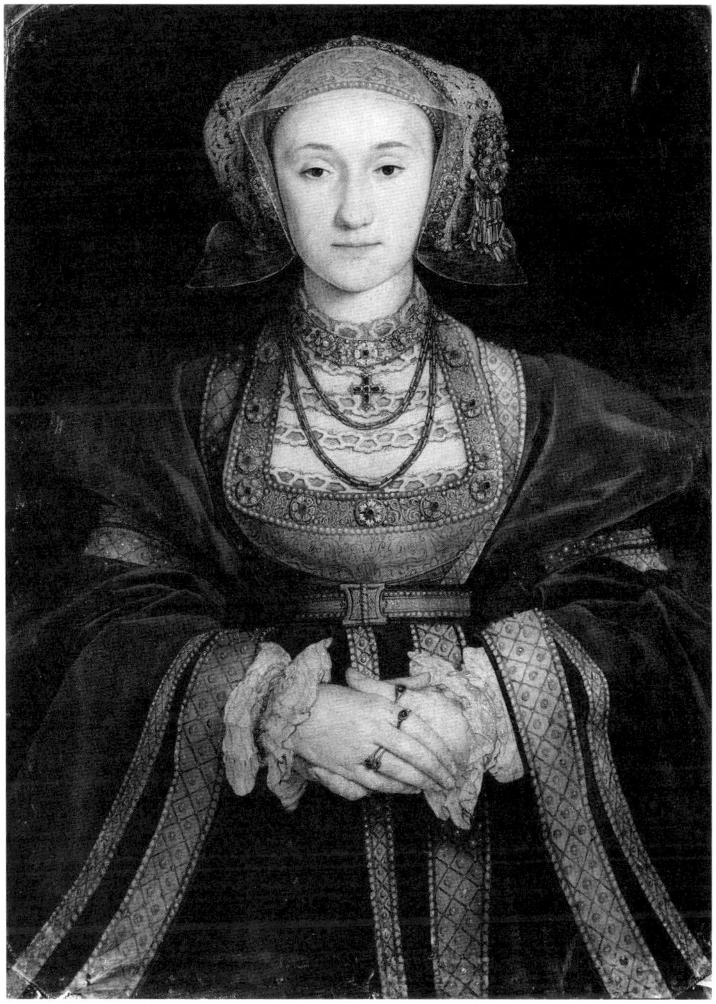

95 Frans Floris, *Lady*, panel, 107 × 83 cm., Musée des Beaux-Arts, Caen (47).

Signed with the artist's monogram and dated 1558, the picture carries an inscription stating that the sitter was forty-eight. The pendant portrait of *A Man with a Falcon* is at Brunswick (39). Though Floris was a remarkable portraitist, he painted very few portraits and may have despised portraiture as an unworthy art form beneath his attention. He specialised in religious and mythological subjects which he treated in the grand Italian manner and which brought him immense success and great wealth. His addiction to drink would in any case have prevented him from becoming a portraitist acceptable in the highest circles of society.

See Van de Velde, 1975, I, pp. 255–6; here p. 81.

96 Hans Holbein the Younger, *Anne of Cleves*, parchment mounted on canvas, 65 × 48 cm., Louvre, Paris (INV. 1348).

When in 1539 Henry VIII of England was planning to marry one of the sisters of the Duke of Cleves, he sent Holbein to Düren to take the likenesses of the two ladies, Anne and Amelia. Holbein's portrait of Amelia is lost; two of his paintings of Anne survive, the Louvre picture and the related miniature in the Victoria and Albert Museum (P. 153–1910). Henry chose Anne (1515–57), whom he married in January 1540. Taking a strong dislike to her, he soon divorced her. The Louvre picture, because its shows Anne dressed in the German and not the English fashion and because it is on parchment and so could easily have been rolled and transported, is thought to have been painted – or at least begun – at Düren. The recent discovery that at least part of Anne's elaborate costume has been drawn from a pricked cartoon does not necessarily invalidate this theory, for Holbein may not have had time to complete his portrait at Düren. Perhaps he concentrated there on the head and worked up the jewellery and clothes later, from rapid sketches made at Düren and subsequently used as a basis for a full size cartoon for the dress. The miniature, showing Anne wearing the same clothes, is not an exact reduction of the Louvre portrait and the differences between the two deserve careful investigation. Anne would appear to have had a long and prominent nose: this defect, not obvious in the full face portrait, may have been the cause of Henry's aversion.

See Foucart-Walter, 1985, pp. 52–64, 76–7; here pp. 65, 84, 197.

draughtsman may place it too far from the nose, too high or too low. In the pure three-quarters-view portrait, the corner of the far eye is tangent to the contour of the nose (plate 80) but otherwise the head may be turned almost into profile (plate 203) or almost into a frontal view (plate 94).

Most artists of the time favoured the three-quarters view, although, as we have seen, in Italy in the fourteenth and fifteenth centuries the profile view was preferred. Castagno, however, in eight of his nine *Famous Men and Women* and in his *Portrait of a Man*, all of about 1450, used the three-quarters view (plates 49, 248), as did Mantegna in his *Cardinal Ludovico Trevisan* of about 1460 (plate 249). The latter two half-length portraits seem to have been influenced by Netherlandish paintings as well as by Roman portrait busts.[16] In Florence during the 1470s, some of the leading painters, almost certainly under Netherlandish influence, began to turn their sitters' heads out of profile: often only slightly (plates 99, 136, 203), sometimes into full three-quarters view.[17] Antonello, strongly influenced by Netherlandish art, preferred the full three-quarters view (plate 100) and, when in Venice in the 1470s, may have helped to encourage Gentile and Giovanni Bellini to emulate the Netherlanders and their brother-in-law Mantegna and to adopt this pose.

The sitter's head might be angled upwards. Francisco de Holanda called this pose 'very difficult and noble':[18] difficult because of the foreshortening of the features, noble presumably because it gives an impression of haughtiness (plate 249). If the head is angled downwards, the sitter, according to his facial expression, may look becomingly modest or else ingratiating (plate 107). If the head is inclined to one side, the sitter may seem either attentive (plate 101) or languorous (plate 102).

The sitter's eyes will normally look in the direction in which his head points or will be turned upon the spectator. If his eyes are not fixed on the spectator, the sitter may appear abstracted (plate 250). If the head is turned away and the pupils are forced to the corners of the eyes so that the sitter may meet the spectator's gaze, the impression may be of shyness or strain (plate 42); or it may seem that the sitter's attention has just been caught and that he has not yet had time to turn to face the spectator (plates 88, 101); or again it may appear that the sitter has turned his eyes on the spectator but is insolent enough not to trouble to turn his head in the same direction (plates 77, 259). If the sitter looks sideways out of the picture away from the spectator, he will seem to avoid the spectator's glance and may appear shifty.[19] A sitter with downcast eyes may look modest or contemplative (plate 136).[20]

The ways in which such poses are interpreted are usually conditioned by the facial expressions of the sitters. The subtleties of facial expressions are difficult to define and to describe, though the English artist Hilliard included in his treatise on the art of limning a beautiful description of smiling:

> the eye changeth and naroweth, houlding the sight yust between the lides as a center . . . the mouth alittel extendeth both ends of the line vpwards, the Cheekes rayse themselues to the eye wards, the nosterels play and are more open, the vaines in the tempel appeare more, and the cullour by degrees increaseth, the necke commonly erecteth it selfe, the eye browes make the straighter arches, and the forhead casteth it selfe in to a plaine as it wear for peace and loue to walke vppon . . .[21]

The trouble with facial expressions is that they are fleeting: a sitter cannot fix an expression without seeming grotesque, and, in any case, with the tedium of sitting, his face will tend to fall into distracted repose. Few portrait-painters have

97 Barthel Beham, '*The Umpire*', limewood panel, 84.8 × 66 cm., Kunsthistorisches Museum, Vienna, Gemäldegalerie (783).

The date 1529 is chalked onto the table-top. Though the sitter's ring carries a coat of arms and the initials HS, he has not yet been identified. The pendant portrait of a woman with a parrot is also at Vienna (3483): there the sitter wears a ring decorated with another unidentified coat of arms and the initials KS. The portraits are attributed to Beham on stylistic grounds. The sitter here may be keeping a score or making a calculation, but why he should be chalking it on a table is not clear. The flies gathering round the slice of fruit suggest decay while the apple and wine refer to Original Sin and the Eucharist. The grapes and probably also the parrot in the pendant portrait are further allusions to sin and Redemption.

See Bergström, 1960, pp. 342–3; Klauner and Heinz, 1963, p. 10; here pp. 74, 81, 98, 134.

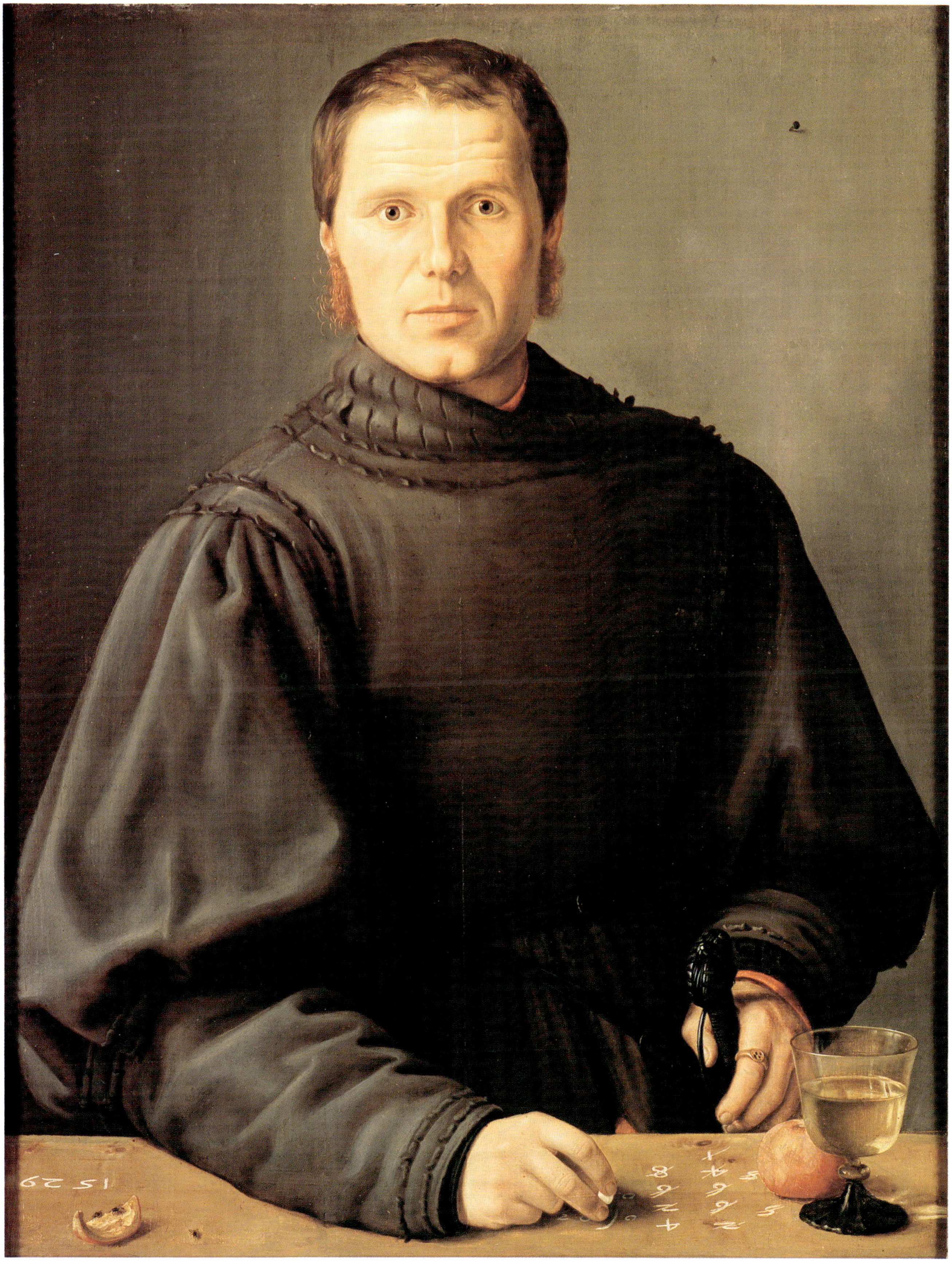

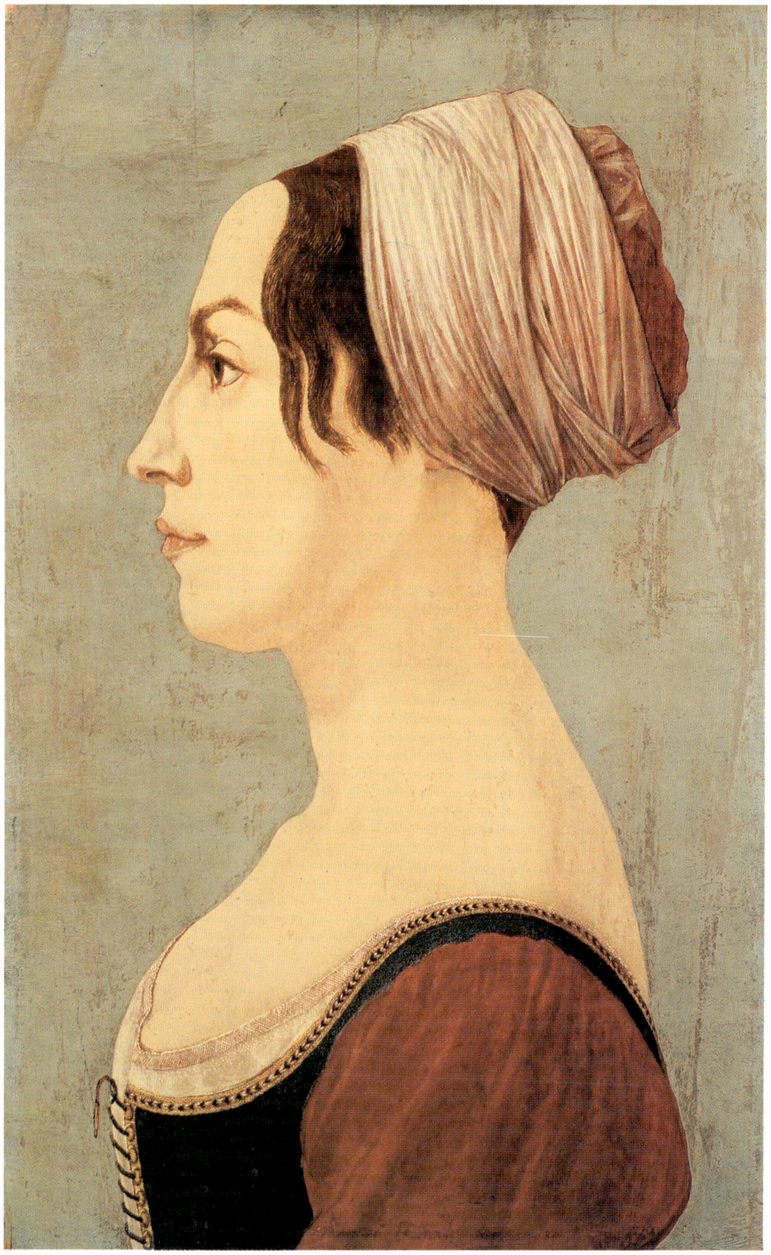

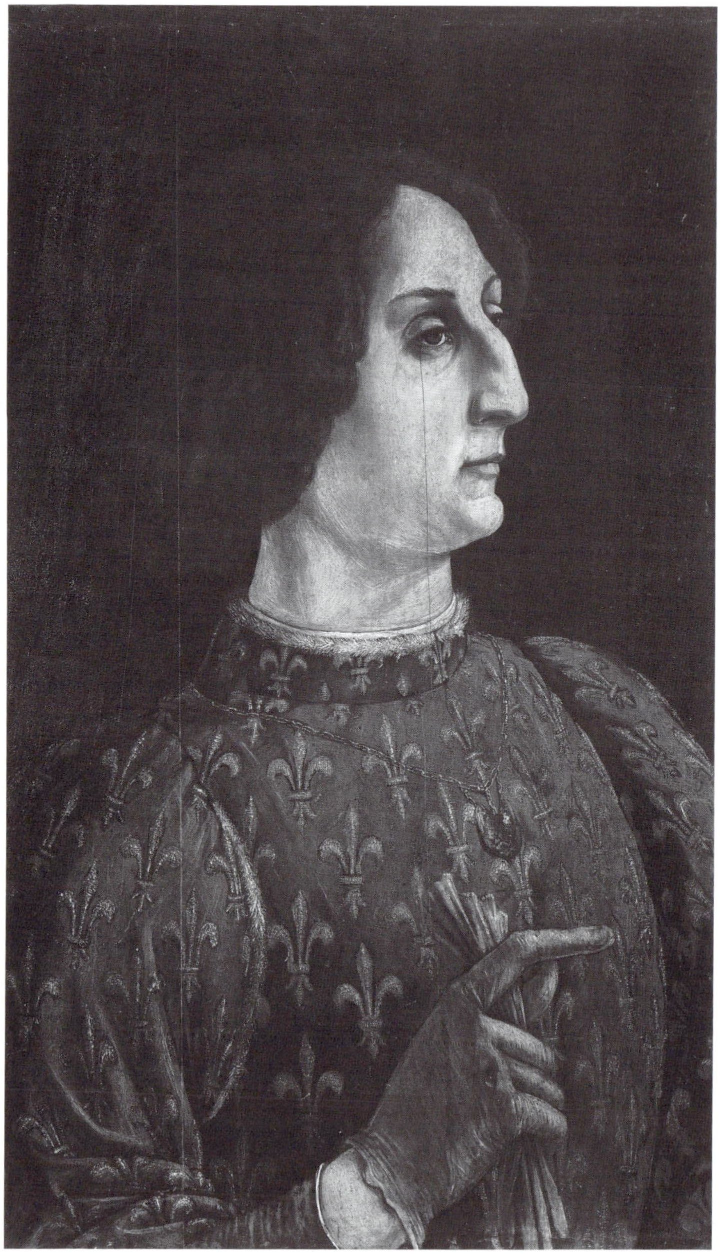

98 (above left) Piero Pollaiuolo, *Lady*, panel, 48 × 30.5 cm., Isabella Stewart Gardner Museum, Boston (P16W7).

The portrait is attributed to Piero Pollaiuolo because of its strong resemblance to his *Galeazzo Maria Sforza* (plate 99) and may have been painted in about 1470. The sitter, not being richly dressed, was probably not of very elevated status.

See Hendy, 1974, pp. 187–8; here p. 120.

99 (above right) Piero Pollaiuolo, *Galeazzo Maria Sforza, Duke of Milan*, panel 65 × 42 cm., Uffizi, Florence (1492).

The portrait, which is not well preserved, was listed in the 1492 inventory of the Medici collections as 'the head of Duke Galeazzo, by the hand of Piero del Pollaiuolo'. It is thought to have been painted when Galeazzo Maria visited Florence in 1471. Galeazzo Maria's dealings with the artists who decorated rooms in his palaces at Milan and Pavia, with Zanetto Bugatto, with Antonello, with Baldassare d'Este and with Mantegna all attest to his strong interest in portraiture (pp. 47, 62, 149, 153–5, 159, 218, 220). It may or may not have been he who persuaded Piero Pollaiuolo to break with Florentine convention by turning his head out of profile and by including the gesturing hand.

See Berti, 1979, p. 425; here pp. 86, 98.

100 (right) Antonello da Messina, '*The Condottiere*', poplar panel, 36.2 × 30 cm., Louvre, Paris (M.I. 693).

The traditional title is fanciful and there are no indications of the sitter's identity. The panel is signed and dated '1475/Antonellus messaneus me pinxit' and was painted during Antonello's stay in Venice.

See the exhibition catalogue Messina, 1981–2, p. 118 (17); here pp. 69, 86, 90, 232.

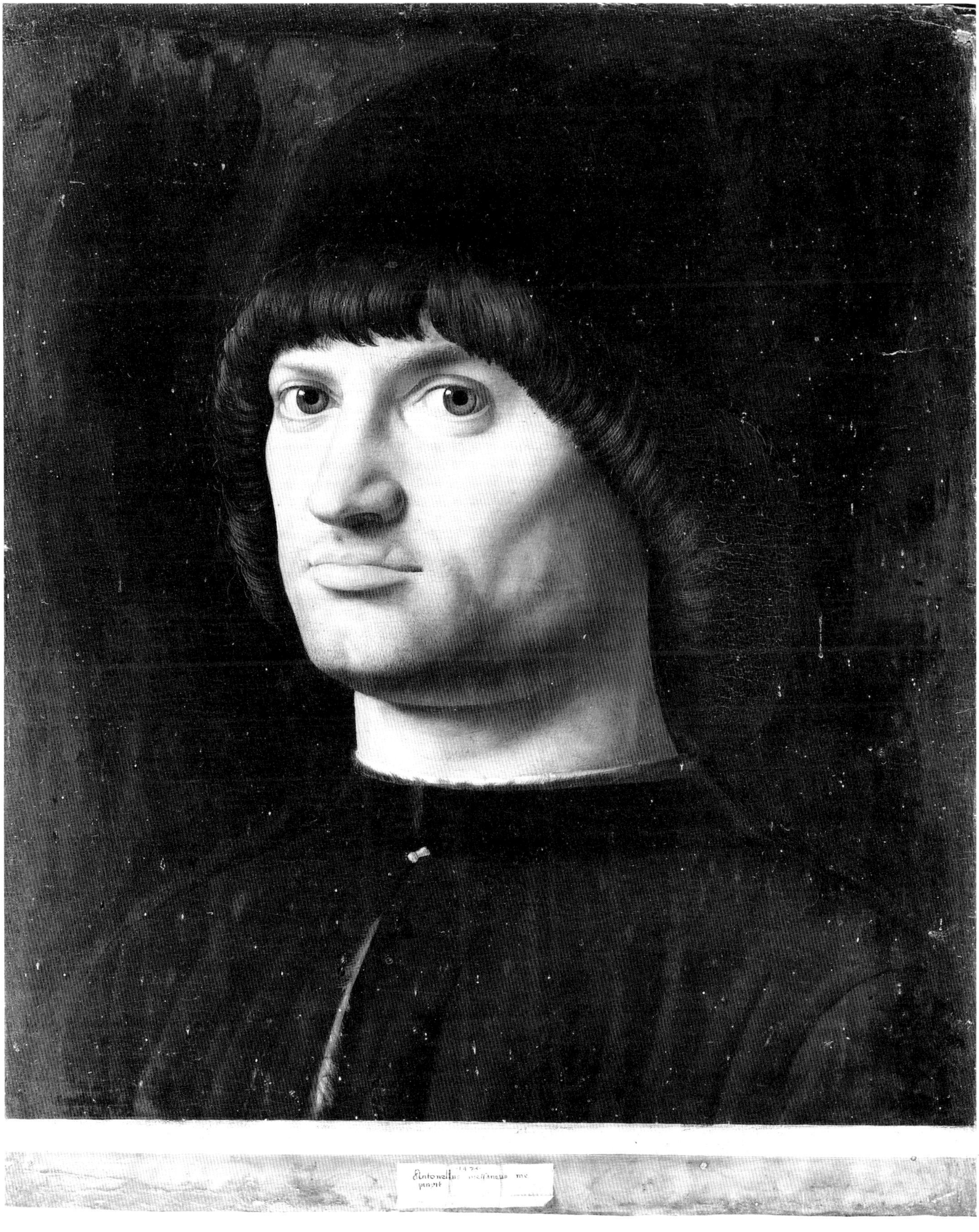
Antonellus messaneus me
pinxit

chosen to give their sitters fixed and well-defined expressions. However cleverly such an expression is caught – for example, that of forceful determination in Antonello's '*Condottiere*' of 1475 (plate 100) – after prolonged contemplation it will seem fatuous and irritating. Though it may be considered very typical, it cannot indicate much about the complexities of the sitter's character and is therefore unnecessarily restricting.

In a pair of portraits by the Master of Flémalle, painted in about 1430, the sitters have definable but not overstressed facial expressions which are contrasted and which the artist doubtless considered typical of the man and woman whom he was depicting (plates 104–5). The man is older and wearier than the woman; his brow is furrowed and the skin of his chin and neck has loosened so that the line of his lower jaw is no longer well marked. His head is lit from above and from our left, and this accentuates the lines of his forehead, chin and neck, the down-turned near corner of his mouth and the sagging folds of skin around and between the eyes. His eyebrows are very close to his eyes and that, according to the treatises on rhetoric, denotes melancholy;[22] in conjunction with the furrowed brow and the lines between the eyes, the eyebrows suggest a slight frown. The weak catchlights make his eyes appear dull, especially in contrast with the sharp catchlights in the woman's liquid eyes, which seem lively and alert. There are no sagging lines in her

101 (below left) Giovanni Battista Moroni, *The Tailor*, canvas, 97 × 74 cm., National Gallery, London (697).

The portrait, showing a tradesman at work, was in the Grimani collection in Venice by 1660. On grounds of style and costume, it is thought to have been painted by Moroni in about 1570.

See Gould, 1975, pp. 165–6; here pp. 74, 86, 98.

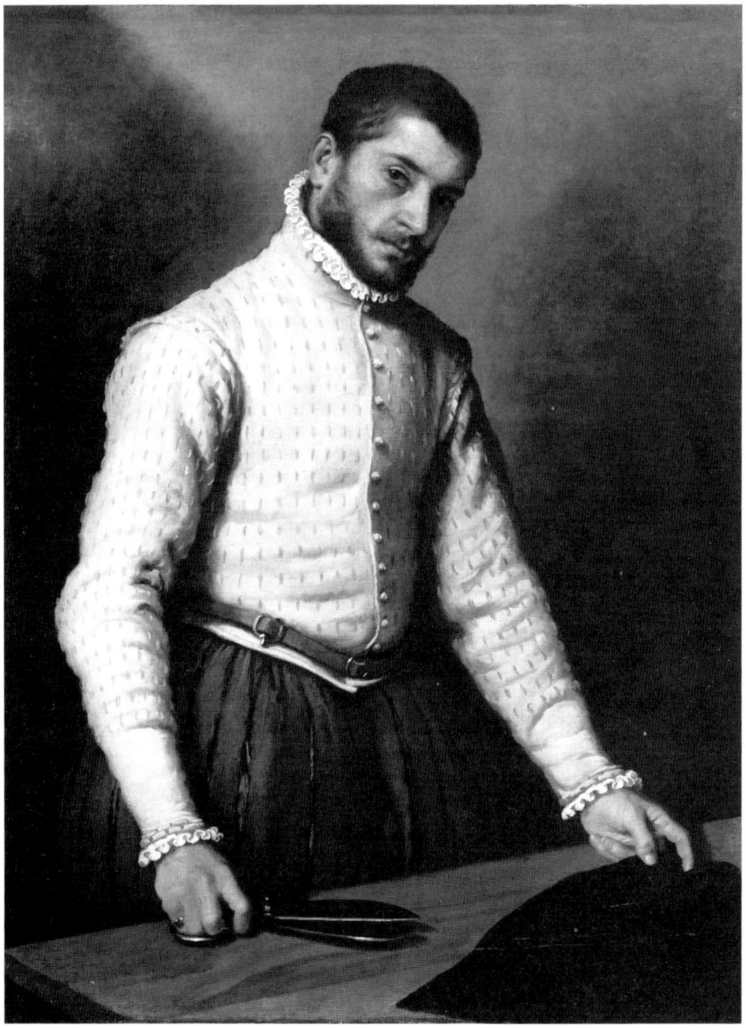

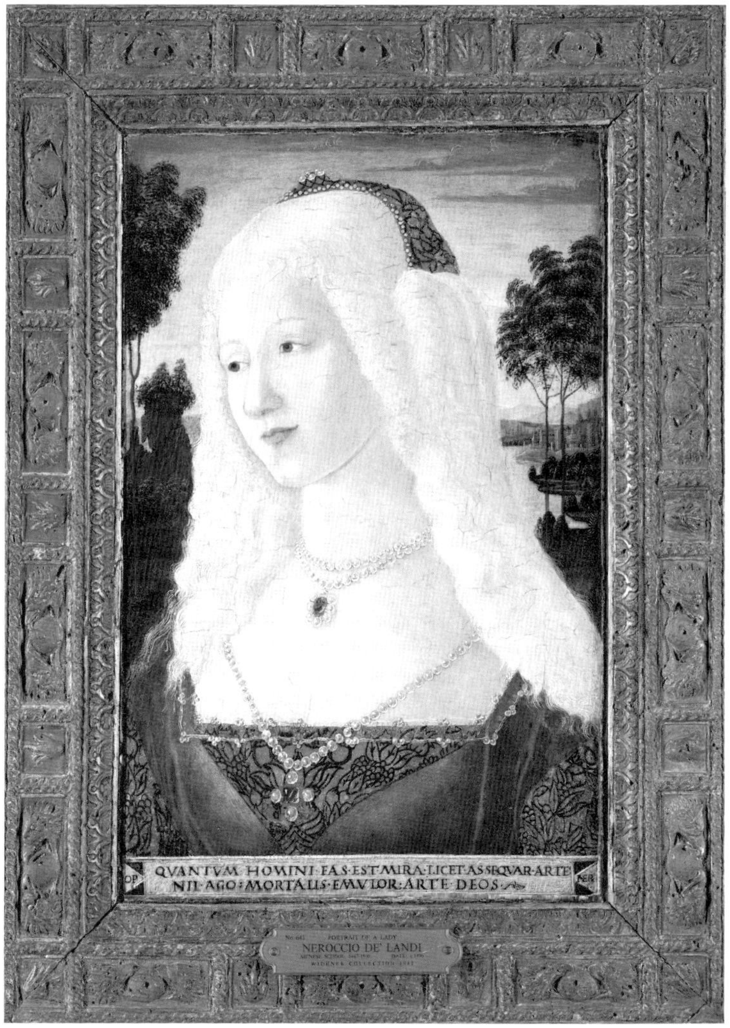

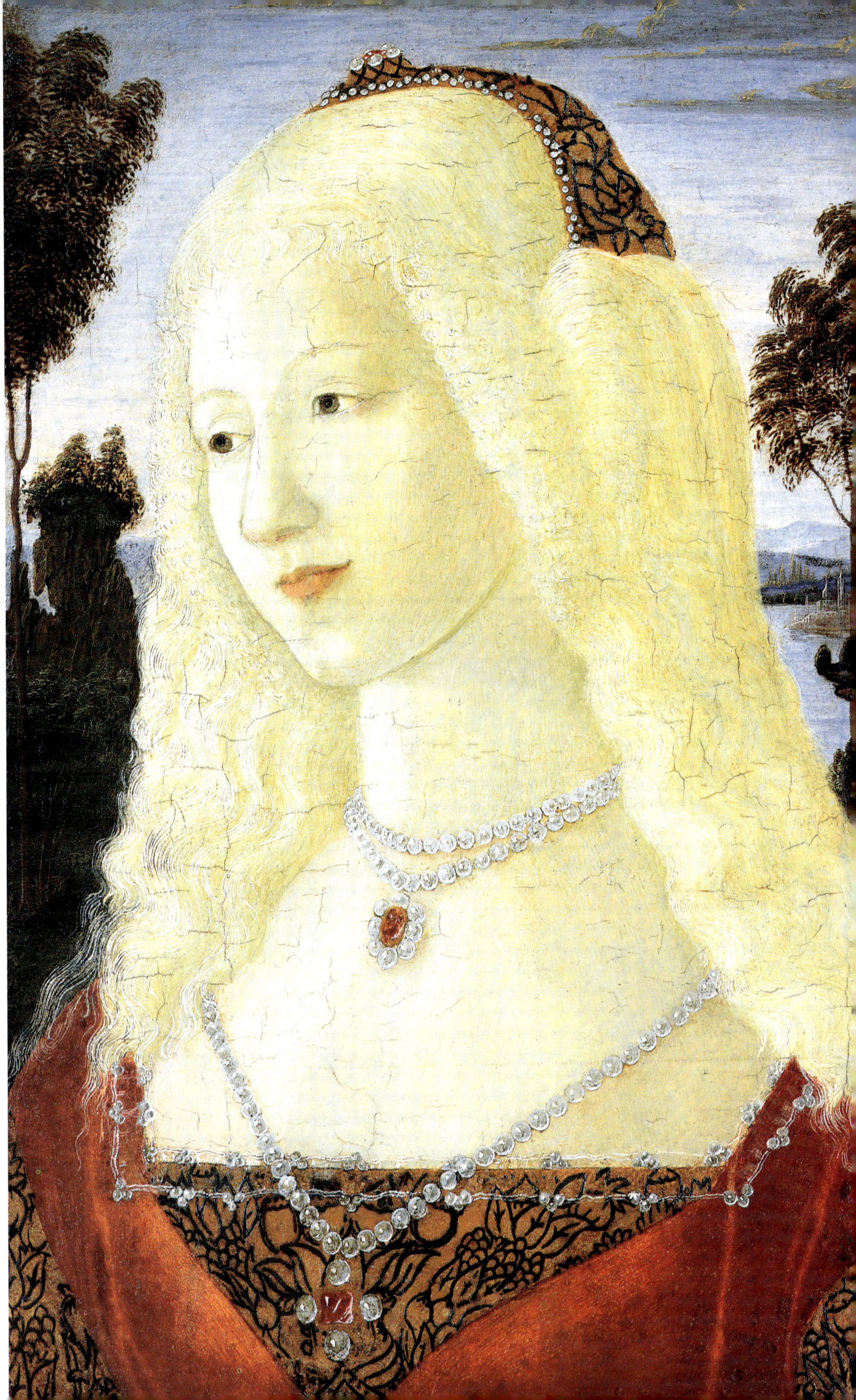

102 (left) Neroccio de' Landi, *Lady*, panel, 46.5 × 30.5 cm., National Gallery of Art, Washington (1942.9.47, Widener Collection).

The picture is signed 'OP NER'; the Latin inscription may be translated 'Whatever a human being is permitted to attain, I attain through my wondrous art. [Yet] I achieve nothing: for I, a [mere] mortal, compete through my art with the gods'. The frame, which is original, is decorated with reliefs showing two eagles' heads biting a sphere: this was a device used by the Bandini family of Siena. The portrait is thought to have been painted in about 1490 and the landscape background betrays strong Netherlandish influence.

See Coor, 1961, pp. 57–61, 191–2; here pp. 65, 69, 86, 121, plate 103.

103 Neroccio de' Landi, *Lady*, detail (see plate 102).

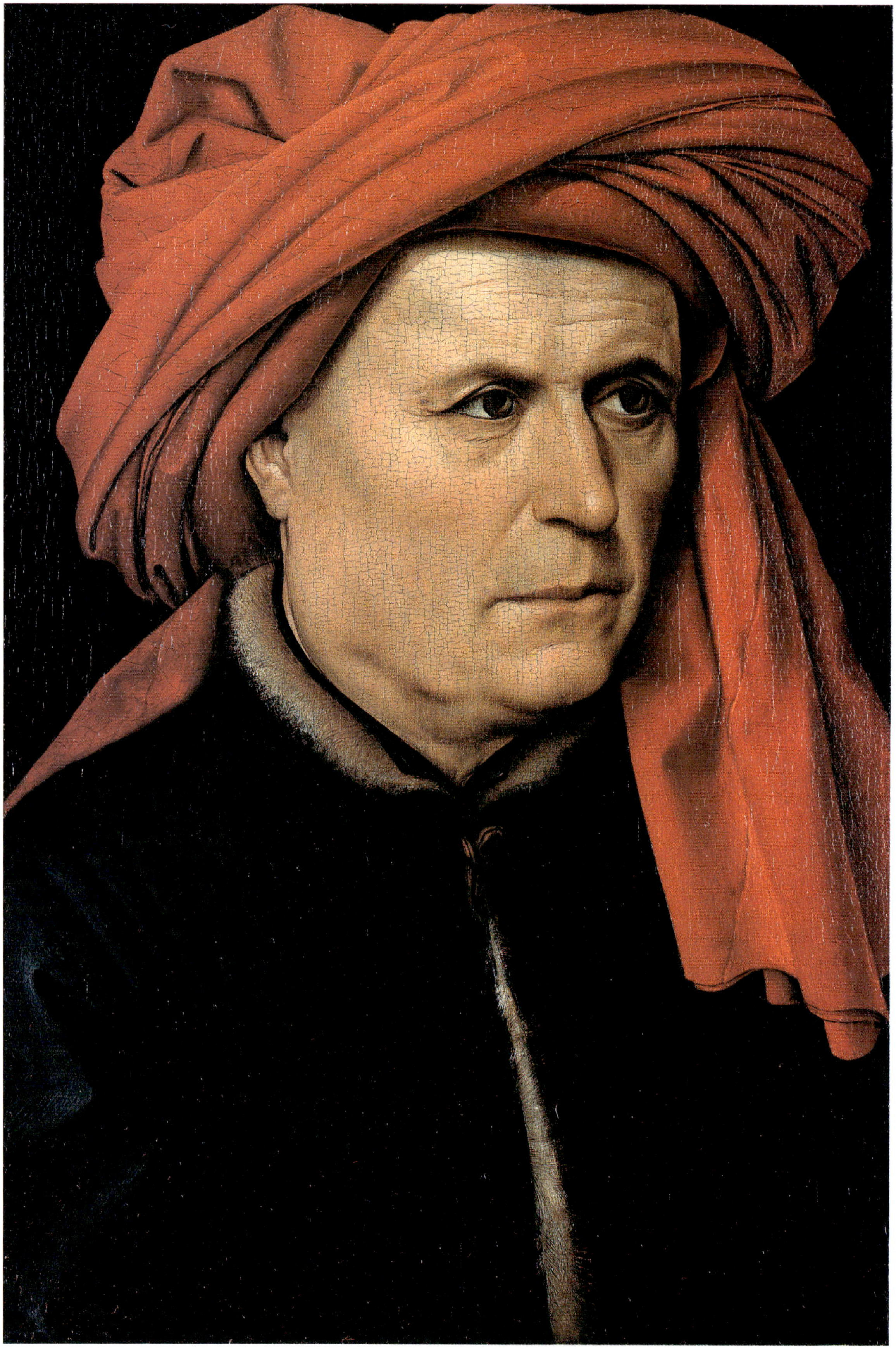

104 Master of Flémalle, *Man*, oak panel, painted surface 40.7 × 27.9 cm., National Gallery, London (653 A).

The pair to the portrait reproduced as plate 105.

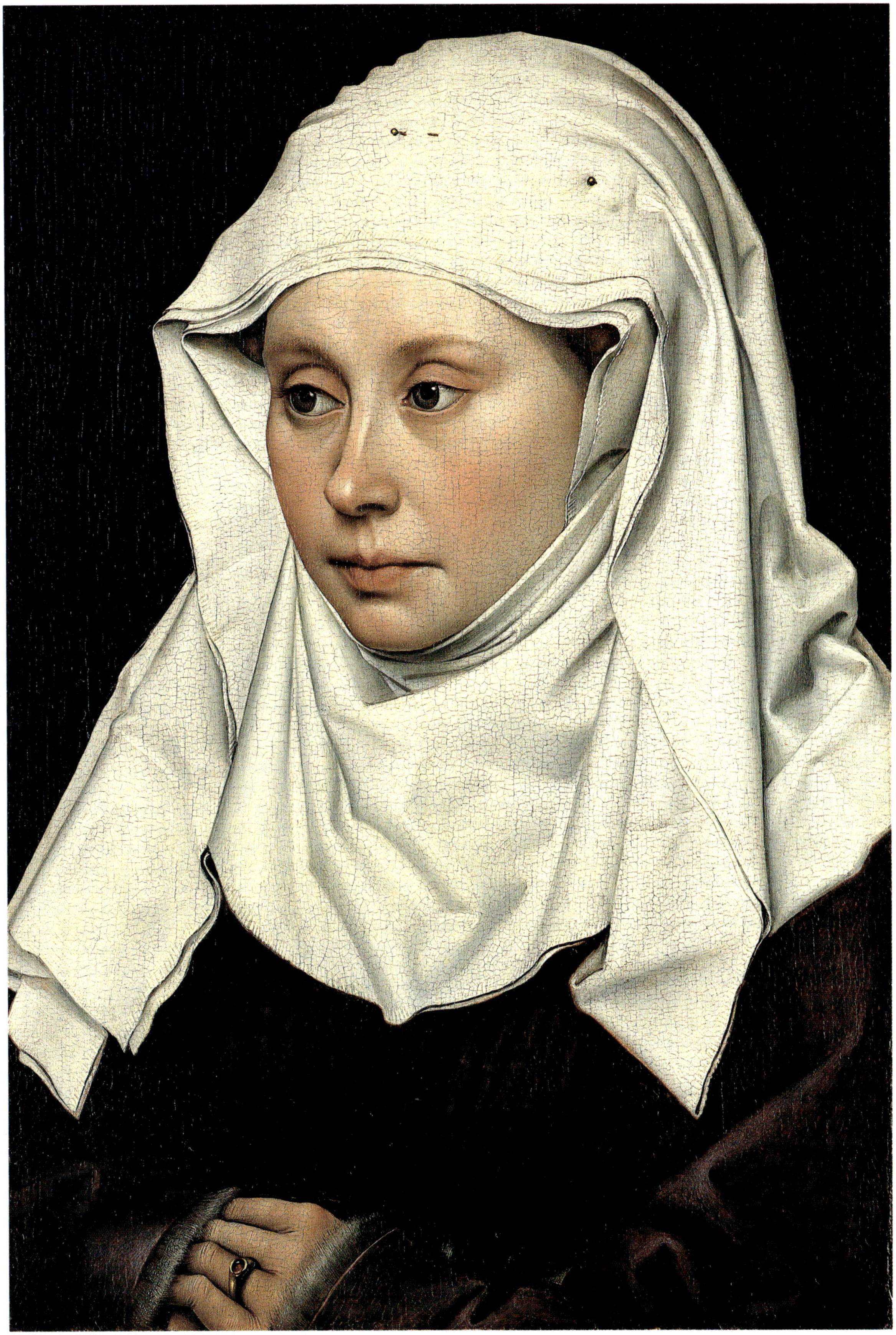

105 Master of Flémalle, *Lady*, oak panel, painted surface 40.7 × 27.9 cm., National Gallery, London (653 B).

The pair to the portrait reproduced as plate 104. The sitters, relatively simply dressed, were evidently man and wife and not persons of very elevated status. In every aspect of their style, the portraits agree closely with the 'Flémalle Panels' at Frankfurt (939, 939 A, 939 B) after which the Master is named. On grounds of style and costume, they may be dated towards 1430. As the man had a head much larger than his wife's, the artist had problems, wonderfully resolved, in maintaining a decorative balance between the portraits. Though he has been criticised for having lit the sitters from different angles, he must have made a deliberate decision to do so and changed his arrangements for sittings accordingly. The varied lighting has allowed him to stress the physical bulk of each sitter and to emphasise the contrasts between their facial expressions.

See Davies, 1968, pp. 27–8; Campbell, 1974, pp. 642–3; here pp. 72, 90–4, 112, 139.

face: the outer corners of her eyes, the far corner of her mouth and the end of her nose turn upwards and her eyebrows are slightly raised. The lighting, here from our right, again stresses the upward movements. In both portraits, the sitters' bodies and clothes are used to complement certain aspects of their faces. The man's hat and scarves are arranged not only to stress his slouched position but also to echo and parallel the downward-turning lines of his eyes and mouth; his hand is not included perhaps because the upward thrust of the arm would have been at variance with the sinking lines of the rest of the figure. The line of the woman's upper lip is repeated in the lower contour of her chin cloth, which arches upwards, and the arrangement of her veils across her temples emphasises the upward slant of the outer corners of her eyes.[23] She is almost smiling.

A smile is perhaps the most easily recognised facial expression. Most sitters will wish to be remembered as benevolent; consequently, smiling sitters constantly appear in portraits. A French-speaking artist of about 1440 painted a smiling portrait of the jester Gonella, a professional buffoon at the court of Ferrara: it was probably essential to show him smiling (plate 106). Parmigianino's *Lady* of about 1530 has a rather obvious and obsequious smile which, with her exotic headgear, has evidently played some part in earning her the title of 'The Turkish Slave' (plate 107). A less marked, more enigmatic smile can hold its fascination, as in Holbein's *Duchess of Milan* of 1538, where the sitter is presented to her suitor Henry VIII of England (plate 1).

Treatises on rhetoric can help in identifying certain less readily understood expressions but can also be misleading, since they deal with the face feature by feature and cannot take account of all the interacting complexities of the movements of the facial muscles. Jodocus Willich, for example, wrote in 1540 of the eyebrows: 'If they are unequal, that is to say if one has been raised and the other has not, they denote cruelty.'[24] It would, however, be ridiculous to claim that Holbein intended the Duchess of Milan, whose right eyebrow is quizzically raised, to look cruel.

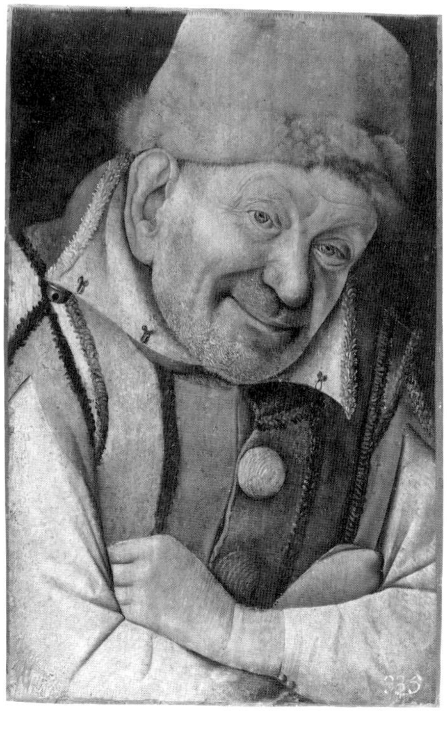

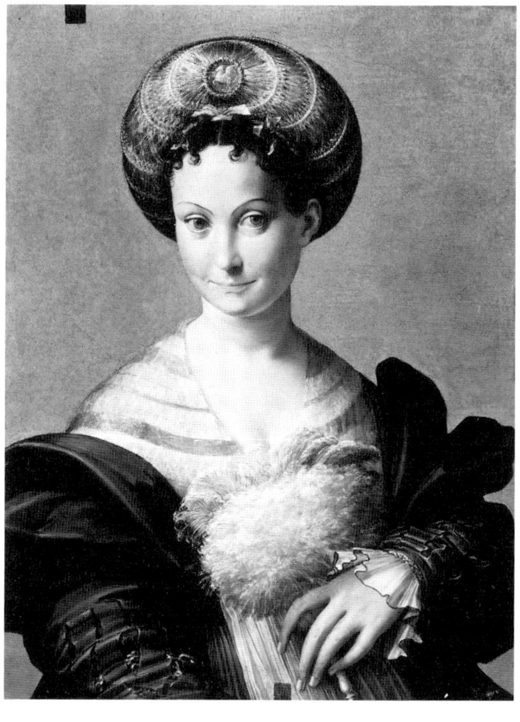

106 (right) French, c. 1440, *The Jester Gonella*, oak panel, 36 × 24 cm., Kunsthistorisches Museum, Vienna, Gemäldegalerie (1840).

The sitter is identified, from an inscription on an old copy and from a description of the original in an inventory of 1659, as the jester Gonella, who was employed at the Ferrarese court. The painter, however, was French-speaking, for infra-red reflectograms reveal that he wrote colour notes in French upon the panel before he began to paint. As the panel is oak, the picture is unlikely to have been painted in Italy. It is now widely regarded as an early work by Fouquet.

See Reynaud, 1981, pp. 6–8; here pp. 69, 94.

107 Parmigianino, '*The Turkish Slave*', panel, 64 × 52.3 cm., Galleria Nazionale, Parma (1147, deposited from the Uffizi, 782).

The traditional title is fanciful and there are no indications of the sitter's identity. On grounds of style and costume, the portrait is attributed to Parmigianino and dated around 1530.

See Berti, 1979, p. 401; here pp. 86, 94, 99.

108 (right) Attributed to Jacques Le Boucq, *Bonne d'Abbeville, Lady of Barbançon*, from the 'Recueil d'Arras', Bibliothèque Municipale, Arras, MS 266, f. 184.

On the 'Recueil d'Arras' see the note to plate 81. The present drawing is a copy made probably in the 1560s after a lost original which, from the costume, would have been produced in about 1460. It would appear that the original was a painting, though the copyist may not have reproduced it in its entirety. Bonne was the wife of Michel de Ligne, Lord of Barbançon, whom she married in 1434. They had eleven children; she was widowed in 1469–70 and died in 1472 (Goethals, 1849–52, III, p. 690).

See p. 95.

109 Paolo Veronese, *Man*, canvas, 99 × 86 cm., Galleria Palatina, Palazzo Pitti, Florence (108).

On grounds of style and costume, the portrait is attributed to Veronese and dated around 1570.

See Marini, 1968, p. 123 (234); here p. 95.

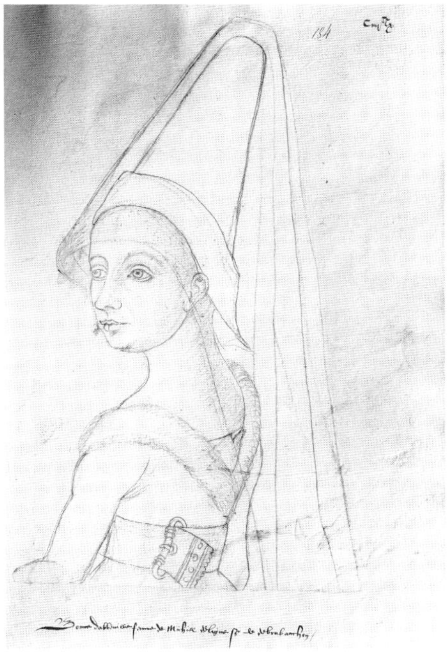

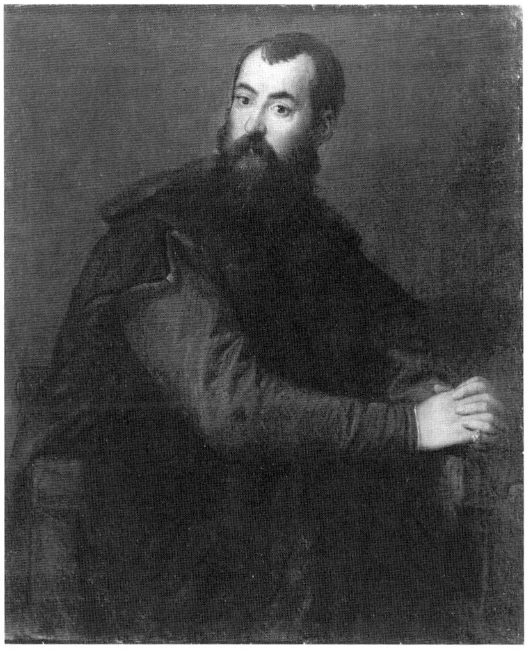

The head and torso are normally turned in approximately the same direction but, at various times and in various areas, certain artists have experimented with complex poses in which the sitters look back over their shoulders towards the spectator. A drawing in the 'Recueil d'Arras' of Bonne d'Abbeville, lady of Barbançon, appears to indicate that a Netherlandish artist of about 1460 tried out a twisting pose, such as was widely used in Italy in the early sixteenth century (plates 77, 88, 108, 118). These dramatic, turning poses clearly appealed to many Italian artists, who perhaps recalled Alberti's advice to include figures looking out of the picture[25] and who obviously liked the impression of immediacy and intimacy conveyed by such elegantly contorted figures. The sitter's chair might be seen from the side, and the sitter made to turn so that his head faced the spectator (plate 89). Other complex, turning poses were used (plates 109, 123) which, though highly decorative, would have been impossible, or at least extremely painful, to hold for long periods. Many of these sitters must have made the same complaint as Samuel Pepys, who, when he was posing in 1666 for John Hayls, wrote: 'I . . . do almost break my neck looking over my shoulder to make the posture for him to work by.'[26]

Unless a symmetrical image was desired, which would give the sitter an air of composure, it was common to show one arm extended and the other bent at the elbow. The hands would then fall at different levels and, especially in full-length portraits, this gave decorative variety to the composition. Similarly, a standing male whose legs were visible was usually shown resting his weight on one leg and bending the other at the knee. It was, besides, considered improper to splay the legs: 'an excessive separation of the feet is blameworthy', wrote Jodocus Willich in 1540 for the benefit of rhetoricians.[27] The straddling posture adopted by Henry VIII of England in Holbein's full-length portrait was doubtless a breach of etiquette that would have been excused only in a monarch (plate 110). Given added respectability by Holbein's image, it was adopted by other artists in their portraits of his son and successor Edward VI.[28]

After the face, the hands are the most interesting and important areas of a

110 Remigius van Leemput, after Hans Holbein the Younger, *Henry VII, King of England, his Wife Elizabeth of York, their Son Henry VIII and his Wife Jane Seymour*, canvas, 88.9 × 98.7 cm., Royal Collection, Hampton Court (308).

Signed and dated 1667, Leemput's copy was made for Charles II and is a faithful reduction of the wall painting by Holbein that decorated the Privy Chamber of the Palace of Whitehall and that was destroyed by fire in 1698. Holbein's original cartoon for the left-hand section has been preserved (National Portrait Gallery, London, 4027). There the life-size figures of Henry VII and Henry VIII are drawn on separate sheets glued onto the paper of the background; the outlines are neatly pricked for transfer to the wall. In the cartoon, the head of Henry VIII corresponds to Holbein's panel of *Henry VIII* in the Thyssen Collection (197) and is turned to our right, whereas in all the copies and versions of the mural his head is seen frontally. The change, at a late stage in the planning of the composition, would probably have made it necessary for Henry to sit again for Holbein. The mural was apparently executed in 1537, for this date appears on the copy in the cartouche above Jane Seymour's head. Henry VIII's parents Henry VII and Elizabeth of York had died in 1509 and 1503 respectively; Holbein based his portraits of them on earlier images. Jane Seymour died in October 1537, a few days after the birth of her son Edward. Holbein's drawing of Jane, on which her portrait in the mural was based, has survived (plate 189). It must have been the birth of Edward, Henry VIII's only son, which prompted him to commission the mural, a compressed dynastic series arranged around an inscription glorifying the House of Tudor. In many respects the composition was a development of that of Holbein's *Ambassadors*, dated 1533 (National Gallery, London, 1314). The fanciful architecture was seen in ingeniously distorted perspective which forced the figures forward so that Henry VIII confronted the spectator with frightening directness.

See Millar, 1963, p. 117 (216); Groos, 1981, p. 57; here pp. 95, 127.

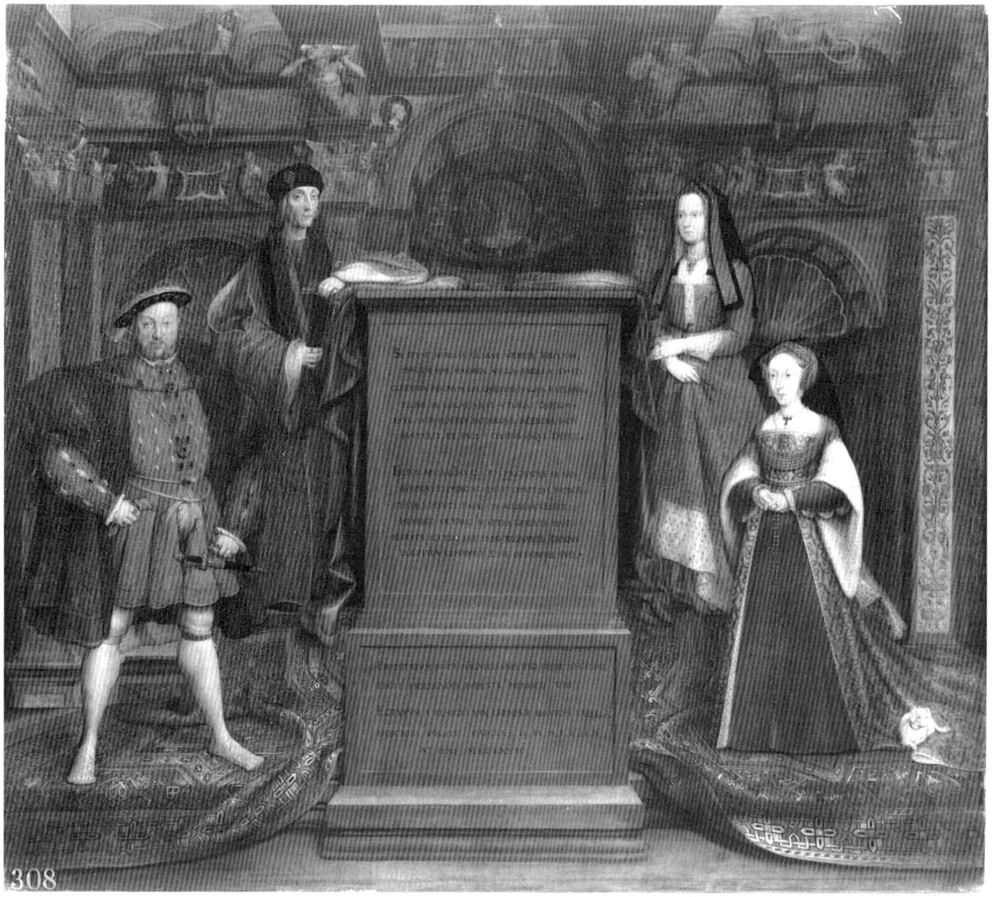

portrait, but are so difficult to draw that some artists have contrived at least partially to hide one or both of them (plate 112). There is another reason for partly concealing the hands: as Francisco de Holanda remarked, each hand is of approximately the same area as the face.[29] The hands, moreover, are of almost exactly the same high tone as the face and a danger therefore arises that the hands may distract attention from the head. In half-length portraits where the sitter is cramped into a small space, it is desirable to conceal one hand, to cover parts of the hands with gloves or drapery or to compress the hands into as restricted an area as possible. In extended half-length and in full-length portraits, the hands may be placed at greater distances from the face and there is less urgent cause to cover them. As the hands cannot be allowed to hang idly by the sitter's sides, they present the portrait-painter with a great number of problems.

Rogier van der Weyden solved these problems by compressing his sitters' hands together at the lower edges of their portraits (plates 80, 111, 154). Helped by a fashion for wearing sleeves that extended almost to the knuckles, he was able to reduce the surfaces of flesh revealed to small pyramids or parallelograms of high tone which echoed in shape the basically pyramidal forms of his compositions and which directed attention towards the head rather than distracted from it. If necessary, the fingers might be entwined around an attribute.

A contemporary of Rogier represented a cleric or academic looking up casually from an open book, as if he had been disturbed while reading (plate 113). The idea of making the sitter perform an action was taken up throughout Europe. At

111 Rogier van der Weyden, *Lady*, oak panel, painted surface 34 × 25.5 cm., National Gallery of Art, Washington (1937.1.44, Andrew W. Mellon Collection).

There are no indications of the identity of the sitter, who is expensively though not very richly dressed. On grounds of costume and style, the portrait is attributed to Van der Weyden and is believed to have been painted shortly before his death in 1464.

See Hand and Wolff, 1986, pp. 241–6; here pp. 61, 72, 96.

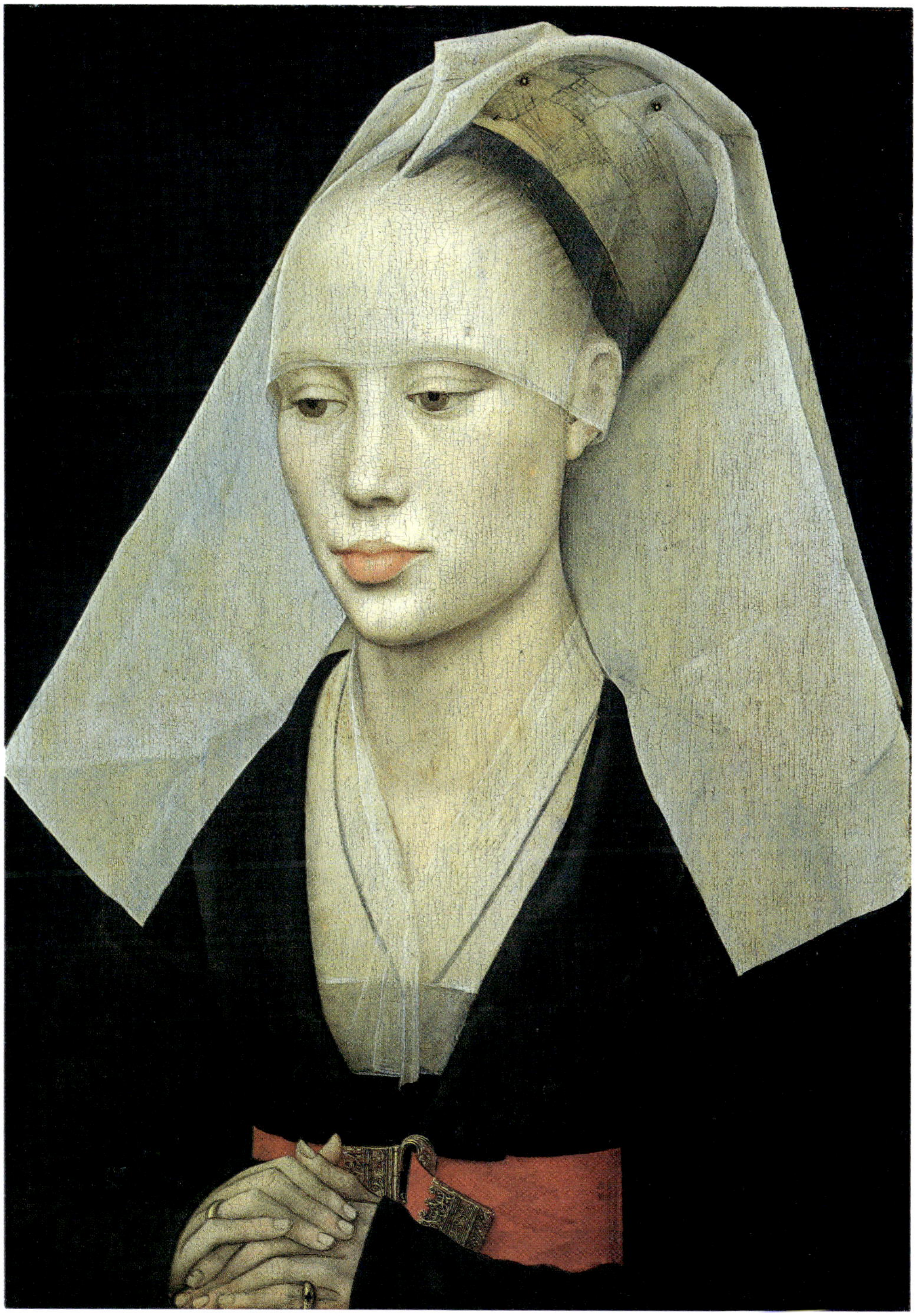

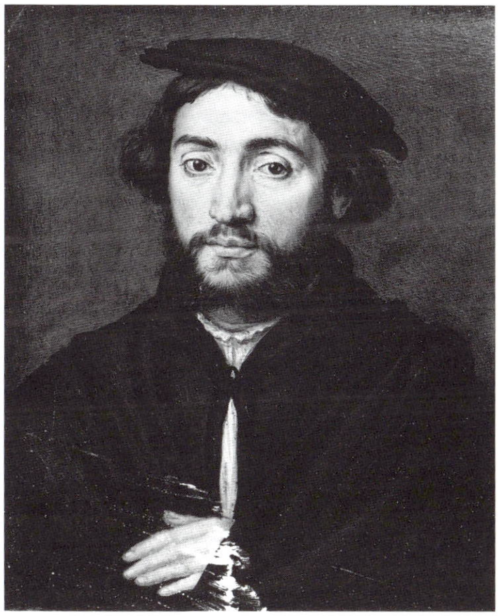

112 Corneille de Lyon, *Pierre Aymeric*, panel, 16.5 × 14 cm., Louvre, Paris (R.F. 1976–15).

On the reverse of the panel is an inscription in French: 'Pierre Aymeric, native of St Flour, residing at Lyons, aged twenty-six or thereby, was painted at Lyons aforesaid by Corneille of The Hague in Flanders [*sic*], painter to the queen, Eleonora, Queen of France, and was finished on 11 April 1534, after Easter. Written and signed by the hand of the said Aymeric on the said day in the said year. P. Aymeric'.

See Béguin and de Groër, 1978, *passim*; here p. 96.

Antwerp in 1517, Quinten Metsys depicted Erasmus standing at his desk and writing the opening passage of his Paraphrase of St Paul's Epistle to the Romans (plate 178). In France in the mid-fifteenth century, an anonymous artist painted a portrait of an unidentified sitter who has evidently been eating bread and cheese and who is about to drink wine (plate 85). In Florence in about 1500, an artist working in a style close to Filippino Lippi's portrayed an unidentified man tuning a musical instrument (plate 114). Lorenzo Lotto in 1527 represented the Venetian

113 Follower of the Master of Flémalle, *Guillaume Fillastre (?)*, panel, painted surface 33.7 × 23.5 cm., Courtauld Institute Galleries, London.

The frame (44.3 × 34.2 cm.) is original: the frame and the painted reverse are discussed in the note to plate 74. The portrait, sadly damaged, bears some resemblance to likenesses of Guillaume Fillastre, who became Bishop of Verdun in 1437, Bishop of Toul in 1448 and Bishop of Tournai in 1460 and who died in 1473. The picture is difficult to date, but may have been painted towards 1440 or 1450.

See Davies, 1972, p. 227; here pp. 65, 66, 96.

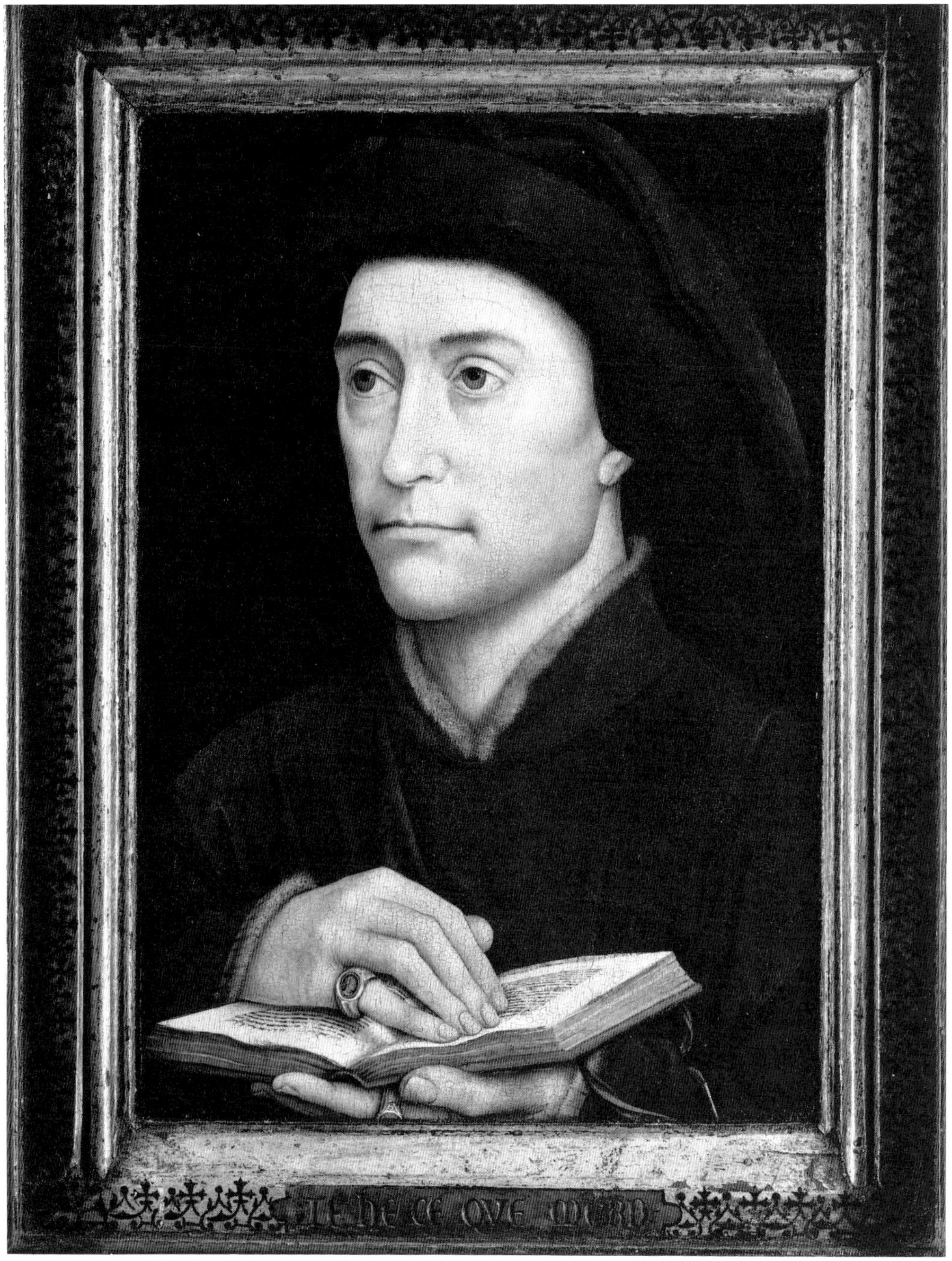

114 Florentine, late fifteenth century, *Man tuning a Viol*, panel, 51 × 36 cm., National Gallery of Ireland, Dublin (470).

The Italian inscription on the viol, partly effaced, has not been fully deciphered and the sitter, perhaps a professional musician, has not been identified. The style is close to that of Filippino Lippi and the artist, like Filippino, has been strongly influenced by Netherlandish painting.

See p. 97.

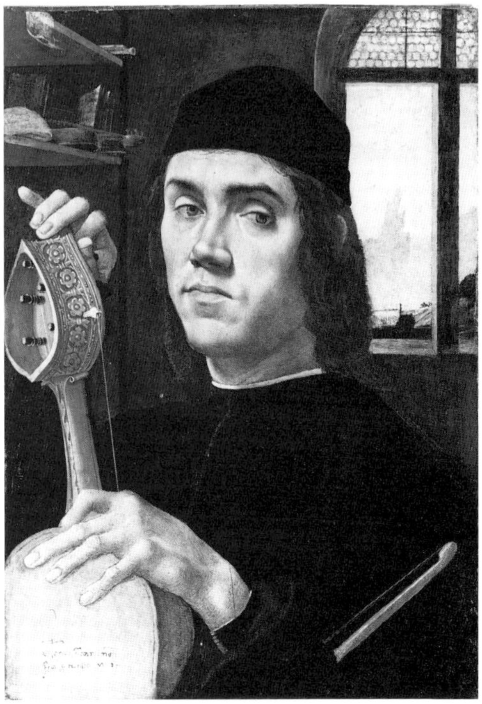

collector Andrea Odoni surrounded by and holding objects from his collection (plate 115). Moroni's *Tailor* of about 1570 apparently shows a tradesman at work (plate 101). A German portrait of 1529, attributed to Barthel Beham, depicts a man chalking numbers onto the surface of a table: he has been said to be an umpire keeping a score, or a merchant performing a calculation (plate 97).

Alternatively, an active sitter might be shown making an eloquent gesture (plates 76, 99). Such gestures occur frequently in portraits of the first half of the sixteenth century: for example, in Dürer's self-portrait of 1500, in which the artist points meaningfully towards his heart;[30] in Raphael's portrait of himself with his 'fencing master' of about 1519, in which the 'fencing master's' dramatically foreshortened right hand points at the spectator (plate 116); or in portraits by the Netherlandish painter Vermeyen, whose sitters often appear to harangue the spectator (plate 117).

Normally, however, the sitter is in repose. A scholar, or someone who wanted to be thought scholarly or pious, might hold, or toy with the pages of, a book (plates 38, 234); a nobleman might rest one hand on his hip (plates 94, 147), or might finger his sword (plates 140, 157, 263) – or might even threaten to unsheath it (plate 145); a person of rank might caress a splendid animal, an attendant slave or a dwarf (plates 87, 119, 159, 255). A seated subject might rest his hands elegantly upon the arms of his chair (plates 38, 89); a seated or a standing subject, supporting his forearm on a chair or desk, might let his hand fall gracefully and limply (plates 33, 131, 158, 261–2). Gloves were useful for occupying the idle hands of men and women, and women might hold handkerchiefs or fans (plates 94, 107, 120). None of these objects seems to have carried any symbolic meaning and they might with relative safety be placed in the hands of any sitter.[31]

The meanings of certain gestures can perhaps be explained by reference to classical and contemporary treatises on rhetoric. Quintilian stated that a pointing index finger could signify affirmation, or, if pointed downwards, insistence:[32] the gestures made with their right hands of Raphael's 'fencing master' and Johannes Münstermann in his portrait by Hermann tom Ring of 1547 are therefore affirmative (plates 116, 245); while Cardinal Granvelle, in Mor's portrait of 1549, may perhaps be indicating insistence (plate 259). Quintilian recommended that, to accompany modest language, the thumb and next three fingers should be gently converged to a point and that the hand should be carried to the neighbourhood of

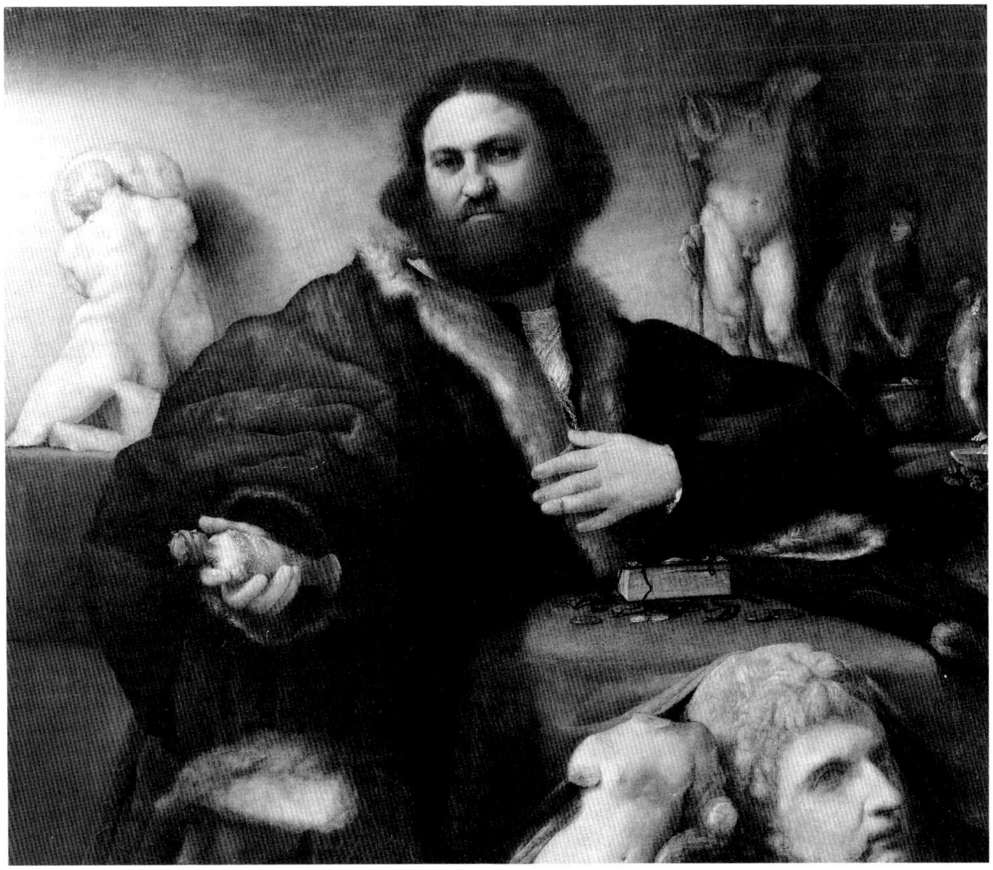

115 Lorenzo Lotto, *Andrea Odoni*, canvas, painted surface 103 × 115.5 cm., Royal Collection, Hampton Court (72).

Signed by Lotto and dated 1527, the portrait represents Andrea Odoni (1488–1545), a Venetian merchant who held various minor offices in the government of the Republic and who owned an important collection of works of art, including the painting reproduced as plate 220.

See Shearman, 1983, pp. 144–8 (143); here p. 98.

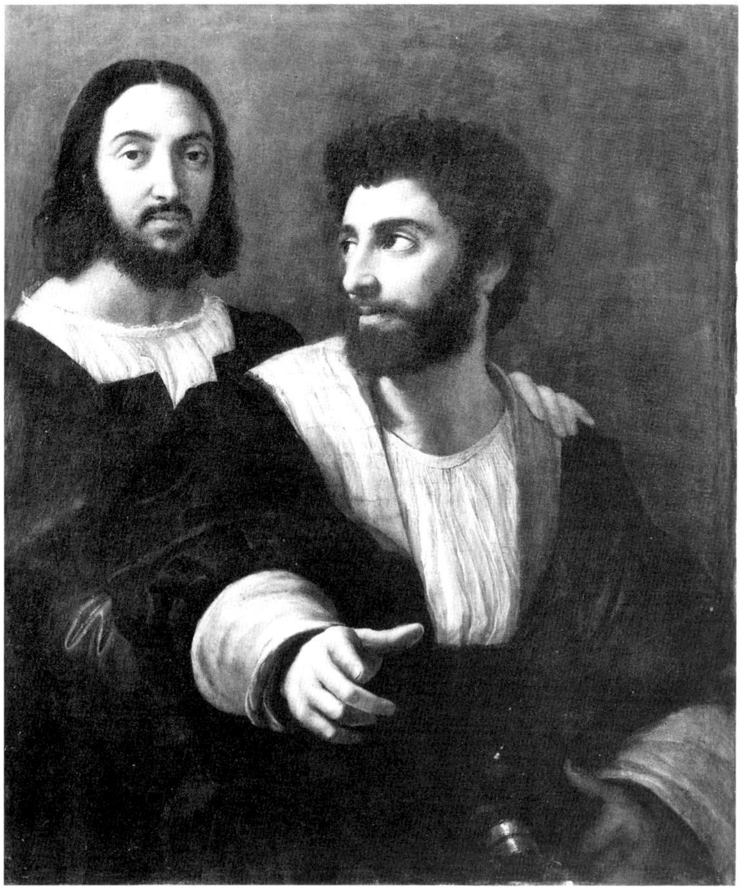

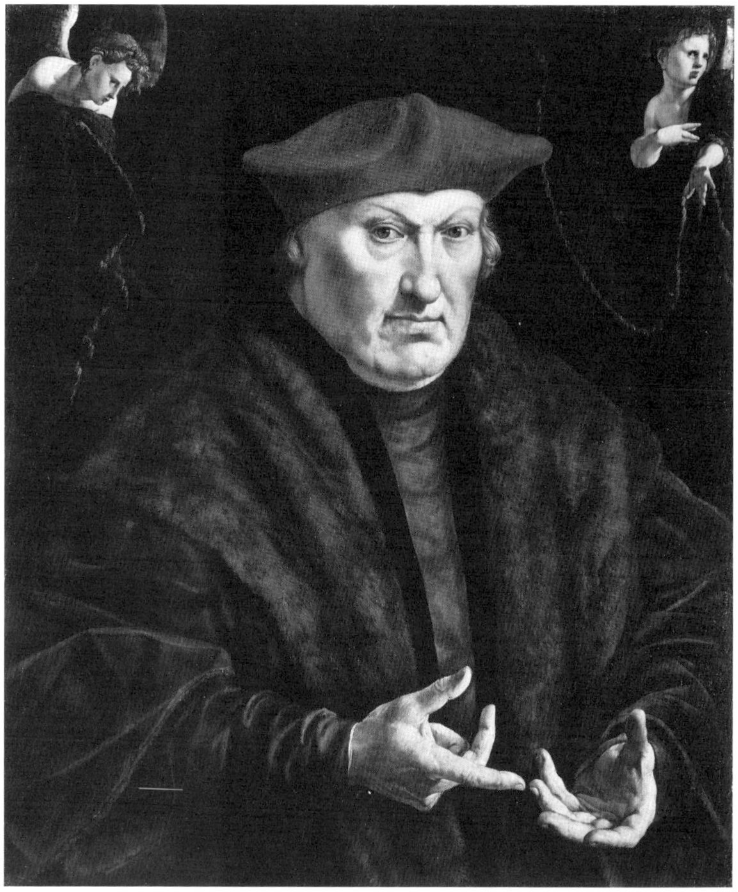

116 (above left) Raphael, *Raphael and his 'Fencing Master'*, canvas, 99 × 83 cm., Louvre, Paris (INV. 614).

The man on our left is Raphael himself; the man on our right, traditionally known as his 'fencing master', has not been identified. The significance of their gestures and the reasons for the painting of the portrait remain totally obscure. It is believed to date from about 1519.

See the exhibition catalogue Paris, 1983–4, pp. 101–4; Béguin, 1984, pp. 58–61; here pp. 98–9.

the mouth or chest, then relaxed palm downwards and slightly advanced.[33] Raphael may have represented Bindo Altoviti making this becoming gesture (plate 118). Again according to Quintilian, when the Romans made vows, they slightly hollowed their hands, presumably to stress their sincerity.[34] In Vermeyen's portrait of Erard de la Marck, the sitter, if he is following Quintilian's precepts, is making an affirmative gesture with his right hand and expressing sincerity with his left (plate 117). It is more probable, however, that he is counting on his fingers and doubtless making rhetorical points.

Certain poses must undoubtedly be understood in relation to the conventions used in religious and secular subjects. It was a time when princes constantly compared themselves, and were compared by others, with characters from the Bible, with saints, with gods or with heroes. Philip the Good, Duke of Burgundy, for example, receiving the fugitive Dauphin of France at Brussels in 1456, said that he could not be more pleased to see him than the Virgin was to encounter the Archangel Gabriel.[35] When Mary Tudor, Queen of England, welcomed Cardinal Pole at Whitehall in 1554, an ambassador imagined that they were re-enacting the Visitation. Mary, believing herself to be pregnant, felt the unborn – and, as it happened, non-existent – child leap in her womb.[36] When a prince was portrayed in a pose and with attributes normally associated with the Virgin, Christ or a saint, a parallel was being deliberately made and was intended to be recognised.

In the triptych of the *Last Judgement* from the town hall of Zierikzee in Zeeland, a Netherlandish artist of about 1505 has represented on the interior faces of the wing panels Philip the Handsome, ruler of the Low Countries, and his wife Joanna

117 (left) Jan Cornelisz. Vermeyen, *Erard de la Marck*, panel, 64 × 54.5 cm., Rijksmuseum, Amsterdam (A 4069).

A closely related etching, inscribed with Erard's name and signed by Vermeyen, provides grounds for identifying artist and sitter. Vermeyen is known to have delivered two portraits of Erard to his employer Margaret of Austria shortly before her death in 1530 (Houdoy, 1872, p. 517). The Amsterdam picture may have been one of them or, at any rate, may have been painted at about that time, when Erard (1472–1538) was approaching sixty. He became Bishop of Liège in 1505 and was made a cardinal in 1521.

See the exhibition catalogue Amsterdam, 1986, pp. 203–4 (78); here pp. 99, 100, 115.

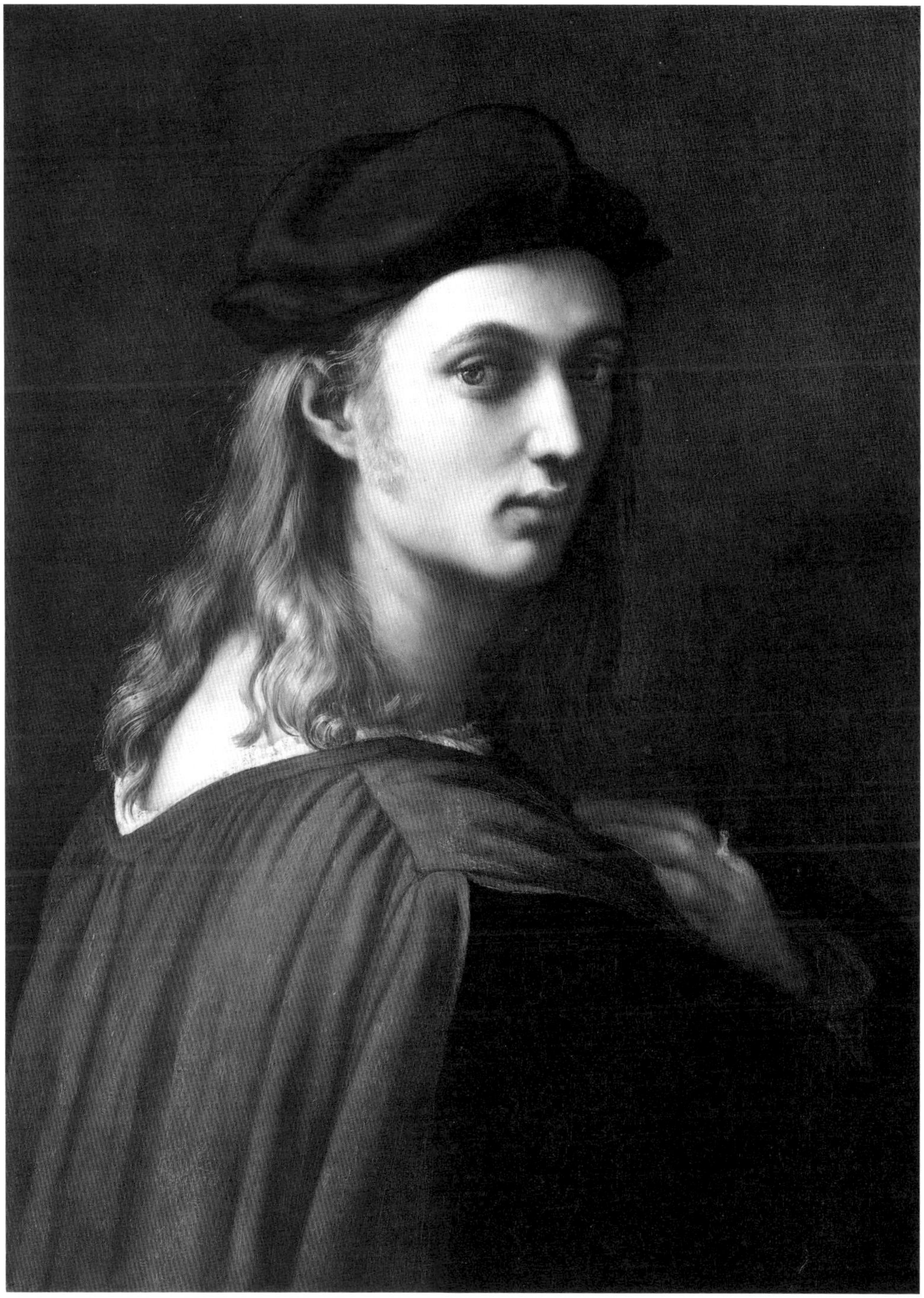

118 Raphael, *Bindo Altoviti*, panel, 59.7 × 43.8 cm., National Gallery of Art, Washington (1943.4.33, Samuel H, Kress Collection).

First traceable in 1767, the picture was then in the possession of the Altoviti family and it seems reasonable to identify it as the portrait of Bindo Altoviti (1491–1557) mentioned in Vasari's life of Raphael. It was probably painted in about 1515 when the young sitter was running the family banking business in Rome. Cellini's bronze bust of Bindo, executed in about 1550, is in the Gardner Museum at Boston.

See Shapley, 1979, pp. 394–6; here pp. 95, 100.

the Mad, Queen of Castile (plate 121). Seen against views of the park of the palace of Brussels, they occupy positions that would normally, in such triptychs, have been allotted to saints; here the saints are relegated to the reverses of the wing panels. Though comparable portraits may be found in the dynastic series (plate 47), the depiction of Philip is similar to an image of a warrior saint, Joanna's, to an image of a virgin saint. In 1508, Burgkmair represented Philip's father, the Emperor Maximilian I, in a woodcut that might easily be mistaken for an image of St George (plate 257). It was not only princes who were so portrayed. When

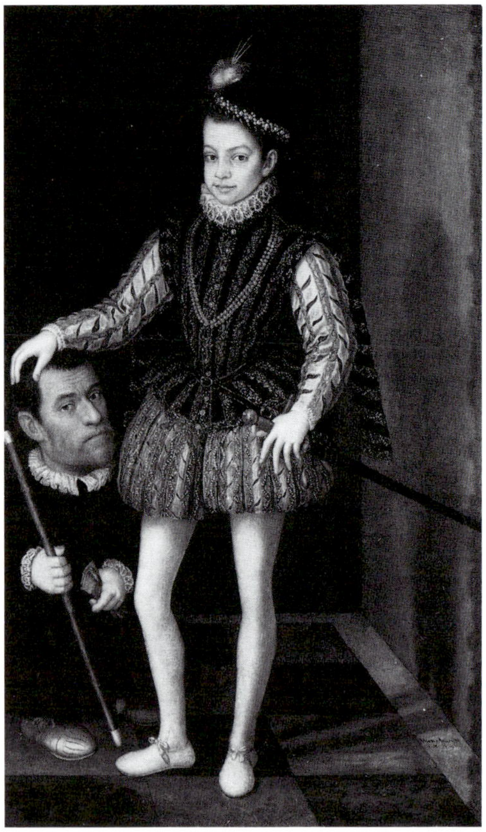

119 Giacomo Vighi, called Argenta, *Charles Emmanuel I of Savoy as a Child, accompanied by a Dwarf*, canvas, 146 × 88 cm., Galleria Sabauda, Turin (18).

Signed in the lower right corner 'IACOBVS ARGENTA', the portrait represents Charles Emmanuel (1562–1630), only child of Emmanuel Philibert, Duke of Savoy, whom he succeeded in 1580. The painter, who came from Argenta near Ferrara, worked at the court of Savoy from 1561 until his death in 1573. The painting would appear to have been executed shortly before he died.

See the exhibition catalogue Turin, 1963, II, Pittura, p. 45 (1); here pp. 54, 99.

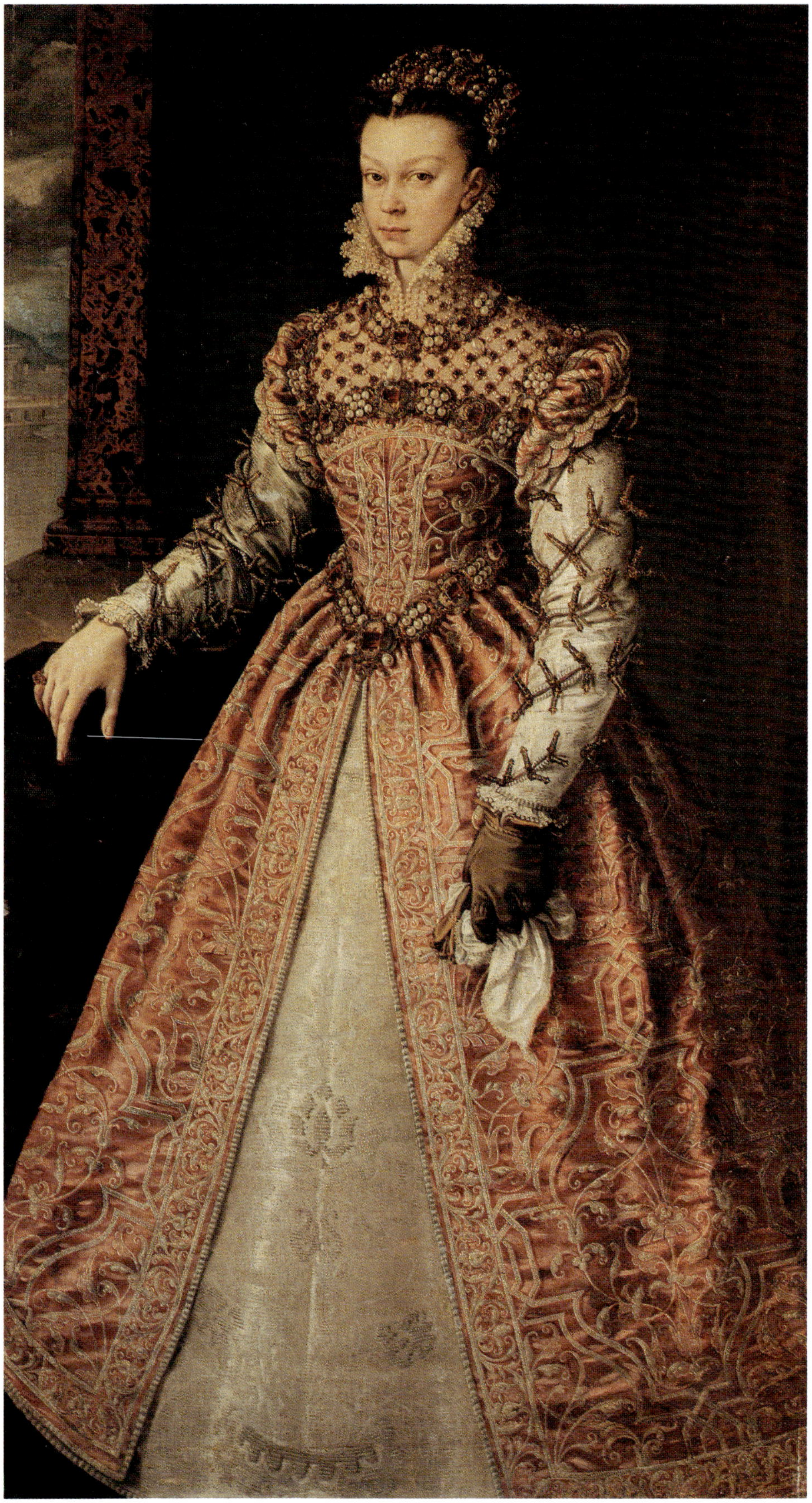

120 Alonso Sánchez Coello, *Elisabeth of Valois, Queen of Spain*, canvas, 163 × 91.5 cm., Kunsthistorisches Museum, Vienna, Gemäldegalerie (3182).

Apparently cut on all four sides, the portrait is attributed on stylistic grounds to Sánchez Coello. The sitter is identified, by comparison with other portraits, as Elisabeth of Valois (1545–68), daughter of Henry II of France and Catherine de' Medici and third wife of Philip II of Spain. Elisabeth was herself an amateur portrait-painter (see p. 151). The Vienna picture was executed in about 1565.

See Klauner, 1961, pp. 143–5; here pp. 99, 120, 208.

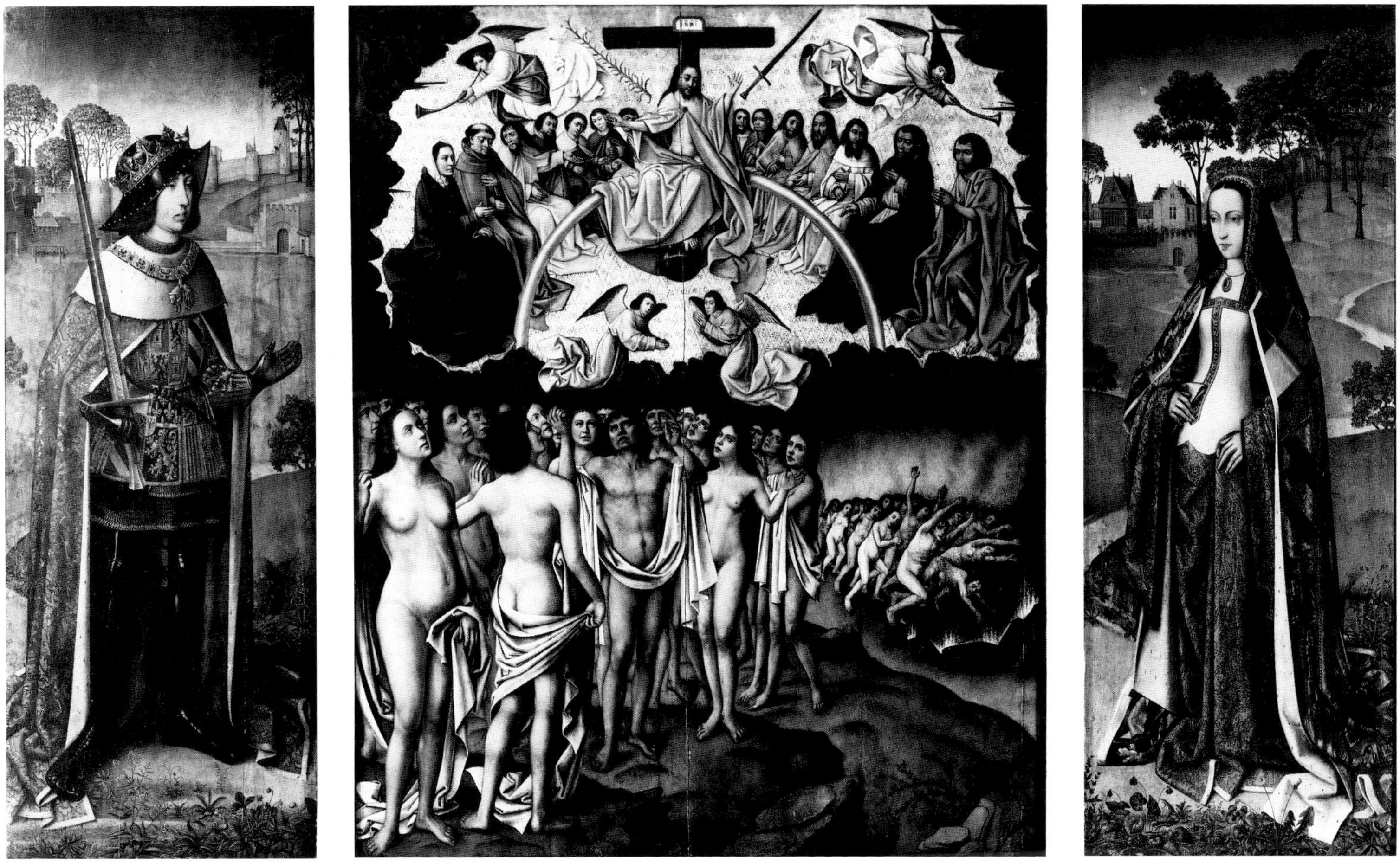

121 Netherlandish, c. 1505, Triptych: *The Last Judgement*, oak panels, painted surfaces 125 × 48 cm., 126 × 105 cm., 124 × 47 cm., Musées Royaux des Beaux-Arts de Belgique, Brussels (2405, 4168, 2406).

In 1731 the triptych was in the town hall at Zierikzee in Zeeland, for which it may well have been painted. On the inside wings are represented Philip the Handsome (1478–1506), ruler of the Low Countries, and his wife Joanna the Mad (1479–1555), Queen of Castile. They are identified by the coats of arms on their embroidered robes and the quarterings of Philip's coat of arms indicate that the panels were painted after 1504, when, on the death of his wife's mother, he took the title King of Castile. On the reverses of the wings are representations of Saints Lieven and Martin. The centre panel and the wing panels appear to be by different artists; the painter of the portraits of Philip and Joanna may have worked in Brussels, for he has set them against views of the park of the palace there.

See the exhibition catalogue Bruges, 1969, pp. 125–7, 256 (59); here pp. 101–3, 128, 236.

in 1517 Quinten Metsys depicted Erasmus according to a compositional scheme normally used for representations of St Jerome in his study, the visual parallel created by the painter between the two scholars, and made very explicit by the inscription HIERONYMVS (Jerome) lettered on the book immediately above his hands, would have been obvious to the educated few who would have seen the portrait in Sir Thomas More's house (plate 178).

Similarly, when Bronzino used the pose of the *Belvedere Torso* for his *Cosimo I de' Medici as Orpheus*, the reference to classical heroes would have been clear to contemporaries.[37] And it was perhaps genre pictures like Lucas van Leyden's of people playing cards or chess that inspired various artists to paint group and double portraits of sitters playing games: for example, Hemessen's *Couple playing Backgammon*, dated 1532; Paris Bordone's *Chess Players*, probably of the 1540s; Sofonisba Anguissola's *The Artist's Sisters playing Chess*, dated 1555; or the mid-sixteenth-century English picture of *Four Gentlemen playing Primero*.[38]

Conversely, court ceremonial and the images of themselves propagated by princes in portraits and at their public appearances unquestionably influenced the ways in which painters visualised the biblical narrative. Some Netherlandish artists found it convenient or interesting to represent one of the Three Kings with the features and ceremonial robes of the Emperor Frederick III, copied from easily available paintings.[39] In a general fashion, devices used by portrait-painters to dignify their sitters were imitated by painters of religious and secular subjects in their images of saints and gods.

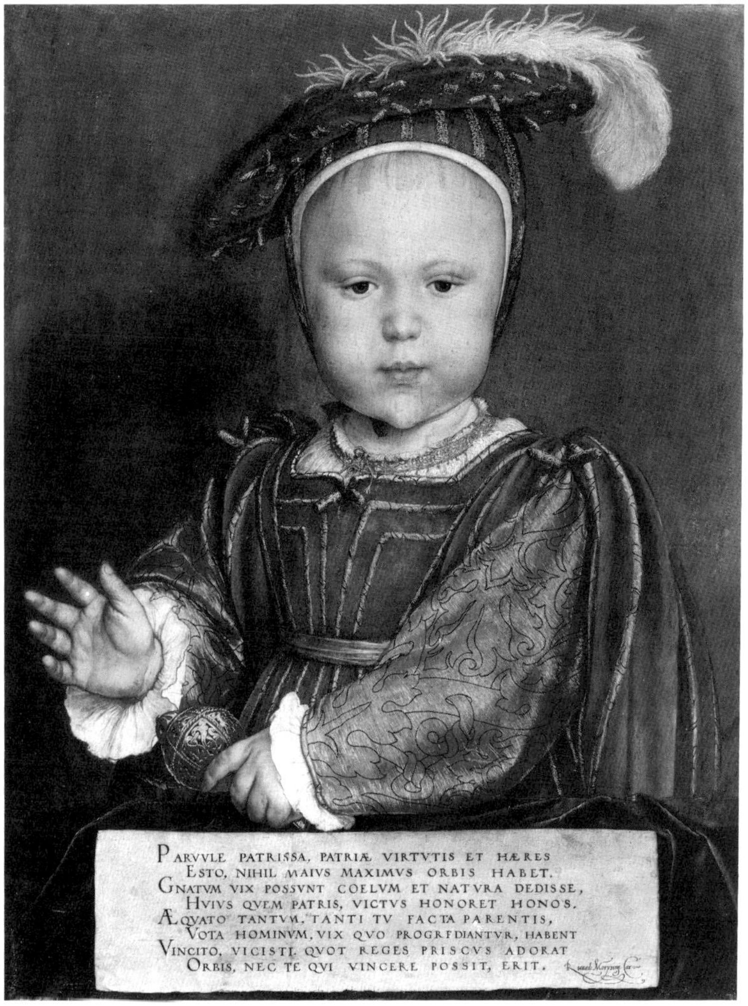

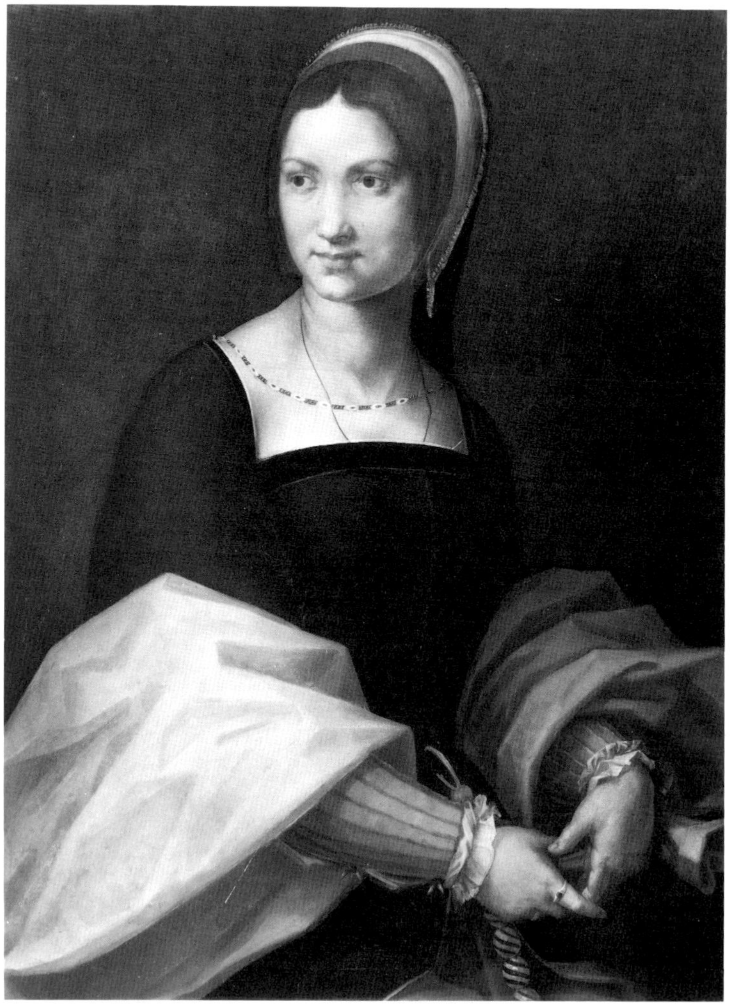

122 (above left) Hans Holbein the Younger, *Edward VI of England as a Child*, panel, 56.8 × 44.1 cm., National Gallery of Art, Washington (1937.1.64, Andrew W. Mellon Collection).

Cleaning tests have revealed that the brown background is painted over the original blue background. Holbein's preliminary drawing for the head, inscribed 'Edward Prince', is at Windsor (Foister, 1983, pp. 21, 43 (46)). The inscription on the painting, composed by Richard Morison, is addressed to Edward and exhorts him to emulate his father Henry VIII; it was copied by a Moravian nobleman who saw the portrait in the Palace of Whitehall in 1600 (Groos, 1981, pp. 46–7). It was evidently the 'table of the pictour of the p'nce grace' which Holbein presented to Henry VIII as a New Year's gift in 1539: Edward, born on 12 October 1537, was then fifteen months old. The object that he holds in his left hand is a gilded rattle.

See Rowlands, 1985, pp. 146–7; here pp. 69, 81, 104.

Conventions of posing certainly existed and many would constantly have changed as artists developed novel poses and as the significance of established conventions became debased by inappropriate imitation and adaptation. Such conventions, rarely described in writing, must normally be deduced from surviving portraits. On a few occasions, a chance reference will bring to light an unexpected convention. In 1606, for example, the future King Louis XIII of France, not yet five, was being painted wearing armour by Charles Martin. While he was posing, he amused himself by playing with paint and with his dog Isabelle, and asked the painter to include the dog beside him in the portrait. One of his ladies remonstrated with him: 'Sir, those who wear armour must not have dogs with them'.[40]

Certain poses became conventional enough to be burlesqued in portraits of children, jesters and freaks. In Holbein's portrait of the baby Edward VI of England, for instance, the child holds his rattle in much the same way as noblemen in grander portraits grasp their swords (plate 122). Mor, in his *Cardinal Granvelle's Dwarf and Dog*, refers back to Seisenegger's and Titian's portraits of Charles V with a dog (plates 124, 255, 256).

At other times, conventions of posing were not so much burlesqued as openly flouted by painters who wanted to enliven their portraits and introduce some sense of movement. They consequently set about destabilising traditional, balanced

123 (left) Andrea del Sarto, *A French Lady*, poplar panel, 82.5 × 62.2 cm., Cleveland Museum of Art, Cleveland (44.82, The Elisabeth Severance Prentiss Collection).

Because the portrait may be attributed, on stylistic grounds, to Andrea del Sarto and because the sitter is dressed in the French and not the Florentine fashion, the painting was probably executed in 1518–19 during Sarto's stay at the court of Francis I of France.

See Stechow et al., 1982, pp. 409–11; here pp. 95, 106.

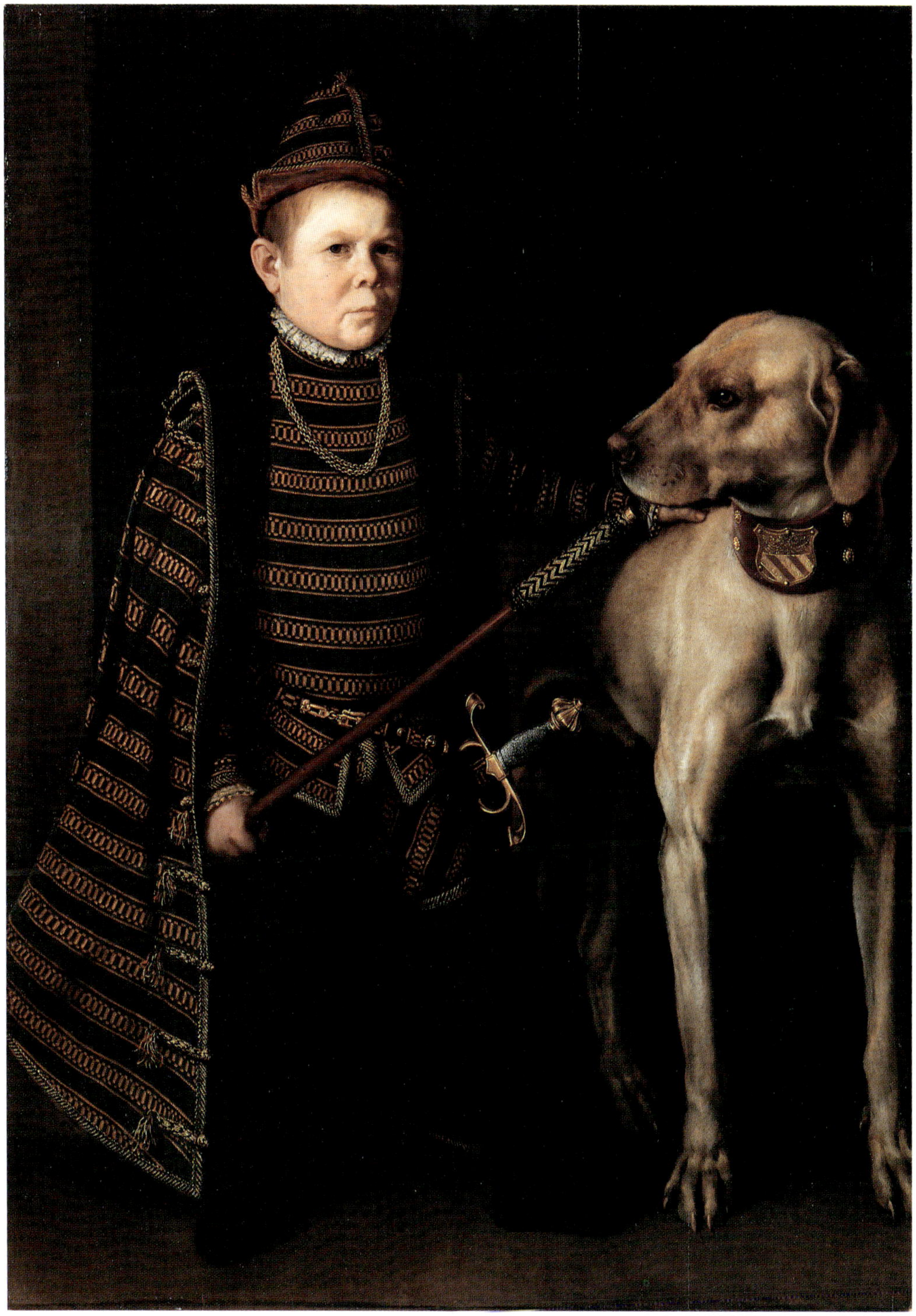

124 Antonis Mor, *Cardinal Granvelle's Dwarf and Dog*, oak panel, 127 × 93 cm., Louvre, Paris (INV. 1538).

The coat of arms on the dog's collar is that of Cardinal Granvelle, who was therefore the owner of the dog and the protector of the dwarf and for whom the picture was almost certainly painted. The dog's portrait doubtless interested him almost as much as the dwarf's. On stylistic grounds the painting is attributed to Antonis Mor, who by 1549 was painter to Granvelle and who lived in his Brussels residence. The dwarf's costume being in the fashion of about 1550, the portrait was perhaps executed before Mor's departure from Brussels in 1550 or soon after his return in 1552–3.

See Michel, 1953, pp. 222–4; here pp. 104, 139, 206.

compositions and employing manifestly strange schemes of lighting. Andrea del Sarto, for example, abandoned in many of his portraits the pyramidal compositions favoured by his predecessors and contrived to introduce diamond-shaped schemes of design (plates 88, 123).[41] The diamond, resting on its point, is a much less stable shape than a pyramid, resting on a horizontal base. This and Sarto's tendency to make his sitters' heads and bodies turn in different directions, give them an air of restlessness. He and certain of his Florentine contemporaries,

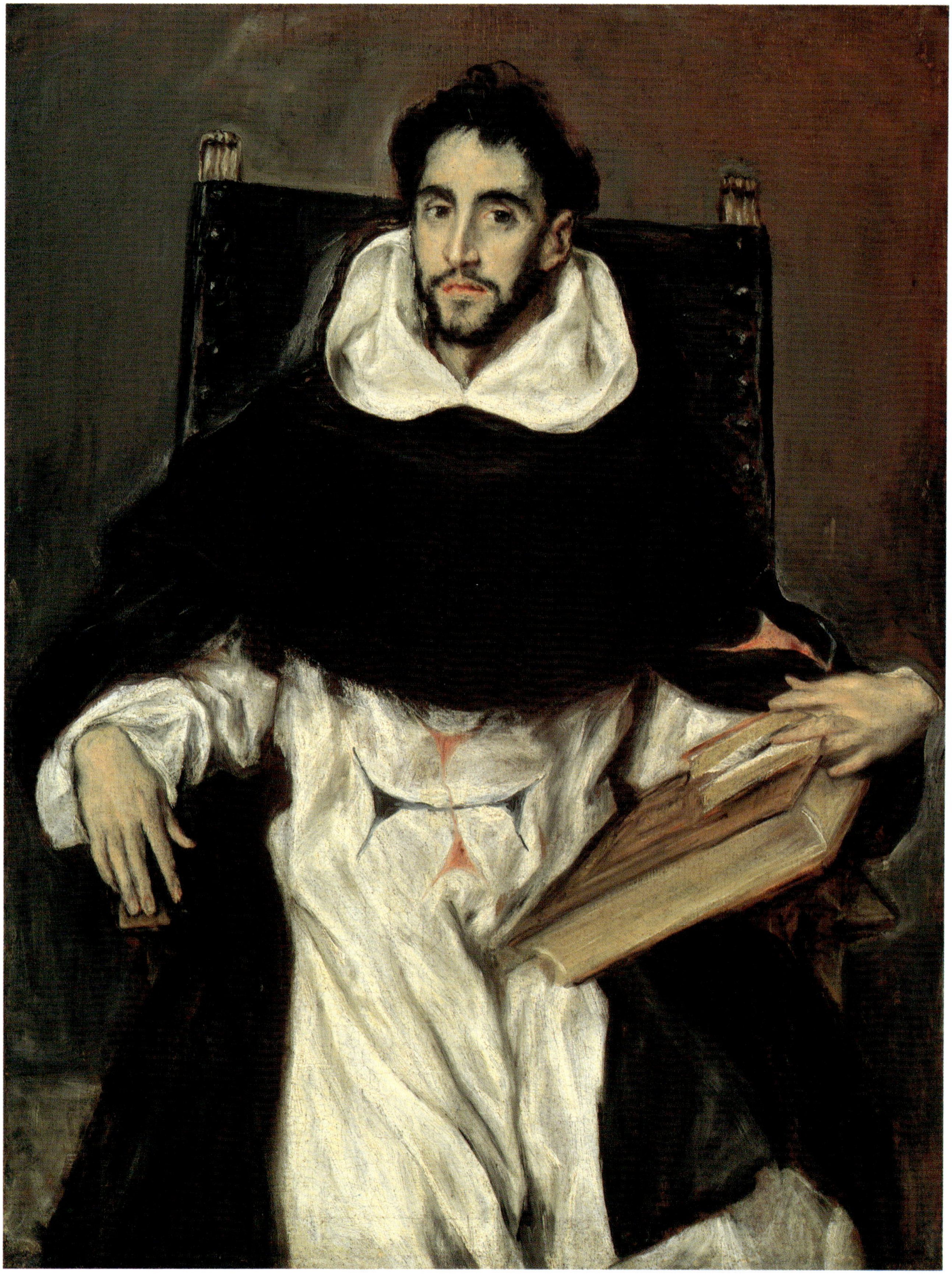

125 El Greco, *Fray Hortensio Felix Paravicino*, canvas, 112 × 86.1 cm., Museum of Fine Arts, Boston (04.234, Isaac Sweetser Fund).

El Greco's signature, in small cursive Greek letters, appears near the books. The sitter (1580–1633), dressed in the habit of the Trinitarian Order, wrote four sonnets addressed to El Greco which were published in 1641 in his *Obras postumas, divinas y humanas*. One of these is on the Boston portrait, stated to have been painted when Paravicino was twenty-nine – therefore in 1609–10. The most renowned orator of his time, he was appointed in 1616 preacher to Philip III of Spain.

See the exhibition catalogue Madrid, Washington, Toledo and Dallas, 1982–3, pp. 261–2 (63); here p. 107.

notably Franciabigio, lit some of their sitters from above so that their eye sockets were in deep shadow. Since their eyes, emerging indistinctly from darkness, are not well-enough defined for their shapes and expressions to be properly registered, they appear romantically enigmatic.[42]

El Greco's portrait of Fray Hortensio Félix Paravicino, painted in about 1609, is odd in that the sitter seems to face the spectator squarely and sit upright in his chair – but in fact he does not (plate 125). The back of the chair is at an angle to the horizontal, and the axis of the head is at an angle to the vertical, but approximately at right angles to the chair back. To someone used to Titian's or Mor's poses, the sitter's right hand may appear to hang elegantly over the arm of the chair, but in truth it floats above it, though conceivably it may support the tips of two fingers. How the two books are held in place is far from clear and the structure of the left upper arm and the relationship between the left elbow and the chair arm are decidedly strange. The sitter's legs do not connect convincingly with the seat of the chair. The pose, seemingly a frontal adaptation from one often used by Titian and Mor (plates 45, 216), is completely illogical and unstable, yet the sitter was so impressed by the likeness and liveliness of the image that he was to write that his soul was perplexed because it no longer knew whether it resided in him or in the picture.[43] The liveliness is at least partly due to the painter's flouting of representational logic and his undermining of established convention.

The interactions that took place between the conventions of portraiture and the conventions of behaviour were no doubt many and complex, but it is often difficult to decide whether portraits showed people acting as they naturally did or whether people came to pretend to be portraits and act out roles created by artists. It is known, from documents and from representations in works of art, that princes made ceremonial appearances at windows, in galleries or on balconies, the sills and balustrades of which were often draped with rich textiles.[44] In portraits, sitters were often depicted behind parapets, and the parallels are striking. A Netherlandish illuminator of about 1470 showed the Virgin and Child appearing to St Luke at a window, the sill of which is draped with figured cloth of gold. St Luke is painting precisely what he sees, the Virgin and Child framed as by the window (plate 191).[45]

At Madrid in 1594, a cleric in the suite of the nuncio Camillo Borghese described the reception of the papal embassy by Philip II: 'He was dressed in black . . . When we entered, His Majesty was seated in a chair of black velvet and, as soon as Monsignor was in the room, he rose to his feet, leaning on a table also covered in black velvet, beneath a canopy . . .'.[46] The description is very reminiscent of Mor's portraits, painted in 1551 and in about 1560, of Philip's sisters Maria and Joanna (plates 262, 266). As versions of such portraits circulated throughout Europe, foreign visitors probably expected princes to appear as they did in their portraits, and, in such a situation, the princes would have been to some degree obliged to conduct themselves as they appeared to behave in their portraits. It is quite possible that Mor's paintings, though indubitably influenced by Spanish ceremonial, may also have exercised a profound effect upon court etiquette.

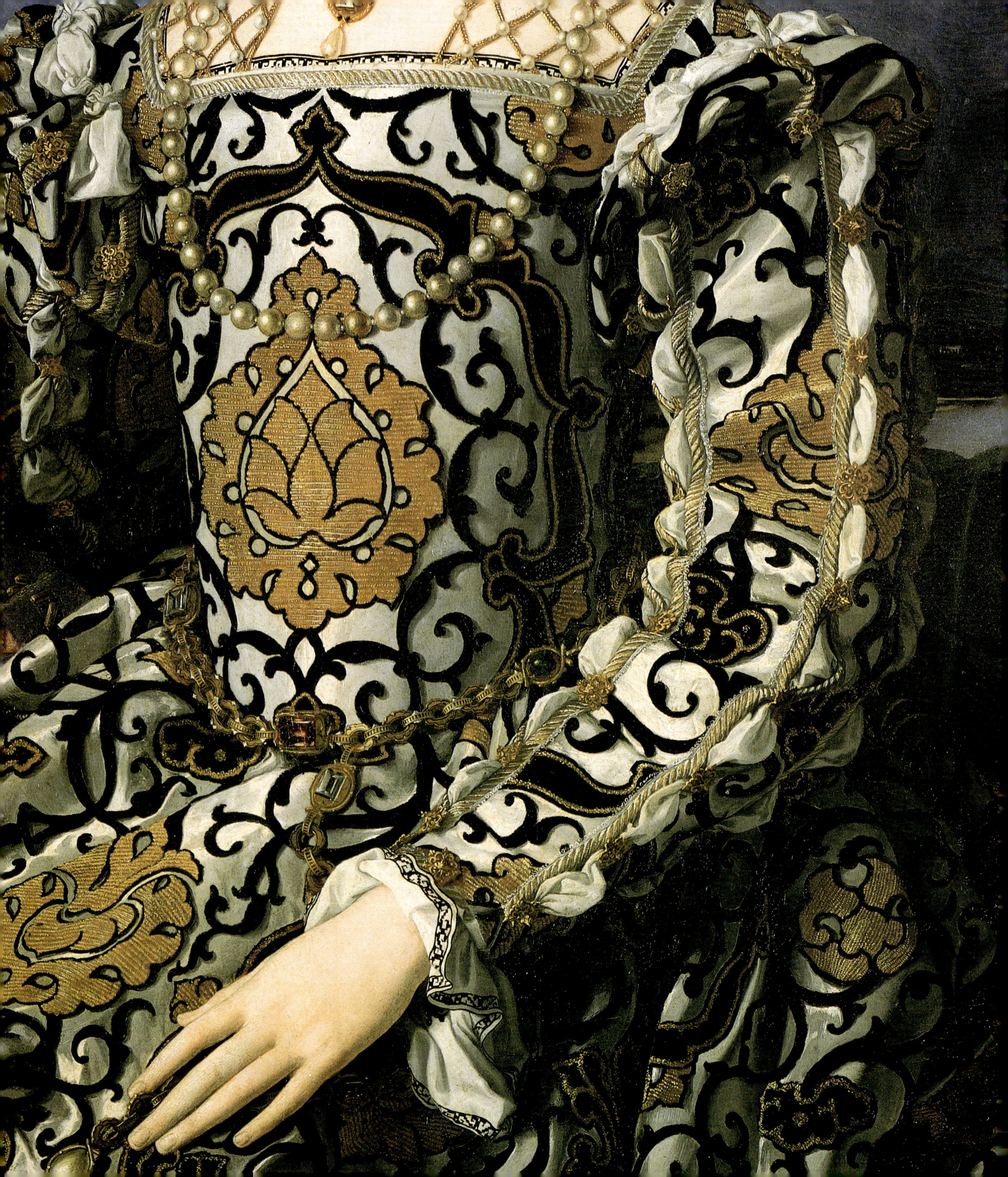

4 Settings, Clothes and Attributes

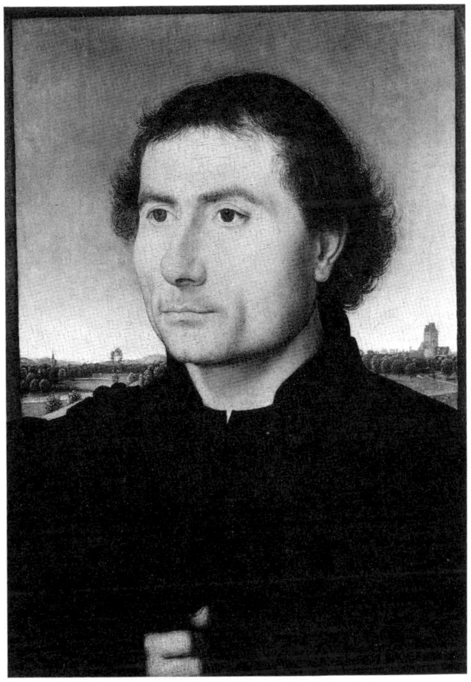

127 Hans Memlinc, *Man*, oak panel, 33.5 × 23.2 cm., The Frick Collection, New York (68.1.169).

There are no indications of the sitter's identity. On grounds of style and costume, the portrait is attributed to Memlinc and dated in the 1470s.

See Friedländer, 1967–76, VIb, p. 109 (Supp. 231); here pp. 109, 120, 233.

The compositional relationship between sitter and frame, besides determining to some degree the sitter's pose, also affected the choice of background. Just as parapets and painted fictive frames were useful in explaining the cutting of figures, so these and similar devices were employed to relate the sitters more securely to the backgrounds and to the actual frames.

Frescoes, which had no real frames, were provided with decorative painted borders, and Castagno, in his series of famous men and women, therefore placed his figures in shallow niches backed with slabs of differently coloured polished stone. Calculated overlaps and foreshortenings allowed some of them to seem to project forward from the picture spaces towards the spectator (plate 49). In the Bruges series of Counts and Countesses of Flanders and in Justus of Ghent's series of famous men, several figures appeared on each panel and simple architectural framing structures were used to confine them neatly in their separate compartments (plates 47, 68). Metsys employed a similar device to divide his sitters in what may originally have been a double portrait (plates 43, 44). Fictive frames painted around the tops and sides of portraits would have seemed to connect with the actual frames; if the sitters overlapped them, they would appear to come forward into the spectator's space (plates 76, 127). In Gossaert's portrait of the children of Christian II of Denmark, the effect is created and simultaneously denied, since the table-top in front of the sitters would seem to be behind the real frame (plate 128). Alternatively, the real frame and the sitter might be made to cast shadows across the background. This idea, which was being implemented in France and the Low Countries in the second half of the fifteenth century,[1] was widely used in northern Europe in the first half of the sixteenth century. It too had the effect of projecting the sitter outwards, in front of the plane of the frame and background (plates 1, 129).

Curtains might serve the same purposes as the fictive painted frames. In Fouquet's portrait of Charles VII of France, the fringe along the top edge of the panel implies that there is a tester above the sitter's head and the two curtains are parted to reveal the king, whose contours they just avoid. Curtains and tester are in the same plane as the frame, to which the curtain on the spectator's left is evidently attached (plate 66). In François Clouet's portrait of Charles IX of France, the tester is no longer visible and the king overlaps the curtain on our left: the impression is now that the curtains have opened to present the monarch and that he has come forward out of the plane which is marked by them and the frame. In the Louvre version, he is still exalted on a level above the spectator's, and distanced from him, by the step that appears in the foreground (plate 131). In Clouet's *Lady in her Bath*, the bath curtains, similarly drawn back, are necessarily in front of the sitter, discovered and displayed in her privacy (plate 15). Such arrangements of canopies and curtains would have brought to mind not only the curtained structures under which princes sat on ceremonial occasions and which were considered appropriate settings for the Virgin as Queen of Heaven,[2] but also the curtained, tent-like constructions in which princes seem to have worshipped in public (plate 173),[3]

126 Bronzino, *Eleonora da Toledo, Grand Duchess of Tuscany, with her Son Giovanni*, detail (see plate 37).

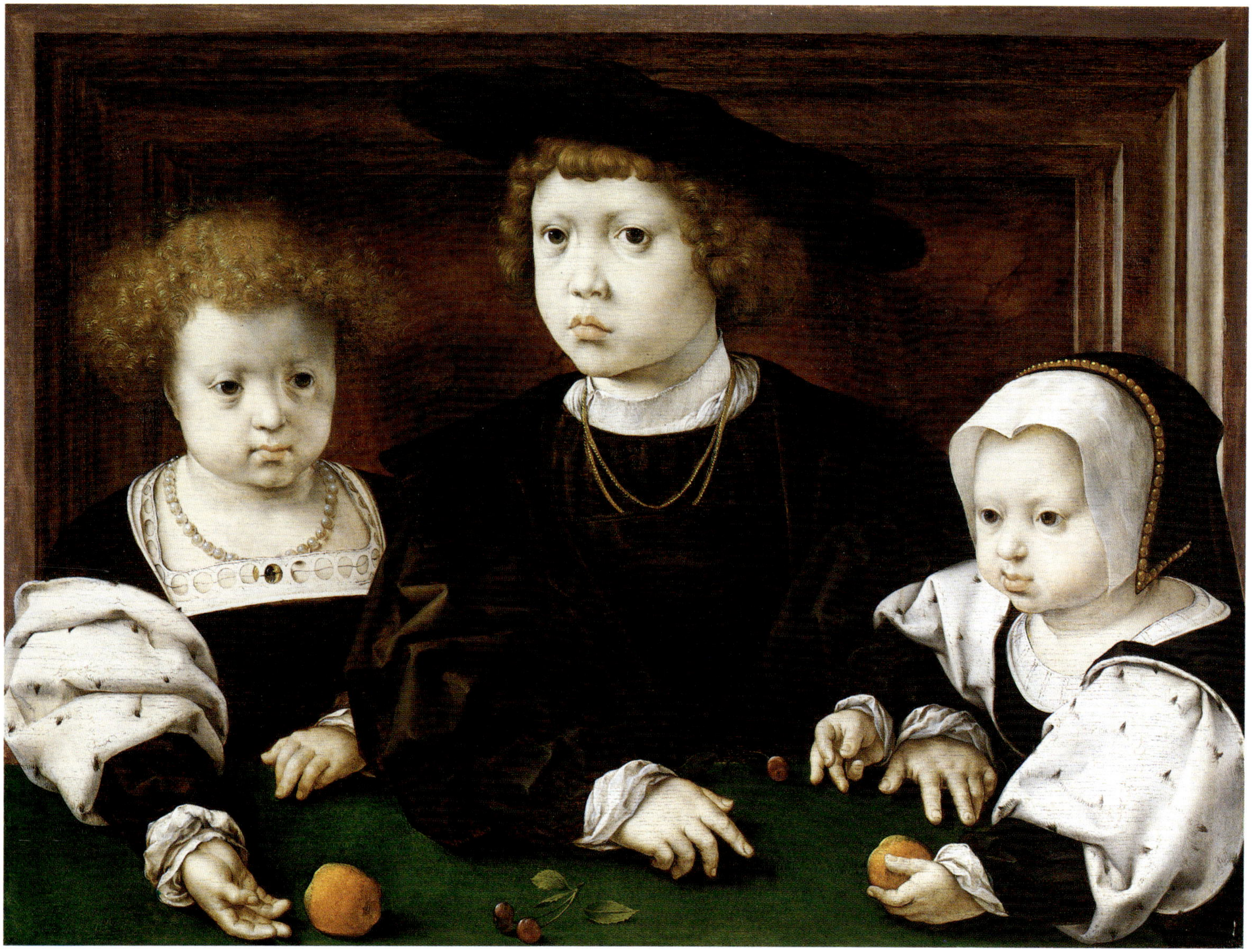

128 Jan Gossaert, *The Children of Christian II of Denmark*, oak panel, 34.2 × 46 cm., Royal Collection, Hampton Court (309).

The boy is identified as John of Denmark (1518–32) by comparison with a drawing in the 'Recueil d'Arras'; the girls are therefore his sisters Dorothea (1520–62) and Christina (1522–90), who in 1538 was to sit to Holbein (plate 1). Henry VIII of England owned in 1542 'oone table with the pictures of the 3 childerne of the King of Denmarks' which would have been either the Hampton Court painting or a version. Christian II and his family were driven out of Scandinavia in 1523; his wife Isabella of Austria died at Ghent in January 1526; Christian left their children in the care of their great-aunt Margaret of Austria at Malines. The portrait is attributed to Gossaert on stylistic grounds. As the children seem to be wearing mourning, it may be dated shortly after their mother's death. It could have been commissioned by Christian or by Margaret of Austria, both of whom were patrons of Gossaert.

See Campbell, 1985, pp. 53–6 (34); here pp. 74, 109, 196.

129 (right) Jan Gossaert, *Man*, oak panel, 56 × 42.5 cm., Staatliche Museen Preussischer Kulturbesitz, Berlin (West), Gemäldegalerie (586 A).

The panel is cradled and an inscription on the cradle, possibly copied from an old inscription on the reverse, covered or planed away when the cradle was applied, identifies the sitter as Baudouin (1445–1508), one of the many illegitimate children of Philip the Good, Duke of Burgundy. As the costume is in the fashion of about 1520–5, however, the sitter cannot be Baudouin. His dagger is inscribed 'ATRE QVE VOV[S]', which is reminiscent of Philip the Good's motto 'Tant que je vive autre n'auray', and the pattern on his collar incorporates saltire crosses very similar to the St Andrew's cross of knotty branches used as a device by the Dukes of Burgundy: it is therefore likely that he is indeed a descendant of Philip the Good. For reasons of style, the portrait is attributed to Gossaert, who worked for another of Philip the Good's bastards, Philip, Bishop of Utrecht, and for the bishop's great-nephew Adolf of Burgundy, Marquis of Veere. The key hanging below the sitter's left wrist may indicate that he held the office of chamberlain; his hat badge bears a representation of Venus and Cupid. The significance of the ring hung from the chain around his neck and of the gilded fish that is attached near the hilt of his dagger and that appears to bite his finger is altogether obscure.

See the exhibition catalogue Rotterdam and Bruges, 1965, pp. 215–16 (38); here pp. 109, 128.

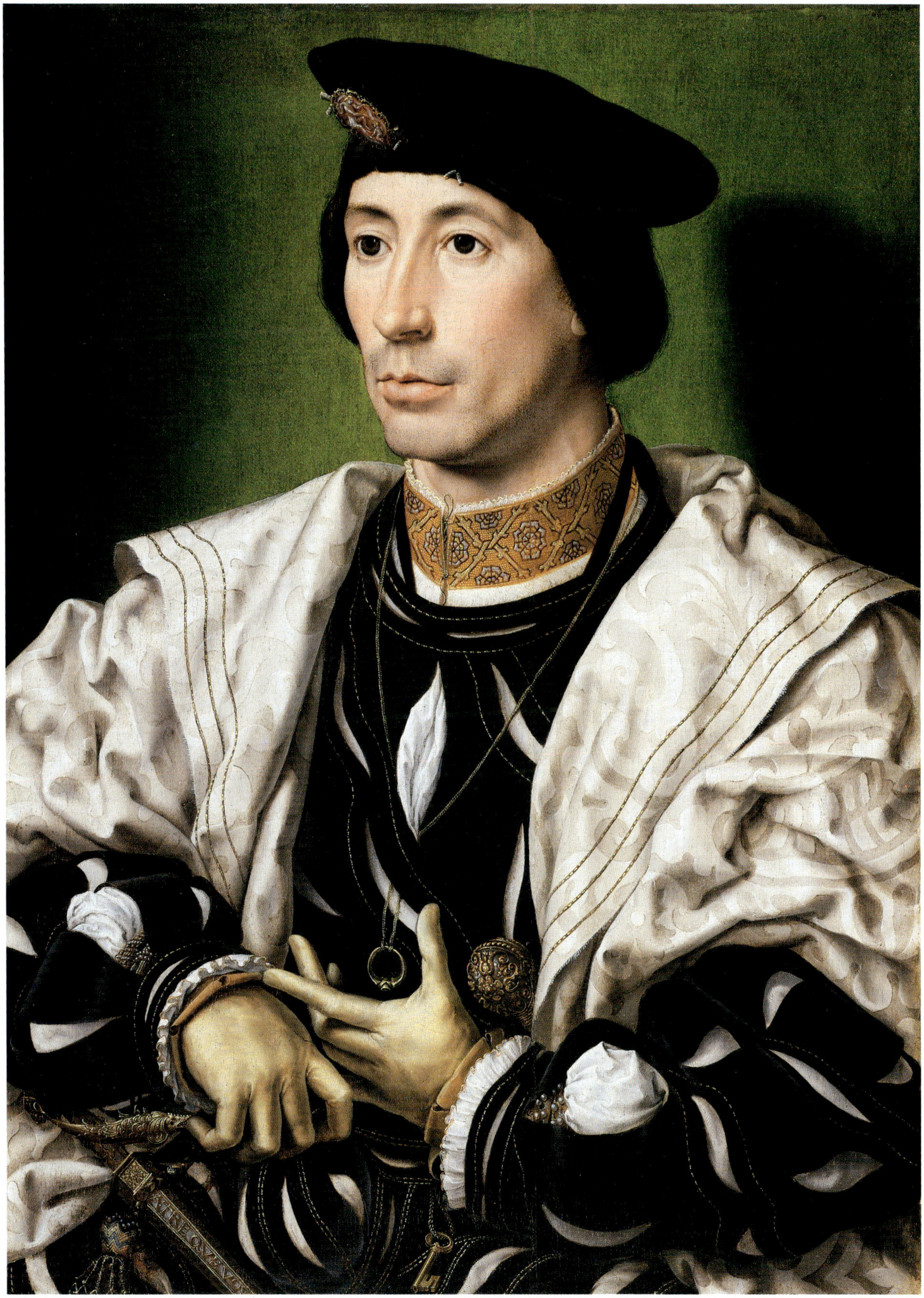

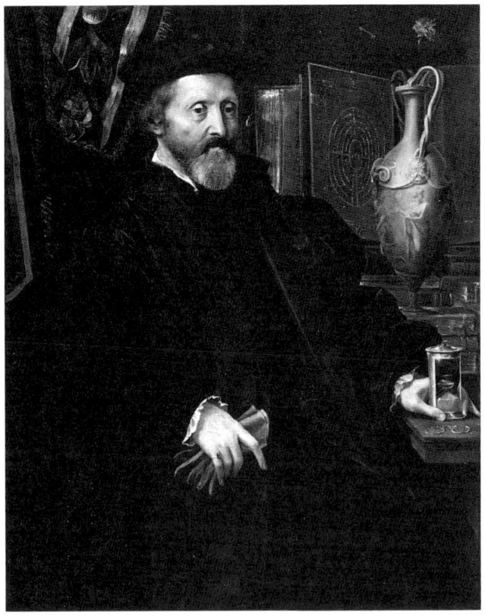

130 Girolamo Mazzola Bedoli, *Man*, canvas, 110 × 90 cm., Galleria Nazionale, Parma (333).

Attributed to Mazzola Bedoli on grounds of style, the portrait is considered to have been painted in about 1545. The sitter, dressed in dark grey and black, holds a gilded hour-glass in which the sand has almost run through; his spectacles lie in front of it, while behind is a vast pile of large books. The vase, inscribed 'ECCE' and decorated with reliefs of the head of Janus and of female figures in the style of Parmigianino, holds an unopened whitish flower, perhaps a lily, and two red carnations. The binding of the book between the sitter and the vase bears the inscription 'E[?X]I': on the rather slight basis of the initials EI, the sitter has been identified as the Parmesan poet Enea Irpino, but he would appear to have been nearing the end of his career in 1520, long before the portrait was painted (Affò, 1791, p. 192).

See pp. 115, 132.

and the proscenium curtains of those *tableaux vivants* that were set up during processions.[4]

Gilded backgrounds were sometimes used in portraits of rulers, exalted by this means like saints. In the portrait of John II of France, a punched pattern round the top and sides of the panel marks a transition between gilded background and gilded frame (plate 63); in the *Richard II of England*, the gilded background, once covered in raised patterns, has been much damaged during restorations (plate 34). After the early fifteenth century, gilded backgrounds became rare in portraits, just as they were less constantly employed in religious paintings; but they did occasionally recur, and were not always restricted to portraits of monarchs (plates 231, 238).[5]

The backgrounds most commonly used were flat areas of one colour, which were obviously the easiest to paint and the cheapest to commission. In the Low Countries in the fifteenth century, dark colours were evidently preferred, though elsewhere, particularly in Germany and Italy, brighter colours were in vogue. Leonardo, Raphael and Titian generally chose dark and unassertive colours, while many of the northern portraitists of the first half of the sixteenth century favoured brilliant blues and greens. Later in the century, more sombre and less striking colours were everywhere the fashion. Plain backgrounds register as flat surfaces or as spaces, according to the lighting of the sitter: if his contours are sharply defined and illuminated, the background will tend to appear as a flat wall or curtain (plates 1, 104, 105); if the contours are less emphatic, the background may seem to be an undefined space (plates 21, 87). If there are slight variations in the

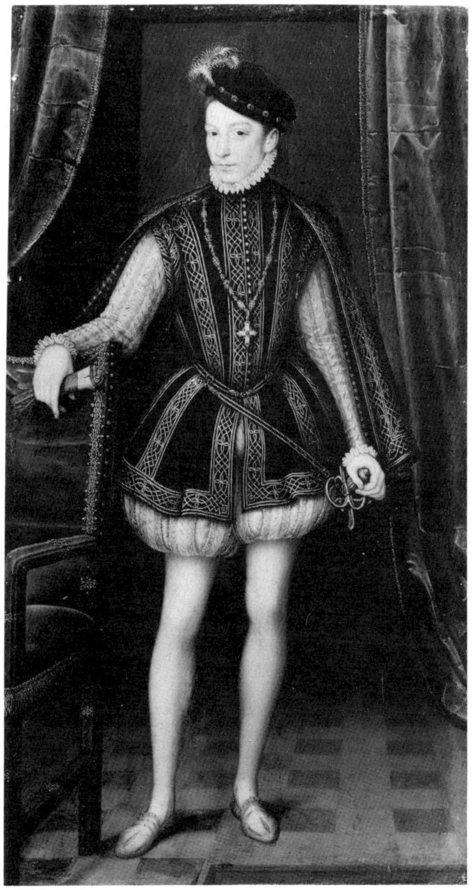

131 (right) After François Clouet, *Charles IX, King of France*, panel, 31.3 × 17.1 cm., Louvre, Paris (INV. 3253).

This is a reduction of Clouet's large portrait on canvas now at Vienna (752: 222 × 115 cm.) which bears the damaged inscription 'CHARLES. VIIII. TRESCHRESTIEN ROY DE FRANCE, EN L'AAGE DE .XX. ANS PEINCT AV VIF PAR IANNET. 1563.'. The date would originally have read 1569.

See Sterling and Adhémar, 1965, p. 26; here pp. 99, 109, 124.

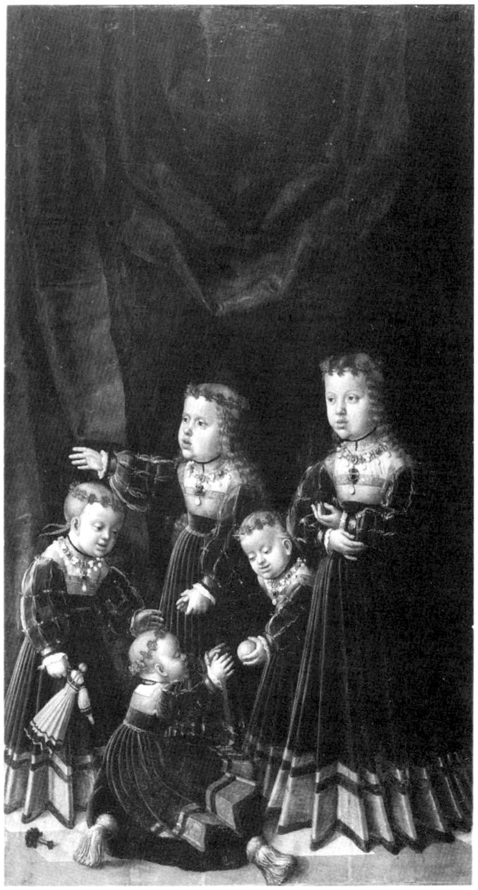

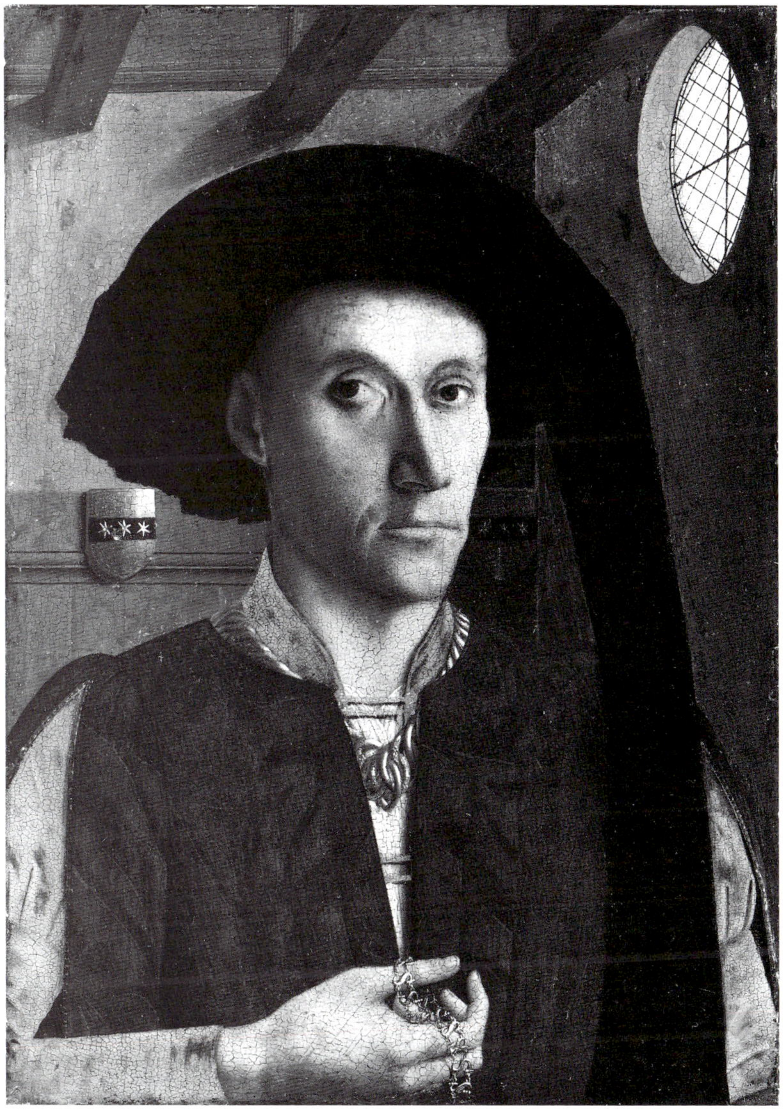

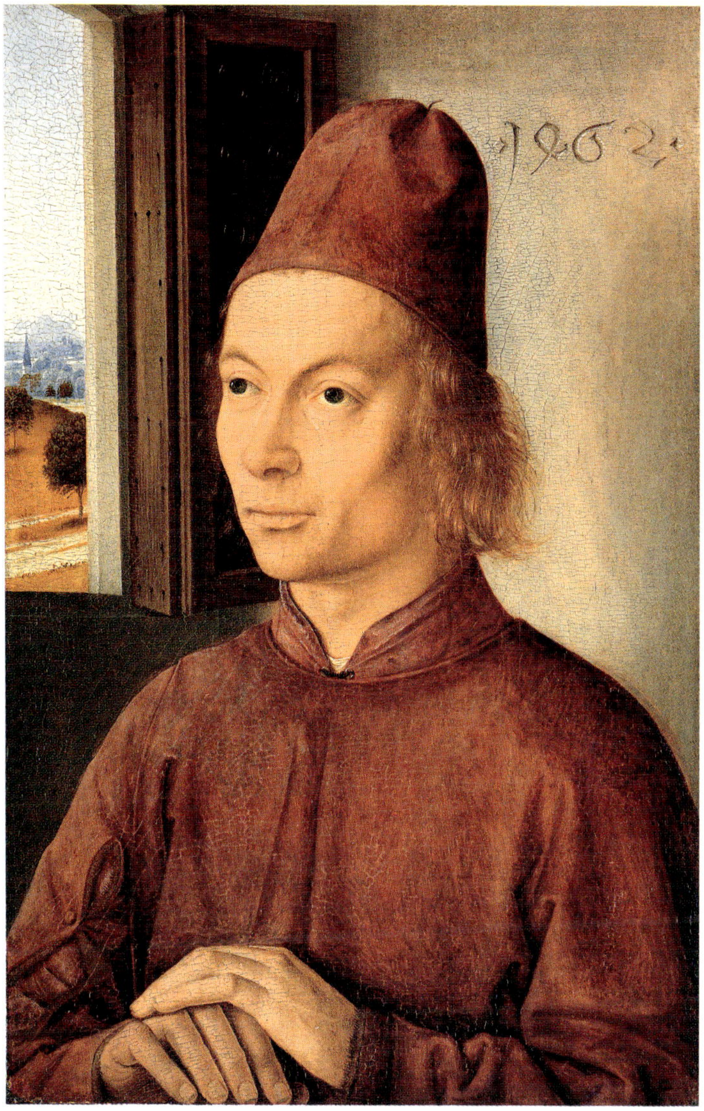

132 (left) Jakob Seisenegger, *The Five Eldest Daughters of the Emperor Ferdinand I*, panel, 220 × 120 cm., Museo Provinciale d'Arte, Trent (Camera del Camin Nero).

The sitters are Elisabeth (1526–45), Anne (1528–90), Maria (1531–81), Magdalena (1532–90) and Catherine (1533–72) of Austria; the portrait was probably painted shortly before the birth on 2 November 1534 of the next sister Eleonora. In a description of the episcopal palace of Trent published in 1539 are mentioned four full-length portraits of Ferdinand, his wife, his sons and his daughters. Only the last, 'another heavenly and exquisite work', has been preserved (Matthioli, 1539, f. Q ii). It is attributed, with every justification, to Seisenegger, who was Ferdinand's court painter; the four pictures were presumably gifts from Ferdinand to Cardinal Bernardo Cles, Bishop of Trent. All five children wear crimson dresses and garlands of red carnations.

See Löcher, 1962, pp. 99, 106; here pp. 115, 120, 132.

133 (above left) Petrus Christus, *Edward Grimston*, panel, 33.6 × 24.7 cm., National Gallery, London (lent by the Earl of Verulam).

On the reverse are the signature of Petrus Christus, the date 1446 and the coat of arms of Grimston, which reappears on the two shields fixed to the panelling behind the sitter. Edward Grimston, who owned the estate of Rishangles in Suffolk, was sent on several occasions during the 1440s by Henry VI of England as his envoy or ambassador to the Burgundian court. He died in 1478. Petrus Christus would have painted his portrait in Bruges during one of his embassies to the Low Countries.

See Scharf, 1866, *passim*; here pp. 115, 128.

134 (above right) Dirk Bouts, *Man*, oak panel, painted surface 31.5 × 20.5 cm., National Gallery, London (943).

Dated 1462, the portrait is attributed to Bouts because of its very close similarities to his documented pictures. The sitter has not been identified. His clothes are unusual in that they are all of one colour and it is possible that he is wearing livery.

See Davies, 1968, pp. 17–18; here pp. 115, 118.

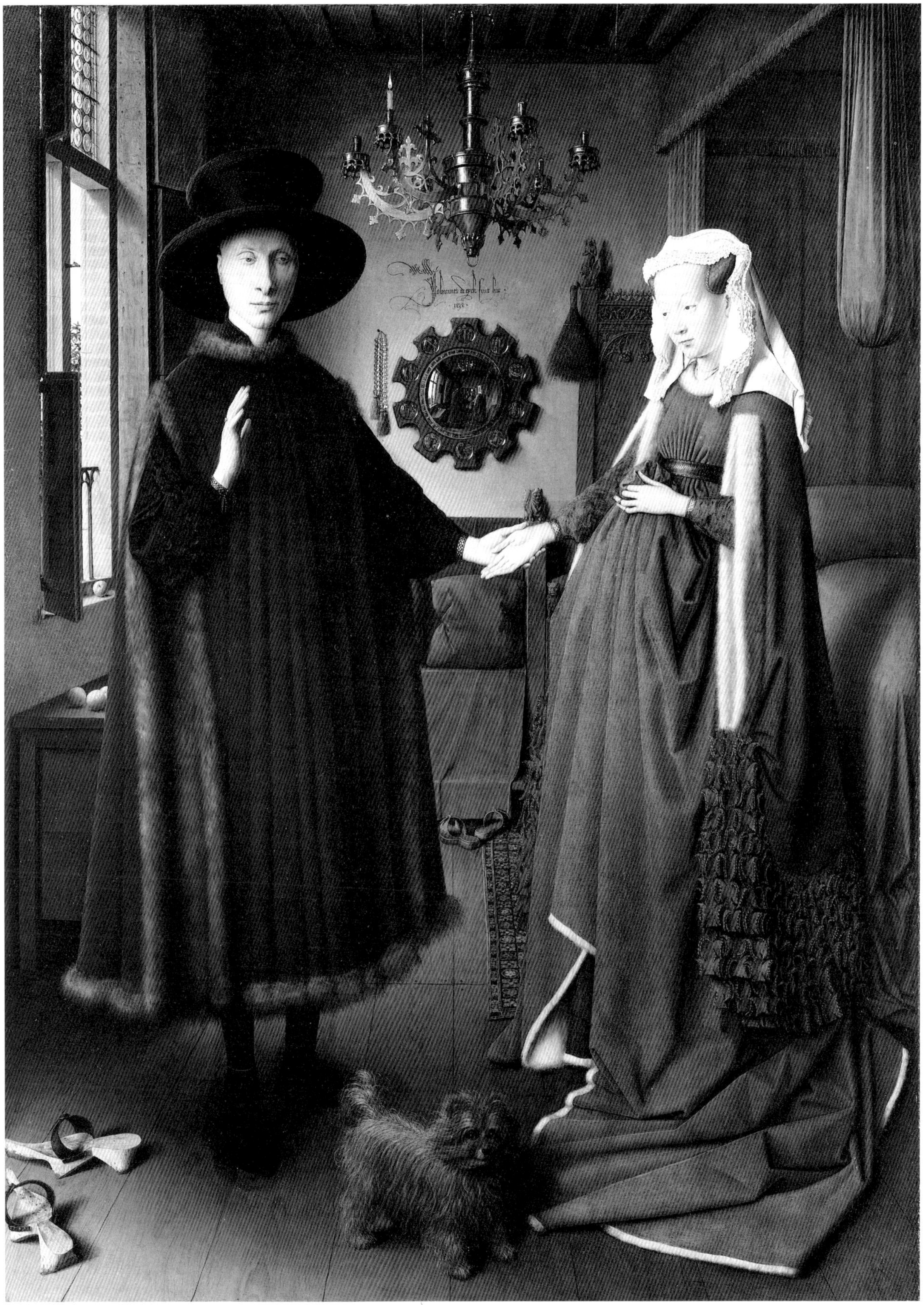

135 Jan van Eyck, *Giovanni Arnolfini and his Wife*, oak panel, painted surface 81.8 × 59.7 cm., National Gallery, London (186).

Signed 'Johannes de eyck fuit hic 1434' ('Jan van Eyck was here 1434'), the picture is first traceable in the 1516 and 1523–4 inventories of the collection of Margaret of Austria at Malines. In the 1516 inventory, it is described as 'a large picture which is called Hernoul le Fin with his wife in a chamber, which was given to My Lady by Don Diego, whose arms are on the cover of the said picture, done by the painter Johannes'. In the 1523–4 inventory, it is listed as 'another very exquisite picture which is protected by two shutters and in which there are painted a man and a woman standing, touching hands, done by the hand of Johannes, the arms and device of the late Don Diego being on the said shutters; the personage is named Arnoult Fin'. 'Hernoul le Fin' and 'Arnoult Fin' are taken to be corruptions of the name Arnolfini and the male subject is identified as Giovanni Arnolfini (died 1472), a Lucchese merchant of great wealth and power settled in Bruges. He was by far the most prominent member of the Arnolfini family who could have encountered Jan van Eyck in 1434, either in Bruges or at the Burgundian court. The lady is consequently his wife Giovanna Cenami (died 1480); the date of their marriage is not known. The portrait may have passed directly from them to Don Diego, the Spanish courtier and collector Diego de Guevara, who gave it to Margaret of Austria. The composition was re-used by various fifteenth-century painters and illuminators and it would be interesting to discover how they knew of it. It is widely believed, though it is by no means certain, that the picture represents the marriage of Giovanni and Giovanna.

See Davies, 1968, pp. 49–52; Dhanens, 1980, pp. 193–205; here pp. 53, 115, 120, 135–6.

tone of the background, the impression of spaciousness will be enhanced, especially if the sitter casts a soft shadow (plate 243).

A flat, patterned textile might function as a backdrop (plate 239).[6] Alternatively, a textile, patterned or undecorated, might be ironed into folds and stretched across the background (plate 215);[7] carved religious images were sometimes displayed against cloths folded in this way, like altar hangings.[8] In English miniatures of the late sixteenth century, backgrounds of folded cloth enjoyed some popularity.[9] Of course, textiles might be draped more realistically to hang in regular, shallow folds (plate 235) or might be suspended in more dramatic loops, knots and swathes (plates 130, 132, 255). Sometimes the textiles were held up by flying genii (plate 117), just as cloths of honour were supported by flying angels behind representations of the Virgin.[10] Very occasionally, draperies might be arranged to give the sitter the appearance of being himself winged (plate 38).[11]

Jan van Eyck in 1434 painted Giovanni Arnolfini and his wife in an expensively furnished interior (plate 135). It is possible, though it cannot be proved, that he was the first portrait-painter to show subjects in a domestic setting, but it may be assumed that the interior, represented with apparent fidelity but distorted with consummate skill to enhance the aesthetic effect of the composition, was intended to be taken for a room in the subjects' mansion. At Bruges in 1446, Petrus Christus, who knew the Van Eyck portrait by report or from versions or in the original, painted a half-length portrait of Edward Grimston, an English visitor to the Low Countries (plate 133). He is set against the background of an interior which is ornamented with shields bearing his coat of arms and which is therefore to be understood as his property, though scarcely as a depiction of an actual room in his English residence. In 1462, Dirk Bouts, whose work has many affinities with that of Christus and who may have seen a portrait similar to the *Grimston*, painted an unidentified sitter placed in the corner of a room (plate 134). In the Van Eyck and Christus portraits, the interiors themselves attract interest and the window openings reveal little in the former and nothing in the latter; whereas, in the Bouts portrait, the sitter's head is silhouetted against a glazed shutter which has been opened to reveal a distant landscape. The recession of the interior has been deliberately obscured and indeed confused by the false horizontal of the window-sill; the room has become little more than a pattern that separates sitter and landscape and creates a subtle alternation of high and low tones across the picture. It is probably no more than a coincidence that these three portraits have survived and that all are dated; they need not necessarily be taken as landmarks in the evolution of Netherlandish portraiture, especially as they do not altogether parallel what can be deduced, from limited evidence, about developments in comparable religious paintings. In the latter, open windows or colonnades commanding views of distant landscapes occur well before 1462 (plate 27).[12]

In Florence, Fra Filippo Lippi's idea of displaying a sitter against an elaborately carved window frame opening onto a distant landscape may have been inspired partly by Netherlandish pictures (plate 138). The idea was taken up by Botticelli, who sometimes placed his sitters between two openings: a window in the plane of the panel, through which the sitter is revealed; and a window or doorway behind the sitter's head (plate 136).[13] Some of Bronzino's sitters are placed against architectural backgrounds that are not strictly interiors: Ugolino Martelli is seated in an outside courtyard of his palace;[14] while Bartolomeo Panciatichi is in a gallery overlooking what would appear to be the entrance courtyard of his house (plate 137). Very occasionally, sitters are placed against the glazed panes of windows;[15]

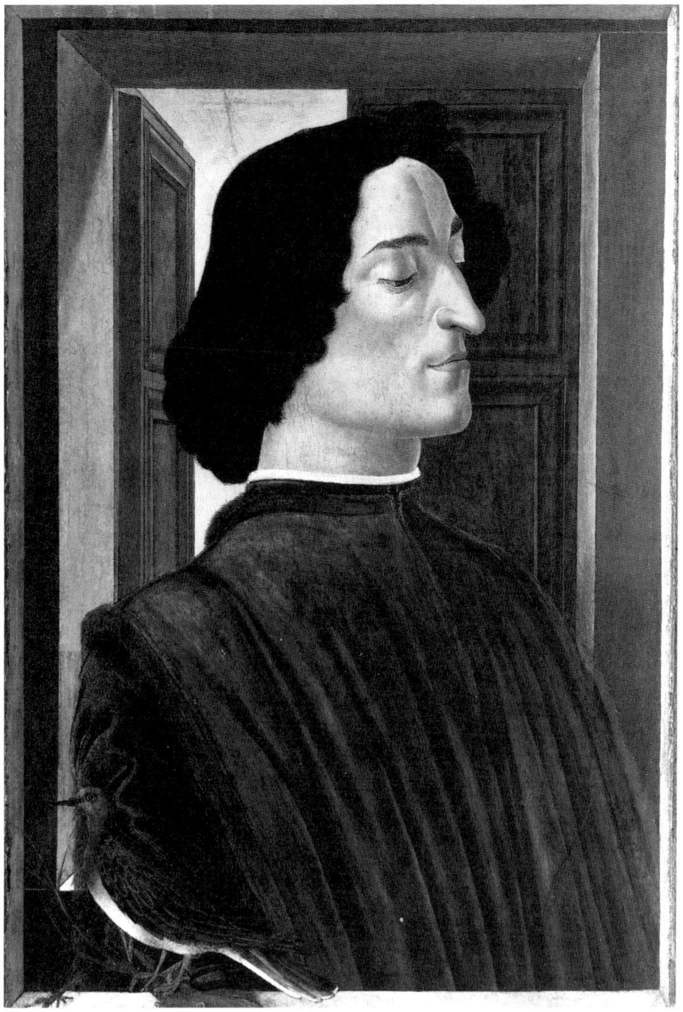

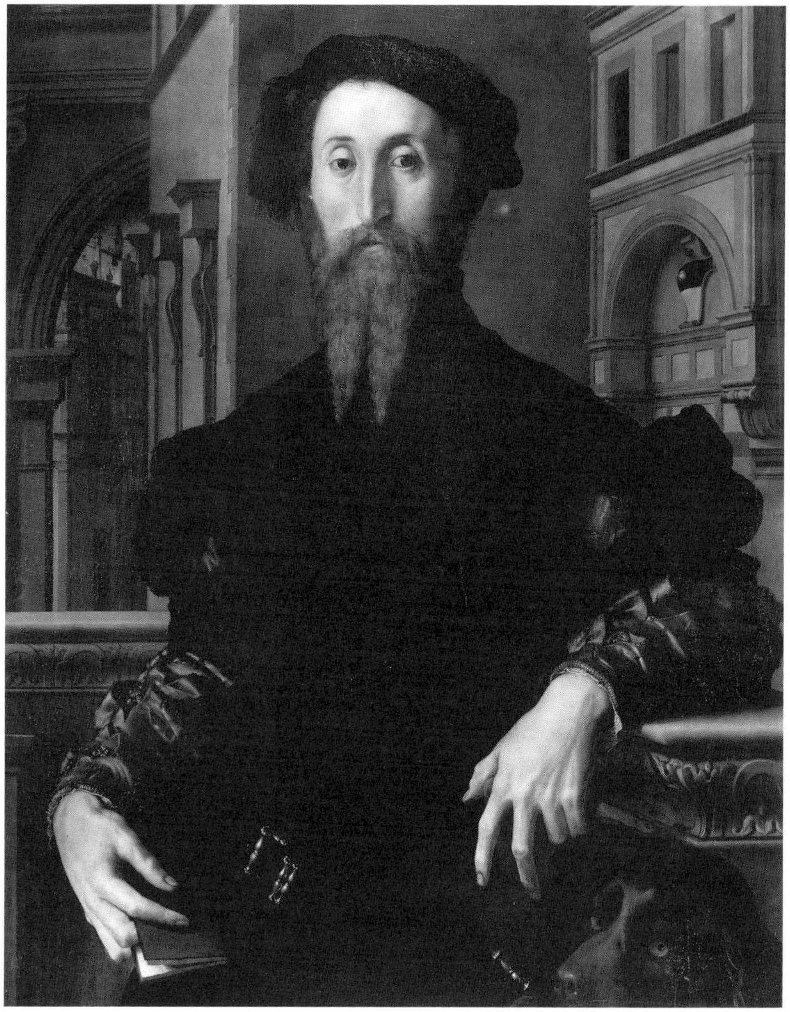

136 Botticelli, *Giuliano de' Medici*, panel, 75.6 × 52.6 cm., National Gallery of Art, Washington (1952.5.56, Samuel H. Kress Collection).

The sitter, identified by comparison with other portraits, was the younger brother of Lorenzo the Magnificent and was murdered by the Pazzi conspirators in 1478, when he was twenty-five. The Washington panel is the most elaborate of several versions of the portrait, some or all of which are considered to have been produced by Botticelli and his workshop. The bird is a bereaved turtle-dove: it was thought that a turtle-dove which had lost its mate would not take another and would perch only on dead branches. The very generalised rendering of the facial anatomy in this and the related portraits suggests that all were painted after Giuliano's murder.

See Shapley, 1979, pp. 83–4; Langedijk, 1981–3, II, p. 1068; here pp. 69, 86, 115.

137 Bronzino, *Bartolomeo Panciatichi*, panel, 104 × 84 cm., Uffizi, Florence (741).

The sitter (1507–82), identified by the coat of arms behind him and from references to the picture by Vasari and Borghini (1584), was born in France and is said to have spent some time as a page at the court of Francis I. He married Lucrezia Pucci, who died in 1572. A man of erudition who wrote and published Latin poetry, he held important state offices in Florence, but he and his wife came under suspicion of heresy and were imprisoned and tortured. In February 1552, they were forced to make public abjurations of their heretical beliefs (Passerini, 1858, pp. 68–72). Bronzino's portrait of his wife is also in the Uffizi (736) but, as the compositions of the two pictures do not balance well, they may not necessarily have been painted as a pair or at the same time. The portrait of Bartolomeo was perhaps executed in about 1540.

See Berti, 1979, p. 188; Plazzotta, 1988, pp. 6–15; here pp. 72, 115.

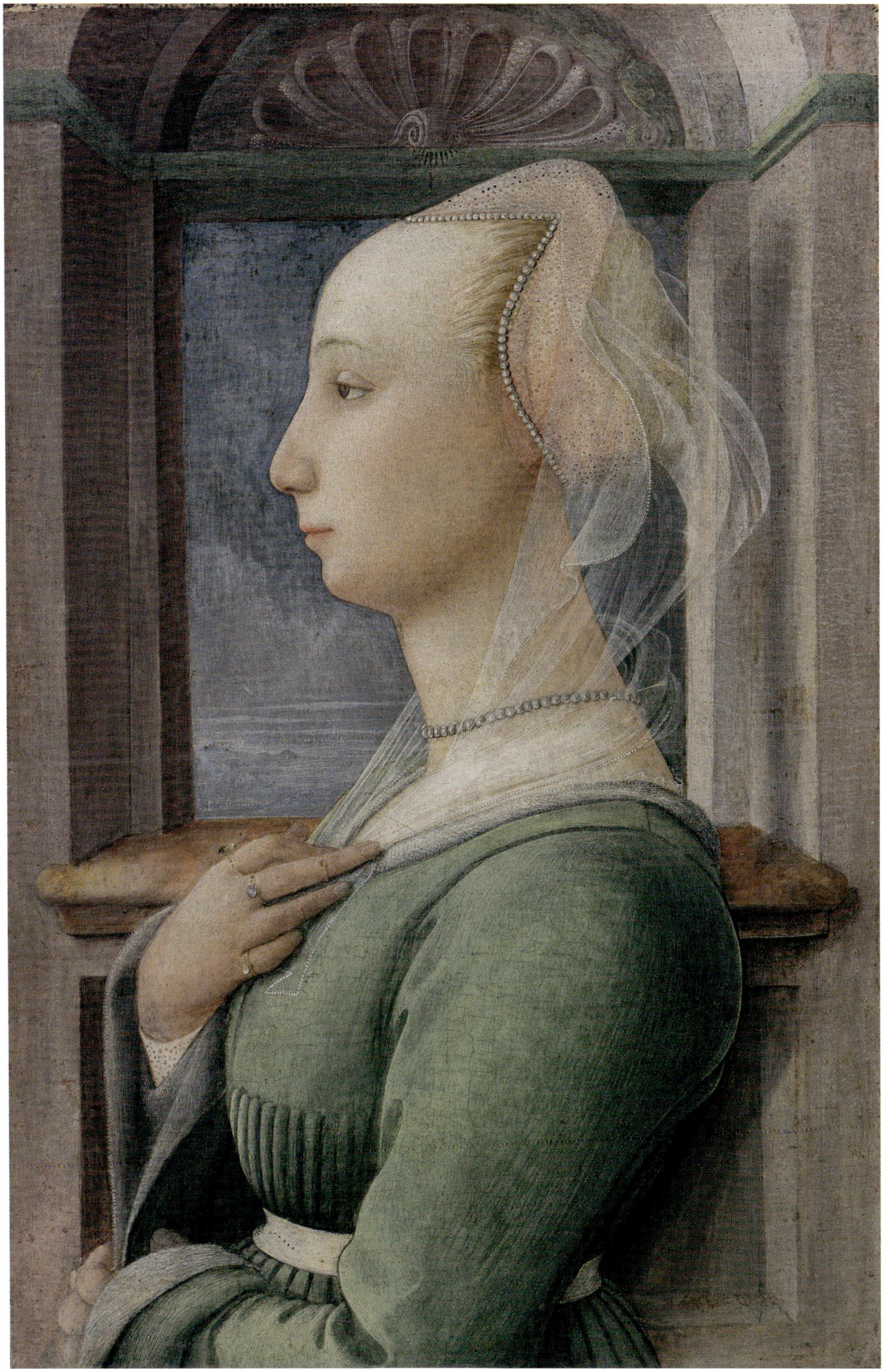

138 Fra Filippo Lippi, *Lady*, poplar panel, 49.3 × 32.7 cm., Staatliche Museen Preussischer Kulturbesitz, Berlin (West), Gemäldegalerie (1700).

There are no indications of the sitter's identity. On grounds of style and costume, the portrait is attributed to Fra Filippo and dated around 1440–50.

See pp. 61, 115.

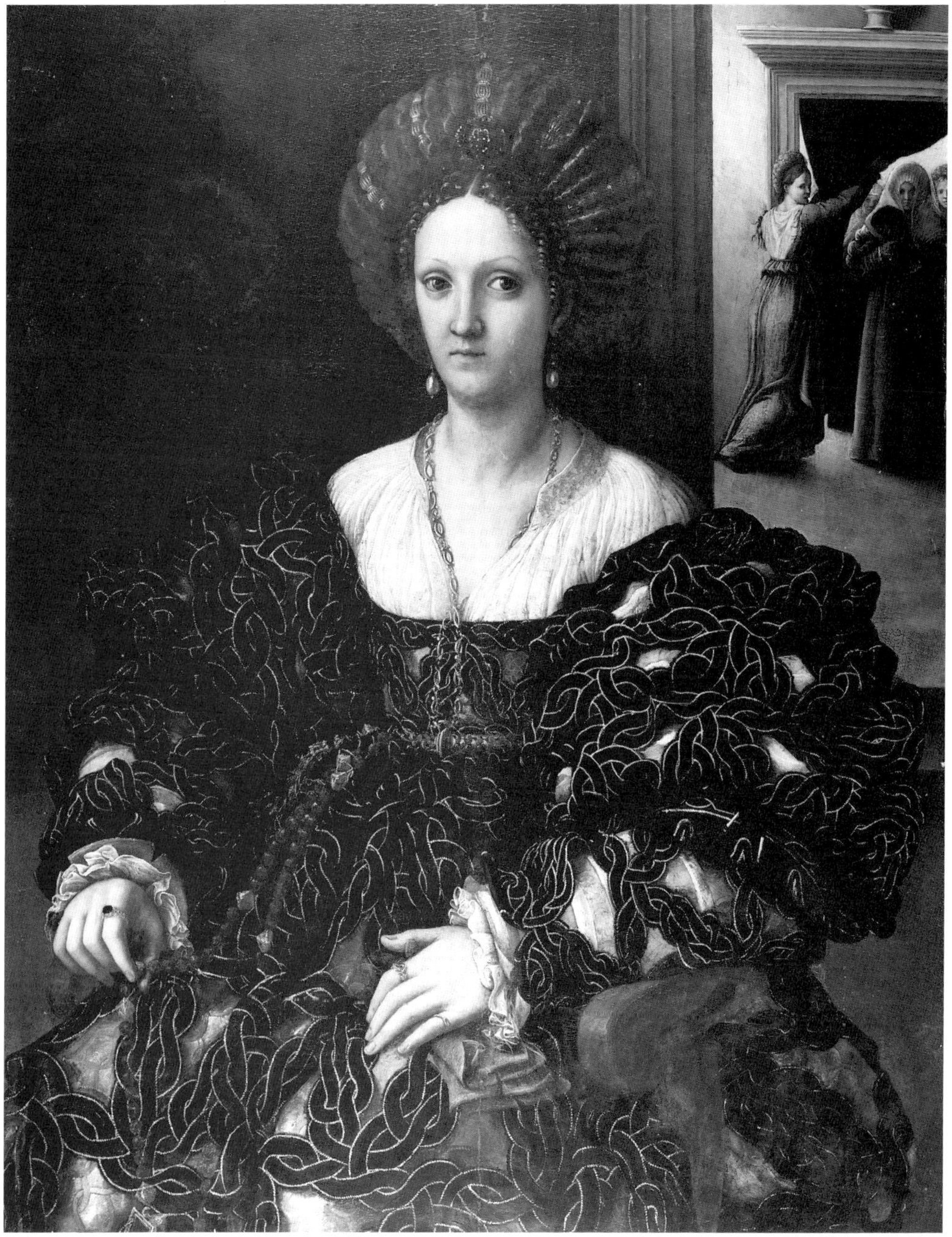

139 Giulio Romano, *Isabella d'Este (?)*, poplar panel, 115.5 × 90.5 cm., Royal Collection, Hampton Court (76).

The attribution to Giulio Romano, made on stylistic grounds, is generally accepted. On the basis of comparisons with other portraits and because the interlace pattern of her dress has been linked with the 'fantasy of knots' which was Isabella's personal device, the sitter has been identified as Isabella d'Este and the portrait has been dated around 1524–5, soon after Giulio settled in Mantua. Though Isabella was then fifty, and the sitter here looks younger, and though certain details do not quite agree with what is known about Isabella's personal appearance, it must be remembered that Isabella refused to sit for her portraits and that she liked to be flattered. Giulio, perhaps nervous of his sitter's reactions, has clearly concentrated on her clothes rather than her face. If she is indeed Isabella, he had every reason to he evasive and to avoid achieving an accurate likeness.

See Shearman, 1983, pp. 118–21 (116); here pp. 118, 124.

more commonly, in Germany and in Italy, they are set against curtains partially drawn across openings through which areas of landscape are visible.[16]

It was, however, the kind of background typified in the Bouts portrait of 1462 that gained favour throughout Europe. The notion of using the corner of a room, with or without a window, was simple and adaptable. The window might become a doorway leading into a secondary space, as in Raphael's *Joanna of Aragon* (plate 71), where the secondary space is a loggia giving onto a landscape, or as in the derivative portrait by Guilio Romano (plate 139), where ladies enter the second room through yet another doorway. It should be recalled that, in palaces, the private apartments or privy chambers of princes were reached through successions of antechambers. Generally, however, the spaces behind the sitters were rather restricted in depth.

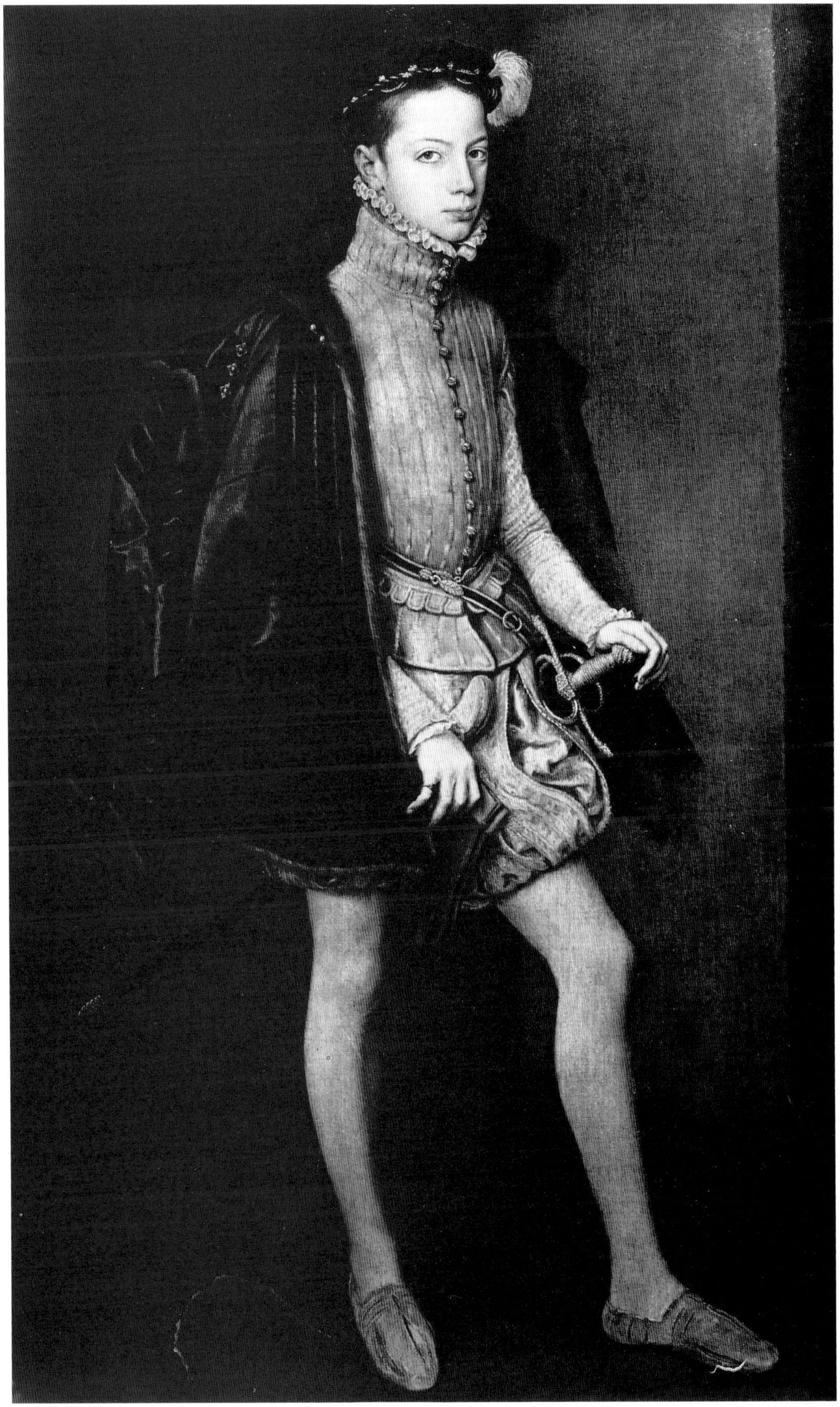

140 Antonis Mor, *Alessandro Farnese*, canvas, 155 × 95 cm., Galleria Nazionale, Parma (300).

In the lower-right corner is the heavily restored signature 'Antonius mor/ m.v.lvii'. By comparison with other portraits, the sitter is identified as Alessandro Farnese (1545–92), afterwards Duke of Parma, whose mother Margaret of Parma was the illegitimate daughter of the Emperor Charles V. Margaret and Alessandro visited the Low Countries and England during the winter of 1556–7 and it was clearly during their visit to the Netherlands that Mor painted Alessandro's portrait.

See pp. 99, 120, 143.

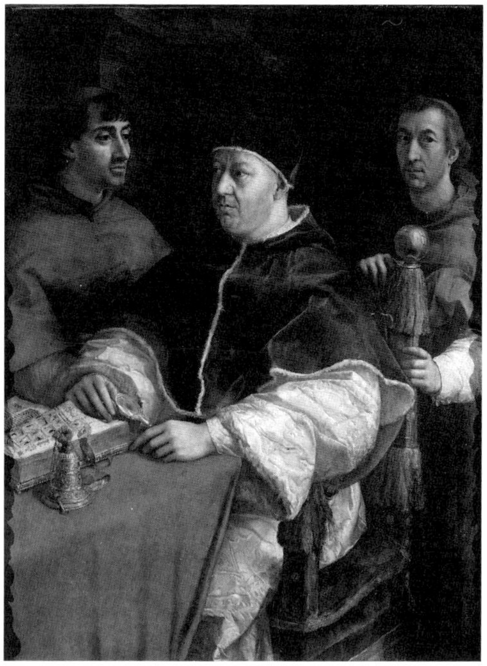

141 Raphael, *Pope Leo X with Cardinals Giulio de' Medici and Luigi de' Rossi*, panel, 155.2 × 118.9 cm., Uffizi, Florence (Palatina 40).

Giovanni de' Medici (1475–1521), a younger son of Lorenzo the Magnificent, was elected Pope in 1513 and took the name Leo X. Giulio de' Medici (1478–1534), his cousin, became a cardinal in 1517 and was later Pope Clement VII. Luigi de' Rossi, another cousin, had been brought up with Leo, also became a cardinal in 1517 and died in 1519. The portrait was sent to Florence and was exhibited at a banquet there in September 1518. Vasari described it at length and was much impressed by its naturalism.

See the exhibition catalogue Florence, 1984, pp. 189–98 (17); here pp. 120, 202, 233.

In life-size, full-length portraits, the areas of background to be covered were often very large. Though on rare occasions elaborately furnished interiors were included (plate 157), it was practical to reduce such interior views to their barest essentials: walls, floors, perhaps curtains, tables or chairs. Seisenegger often included a curtain and a floor with a simple tiled pattern (plates 132, 255), while Mor used highly simplified architectural backgrounds, where the junctions between floors and walls are barely discernible in dimly lit interiors (plates 140, 264). Sánchez Coello sometimes followed this practice but at other times introduced a balustrade or a doorway giving onto a balcony (plates 120, 217, 223).

The grandeur of an interior setting might be enhanced by including columns of expensively polished or carved stone. The small columns that Memlinc frequently employed to frame views from window openings (plate 59) were imitated in Italy[17] and may have inspired Raphael and Titian to experiment with columns and pilasters of huge proportions. Both used immense columns bases which implied that their sitters inhabited palaces unimaginably lofty and vast but which avoided the fatal error of making them seem dwarfed by their surroundings. In Raphael's portrait of Pope Leo X with two cardinals, the sitters do not seem to relate very comfortably or convincingly to one another or to their setting and the horizontal lines of the architecture, continuing above the head of the seated pope, are oppressive rather than exhilarating (plate 141). In Titian's portrait of Philip II of Spain in armour, however, the single column base is exploited to magnificent effect (plate 263), and Mor – and afterwards Van Dyck – developed the idea with enthusiasm (plates 262, 267). The triumphal arch placed behind the sitter, another idea that found much favour with Baroque portraitists, was occasionally employed in sixteenth-century Germany (plate 257).[18] Moroni had an unusual fondness for placing his sitters in the ruins of classical buildings.[19]

A device much used by later portraitists, but surprisingly seldom by Renaissance painters, was to place a mirror behind or beside the sitter to reflect a different view of his head and body. The convex mirror in the background of Jan van Eyck's *Giovanni Arnolfini and his Wife* reflects the subjects and their setting (plate 135). In 1562, Mazzola Bedoli filled much of the background of his *Anna Eleonora Sanvitale* with a large mirror which reflects the back view of the child subject (plate 153).[20]

Landscape backgrounds occur from an early date. Many of the northern and North-Italian group portraits of around 1400 represented outdoor scenes and the sitters were presumably depicted in stylised landscapes like those in tapestries of the period.[21] The copyist has probably transformed the landscape of the *Hunting Festival of Philip the Good* in accordance with sixteenth-century conventions of landscape painting (plate 50), but Pisanello's portrait of Ginevra d'Este, in which a decorative bush sprouting roses, columbines and pinks intervenes between the sitter and the sky (plate 92), and a German double portrait of about 1480, in which no sky is visible (plate 58), show the decorative potentialities of this kind of abstracted landscape. In certain Netherlandish and Italian portraits of the fifteenth and early sixteenth centuries, the sitters are silhouetted against the sky (plates 39, 98, 248).[22] The highly artificial idea of placing a figure in front of a distant landscape, developed in religious paintings like Van der Weyden's *Braque Triptych* of about 1450, where five half-length figures are set in front of panoramic landscapes,[23] may first have been used in portraiture by Memlinc: his, at least, are the earliest-known Netherlandish portraits in which the idea is applied (plates 127, 142), while Piero della Francesca's are the first surviving Italian portraits in which

142 Hans Memlinc, *Man*, panel, 35 × 26 cm., Palazzo Vecchio, Florence, Opere d'arte recuperate (86).

On grounds of costume and style, the portrait is attributed to Memlinc and dated to the 1470s. Though there are no indications of the sitter's identity, a copy in tempera, now at Petworth, is clearly the work of an Italian artist of the late fifteenth century and indicates that the original must have been taken to Italy soon after it was painted.

See Friedländer, 1967–76, VIA, p. 56 (86); here p. 120.

143 (foll. page) Lucas Cranach the Elder, *Johannes Cuspinian*, panel, 59 × 45 cm., Sammlung Oskar Reinhart 'Am Römerholz', Winterthur (36).

The pair to the portrait reproduced as plate 144.

144 (p. 123) Lucas Cranach the Elder, *Anna Putsch, First Wife of Johannes Cuspinian*, panel, 59 × 45 cm., Sammlung Oskar Reinhart 'Am Römerholz', Winterthur (37).

The pair to the portrait reproduced as plate 143. The sitters are identified by the (damaged) coats of arms of Cuspinian and Putsch which appear on the reverse of the portrait of Johannes and from a woodcut copy of the *Johannes* which is inscribed with his name and which he used as a book-plate. Johannes Cuspinian (1473–1529) was a doctor, an important humanist poet and philosopher, a dignitary of the university of Vienna and a favoured official of the Emperor Maximilian I. His first wife Anna (1485–1513) was the daughter of Ulrich Putsch, barber and chamberlain to Maximilian. They were married in 1502 or early in 1503 and the portraits, attributed to Cranach on stylistic grounds, would have been painted at the time of the marriage. The backgrounds are full of erudite symbolism, no doubt devised by Cuspinian himself. The god Apollo appears behind his right shoulder; the star above his head apparently refers to the coming of Christ; the owl may denote evil. Other details may allude to the physiological and psychological theory of the four humours and to astrology, while the significance of the women in and near the lake remains to be explained.

See Koepplin, 1973, *passim*; here pp. 25, 61, 121–4.

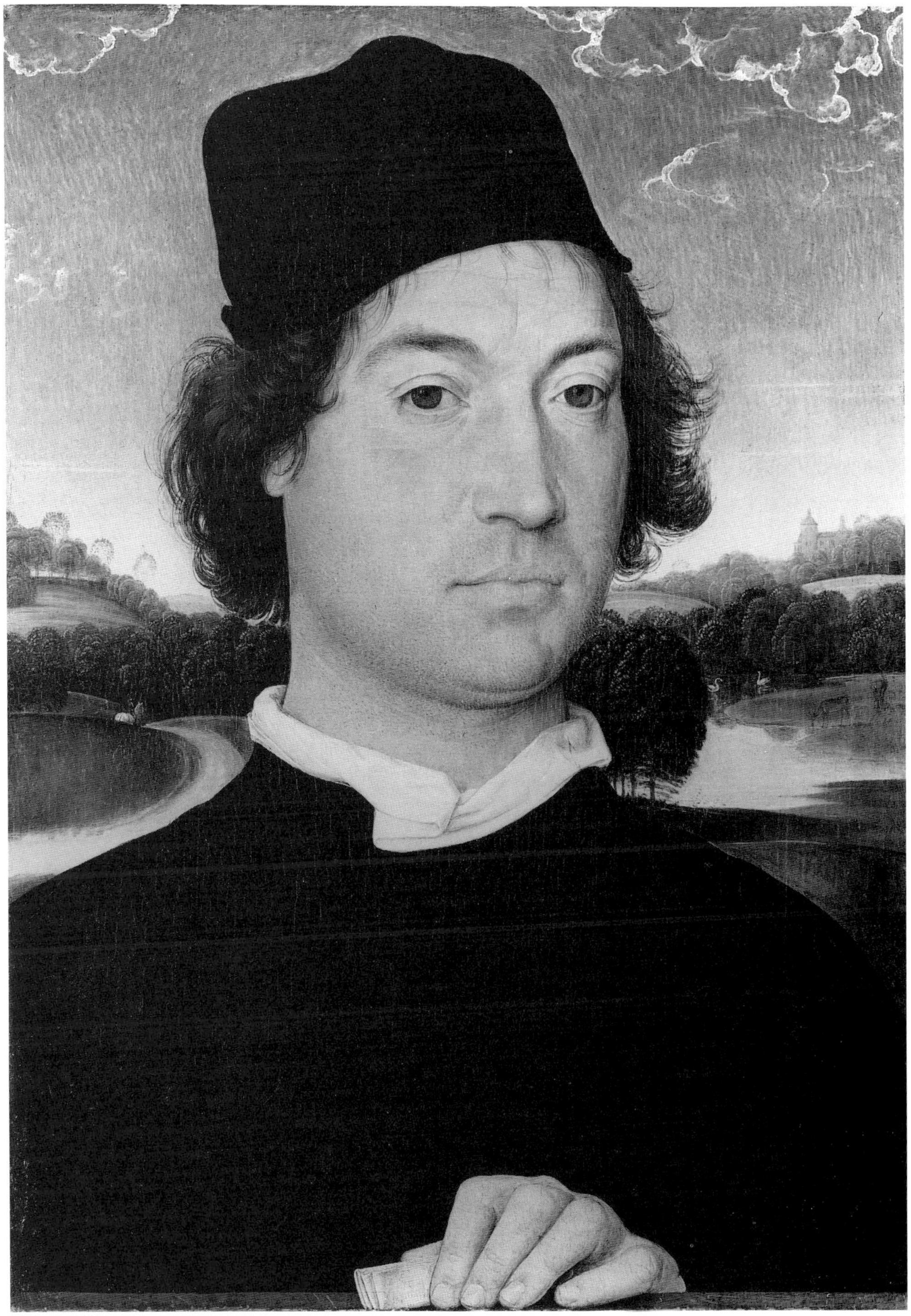

the compositional scheme is adopted. For a time it was taken up with enthusiasm throughout Europe (plates 102, 252).[24] Some artists introduced balustrades behind the sitters to explain their situation on eminences, from which alone panoramic views can be obtained (plate 59).[25] When Bronzino painted his portrait of Eleonora da Toledo, the arrangement was becoming dated (plate 37): here Bronzino may have been almost parodying an archaic and expensive convention.

Cranach's portraits of Johannes Cuspinian and his wife, of about 1502–3, are

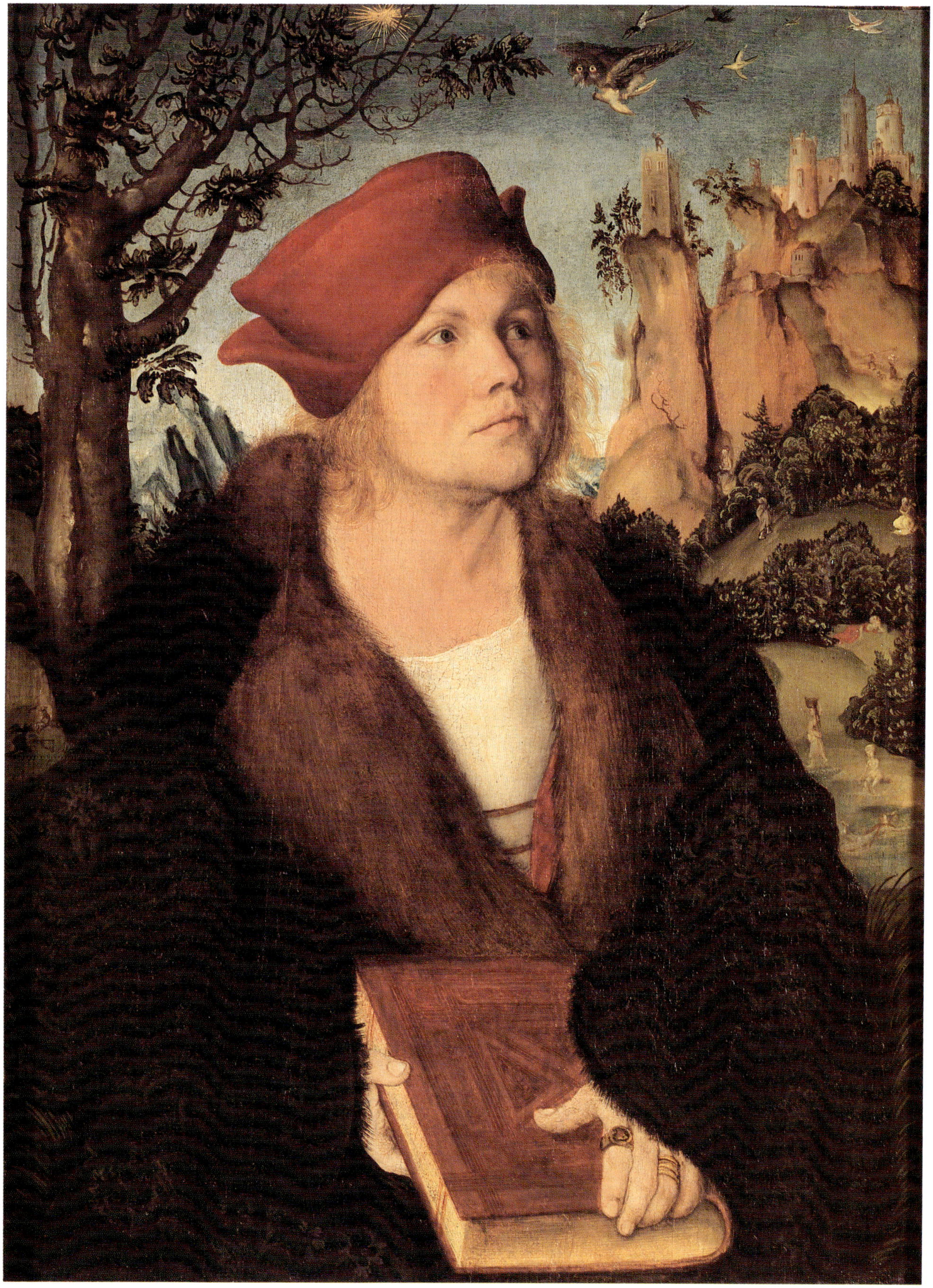

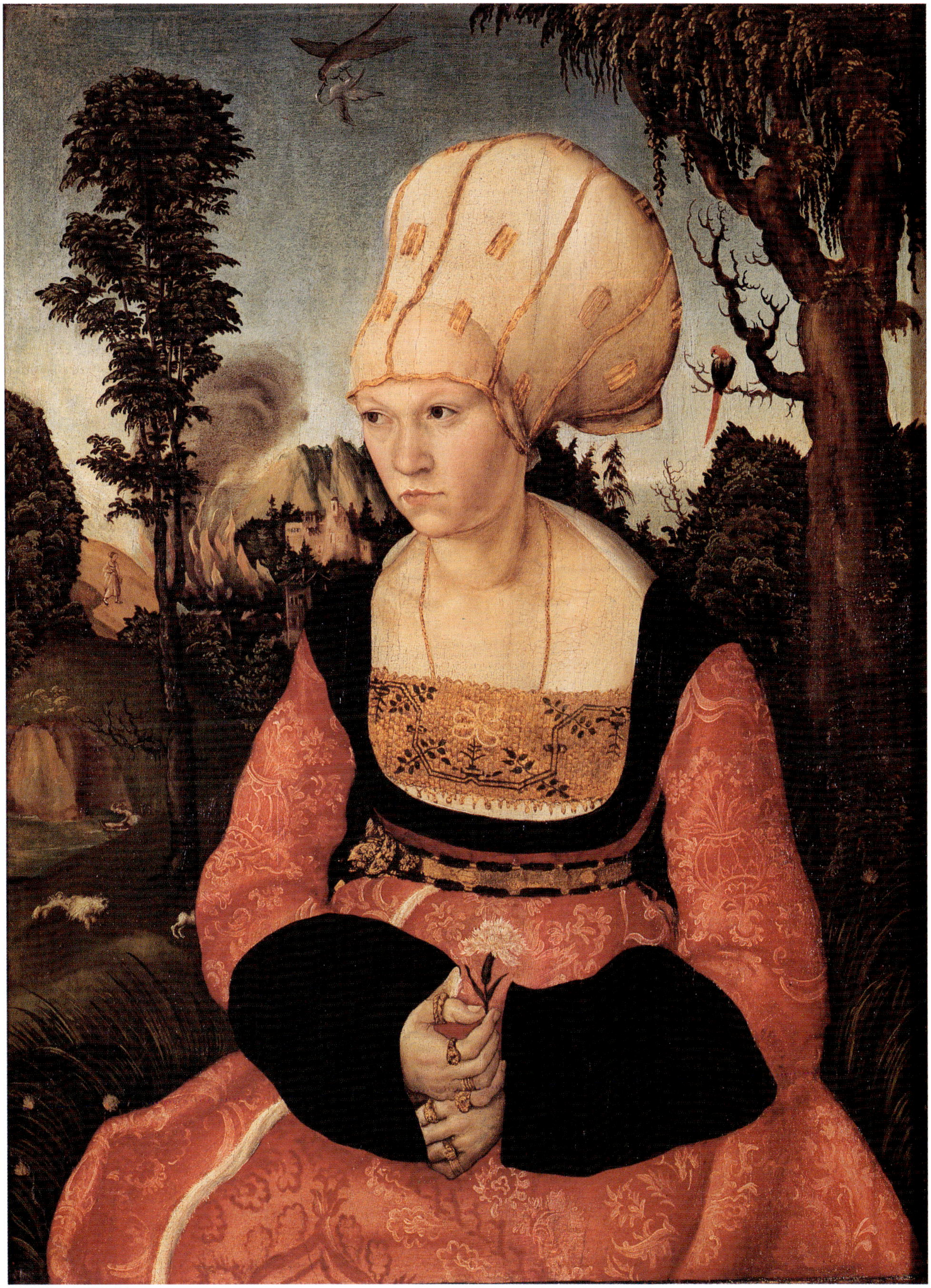

unusual in that the sitters are very obviously seated in their landscapes, even if the grassy banks that serve them as benches seem rather contrived (plates 143, 144). Generally some real or implied barrier separated sitter from landscape, but in equestrian portraiture there was no reason to make such a division (plate 48). Unless the horses were placed on eminences, panoramic views could be justified only with difficulty (plate 258).[26]

In full-length portraits with landscape backgrounds, the landscape was often reduced to a rudimentary strip of ground so that most of the background area was taken up with sky, which could be painted more easily and quickly than vegetation. In Cranach's portraits of Henry the Pious, Duke of Saxony, and his wife (plates 145, 146) and in Mor's portrait of Philip II of Spain (plate 219), the skies are black – as in pictures of Venus by certain Italian artists and by Cranach himself.[27] Venus, a planetary deity, herself lights the night sky; a parallel between princes and stars is perhaps implicit in Cranach's and Mor's portraits.

At court, who might remain seated in whose presence was a question that gave much concern, assuredly to courtiers as well as to writers on etiquette, and when chairs with upholstered seats and arms came into general use, the regulation of seating arrangements became still more complicated. In fourteenth- and fifteenth-century portraits, however, the chairs in which seated subjects were posed were almost never made visible, and even in the sixteenth century chairs were usually discreetly hidden by the sitter's draperies and hands. Infrequently, simple benches draped with cloth replaced chairs (plates 37, 147). Only on rare occasions, as in Mor's portrait of Mary I of England (plate 216), was a magnificently embroidered and fringed chair obviously displayed. In some Italian portraits where unusually contorted poses were adopted, chairs were necessarily made visible (plate 89). There the arms of the chairs might be parallel, or nearly parallel, to the horizontals of the frames; but in a three-quarters-view portrait, the chair was normally at an angle to the picture plane and its arms, if not concealed, might create discordant diagonal accents. Some painters chose to distort the perspective so that the visible chair arm or arms might be more easily integrated with the other diagonals of the composition (plate 38).

Paradoxically, chairs often appeared in portraits of standing subjects, for a chair back or arm might provide a useful resting place for the subject's arm or hand (plates 131, 266). Tables might serve the same purpose and were in general serviceable for closing gaps in compositions and for displaying small objects of personal, social or symbolic significance (plates 45, 259–63). In full-length portraits, tables and chair backs created horizontal accents in compositions where verticals might very easily have become too dominant. Placed in front of the subjects they broke the verticals of their contours and distanced them slightly from the spectator, in case a sense of intimacy might threaten their dignity (plates 262, 266).

Clothes were of enormous importance to many sitters, some of whom spent immense sums of money upon them, were often justifiably proud of them and were anxious to show them off. Certain princes dressed in such a way that they might be recognised by their clothes alone.[28] Perhaps from an excess of tact or caution, a portraitist might concentrate on the clothes rather than the head (plate 139). Seventeenth-century portrait miniatures survive in which the sitters have been equipped with two sets of clothes: one painted in the miniature, the other, on a talc overlay which could be inserted into the frame.[29] Similar contrivances might have been used earlier. At least one sixteenth-century portrait sculpture was con-

145 Lucas Cranach the Elder, *Henry the Pious, Duke of Saxony*, limewood panel transferred to canvas, 184 × 82.5 cm., Staatliche Kunstsammlungen, Dresden, Gemäldegalerie (1906 G).

The pair to the portrait reproduced as plate 146.

146 Lucas Cranach the Elder, *Catherine of Mecklenburg, Duchess of Saxony*, limewood panel transferred to canvas, 184 × 82.5 cm., Staatliche Kunstsammlungen, Dresden, Gemäldegalerie (1906 H).

The pair to the portrait reproduced as plate 145. The painting of Catherine is signed with Cranach's initials and the winged serpent that formed part of his coat of arms and is dated 1514. The portraits remained with the descendants of the sitters, whose identities are established by descriptions in early inventories. Henry the Pious (1473–1541) married in 1512 Catherine (1487–1561), daughter of Magnus II of Mecklenburg; they were the parents of Maurice and Augustus, Electors of Saxony. The yellow areas of the sitters' costumes are gilded and glazed. As Henry's scabbard continues into Catherine's portrait, it is possible that the two pictures were originally on one support and that they were separated when they were transferred to canvas.

See Schade, 1980, p. 55; here pp. 56, 99, 124, 139, 236.

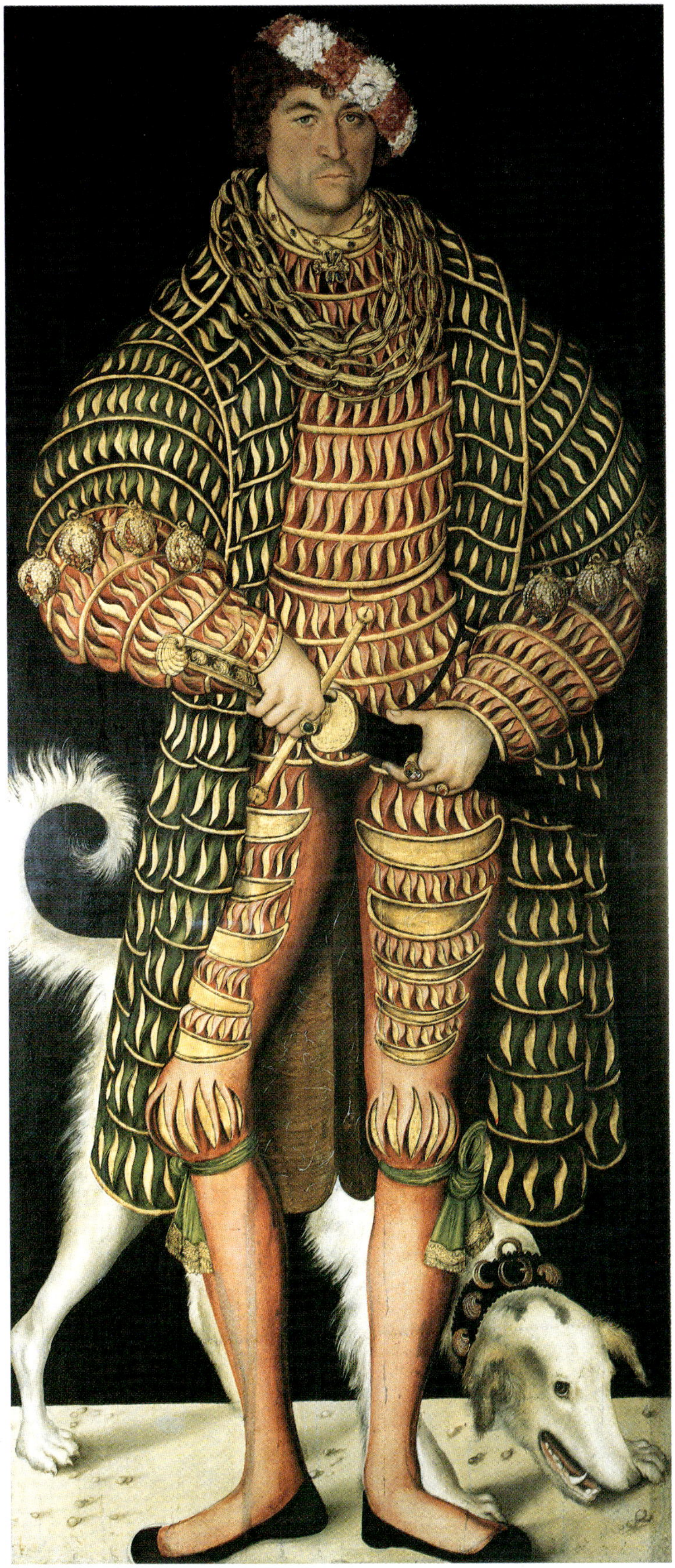

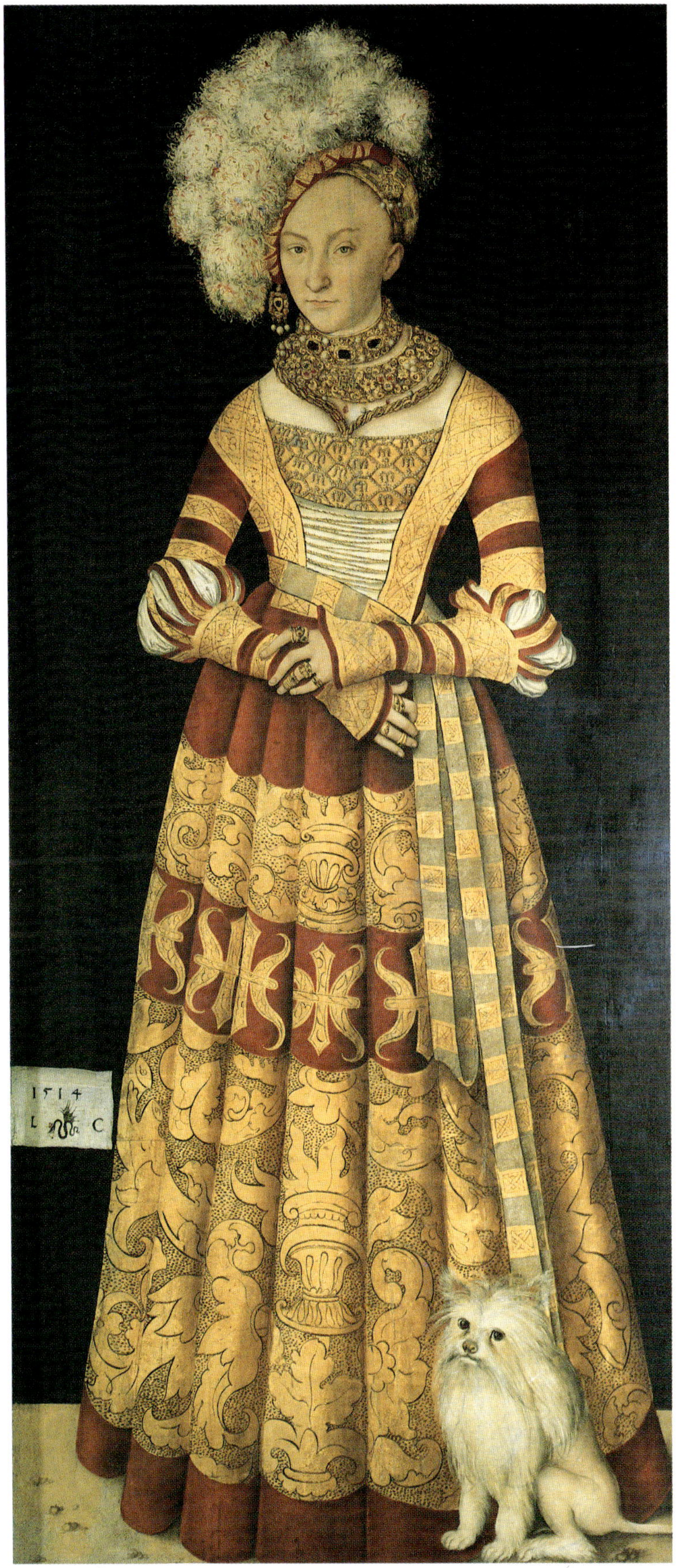
1514
L C

147 Attributed to Guillaume Scrots, *Maximilian of Austria*, oak panel, 92 × 74 cm., Kunsthistorisches Museum, Vienna, Gemäldegalerie (2749, exhibited at Schloss Ambras, Innsbruck).

The companion picture is in the same collection (2603); both show youths dressed in black seated on pink benches before intense green backgrounds. The sitters are identified, by comparison with other portraits, as Maximilian (1527–76) and Ferdinand (1529–96), sons of the Emperor Ferdinand I. Maximilian succeeded his father as emperor; Ferdinand ruled the Tyrol and was an avid and celebrated collector of portraits. The two paintings are thought to have been executed in about 1544, possibly by the Netherlandish painter Guillaume Scrots, who since 1537 had been in the service of Mary of Hungary and who in 1546 entered the employ of Henry VIII, King of England.

See Heinz and Schütz, 1976, pp. 87–8; here pp. 99, 124.

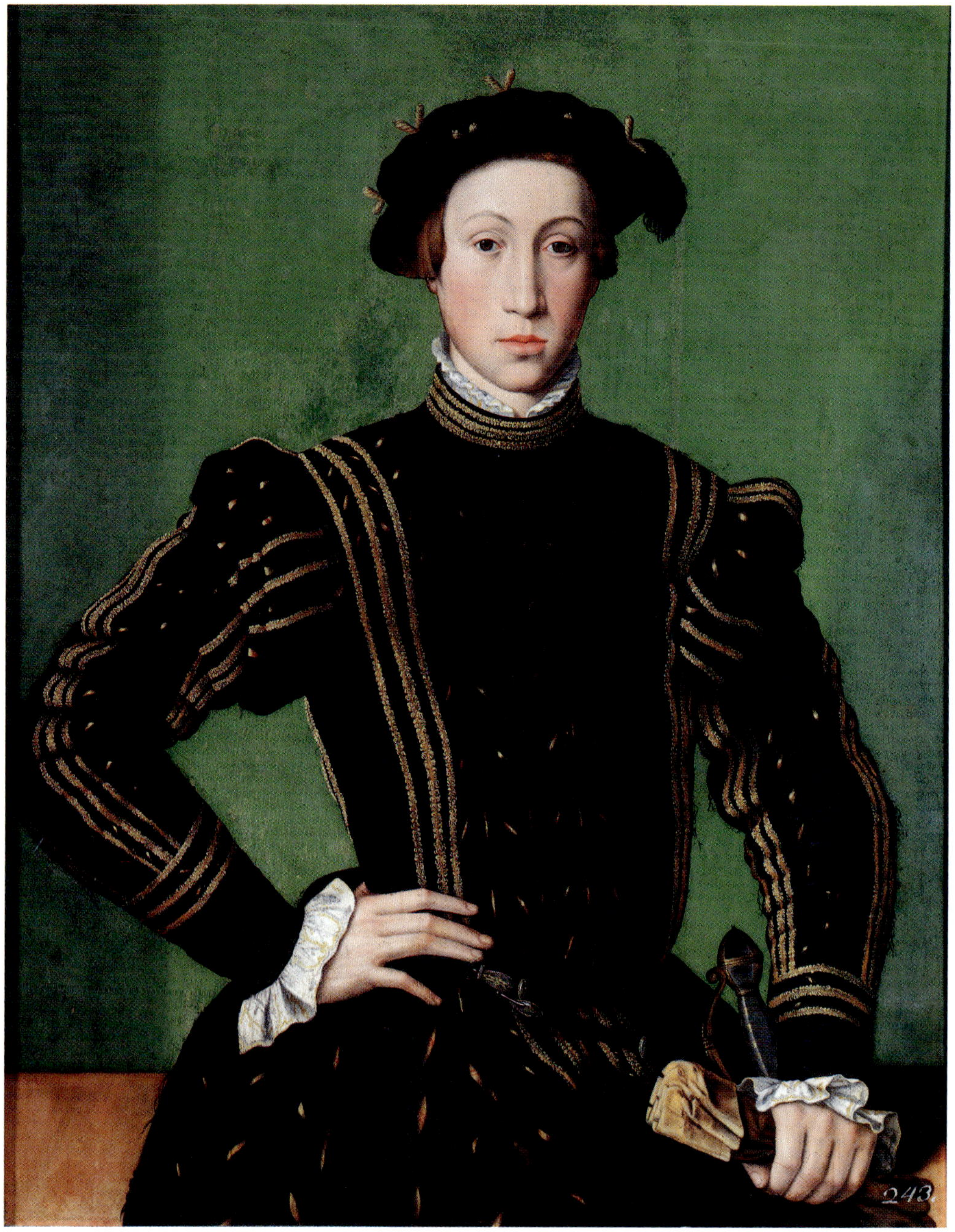

structed so that the subject might be viewed nude or clothed. This was Leone Leoni's bronze statue of Charles V overcoming Fury, where the making of the removeable armour was a feat of great technical skill (plates 148, 149). The emperor appeared nude in order to demonstrate the impartiality with which he wielded power: like the Roman emperors, he had to 'show openly to the populace what he is, so that he is revered for his virtue and feared for the justice which he ministers'.[30] In a pair of portraits of the son and daughter of the Florentine collector Niccolò di Sinibaldo Gaddi, the little boy, not yet breeched, wears his skirts kilted up to reveal his genitals, so that there can be no doubt about his sex (plates 150, 151).

Many patrons were anxious that the portraits they commissioned should be

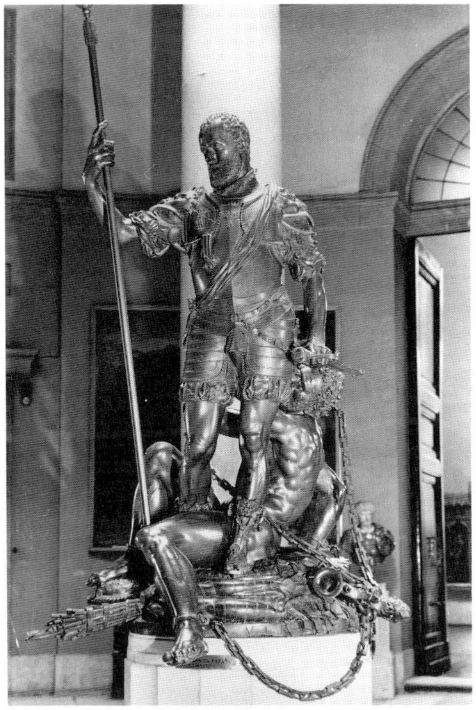

148 Leone Leoni, *The Emperor Charles V overcoming Fury* (with armour), Museo del Prado, Madrid (Esc. 273).

See plate 149.

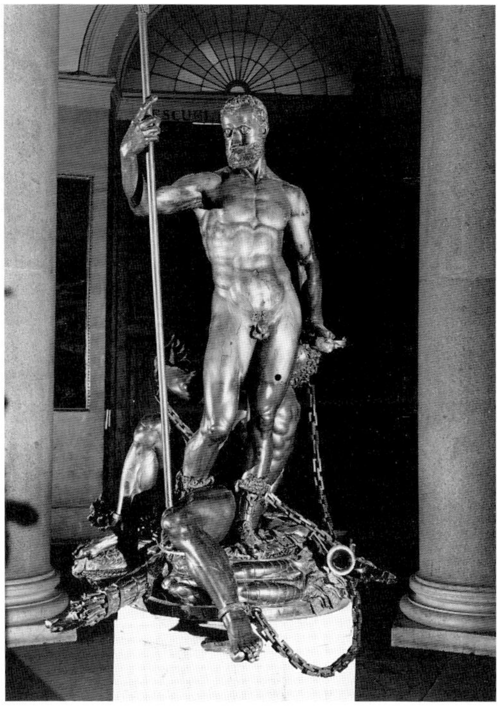

149 Leone Leoni, *The Emperor Charles V overcoming Fury* (without armour), bronze, 251 cm. high, Museo del Prado, Madrid (Esc. 273).

The statue is inscribed 'CAESARIS VIRTVTE DOMITVS FVROR/LEO. P. POMP. F. ARET. F. 1564': 'Fury tamed by the virtue of the emperor/ Leone, the father, and Pompeo, the son, of Arezzo, made this. 1564'. The figure of Charles was cast in 1551, that of Fury in 1553; the removable armour was added later and the group was not finished until 1564, six years after Charles's death. The figure of the emperor was made with the assistance of a set of Charles's measurements obtained from Brussels in 1550.

See Plon, 1887, pp. 281–4; here pp. 126, 162.

clearly inscribed with the names and ages of the sitters and the dates of painting. Some artists were content to letter such inscriptions boldly across the backgrounds of portraits (plates 40, 150–2); others confined them to the frames, to fictive frames or to parapets, or found more discreet ways of including them within the picture (plates 65, 200). A paper bearing the sitter's name, or a letter addressed to him might be introduced (plates 42, 179), or the presence of an inscription might be excused by placing it on a tablet (plates 110, 153). Mottoes or even horoscopes

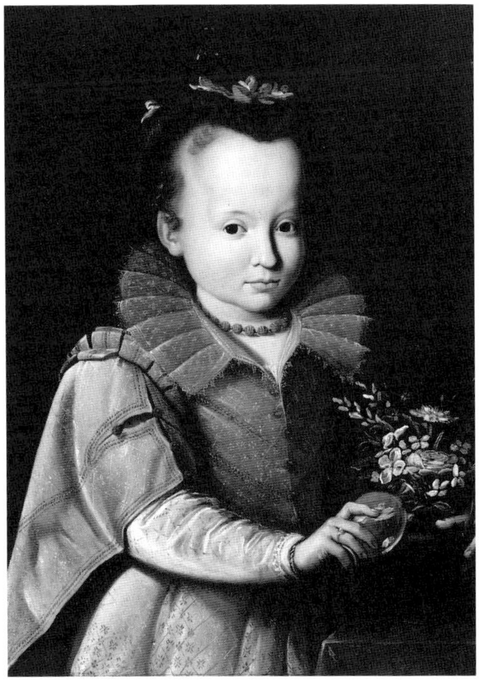

150 Florentine, 1564(?), *Emilia Gaddi*, panel, 61 × 43 cm., sold at Christie's, London, 11 December 1987 (123).

Inscribed with the sitter's name, 'Emilia, daughter of Niccolò di Sinibaldo Gaddi', the portrait is the pair to that reproduced as plate 151.

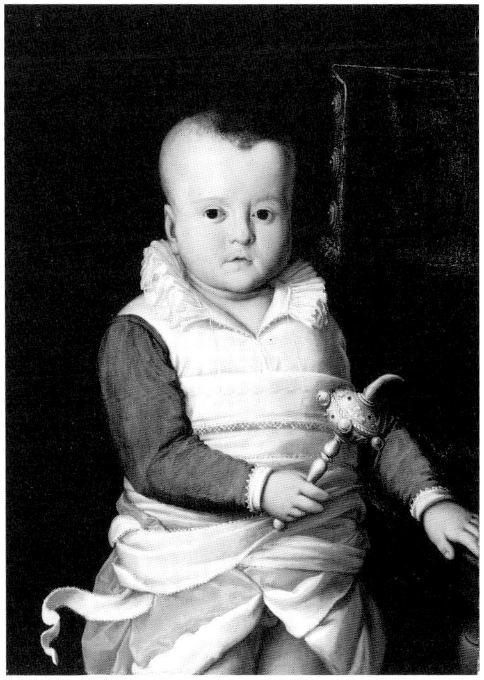

151 Florentine, 1564(?), *Sinibaldo Gaddi*, panel, 61 × 43 cm., sold at Christie's, London, 11 December 1987 (124).

Inscribed with the sitter's name, the portrait is the pair to that reproduced as plate 150. The sitters were the children of Niccolò di Sinibaldo Gaddi, an erudite and important Florentine collector (Vignau-Wilberg, 1987, *passim*). Nothing is known about Emilia; Sinibaldo was six months old when he died in March 1564.

See pp. 126–7.

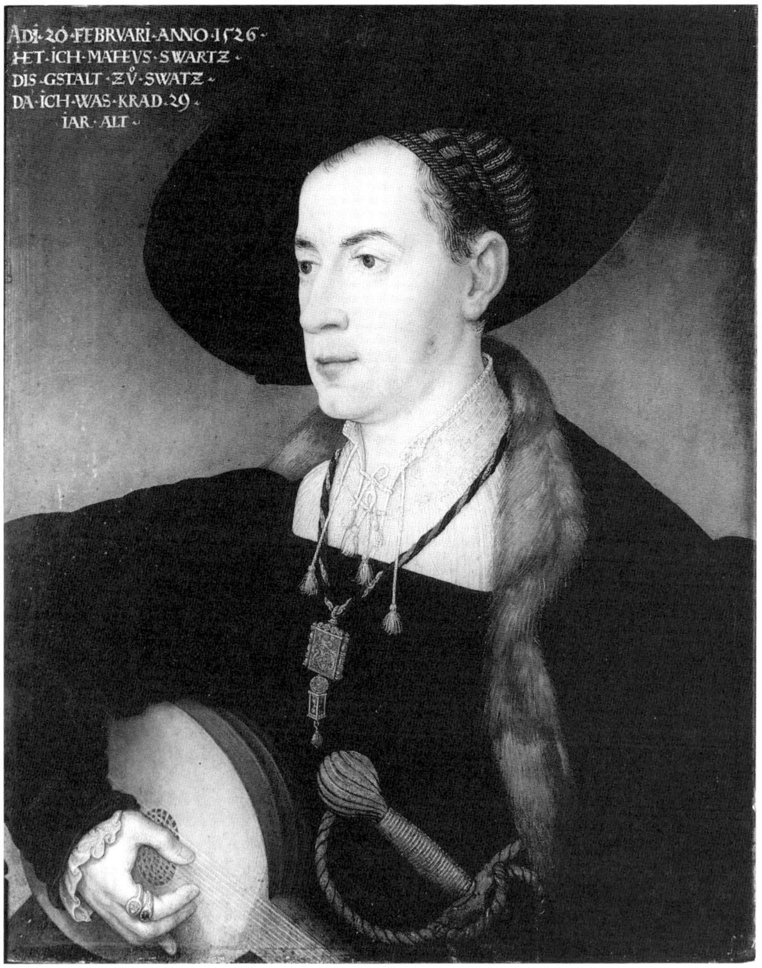

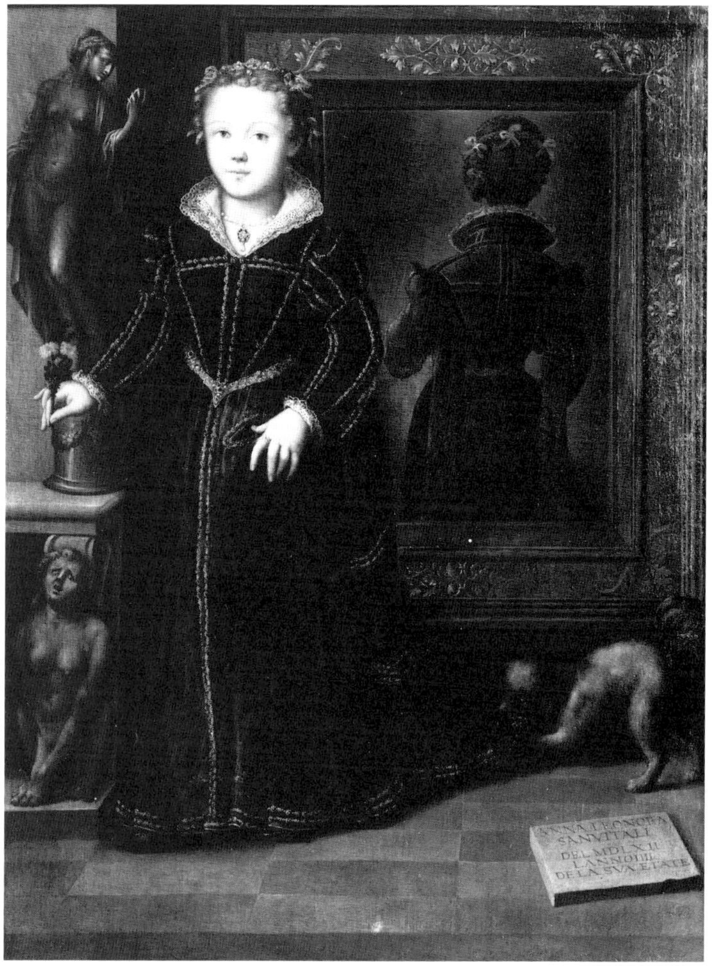

152 (above left) Hans Maler, *Matthäus Schwarz*, panel, 41 × 33 cm., Louvre, Paris (R.F. 1958–8).

The inscription may be translated: 'On 20 February 1526 I Matthäus Schwarz had this form at Schwaz. I was then exactly twenty-nine years old'. On the reverse is the sitter's coat of arms, which reappears on the pendant around his neck, from which hang a watch and an hour-glass. The portrait is attributed on stylistic grounds to Hans Maler, who indeed worked at Schwaz near Innsbruck. On the sitter and his interest in portraits, see the note to plate 33.

See Fink, 1963, p. 13; here p. 127.

might also be included, while a coat of arms or heraldic emblem might be painted on the frame or on an architectural detail in the background (plates 33, 133, 245). Indeed, heraldic devices might decorate the sitters' clothes in the form of embroidery or jewellery (plates 92, 121, 262); signet rings were useful for making discreet displays of coats of arms or merchants' marks (plates 40, 245).

Objects placed in the sitter's hands, or close to him, might indicate his real or assumed status or interests. The small hammer held by Francesco d'Este in Van der Weyden's portrait of about 1460 is an emblem of authority, but its exact significance, and that of the ring which he also holds, have not been fully clarified (plate 154).[31] It is not known why the *Grand Bâtard* of Burgundy, in another Van der Weyden portrait of about 1460, should be clasping an arrow to his heart (plate 250) or why, in Gossaert's portrait of about 1520, the unidentified nobleman should have his finger bitten by the gilded fish attached to his sleeve (plate 129). In an Italian portrait dated 1536, a gentleman stands in front of a picture of an hour-glass and a hare or rabbit playing dice (plate 196). The hour-glass is an obvious reference to the passage of time, but the dice-playing rabbit is more difficult to explain.[32] Some symbolic allusions may have been of a significance so private that the sitters may never have wished their meanings to be widely understood, while others may have been deliberately obscure in order to show off the erudition of the sitter who, by explaining them to his acquaintances, might use his portrait to demonstrate his learning.

153 (left) Girolamo Mazzola Bedoli, *Anna Eleonora Sanvitale*, canvas, 121.5 × 92.2 cm., Galleria Nazionale, Parma (1471).

The inscription on the plaque in the foreground gives the child's name, the date 1562 and her age, which is four. The portrait was among pictures at Sala confiscated from the Sanvitale family in 1612 by Ranuccio I Farnese, Duke of Parma. It was listed as by Mazzola Bedoli in an inventory of 1708 and there seems no reason to question the attribution. The sitter was evidently the same Eleonora Sanvitale, daughter of Giberto, Count of Sala, who married in 1576 Giulio Thiene, Count of Scandiano, and to whom Torquato Tasso addressed poems (Solerti, 1891, pp. CXI–CXXV).

See Bertini, 1987, pp. 42, 113; here pp. 120, 127, 132.

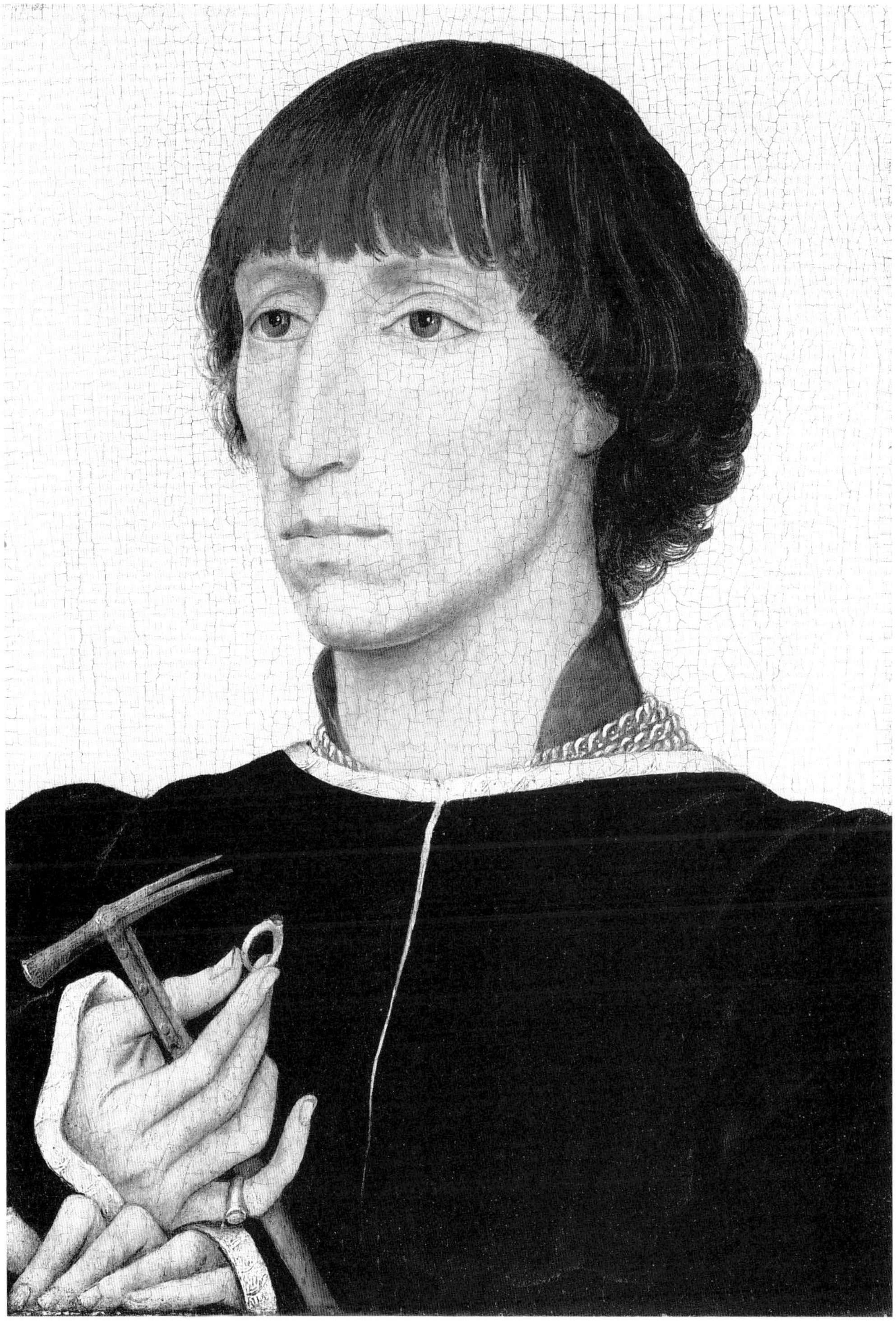

154 Rogier van der Weyden, *Francesco d'Este*, panel, 29.8 × 20.4 cm., Metropolitan Museum of Art, New York (32.100.43).

The sitter is identified by the coat of arms and the inscription 'francisque' on the reverse of the panel. He was an illegitimate son of Lionello d'Este, Marquis of Ferrara, was born in about 1430 and in 1444 was sent to the Burgundian court, where he was educated with the young Charles the Bold. Though he revisited Italy on several occasions, he lived mainly in the Netherlands, where he is last mentioned in 1475. The portrait is attributed to Van der Weyden on grounds of style and may be dated around 1460 on the basis of style, the sitter's costume and his apparent age.

See Davies, 1972, p. 299; here pp. 16, 37, 61, 72, 96, 128.

Painters, too, might make displays of erudition in their portraits. Vasari in 1534 executed a full-length portrait of Alessandro de' Medici, Duke of Florence, which he afterwards claimed to have painted from life and to have presented to the duke, who gave it to Ottaviano de' Medici (plate 155). In fact it seems to have been based on a medal and was sent to Ottaviano himself, to whom Vasari wrote a letter in which he explained the meaning of his picture. Having been permitted to paint 'an

155 Giorgio Vasari, *Alessandro de' Medici, Duke of Florence*, panel, 158 × 115 cm., Uffizi, Florence (1563).

Vasari received the commission and began the portrait on 8 January 1534. When he had finished it, he sent it to Ottaviano de' Medici with an undated letter in which he explained its iconography. The composition is adapted from Michelangelo's statue of one of the Medici dukes on their tombs at San Lorenzo in Florence and from Dürer's woodcut portrait of the Emperor Maximilian I enthroned from his *Triumphal Arch*. Alessandro, the illegitimate son of Pope Clement VII, was created Duke of Florence in 1532 and was murdered in 1537.

See Langedijk, 1981–3, I, pp. 70–5, 226–7; here pp. 81, 128–32.

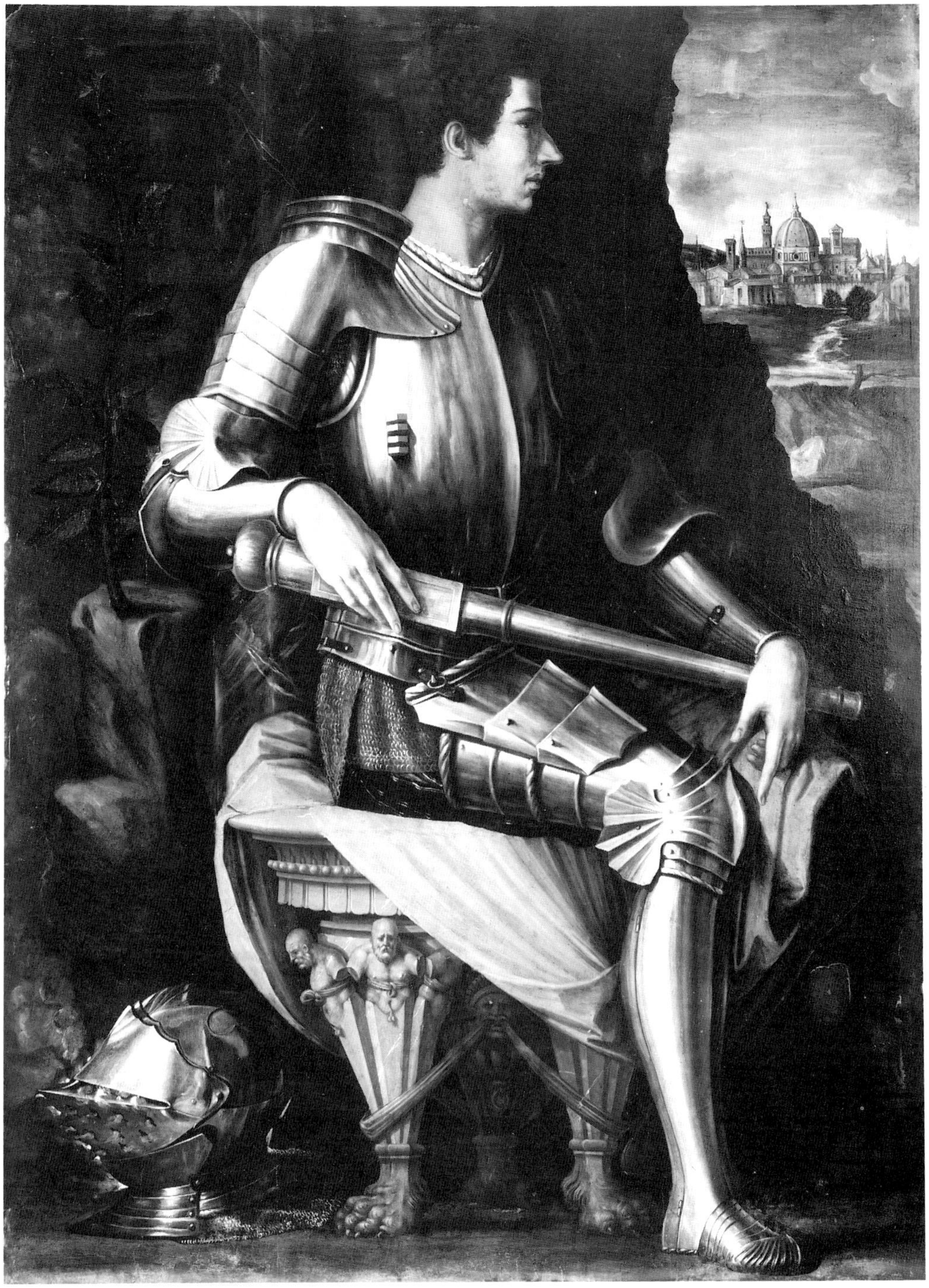

156 Hans Holbein the Younger, *Georg Gisze*, detail (see plate 42).

invention according to my caprice', he felt obliged to send a written account of the iconography. The duke's armour is the prince's mirror, 'such that his people may be able, in the actions of their lives, to reflect themselves in him'; he is fully armed to show that he is prepared, for love of his country, to defend all public and private causes. He is seated, to demonstrate that he has taken possession of his duchy, and he holds the golden baton of power to rule as prince and to command as captain. The ruins behind him refer to the siege of Florence in 1530, while he faces a view of the city in serene prosperity. The round seat, without beginning or end, shows that his reign is perpetual. It has three legs, three being the perfect

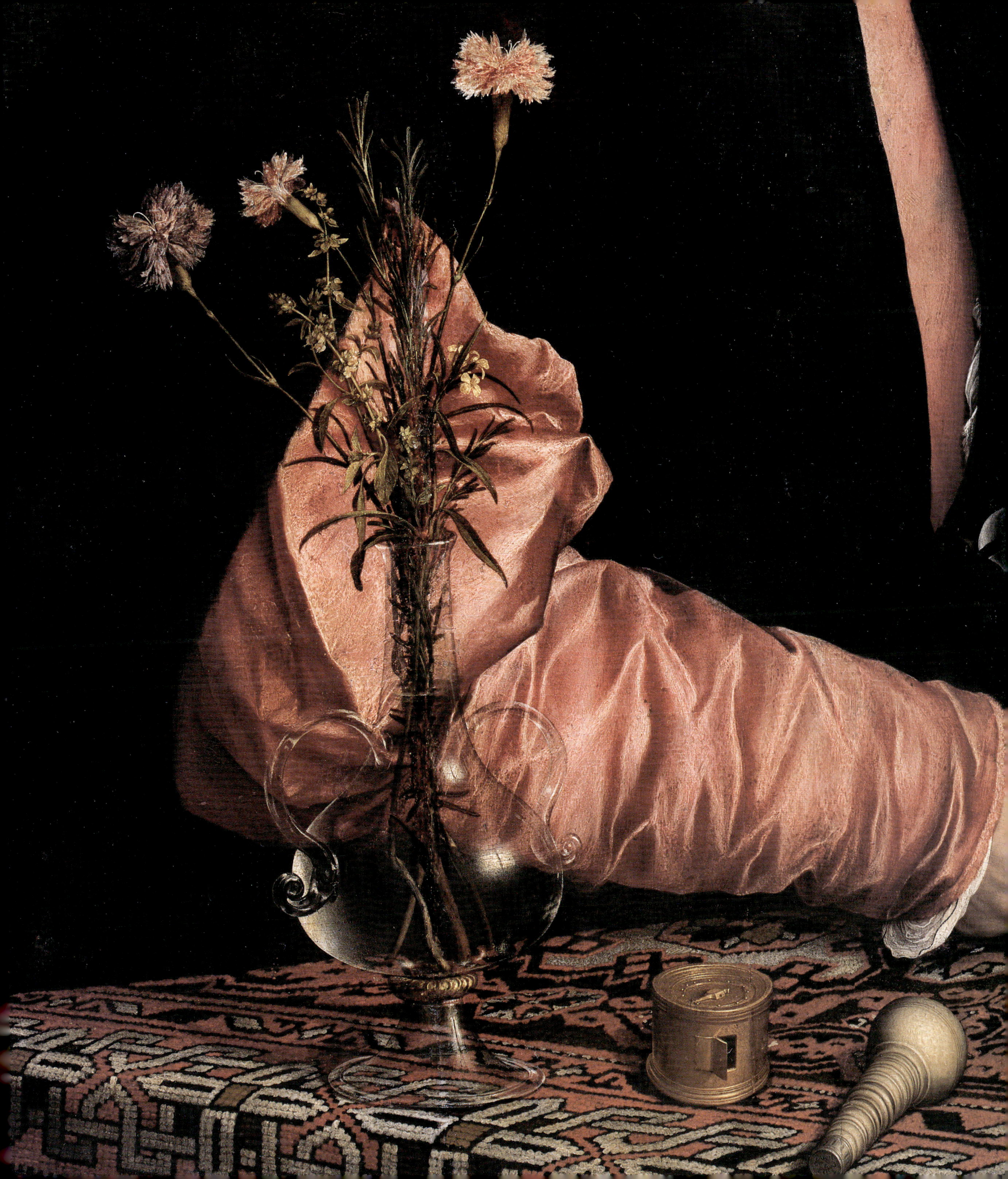

number, and they are his people, who have no limbs: they need none, as they are guided by their ruler. The chair legs end in lions' paws referring to the lion of Florence. The mask, bridled by bands, stands for Volubility, and shows that the unstable populace is kept under control from the fortress and by the love that the people bear to the duke. The red drapery represents the blood shed by the enemies of the Medici family; the part covering Alessandro's leg shows that the Medici themselves have shed blood. The dead branch of laurel sprouting forth a new, straight shoot is the Medici dynasty regenerated in the person of Alessandro. The flaming helmet, placed on the ground, is eternal peace, proceeding from the prince's head by his good government and overwhelming his people with joy and love. Vasari was realistic enough to admit that 'because of the obscurity of the thing, many would not understand it'. He therefore appended six lines of explanatory Latin verse which a friend had composed.[33]

This letter, and another from Vasari to Alessandro himself in which he explained the iconography of his posthumous portrait of Lorenzo the Magnificent,[34] are the only known documents in which an artist elucidates the meanings of his portraits. The two paintings, however, were of exceptional complexity and pretension. Vasari was a young artist ambitious to impress the Medici family. His portraits, ridiculous in their portentous obscurity, might have been laughed at if he had not made careful efforts to give them intellectual respectability.

The symbolism in Hans Mielich's portrait of Ladislas of Fraunberg, Count of Haag, is more readily interpreted (plate 157). Painted at Munich in 1557, it shows the count richly dressed in an expensively appointed interior. His coat of arms, rendered in stained glass, dominates the upper window, while the lower window opens onto a view of his castle at Haag. The trophy refers to his military career; the crucifix, skull and hour-glass indicate his piety and seemly awareness of the inevitability of death and judgement. The leopard behind the count, poorly drawn and resembling a badly stuffed rather than a real animal, might also be thought to have symbolic significance but was in fact his pet and constant companion. On the table beside him is a costly glass vase containing a single stem from a carnation plant. Carnations often referred to matrimony and indeed in 1557 the count, though already married to, and separated from, an Italian wife, was courting a local noblewoman.[35]

Certain objects, however, could have different meanings in different contexts, in different areas and at different periods. Flower symbolism and colour symbolism raise particularly complicated issues. Carnations, for example, might normally have referred to matrimony, but it is difficult to make direct connections between marriage and the red carnations in the garlands worn by Emperor Ferdinand I's young daughters in a group portrait by Seisenegger (plate 132), or the carnations held by the four-year-old Anna Eleonora Sanvitale in her portrait by Mazzola Bedoli (plate 153), or the carnations in the vase next to the elderly man in clerical dress in his portrait by the same artist (plate 130).[36] Flowers and vases of flowers may sometimes have been included in portraits because the sitters were fond of flowers, or proud of their vases, or because the painters wished to fill gaps with suitably decorative objects. Similarly, while it is known that colour symbolism was a subject which intrigued many,[37] and that Lionello d'Este, Marquis of Ferrara, who died in 1450, dressed in colours selected according to astrological criteria,[38] it is not necessary to assume that all sitters had symbolic reasons for choosing the colours of the clothes in which they appeared in their portraits.

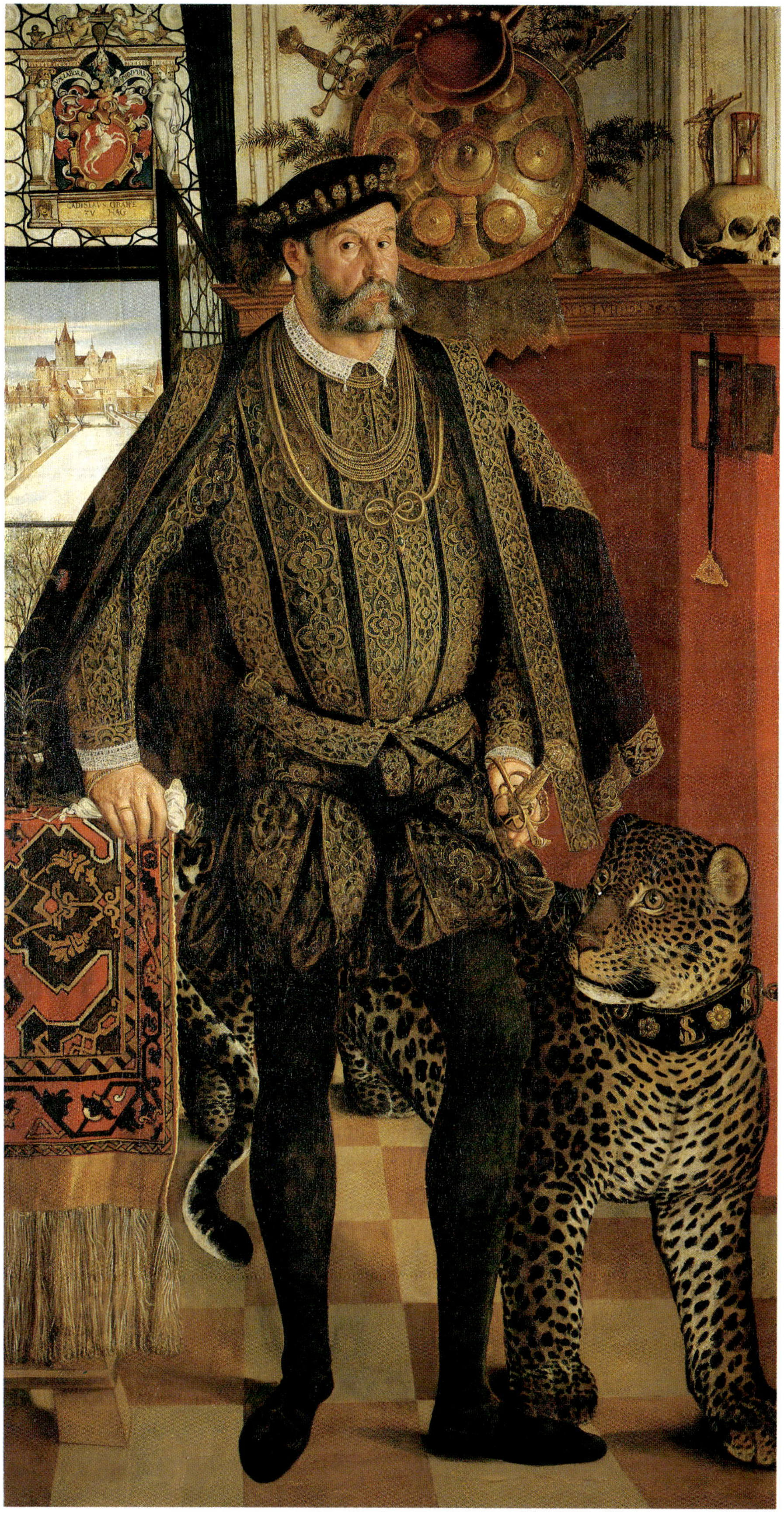

157 Hans Mielich, *Ladislas of Fraunberg, Count of Haag*, canvas, 211 × 111.5 cm., Sammlungen des Regierenden Fürsten von Liechtenstein, Vaduz (1065).

The painting is signed and dated: 'In the year of Our Lord 1557 Hans Mielich made this at Munich'. The subject is identified by the coat of arms in the stained glass window, beneath which is the inscription 'LADISLAVS GRAFFE ZV HAG'. Through the open window is seen a view of his castle at Haag, east of Munich. Hans Mielich was court painter to Albert V, Duke of Bavaria, who had Ladislas arrested in September 1557 and detained him in Munich until the following November. The portrait was evidently painted or at least started during those months. Ladislas (1505–66), the last of the Counts of Haag, had been a soldier in the service of the Emperor Charles V and of Francis I, King of France.

See the exhibition catalogue New York, 1985, pp. 241–2 (153); here pp. 99, 120, 132.

158 (facing page, left) Titian, *Young Man with a Tattered Glove*, canvas, 100 × 89 cm., Louvre, Paris (INV. 757).

Signed in the lower right corner 'TITIANVS. F', the portrait is believed to have been painted in the early 1520s. The sitter, dressed in dark grey and black, has not been identified and the paint surface is so obscured by dirt and discoloured varnishes that it is difficult to make sense of the structure of his costume.

See Wethey, 1971, p. 118; Hope, 1980, p. 64; here pp. 69, 99, 134.

Gloves were extremely serviceable to portrait-painters, for they were often used to occupy the idle hands of sitters. Because they were difficult to make and to clean, they were expensive items which had to be frequently discarded and replaced, and those who wore gloves were unable to do many kinds of manual work. Gloves therefore indicated that their wearer had a certain social status, and they might also draw attention to beautiful hands. As Castiglione observed of ladies' hands:

> they leave a very great desire of them selves, and especially after they are covered with gloves againe, for a man woulde judge that in putting them on again she passeth not and litle regardeth whether they be in sight or no, and that they are so faire rather by nature, than by any studie or diligence.[39]

Earlier, however, gloves had been regarded with some suspicion as the means by which the rich kept their hands soft for lascivious purposes.[40] It was probably for this reason that a fifteenth-century illuminator represented Frivolity as a damsel 'who wishes only to play and waste time, and that she demonstrates by placing one hand in her bosom and by fiddling with her glove with the other'.[41] At the Burgundian court in the fifteenth century, those in deep mourning wore 'neither rings nor gloves'.[42] When Mary Tudor and Philip II of Spain entered London in 1554, the route along which they passed was hung with pictures, including portraits. One was of Henry VIII,

> having in one hand a cepter and in the other hande a booke, whereon was wrytten *Verbum Dei*; but after the king was passed, the bushoppe of Winchester, noting the book . . . shortely afterwards called the paynter before him . . . and . . . askte why and who bad him describe king Henry with a boke in his hande . . . And so he paynted him shortly after, in the sted of the booke of *Verbum Dei*, to have in his handes a new payre of gloves.[43]

Gloves had apparently come to be considered inoffensive and insignificant.

Tattered old gloves, however, were a different matter, and in Titian's *Young Man with a Tattered Glove*, artist and sitter must have had some definite reason for placing a badly torn glove on the sitter's left hand (plate 158). In other Venetian pictures of the time, for example the several paintings of *Lovers*, all thought to be versions of a lost Giorgione,[44] a finger end protruding through a hole in a glove seems intended to look phallic. It would be rash, however, to assume that there is necessarily any sexual reference in Titian's portrait.

In certain portraits flies are placed on or near the sitters (plates 61, 97). In some cases, especially where they are associated with food, the flies may refer to the processes of natural decay; in others, they may be displays of the artist's virtuosity in enhancing the sense of actuality in his picture.[45]

Servants, slaves and dwarfs were represented next to some sitters in order to demonstrate their social ascendancy (plate 159). Brantôme, nevertheless, could envisage a situation in which

> an excellent painter . . . , having executed the portrait of a very beautiful and pleasant-looking lady, places next to her an old hag, a moorish slave or a hideous dwarf, so that their ugliness and blackness may give greater lustre and brilliance to her great beauty and fairness.[46]

Presumably it was vanity that prompted ladies and men to keep, and to appear in public with, attendants who would have been considered ugly.

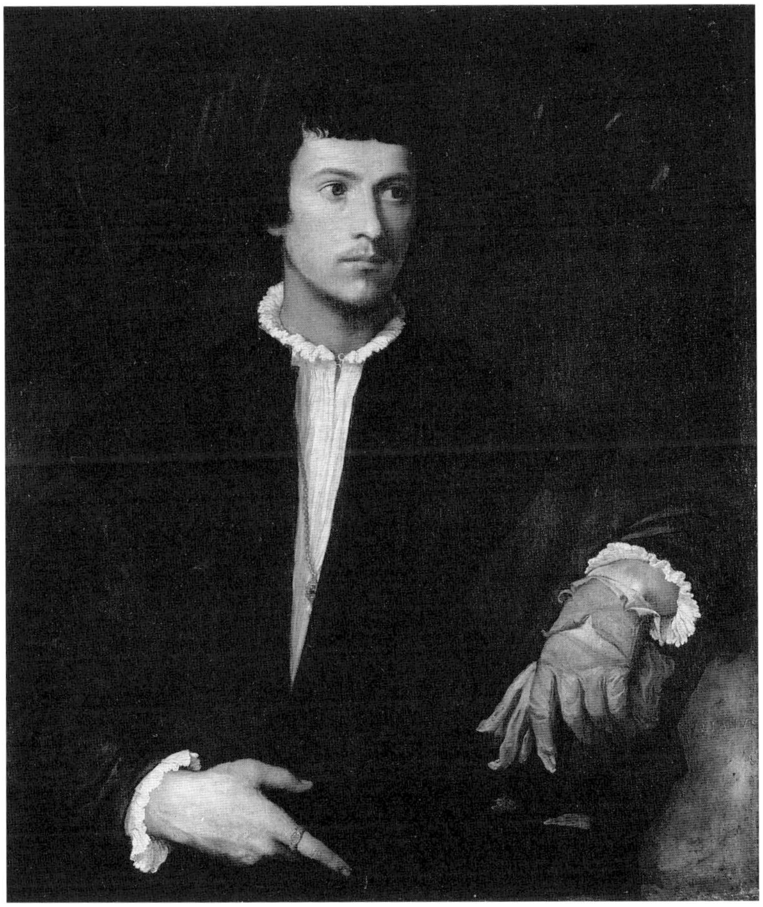

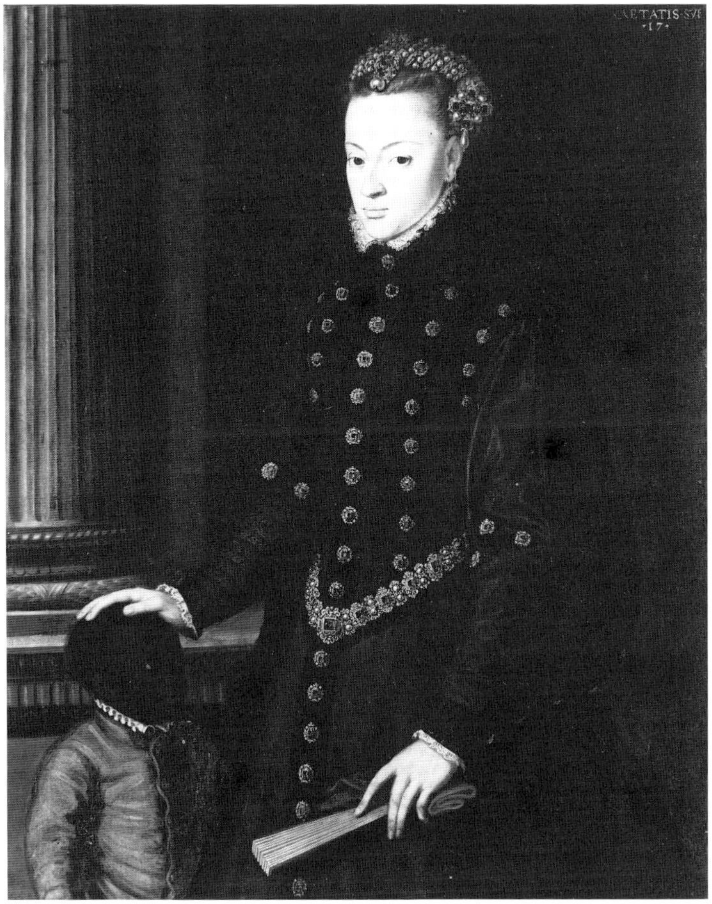

159 (above right) After Antonis Mor, *Joanna of Austria with a Slave*, canvas, 99 × 81.5 cm., Musées Royaux des Beaux-Arts de Belgique, Brussels (1296).

In the upper-right corner is the inscription '.AETATIS. SVE/ .17.'. The sitter (1537–73), daughter of the Emperor Charles V, is easily recognised from other portraits and the Brussels picture was evidently in her possession when she died (Campbell, 1985, p. 103). In the inventory taken after her death was listed 'A half-length portrait of the said Most Serene Princess, our lady, painted on canvas, in a plain wooden frame, with her hand on the head of a little black girl . . .' (Pérez Pastor, 1914, p. 364). Joanna married in December 1552 John, Prince of Portugal (1537–54). The inscription on the Brussels portrait may mean that she is seventeen or that she is in her seventeenth year, which began on 27 June 1553. The painting is apparently based on a portrait executed by Mor during his visits to the Spanish and Portuguese courts between 1550 and 1552–3.

See Breuer, 1984, pp. 315–16; here pp. 54, 61, 99, 134.

Jan van Eyck's portrait of Giovanni Arnolfini and his wife, dated 1434, has been thought to be full of symbols indicating that a marriage ceremony is taking place (plate 135).[47] In inventories of 1516 and 1524, it is described simply as a double portrait; the notion that a marriage is represented seems to have arisen in the mid-sixteenth century and might have been evolved by someone who, believing that the lady was pregnant, was attempting to explain her apparent pregnancy, the prominence of the bed and the solemnity of both sitters' gestures.[48] The lady is not pregnant, but is standing in an attitude fashionable in 1434 but no longer modish in the mid-sixteenth century: in a triptych by Van Eyck dated 1437, the virgin St Catherine stands in an almost identical posture and there again her heavy, fur-lined dress emphasises the swelling contour of her belly.[49] Magnificent beds were expensive items of furniture and in the fifteenth century were displayed prominently in reception rooms.[50] The bed in the portrait may be another indication of the sitters' affluence, like the oriental rug and the oranges carelessly arranged on the chest: for in Bruges in the fifteenth century, oranges were exceedingly expensive.[51] The solemn gestures, seen in the context of Van Eyck's other paintings, would have appeared less extraordinary to his contemporaries than to mid-sixteenth-century observers: Giovanni Arnolfini may be raising his right hand to greet the two men who are entering the room and who are reflected in the mirror.

It might be asserted with some confidence that the picture is a straightforward double portrait which has been misinterpreted by mid-sixteenth-century and later writers, if it were not for the presence of three details that seem to demand further

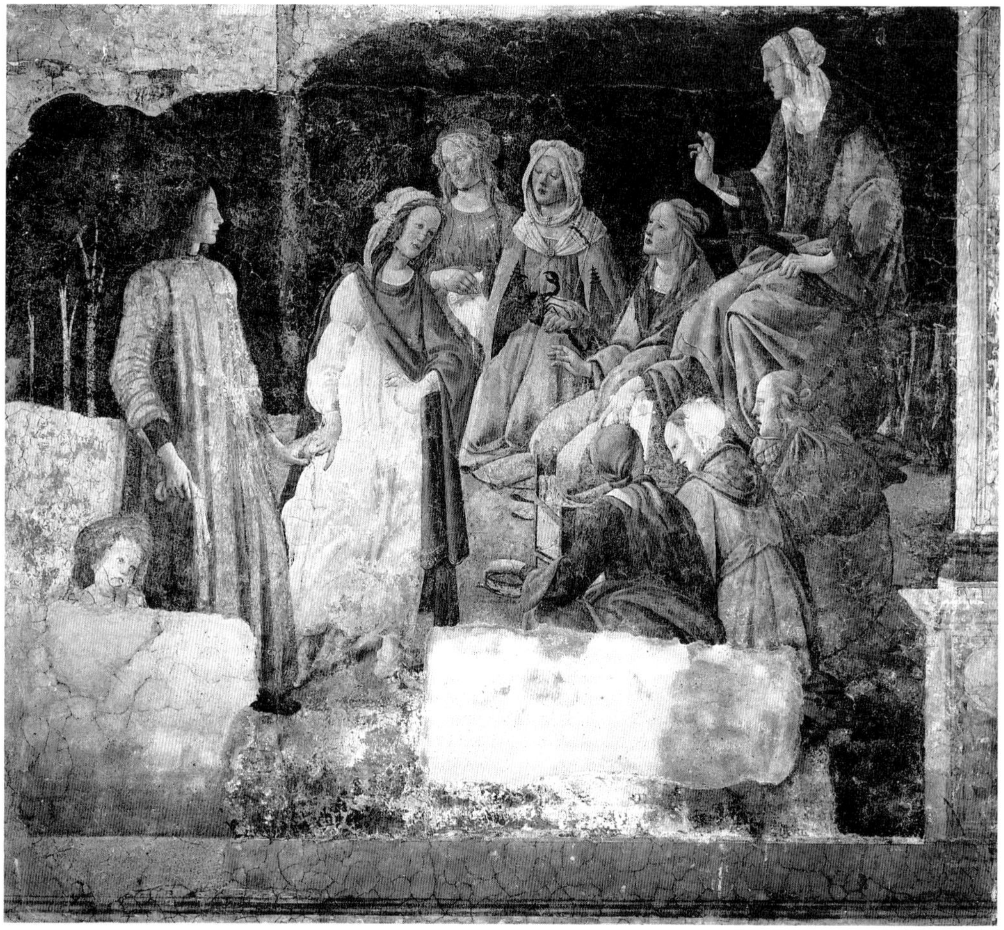

160 Botticelli, *Lorenzo Tornabuoni and the Liberal Arts*, detached fresco, 237 × 269.5 cm., Louvre, Paris (R.F. 322).

Discovered in 1873 in a large upper room in a villa near Florence, this fresco and its pair, *Giovanna degli Albizzi with Venus and the Graces*, were subsequently detached and sold; a fragment from another fresco, found on the opposite wall of the same room, apparently represented *Giovanni Tornabuoni with his Daughter Ludovica* and had disappeared by 1913. The villa belonged to Giovanni Tornabuoni (1428–97), uncle of Lorenzo the Magnificent de' Medici and father of Lorenzo Tornabuoni (1468–97) who married in 1486 Giovanna degli Albizzi (1468–88). The portraits of Lorenzo and Giovanna are identified by comparison with medals and from the information that, in 1873, the Albizzi coat of arms appeared in the lower-right corner of the fresco reproduced. It is possible that the entire room was decorated with fresco portraits of members of the Tornabuoni family and it is likely that the frescoes were painted shortly after Lorenzo's marriage in 1486. They are attributed to Botticelli on stylistic grounds. Here night has fallen; against a background of trees, Lorenzo is presented by Grammar to the other Liberal Arts, over whom Prudentia presides.

See Horne, 1908, pp. 142–8; Lightbown, 1978, I, pp. 94–7, II, pp. 60–3; here pp. 56, 137.

explanation: the two visitors; the odd signature 'Jan van Eyck was here/1434', prominently written across the centre of the composition; and the unnecessary lit candle. The signature may indicate that one of the visitors is Van Eyck himself; if anything were known about the personal relationship between him and Arnolfini, it would be easier to attempt to elucidate its significance. Van Eyck and Arnolfini, who would have been in contact both in Bruges and at the Burgundian court, might have been close friends, and it is even possible that the portrait was not commissioned but was a gift from the painter to the sitters. Though candles were frequently used in various religious rituals, no certain link has been made between the single burning candle and marriage ceremonies. The significance of the candle remains unexplained.

As the evidence is incomplete and inconclusive, it would seem unwise to dismiss as irrelevant or ill-informed the inventories of 1516 and 1524 where the picture is described simply as a double portrait. It would be inadvisable to conclude that a marriage ceremony is taking place, or that every detail has symbolic connotations. It is still more inadvisable to assume that the painting, like a photograph, was a totally objective record of a significant moment during the marriage ceremony, or that it was made as a 'pictorial marriage certificate'.[52] It is an insult to Van Eyck to treat his picture as if it were a painted substitute for a marriage contract, or a snapshot or a puzzle to be unriddled by analysing its symbolism. The extent to which Van Eyck has here used symbolism must remain a debatable question.

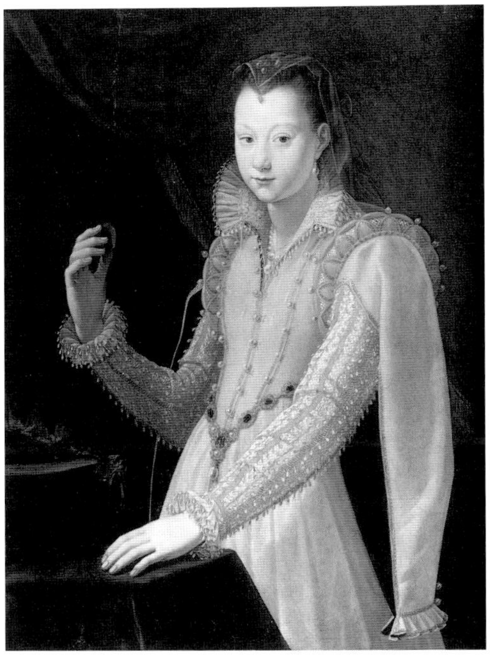

161 Follower of Bronzino, *Lady as Portia the Wife of Brutus*, panel, 100 × 77 cm., Statens Museum for Kunst, Copenhagen (3623).

From the costume, the portrait may be dated around 1560–70.

See Langedijk, 1981–3, I, pp. 675–6; here p. 137.

Some sitters had themselves portrayed accompanied by allegorical figures. In a fresco by Botticelli, Lorenzo Tornabuoni is led into the presence of the Seven Liberal Arts (plate 160). Parmigianino chose to represent the Emperor Charles V with Fame, who crowns him with laurels; the infant Hercules offers him the world (plate 177).

Other sitters had themselves painted in the guise of heroes, gods or saints. Gossaert, for example, depicted the wife of his patron, the Marquis of Veere, as the Virgin, with one of their sons as the Christ Child. The number of surviving versions of Gossaert's composition suggests that it interested a great many people, not just the Veere family; the reasons can only be guessed at.[53] Bronzino showed the admiral Andrea Doria as Neptune, and one version of his portrait was exhibited in the museum of portraits established at Como by Paolo Giovio (plate 8). A follower of Bronzino represented a lady holding, and apparently about to eat, a burning coal (plate 161). She is enacting the part of Portia, the wife of Brutus, who, according to Valerius Maximus and Boccaccio, demonstrated her fidelity to her husband by committing suicide when she heard of his death. Not finding a more convenient way of killing herself, she swallowed burning coals.[54] By casting herself as Portia, the lady in the portrait is demonstrating that she is an exemplary wife.

Group and double portraits were executed in which families masqueraded as members of the Holy Family. In a diptych commissioned by Johannes Cuspinian and dated 1520, Bernhard Strigel depicted the Emperor Maximilian I and members of his family as Cleophas, the Virgin's brother-in-law, his wife and children; he portrayed Cuspinian himself as Zebedee, his wife as Mary Salome and their sons as Saints James the Great and John the Evangelist. Without the inscriptions giving these identifications, however, the two panels would be taken for ordinary group portraits.[55] Later, such images were better disguised. In about 1580, the Bavarian court painter Engelhard de Pee painted a *Presentation in the Temple* in which the protagonists are members of the Bavarian ducal family,[56] while in the 1600s Pantoja painted an *Annunciation* in which the Virgin is a portrait of Margaret of Austria, Queen of Spain, and the Archangel Gabriel is a portrait of her daughter Anne of Austria.[57]

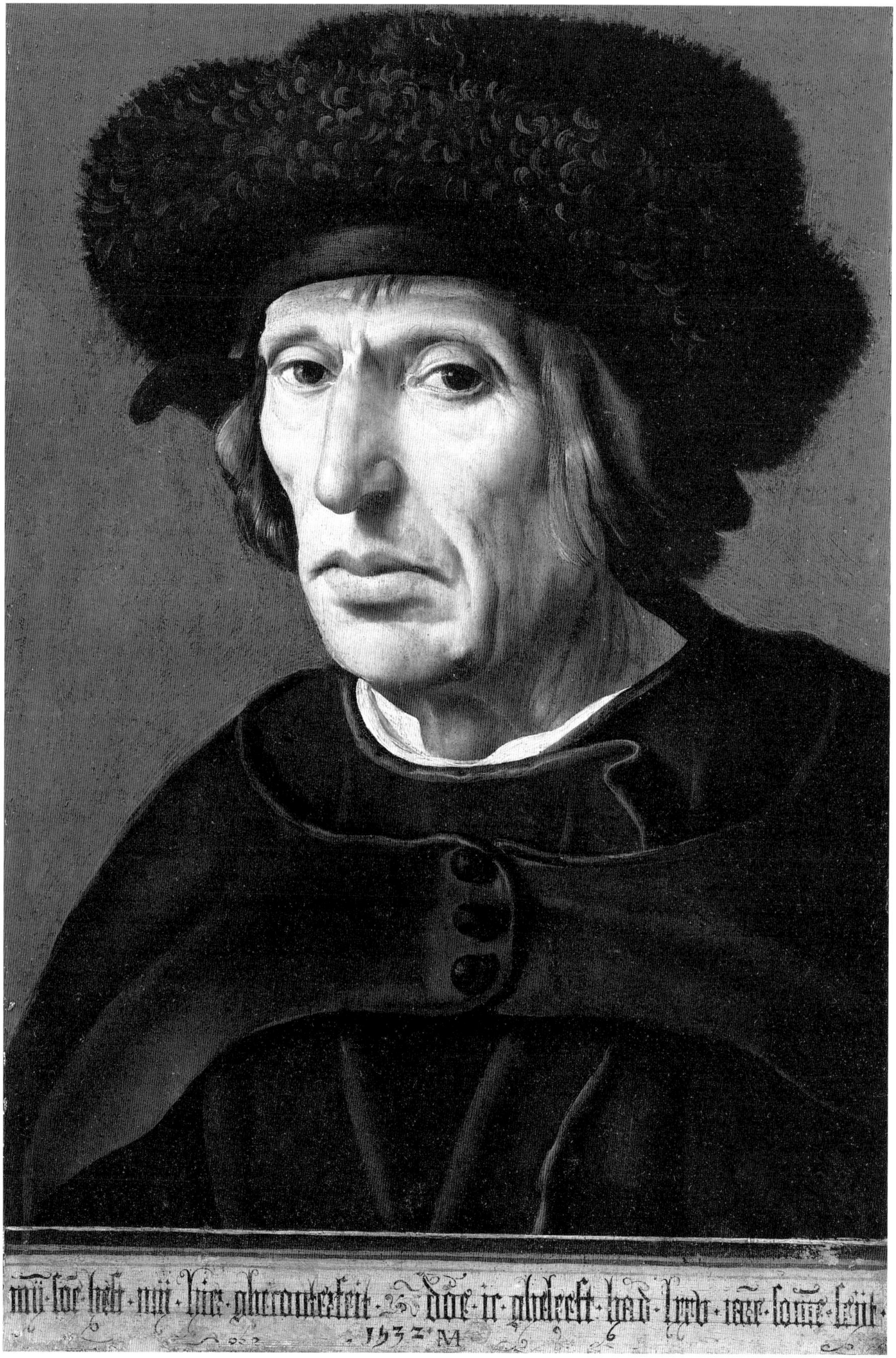
1532 M

5 The Sitters

The sitter and the patron who paid the painter for the portrait were often the same person, but frequently the sitter was the patron's wife, a member of his family or household, a friend or someone whom he admired or who otherwise intrigued him. Portraits of dwarfs and jesters were normally commissioned by their employers (plates 124, 167–8) but there was a wider market for portraits of those celebrated for their freakishness (plate 166), their beauty, their heroism, their political importance or their intellectual attainments.

It must once again be stressed that the available evidence is heavily biassed towards portraits of princes and great lords which are much more likely to have been preserved, copied or mentioned in surviving documents. Many portraits are of unidentified sitters and, even if the sitter can be named, it may be difficult or impossible to discover much about him or his social status. Though the dress and jewellery worn by an unidentified sitter may give indications of his rank and wealth, it is dangerous to rely overmuch on costume. Certain identified sitters of immense riches and power appear in their portraits relatively simply dressed;[1] while less affluent sitters might have hired the clothes in which they were to be painted,[2] or simply persuaded the painters to array their images in clothes and jewels that were not their own.[3] It is therefore exceedingly difficult to say whether portraiture was an art form that was becoming increasingly available to a widening social range of sitters. A casual consideration of the visual and documentary evidence might suggest that this was so; the impression, however, may result largely from the increasing volume of evidence, infinitely richer for the sixteenth century than for the fourteenth.

The couple who sat to the Master of Flémalle in about 1430 would seem, from their clothes, to have been prosperous townspeople, but not persons of great wealth (plates 104–5). Jacob Willemsz. van Veen, who sat for his portrait in 1532, was a farmer (plate 162). Jacob, however, was the father of Marten van Heemskerck, the artist who executed his portrait; the Master of Flémalle's sitters might conceivably have been relatives or friends of the painter. It would be dangerous to suppose that those in humble life could never have aspired to have portraits of themselves. Equally, it would be rash to assume that all princes and courtiers were constantly having themselves painted, while those outside the courts would have had more limited opportunities to commission portraits. It is true that Louis XIII of France had been painted or drawn on at least three occasions before his first birthday in 1602, and that, by the time of his sixth birthday in 1607, he had sat at least seventeen times to various artists.[4] In 1572, however, Augustus, Elector of Saxony, was unable to lay his hands on portraits of his father, his grandfather or his uncle,[5] in spite of the fact that his father, Henry the Pious, had been one of the elder Cranach's patrons (plate 145). On the other hand, between about 1549 and 1569, the English musician Thomas Whythorne sat for at least four painted portraits.[6]

Inevitably an artist will find it easier to paint beautiful portraits of handsome or striking and elegantly dressed sitters than of plain, insignificant and dowdy sitters. He may also find it hard to form sympathetic relationships with certain sitters,

162 Marten van Heemskerck, *Jacob Willemsz. van Veen*, panel, 51.9 × 34.8 cm., Metropolitan Museum of Art, New York (71.36).

Signed with the artist's monogram and dated 1532, the picture is inscribed: 'My son has counterfeited me here when I had lived for seventy-five years, so they say'. Heemskerck's father, a prosperous farmer, opposed with some severity his son's ambitions to be a painter. The monument which in 1570 Marten erected in his memory still stands in the cemetery at Heemskerk and bears a profile portrait relief of Jacob, who died on 16 September 1535 aged seventy-nine.

See Veldman, 1977, pp. 144–55; here pp. 61, 69, 139, 140, 225.

who may behave towards him in a difficult or unpleasant manner. Only rarely is it known what a painter thought of his sitter. Heemskerck had every reason to dislike his father, who had treated him with great harshness (plate 162);[7] Titian was reported to have called Jacopo Strada an ignorant confidence trickster whose success was due to luck as well as duplicity.[8] Personal dislike might lead to an unsympathetic, yet wonderfully analytical and critical portrait, but constant annoyance of the artist by the sitter might induce the painter simply to lose interest in his portrait.

Capricious or indecisive sitters might be extremely irritating. Tito Vespasiano Strozzi wrote a poem in which he satirised a young woman named Helen, who wished to be painted by Cosimo Tura but who could not make up her mind which season was the most suitable, which clothes she should wear or whether her hair should be covered or unbound: 'And while the silly girl shifts the day and different forms of dress, she drags out what she wants in long delays . . .'.[9] Fortunately, perhaps, for Tura, Helen may never have existed; even if she did, her vacillation seems to have prevented her from placing a commission with him. Many artists, nevertheless, must have had to deal with sitters who commissioned portraits and then behaved like Helen. Other sitters were quite unpredictable. Isabella d'Este, for example, was completely inconsistent in her treatment of her portraitists. In 1504, as we have seen, she wrote to Leonardo to remind him that, when he had visited Mantua, he had made a drawing of her and had promised to base a painted portrait upon it (plate 93). She realised, however, that this was now 'nearly impossible' as he could not return to Mantua:[10] in other words she did not expect him to work up his drawn into a painted portrait without further sittings. But she was quite content to allow Francia in 1511 and Titian in 1534–6 to paint portraits of her without sittings: indeed she refused to allow Francia even to see her.[11]

Sitters who used cosmetics also presented problems. Castiglione was critical of the lady 'so bedawbed, that a man would wene she had a viser on her face, and dareth not laugh for making it chappe . . . [she] standeth like an image of woode without moving, shewing her selfe onely in torche light, as craftie marchantmen doe their clothes in their darke lights'.[12] There would be difficulties, too, with Castiglione's 'soft and womanish' courtiers, who

> doe not onely courle the haire, and picke the browes, but also pampre them selves in everie point like the most wanton and dishonest women in the world: and a man would thinke them in going, in standing, and in all their gestures so tender and faint, that their members were readie to flee one from an other, and their wordes they pronounce so drawningly, that a man woulde weene they were at that instant yeelding up the ghost . . .[13]

Francisco de Holanda in his dialogue on portraiture fulminated against eyebrow-plucking.[14]

The ways in which artists managed sittings and dealt with bored or restive sitters will be considered in the chapter on portrait method.

When a portrait was commissioned, artist and patron must normally have agreed on its size, general appearance and price. Even Lorenzo Lotto, not the most businesslike of portraitists, usually settled a price when he accepted a portrait commission. Formal contracts for portraits seem to have been drawn up very rarely;[15] usually patron, sitter and artist would have been in such constant contact that there was no need to spend money on drawing up a legally binding document. The price of a portrait would have depended on its size and the amount of detail to be included in the sitter's costume, in the background and in accessory objects, and many or most painters would have had a sliding scale of standard charges according to size. Vasari stated that Tintoretto painted 'portraits in oils at every price';[16] Frans Pourbus the Younger was evidently delighted to discover that, in Paris in 1610, he could charge 20 *pistoles* for a portrait without hands and 10 *pistoles* for a very small portrait. His prices were high because his exceptional ability was recognised: a 'distinction is made between my work and that of all the other painters in France'.[17] The Scottish painter George Jamesone was to write in 1636 to a patron: 'The pryce quhilk ewerie one payes to me, abowe the west, is twentie merkis, I furnishing claith and coulleris; bot iff I furniss ane double gilt muller, then it is twentie poundis.'[18] Seisenegger, in the bills that he made up for his patron the Emperor Ferdinand I, described in great detail the costumes worn by his sitters and mentioned when he had included elaborate architectural or landscape backgrounds.[19] In so doing, he was evidently justifying the prices he was charging and his departures from his standard rates. At Berlin in 1580, the court painter Johann Baptista wrote that he had always charged 30 *thalers* for a portrait of a prince and 20 *thalers* for a portrait of a commoner.[20] This was presumably because of the extra work required on the prince's clothing.

It is probable that, when portraits were commissioned, painters would often have shown to their clients rough sketches to demonstrate what their finished portraits would look like. In the cases of large, elaborate and expensive portraits, particularly group portraits, the artists might have made several sketches of different compositions and asked their patrons to select the ones they preferred. As will be discussed below, Holbein's drawing of the More family was evidently, submitted to the sitters for their approval before he began his painted portrait (plate 164); while in about 1582, Friedrich Sustris seems to have executed for William, Duke of Bavaria, two alternative projects for a group portrait of William with his wife and children. In one, the duke and duchess were shown seated; in the other they were represented standing.[21]

One of the dangers in not having a formal contract was that the patron might refuse to accept and pay for the finished portrait. That may not have happened often, because the close contacts between artist and sitter would normally have allowed problems to be solved while the portrait was being painted or because the crisis would have arisen before the portrait was finished and work on it would have stopped. On occasion, however, patrons did refuse to pay. In January 1545, Lorenzo Lotto agreed to paint a life-size portrait of Tommaso Costanzo in armour. The price agreed was 10 *scudi*, which Lotto thought too low but which he was prepared to accept in the hope that Costanzo would offer him an additional 'courtesy' payment. In October 1548, Lotto wrote to remind Costanzo that he had not collected or paid for his portrait, but he received only 'fine words' in reply. Lotto wrote again, and Costanzo answered that he did not want the picture because it was not a good likeness; he conceded that he did not wish Lotto to return the advance payment which he had made. The 'discourtesy' distressed Lotto, who noted in his account book that the painting was unsaleable. Eventually, in 1553, after Tommaso Costanzo's death, Lotto contrived to sell the portrait to his son.[22]

In 1579, George Frederick, Margrave of Brandenburg-Ansbach and Bayreuth, commissioned several portraits from Lucas Cranach the Younger, who executed them with obliging speed and sent them to Ansbach with his bill. Three of them, small posthumous portraits of the Margrave's first wife, failed to please because

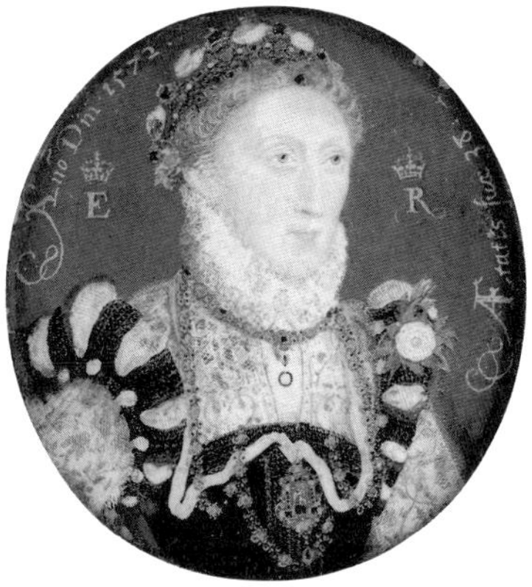

163 Nicholas Hilliard, *Elizabeth I, Queen of England*, parchment mounted on a playing card (part of a queen showing on the reverse), oval, 5.2 × 4.7 cm., National Portrait Gallery, London (108).

Inscribed with the crowned initials ER, for Elizabeth Regina, and the words 'Año Dñi .1572./Ætatis suae 38', the miniature is attributed to Hilliard on stylistic grounds and is believed to be his earliest portrait of the queen, which he painted in a garden (Hilliard, 1981 edn, pp. 84–6). The face and ruff are much restored.

See the exhibition catalogue London, 1983, pp. 117–18 (182); here pp. 64, 142.

they were not 'quite like' the lady. They were returned to Lucas, and their price was deducted from his account.[23] Some artists had to go to great lengths to make their clients pay for portraits. According to Van Mander, an English captain commissioned his portrait from Jacques de Poindre and then refused to collect or pay for the picture. Jacques therefore painted, in water-colour, bars across the sitter's face, to make it appear that he was in prison, and placed the portrait on public exhibition. When the Englishman heard of this and went to complain to the painter, he told him that he had to remain in his pictorial prison until he settled his account. The Englishman paid, and Jacques, taking up a sponge, wiped away the bars.[24]

The patron, who had the ultimate sanction of withholding payment, was in a position to exercise complete control over the painter and many patrons dictated to their artists. In 1547, Catherine de' Medici, Queen of France, asked for portraits of all her children and insisted that they should not be done from the painter's 'usual angle'.[25] In 1551, Philip II of Spain wrote to his aunt that he was dissatisfied with the haste with which Titian had painted his portrait in armour; if there had been time, he would have made him go over it again (plate 263).[26] When Hilliard first painted Elizabeth I of England, probably in 1572 (plate 163), she 'chosse her place to sit in for that porposse in the open ally of a goodly garden, where no tree was neere, nor anye shadowe at all'.[27] Hilliard usually, and not unreasonably, posed his sitters in his studio and would undoubtedly have preferred to paint Elizabeth indoors.

From the preliminary drawings and from copies of the lost painting, much can be deduced about the genesis of Holbein's portrait of the family of Sir Thomas More. Holbein, who had come to London with a letter of introduction from Erasmus to More, must have discussed the project with the Mores before beginning work on the preliminary portrait drawings, which were executed in coloured chalks. He must then have produced his careful pen drawing of the whole group (plate 164). When he made the pen drawing, he had evidently not yet seen More's adopted daughter Margaret Giggs, whose head is done in a rather more summary and tentative way than the others and bears no resemblance to the chalk drawing finally used in the painting. She clearly sat to Holbein after he had shown his pen drawing to the Mores and discussed it with them. The results of their discussions are partly incorporated in the notes scribbled by Holbein himself across the drawing: 'she will sit', next to the kneeling figure of Lady More, and 'clavichords and other instruments on the sideboard'. Using the same ink, he has crossed out the candlestick behind Lady More and sketched a monkey at her skirts, a viol hanging above Margaret Giggs and various books scattered across the floor. Margaret Roper's dress has been given a laced instead of a closed front, and a slight scribble of a head indicates the position of a figure to be added in the doorway behind Lady More. Most of these changes were indeed made in the painted portrait, while further alterations to Holbein's original plan, not noted on the drawing, may have been made either at this or at a subsequent consultation. In the painting, the clock was brought to a position directly above Sir Thomas More, to stress his central importance. Margaret Giggs, the adopted daughter, no longer leant over to converse with More's father but was removed to the extreme left of the composition while the figure of More's own daughter, Elizabeth Dauncey, was shifted across to take her place beside Judge More. Cicely Heron's prayer beads were omitted and the positions of her hands slightly changed so that she appeared to be counting on her fingers and doubtless making rhetorical points. Magnificent vases of

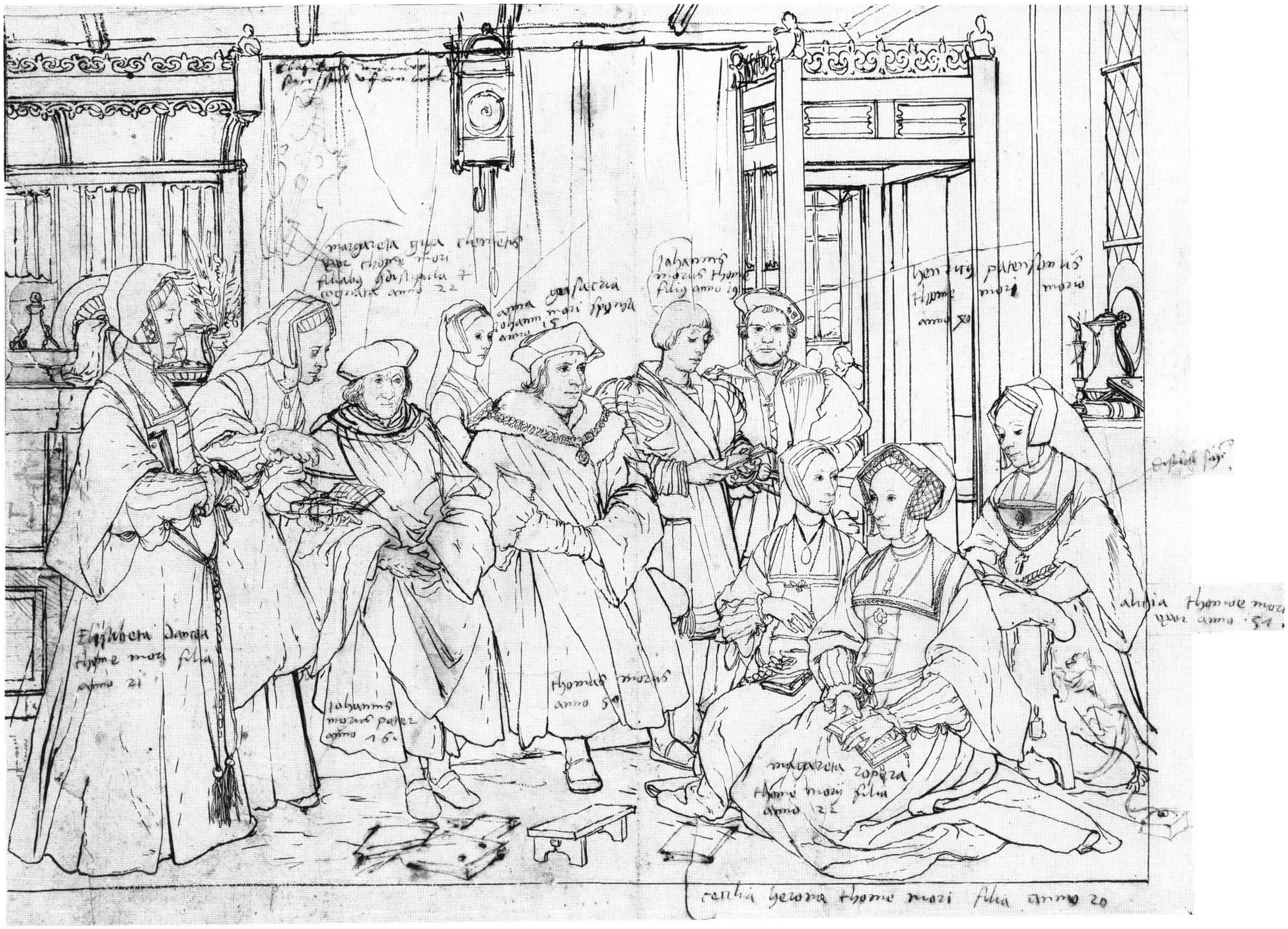

164 Hans Holbein the Younger, *Sir Thomas More and his Family*, pen, brush and ink over chalk on paper, 38.9 × 52.4 cm., Öffentliche Kunstsammlung, Basle, Kupferstichkabinett (1662.31).

The Latin inscriptions, in handwriting identified as that of the astronomer Nikolaus Kratzer, give the names and ages of the sitters who are, from left to right: Elizabeth Dauncey, More's second daughter; Margaret Giggs, Mrs Clement, his adopted daughter; Sir John More, his father; Anne Cresacre, his daughter-in-law; Sir Thomas himself; John More, his son; Henry Patenson, his jester; Cicely Heron, his youngest daughter; Margaret Roper, his eldest daughter; and Alice, his second wife. The German inscriptions are notes by Holbein himself. Sir Thomas gave the drawing to Erasmus, to whom it was delivered by Holbein after his return from London to Basle in 1528. Erasmus's letters of thanks to More and to Margaret Roper were written on 5 and 6 September 1529; in the second, he remarked that 'if I had been among you, I would not have seen you more clearly'. The drawing is one of Holbein's preliminary drawings for his large painting of the More family, which was on canvas and which was detroyed by fire in 1752. Holbein's drawings of the heads of all the sitters except Patenson, Margaret Roper and Lady More are preserved at Windsor (Foister, 1983, pp. 16–17, 39 (1–8)). Several versions of the lost painting are known: that in the collection of Lord St Oswald at Nostell Priory, signed by Rowland Lockey and dated 1592, is considered to be a reliable copy of the lost original and is the only version in which Holbein's finished composition is reproduced in its entirety and without added figures by the copyists. When he made the Basle drawing, Holbein had evidently decided exactly how he wished to paint the group portrait and the drawing was presumably executed to be presented to the Mores for their final approval. It would appear that it was interference from them which prevented him from carrying out his original scheme and which forced him to depart from it in several important respects. In style and technique, the drawing is close to Holbein's *Sapor and Valerian* of about 1521, a preliminary study for one of his murals in the Town Hall at Basle (Basle, 1662.127).

See the exhibition catalogue Basle, 1988, pp. 209–12 (65); here pp. 53, 65, 141–5.

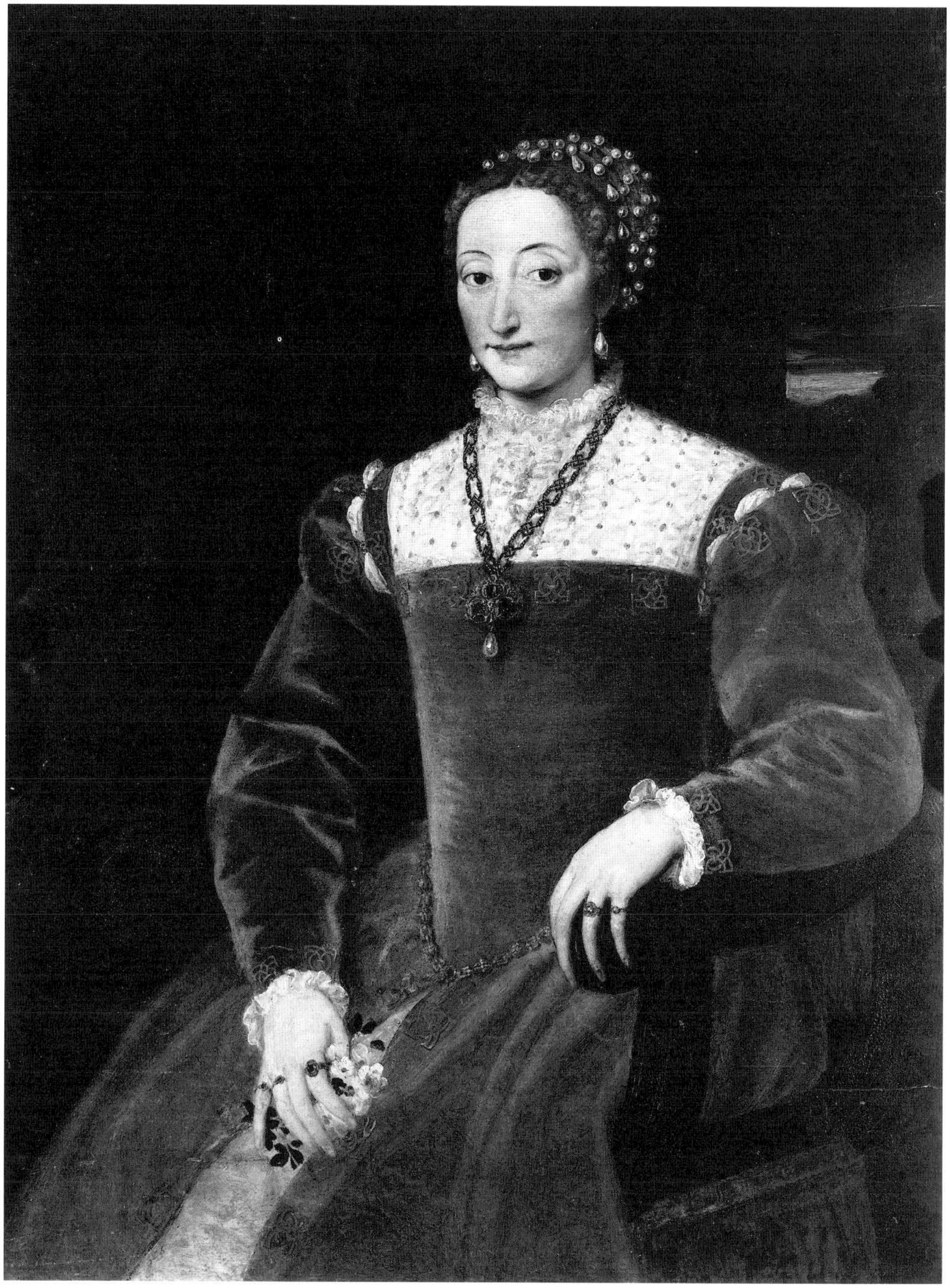

165 Titian, *Giulia Varano, Duchess of Urbino*, panel, 113.5 × 88 cm., Palazzo Pitti, Florence, Appartamenti (Oggetti d'Arte 764).

Giulia Varano (1523–47) married in 1536 Guidobaldo della Rovere, Duke of Urbino. In October 1545, Aretino wrote to tell her that Titian was painting her portrait from her husband's verbal description and that his portrait was as life-like as if she had been sitting for him. Titian seems to have taken a long time to finish his picture for in November 1546 and February 1547 clothes belonging to the duchess were being sent to him: sleeves and then a dress of crimson damask. The Pitti portrait, though damaged and dirty, is clearly by Titian and is identified as his portrait of Giulia because it came from Urbino, because the sitter's dress is decorated with GG monograms – for Giulia and Guidobaldo – and because she wears crimson.

See the exhibition catalogue Florence, 1978–9, pp. 144–8 (33); here pp. 145, 190.

remarkably large flowers were introduced, and the sideboard, draped with a rich cloth and a carpet, was extended far to the right of its position in the drawing.

That most of the changes were made at the instance of the Mores, rather than by Holbein on his own initiative, seems clear. The suppression of the references to the piety of Lady More and Cicely Heron is so radical an alteration that it can scarcely have been Holbein's idea; the composition works more successfully in Holbein's pen drawing than in the copies of his finished painting, where the interchanged figures of Margaret Giggs and Elizabeth Dauncey create a less satisfactory decorative rhythm. That suggests a patron's interference rather than an artist's change of mind. It may be argued that, if Holbein had been allowed to stick to his original plan as expressed in the pen drawing, his painted portrait would have been more coherent in design and that in this case the controls exerted by the patrons were detrimental to the painter's achievement.

Some patrons allowed their painters a degree of discretion. In 1549, Cosimo I de' Medici, Duke of Florence, and his wife Eleonora da Toledo ordered portraits from Bronzino which were to be sent to Cardinal Granvelle. They allowed that, for Bronzino's convenience and for the sake of speed, Eleonora should not be shown wearing rich brocade, but that her dress might be of 'some other patterned cloth which will make a fine show'.[28] In 1547, Titian was painting Giulia Varano, Duchess of Urbino. According to Aretino, the head was painted from her husband's verbal description, but the clothes were sent from the duchy to Titian in Venice (plate 165). A disgruntled courtier wrote that he would have dispatched a more magnificent dress 'if Titian had not insisted on crimson or rose velvet. Since Her Excellency does not have a dress like that, she has decided that this one, of damask of the same colour, may suit his purpose.'[29] Perhaps only an artist of Titian's standing could have specified that a sitter of high rank should appear dressed in a certain colour and fabric, but, according to Francisco de Holanda, not even the pose was to be decided by the sitter. He recommended that the artist should persuade the sitter to adopt the desired position, that the sitter should then be told to look at a fixed point and not to move, and that the artist should then determine whether he would execute a full face, profile or three-quarters-view portrait. As he was adamant that no sitter should see his portrait before it was finished, the sitter's opportunities to interfere were very effectively limited.[30] How many sitters were amenable to such treatment is another question.

When a patron commissioned portraits of people who were not members of his family, arrangements had to be made to gain the painter access to the sitters or to other portraits that he would copy. Travelling might be involved. Van Orley in 1532 sent to Mencía de Mendoza, Countess of Nassau, a bill for fifteen portraits: three of herself, three of members of the Nassau family, four of members of the imperial family and the remaining four of noble ladies. Two of the subjects were dead; at least one of the portraits of noble ladies was copied from 'the large picture in the gallery'. Van Orley asked for an additional payment for having spent several days at court and with Mencía, 'in order to take accurately the true likenesses of the said faces. On this he has spent much time, which he could have employed at home on several other projects from which he could have had great profit and advantage.' Mencía's officials not only failed to make any additional payment but also reduced his prices for all but two of the portraits.[31] Jamesone was clearly aware that problems might well arise over such arrangements. In 1636, he had agreed to paint sixteen portraits of noblemen for Sir Colin Campbell of Glenorchy, to whom he wrote, 'your worship wold resolwe at quhois charges I mist go throwe the countrey to maik thir picturis, for all that are heir in town neidis onlie yowr worships letter to theam to causs theam sitt . . .'.[32]

The physical freaks, whose portraits were much in demand, would not have had much control over the manufacture of their likenesses, which were commissioned and distributed by their protectors. They kept these freaks only so that they might be displayed in person, and doubtless they tried to regulate their display in image. Cosimo I, Grand Duke of Tuscany, commissioned Bronzino to paint two nude, full-length portraits of his dwarf Morgante, who presumably had to sit for them. Bronzino's canvases, framed back to back, remained in the Medici collection (plates 167–8).[33] Petrus Gonsalvus, whose head and body were entirely

166 Bavarian, c. 1582, *A Daughter of Petrus Gonsalvus*, canvas, 122 × 85 cm., Kunsthistorisches Museum, Vienna (8331: exhibited in the Kunstkammer, Schloss Ambras, Innsbruck).

This is one of a series of four full-length portraits of Petrus Gonsalvus, the 'Hairy Man of the Canaries', his (normal) wife, their eldest hairy daughter and their hairy son. The pictures are from the collection of the Archduke Ferdinand of Tyrol, who also owned small versions of the heads, incorporated into his 'Ambras Collection' of portraits now exhibited in the Münzkabinett of the Kunsthistorisches Museum. Miniature versions of the four pictures are in Hoefnagel's manuscript of *The Four Elements* (lent by Mrs Lessing J. Rosenwald to the National Gallery of Art, Washington) and are accompanied by an inscription composed at Munich in 1582 (exhibition catalogue Washington and New York, 1986–7, p. 200). The daughter, whose name is not known but who was born in about 1574, appears to have died young. Here she is fashionably dressed in grey. Like her father and brother, but unlike her mother, she is placed in front of rocks and a cave.

See Scheicher, 1977, p. 150 (390); here pp. 139, 145–7, 206.

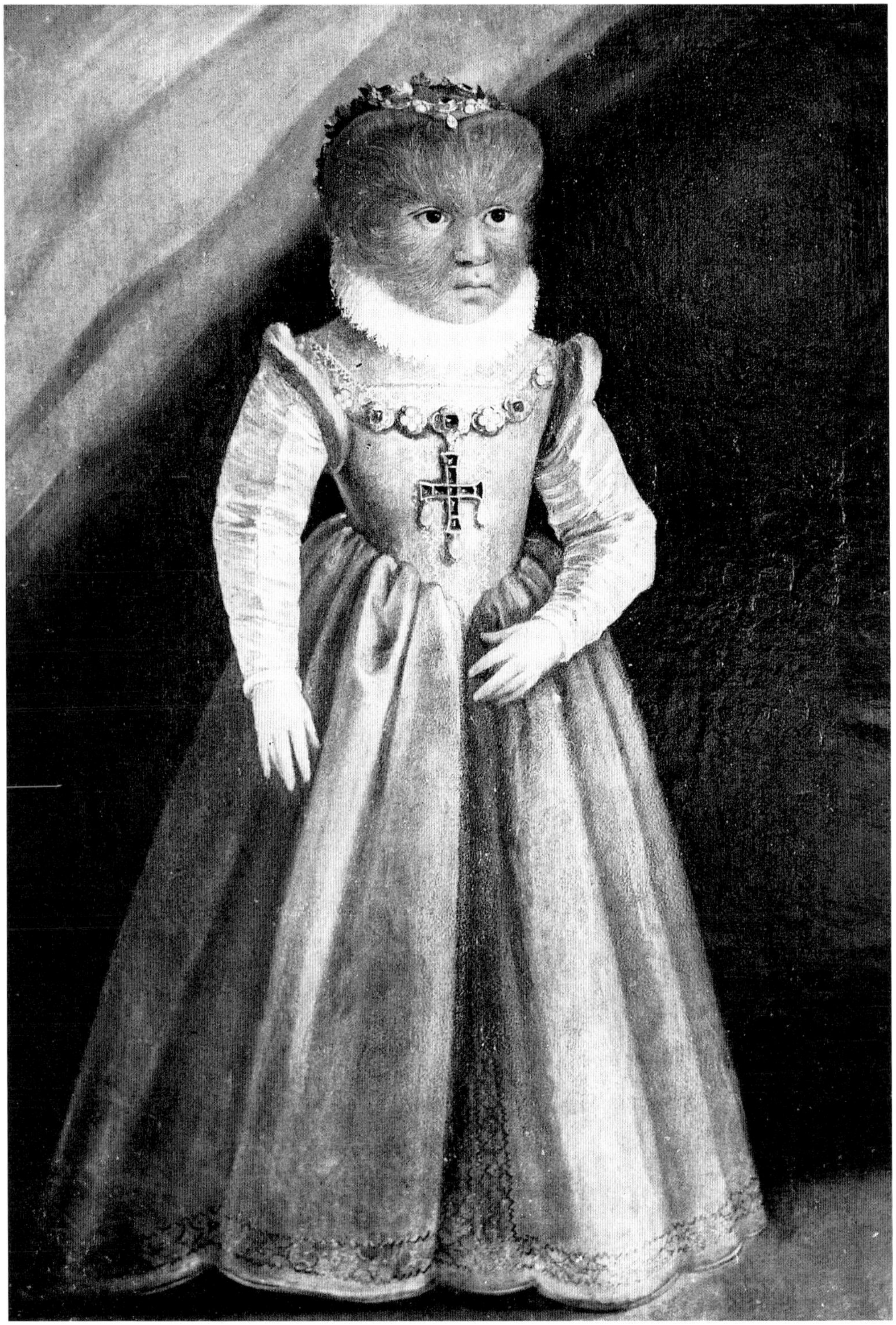

167 (facing page, left) Bronzino, *The Dwarf Morgante, seen from the Front.*

See the note to plate 168.

168 (facing page, right) Bronzino, *The Dwarf Morgante, seen from the Back*, both this and 167 on canvas, 150 × 100 cm., Deposito della Soprintendenza, Florence (5959).

Morgante (c. 1535–after 1594), so named after a giant, was employed at the Medici court and was frequently portrayed by sculptors. Bronzino's paintings, now much damaged, were and are placed back to back in the same frame. Listed in the 1553 inventory of the Medici collections and described by Vasari, they show the nude dwarf as Bacchus and as a huntsman, doubtless a classical god or hero; they were probably painted shortly before 1553.

See the exhibition catalogue Florence, 1980, pp. 273–4 (513); here pp. 65, 139, 145.

covered in hair, came as a boy from the Canary Islands to the French court, where he was educated and learned Latin. He spent some time at the court of Margaret of Parma, Regent of the Netherlands, and married a lady of the Low Countries who bore him several children, some hairy and some normal. The family lived for a while at the court of Munich, where the Duke of Bavaria commissioned various

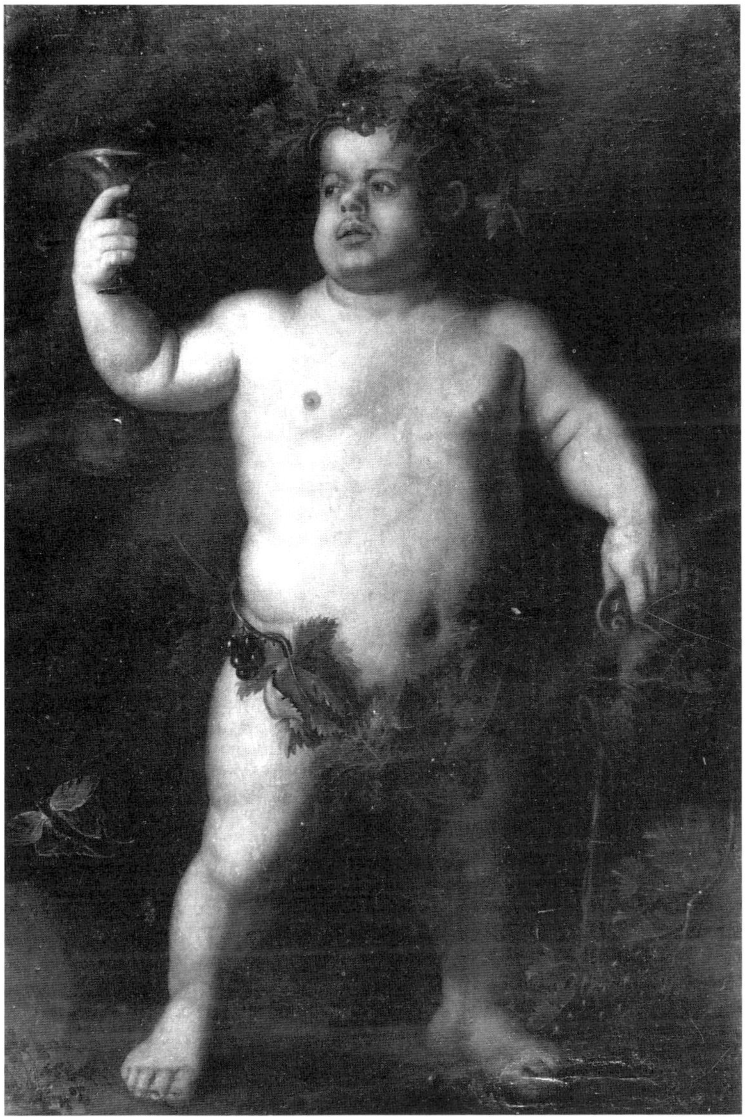

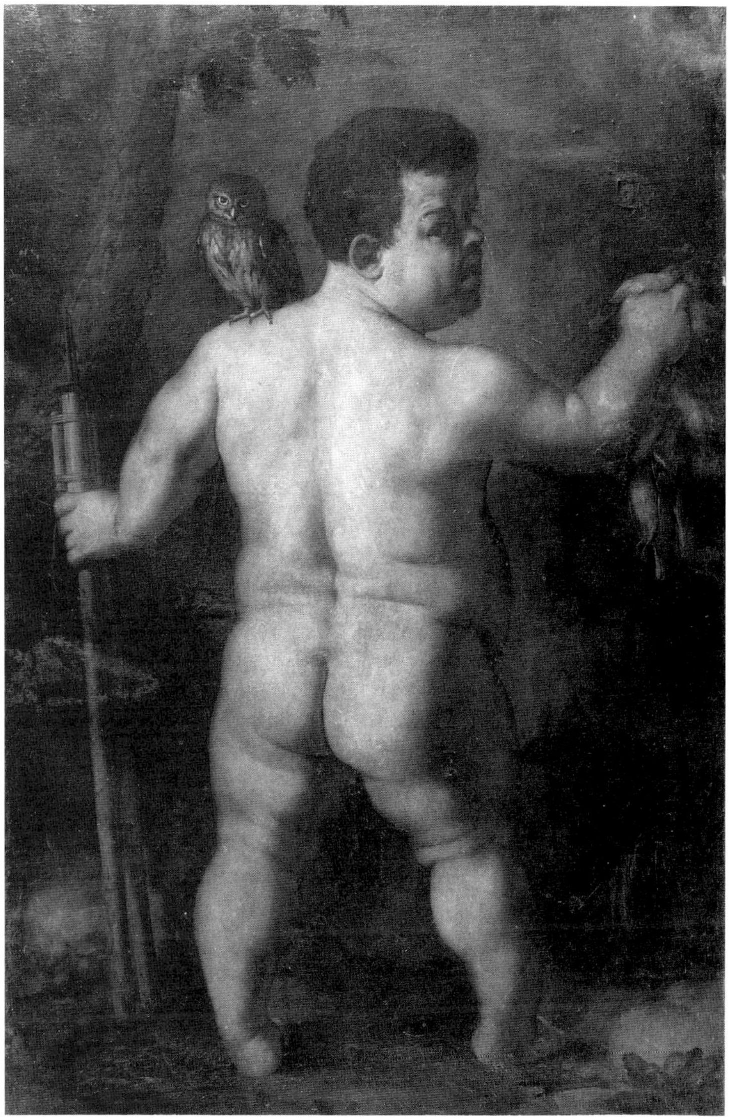

group and single portraits of them (plate 166).[34] When Gonsalvus's children passed through Basle in 1583, a doctor, Felix Plater, saw them and had them painted:[35] it is not clear whether he persuaded them to sit to a local painter, whether portraits were painted without sittings, or whether he was able to procure copies of portraits executed at the Bavarian court.

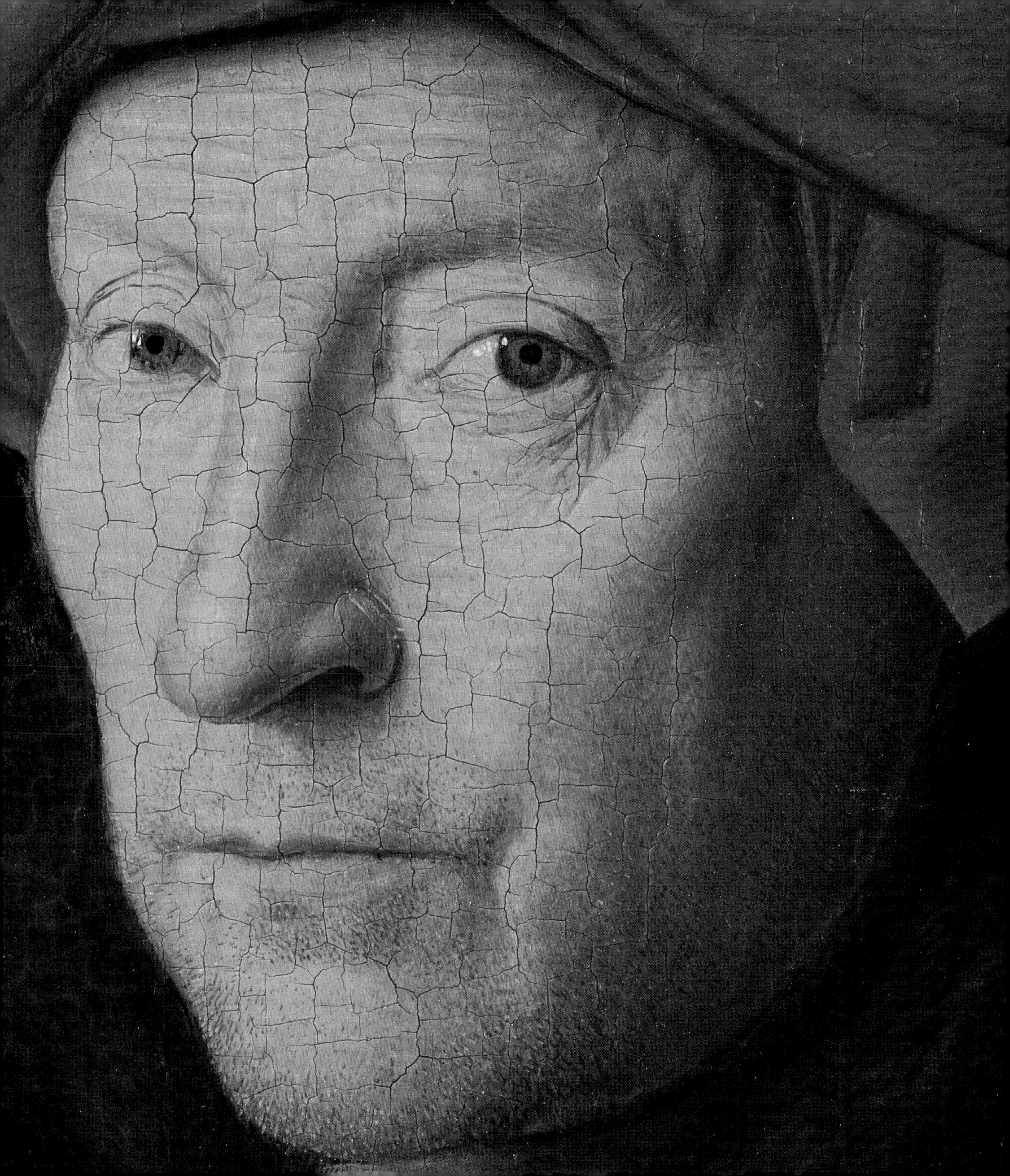

6 The Painters

Though most painters were expected, and prepared, to execute portraits, some specialised to a large extent in portraiture, and good portrait specialists seem to have been hard to find. Zanetto Bugatto, for example, from 1460 until his death, appears to have been the preferred portraitist of the Dukes of Milan and on 9 March 1476, Galeazzo Maria Sforza wrote to his representative in Venice: 'Master Zanetto our painter, who did portraits of singular perfection [*quale retraseva dal naturale in singulare perfectione*], has died; we wish to have another who will satisfy us with similar ability.' Having seen a portrait by Antonello da Messina, described in the letter as 'a Sicilian painter residing in Venice', and having been greatly impressed by it, Galeazzo Maria wanted him to come to the Milanese court.[1]

In a letter of 1493, Isabella d'Este complained of the difficulty in finding 'painters who can perfectly counterfeit the natural face'.[2] The Duchess of Guise, writing to her daughter in 1539, apologised for not sending a portrait of her daughter's son, 'but I cannot find a good painter to my taste'.[3] A papal nuncio, asked in 1573 to send portraits from France to Rome, wrote that 'it will be difficult to get totally natural ones, as in France they know so little of portraiture that one hardly ever sees here a portrait which has style . . .'.[4] In 1577, the Electress of Saxony wrote to the Duchess of Bavaria: 'Truly we lack in this country such good painters as are to be found abroad who can make really good likenesses.'[5]

Despite the nuncio's low opinion of French portraiture, in the later fifteenth century and throughout the sixteenth century, many Italians seem to have acknowledged that northern artists were good portraitists. In August 1460, Francesco Sforza, Duke of Milan, commissioned Zanetto Bugatto to paint a portrait of his daughter Ippolita;[6] in the following December, the duchess, recognising Zanetto's 'singular ability in the art of painting', sent him to Brussels to be instructed by Rogier van der Weyden.[7] Initial difficulties between Rogier and Zanetto were allayed when the Dauphin of France intervened to settle a quarrel,[8] and Zanetto had returned to Milan by May 1463, when the duchess wrote to Van der Weyden to thank him for having taught Zanetto.[9] Thereafter, he was employed at the Milanese court mainly to paint portraits,[10] and it seems likely that he had been sent to Brussels to learn about Netherlandish portraiture. It can be no coincidence that, when he died, Galeazzo Maria Sforza wished to replace him as portrait specialist with Antonello, who also knew a great deal about Netherlandish techniques and styles.[11] When in 1477 Galeazzo Maria's widow wanted a portrait of their four-year-old daughter Anna to send to Ferrara, it was commissioned from a 'French' painter, who made difficulties about completing it.[12] Apparently in the 1500s, 'a Fleming brought to Milan a head of a youth, painted in oils, which was much admired by all'. Giovanni Francesco Caroto wagered that he could do better, but lost the competition.[13] The Antwerp painter Louis van Oort settled during the 1550s in Florence, where he was known as Luigi Fiammingo and where he executed many portraits for the Medici family.[14] At Mantua Giannino Bahuet and later Frans Pourbus the Younger were employed as portraitists at the Gonzaga court.[15]

169 Jan van Eyck, *Man in a Red Turban*, detail (larger than actual size; see plate 22).

Paradoxically, in the Low Countries themselves, few painters seem to have specialised exclusively in portraiture and at the Netherlandish court the idea of employing specialist portraitists as salaried court painters appears to have arisen only in the sixteenth century. In the fifteenth century, varying numbers of painters were retained at the Burgundian court, but their principal occupation was to paint 'coats of arms, banners and standards'.[16] One of them was Jan van Eyck, who was, of course, an outstanding portrait-painter and whom Philip the Good sent to Portugal in 1428–9 to paint the Infanta Isabella, his future wife; but Van Eyck's position as court painter was exceptional.[17] Rogier van der Weyden, who painted many portraits of members of the ducal family and several of the great nobles and court officials, never held a salaried post at court.[18] The situation changed only under the rule of Margaret of Austria, who attached a larger number of painters to the court. Two of them – Van Orley, salaried from 1518, and Vermeyen, salaried from about 1525 – to some extent specialised in portraiture and continued to work for Margaret's successor Mary of Hungary; but they also produced for the court paintings that were not portraits.[19]

Certain painters were thought to be unsatisfactory portraitists, and some even refused to execute portraits. In 1475, the Marquis of Mantua wrote of his painter Mantegna: 'And it is true that Andrea is a good master in other things, but in portraits he could have more grace and does not do so well.'[20] In January 1493, Isabella d'Este announced that she had commissioned from Mantegna a portrait of herself, on panel; it would appear to have been the portrait that she criticised in the following April: 'the painter has portrayed us so badly that it is nothing like us: we have sent for a painter from outside Mantua who is reputed to be good at counterfeiting from life . . .'. The second painter was Giovanni Santi.[21] Michelangelo, it will be recalled, was said to have drawn only one portrait, 'for he abhorred drawing anything from life unless it was of the utmost beauty'.[22] Michelangelo's dislike of portraiture, and the reasons for his dislike, encouraged in his followers a distaste for portrait-painting for which they sought theoretical justification. Naïve enough to believe that artists should constantly strive to create ideally beautiful figures, they could look down upon the portraitists, compelled to take account of the physical imperfections of their sitters. A patronising attitude to portraiture as mere representation had come into being, and indeed still persists.

Vasari in his autobiography wrote: 'I will make no mention of the numerous portraits I have painted, as it would only be wearisome and, to tell the truth, I have avoided doing them whenever possible.'[23] He stated that Jacopino del Conte, 'being much inclined from his youth to making portraits, wished to make portraiture his principal profession . . . He designed so well as a boy that great expectations were entertained of him, if he studied, but he preferred to follow his natural bent.'[24] According to Vasari, Girolamo da Carpi 'was better at portraits and single things than at striking scenes demanding artistic power and design'.[25]

Strongly influenced by Vasari and other Italian theorists, the Fleming Carel van Mander concluded that portraiture was a 'bypath' of art:

> most [painters], lured by profit or simply in order to make a living, start and continue on that bypath of the arts (that is, portraiture from life) without having the time or desire to look and search for the road of historical or figure painting which leads to the highest perfection. Thus many a fine and noble mind has remained without fruit and quenched, to the great detriment of art.[26]

The fact that many theorists did not think portraiture quite intellectually respectable must have been irksome to the portrait specialists but it can have had little real impact upon them, for successful portrait-painters were treated with great respect in the highest society, where their paintings were eagerly sought after and discussed. Their social and financial success would have caused them to be envied and jealousy may have played a large part when their rival painters tried to belittle their talents and achievements.

The social, as opposed to the intellectual, respectability of portraiture is demonstrated by the fact that several princes became amateur portrait-painters. Elisabeth of Valois, Queen of Spain, was a proficient portraitist and her husband Philip II employed Sofonisba Anguissola to tutor her. In February 1560, immediately after her marriage, a French courtier reported from Toledo to her mother Catherine de' Medici:

> I found her passing her time sketching a portrait . . . It is incredible how, having learned a little from one of her Italian ladies whom the king has given to her, she has advanced in her painting . . . She has commanded me to ask you to send, at the first opportunity, well-made crayons of every colour which, she knows, François Clouet can prepare skilfully for her.[27]

In February 1561, an Italian observer reported: 'she has begun to paint, and Sofonisba of Cremona, who is her teacher, says . . . that she draws in charcoal in such a way that the person portrayed is immediately recognisable'.[28] In the following March, she sent to the Cardinal of Lorraine a portrait of a Spanish lady, and asked him, 'I don't know if you recognise her?'[29] In September 1561, one of her ladies wrote to her mother, 'She spends most of her time painting, in which she takes great pleasure, and I think that, before a year is out, she will be as good as her teacher, who is one of the best in the world.'[30] Louis XIII of France was very young when he began to draw and paint. In January 1609, when he was seven, he copied 'in oils the portrait of the king [his father, Henry IV] which was in front of him: the copy was quite recognisable'.[31] Such statements by obsequious courtiers need not be taken too literally.

In *Méliador*, as we have seen, Froissart imagined the knight Agamanor taking oil- and gum-based colours and painting on canvas a grisaille picture of his exploits at the tournament of Tarbonne and a representation of himself offering an amorous rondeau to his beloved Phénonée. These he presented to Phénonée, who placed them in her chamber, looked at them, touched them and said that they were well done. He felt obliged to explain to her that he had learned to paint when he was a boy, from artists working in his father's house, and that his parents had allowed him to spend three years studying painting. It was, he said, a noble art which had been practised by a son of one of the Byzantine emperors and by many knights.[32] Pontormo's portrait of Alessandro de' Medici, Duke of Florence, painted in 1534 for one of his mistresses, shows Alessandro drawing a lady's profile (see plate 170). In 1550, Catherine de' Medici, Queen of France, presented to an ambassador a portrait of her daughter Elisabeth, 'drawn to the life by a young lady named Elizabeth, who is in the queen's service'.[33] Pierre Mertens, Prior of the Charterhouse of Scheut near Brussels during the 1550s, painted a self-portrait which was still preserved by the Carthusians of Scheut in 1691.[34]

A successful professional portraitist had to be not only a good painter, skilled in getting likenesses, but also a man of tact and discretion. A great lord would hardly have been inclined to leave his wife or child in the company of an uncouth artist, and the painters to whom their sitters lent expensive clothes, armour or jewellery

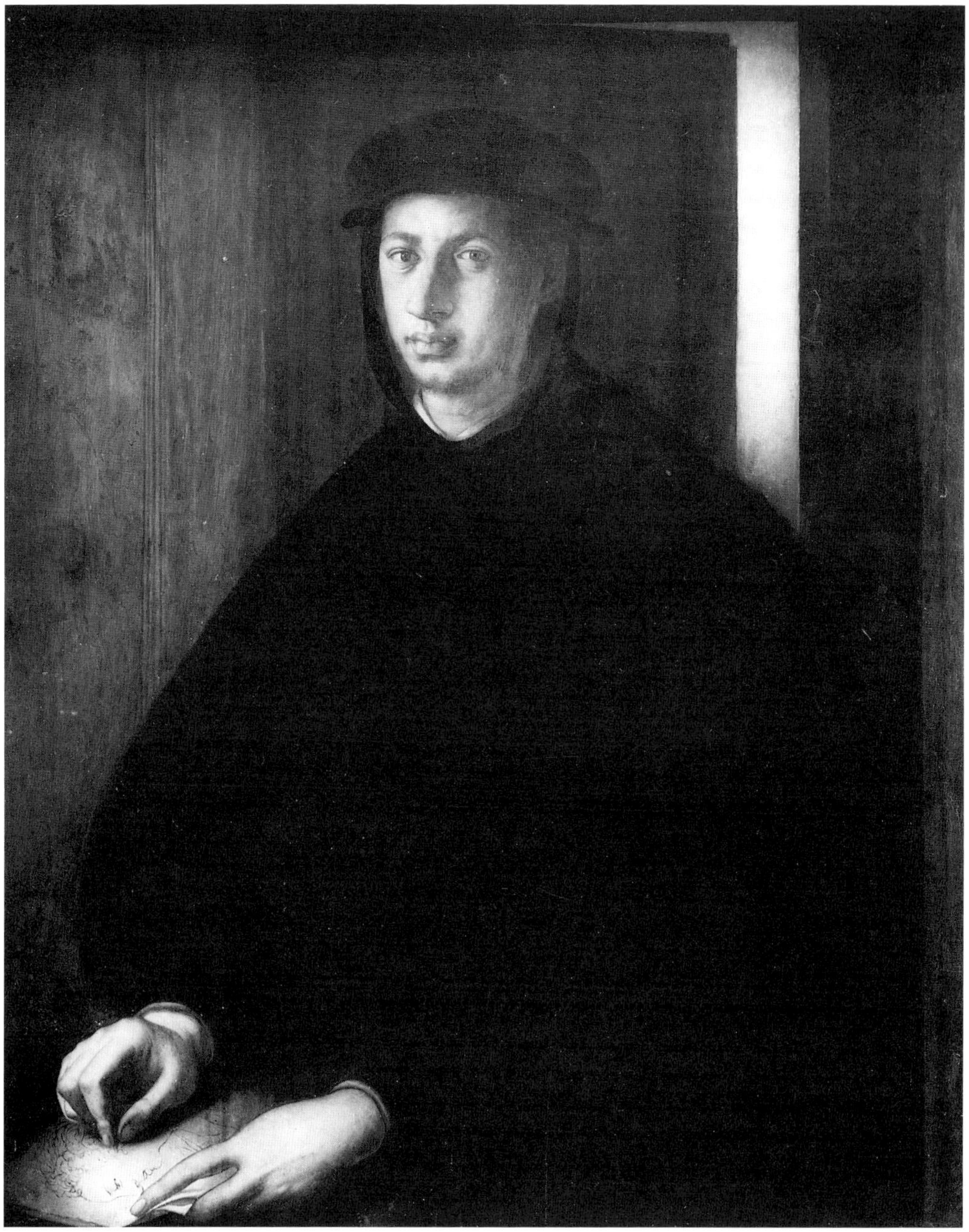

170 After Pontormo, *Alessandro de' Medici, Duke of Florence*, poplar panel, 101 × 82 cm., Museu Nacional de Arte Antiga, Lisbon (607).

Pontormo's damaged original is at Philadelphia (83) and was mentioned by Vasari, who stated that it showed the duke drawing the head of a woman and that he gave it to Taddea Malaspina. In the original, the duke's drawing is much abraded but in the Lisbon picture, an old and good copy, the profile of a lady, possibly Taddea herself, is clearly visible. Pontormo's portrait was painted when Alessandro was in mourning for Pope Clement VII, who died in September 1534 and who was probably his father. A recent technical examination of the Philadelphia picture shows that Pontormo flattered Alessandro, for in the underdrawing the face and neck are considerably fatter, and apparently more truthfully rendered, than in the finished painting.

See Strehlke, 1985, *passim*; here p. 151.

must have been considered totally trustworthy. Harmless eccentricities might be tolerated in able painters, especially those with established reputations. Cornelis Ketel, for example, would on occasion lay aside his brushes and paint portraits with his fingers or even his toes.[35] In 1602, it was reported that the Duke of Mantua's painter was late in delivering certain portraits: he was 'something of a humourist' who worked when he pleased, 'now pretending to be ill, now inventing some other impediment, but all is excused because of the excellence of his work'.[36] The portraitist Daniel Dumoustier, whose 'manner of living attracted more people than his work', was celebrated for being outspoken. On one occasion he received in his studio a papal legate and in his suite a young cleric who was afterwards to become Pope Innocent X. He attempted to steal a valuable book from Dumoustier who, seizing him by the shoulders, snatched back the book, called him 'burgomaster of Sodom' and threw him out.[37]

In 1469, Galeazzo Maria Sforza, Duke of Milan, wrote to Borso d'Este, Duke of Ferrara, about the painter Baldassare d'Este, who worked mainly as a portraitist. He recommended him as: 'a suitable and respectable kind of person and also because he is good at his craft, in which he has given us every satisfaction and for which he has received much commendation from us'.[38] It seems significant that his personal qualities were praised before his artistic skills were mentioned. Baldassare claimed to be Borso's brother, and Borso accepted him as such,[39] but the succeeding duke, Ercole, does not appear to have acknowledged any relationship. In 1493, Baldassare, whose daughter had been abducted by three noblemen of Reggio and who himself had been imprisoned, signed a petition addressed to Ercole: 'Your servant Baldassare d'Este, the slave of your slaves.'[40] His claims to noble birth had no doubt helped him to fame but, when they were denied, he accepted the inevitable, behaved with propriety and again demonstrated that he was 'a suitable kind of person'.

The most successful portrait-painters of the sixteenth century were noted for their abilities to please their patrons. Mor, for instance, was 'most courteous and beloved',[41] while Bronzino could compose letters that were masterpieces of courtly sycophancy and he contrived to avoid quarrelling with exceedingly difficult colleagues at the Medici court.[42] When Titian was painting Charles V at Augsburg in 1548, he had every opportunity to speak to the emperor. On his return to Venice, he reported that Charles was in good health, but thoughtful and melancholy beyond measure.[43] At Brussels in 1549, the portrait sculptor Leone Leoni claimed to be on similar terms of easy intimacy with Charles, who 'often spends two or three hours chatting to me and to my [son] Pompeo'.[44]

Charles would have addressed these artists in Italian, for he was a excellent linguist. His son, Philip II of Spain, was not, and would speak no language but Spanish, though he understood others.[45] Titian must have found it difficult to communicate with Philip and cannot have formed as easy a personal relationship when he was painting Philip's portraits as he had done when painting Charles's. Mor, however, must have spoken Spanish and, if Van Mander is to be believed, entered into too relaxed an intimacy with Philip.[46] Mor's international success would not, perhaps, have been possible if he had not been a proficient linguist: he presumably knew French, Spanish and Italian as well as his native Dutch and, in the inscriptions on his *Self-Portrait*, he proclaimed that he was conversant with Latin and Greek (plate 171). Mor's position was exceptional, for he spent some time in Italy and worked at the French-speaking court of Brussels as well as at the Portuguese, Spanish and English courts. No other portraitist of the time would have needed to develop to the same extent his skills as a linguist.

The successful portraitist had to have the tact and intelligence not only to manage difficult sitters but also to parry criticism from his sitters' obsequious friends and hangers-on, who would try to flatter the sitter by insulting his picture. When Galeazzo Maria Sforza was thinking of marrying Bonne of Savoy, he sent his painter Zanetto Bugatto to the French court where Bonne was then residing. Zanetto painted her portrait, which delighted the duke: in a letter of 1468, which Zanetto delivered to his mother, he wrote that Bonne 'appears to me to be not just beautiful, but most beautiful'.[47] He therefore arranged that they should be married by proxy in France. Bonne then travelled to Italy and on her arrival at Genoa was seen by a courtier, who wrote to Galeazzo Maria: 'Your lordship can

171 Antonis Mor, *Self-Portrait*, panel, 113 × 84 cm., Uffizi, Florence (1637).

On the ledge of the easel is the Latin inscription 'Antonis Mor, painter to Philip, King of Spain, painted by his own hand in the year 1558'. Fixed with a golden pin to the prepared panel that rests on the easel is a paper inscribed with a poem written in Greek by his friend the humanist Lampsonius. In it Mor is praised as the best of painters who has excelled Apelles and Zeuxis; it ends with the lines 'The false Mor who is here will presently speak'. Mor is comfortably seated on a red cushion and wears elegant dark grey and black clothes trimmed and lined with brown fur. In his left hand he holds his maulstick, three well-pointed brushes of different sizes, a small palette, which seems to be prepared for painting flesh and on which he has mixed some pink paint, and a cloth, apparently the rag on which he wipes his brushes.

See Berti, 1979, p. 939; here pp. 153, 155, 216.

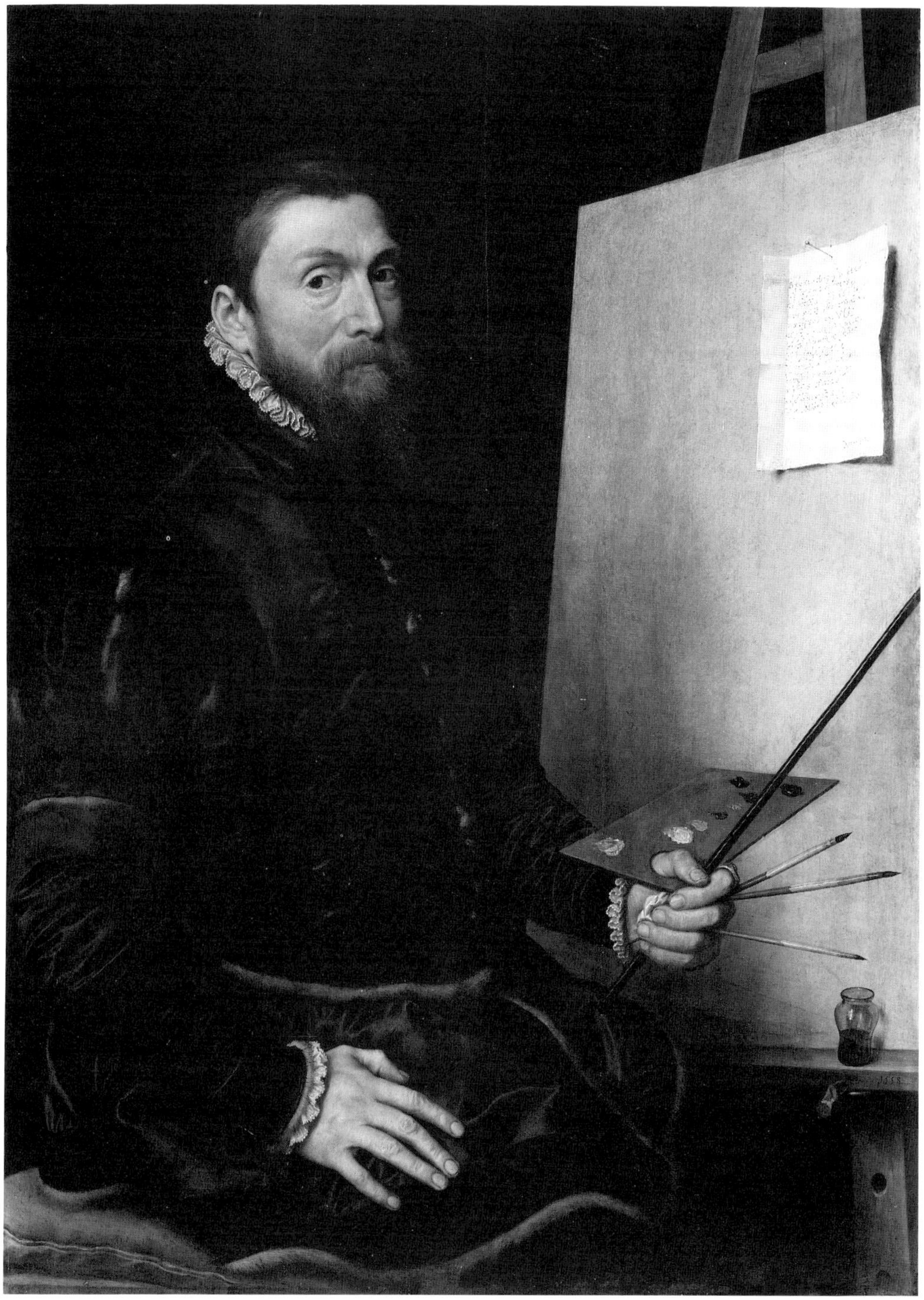

give away Master Zanetto's picture, for it does not match the living lady and makes her appear rather older than she is.'[48]

It was desirable that a portrait-painter should have an elegantly appointed establishment in which to receive his sitters and a comfortable studio in which they could feel at ease. The court painters were sometimes given accommodation in or near the royal palaces. Sánchez Coello, for example, lived in a large house adjoining the palace in Madrid and often both its large courtyards were filled with the horses, litters, carriages and chairs of his noble visitors.[49] Cranach's house in

Wittenberg was so grand that, when Christian II, the exiled King of Denmark, visited the town in 1523, he was lodged with Cranach.[50] Hilliard, thinking not only of the artist's convenience but also of his sitters' comfort, advised that the studio should be in a place 'wher neither dust, smoak, noisse, nor steanche may ofend' and stressed the importance of cleanliness.[51]

Not all portraits could be painted in the studio and many artists had to go to the sitters in their residences. Hans the painter, sent by Henry VI of England in the winter of 1442–3 to paint the three daughters of the Count of Armagnac, encountered problems. On 3 January 1443, it was reported:

> Hans has finished one of the three likenesses. From the severe coldness of the weather, which has prevented his colours from working, he could not finish it sooner, though he laboured with constant diligence. He is beginning to proceed with the other two, which . . . he will finish in a shorter time, especially if the cold weather should subside . . .[52]

On 15 August 1472, Galeazzo Maria Sforza wrote to Zanetto Bugatto, then in Milan: 'As soon as you receive this, you will go to Pavia and will take with you the things necessary for depicting persons from life and you will await our coming'.[53] In 1518, a Florentine agent in France was attempting to obtain a good portrait of Madeleine de la Tour, who was about to marry Lorenzo de' Medici, Duke of Urbino. She was then in the Auvergne, and the agent observed:

> When I went to the Auvergne, I would have liked to take with me one of the pupils of Leonardo da Vinci, who is here; but they ask for hundreds of ducats and I know that His Excellency the Duke has so many expenses in the matter of this marriage that I would not add to them; but someone will be found who will go for a more convenient sum . . . and when the lady is at court, it will be easy to have a good portrait . . .[54]

It would be interesting to know exactly what equipment travelling portraitists carried with them, but evidence on this question is lacking. Antonio de Holanda, who in 1528 or 1529 journeyed from Lisbon to Toledo to paint Charles V, used an adjustable table. As he had difficulty with the straps that altered its angle, the emperor had to help him by making new holes in them with his dagger.[55] It was presumably a borrowed table rather than one specially brought from Lisbon. Hilliard, who had to paint Elizabeth I of England in a garden, would have needed portable equipment.[56]

Hilliard advised the limner to dress in silk, 'such as sheadeth lest dust or haires'.[57] It was also important for the portraitist to appear, in his clothing as in his manners, as a gentleman. In 1502, Baldassare d'Este had to ask the Duke of Ferrara for money to buy clothes so that he could appear before him suitably dressed; he was 'ashamed to ask for this charity'.[58] The elegant, dark-grey silk clothes worn by Mor in his self-portrait of 1558 show how he dressed to demonstrate his respectability (plate 171).

Speed and efficiency were eminently desirable qualities in a portrait-painter. Pisanello was blamed for having taken six months to paint his portrait of Lionello d'Este, Marquis of Ferrara.[59] Even Cranach, renowned as the 'swiftest of painters',[60] delayed in delivering a portrait of one of the Duchesses of Saxony. On 2 August 1529, her husband, Henry the Pious, wrote to Cranach: 'About three years ago we ordered you to paint a portrait of our beloved wife . . . which we have not as yet seen or received. We desire therefore that you execute such a portrait – if it has not already been painted, for which you have received payment, and send it to us'.[61] An efficient portraitist worked to a demanding timetable. On 20 August 1606, Frans Pourbus the Younger wrote to his employer the Duke of Mantua that he had on the previous day begun a portrait of Marie de' Medici, Queen of France, 'to the greatest satisfaction of Her Majesty and to the applause of the other princesses, and this afternoon I must go to St Germain to paint the Dauphin's portrait and I believe that I will also paint the King's, all of which are to be sent to Your Highness'.[62] As the Dauphin's doctor recorded, on that day Pourbus made a full-length portrait of the four-year-old boy.[63]

Like most artists, many portrait-painters employed assistants. Pourbus, returning from Paris to Mantua, was overwhelmed with requests for versions of his portraits of the King and Queen of France. When he was driven to say that he had only one pair of hands, Ferdinando Gonzaga disagreed, 'for he has pupils whose hands are at his disposition along with his own'. Pourbus rejoined that he could hardly expect his pupils to make copies of his portraits before the originals had been finished.[64]

It was reported from Florence in April 1501 that two of Leonardo's assistants were doing portraits and that he occasionally put his hand to some of them.[65] Alessandro Allori recorded in 1582: 'I have retouched a head for the said Messer Raffaello [Torrigiani] of Messer Luchino his son in a picture which my pupil Alessandro Pieroni had done.'[66] These experienced assistants would have been journeymen; apprentices would presumably not have been entrusted with responsible tasks of such a kind.

The career of one of Mor's journeymen, Conrad Schot, was described in some detail in legal documents of 1553. Schot, who was then aged about twenty-six, had been taught to read and write and then to read and speak Latin; he had spent some time working as a clerk with a gentleman of Bergen-op-Zoom and then with his father in Brussels; after a four-year apprenticeship with an Italian painter established in Brussels, he entered Mor's service, in which he remained for almost eighteen months. Mor was at that time painter to Cardinal Granvelle and was living in his Brussels residence. Schot lodged there with Mor and worked under his direction. When the future Philip II of Spain was in Brussels, Schot went to his apartments; Philip spoke to him on several occasions and, when Mor was painting Philip's portrait, Philip entrusted into Schot's keeping his rings, chains, jewels and precious garments. Schot also visited the apartments of Eleonora of Austria, the widowed Queen of France, and of many other great ladies whose portraits Mor and his assistants were painting; he was daily admitted to the great houses of Brussels. When Mor was sent to Portugal in 1550, he wished to take Schot with him, but Schot's father did not want him to travel abroad and he therefore entered the workshop of Jan Maes, who had been one of Mor's principal assistants. Maes was born in about 1533, became a master of the Antwerp guild in 1550 and settled in Malines in or before 1553. In the service of Maes at Antwerp, Schot had been in contact with the great merchants and with the English ambassador, in whose residence they painted a portrait of Edward VI of England. There Schot had been left alone in a chamber where all the ambassador's jewels were kept.[67]

Mor evidently employed other assistants, as Jan Maes had been only one of his 'principal' assistants and Schot, although he had served his apprenticeship, did not rank as a 'principal' assistant. One of Mor's other 'principal' assistants may have been the young Sánchez Coello, who was born in 1531 or 1532, who was sent by the King of Portugal to study painting in the Netherlands and who spent 'some years' with Mor when he was residing with Cardinal Granvelle.[68] Mor clearly wished to take assistants with him to Portugal and, though he was unable to persuade Schot to accompany him and though Maes remained in the Low Countries, he very probably went with other trained assistants.[69]

When Mor finally settled in Antwerp, he employed on a daily basis Joachim Beuckelaer, who was already a master but who was an inefficient businessman and had to hire out his services to other master painters in order to make a living. Beuckelaer, who himself is not known to have executed portraits but who specialised in still life and genre scenes, worked as Mor's drapery-painter.[70] Sánchez Coello, in his early years at the Spanish court, worked from time to time as drapery-painter and copyist for Sofonisba Anguissola. In 1564, he was paid for a portrait of the queen, Elisabeth of Valois, in which Sofonisba had painted the head.[71] According to a bill of 1568, he had painted six copies of a portrait by Sofonisba of Don Carlos, Elisabeth's stepson.[72] Drapery-painters were also to be found in Florence, where in 1603, Valerio Marucelli sent in a bill for painting 'two dresses, from the middle upwards, and the hands, in the portraits of the princesses where the heads were done by S. Costantino de' Servi'. The princesses were Eleonora and Catherine, daughters of Ferdinando I, Grand Duke of Tuscany.[73]

Seisenegger and Vermeyen, like other successful portraitists, would have had assistants; unlike Mor, they do not seem to have been able to take them with them when they travelled over long distances. When Vermeyen was sent in 1530 from Malines to Augsburg to paint various members of the imperial family, he was allowed only one horse;[74] similarly, when in the 1530s Seisenegger was ordered to go from Prague to Brno, he was allowed funds to buy only one horse and one saddle.[75] This suggests that they travelled unaccompanied. Seisenegger, however, required assistance on several of the projects that he undertook when he was away from home, and entered the cost in his accounts. At the Diet of Augsburg in 1530, he was so busy that he had to employ other artists to prepare some of his panels – which he bought, already framed, from a carpenter – and to grind his colours. At Regensburg in 1532, he had to engage 'the two best masters to be found in Germany' to help him with two group portraits of the Habsburg children.[76]

Though any successful painter would have had to develop skills in selecting, training and managing assistants, portrait specialists would perhaps have had to master such skills to a higher degree. Some at least of their assistants would have been more likely than assistants to other painters to encounter and converse with their clients, while travelling portrait-painters must have been prepared to take on foreign assistants and train them at great speed.

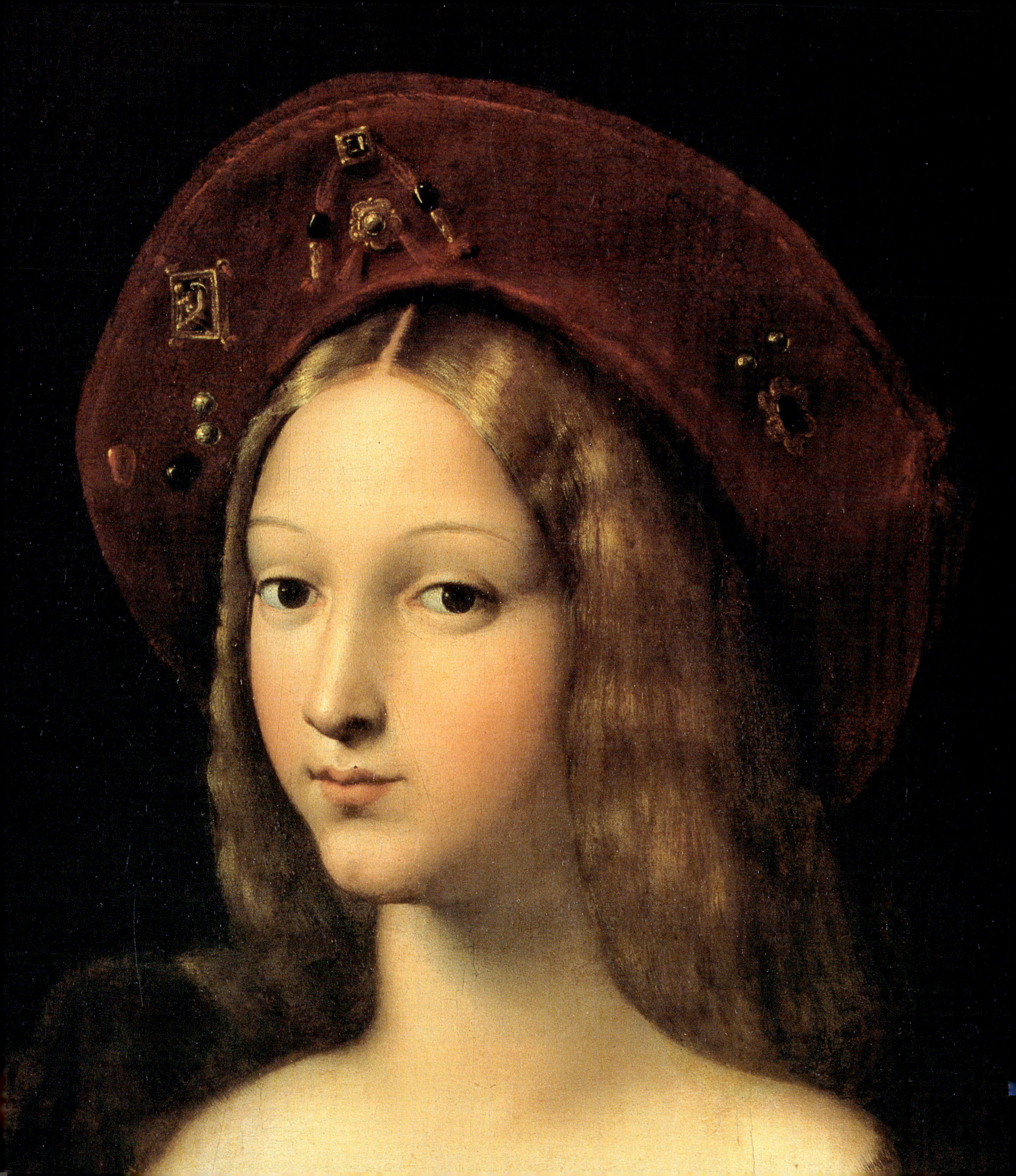

7 Portrait Method

By the second half of the fifteenth century, recognisable portraits even of animals were being produced. In 1469, Bonifacio Bembo prepared an estimate for paintings that were to be executed in the castle of Pavia, many of which were group portraits. He itemised the cost for each room to be decorated, but a separate charge of 500 ducats, out of a total of 7,880 ducats, was to be made 'for portraying to the life men, horses and dogs'.[1] That was presumably to cover Bembo's expenses in procuring the necessary likenesses. In an undated account sent to Galeazzo Maria Sforza, Duke of Milan, by Zanetto Bugatto, who died between 1474 and 1476, one of the items to be paid for was 'a portrait of the dog called Bareta'.[2] Bonsignori painted for the Marquis of Mantua a dog, bow and quiver which had been presented to him by the Ottoman Emperor and which were depicted with the Turk who had brought them. The dog's portrait was so convincing a likeness that one of the marquis's own dogs, the mortal enemy of the Turkish dog, was said to have attacked the painting.[3] Margaret of Austria owned in 1516 'a well-painted picture of a beautiful slave girl, on the cover of which are Charles Ourssin, comptroller to my lady, and his father and also my lady's dog which is called Bonté'.[4] The most celebrated surviving portraits of animals are perhaps the frescoes by Giulio Romano in the 'Sala grande dei cavalli' of the Palazzo del Te at Mantua: 'the walls bear representations of all the best horses of the marquis's breed and the dogs also, which are marked, like the horses, each with its name, all being designed by Giulio and executed in fresco by his pupils Benedetto Pagni and Rinaldo Mantovano, so well that they seem alive'.[5]

If portraits of animals were intended to be instantly recognisable, portraits of humans were evidently expected to be extremely accurate likenesses. When Henry VII of England was thinking of marrying the widowed Queen of Naples, he sent ambassadors in 1505 to Spain with an elaborate questionnaire on her physique. They were to 'marke the favor of hir visage whether she bee paynted or not . . . To marke whether there appere any here aboutes hir lippes or not' and to

> endevor theym to speke with the said yong quene fasting . . . and to approche as nere to hir mouthe as they honestly maye to thentent that they may fele the condicion of hir brethe whether it be swete or not . . . *Item*, The kyngs said servauntes shall also at their commyng to the parties of Spayne Diligently enquere for some conynge paynter havyng good experience in making and paynting of visages and portretures and suche a oon they shall take with theym to the place Wher the said quenes make their abode to thentent that the said paynter maye drawe a picture of the visage and semblance of the said yonge quene as like unto hir as it can or maye bee conveniently doonn. Whiche picture and Image they shall substancially note and marke in every pointe and circumstance soo that it agree in similitude and likenesse as nere as it may possible to the veray visage countenaunce and semblance of the said Quene. And in case they may perceyve that the paynter at the furst or seconde making therof hath not made the same perfaite to hir similitude and likenesse or that he hath omitted any feture or circumstance either in colours or other propor-

172 Raphael, *Joanna of Aragon*, detail (see plate 71).

cions of the said visage then they shall cause the same paynter or some other the most conyng paynter that they can gete soo oftentymes to renewe and reforme the same picture till it be made perfaite and agreable in every behalf with the veray Image and visage of the said Quene.[6]

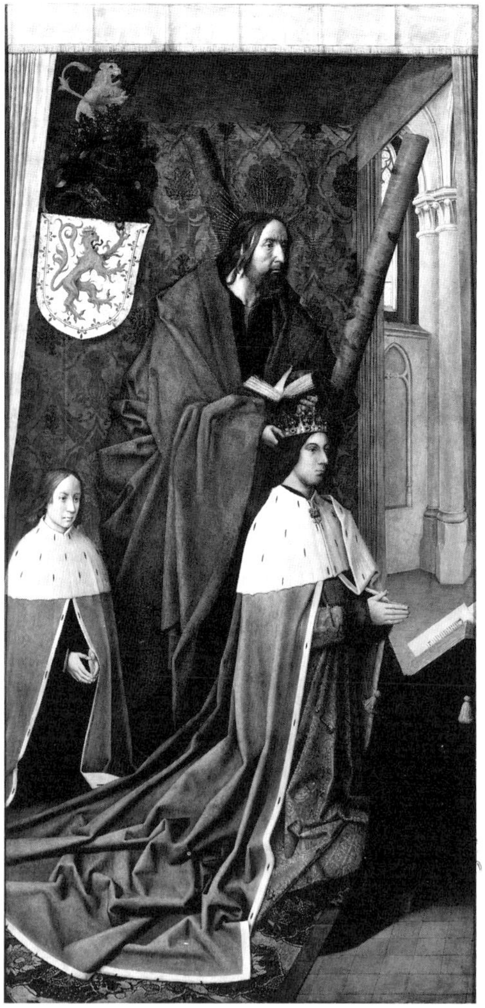

173 Hugo van der Goes, *James III, King of Scots, accompanied by his Son James, presented by St Andrew*, oak panel, painted surface 198.7 × 97.1 cm., National Gallery of Scotland, Edinburgh, lent by Her Majesty The Queen.

The painting is the obverse of the left wing of a triptych, of which the centre panel is lost. On the obverse of the right wing is James III's queen, Margaret of Denmark, presented by St George. On the reverses of the wings are representations of the Trinity and of Edward Bonkil, provost of the Collegiate Church of the Holy Trinity in Edinburgh, who evidently commissioned the triptych for his church. The panels are attributed to Van der Goes because of their close similarity to his 'Portinari Triptych' (see plates 32, 192) and were commissioned in or after 1473, when the prince was born, and probably before 1478, when the queen gave birth to a second son.

See Campbell, 1985, pp. 42–7 (30); here pp. 109, 160.

Baldassare d'Este was employed in 1470–1 to 'improve' thirty-six heads in the Palazzo Schifanoia at Ferrara: he was evidently correcting the likenesses in the portrait heads of the frescoes in the 'Hall of the Months', executed by Francesco del Cossa and others (plate 51).[7] During the 1470s, Hugo van der Goes had to paint James III of Scotland without seeing his sitter. His portrait was clearly considered unsatisfactory when it arrived in Edinburgh and was replaced with a head that, by comparison with a contemporary coin portrait, is demonstrably a likeness (plate 173).[8] The Emperor Charles V was not quite happy with the nose in one of Titian's posthumous portraits of the empress and intended to make the artist change it.[9] In 1571, Catherine de' Medici sent to Elizabeth I of England two drawings of her son Henry. One was of his head, which Catherine praised as very good and true to life,[10] and which Elizabeth liked 'though it is only a crayon and though his face is almost completely smeared over with charcoal'. The other was a full-length portrait, about which Catherine warned: 'the other will serve only for the body, where it is also truly like my said son; but here he [François Clouet] has not bothered to make the face perfectly, since the other was already done and I was in a hurry to send off this messenger'.[11]

The importance of accurate likenesses is stressed in a letter written in 1577 to the Duke of Nevers by one of his officials:

> there is scarcely anything that touches the hearts of simple people so much as portraits of their princes and lords, which are recognised by the living and which perpetuate their memory for posterity; if they see them well done, they honour and bless them, but, if they are not like or are done by some inferior painter, they renounce and disdain them.[12]

In order to ensure accuracy of reproduction, mechanical devices might be used. Pliny believed that the practice of painting had originated when someone traced an outline round a man's shadow and he recounted the story of a lady who had drawn a line round the shadow cast by her lover's face.[13] The shadow profile was a simple trick and may have been widely used to obtain or to check likenesses. Dürer described and illustrated the much more sophisticated device of the pane of glass and peep-hole, which must have had the disadvantage of producing rather a small image (plate 174). Dürer recommended this device to artists who were uncertain of their draughtsmanship;[14] it has been suggested, though it seems most unlikely, that Holbein used such a machine.[15] Devices of the kind, however, were used, and, for all their limitations, produced manifestly objective and accurate likenesses.

Cennino Cennini recommended that life masks might be taken. By using them, the painter might acquire a 'great reputation in drawing, for copying and imitating things from nature'.[16] Another check on accuracy was by measurement. In 1493, Beatrice d'Este, Duchess of Milan, wrote to her mother the Duchess of Ferrara:

> I have been hoping that the painter would bring me the portrait of Ercole [her son, then three months old] which my husband and I now send to you by this post. And, I can assure you, he is much bigger than this portrait makes him appear, for it is already more than a week since it was done. But I do not send

174 Albrecht Dürer, *An Artist drawing a seated Man*, woodcut, 12.9 × 14.8 cm., British Museum, London, Department of Prints and Drawings (1895–1–22–730).

One of the illustrations published in Dürer's *Vnderweysung der messung* (Nuremberg, 1525), the wooduct shows an artist viewing a model through a peep-hole and a framed sheet of glass, on which he traces with a brush the outlines of the model.

See the exhibition catalogue Nuremberg, 1971, pp. 352–4 (641); here p. 160.

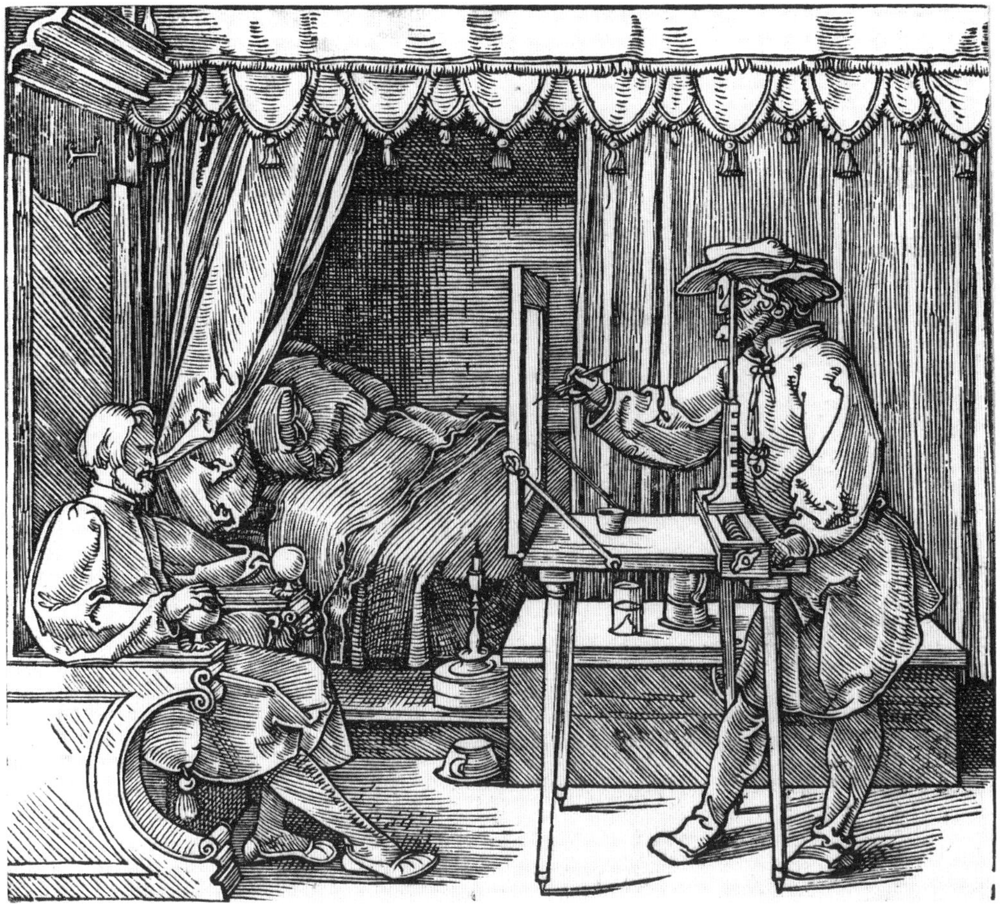

you the measure of his height, because people say that if I measure him he will never grow.[17]

Barthel Beham's portrait of the Archduke Maximilian, dated 1529, is inscribed:

When I was two years old
Then I had this height and form.[18]

In 1535, Van Orley was paid for a life-size portrait of the Duchess of Milan,[19] and life size evidently meant exactly life size. A Pontormo drawing of the head of Cosimo de' Medici, Grand Duke of Tuscany, is life size and the scale of marks and numbers up the left-hand side of the sheet seems to indicate that Pontormo took measurements from the sitter's head, with a rule or perhaps even with callipers (plate 175).[20] The sculptor Leone Leoni, summoned to Brussels, there executed a bust of the Emperor Charles V and in a letter of June 1549 boasted that it 'is so exactly measured that there is not a hair's difference [between bust and sitter] . . . it has not a line more or less than His Majesty's head . . .'.[21] Leoni disliked Brussels and, though he was to continue to make images of the imperial family, he finally received permission to return to Milan. On the way back, there was an accident: Leoni's servant fell off his horse and broke the staff on which Charles V's measurements were marked. Unable to repair the staff, Leoni wrote to Brussels for a new set of measurements. They were to be made from measurements that were kept in a foundry at Brussels and that had presumably been taken by armourers, who would have needed extremely elaborate and accurate ones. Leoni

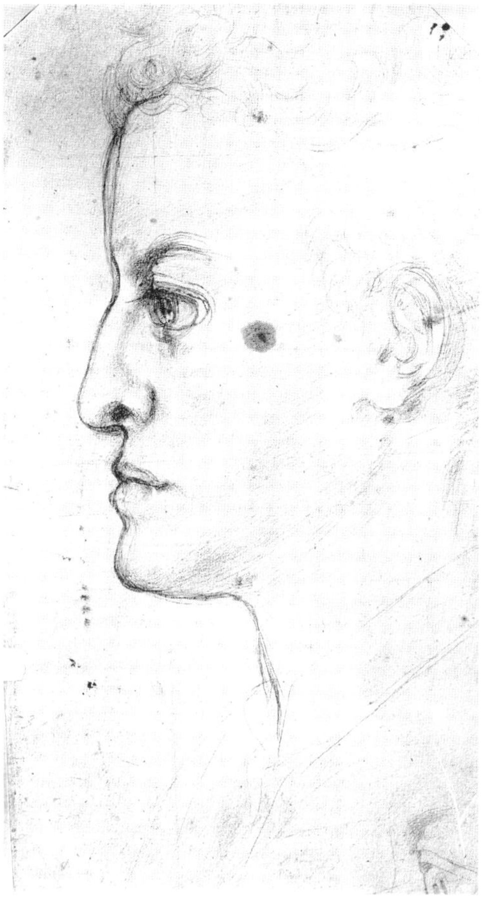

175 Pontormo, *Cosimo de' Medici, Grand Duke of Tuscany*, black chalk on paper, 42.1 × 21.5 cm., Uffizi, Florence, Gabinetto dei disegni (6528 F verso).

On the recto is a study for Pontormo's *Resurrection of the Dead* once in San Lorenzo in Florence. The grid of ruled lines and the numbers written at the left side of the sheet would appear to indicate that this life-size drawing is based on measurements taken from the sitter. The numerous changes, for example in the line of the forehead, the contours of the eye and the position of the ear, are a little surprising and suggest that Pontormo was not accustomed to making measured portrait drawings or that he was nervous of the sitter. Cosimo, easily recognised from other portraits, was born in 1519 and became Duke of Florence in 1537; the drawing is thought to date from that time.

See Langedijk, 1981–3, I, pp. 438–9; here p. 161.

asked that they should be copied onto another strip of wood and posted to him.[22] They arrived after a delay of three months and were apparently used for his *Charles V overcoming Fury* (plates 148–9); the emperor's figure was finally cast in bronze over a year later, in July 1551.[23]

In May 1560, Philip II of Spain, his wife Elisabeth of Valois and his sister Joanna dined together and afterwards looked at a portrait of Elisabeth's dead father, Henry II of France. Philip asked 'if it was well done and if it was life size'.[24] In 1578, the Venetian ambassador in France reported that Elisabeth's brother Francis, Duke of Anjou, 'has sent a portrait of his exact size and stature to the Queen of England, as she has sent him hers'.[25]

Despite the concern for exact likenesses, drawing and painting from life do not seem to have been concepts very familiar to some patrons or to compilers of accounts and inventories. This impression results partly from the carelessness of modern authors, who have often translated terms like *ad vivum, au vif* and *al naturale* as 'from life', whereas they clearly mean 'to the life' or life-like. In 1477, Mantegna wrote to the Marquis of Mantua: 'one cannot do someone well from life [*dal naturale*] if one has not the opportunity to see him'.[26] Dürer's engraving of Erasmus, dated 1526, is described in the inscription as 'the image of Erasmus . . . delineated according to his living appearance [*ad vivam effigiem deliniata*]': but Dürer had not seen Erasmus since 1520 and had based his engraving on a drawing made at Brussels in that year (plate 210).[27]

In 1462, Franceso Sforza, Duke of Milan, wrote to a correspondent in Viterbo:

> Having heard that there is in Viterbo . . . a portrait of our late most illustrious father [who had died in 1424] done from life [*tracta dal naturale*], we . . . charge you . . . to have it copied on panel or on paper in that same form and to the life [*al naturale*] . . . and to send it to us . . .[28]

In 1535, Van Orley was paid for a portrait of the late King Louis of Hungary, 'to the life [*au vif*]' and 'of the length which he was in his lifetime':[29] Louis had been killed nine years before. In 1530, Van Orley's colleague Vermeyen was sent to Augsburg to paint members of the imperial family 'as close to the life as he could manage [*au plus près du vif que possible luy seroit*]'.[30] Tintoretto was asked in 1579 to include in a painting of a historical subject 'portraits to the life [*ritratti al naturale*]' of the Emperor Sigismund, who had died in 1437, and of Gianfrancesco Gonzaga, the first Marquis of Mantua, who had died in 1444.[31] Van Orley, Vermeyen and Tintoretto were expected to paint portraits that were as exact as possible in terms of likeness; the posthumous portraits would have been taken from originals that were considered to be reliable.

The French painter Colin d'Amiens received in about 1481 a paper instructing him to prepare a painted design for the tomb of Louis XI (plate 176): 'you must make the representation of the king our lord: he is to be kneeling on a cushion, as below . . . with the most handsome face that you can do, young and full, the nose rather long and fairly high, as you know, and on no account make him bald'. Below the drawing is a series of notes: 'The nose aquiline, the hair longer at the back . . .'.[32] It seems that Colin d'Amiens was to execute his painting from memory and without recourse to the sitter – which, as he was to introduce gross flattery into his image of the fifty-eight-year-old king, was perhaps just as well.

Parmigianino painted his portrait of the Emperor Charles V at Bologna in the winter of 1529–30 (see plate 177). According to Vasari, Parmigianino sometimes went to watch Charles dining and then painted the portrait from memory. His

176 French, c. 1481, Instructions to the painter Colin d'Amiens, Bibliothèque Nationale, Paris, MS fr. 20493, f. 5.

On this sheet, preserved among papers of Jean Bourré, Treasurer of France, are instructions given to Colin d'Amiens when he was commissioned to design an effigy for the tomb of Louis XI (1423–83). The amateurish drawing is probably by an official of the Treasury and is certainly not by Colin, a celebrated painter in his time; below is a series of notes on how the image of Louis in his hunting clothes is to be altered and improved. Colin made a design or '*patron*'. Bourré finally engaged a goldsmith and a cannon-founder to make the bronze figure and by a contract signed at Amboise on 24 January 1482 they agreed to make the effigy 'as close to the life as will be possible' and 'according to the painted device and *patron*' which had been delivered to them and which they promised to return. The tomb, in the church of Notre Dame at Cléry near Tours, was destroyed during the sixteenth century.

See Laborde, 1850–5, I, pp. 59–61; here p. 162.

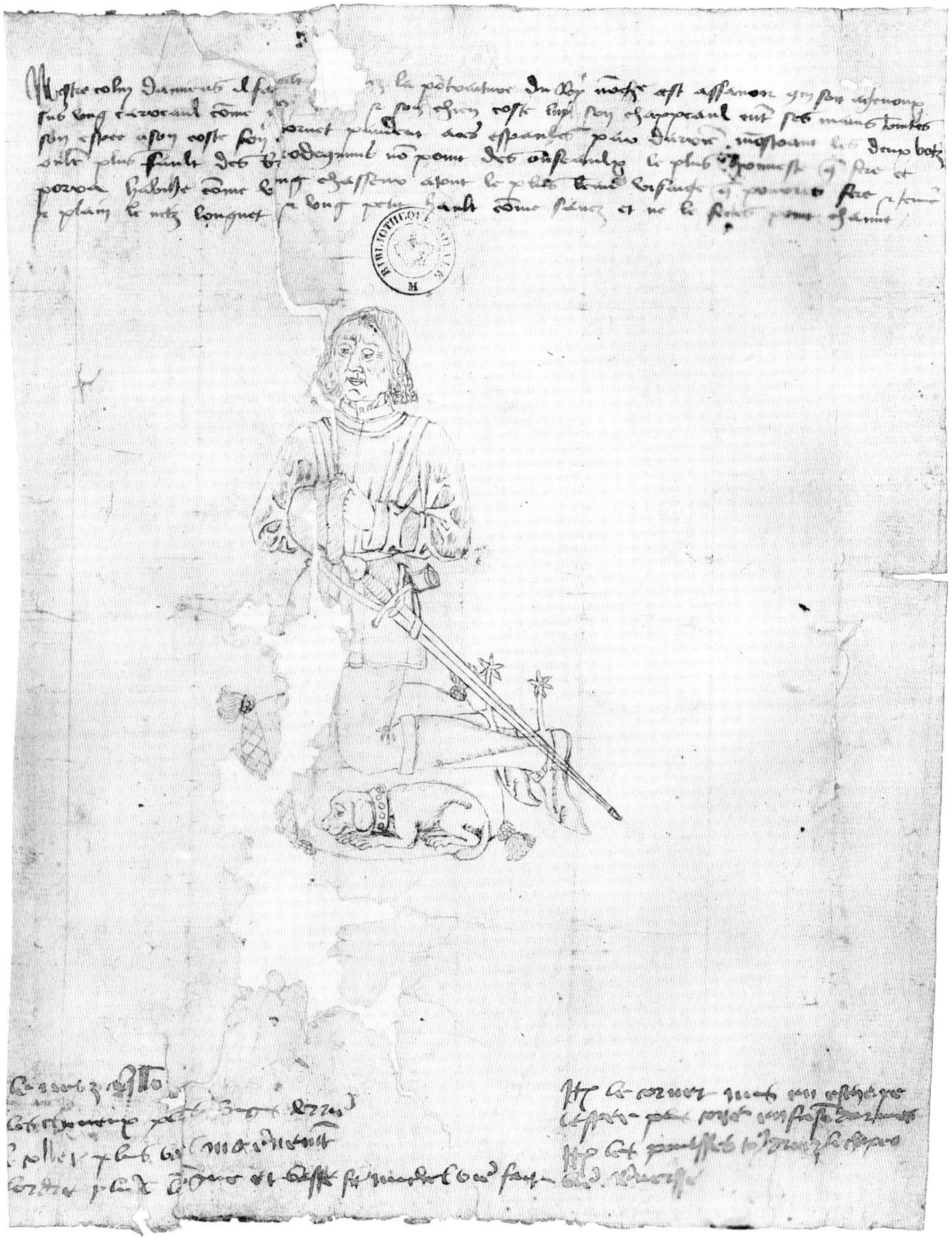

picture was shown to Charles, who liked it and wanted to have it; but Parmigianino unwisely protested that it was not quite finished, took it away and apparently received no reward, as he would no doubt have done had he given it to Charles.[33] Significantly, Charles did not offer to sit for him to help him to finish the painting.

In 1569, the authorities of the French royal mint decided that a new coinage should be struck bearing an up-to-date portrait of King Charles IX, then aged nineteen. The previous coinage had been struck at the time of his accession in 1560, when he was ten. A new design was made and approved by François Clouet, who said that it was very like the king;[34] but, when it was sent to Charles for his approval, he himself wrote from Angers:

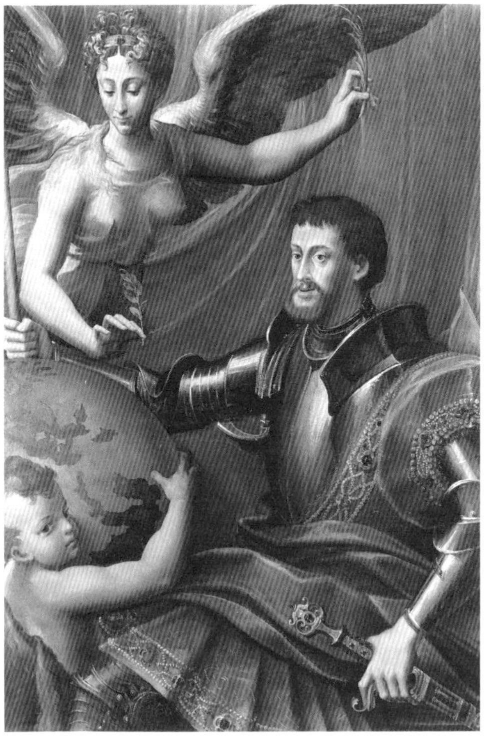

177 After (?) Parmigianino, *Allegorical Portrait of the Emperor Charles V*, canvas, 172.7 × 119.4 cm., Rosenberg & Stiebel, Inc., New York.

This is either the damaged original, or an old copy, of the portrait of Charles discussed at some length in Vasari's life of Parmigianino. Fame crowns the emperor while the infant Hercules offers him the world. Parmigianino's portrait was painted, without sittings, at Bologna in 1529–30. Two preliminary drawings for the composition are in the Morgan Library, New York (IV.43 recto and verso: Popham, 1971, I, p. 124; II, pl. 233).

See the exhibition catalogue Bologna, 1986, pp. 172–4 (62); here pp. 1, 137, 162–3, 185.

> the portrait in no way corresponds with our age, our face or our size and we imagine that the cause is that it is a long time since you have seen us; we wish you to defer making new dies for the coinage until we return to Paris, when it will be easier to make them properly and to represent our person in a more life-like way . . .[35]

He did not directly offer to sit for the coin portrait.

It is nevertheless clear that most people were willing to sit for portraits which they or their families commissioned, though information on sittings, their lengths and their frequency is extremely hard to find. In 1493, Giovanni Ambrogio Preda was at Innsbruck in the suite of Bianca Maria Sforza, who had married the Emperor Maximilian I. One afternoon, Catherine of Saxony, Duchess of Tyrol, said to Bianca Maria that she understood that she was having a portrait done of her by Giovanni Ambrogio to send to Milan. The duchess 'did not want it sent if it was not well rendered; and Giovanni Ambrogio was sent for and came to portray her and she had the patience to sit for perhaps two hours until her portrait was done . . .'.[36]

In 1517, Erasmus and Pieter Gillis commissioned their portraits from Quinten Metsys as a gift for their friend Sir Thomas More. On 30 May, Erasmus wrote to tell More that his portrait had been started but that there had been delays. Gillis had been ill, and then Erasmus, though perfectly well, had foolishly followed his doctor's advice and taken some purgative pills. The result had been that Metsys had complained that his appearance had altered, and work on his portrait had been suspended. He nevertheless hoped that the portraits would be ready within a month. Possibly because Gillis took a long time to recover from his illness, there were further delays and the portraits were not sent off to More until 8 September (plates 178–9).[37] At Antwerp on 2 July 1521, Christian II of Denmark sent for Dürer and asked him to take his portrait in charcoal. Dürer also drew one of the king's servants and dined with Christian. The next day, at Christian's command, Dürer travelled with him to Brussels, as he now wanted a painted portrait. Soon after their arrival in Brussels, Dürer bought a panel and paint; by the time he left Brussels on 12 July, he had finished and framed the portrait, presumably after he had had further sittings.[38]

On 8 June 1532, Sebastiano del Piombo wrote to Michelangelo: 'I think that tomorrow I will leave Rome for Fondi to paint a lady's portrait and I believe that I will stay for a fortnight.'[39] The lady was Giulia Gonzaga. According to Vasari, Sebastiano completed the portrait in a month; he was certainly back in Rome by 15 July.[40] In October 1535, the Bishop of Ermland reported that the Prussian court painter had been with him for three days and had painted his portrait, which he had taken away with him, though he had promised to send the bishop a copy.[41] Holbein was sent to Brussels in 1538 to paint the Duchess of Milan. He saw her only once, for one sitting of three hours, after which he immediately set out on his return journey to London. It is not known whether, during the sitting, he made a drawing or a coloured sketch, but it is altogether improbable that he began work on the panel of the finished portrait while he was in Brussels (plate 1).[42] Titian painted one of his portraits of Aretino in 'three days',[43] though presumably not on three consecutive days, for he could not very well have worked over paint that was still wet. In the case of Mor's portrait of Hubert Goltzius (plate 181), which was painted in gratitude because Goltzius had given Mor a copy of one of his books, we have Van Mander's presumably accurate account of its execution. Mor

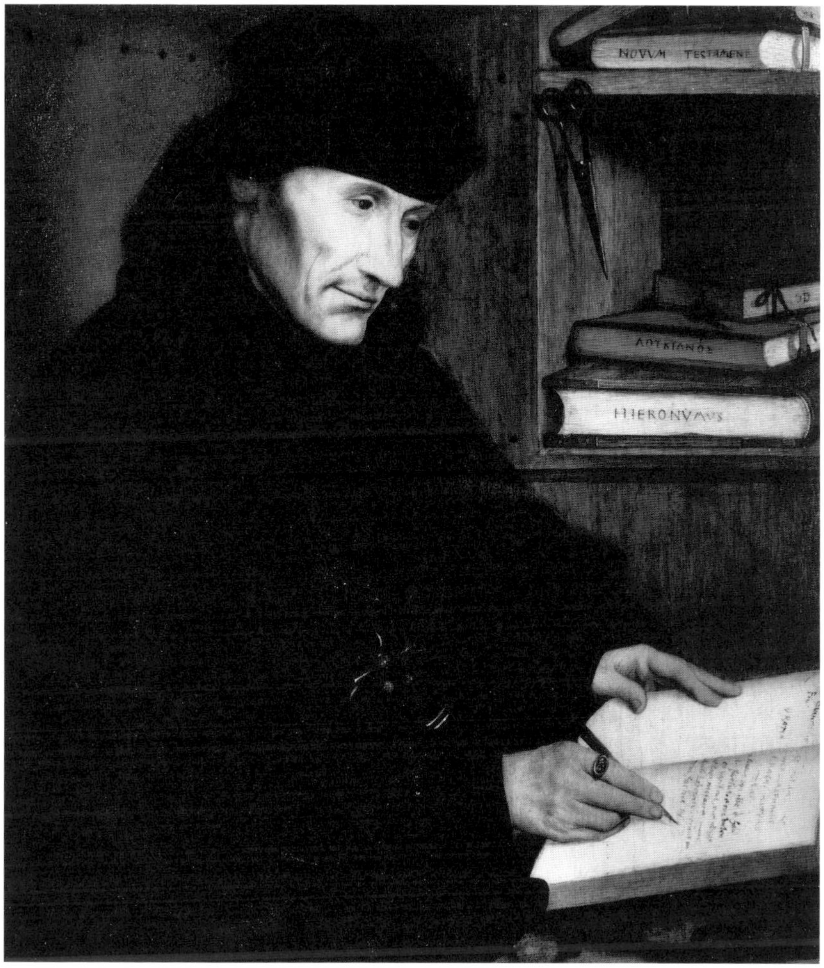

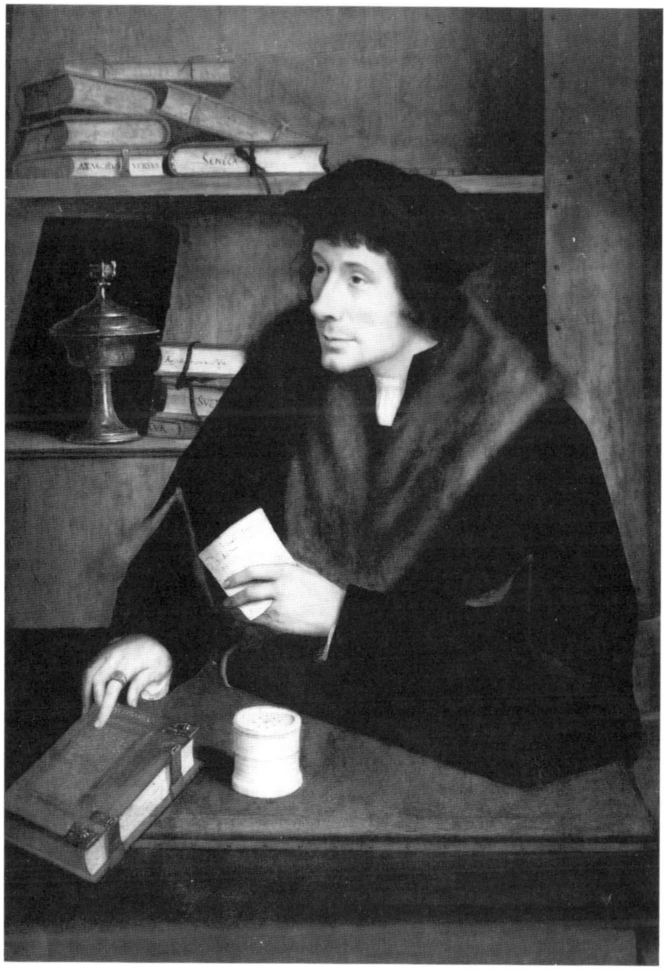

178 Quinten Metsys, *Erasmus*, oak panel, 50.4 × 45 cm., Royal Collection, Hampton Court (331).

The pair to the portrait reproduced as plate 179.

179 Quinten Metsys, *Pieter Gillis*, panel, 74.6 × 53.4 cm., Private Collection, United Kingdom.

The pair to the portrait reproduced as plate 178. The painting has been enlarged on all four sides; the original section is an oak panel that measures 50.6 × 44 cm. Early in 1517, Erasmus and Gillis, the learned town clerk of Antwerp, commissioned their portraits from Metsys as gifts for Sir Thomas More. On 30 May 1517, Erasmus wrote to More to tell him that his own portrait had been begun and that he hoped that both pictures would be completed within a month. Gillis, however, had been ill and Erasmus himself had taken some pills which had so altered his appearance that work on his portrait had had to be interrupted. It was probably completed when he left Antwerp and on or about 1 August he wrote from Louvain to Gillis in Antwerp asking him to 'urge Quinten to finish'. On 8 September Erasmus wrote to inform More that he was sending the portraits 'so that, if fate should carry both of us off, we can in some form at least be with you. Pieter and I have halved the painter's bill, not because either of us would not have been happy to pay the lot, but so that we could make you a joint gift'. At Calais on 7 October More wrote to both sitters to thank them for their present. In his letter to Gillis, he expressed his admiration for Metsys's skill in imitating his handwriting on the letter addressed to Gillis which he held in his left hand and asked for the original letter to be returned to him. 'Put up beside the picture, it will make it seem more wonderful than ever'. The portrait of Erasmus shows him writing the opening passage of his *Paraphrase of St Paul's Epistle to the Romans* and is deliberately reminiscent of images of St Jerome in his study.

See Campbell, 1985, pp. 86–9 (54); here pp. 74, 97, 103, 127, 164, 210–11.

180 Juan Pantoja de la Cruz, *The Infanta Maria in her Coffin*, canvas, 95 × 100 cm., Monasterio de las Descalzas Reales, Madrid.

Maria, second daughter of Philip III of Spain, was born on 1 February 1603 and died on 1 March 1603. On 9 March 1603 and on the following 12 May, Pantoja delivered to her mother three portraits of the baby lying in a coffin of crimson velvet, trimmed with gold, and dressed in the habit of the Order of the Immaculate Conception, with a garland on her head and a cross in her hands. One portrait was sent to Germany, the second, to Flanders; the third remained in the palace. On 1 and 23 September 1603, Pantoja delivered another two versions of the picture and on 7 April 1607, he delivered a sixth version to the queen. The painting reproduced is presumably one of the six documented portraits.

See Kusche, 1964, pp. 162–3, 237, 241; here pp. 55, 166.

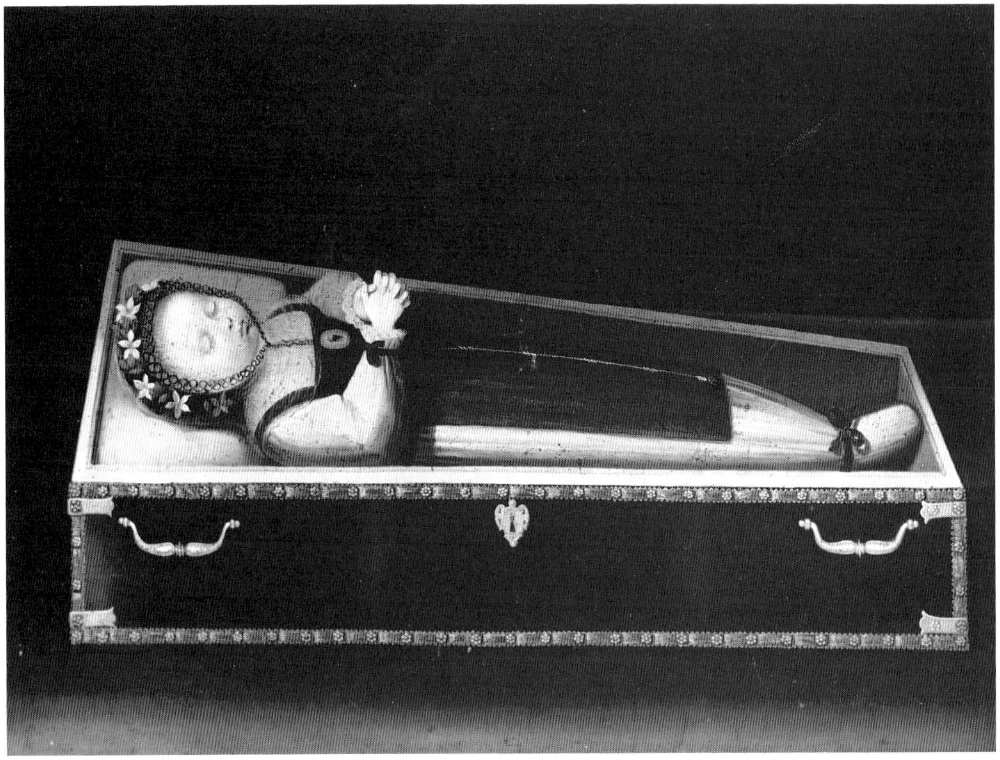

181 (facing page) Antonis Mor, *Hubert Goltzius*, panel, 66 × 50 cm., Musées Royaux des Beaux-Arts de Belgique, Brussels (1253).

The Latin inscription, which is a later addition, identifies sitter and artist. Hubert Goltzius (1526–83) was a painter and numismatist. According to Van Mander, the portrait, painted in an hour or less, was given by Mor to the sitter out of gratitude because Goltzius had presented to him a copy of his book on Roman coins, *Caesar Augustus*, printed in January 1574. Mor's copy, with Goltzius's dedication to him and his signature, is preserved with the portrait in the Musées Royaux. Goltzius mentioned Mor's portrait in a letter dated 21 February 1574 and an engraving of it, accompanied by six poems by different authors, appeared in Goltzius's *Sicilia et Magna Graecia*, printed in 1576. The face in Mor's picture, painted with consummate skill, is boldly and rapidly executed and could well be the work of an hour.

See Monballieu, 1984, pp. 210–11; here pp. 61, 164–6, 246.

invited Goltzius to breakfast, entertained and conversed with him, but did not start the picture. The next day, the same thing happened. On the third day, after breakfast, Mor took up his brushes and completed the portrait within an hour.[44]

In 1573, the papal nuncio Antonio Maria Salviati wrote from France that the poor results obtained by French portrait-painters were not altogether unexpected, since 'the French princes, when they want portraits, given them so little time that they cannot possibly do anything good'.[45] Christina of Lorraine, Grand Duchess of Tuscany, after her arrival in Florence in 1589, refused to sit unless to a Frenchman; but she was delighted to discover the speed at which at least one Florentine portraitist could work. Santi di Tito told a courtier 'that he would make the Grand Duchess happy and would make her laugh. And he took her portrait in half an hour and her Most Serene Highness was astonished that he had done such a portrait so quickly and well, because the French painters used to detain her for three or four hours of inconvenience.'[46] The Spanish court painter Juan Pantoja could also work at speed. Philip III's daughter Maria died on 1 March 1603 and by 9 March, Pantoja had supplied one and perhaps two portraits of the child in her coffin (plate 180).[47] Pantoja normally worked more slowly. In February 1607, he was paid for a picture of the queen, and the royal accounts record that he had gone to the Escorial for a month to paint this portrait. But he had also been working there on three full lengths of the royal children.[48]

Sitting for an English painter or miniaturist must have been uncommonly tedious. Norgate, writing in the 1620s, advised the limner 'to observe the Manner of the Oyle paynters in theire ordinary Pictures', and suggested three sittings: the first of two to four hours; the second of four to six hours, after which, not surprisingly, the subject might be 'weary with Sitting (as comonly they are)'. The third sitting should be of two to three hours. At the first sitting, the artist was

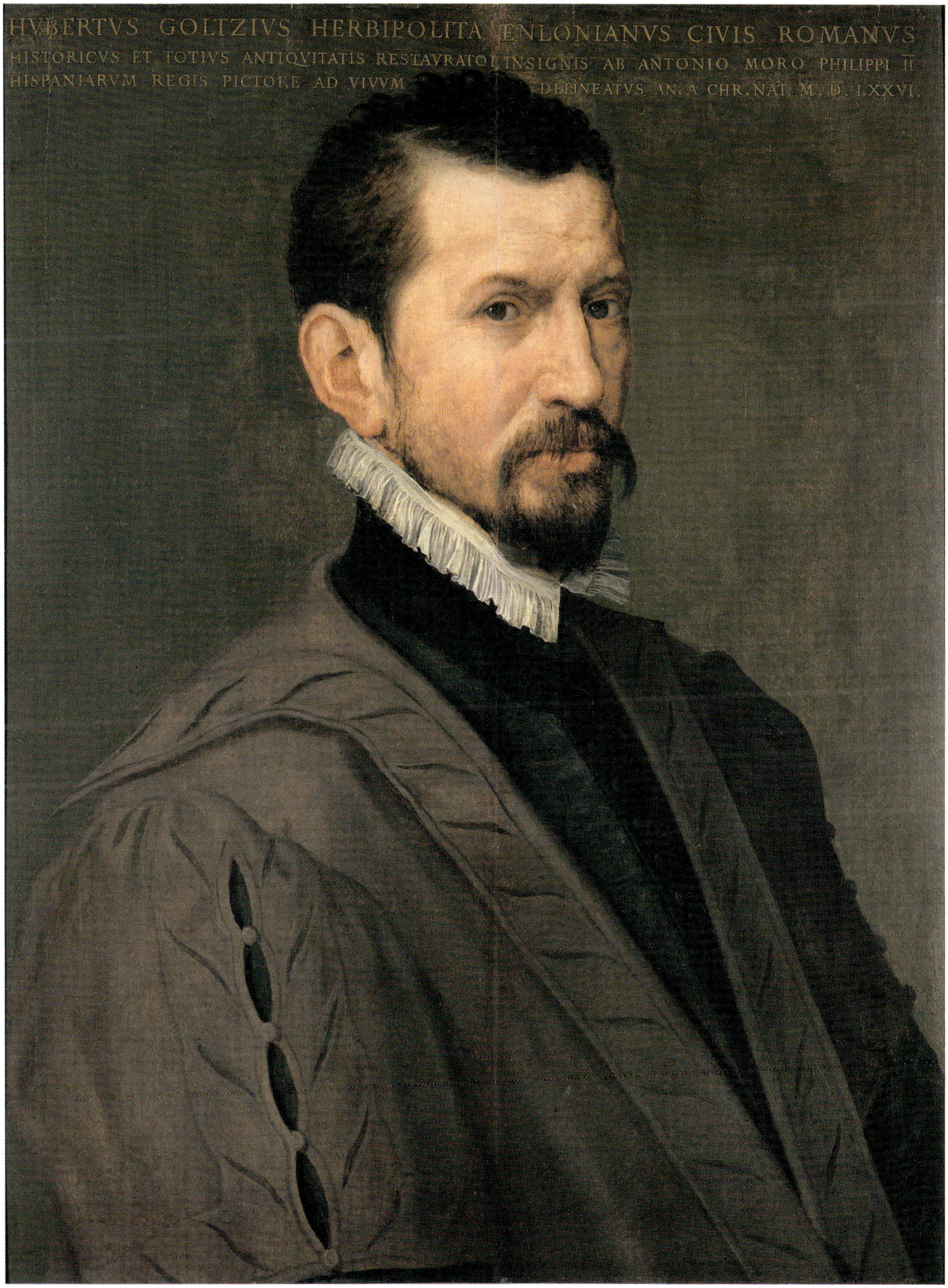
HVBERTVS GOLTZIVS HERBIPOLITA ENLONIANVS CIVIS ROMANVS
HISTORICVS ET TOTIVS ANTIQVITATIS RESTAVRATOR INSIGNIS AB ANTONIO MORO PHILIPPI II
HISPANIARVM REGIS PICTORE AD VIVVM
DELINEATVS AN. A CHR. NAT. M. D. LXXVI.

182 Follower of Dirk Bouts, *St Luke drawing the Virgin*, panel transferred to canvas, 109.2 × 86.4 cm., Collection of Lady Janet Douglas-Pennant, Penrhyn Castle, Bangor.

First traceable in 1818, when it was in a private collection at Louvain, the picture may have been painted towards 1470 or 1480. It is particularly interesting because of the depiction on the right of the painter-saint's workshop, where his painting materials are carefully arranged.

See Friedländer, 1967–76, III, p. 71 (84); here pp. 65, 169.

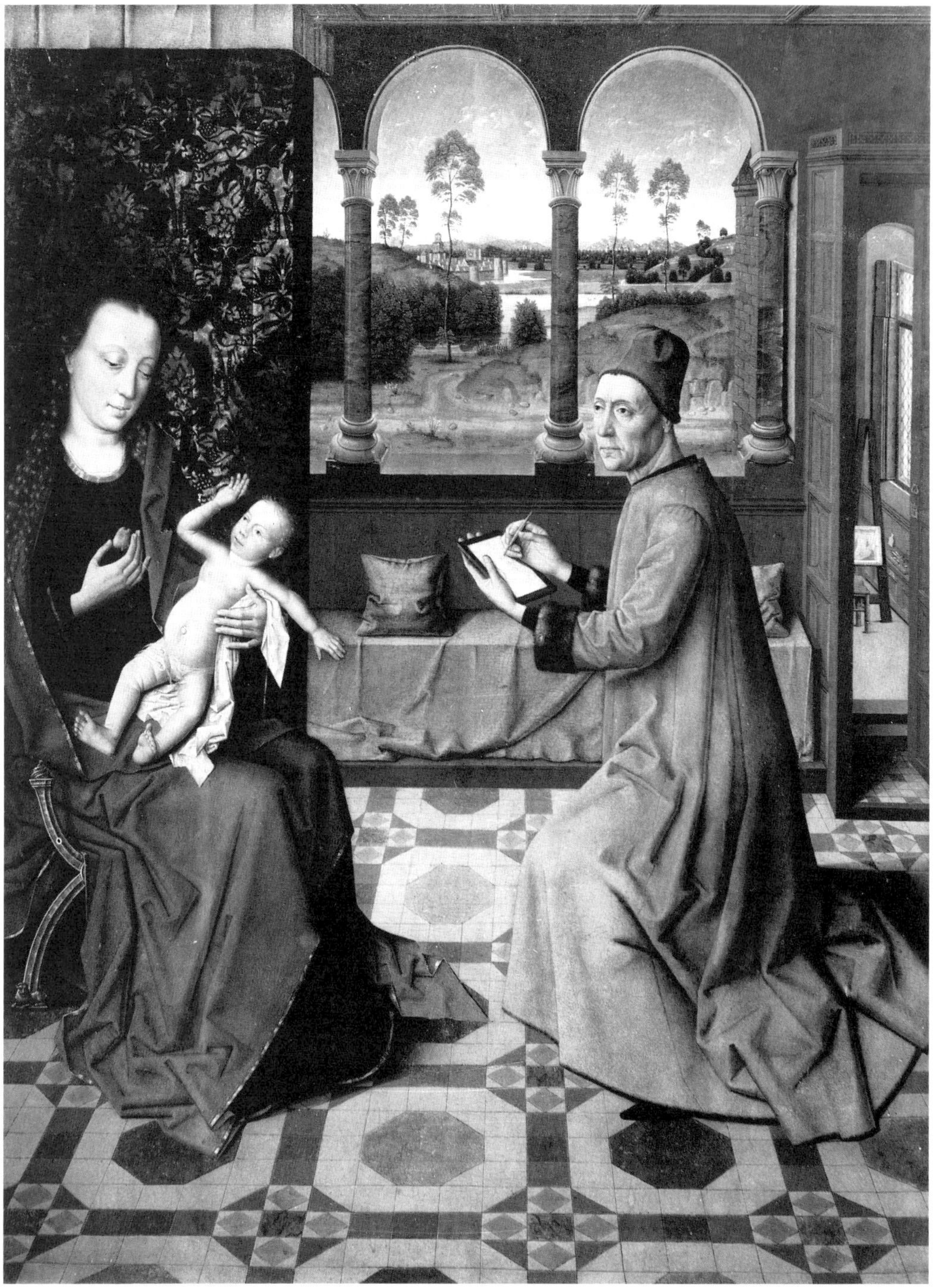

to 'deade Colour the fface' with red lake and white; at the second, he was to 'goe ouer the fface very curiously' and lay in the background and costume; at the third, he was to add finishing details, such as 'Scarrs, Moles, Sunleavings', catch the expression and intensify the shadows in the flesh.[49]

It is often assumed that painters usually began work on a painted portrait by making a detailed drawing of the sitter. The painted portrait might then be executed from the drawing, without troubling the subject for many, or if necessary any, more sittings. This theory is to some extent borne out by various representations of *St Luke drawing the Virgin*, for example the picture from the circle of Dirk Bouts, where St Luke's unfinished painting of the Virgin is seen on his easel in the background (plate 182). The head has been left blank, and will apparently be completed from the metalpoint drawing that the saint is making. There is of course no guarantee that artists showed St Luke using the same methods as they

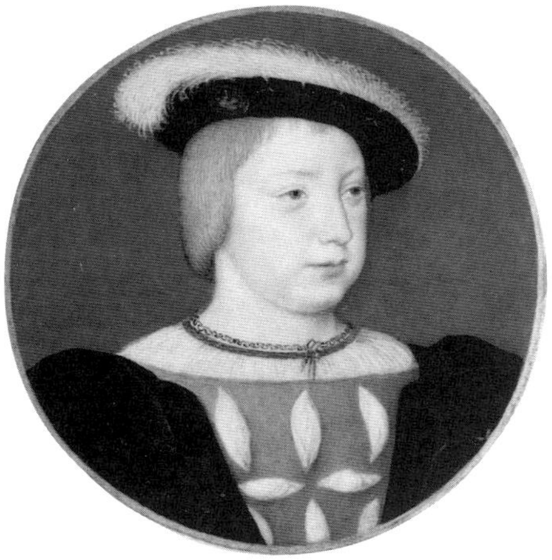

183 Jean Clouet, *Francis, Dauphin of France*, parchment, diameter 6 cm., Royal Collection, Windsor Castle (Vitrine I, 49).

Based on the drawing reproduced as plate 184 and related to the painting at Antwerp (33), the miniature, like the painting, shows the child grandly dressed whereas in the drawing he wears less expensive and less elaborate clothes. Evidently, he sat to Clouet in his everyday attire; Clouet then used the drawing as a basis for painted images, which he may well have reproduced without further sittings and in which he arrayed his sitter in rich and fashionable garments. The clothes in the miniature and the painting do not correspond: it is possible that the drawing was reproduced over a period of many months during which fashions changed.

See the exhibition catalogue London, 1988–9, p. 85 (74); here pp. 64, 175.

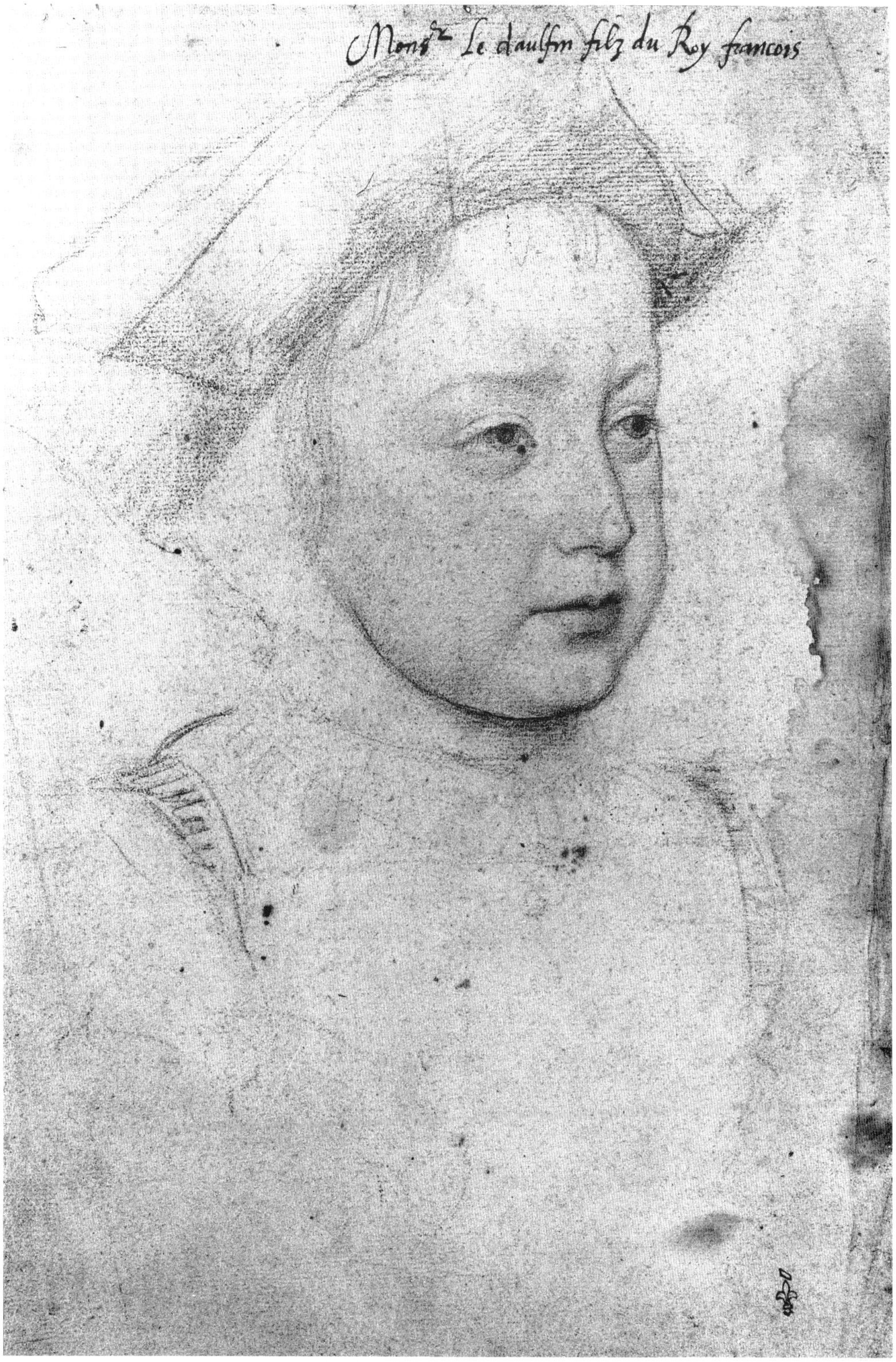

184 Jean Clouet, *Francis, Dauphin of France*, black and red chalks on paper, 26.4 × 17.7 cm. Musée Condé, Chantilly (MN 5).

The inscription identifies the sitter as Francis (1517–36), eldest son of Francis I of France. He died before his father. As he appears to be about five years old, the drawing is dated around 1523. On stylistic grounds it is attributed to Jean Clouet, one of the principal painters to Francis I; a painting at Antwerp (33) and a miniature at Windsor (plate 183) are based upon it.

See Mellen, 1971, p. 217; here p. 175.

185 (right) Jan van Eyck, *Cardinal Albergati*, silverpoint on whitish prepared paper, 21.4 × 18.8 cm., Staatliche Kunstsammlungen, Dresden, Kupferstichkabinett (C 775).

The inscriptions, so minute as to be barely legible, are the artist's colour notes; the stains along the left edge are paint. When making his drawing, Van Eyck must have placed his sitter and himself in a very strong light, which has caused the pupils of his sitter's eyes to contract and which would have been necessary for the artist to see his drawing and his notes. The face is of quite exceptional delicacy: it should be remembered that the head is only about 4 inches high and that, in photographs and reproductions of silverpoint drawings, the tonal contrasts are inevitably heightened so that the lines are coarsened. The sheet is clearly the preparatory study from which the painted portrait reproduced as plate 186 was taken.

See Dhanens, 1980, pp. 282–91; here pp. 65, 174–5.

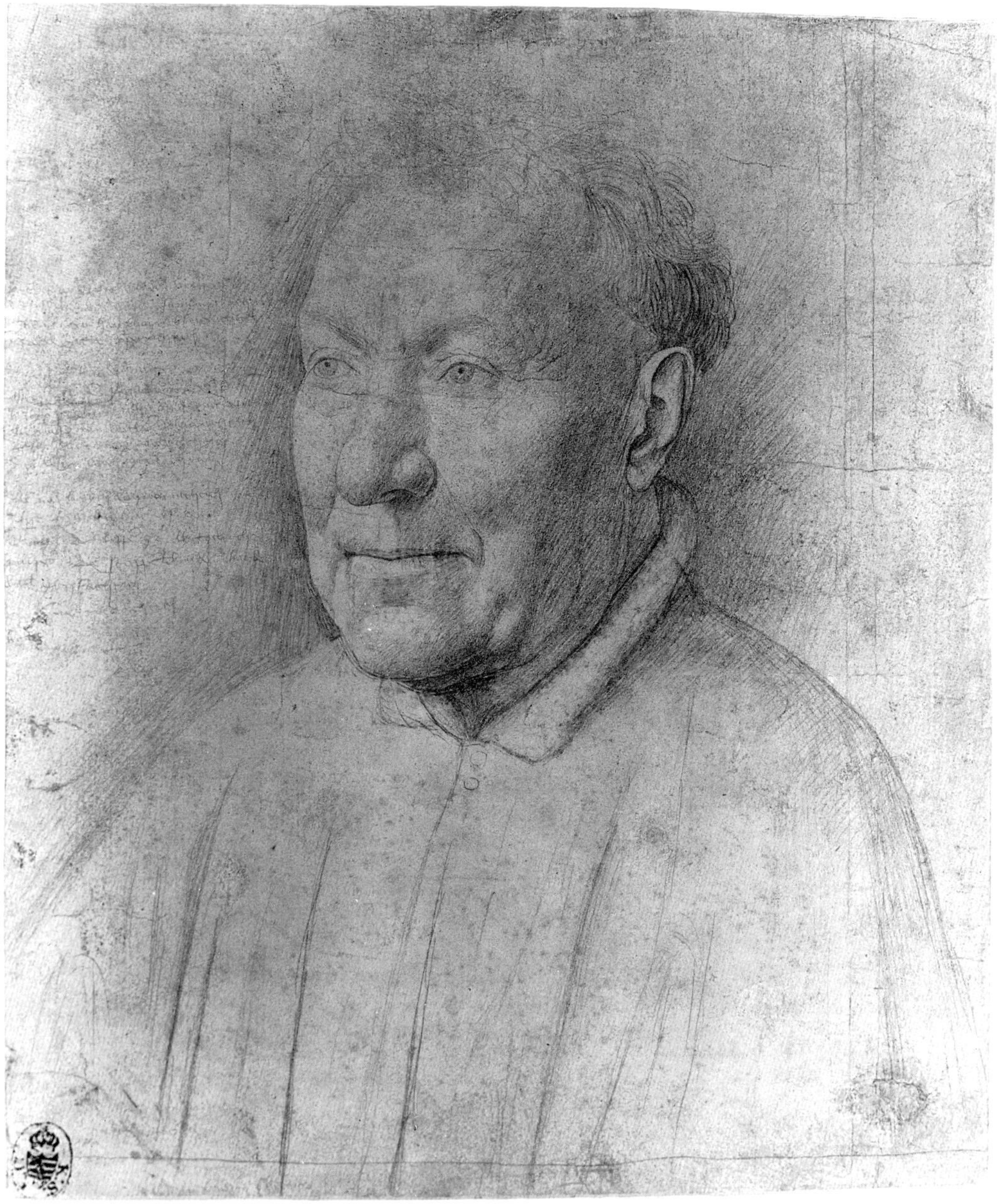

186 (facing page) Jan van Eyck, *Cardinal Albergati*, oak panel, 34.1 × 27.3 cm., Kunsthistorisches Museum, Vienna, Gemäldegalerie (975).

The panel has been cut to an oval, but the corners have been replaced; there are narrow additions at both sides. First traceable in the 1640s, the portrait then belonged to the Antwerp collector Pieter Stevens, who stated that the artist was Jan van Eyck, that the sitter was the Cardinal of S. Croce and that the picture was painted in 1438. His information may have been taken from an inscription on the original frame, lost probably when the panel was cut to an oval. The Cardinal of S. Croce was Niccolò Albergati (1375–1443), who became a cardinal in 1426 and who visited the Low Countries in 1431 and 1435. Unless Stevens misread 1435 as 1438, the portrait must have been executed long after Jan van Eyck had seen the cardinal. The picture is obviously based on the silverpoint drawing reproduced as plate 185. The colour notes on the drawing are followed with meticulous care in the painting and it would appear that the drawing was made from life and that the painting was made from the drawing, without further recourse to the sitter. In the drawing, Van Eyck has concentrated on the features, in relation to which the top and back of the head and the torso are diminished in scale. Enlarging his drawing onto the panel, he has increased the height and breadth of the cranium and has put less tonal emphasis on the bulges formed by the point of the nose. The facial expression has altered a little because of these changes and because he has dilated slightly the pupils of his sitter's eyes. Extremely small and clearly defined in the drawing, the pupils are less striking in the painting because of the catchlights and the colouring of the irises, where Van Eyck has followed his detailed notes made on the drawing.

See Dhanens, 1980, pp. 282–91; Demus, Klauner and Schütz, 1981, pp. 169–73; here pp. 174–5.

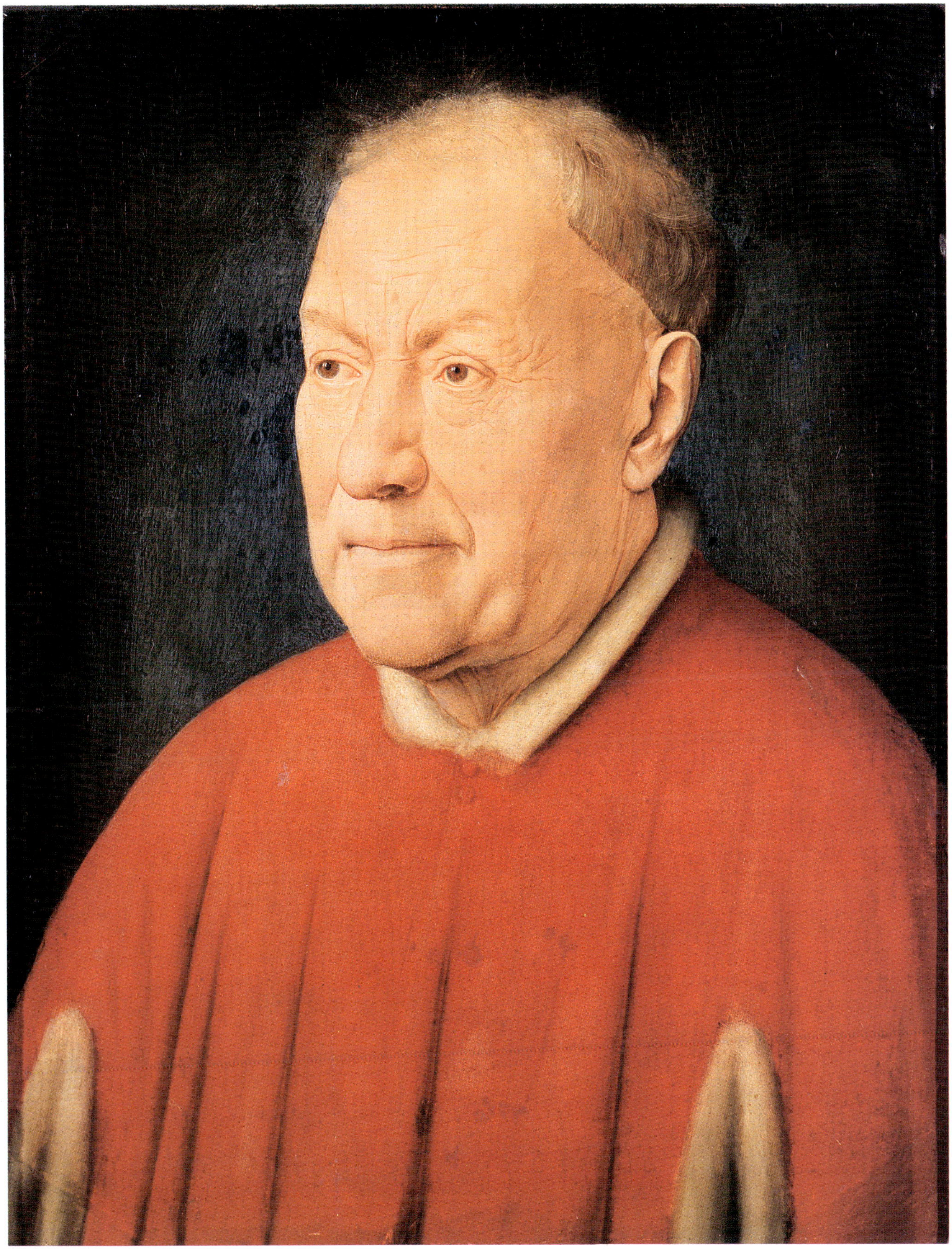

187 (right) Jean Fouquet, *Guillaume Jouvenel des Ursins*, black and coloured chalks on grey prepared paper, 26.7 × 19.5 cm., Staatliche Museen Preussischer Kulturbesitz, Berlin (West), Kupferstichkabinett (KdZ 4367).

Obviously the preliminary study for the painting reproduced as plate 188, the drawing is much larger in scale and considerably less refined in technique than Van Eyck's silverpoint of Cardinal Albergati (plate 185). The paper has quite a marked grain and the chalks, sometimes dragged across the the grain, produce softer, less precise lines than the silverpoint. Fouquet has begun by sketching the head lightly in black chalk and has then reinforced the contours in black, making and then correcting mistakes in the outline of the face opposite the mouth and in the line of the point of the nose. Hatching in black chalk indicates the principal areas of shadow. Very soft red chalk has been used to suffuse with colour certain areas of the head and white chalk has been sparingly employed in the whites of the eyes and in the highlights on the skin. The hair has been coloured with brown chalk, presumably applied over the black chalk lines. The drawing is relatively schematic in detail and in tone: the pupils of the eyes, for example, are differently and irregularly shaped. The colouring, though increasing the tonal range available to the draughtsman, does not correspond at all closely to the appearance of the skin and cannot have been of great assistance to Fouquet when he came to execute his painted portrait.

See Reynaud, 1981, pp. 29–30 (8); here pp. 65, 175.

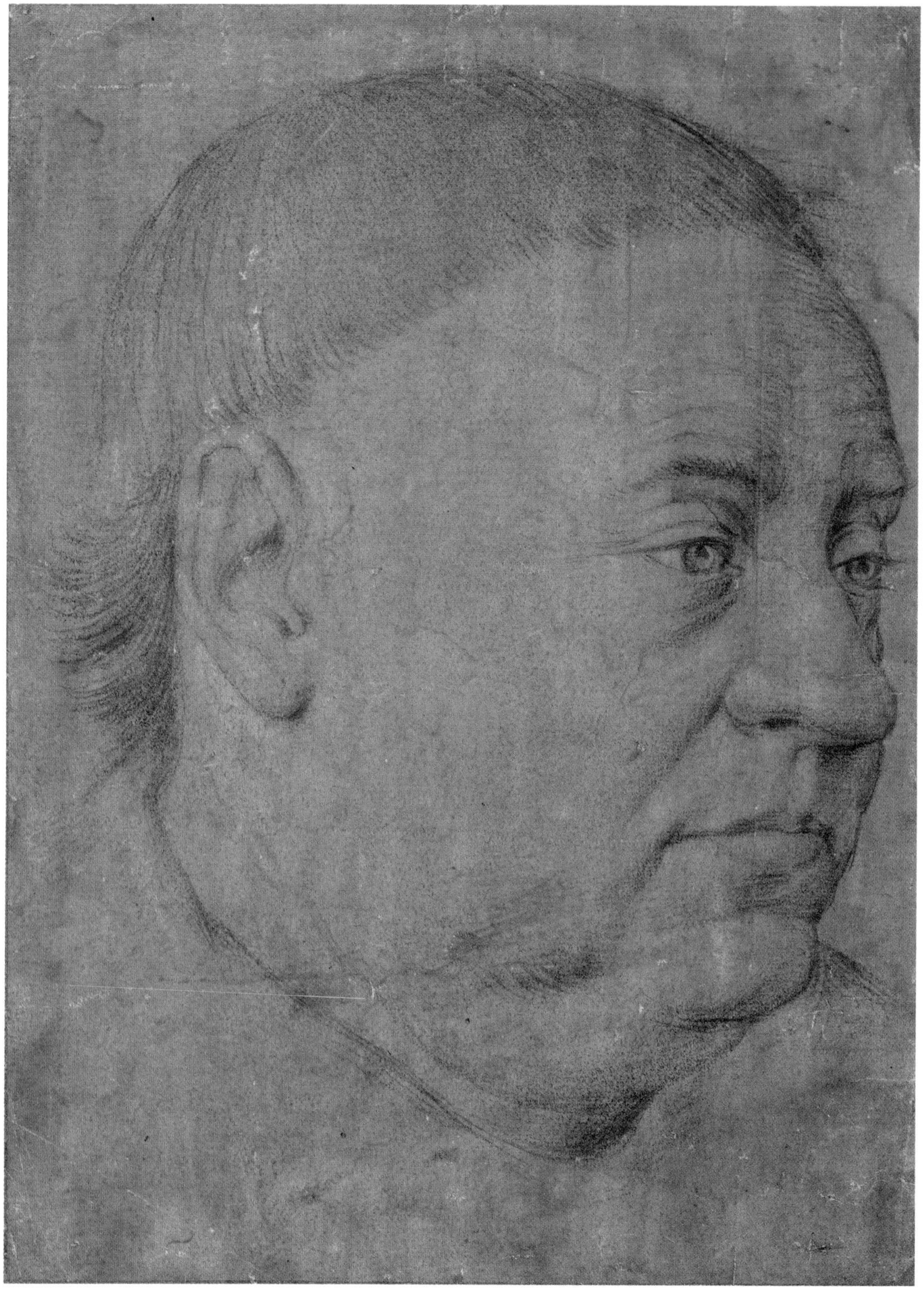

188 (facing page) Jean Fouquet, *Guillaume Jouvenel des Ursins*, oak panel, 96 × 73 cm., Louvre, Paris (INV. 9619).

The panel was the wing of a diptych or triptych. The sitter, identified by the coats of arms, was born in 1401 and was Chancellor of France from 1445 to 1461 and from 1465 until his death in 1472. The portrait is attributed to Fouquet on stylistic grounds and, on the basis of style, the sitter's apparent age and his costume, may be dated towards 1460. The preliminary drawing is reproduced as plate 187. The painted head is slightly larger than the drawn head, but Fouquet has followed rather exactly in his painting the shapes and proportions established in the drawing and has constructed from the gilded architectural ornament a 'frame' for the head which approximates to the edges of the drawing. In the painting, Fouquet has further simplified the contours in terms of geometric curves and has adjusted the shapes of the sitter's right eyelids and eyebrow to give him a more suitably pious expression. In both the drawing and the painting, Fouquet has followed his usual practice in exaggerating the distance between the ear and the eye. It seems impossible that he executed his painting from the drawing alone: in order to reproduce the wide range of tonal and colour transitions in the flesh, he must have had further sittings.

See Reynaud, 1981, pp. 31–4; here p. 175.

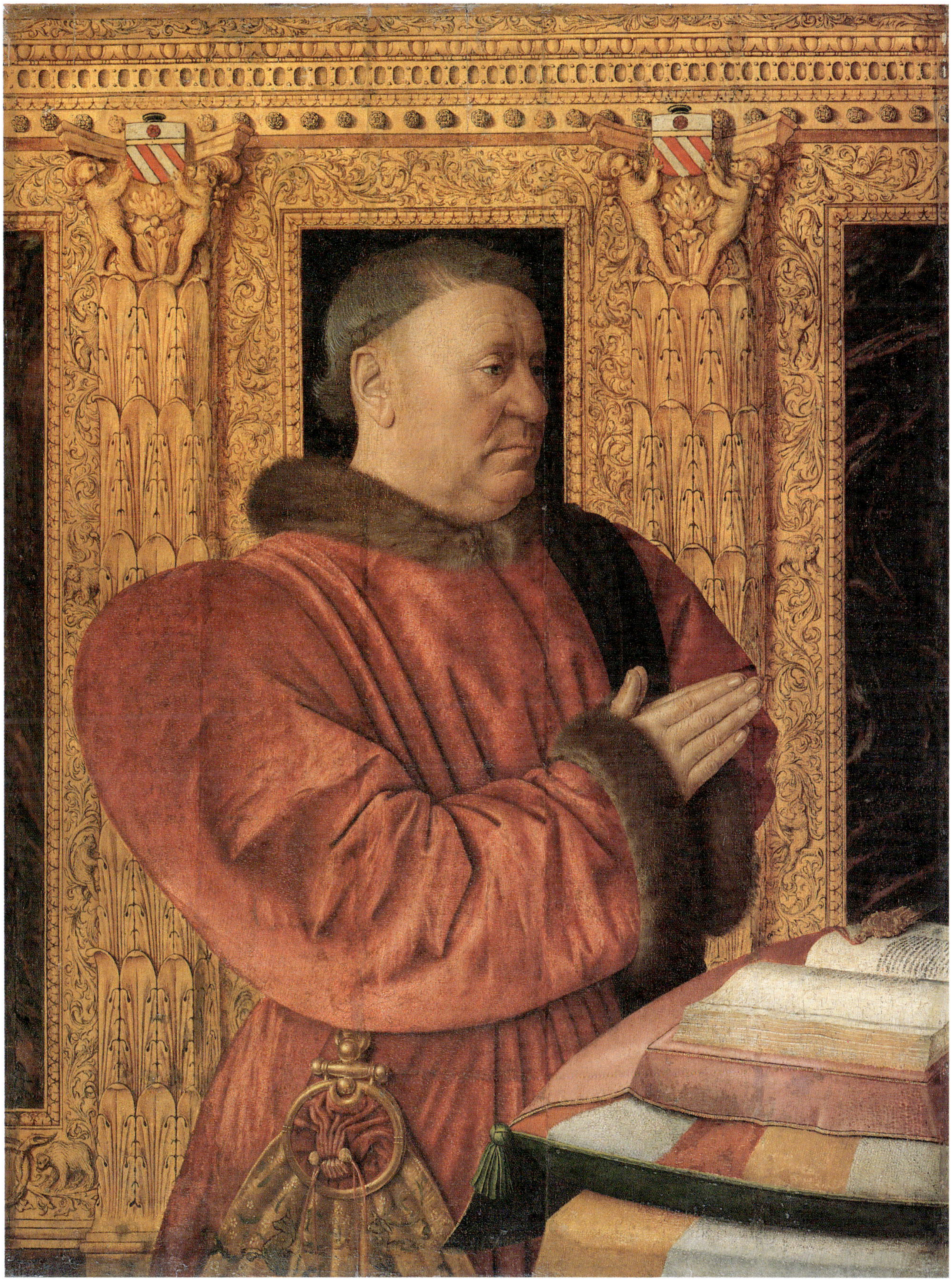

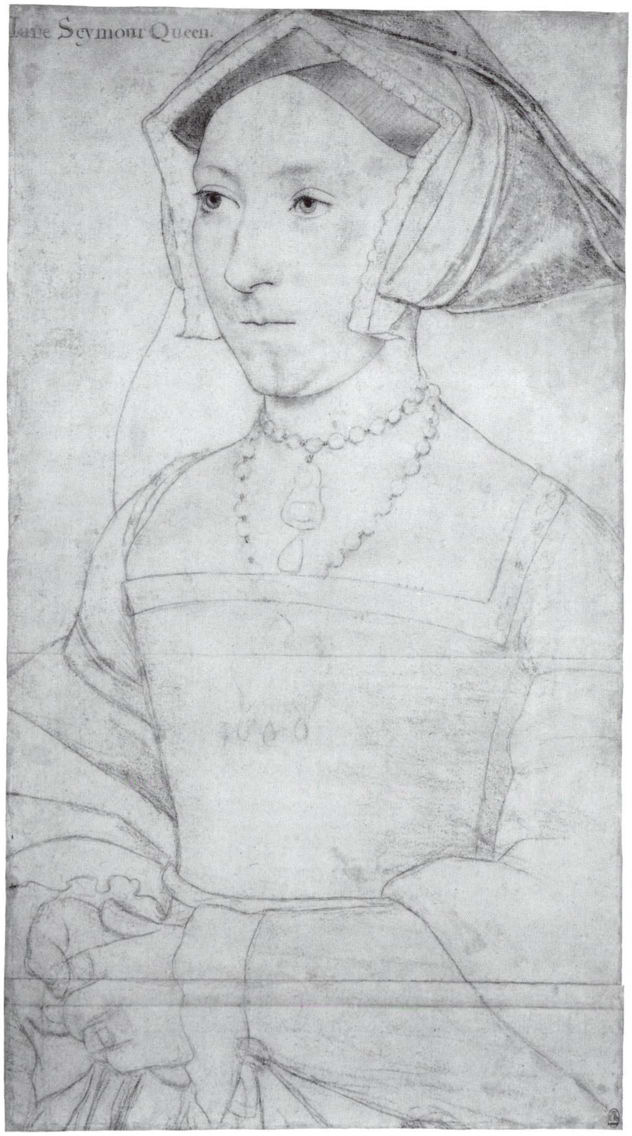

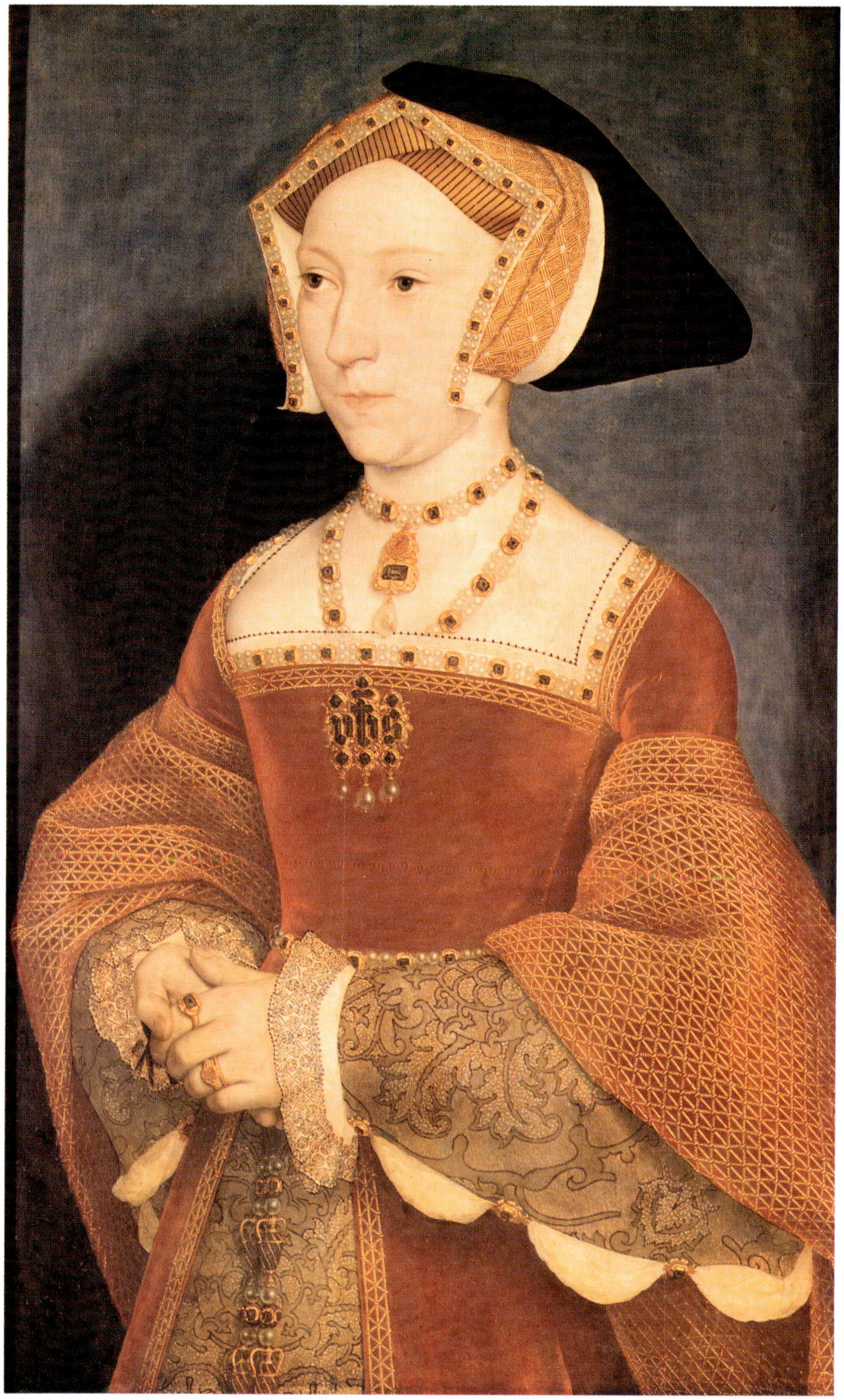

themselves employed, yet it seems likely that they did. Van Eyck's *Portrait of Cardinal Albergati* (plate 186) was certainly executed from the meticulous silverpoint now at Dresden (plate 185), which is covered with elaborate colour notes followed with precision in the painting: 'the iris of the eye, near the pupil . . . brownish yellowish, bluish at the contour near the white . . . the white also yellowish, the nose a sanguine-brownish colour . . . the lips very whitish-purple,

189 (far left) Hans Holbein the Younger, *Jane Seymour*, black and coloured chalks, reinforced with pen and ink and metalpoint, on pink prepared paper, 50 × 28.5 cm., Royal Library, Windsor Castle, Print Room (RL 12267).

The sitter is identified in the inscription as Jane Seymour, the third wife of Henry VIII of England, whom Henry married in May 1536 and who died in October 1537. The drawing would have been executed between those dates. Now rather damaged, it was the basis for the painting by Holbein reproduced as plate 190; for his full length portrait of Jane in the lost Whitehall mural (see the copy reproduced as plate 110); and for a small painting at The Hague (278), thought to have been executed in his workshop.

See Foister, 1983, pp. 21, 42–3 (39); here pp. 175–7.

190 (left) Hans Holbein the Younger, *Jane Seymour*, oak panel, 65.4 × 40.7 cm., Kunsthistorisches Museum, Vienna, Gemäldegalerie (881).

The portrait is based on the drawing reproduced as plate 189; measurements taken from the drawing and from the painting correspond so exactly that a tracing process must have been used to transfer a precise reproduction of the drawing onto the panel (Foister, 1983, p. 21).

See Rowlands, 1985, p. 144; here pp. 175–7.

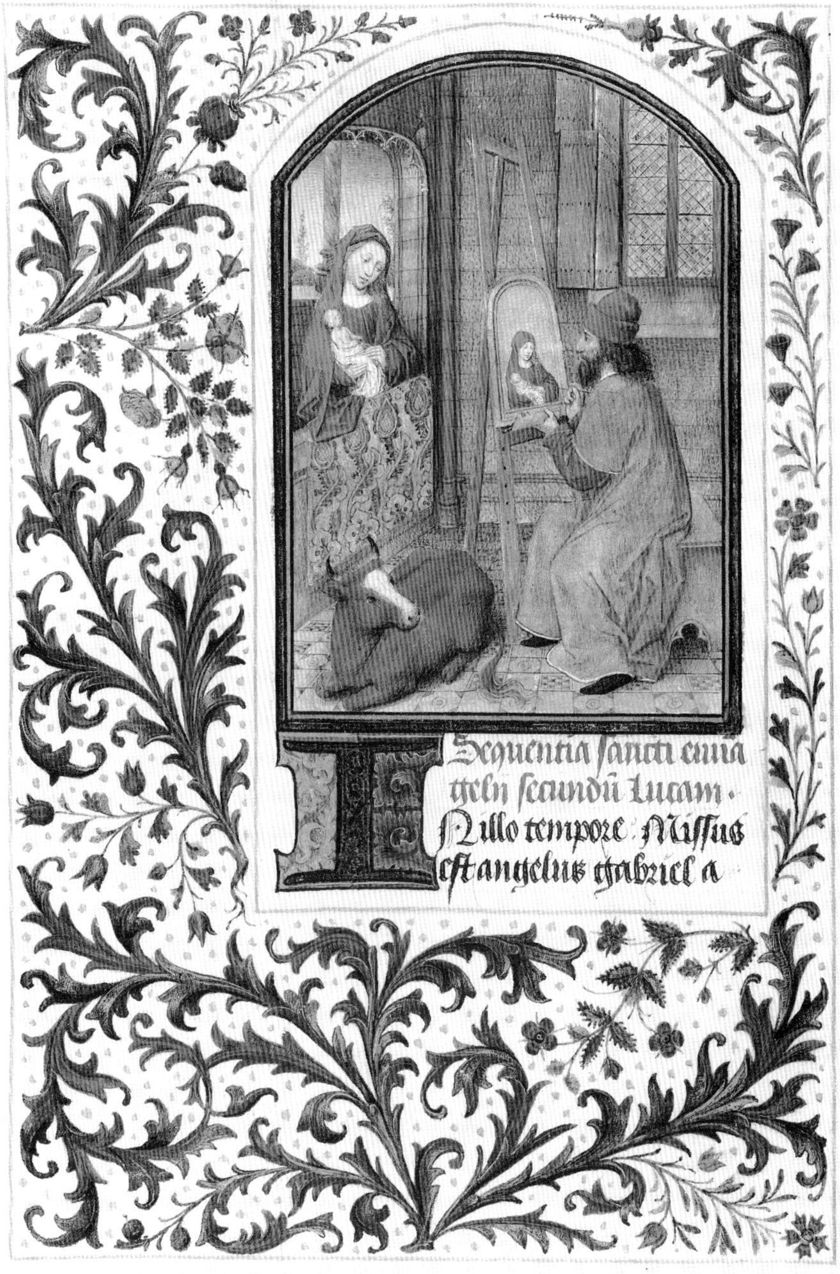

191 Attributed to Simon Marmion, *St Luke painting the Virgin*, parchment, 21 × 14 cm., from a Book of Hours, Henry E. Huntington Library and Art Gallery, San Marino (California), HM 1173, f. 15v.

On grounds of style, the illumination and decoration of the book may be dated towards 1470. The miniatures belong to a group of stylistically related illuminations and panel paintings which are generally attributed to Simon Marmion, a celebrated artist who worked at Amiens, Valenciennes and Tournai. As no securely documented works by Marmion have been discovered, it is not possible to confirm or reject this hypothesis.

See Thorpe, 1977, pl. 2; here pp. 65, 107, 177.

the stubble of the beard quite greyish, the chin reddish . . .'.[50] It may be, however, that the *Albergati* is an exceptional case and that the method was adopted because the cardinal was able to give only one sitting. Fouquet and Jean Clouet also made elaborate preparatory drawings, but they may well have had subsequent sittings (plates 183–4, 187–8). Holbein's preliminary drawings are generally of exactly the same size as the painted heads in his finished portraits, and he must therefore have

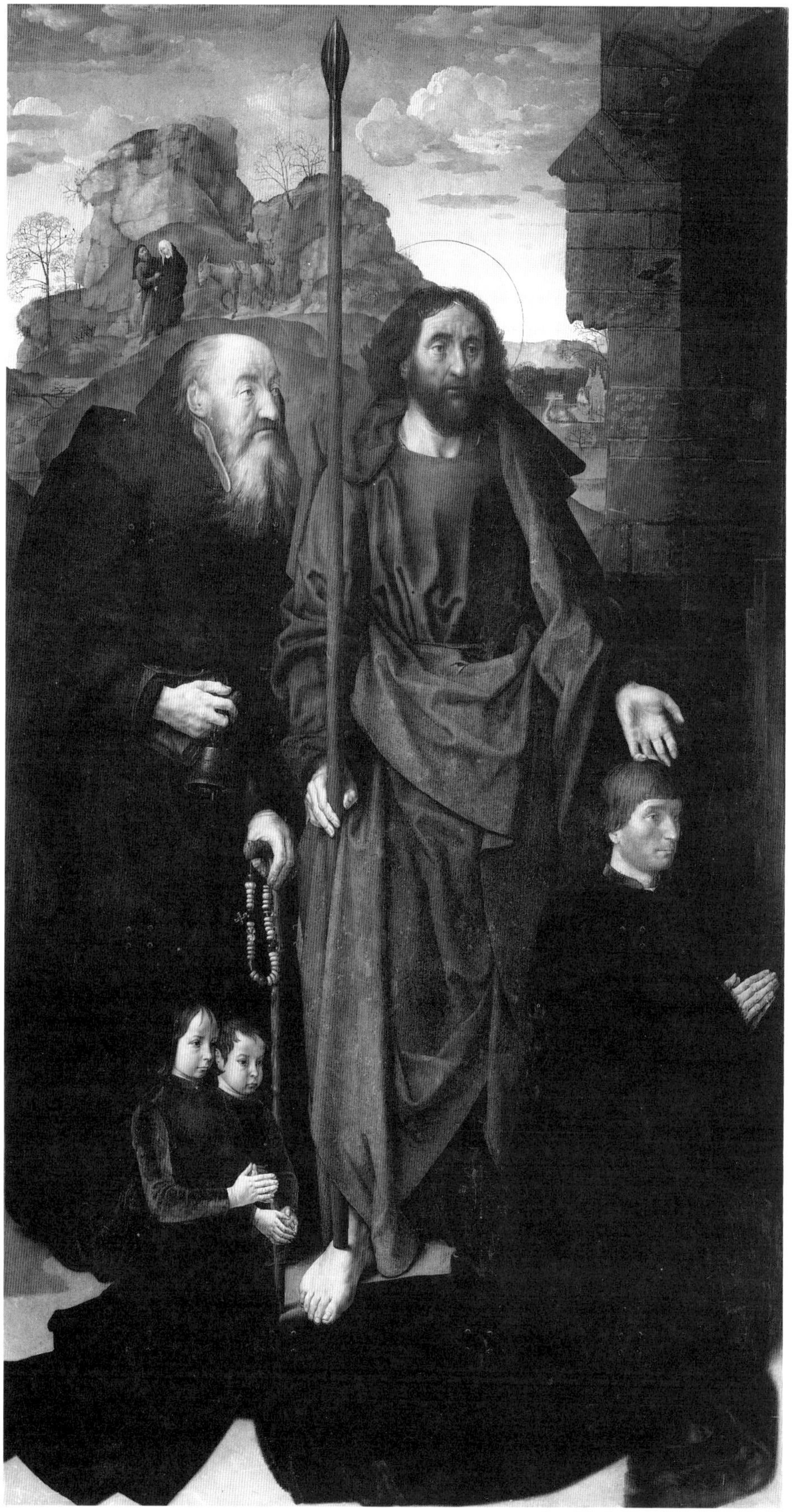

192 Hugo van der Goes, *Tommaso Portinari and his Sons Antonio and Pigello presented by Saints Anthony and Thomas*, left wing of the 'Portinari Triptych', oak panel, 253 × 141 cm., Uffizi, Florence (3191).

For the right wing, see plates 30, 32. The fact that Tommaso's head differs in colour and texture from the other areas of flesh in the altarpiece, including Tommaso's hands, used to be explained in terms of damage. Recently, however, it has been discovered, from an examination of the X-radiographs, that it is painted on a separate support, perhaps of metal foil or parchment, and glued into place on the panel. Van der Goes must have had particular reasons for resorting to this strange, technically unsatisfactory yet not unparalleled procedure, which has caused the paint of Tommaso's head to deteriorate. It seems likely that, when Tommaso left the Netherlands for Italy in 1477, the wing panels of the triptych had not been started but that Tommaso was anxious to speed progress and doubtless wanted to supervise the installation of the altarpiece in Florence. Van der Goes must have insisted that his portrait head had to be painted from life and must have refused to work from a drawing or to make a separate painted portrait which he might afterwards have copied in the finished triptych. He would therefore have adopted the expedient of a separate support, painted Tommaso's head upon it before he left for Italy and kept the painting aside until it could be incorporated in the altarpiece. The portraits of Tommaso's wife and children, who remained in the Low Countries until 1478, were executed in the usual way, directly upon the panels.

See Marijnissen and Van de Voorde, 1983, p. 46; here pp. 177, 232.

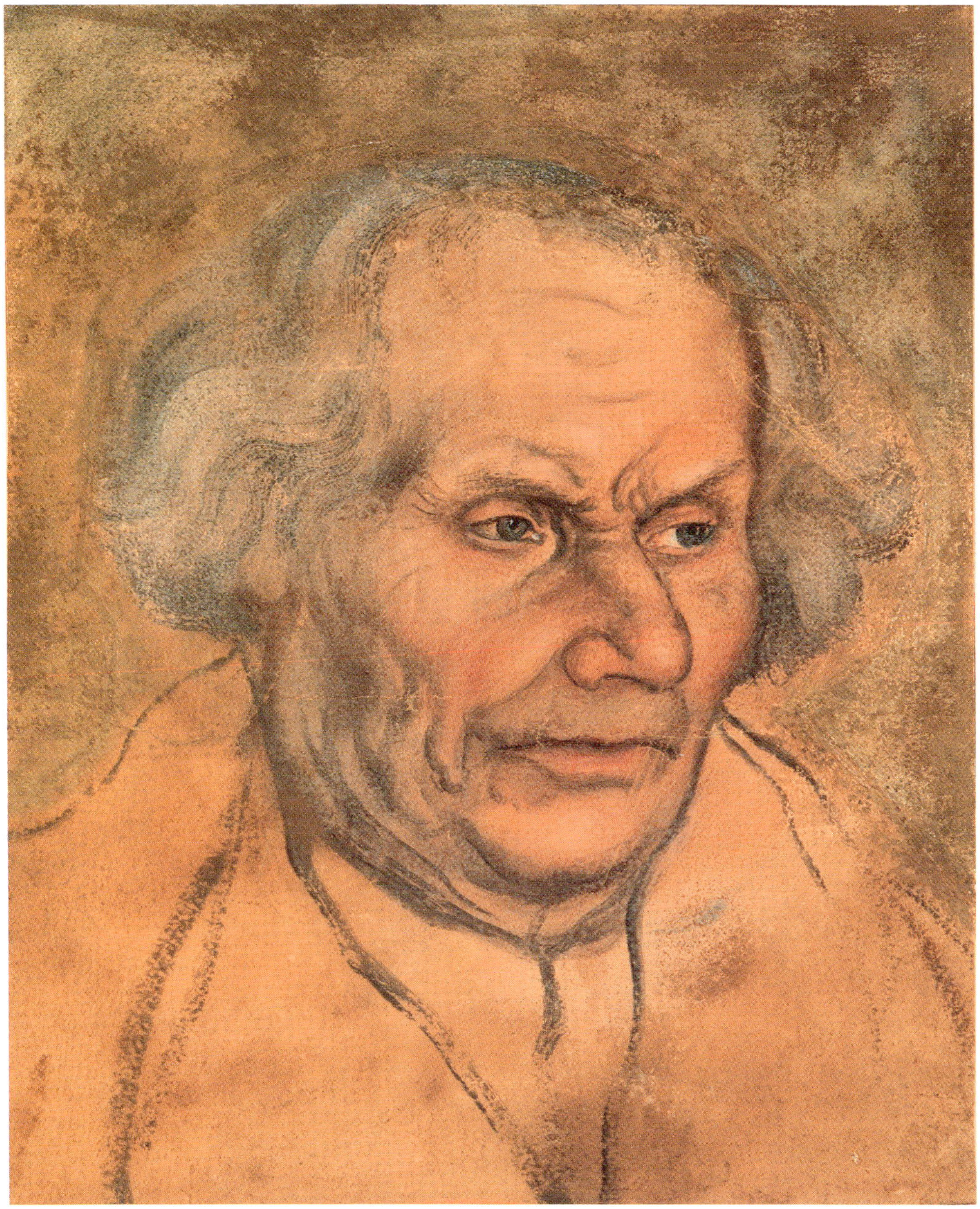

193 Lucas Cranach the Elder, *Hans Luther*, body-colour on oiled paper, cut round the contour and mounted on paper, 21.8 × 18.3 cm., Graphische Sammlung Albertina, Vienna (26156).

The drawing is the preliminary study for a painted portrait (copper-beech panel, 39 × 26 cm., Wartburg Stiftung, Eisenach) inscribed with the sitter's name, signed with the winged serpent that formed part of Cranach's coat of arms and dated 1527. Hans, the father of Martin Luther, died in 1530. Cranach's portrait studies are executed with wonderful freedom and assurance and were probably made at great speed. He put in the dark lines stressing the salient features as final touches and sometimes made important revisions at this last stage. The finished paintings are much less bold: the contrasts of tone and colour are less extreme; details are suppressed or stylised; lines become more calligraphically elegant.

See the exhibition catalogue Basle, 1974, II, p. 693 (615); here pp. 65, 177–8.

used a tracing process to transfer his drawing to the panel;[51] but again, there is no proof that he did not normally ask his subjects to return for further sittings (plates 189–90).

Painting from life was far from an unknown concept: representations of *St Luke painting the Virgin* do exist (plate 191). Furthermore, it has recently been discovered that certain portrait heads in fifteenth-century Netherlandish pictures are painted on separate supports and glued into place on the panels: for example the head of Tommaso Portinari in the *Portinari Altarpiece* by Van der Goes (plate 192). It appears that artists who were unable to bring their sitters to the panels were forced to adopt this technically unsatisfactory expedient in order to obtain portraits painted from life.[52] The Cranachs compromised by making preliminary studies on paper in ink, water-colour and body-colour, and may often have worked up their panel portraits from such studies and without further recourse to the sitters (plate 193). On the other hand, Titian's portrait of Ranuccio Farnese was admired 'especially since he executed it partly in the presence of the sitter and partly in his absence' (plate 194).[53]

The method adopted probably depended as much on the sitter, and his ability or willingness to pose, as on the individual artist's preferences. Persons of high rank would have had less time to sit, and the court painters were perhaps constrained to rely heavily on preliminary drawings. If a portrait were to be worked up from a drawing, even a coloured drawing, abrupt contrasts of light and shade would have been avoided from the start, since, in the absence of a model, no painter can render with complete success the subtleties of the tonal transitions in the flesh.

Hilliard advised: 'In drawing after the life, site not nearer then too yards from the partye, and sit as euen of height as possible yo maye . . . If yo drawe frome head to foote, lett the party stand at least sixe yards frome yo, when yo take the discription of his whole stature . . .'.[54] Hilliard clearly had quite a large studio. Francisco de Holanda advised the painter to converse with the sitter until he adopted the desired pose and then to tell him to look at a fixed point and not to move.[55] A barely perceptible movement of the sitter's head might have disastrous results. As Hilliard remarked, 'the littele mouing, leadeth yo to a great error, if yo perceiue it not quickly, soe that they sometime make the eyes at one position or standing, the nosse at ane other, the mouth at an other, the eare at an other, I amonish yo of that fault both Sitter and drawer, wch is the greatest cause of leesinge the liknes in pictures'.[56] Hilliard thought that, for the painting of the body, the subject should stand: 'for in sitting, fewe cane sit very vpright as they stand, wherby the *Drawer* is greatly deceiued commonly, and the party drawne disgraced'.[57] He further recommended: 'tell not a body when yo drawe the hands, but when yo spie a good grace in theire hand take it quickly, or praye them to stand but still/for commonly when they are towld, they giue the hand the worse and more vnnaturall or affected grace'.[58] Norgate developed Hilliard's line of thought:

> it wilbe very necessary that you finde or make occasion by discourse or otherwise to cause the party you drawe to speake and bee in accon, and to regard you with a Joviall, merry and discoursive aspecte, wherin you must be sudden and ready, to catch or steale your observations, and to expresse them with a quicke, bould and constante hand . . .[59]

A bored sitter obviously presented problems and not all portraitists were able to paint and at the same time to keep the sitters entertained. In 1494, Cardinal Ippolito d'Este informed his sister Isabella that it was only for love of her that he would submit to the tedium of sitting, 'a thing which he would not have done for any of his brothers'.[60] Isabella herself found the patience involved in staying still so much of an annoyance that she resolved in 1511 never again to make the sacrifice of sitting for her portrait.[61] In 1516, she wrote that 'we no longer wish to endure that boredom of staying patient and sitting for our portrait'.[62] Vasari was conscious of the 'melancholy' frequently found in portraits of abstracted sitters and claimed that 'while Leonardo was painting Mona Lisa's portrait, he engaged people to play and sing, and jesters to keep her cheerful and remove that melancholy which painting usually gives to portraits'.[63]

It was particularly difficult to keep babies and children entertained. On 14 March 1494, Bonsignori began a portrait of Isabella d'Este's daughter Eleonora

194 Titian, *Ranuccio Farnese*, canvas, 89.7 × 73.6 cm., National Gallery of Art, Washington (1952.2.11, Samuel H. Kress Collection)

Signed 'TITIANVS/.F.', the picture represents a boy wearing a robe decorated with a Maltese cross. He is identified, by comparison with another portrait, as Ranuccio Farnese (1530–65), a grandson of Pope Paul III and Prior of San Giovanni dei Forlani in Venice, a rich property that belonged to the Knights of Malta. Titian painted Ranuccio's portrait in 1542, 'partly in the presence of the sitter and partly in his absence'.

See Shapley, 1979, pp. 483–5; here pp. 61, 178, 243, plate 195.

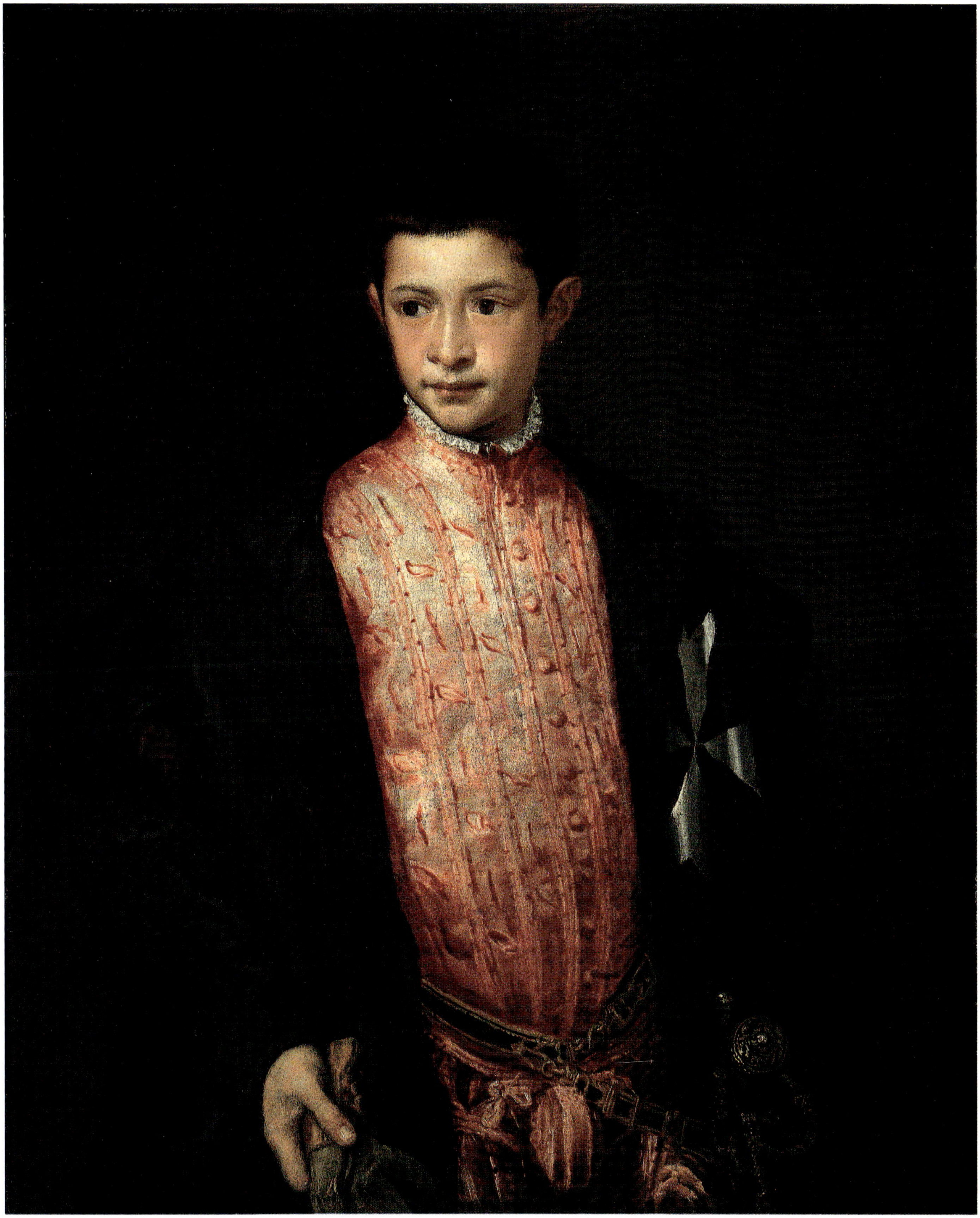

Gonzaga, 'but could not finish it, because she went to sleep; he has put off [completing it] until tomorrow'.[64] When the Emperor Charles V met Cranach the Elder in 1547, they recalled how, when Charles was a boy of eight, Cranach had painted his portrait. They discussed how Cranach had contrived to make him sit still and Cranach said that, on the advice of Charles's tutor, a polished weapon had been hung on the wall and this had held Charles's attention, for he was interested in such things: fixing his eyes upon it, he had sat until Cranach had finished his painting.[65] At Innsbruck in 1548, Titian painted the Archduchess Catherine, then aged fifteen. They may have had problems in communicating with each other and, in any case, the girl was bored. It was reported:

> although the archpainter signor Titian has portrayed her in as natural a way as possible, in one respect alone the likeness is slightly less than perfect, that is to say, in the picture the face is somewhat more severe than in life; this is not the fault of the painter, for it seems that when Her Serenity had to sit for a long and tedious period, she became pensive, and as a result her face appears less cheerful, gentle and sweet than it really is; but otherwise it is so natural that it lacks nothing except the living spirit.[66]

Bronzino, executing portraits of the Medici children at Pisa in 1551, painted them while they were having lessons in Latin and Greek.[67] The artists who had to draw or paint the future Louis XIII of France observed the little boy playing or eating, but it soon emerged that the best way to amuse him was to let him draw too, or play with paint.[68]

It was obviously impossible to make a baby or child sit perfectly still. Some painters did not insist that adult sitters should remain immobile. Hilliard, for example, though stressing the importance of maintaining the pose of the head, allowed his subjects at least to move their hands;[69] while Daniel Dumoustier's sitters were allowed to do as they liked. Only occasionally did he ask them to turn round.[70]

There were dangers in bringing others to entertain the sitter. Francisco de Holanda thought that the painter should be alone with the sitter, to avoid distraction and the risk that the appearances of others present should contaminate the likeness of the sitter. He related how, when he had been painting the King of Portugal, a count, standing beside Francisco, had insisted on conversing with the king. Francisco, unable to work, had asked the king to dismiss the count, and the queen, who was also present, had had to excuse Francisco to the count.[71] Hilliard advised: 'shut out questioners or busi fingers', but recommended that '*Discret* talke or reading, quiet merth or musike ofendeth not, but shortneth the time, and quickneth the sperit both in the drawer, and he which is drawne.'[72]

Lighting was a constant problem and, not surprisingly, artists from different areas of Europe offered differing advice on how to control natural light. Leonardo advocated painting portraits in dull weather, or at dusk, or in courtyards with blackened walls which might be covered in with linen awnings when the sun shone.[73] Francisco de Holanda recommended that light from windows should be moderated and 'musical'[74] and presumably would have employed blinds or curtains to achieve such an effect. Though Hilliard had on one occasion to paint Elizabeth I of England in a garden, he clearly preferred to paint in a studio with a good north light: 'let yr light be northword, somwhat toward the east which comonly is without sune, *Shininge* in. on only light great and faire let it be, and without impeachment, or reflections, of walls, or trees, a free sky light the dieper

195 Titian, *Ranuccio Farnese*, detail (see plate 194).

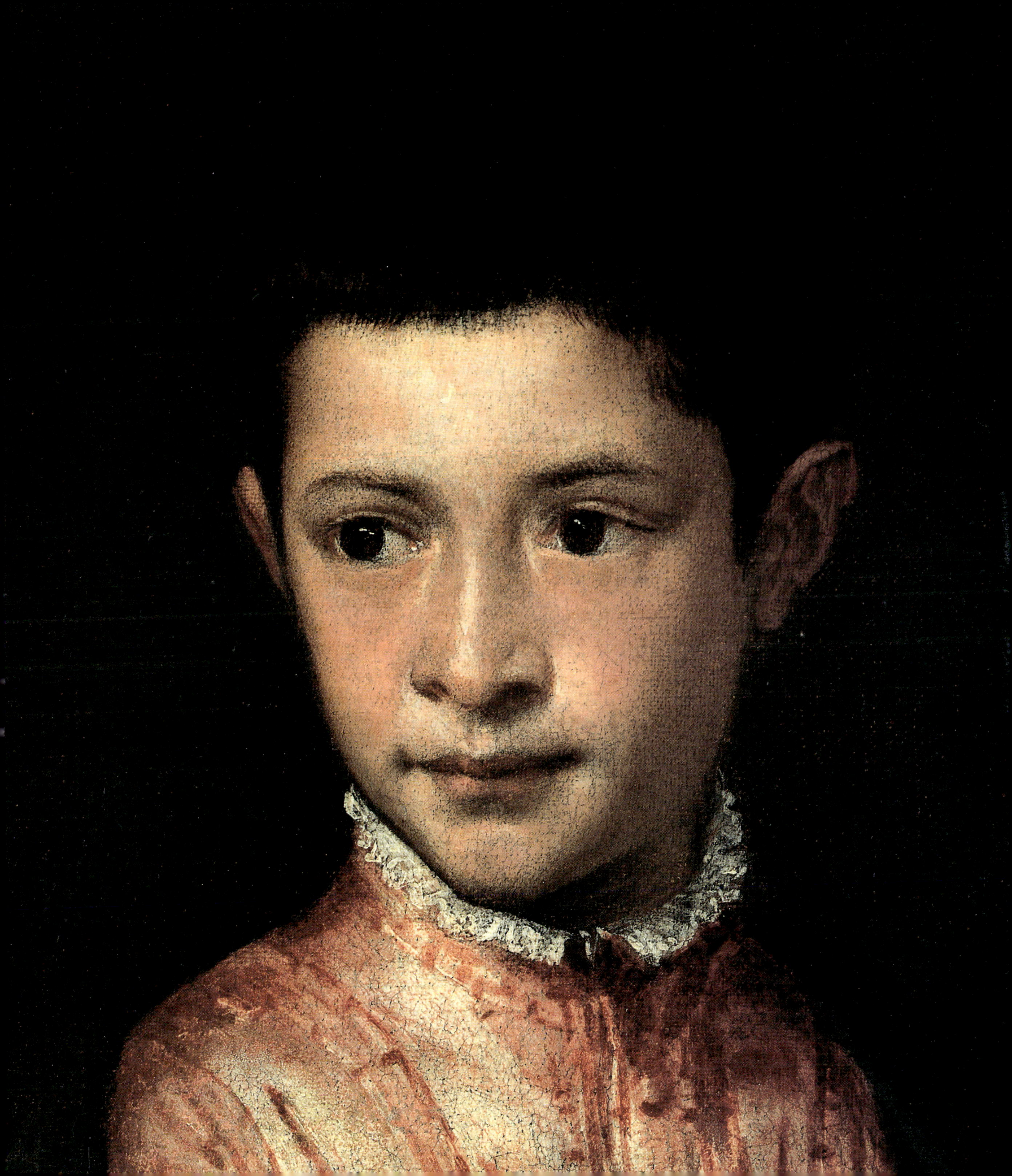

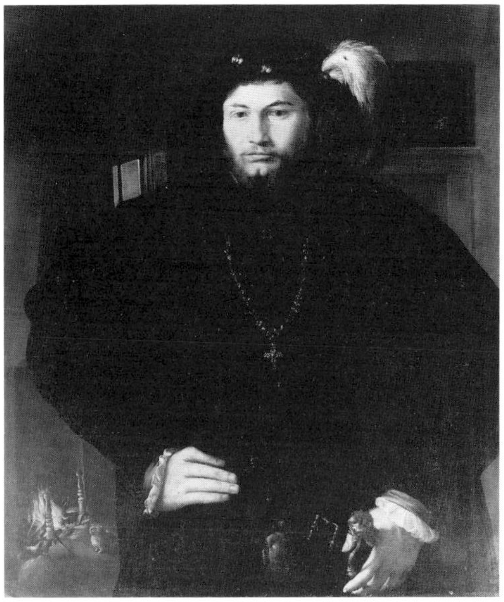

196 Italian, 1536, *Man*, canvas, 92 × 81 cm., Museo di Capodimonte, Naples, Pinacoteca (IC 214).

The date MDXXXVI appears behind the sitter's head on the door frame, above which is a picture of an hour-glass and a rabbit or hare holding one of a pair of dice. On the left, a small dog sits before a fire. The paint surface is so obscured by dirt and old varnishes that further interesting details may lie concealed. The sitter has not been identified but the portrait was in the collection of the Dukes of Parma by about 1680 and was attributed to Parmigianino. It has also been ascribed to Lotto, to Girolamo da Carpi and to an anonymous Netherlander working in Italy, but none of these proposals has much to recommend it.

See Bertini, 1987, pp. 86–7; here pp. 128, 182.

197 (facing page, left) Titian, *Man wearing the Armour of Francesco Maria della Rovere, Duke of Urbino*, pen and brown ink on paper, 23.7 × 14.1 cm., Uffizi, Florence, Gabinetto dei Disegni (20767 F).

A preparatory study for the portrait reproduced as plate 198, the drawing is puzzling in many respects: the squaring, for example, is untidily done and seems to have no useful function. Titian borrowed the duke's armour which is here worn by a model whose legs and feet are bare. The head resembles the duke's but it is hardly likely that Francesco Maria posed bare-legged for Titian. The head, which is less boldly drawn than the body and which is apparently in a different ink, was probably not taken from the model who wore the armour. Titian could have sketched the head from his memory of the duke's appearance either before or after he drew the body.

See the exhibition catalogue London, 1983–4, pp. 291–2 (D 71); here p. 182.

the window and farer, the better, and no by window . . .'.[75] Dürer would appear to have placed some of his sitters very close to large windows, which are reflected in their eyes. The harsh illumination allowed him to record in meticulous detail all their physical peculiarities, but, if they were made to stare for long periods into a strong light, that might account for their rather strained, sometimes scowling, expressions and their contracted pupils.[76]

Some painters worked by artificial light. At Brussels in 1520, Dürer 'took a portrait at night by candlelight of Master Konrad of Brussels, who was my host; I drew at the same time Doctor Lamparter's son in charcoal, also the hostess'.[77] Vermeyen painted for Margaret of Austria a portrait of Jean Denis 'done by candlelight'.[78] In 1532, Heemskerck depicted St Luke painting the Virgin, who is illuminated by the light of a torch;[79] and Francisco de Holanda reported that Italian portrait-painters used candlelight to obtain strong contrasts of light and shade and so more force and more emphatic 'senses and sentiments'.[80] According to Vasari, Orlando Fiacco made a portrait of Cardinal Caraffa 'by torchlight as he dined in the bishop's palace at Verona'.[81] In an Italian portrait of 1536, the dog in the background is illuminated by firelight; the interior is dimly lit from the window behind the sitter; the rather sharp tonal contrasts in the sitter's face and hands may have been obtained by artificial lighting (plate 196). Candles would have provided useful secondary sources of light; mirrors and other reflecting surfaces may well have been employed to control the illumination of the sitter.

In order to save the sitter time and trouble, his clothes could be lent to the artist and draped on another model or on a dummy. In 1549, the rings, chains, jewels and precious garments belonging to Philip II of Spain which were entrusted to Mor's assistant Conrad Schot, were clearly left in Mor's workshop so that he and his assistants might reproduce them in the portraits of Philip that they were executing.[82] In November 1580, Alessandro Allori returned to the Wardrobe officials of Bianca Capello, Grand Duchess of Tuscany, various rich garments that she had lent to him; and in January 1581, he returned to one of her ladies a pearl and diamond head-dress which Bianca had entrusted to him with her own hands to be used in a portrait that she intended to send to Venice.[83] When in 1536 Titian was painting the Duke of Urbino's portrait, he borrowed the duke's armour[84] and put it on another model whom he drew with bare legs and feet (plate 197). As Titian's painting was a half-length portrait, there was no need to bother with the leg-armour or other clothing for the legs (plate 198), and the full-length drawing seems to have been made merely to rationalise the pose of the upper part of the body. In 1547, when Titian was painting the duke's daughter-in-law Giulia Varano, he borrowed her clothes and specified that he wanted a dress of crimson or rose velvet.[85] François Clouet and Cornelis Ketel made separate costume drawings for some of their portraits in which the heads were sketched in only the most summary manner.[86] Perhaps they, too, had borrowed their sitter's clothes and put them on professional models.

In some circles, demand for portraits was so great that artists had to be prepared to turn out replicas in considerable quantities. In 1533, for example, Cranach the Elder was paid for sixty pairs of portraits of the late Electors of Saxony.[87] The Cranach workshop was apparently organised for this kind of mass production: the long inscriptions that often accompanied such portraits were printed on paper and then glued to the panels (plate 199). A Milanese official wrote to Cardinal Granvelle in 1550 to say that he had heard from Leone Leoni that the cardinal had many portraits of himself. He asked for one, and eleven days later wrote again

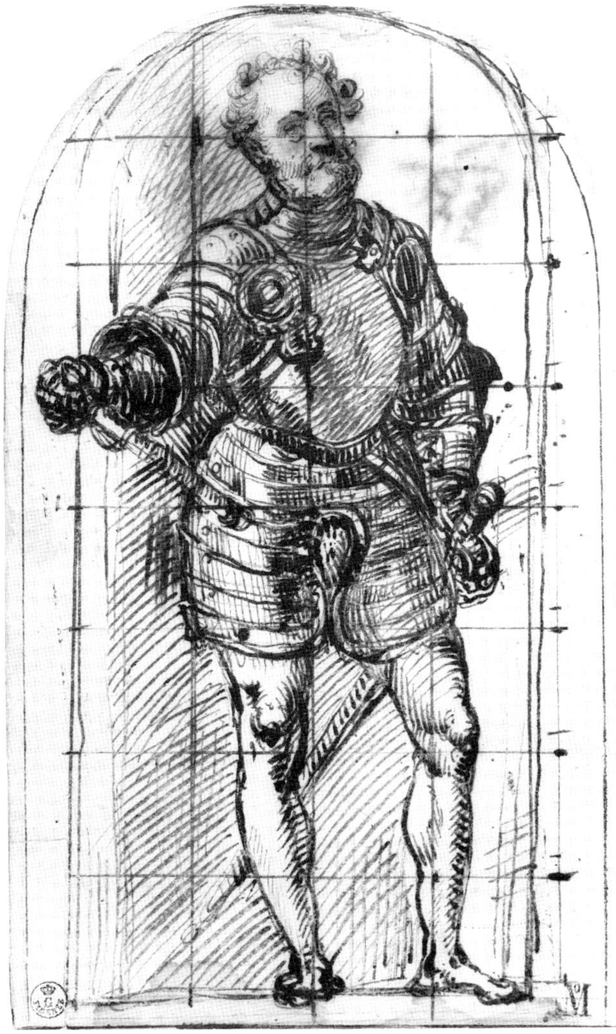 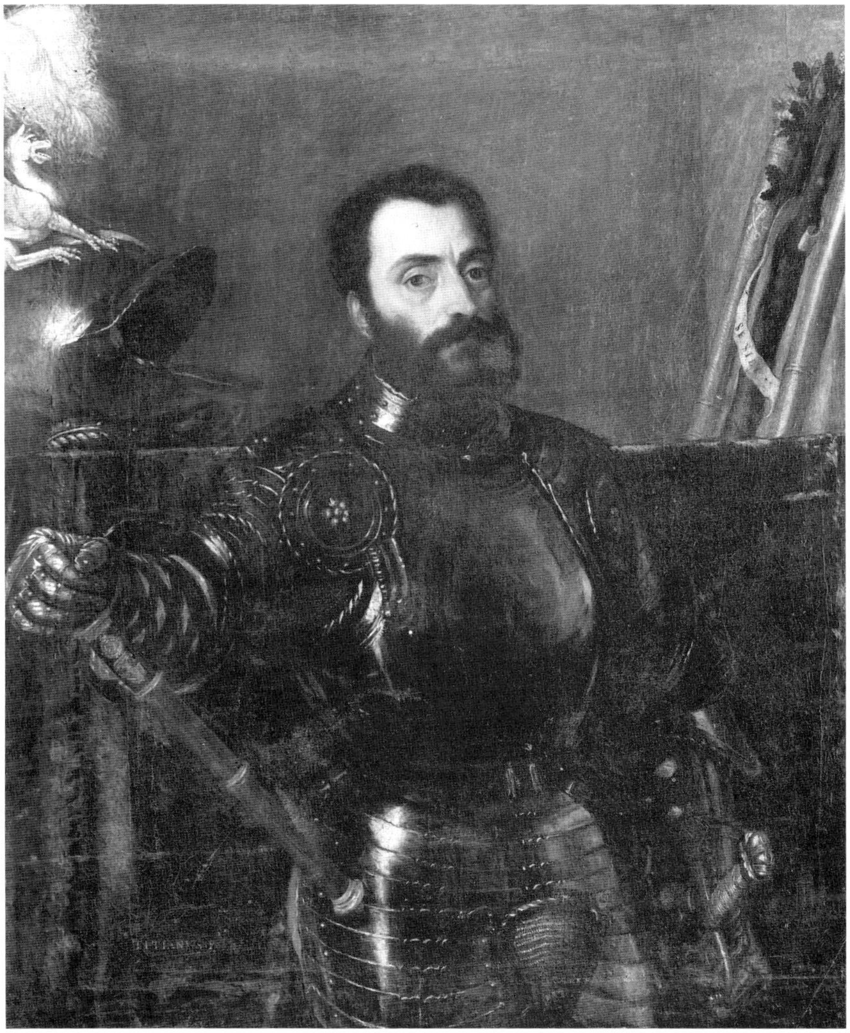

198 (above right) Titian, *Francesco Maria della Rovere, Duke of Urbino*, canvas, 114 × 103 cm., Uffizi, Florence (926).

The pair to the portrait reproduced as plate 45. Titian painted the two pictures in 1536–8. Behind the duke (1490–1538) are a commander's baton with the papal insignia and a branch of oak, referring to his surname (*rovere* meaning oak) and entwined with a scroll inscribed 'SE SIBI', apparently indicating that the duke fights also for himself and the glory of his family. For a preparatory drawing, see plate 197.

See the exhibition catalogue Florence, 1978–9, pp. 116–21 (28); here pp. 182, 220–2.

to ask for a portrait 'by your most excellent painter', which he would keep 'for my contemplation and for the decoration of my house'.[88] Granvelle's excellent painter was Mor, whose signed portrait of him is dated 1549 (plate 259). Evidently Mor's assistants were producing quantities of copies.

In 1585, the Venetian nobleman Francesco Bembo visited Bianca Capello, the Grand Duchess of Tuscany. In Florence, he saw and admired a portrait of her by Scipione Pulzone. He went on to Rome, where Pulzone resided, and commissioned him to execute a replica of the portrait. The copy was sent to him in Venice, where it was much admired, and on the Feast of St Apollonia, 9 February 1586, he arranged for it to be exhibited. It was seen by over three hundred people and praised by all. In April, he took it to the Capello family residence, where it was lauded and kissed. As several people wanted copies of it, Tintoretto was commissioned to paint two or three and others were ordered from Bassano, Palma Giovane and Veronese.[89]

Since Pulzone was able to produce in Rome a replica of his portrait in Florence, he must have kept some painted or drawn record of the original in anticipation that he might be required to execute replicas and versions. Most portraitists, indeed, appear to have retained portrait 'patterns' from which more portraits might be made if and when they were needed. Among Baldovinetti's possessions

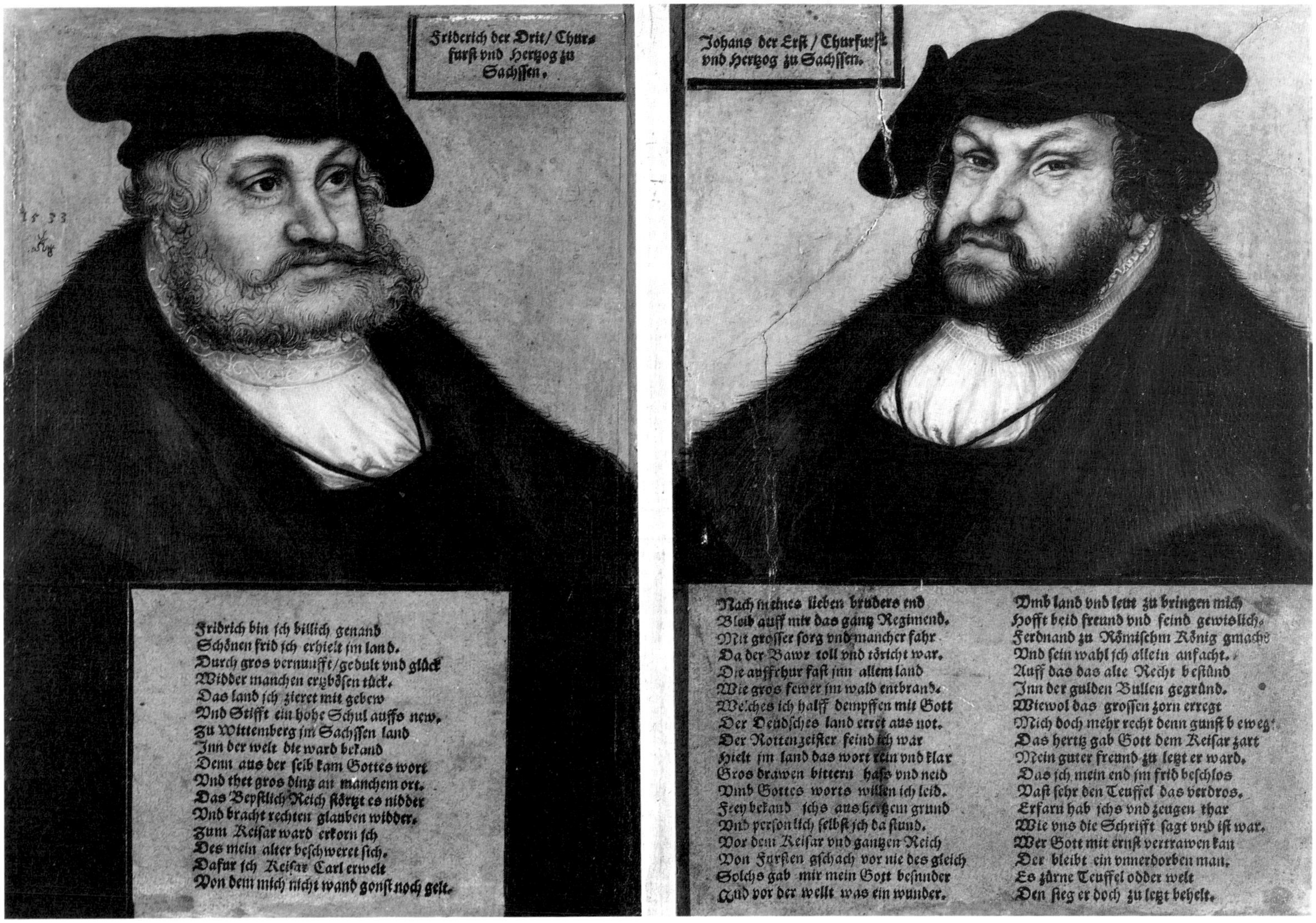

199 Lucas Cranach the Elder, *Frederick the Wise and John the Constant, Electors of Saxony*, panel, each 20 × 15 cm., Uffizi, Florence (1150, 1149).

The portrait of Frederick is dated 1533 and signed with the winged serpent that formed part of Cranach's coat of arms. In the upper inscriptions the names and titles of the sitters are given; in the lower inscriptions the laudatory verses are written as if by the sitters themselves. Cranach had been employed by both Frederick (1463–1525) and John (1468–1532) and in 1533 was in the service of John's son the Elector John Frederick. In that year he was paid for sixty pairs of small portraits of the two deceased electors, among which would have been the Uffizi panels and several other similar portraits.

See Berti, 1979, p. 230; here pp. 61, 182.

at the time of his death in 1499 were 'drawings of portraits';[90] Francesco Bonsignori kept black-and-white copies of his portraits – clearly drawings in black chalk – which his descendants inherited and showed to Vasari (plates 200–1).[91] Corneille de Lyon opened to the public in Lyons a large room in which were small portraits of all the gentlemen and ladies of the French court: it seems safe to assume that visitors could order replicas.[92] In 1549, Cardinal Granvelle wrote to Titian to say that he wanted a copy of the portrait of Philip II of Spain which Titian had executed at Milan: 'if you have retained a drawing of it, let me have a version'.[93] In 1561, Sofonisba Anguissola painted a portrait of Elisabeth of Valois, Philip II's third wife; it was sent to the pope with a letter from the artist dated 16 September 1561.[94] A fortnight later, one of Elisabeth's ladies wrote to her mother, Catherine de' Medici, and reported that the picture was on its way to Rome: 'I think, madam, that another will be commissioned for you and sent to you: and this I strongly desire for the pleasure which you will receive from it.'[95] The 'thirty five roughly sketched portraits of different persons' that were in Pantoja's studio at the time of his death in 1608 may have been portrait patterns.[96] Jamesone, writing in 1636 to a patron who had commissioned sixteen portraits of noblemen, stated: 'for theam quhois picturis I hawe allreadie, I shall double theam, or then giwe

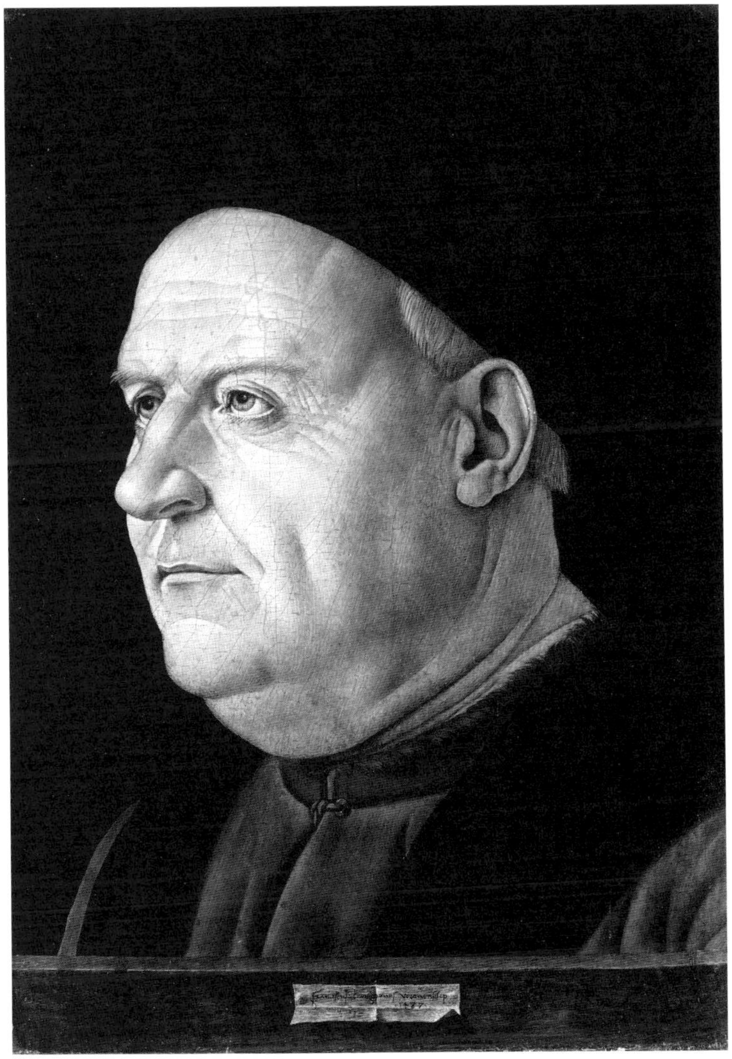

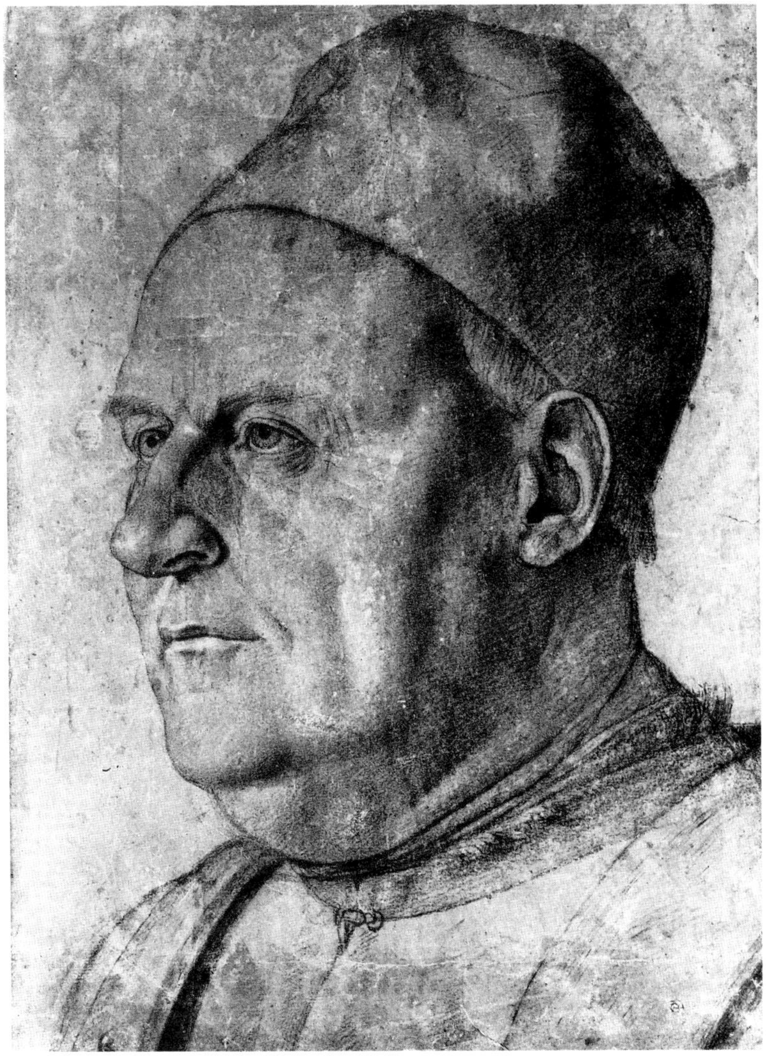

200 Francesco Bonsignori, *Man*, panel, painted surface 42 × 29.5 cm., National Gallery, London (736).

The painting is signed and dated on the paper fixed to the parapet: 'Franciscus. Bonsignorius. Veronensis. p/.1487.' The sitter has not been identified.

See Davies, 1961, p. 95; here pp. 69, 127, 184.

201 Francesco Bonsignori, *Man*, black chalk, heightened with white, on brownish paper, 36 × 26.2 cm., Graphische Sammlung Albertina, Vienna (17672).

The drawing is generally believed to be the preliminary study for Bonsignori's portrait of 1487 reproduced as plate 200. It is, however, a full-size copy executed by Bonsignori himself after his painting and would have been one of the collection of such copies which, according to Vasari, Bonsignori's heirs preserved at Mantua.

See pp. 62, 184.

yowr worship the principall'.[97] Clearly different artists used different techniques for making and using such patterns, but keeping copies of portraits was evidently standard practice.

If the subject was unable or unwilling to sit, the painter had to work from casual observation – as Parmigianino did when he painted the Emperor Charles V (plate 177) – from other portraits or even from verbal descriptions. When in 1511 Lucrezia Bentivoglio wanted a portrait of Isabella d'Este by Francia, Isabella had already resolved that she would never again sit to a painter; she also refused to let Francia come to Mantua and he had to execute his portrait in Bologna with the help of an old portrait of Isabella and under the guidance of Lucrezia, who claimed to have a lively memory of Isabella and to be able to correct the shortcomings of the old portrait. Francia had difficulties, but, as Isabella continued to refuse to allow him to come to Mantua and see her, he had to persevere and eventually completed a picture that satisfied Lucrezia and was sent to Isabella. Isabella thought that Francia had made her 'rather more beautiful than had Nature' and complained that the eyes in his portrait were too dark. Francia refused to change them. Isabella gave away the portrait almost immediately, but in 1534 borrowed it back and sent it to Titian, whom she had commissioned to paint a retrospective

202 Titian, *Isabella d'Este*, canvas, 102 × 64 cm., Kunsthistorisches Museum, Vienna, Gemäldegalerie (83).

Cut down at both sides, the picture may be identified as the portrait of Isabella (1474–1539) that Titian painted between 1534 and 1536. He copied a painting executed in 1511 by Francia, who had in turn copied an earlier portrait by an artist still to be identified.

See Wethey, 1971, pp. 95–6; here pp. 185–90.

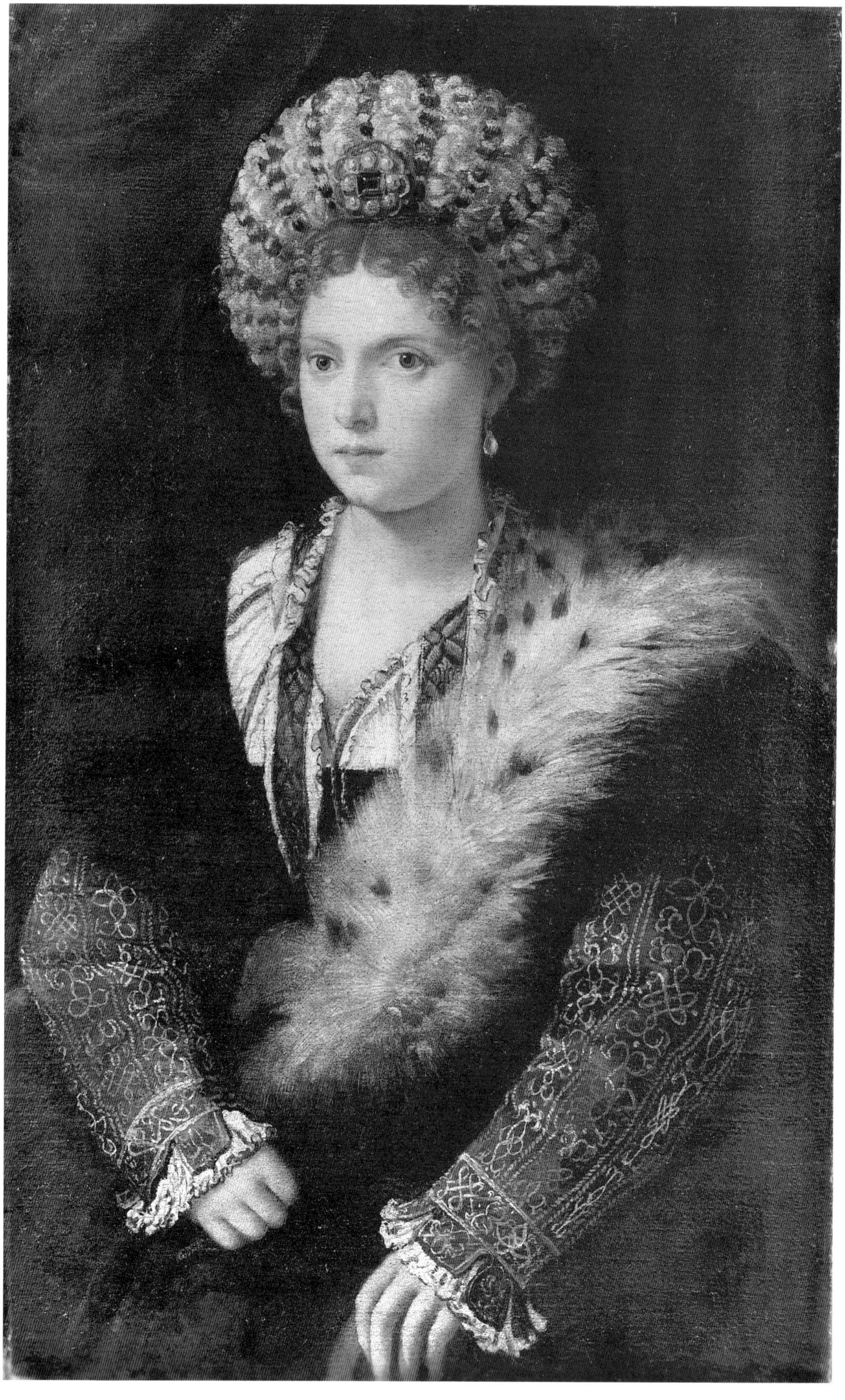

203 (facing page) Domenico Ghirlandaio, *Old Man and Child*, poplar panel, 62.7 × 46.3 cm., Louvre, Paris (R.F. 266).

The preliminary drawing for the old man's head (Stockholm, 1/1863) shows him with closed eyes and downturned mouth and was evidently made from his corpse. He suffered from rhinophyma: the growths on his nose, observed with clinical exactitude in the drawing, have been modified and stylised in the painting. The sitters have not been identified; from the style and from the fashions of their costumes, the portrait is attributed to Ghirlandaio and dated around 1490. Strongly influenced by Netherlandish painting, Ghirlandaio has here imitated a Netherlandish portrait type and has striven to emulate, in details such as the hair, the fur and the foliage of the trees in the background, effects obtained by artists like Memlinc. As he was working in tempera and they in oil, his efforts could not succeed.

See pp. 86, 190.

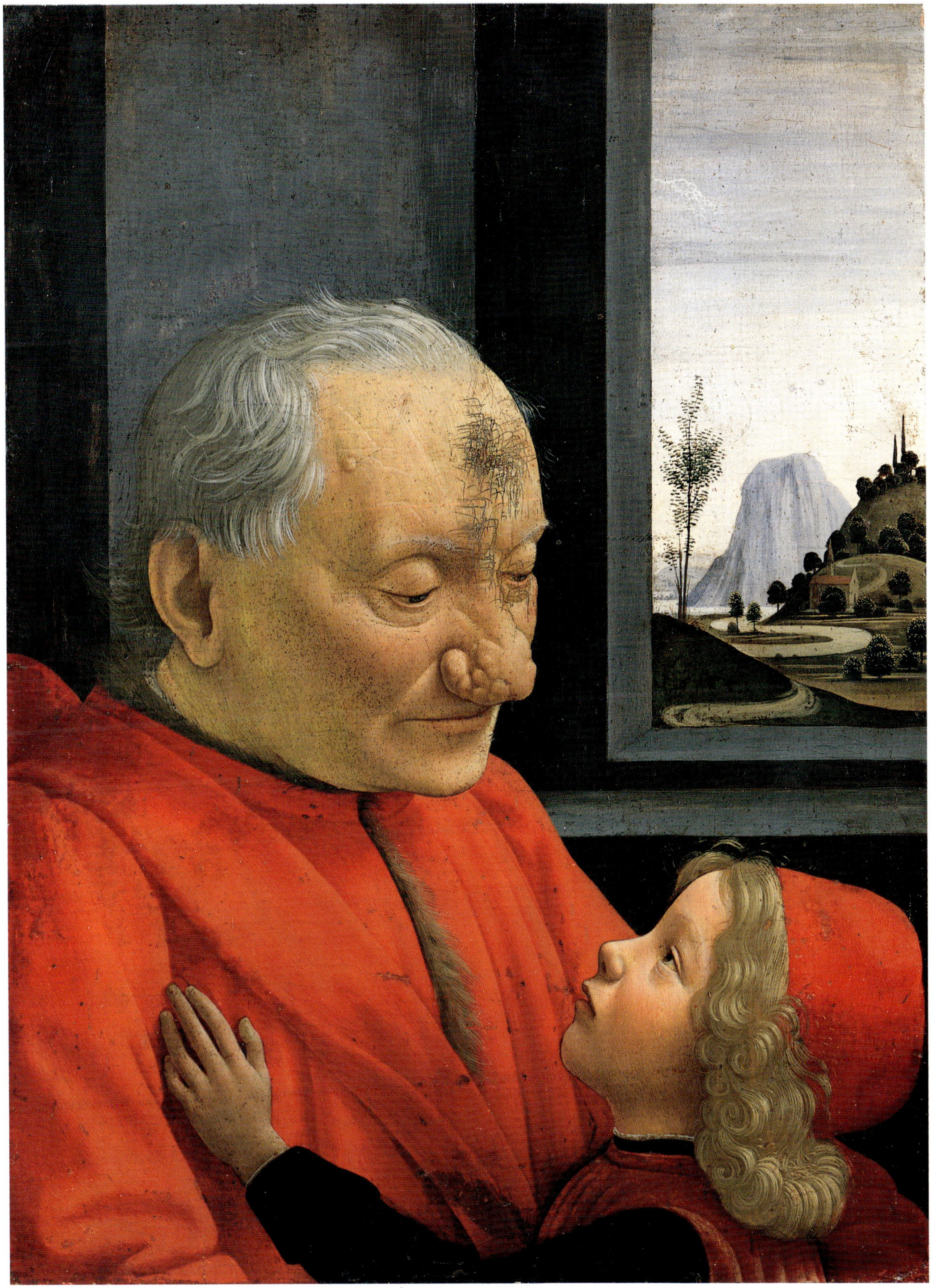

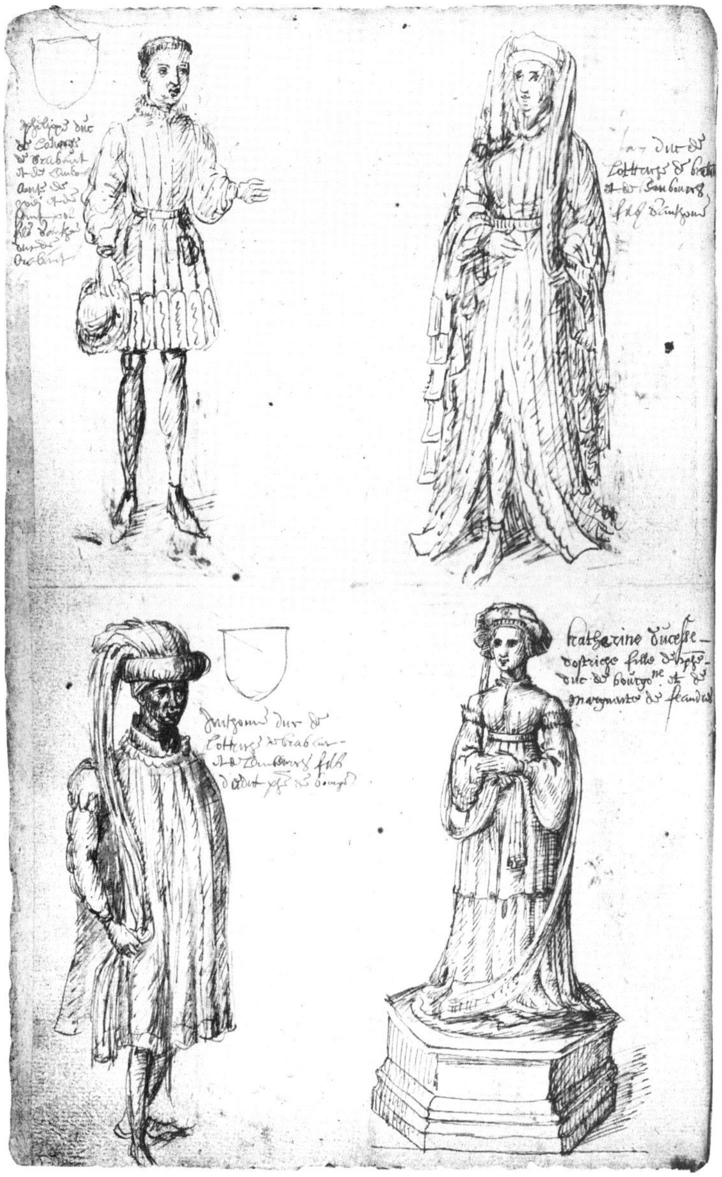

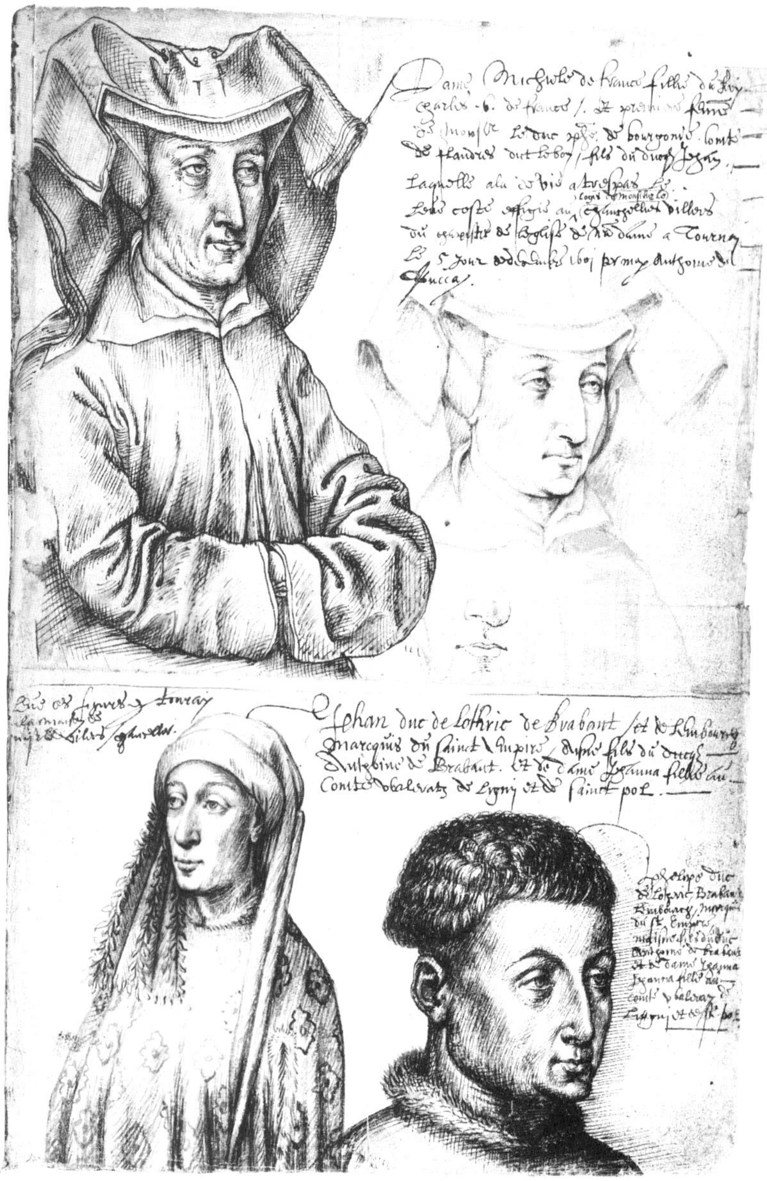

204 (above left) Antoine de Succa, *Four Weepers from the Tomb of Louis of Male, Count of Flanders* from his 'Mémoriaux', Bibliothèque Royale, Brussels, MS II 1862/1, f. 56 v.

Louis of Male, who died in 1384, was buried in the Collegiate Church of St Peter at Lille. His great-grandson Philip the Good, Duke of Burgundy, paid for the magnificent bronze tomb erected in his memory: this was completed in 1455 and destroyed at the end of the eighteenth century. Its appearance is recorded in several drawings and engravings. The Brussels founder Jacob van Gerines contracted in 1453 to construct the monument, upon which he placed his name, but the artists responsible for its design are not named in the available documents. The base of the tomb was surrounded by twenty-four weepers or *pleurants*, representing descendants of Louis; each was identified by his coat of arms, placed on the plinth on which he stood. Philip the Good had made elaborate arrangements to ensure that the tomb would be cleaned four times a year and it was perhaps during cleanings that the *pleurants* were moved about. It is in any case evident that between 1455 and 1602, when Succa made his drawings of the tomb, the *pleurants* had been taken from their plinths and coats of arms and replaced seemingly at random. Succa's identifications of the *pleurants*, made from the coats of arms, are consequently unreliable; some, but not all, can be checked from other sources. In the sheet reproduced, the two figures at the top are correctly identified as Philip of St Pol (1404–30) and John IV (1403–27), Dukes of Brabant; the figure below on the left, called by Succa Antoine, Duke of Brabant, is in fact Louis, Duke of Savoy (1402–65); the figure below on the right is identified by Succa as Catherine of Burgundy, Duchess of Austria (1378–1425). Most or all of the twenty-four figures were based on old portraits (see plate 205). The *pleurants*, or the designs from which they were made, were often imitated by artists responsible for creating portraits of the illustrious dead (see plates 47, 206–7). The copyist Succa (c. 1566–1620), an indifferent draughtsman, was a painter who specialised in historical portraits, over which he endeavoured to enforce copyright restrictions.

See Comblen-Sonkes and Van den Bergen-Pantens, 1977, pp. 166–9; here p. 191.

205 (left) Antoine de Succa, *Three Portraits from the Collection of Denis de Villers* from Succa's 'Mémoriaux', Biblothèque Royale, Brussels, MS II 1862/1, f. 2.

In 1601, Succa copied five portraits then in the collection of Denis de Villers (1546–1620), canon of Tournai cathedral. The three copies on the sheet reproduced are after portraits of Michelle of France (1395–1422), Duchess of Burgundy, and John IV (1403–27) and Philip of St Pol (1404–30), Dukes of Brabant. Versions of these three portraits were known to the Master of the Legend of St Catherine (see plate 11) and to the designer of the *pleurants* on the tomb of Louis of Male (see plate 204). The portraits of John and Philip provided bases for the *pleurants* representing these princes (plate 204) while the portrait of Michelle, who was not represented on the tomb, was used as a source for the *pleurante* identified by Succa as Isabella of Burgundy, Countess of Penthièvre.

See Comblen-Sonkes and Van den Bergen-Pantens, 1977, pp. 98–9; here pp. 5, 191.

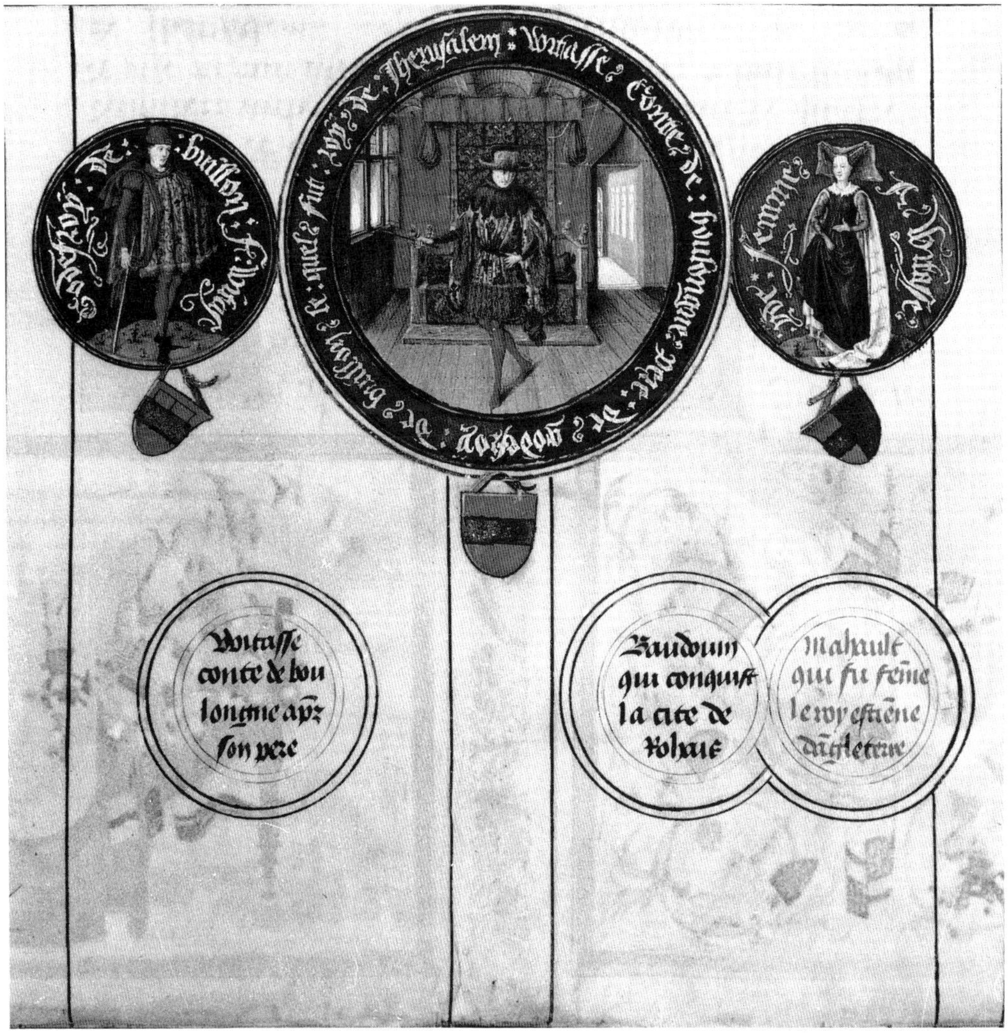

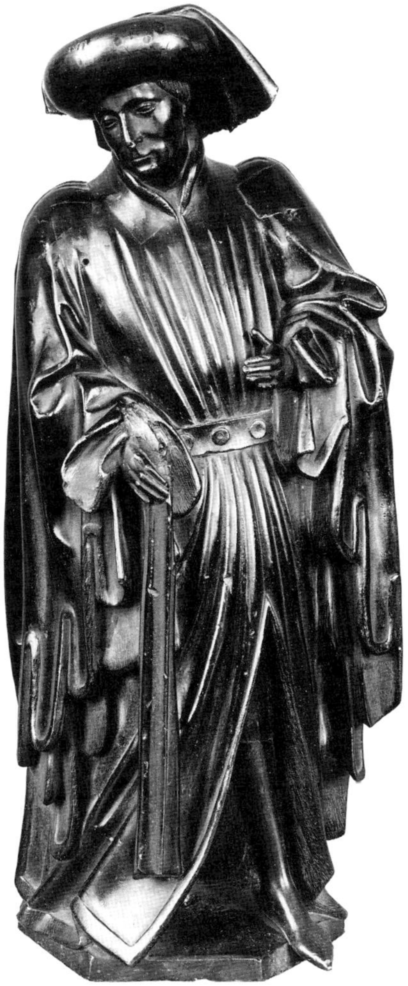

207 (left) Netherlandish, 1476, *Weeper from the Tomb of Isabella of Bourbon, Countess of Charolais*, bronze, 55 cm. high, Rijksmuseum, Amsterdam (Am.33-d).

Isabella, who died in 1465, was the second wife of Charles the Bold, afterwards Duke of Burgundy, and the mother of Mary of Burgundy. She was buried in the church of the abbey of St Michael at Antwerp; her tomb, set up there in 1476, was surrounded by twenty-four bronze *pleurants* representing her ancestors. Ten of them are preserved, all in the Rijksmuseum. Many of them are reversed copies of *pleurants* from the tomb of Louis of Male at Lille. The *pleurant* reproduced, an unidentified ancestor of Isabella, is a reversed copy of the Lille figure of John IV of Brabant (see plate 204), but John was not an ancestor of Isabella and so was not represented on the Antwerp tomb.

See Leeuwenberg and Halsema-Kubes, 1973, pp. 40–5; here p. 191.

206 (above) Netherlandish, c. 1456, *Godfrey of Bouillon, King of Jerusalem, and his Parents the Count and Countess of Boulogne*, parchment, 54.4 × 28.2 cm., from the 'Chroniques de Jérusalem abrégées', Österreichische Nationalbibliothek, Vienna, cod. 2533, f. 2 v.

The manuscript was illuminated shortly after December 1455 for Philip the Good, Duke of Burgundy. The miniatures reproduced are from a family tree of the Kings of Jerusalem and represent Godfrey of Bouillon (died 1100) and his parents Eustace II ('Witasse'), Count of Boulogne (died 1086/8), and his wife Ida of Lower Lorraine. All three correspond to *pleurant* figures on the tomb of Louis of Male: the figure of Godfrey, for example, is based on the same design as the *pleurant* representing Louis, Duke of Savoy (see plate 204).

See Pächt, Jenni and Thoss, 1983, pp. 61–77; here pp. 64, 191.

208 (facing page) Cristofano dell'Altissimo after Jean Fouquet, *Pope Eugenius IV*, panel, 60 × 45 cm., Uffizi, Florence (2982).

The Venetian Gabriele Condulmer (1383–1447) was elected Pope in 1431 and took the name Eugenius IV. Fouquet's lost portrait was described by Filarete and by Francesco Florio, who stated that it was painted on canvas, that it showed Eugenius with two of his familiars and that it was placed in the sacristy of Santa Maria sopra Minerva at Rome (the texts are quoted below, Chapter 9 n. 6). It was probably painted between 1443, when Eugenius returned to Rome from Florence, and January 1447, when he fell gravely ill. An Italian engraving published in 1568 is believed to be a reversed copy of the figure of Eugenius (see Reynaud, 1981, pp. 9–10); nothing further is known about Fouquet's picture. In an inventory taken in 1653 of paintings in the Palazzo Farnese in Rome were listed 'a large portrait of Pope Eugenius IV with two friars' and 'a large picture on canvas with Pope Eugenius IV and two monks' ('Un ritratto di Papa Eugenio 4° in grande con dui frati cornice di noce'; 'Un quadro in tela con Papa Eugenio 4° e due Monici grande con cornice di noce': Bertini, 1987, p. 208 (56, 66)). The same two paintings were listed in another inventory of the palace taken between 1662 and 1680 (*ibid.*, pp. 228 (57), 229 (96), similarly described); nothing further is known about them. One may well have been Fouquet's missing portrait, which a member of the Farnese family might, without much difficulty, have removed from Santa Maria sopra Minerva; the other would have been a copy. Even if the Farnese pictures were both copies, the fact that they were described as 'large' suggests that they were full-lengths. As Fouquet seems normally to have painted on wood, his decision to paint his portrait of Eugenius on canvas may also indicate that it was a large picture and therefore a full-length portrait.

The painting reproduced is one of a series of copies made after pictures in the museum of portraits established at Como by Paolo Giovio (1483–1552). In 1552, Cosimo I de' Medici, Grand Duke of Tuscany, sent Cristofano dell'Altissimo to Como to copy the collection and by 1568 he had dispatched to Florence 280 such copies, including the *Eugenius*. The *Eugenius* at Como must itself have been a copy after the lost Fouquet; Cristofano's copy corresponds with the engraving of 1568 and, though painted at one remove from the original, preserves something of Fouquet's style.

See Berti, 1979, pp. 603, 626; here pp. 52, 191, 228, 233.

portrait. Titian's painting was delivered in 1536 and Isabella was pleased with it (plate 202): 'We doubt whether, at the age at which he represents us, we were as beautiful as the picture.' Isabella was then sixty-two.[98]

Titian was prepared to work not only from other paintings but also from portrait miniatures and medals.[99] According to Aretino, his portrait of Giulia Varano, Duchess of Urbino, was executed from a verbal description given by her husband;[100] he may possibly have referred also to another portrait of Giulia (plate 165). Paleotti, however, affirmed in 1582 that certain artists were able to work solely from verbal descriptions of people whom they had never seen and to execute portraits as marvellous as if they had had long sittings.[101]

Posthumous portraits might be executed from corpses. Ghirlandaio's *Old Man with a Child* may be a case in point (plate 203), as the preliminary drawing of the old man's head seems certainly to have been made after he was dead.[102] During the Sack of Rome in 1527, Baldassare Peruzzi was forced to paint a portrait of the Constable of Bourbon 'either from his corpse or from sketches or descriptions'.[103] Other portraits were made from death masks which, in Florence at least, were much in vogue. According to Vasari, 'infinite numbers, so well made and natural that they seem alive, are to be seen in every house in Florence, over chimney-pieces, doors, windows and cornices'.[104] In 1507, on the death of St Francis of Paola, the French court painter Bourdichon made a death mask, 'so that he might paint a representation of his face according to its true form'. When the saint's body was exhumed later in the same year, he made a second death mask, 'so that he might paint him better and with more certainty'. All this was recorded at the inquest which took place prior to the saint's canonisation.[105] On the death in 1526 of Giovanni de' Medici '*delle bande nere*', Aretino requested Giulio Romano to make a death mask, from which Giulio executed a painted portrait. Titian was later asked to paint a portrait from the same death mask and a painting supposedly by Titian was presented to Giovanni's son Cosimo, Grand Duke of Tuscany.[106] Alessandro Allori charged extra for such portraits. He wrote in his memorandum book on 29 July 1583:

> I have delievered to M^{a}. Lucretia Capponi de' Torrigiani a portrait of her husband Messer Raffaello done after his death, two *braccia* square, with much time put in as well on the clothes as on the head, for which I had nothing but a small clay mould. This I made several months after his death, and the price of the said portrait, given all the labour and time, is 30 gold *scudi*.[107]

In 1549, having heard of the death of the Nuremberg scholar Veit Dietrich, the Duke of Prussia wrote to his widow to say that he had been told that a death mask had been taken and to ask for a cast. In 1550, he wrote to her again, requesting a painted portrait. She commissioned from the Cranach workshop a painting based on the death mask but, when it arrived, she thought it so formless that it was scarcely worth sending to Prussia.[108]

The Duke of Prussia was an avid collector of portraits and spent a great deal of his time writing to correspondents all over Europe to ask for portraits of princes and other notables.[109] In 1546, hearing that the King of Poland was forming a similar collection, he wrote to offer to have any of his own portraits copied and sent to Poland.[110] The most celebrated Italian collection of portraits was that of Paolo Giovio, Bishop of Nocera, who in a letter of 1521 expressed his intention of bringing together 'true portraits of men of letters, the sight of which will stimulate men to virtue'.[111] He was to add portraits of artists, popes and princes and

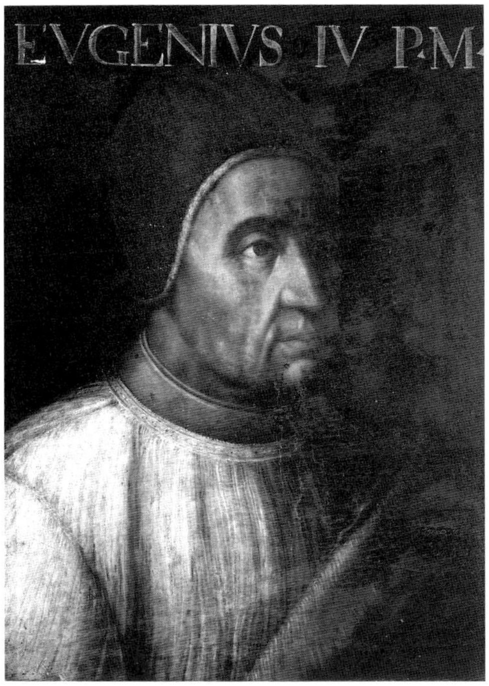

in 1537–43 built a public museum at Como to house the pictures. Giovio persuaded people to send him their portraits by promising that, in his museum, they would be immortalised for posterity.[112] The Medici sent a painter to Como to copy the collection, and hundreds of copies survive in the Uffizi (plate 208).[113] In the 1600s the Florentine copies were themselves copied for the Petitie Galerie of the Louvre.[114]

The collections of Giovio, the Duke of Prussia and many more were continuing, elaborating and systematising an ancient tradition of gathering together series of portraits of princes and famous men.[115] Those patrons who commissioned such series were not all as scrupulous as Giovio in attempting to secure reliable likenesses, which, in any case, were not always available. Even the Electors of Saxony failed to keep up a complete series of family portraits, and when, in 1571–2, the younger Cranach was working on a set of forty-eight full-length portraits of the Saxon family for the Elector Augustus, he could not complete the series because he did not have access to likenesses of the father, grandfather and uncles of Augustus. The Elector wrote that he was unable to supply them, but that he hoped to be able to buy them at the next Leipzig Fair.[116]

Sodoma in the 1500s included in the frescoes he was painting at Monte Oliveto medallions representing all the generals of the Olivetan Order. 'As he had not their portraits, he drew most of them from fancy and from some of the old friars then in the monastery . . .'.[117] Indeed, if genuine likenesses could not be found, portraits of completely different people were frequently used. The tomb of Louis of Male, Count of Flanders, who died in 1384, was set up at Lille in 1455. The base was surrounded by twenty-four bronze figures of 'weepers' representing descendants of Louis, most of whom were long dead. Some at least of the figures were designed after old portraits and, if a reliable likeness was not obtainable, an approximately contemporary portrait of another sitter was used (plates 204, 205). Most of the 'weeper' figures were copied for the tomb of Isabella of Bourbon, Countess of Charolais, erected at Antwerp in 1476: there they represented Isabella's ancestors – a completely different set of people (plate 207). The figures from the tomb of Louis of Male, or the designs from which they were made, served as models for representations of notables of the Crusades in a manuscript of the later 1450s (plate 206) and for some of the countesses in the Bruges series of Counts and Countesses of Flanders (plate 47). They continued until the seventeenth century to provide a repertoire of models for designers of fanciful historical portraits.[118]

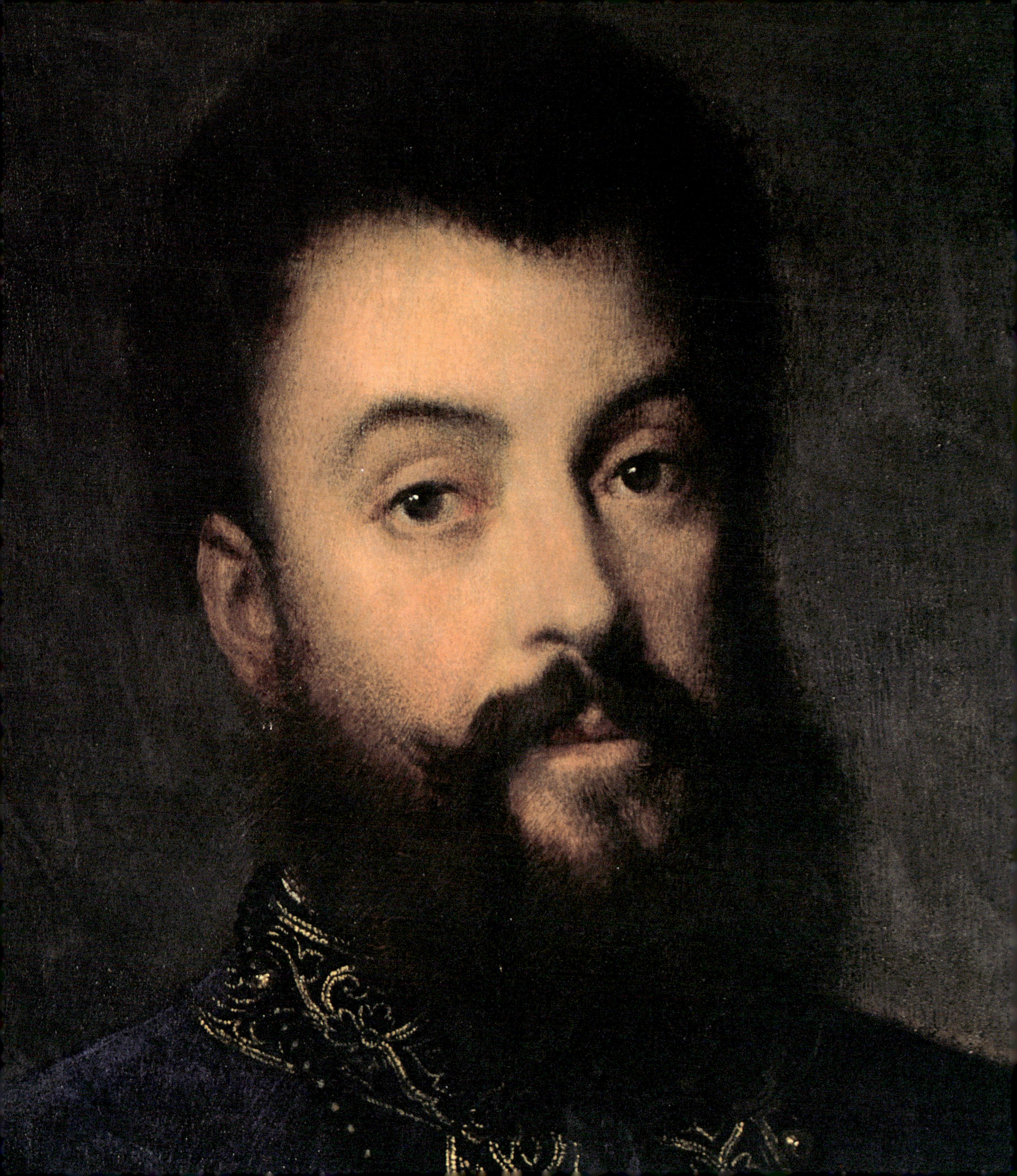

8 The Functions and Uses of Portraits

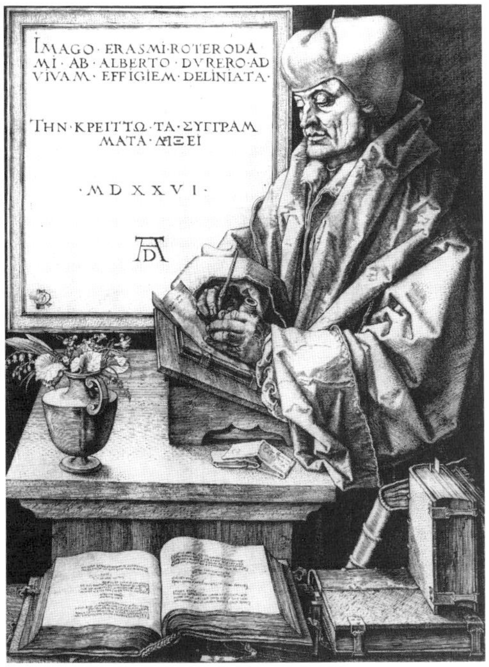

210 Albrecht Dürer, *Erasmus*, engraving, 24.9 × 19.3 cm., British Museum, London, Department of Prints and Drawings (E.3–30).

The Latin inscription identifies sitter and artist and states that the engraving was 'delineated according to his living appearance'; the Greek inscription may be translated 'the better image will his writings show'; below are the date 1526 and Dürer's monogram.

See White, 1971, pp. 178–9; here pp. 162, 193.

209 Titian, *Federico Gonzaga, Duke of Mantua*, detail (see plate 87).

The basic function of portraiture was and is commemorative. Dürer saw in portraiture one of the principal purposes of art: 'It preserves the likenesses of men after their deaths.'[1] In 1526, he decided so to immortalise Erasmus in an engraving (plate 210). Basing his print on a drawing made during an interrupted sitting at Brussels in 1520, he placed on the engraving the modest inscription 'the better image will his writings show'. Erasmus was not altogether satisfied with the portrait which, he thought, was not a striking likeness: 'but that is not suprising for I am not the man I was five [*sic*] years ago'.[2] A portrait of Mario Beltramini, painted in fresco on tile in about 1521 at Colle di Val d'Elsa by Ridolfo Ghirlandaio, had, according to the sitter's son, been kept over a doorway in their house; but 'after his death it was taken down, so that it would not act as a constant reminder of the death of one so much loved by all the family; and through neglect it was broken, to my infinite displeasure . . . If it were possible, I would purchase it again, however high the price.'[3] Leonardo stated that, in portraits, beauty is preserved which otherwise Nature and Time would destroy;[4] and the poet Bernardino Bellincioni, who died in 1492, expressed similar thoughts in a sonnet on Leonardo's portrait of Cecilia Gallerani (see plate 67).[5]

Christopher Hales, attempting to obtain from Zürich portraits of six Protestant divines, was obliged to explain, in a letter of 1550, his reasons for wanting them:

> I desired to have them on this account, that they might be an ornament to my library and so that your images might be beheld in pictures, as in mirrors, by those who, because of distance, are prevented from seeing you in person. This is not done . . . with a view to making idols of you; they are desired for the reasons which I have mentioned and not for the sake of honour or veneration.[6]

In 1574, Hortensia Borromeo, Countess of Hohenems, wrote to her husband, then campaigning in the Low Countries, to thank him for a portrait which she had just received:

> I experienced so much sweet emotion when I saw this picture, for which I had waited so yearningly and fervently, that I no longer knew whether I was on earth or in heaven. Marvelling, and repeatedly looking, at the beautiful face, I . . . lost recollection of all else in the world . . . For me, the time of your absence now passes with far less pain that at first, for I will now delight in this image until your homecoming.[7]

Gabriele Paleotti allowed that people might ask for a portrait of a relative or friend from whom they were separated, 'in order to be able, by this means of keeping a picture, to alleviate the hurts brought about by his absence'.[8]

Many authors mentioned the practice of keeping family portraits, for example Vasari in his life of Giovanni Bellini:

> It became customary in that city [Venice] that every man of any note should have his portrait painted either by Giovanni or by some other. In all the houses of Venice are many portraits and several gentlemen have those of their ancestors to the fourth generation while some of the noblest go even further back. The

custom is a most admirable one and was in use among the ancients. And who does not experience the utmost satisfaction in seeing the likenesses of his ancestors, especially of those who have been distinguished in politics, for worthy deeds in war and peace, in letters or for other honourable qualities? Moreover the portraits are themselves ornamental.[9]

If a sitter had neglected to have his portrait taken during his lifetime, a death mask could be made or an artist could be employed to execute a representation of the corpse on which posthumous portraits might be based. It may be assumed that, normally, such portraits of corpses would have been transformed into life-like images for public presentation, but in certain circles there was a demand for uncompromising depictions of corpses. It was said of Signorelli that

> when a much-loved son, very handsome in face and figure, was killed at Cortona, he had him stripped naked and, with extraordinary strength of mind and without shedding a tear, made a representation of the body, because he wished always to be able to see, in the work of his own hands, what Nature had given to him and what cruel Fortune had taken away.[10]

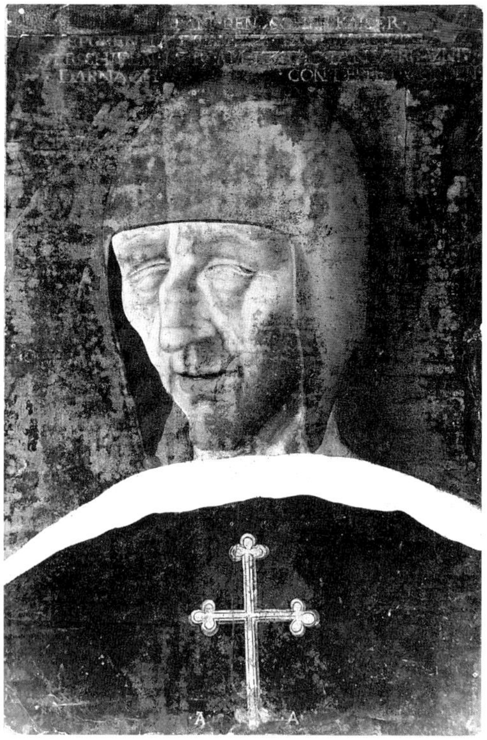

211 Monogrammist AA, *The Corpse of the Emperor Maximilian I*, paper, 43 × 28 cm., Landesmuseum Joanneum, Graz, Alte Galerie (392).

The inscription records that Maximilian was born on 22 March 1459 and died on 12 January 1519 'and thereafter has been counterfeited'. The initials AA are on either side of the cross. Several versions are known but the Graz painting is believed to be the original, executed by the unidentified monogrammist immediately after the emperor's death at Wels, near Linz.

See Biedermann, 1982, pp. 171–3; here pp. 14, 194.

212 (facing page, left) Netherlandish, c. 1450, *Man with an Arrow*, panel, 75 × 50 cm., Koninklijk Museum voor Schone Kunsten, Antwerp (539).

The Latin inscriptions on the black scroll are from St Paul's Epistle to the Romans 13:11: 'Now it is high time to awake out of sleep' and from the First Epistle of St John 2:18: 'because it is the last hour'. On the clock face are written 'Tant que je viue' and 'Aut[re] Nauray' ('As long as I live, I will have no other'), a motto used by Philip the Good, Duke of Burgundy; the hand of the clock is about to point to twelve. The sitter has not been identified but the style of the painting and the sitter's costume indicate that the portrait was executed in about 1450 by a follower of Rogier van der Weyden.

See Vandenbroeck, 1985, pp. 158–61; here pp. 61, 196.

The Emperor Maximilian I, who died in 1519, was depicted as he lay on his death-bed by the Monogrammist AA (plate 211); in 1564, on the death of the Emperor Ferdinand I, a painter was employed to portray the corpse, and his painting was sent to the emperor's daughter, the Duchess of Mantua.[11] Elisabeth of Austria, Queen of France, owned at the time of her death in 1592 a version of the picture of Maximilian I's corpse and a companion painting of the corpse of her father Maximilian II, who had died in 1576.[12] Two painters are known to have made representations of Luther's corpse on his death in 1546: the first, when the body was still in the death-bed; the second, Furtenagel, when the corpse had already lain a night in the coffin.[13]

Some, like the boastful Aretino in letters of 1544 and 1545, gloried in the fact that their portraits, in all conceivable media, were scattered about the world like those of Alexander the Great, Julius Caesar and Scipio.[14] In 1499, however, Isabella d'Este wrote, though without much sincerity, of her concern that she would 'weary . . . all Italy with sending out my portraits'.[15]

Many people were clearly worried that commissioning a portrait might be taken as a mark of ostentation and self-satisfaction, and some philosophers and art theorists were anxious to provide portraiture with a moral justification. Sir Thomas More, for instance, wanted 'the ymages [*statuas*] of notable men' to be set up in the market-places of his Utopia, 'for the perpetual memorie of their good actes; and also that the glory and renowne of the auncestors may sturre and prouoke their posteritie to vertue'.[16] This view was widely shared. The Italian theologian Gabriele Paleotti, writing in 1582, agreed that people might benefit from contemplating portraits of the virtuous, but was suspicious of the motives of those who commissioned portraits of themselves and utterly against portraits of those whom he considered vicious. He objected to flattering portraits and to frivolous accessories like pet dogs, flowers or fans; and he particularly condemned the exchange of portraits by illicit lovers. He praised a Bolognese painter who, commissioned to execute portraits of such a kind, supplied instead images of Christ at the Column or of the Madonna. According to Paleotti, his clients were 'stupefied' with religious emotion and highly satisfied by the edifying substitution.[17]

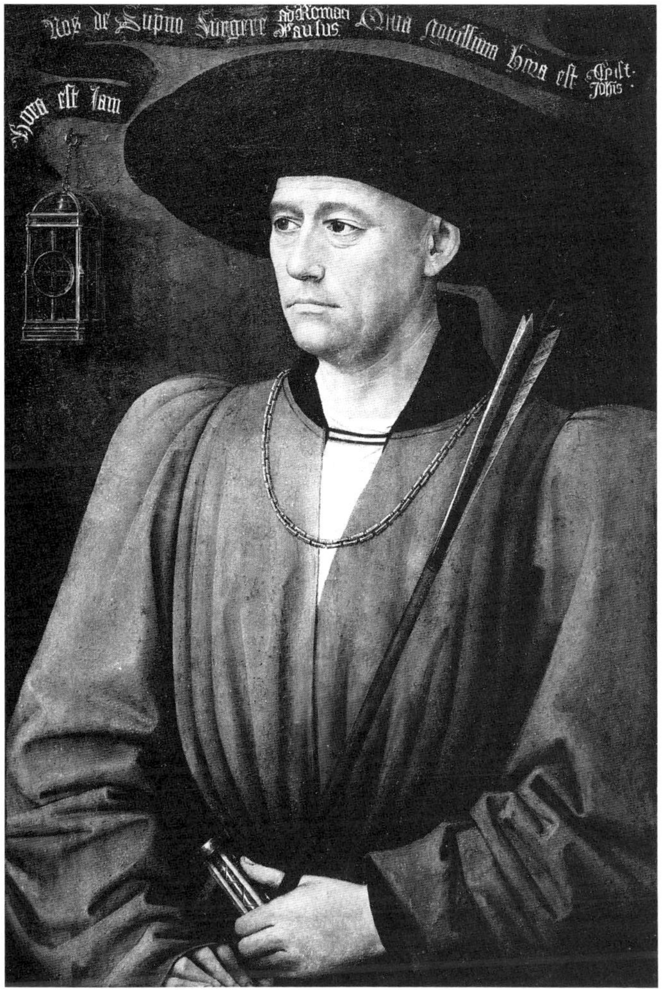

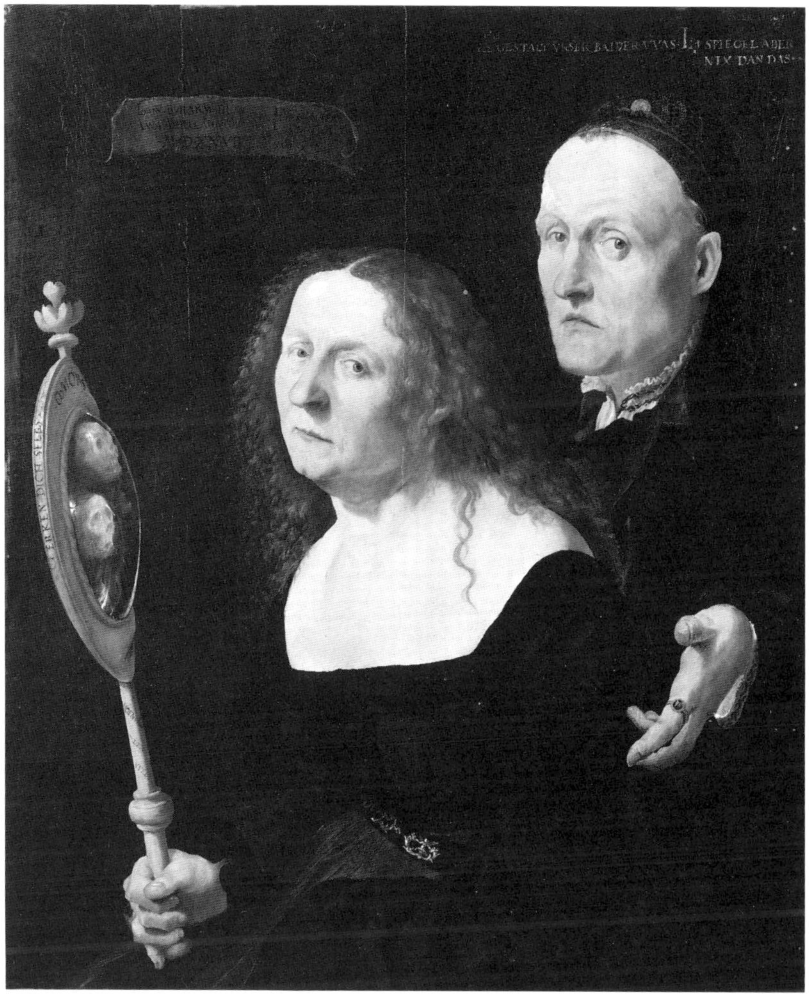

213 (above right) Lucas Furtenagel, *Hans Burgkmair and his Wife*, limewood panel, 60 × 52 cm., Kunsthistorisches Museum, Vienna, Gemäldegalerie (924).

The artist's signature is in the top-right corner; below is a German inscription in which the sitters address the spectator: 'Such was our shape in life; in the mirror remains nothing but this'. On the paper in the top-left corner is written, in German: 'Hans Burgkmair, painter, 56 years old/Anna Allerlay, his wife, 52 years old/10 May 152[?9]'. On the frame of the mirror are inscriptions in Latin: 'O Death', and in German: 'Know thyself'; on its handle is written, in German: 'hope of the world'. For a print by Burgkmair, see plate 257.

See Klauner and Heinz, 1963, pp. 58–9; here p. 196.

Painters, too, worried over the ethics of portraiture. Francisco de Holanda justified it by saying that, as an imitation of God's work of creation, it was the highest of the arts. Only famous princes deserved to be portrayed and so commemorated, or princesses who, by their virtue and wisdom, were worthy to be remembered, or famous men distinguished in war, art or letters or in liberality and virtue. It was right for children to keep portraits of their parents and ancestors, so that they were always present for the emulation of their virtues and the honour of the family, 'and if someone loves very faithfully and chastely, he is worthy to have the portrait of the face that he loves, as well for its absences in life as for its commemoration after death'.[18]

The sitters were occasionally moved to justify the fact that they commissioned portraits. In 1494, Isabella d'Este, giving her portrait by Giovanni Santi to the Countess of Acerra, wrote that she was sending it 'to satisfy your ladyship's wish, not because my appearance is of such beauty that it deserves to be painted . . .'.[19] In 1543, Claudio Tolomei wrote to Sebastiano del Piombo to ask him whether he would paint his portrait. He would never have dared to make the request in person, and did not know whether he was prompted by ambition, or vanity, or both, but Sebastiano had often offered to paint him. If he now agreed to fulfil his promise, Tolomei would have a 'divine mirror' in which he would see Sebastiano and himself together: 'you, because I will perceive in my image your singular ability and your marvellous skill; me, because I will see my image . . . which will constantly stimulate me to purge my soul of its many shortcomings . . . it will fire my soul with a fine desire for honour and glory'.[20] The English musician Thomas Whythorne, who died in 1596, thought that portraits should be contemplated by the sitters to inspire them to consider 'how they ought to alter their conditions' and prepare for death. He believed that people should leave portraits to their friends, and especially to their children, to encourage them to learn from their moral examples.[21]

The moralising purpose of some portraits is very obvious, for example the *Man with an Arrow*, painted in about 1450 by a follower of Van der Weyden, with its inscriptions warning that the 'hour is come' and with its clock, the hand of which is just about to point to twelve (plate 212), or the *Man with a Pansy and a Skull*, painted in the Netherlands in about 1535, in which the pansy stands for thought and the sitter is clearly meditating upon death.[22] Lucas Furtenagel's portrait of the painter Hans Burgkmair and his wife, which is dated 1529, shows the sitters' heads reflected as skulls in the mirror, and the mirror frame is inscribed 'know thyself' (plate 213).

The evidence concerning portraits of members of royal and princely families is inevitably much more informative than that for other social groups, and it is as well to concentrate first on royal and princely portraits. The princes of Europe used portraits to keep themselves and their families in the public eye and to let foreign courts know what they looked like and how they were all getting on. In 1514, for example, an English ambassador at Mantua asked for, and received, portraits of the marquis and his wife Isabella d'Este, which were to be presented to Henry VIII.[23] Henry owned also a portrait of the three children of Christian II, the exiled King of Denmark, which was painted in about 1526. The children were the great-nieces and great-nephew of Henry's wife Catherine of Aragon; otherwise there seems to have been no specific reason for sending the portrait to England (plate 128). In 1580, Philip II of Spain sent to the Emperor of China equestrian portraits of himself and his father the Emperor Charles V.[24] In 1606, Marie de' Medici, Queen of France, dispatched to Italy a case that contained, as she wrote to a cousin: 'our portraits, which I send to you in order to refresh your memory of us'.[25]

Princesses who were forced to live at great distances from their children were naturally anxious to have portraits of them. In the winter of 1541–2, Eleonora of Austria, Queen of France, wrote to her only child Maria of Portugal, her daughter by her first husband. Maria was then twenty, and had not seen her mother for many years: 'With your picture, daughter, I have idled much, since I am unable to see the original . . .'.[26] In about 1541, the Duke of Longueville, then six, wrote to his mother Mary of Guise, who had left him in France when she went to Scotland in 1538 to marry James V: 'My lady my granny will send me to my lady the Queen, but painted on a canvas and as big as I am and I am so very pretty now that I have my hair cut like my uncles'.'[27]

Portraits were used to check on the health of absent members of princely families. Catherine de' Medici, Queen of France, generally lived apart from her children, who had their own household and their own painter. In 1548, she wrote to their governor: 'I have received the pictures of my children which you had done for me . . . and I see that they are much recovered since I saw them.'[28] Four years later, she wrote urgently requesting more portraits of the royal children, which were to be 'as they are without omitting anything of their countenances', to be in

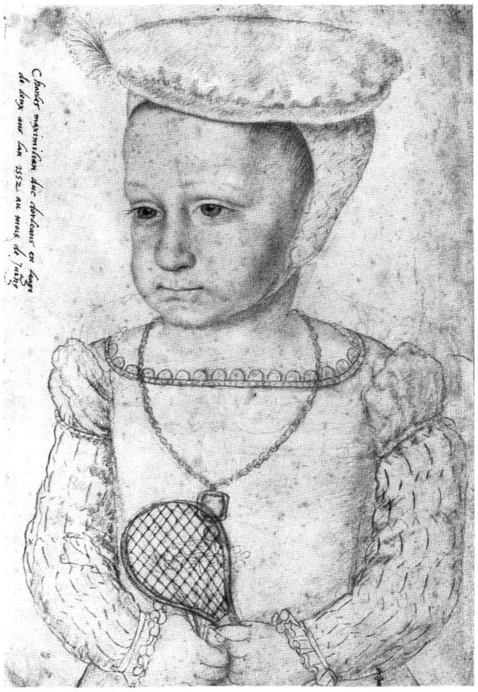

214 Germain Le Mannier, *Charles IX, King of France, aged Two*, black, red and yellow chalks on paper, 33.5 × 23.4 cm., Musée Condé, Chantilly (MN 39).

The inscription may be translated 'Charles Maximilian, Duke of Orléans, at the age of two in the month of June 1552'. The sitter, born on 27 June 1550, was a younger son of Henry II of France and Catherine de' Medici and succeeded to the throne on the death of his brother Francis II in 1560. He holds flowers in his right hand; the small racket in his left hand is drawn across the flowers and the pendant jewel. The drawing may be grouped with two others, also at Chantilly, representing Charles's brother Francis and Francis's future wife Mary, Queen of Scots: they are dated July 1552. All three may be associated with letters written on 1 and 16 June by Catherine de' Medici to her children's governess in which she asked for crayon portraits by 'the painter whom you have there' of all her children and the Queen of Scots. They were to be posted to her and the three drawings have been folded, perhaps to facilitate their transport by post. The 'painter whom you have there' was apparently Germain Le Mannier, who had been appointed painter to the royal children in 1547.

See Moreau-Nélaton, 1901, pp. 35–8; here pp. 196–7.

crayon, for the sake of speed, and to be sent to her by post.[29] Three of the drawings survive (plate 214). In 1586, the Grand Duke of Tuscany wrote to his son-in-law the Duke of Mantua to congratulate him on the birth of his first child, a son born just over a fortnight previously. 'Seeing from the portrait, and hearing from everyone, that the baby . . . is so fat and large and bouncing', he proposed that he should undergo a cauterising operation and offered to send a surgeon from Florence.[30] In 1626, Sustermans was to record the sufferings of the sixteen-year-old Ferdinando II, Grand Duke of Tuscany, during an attack of smallpox: he painted his portrait on the seventh and ninth days of his illness.[31]

When a marriage between princes was being negotiated, a portrait of the lady was often sent to the man so that he might have some advance knowledge of her appearance. In 1442, for example, when Henry VI of England was thinking of marrying one of the daughters of the Count of Armagnac, Hans the painter was sent in all haste to execute portraits of the ladies: 'in their kertelles simple, and their visages, lyk as ye see their stature and their beaulte and color of skynne and their countenaunces, with al maner of features'.[32] Charles VI of France, hearing of the beauty of Egidia, daughter of Robert II of Scotland, sent a painter in secret to take her portrait and intended, if it pleased him, to marry her. Before the painter arrived in Scotland, however, the lady married Sir William Douglas of Nithsdale.[33] A 'most expert' painter was sent to the courts of Bavaria, Austria and Lorraine to execute portraits of three other eligible ladies: Charles, seeing the three pictures, chose Isabella of Bavaria, whom he married in 1385.[34] The beauty of the woman as she appeared in her portrait seems often to have been an important factor in determining a prince's choice of consort. Holbein's portraits of the prospective wives of Henry VIII or England are the best-known surviving examples of such pictures: his *Duchess of Milan*, painted in 1538, and his *Anne of Cleves*, painted in 1539 (plates 1, 96).

The lady was not expected to take so strong an interest in her future husband's appearance but often did receive a portrait as marriage negotiations went forward. Before her marriage in 1473 to Ercole d'Este, Duke of Ferrara, Eleonora of Naples received from her betrothed two portraits by Cosimo Tura: one was of Ercole himself, while the other was of his illegitimate daughter Lucrezia.[35] Even if an intended couple were babies, portraits might be exchanged. In 1477, Tura was paid for three portraits of the one-year-old Alfonso d'Este, Ercole's son and heir.[36] One of them was sent to Milan and a portrait of Alfonso's betrothed, Anna Sforza, then aged four, which was completed after some delays by a French painter, was then dispatched to Ferrara.[37] Such exchanges of portraits became to some extent formalities. Elizabeth I of England, however, found it convenient to say that she refused to put her trust in portraits and insisted on seeing her suitors in person. As she told an Austrian ambassador in 1565, she knew very well 'how the King of Spain had cursed the painters and envoys when he first beheld Queen Mary', her sister; Elizabeth had no wish to give her suitors cause to curse.[38] Philip II had perhaps seen one of Eworth's numerous portraits of Mary (plate 215); whereas Mor's portrait of the queen, painted in 1554 after she had married Philip, must undoubtedly have been a more uncompromising likeness (plate 216).

In 1564, there were plans to marry Philip II's son Don Carlos to his cousin the Archduchess Anne, and the Austrian ambassador in Madrid sent to Vienna a superficially flattering, but in fact devastatingly critical, description of Carlos's physique.[39] He then sent a painted portrait by Sánchez Coello (plate 217), with a covering letter in which he noted that the prince's mouth always hung open,

215 Hans Eworth, *Mary I, Queen of England*, panel, 20.4 × 15.3 cm., National Portrait Gallery, London (4861).

The painter's monogram HE and the date 1554 appear in the upper-left corner. The sitter (1516–58) is identified by comparison with other portraits and holds a rose, one of the emblems of the Tudor dynasty. The portrait is one of several similar paintings of Mary; Eworth was apparently supplying a lively demand for them.

See Strong, 1969[2], p. 87; here pp. 115, 197.

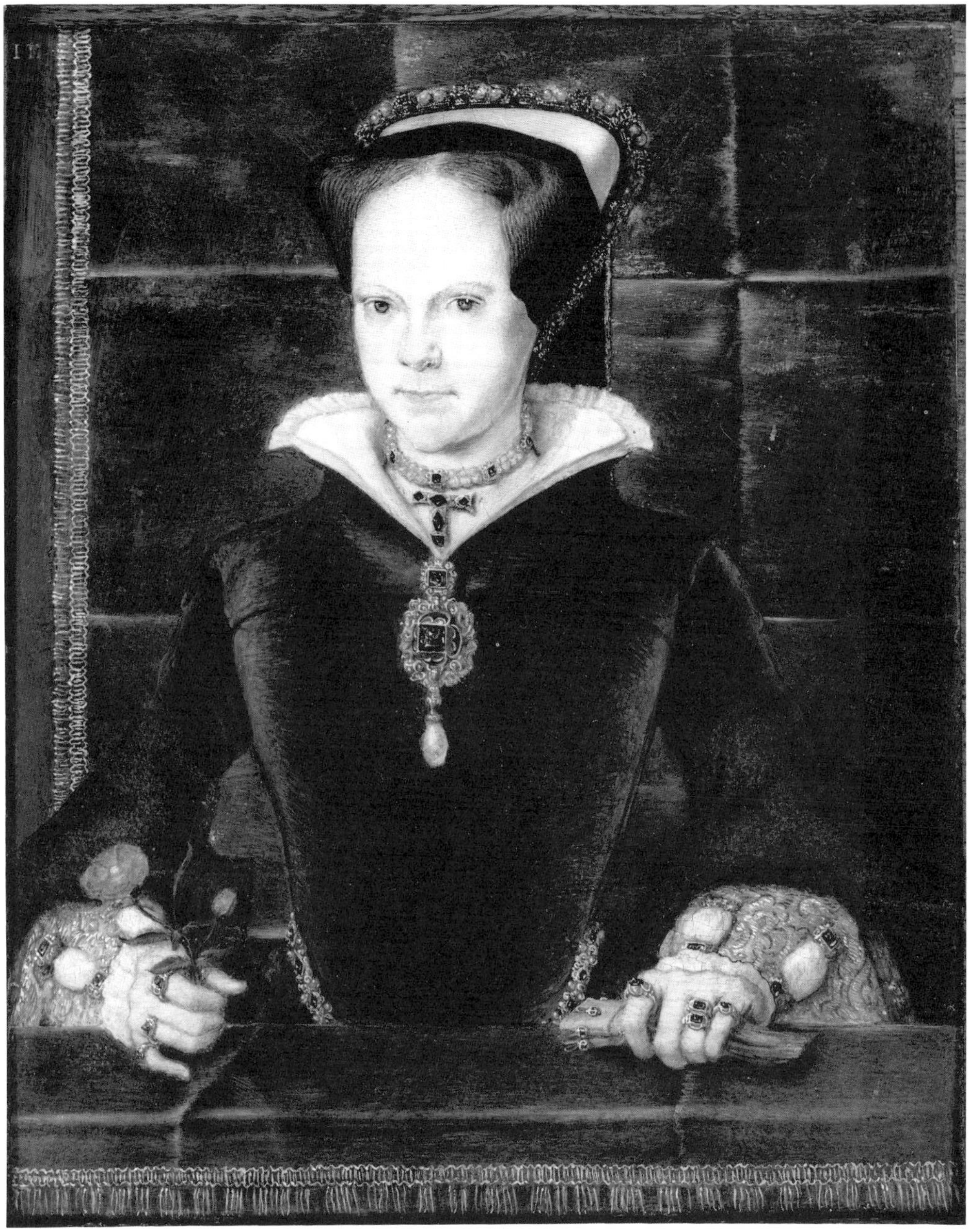

216 (facing page) Antonis Mor, *Mary I, Queen of England,* panel, 109 × 84 cm., Museo del Prado, Madrid (2108).

The picture is signed and dated 'Antonius mor pingebat 1554'. In July 1554, Mary married Philip II of Spain. Mor went to England at the end of that year and in December, in London, Philip granted him an annual pension. According to Van Mander, Mor travelled to England at the command of Philip's father, Charles V, who retained the original portrait of Mary. A second signed version, inscribed 'Antonius mor pinxit 1554', is in the collection of the Marquess of Northampton; a third version of good quality is in the Gardner Museum at Boston. There are numerous other copies: Van Mander stated that Mor made several replicas of the head, which were given to the great nobles of the Low Countries.

See Campbell, 1985, p. xxvi; here pp. 61, 107, 124, 197, plate 2.

that his face was less full and that his eyes were less open than the painter had represented them.[40] Sánchez Coello had not been able to conceal the fact, already mentioned by the ambassador, that Carlos's shoulders were unequal in height and that his left leg was considerably longer than his right. A miniature of Anne, set in a diamond cross 'worth over a thousand ducats', was sent to Carlos and it was reported in 1567 that he always wore it.[41]

Portraits of foreign princes, accumulating in royal collections, could be put to political use. In 1559, the French ambassador in England reported that Queen Elizabeth had taken him into her 'gallery' at Hampton Court where she had shown him a portrait of Mary of Guise, Queen Regent of Scotland, and used the occasion to protest her affection for Mary.[42]

Some portraits were, of course, expressly designed for propaganda purposes. It

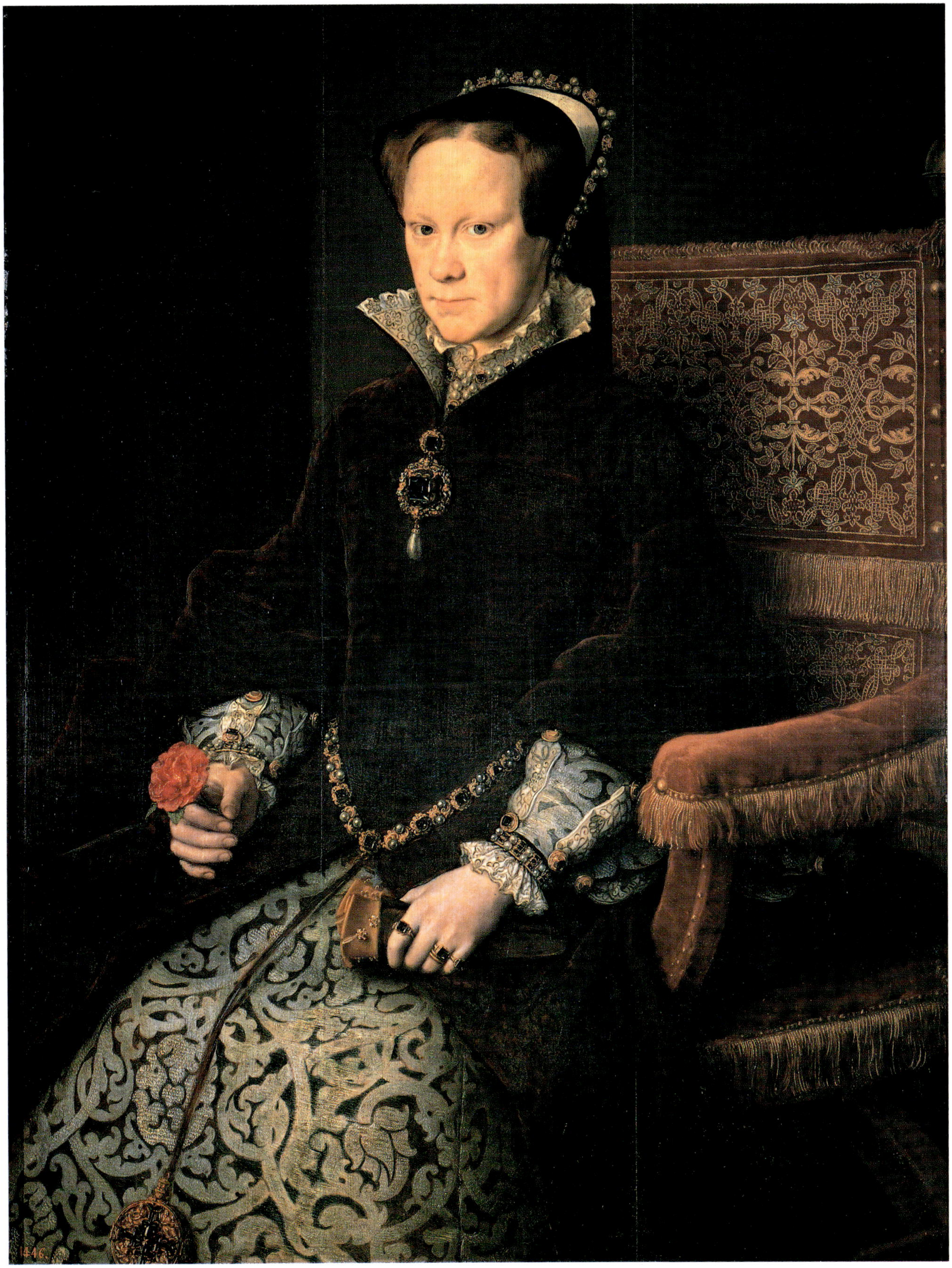
1446.

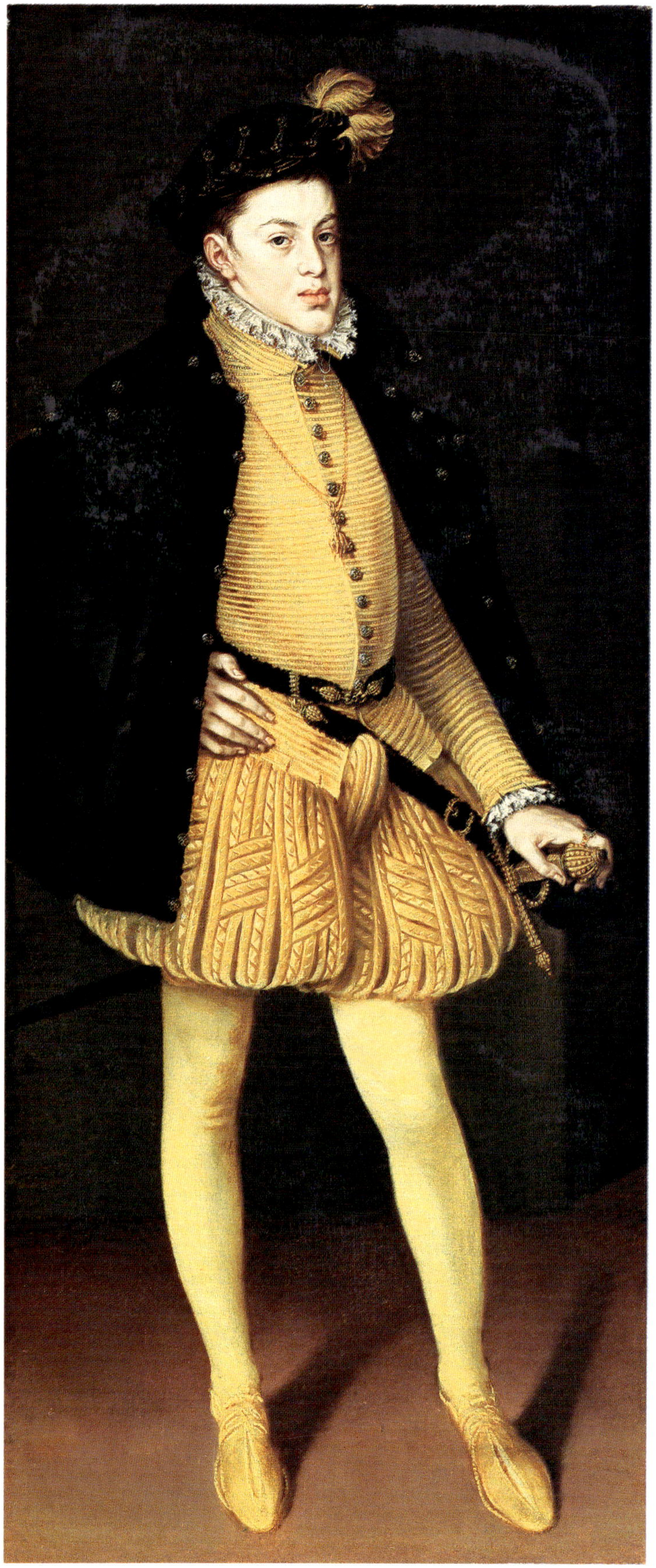

217 Alonso Sánchez Coello, *Don Carlos*, canvas, 186 × 82.5 cm., Kunsthistorisches Museum, Vienna, Gemäldegalerie (3235).

The sitter (1545–68) was the eldest son of Philip II of Spain and the portrait, signed and dated 'A. Sanchez F. 1564', was painted during negotiations for a marriage between Carlos and his cousin Anne of Austria (who afterwards married his father). On 29 June 1564, the Austrian ambassador in Madrid reported that the picture was not quite ready, but on 4 July, he was able to announce that it was being dispatched to the emperor.

See Zimmermann, 1909–10, *passim*; here pp. 120, 197–8.

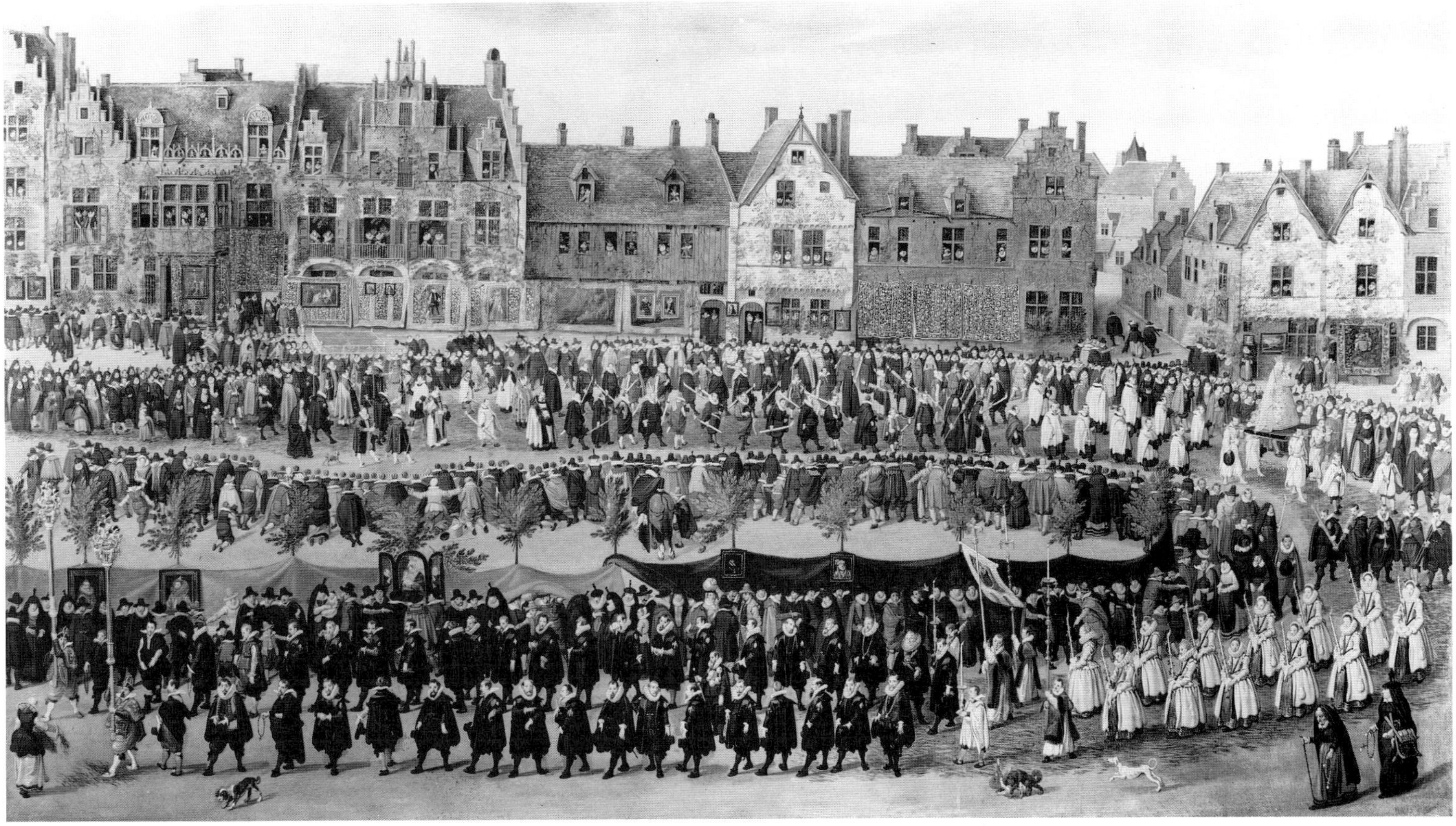

218 Anthonie Sallaert, *Procession in the Place du Grand Sablon at Brussels*, panel, 56 × 99 cm., Galleria Sabauda, Turin (296).

The painter's monogram AS appears on the figure in the lower-right corner; the picture may be dated around 1620. The route of the procession is hung with rich textiles and with pictures, many of which are portraits. In the foreground on the left, suspended from trees against a red drapery, are half-length paintings of Albert and Isabella, rulers of the Spanish Netherlands. The two smaller portraits in the centre are probably of Isabella's father, Philip II of Spain, and of a Knight of the Golden Fleece in full ceremonial attire – he is possibly one of Albert's brothers, the Emperors Rudolf II and Matthias. In the background, hung against patterned cloths from the façade of one of the houses, are life-size full-length portraits, apparently again representing Albert and Isabella. Other portraits decorating the façades depict more simply dressed sitters, perhaps ancestors or relations of the inhabitants of the houses. The picture itself is, of course, a group portrait.

See Bernardi, 1968, pp. 210–11; here p. 201.

was common for portraits to be publicly displayed at ceremonies such as 'joyous entries' and during processions. Among the painted decorations prepared in 1398 for display at one of the Antwerp *ommegangen* was a float showing the Dukes of Brabant.[43] Louis XII of France, entering Paris in 1498, was greeted at the Châtelet by images of himself and eight of his ancestors, back to St Louis.[44] Queen Mary I, entering London in 1554, found the streets hung with images of her predecessors.[45] An early-seventeenth-century picture by the Brussels painter Anthonie Sallaert shows such a procession (plate 218). When in 1615 the Infanta Isabella, Regent of the Netherlands, had won 25,000 florins in an archery competition by shooting a stuffed bird off the top of the Sablon church in Brussels, she had invested the prize money to provide dowries for six poor virgins every year. The painting shows twelve of the virgins in procession, and the route is hung with painted portraits of Isabella and her family.[46]

The monarch most keenly aware of the value of portraits in propaganda was probably the Emperor Maximilian I, who wrote: 'He who during his lifetime provides no remembrance for himself has no remembrance after his death and the same is forgotten with his passing bell, and therefore the money that I spend on my remembrance is not lost . . .'.[47] Not being well supplied with money, Maximilian wisely concentrated on prints and illustrated books, which were cheaper than paintings and could be widely disseminated. His *Triumphal Arch*, printed from 192 woodcut blocks, over eleven feet in height and designed by Dürer, was a vast glorification of Maximilian and his dynasty and was completed in 1515.[48] The more portable *Weisskunig*, a sort of autobiography, was never finished but was to have had over two hundred woodcut illustrations.[49]

Raphael's portrait of the Medici pope, Leo X (plate 141), was sent to Florence in 1518, just in time to be hung over the duchess's table at the banquet following her entry into Florence with her husband Lorenzo de' Medici, Duke of Urbino. This was an important political event, and the display of Raphael's portrait in so prominent a position was obviously intended to stress the power and connections of the Medici family.[50]

Painted propaganda could, of course, be wilfully misleading. Mor's great portrait of Philip II was described in the Escorial inventory of 1576 as showing the king as he was during the 'war of St Quentin' in 1557.[51] The implication of the portrait is that it represents Philip commanding his troops at the Battle of St Quentin; but in fact he was not present and, though dressed that day in the armour shown in the painting, he kept at a safe distance (plate 219). Portraits were also used in hostile propaganda. In 1583, a 'fowle picture' of Elizabeth I of England was displayed in Paris: 'she beinge on horsback her left hande holdinge the brydell of the horse, with her right hande pullynge vpp her clothes shewing her hind-parts... Vnder ytt was a picture of Mons[r] [Francis, Duke of Anjou] verie well drawen in his best apparell ...'.[52]

If it was in the princes' interests to encourage the diffusion of their portraits at home and abroad, it was also essential for them to censor the portraits and to attempt to exert some sort of control over their production. In 1541, the French ambassador in London reported that no painter was permitted to execute a portrait of Princess Mary without the permission of her father Henry VIII.[53] During Elizabeth's reign, there were repeated attempts to control production of portraits of the queen. In 1563, a proclamation was drafted in which it was stated that

> all manner of painters have already and do daily attempt to make in short manner portraiture of her majesty in painting, graving, and printing, wherein is evidently seen that hitherto none hath sufficiently expressed the natural representation of her majesty's person, favour or grace, but that most have so far erred therein as thereof daily are heard complaints among her loving subjects ...

Consequently Elizabeth was

> content that some special commission painter might be permitted, by access to her majesty, to take the natural representation of her majesty, whereof she hath been always of her own disposition very unwilling, but also to prohibit all manner of other persons to draw, paint, grave, or portray her majesty's personage or visage for a time until, by some perfect patron and example, the same may be by others followed ...[54]

In 1596, the Privy Council issued

> A warant for her Majesty's Serjeant Painter and to all publicke officers to yelde him their assistance touching the abuse committed by divers unskillfull artizans in unseemly and improperly paintinge, gravinge and printing of her Majesty's person and vysage, to her Majesty's great offence and disgrace of that beutyfull and magnanimious Majesty wherwith God hathe blessed her, requiring them to cause all suche to be defaced and none to be allowed but suche as her Majesty's Serjant Paynter shall first have sight of.[55]

Walsingham wrote from Paris on 28 January 1572 to the Earl of Leicester: 'Touching the pictures your Lordship desired, they can by no means be gotten, for

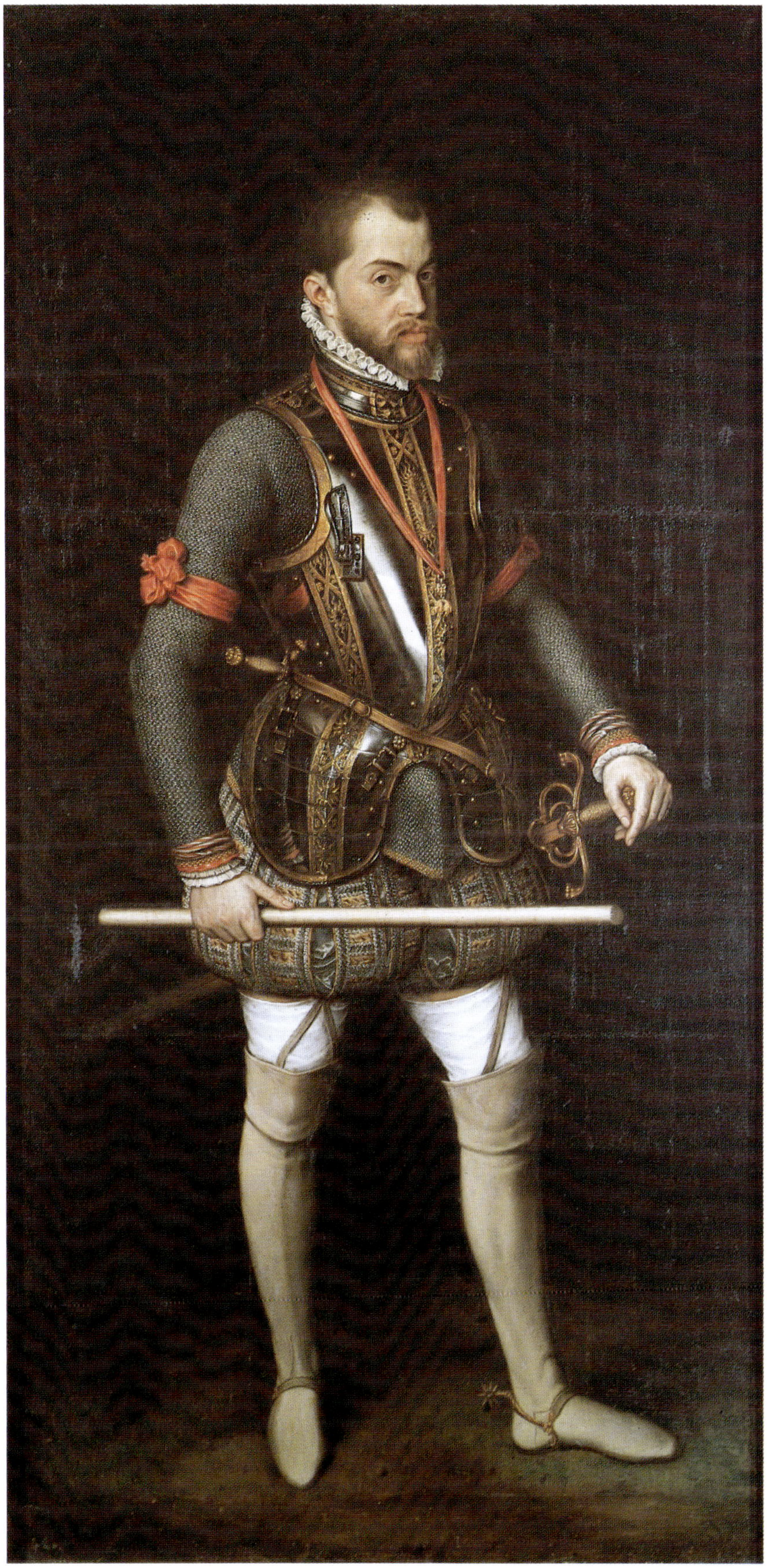

219 Antonis Mor, *Philip II, King of Spain*, canvas, 138 × 125 cm., Monasterio de San Lorenzo, El Escorial (1653).

The inscription 'A. Moro f.^o' which appears in the lower-right corner is an addition and not a signature. The portrait was given by the king to the Escorial in 1576, when it was described as by Mor and as representing Philip as he was during the 'war of St Quentin' in 1557.

See pp. 124, 202, 239–43.

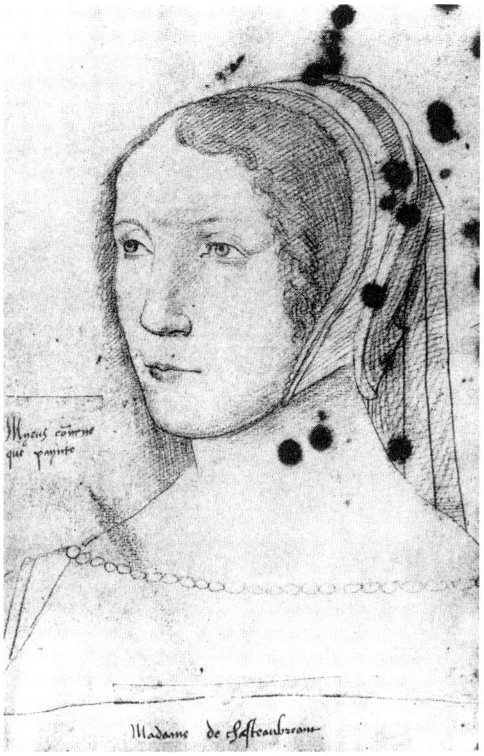

220 After Jean Clouet, *Françoise of Foix, Countess of Châteaubriant* from the 'Recueil Montmor', Bibliothèque Méjanès, Aix-en-Provence, Rés. MS 20, f. 13.

The inscriptions read 'Madame de chasteaubreant' and 'Myeus cõurne que paynte', 'better contoured than painted': this seems to suggest that the sitter was more shapely than she appeared in the drawing. Françoise (1495–1537), the wife of Jean de Laval, Count of Châteaubriant, was one of the mistresses of Francis I of France. The 'Recueil Montmor' is an album of fifty-one drawn portraits all but five of which bear inscriptions in an early-sixteenth-century hand identifying the sitters. Twenty-one carry epigrammatic, and often unflattering, descriptions, written in the same hand. Both sets of inscriptions were once covered by flaps of paper glued to the drawings: only one survives, but the marks left by the others are easily seen. Those who looked at the album were evidently expected to guess the name of each sitter and the drift of the epigram. The flaps might then be raised to prove them right or wrong. The 'Recueil Montmor', the only surviving album with such epigrams, is thought to have been put together in about 1523, because of the identities of the persons represented. The drawings are amateurish copies. That reproduced derives ultimately from a lost drawing by Jean Clouet, whose distinctive, Leonardesque technique of hatching the copyist has tried to imitate.

See Moreau-Nélaton, 1924, II, p. 158; Dimier, 1924–7, III, pp. 9, 10; here p. 205.

no man may make any counterfeit of the King or his Brother, without license; if he do, the punishment is great.'[56]

Perhaps because of anxieties over uncontrolled production, a notion that approved portraits might almost be 'published' seems to have arisen. A French ambassador in London noted in 1553 that Mary I had had her portrait painted and that 'she desires soon to cause it to appear'.[57] In 1579, the Elector of Saxony sent to Cranach the Younger 'models' for portraits of two of his sons, but instructed him 'not to make them public, and send them back as soon as you have no more need of them'.[58]

At the courts of Europe, portraits were everywhere. Royal portraits decorated such objects as gaming boards and the cases of lutes,[59] and they often provided diversion during idle moments of court routine. In 1498, Isabella d'Este wrote from Mantua to Cecilia Gallerani in Milan:

> Today we happened to be looking at certain fine portraits by the hand of Giovanni Bellini and we came to discuss the works of Leonardo, and wished that we could compare them with these pictures. Remembering that Leonardo has painted your portrait, we ask if you would be good enough to send us your portrait by this messenger so that we may be able not only to compare the works of the two artists but also to have the pleasure of seeing your face again. As soon as the comparison has been made, we will return it to you.[60]

In 1532, a correspondent in Ferrara wrote to Isabella d'Este to tell her that he had been discussing with the Duchess of Ferrara a resemblance between her two-month-old daughter Anna and Isabella, the baby's great aunt. He remembered having seen a portrait of Isabella as a child, and asked Isabella if she would send it to Ferrara.[61] Isabella replied immediately:

> I am sending, for the pleasure of the duchess, my portrait, which is, I think, the one about which you wrote to me and which was done when I was about three . . . I have given to the painter, to have it restored, another portrait of myself which was done after I was married. When it is ready, I will send it to you.[62]

As soon as the pictures arrived in Ferrara, they were taken to the duchess, 'and they pleased her more than I can say, and we went immediately to see the baby. My lady, the child portrait is most certainly like her . . .'.[63] The duke and duchess had both portraits copied before returning them to Isabella.[64]

In 1507, Louis XII of France wrote from Italy, where he was campaigning, to Guillaume de Montmorency: 'when Perréal has done your portraits, have them sent to me, to show to the ladies of this country . . .'.[65] In 1566, Mary, Queen of Scots, visited a merchant's house in Edinburgh, where there was a portrait of the Queen of England. As the company discussed the likeness, Mary took this improbable opportunity to assert her claim to the English throne: 'Nay, quoth she, it is not like her, for I am Queen of England.'[66] From Antwerp in 1567, the Earl of Sussex wrote to Elizabeth I to give an account of an interview with Margaret of Parma, Regent of the Netherlands:

> she desired moche to see your picture, which with some travell she recovered, and for that it was drawen in black with a hoode and a cornet which she perceived was not the attire Your Majestie now used to were, she desired me, if I had your picture, that she might see it . . . I answered at the first that the picture commonly made to be solde did nothing resemble Your Majestie . . . I

coulde not denye the havinge of your picture, which she sawe with the Duchesse of Askott and the Countesse of Mansfelde and certen other lordes and ladyes, in whose presence Monsr de Maldingham affirmed it to be so like unto you as ther lacked but speche . . .[67]

Dr Wilson, another English ambassador, reported in 1577 to Elizabeth a conversation he had had with Don John of Austria:

> And then, somewhat to please hym for the tyme, I shewed hym Your Majesties picture . . . And suerlie, Madame, Don Jhon was moche pleased with the sight of it, and perused it verie curioslie a good longe tyme . . . he desired earnestlie of me to have Your Majesties entier stature and makinge, and the sooner the better. I towlde him I woulde doe my best upon my retorne . . . but, in the meane season, I desired his whole picture, whiche he promysed I showlde have . . . if I cawse any paynter cumme to hym in my name, he wil sytte him for my sake, and so I shal have hym.[68]

Whether Dr Wilson really wanted a full-length portrait of Don John seems doubtful. In 1582, Catherine de' Medici exhibited to the French court a portrait of Elizabeth:

> The Quene moother this other daie shoed in Courte her Ma^{ts} picture made in full length and p[ro]portion by her owne frenche painter wch was lately in England, of the wch picture this Quene semeth to make great est'macione . . . The great princesses did note, and weare very much satisfied to see her ma^{tie} appareled and attyred all over alla françoyse.[69]

Courtiers also played games with portraits. In France in the early sixteenth century, albums of drawn portraits were manufactured in which inscriptions giving the sitters' names and epigrammatic descriptions might be covered with flaps of paper: these albums were used in guessing contests (plate 220).[70] Brantôme recalled that, during the reign of Henry III of France (1574–89), a gentleman gave to his mistress a costly manuscript in which there were illuminated portraits of thirty-two ladies of the court. They were represented in various states of dress or undress, engaging in amorous pursuits with one or several lovers, and 'over a hundred and forty' of Aretino's positions were depicted. The book was shown round the court. While some ladies took at least two hours to peruse it, another 'conceived so ardent a desire to imitate these lascivious paintings that she was unable to get beyond the fourth folio, and at the fifth she fell down in a swoon'.[71]

The anamorphosis of Edward VI of England, painted in 1546, delighted generations of visitors to Whitehall, who viewed it through a special apparatus (plate 221).[72] In 1592, Ludovico Buti was paid for having constructed an elaborate trick portrait, on a panel of triangular facets, of the Grand Duchess of Tuscany and her

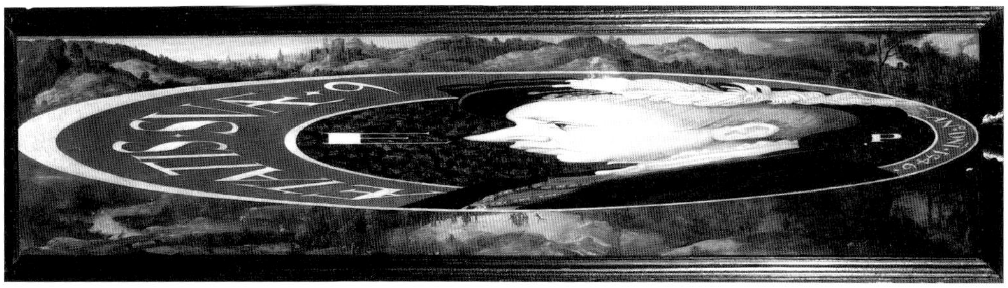

221 Guillaume Scrots, *Edward VI of England aged Nine*, panel, in its original frame, 42.5 × 160 cm., National Portrait Gallery, London (1299).

In 1713, the frame bore the inscription 'Guilhelmus pingebat', which has subsequently disappeared but which was evidently the signature of Guillaume Scrots, a Netherlandish artist who in 1546 entered the service of Edward's father Henry VIII. The sitter is identified by the initials EP, for Edwardus Princeps; he was born on 12 October 1537 and the Latin inscription records that the portrait was painted in 1546 when he was nine. The landscape is a later addition. The portrait is an anamorphosis and the distortions are resolved when it is viewed from the correct angle.

See Strong, 1969[1], pp. 88–90; here p. 205.

222 Ludovico Buti, *Charles II, Duke of Lorraine, and his Daughter Christina, Grand Duchess of Tuscany*, panel, 87 × 70 cm., Museo di Storia della Scienza, Florence (3197).

Buti's bill for the object, dated 26 February 1592, was addressed to Christina's husband, Ferdinando I de' Medici. The smaller rectangle is a mirror, secured at ninety degrees to the edge of the larger rectangle. This is a panel, across the surface of which are laid horizontally thirty-seven lengths of wood, triangular in section. The two portraits, copied from other images, are painted in horizontal strips on the two exposed sides of each of the thirty-seven triangular pieces of wood – that of Charles on the forward-facing facets, that of Christina on the opposite facets. The panel normally hangs vertically in its mounting but, if it is turned as in the reproduction, the spectator will see at the same time the portrait of Charles on the panel and the portrait of Christina reflected in the mirror.

See Langedijk, 1981–3, I, pp. 657–8; here pp. 205–6.

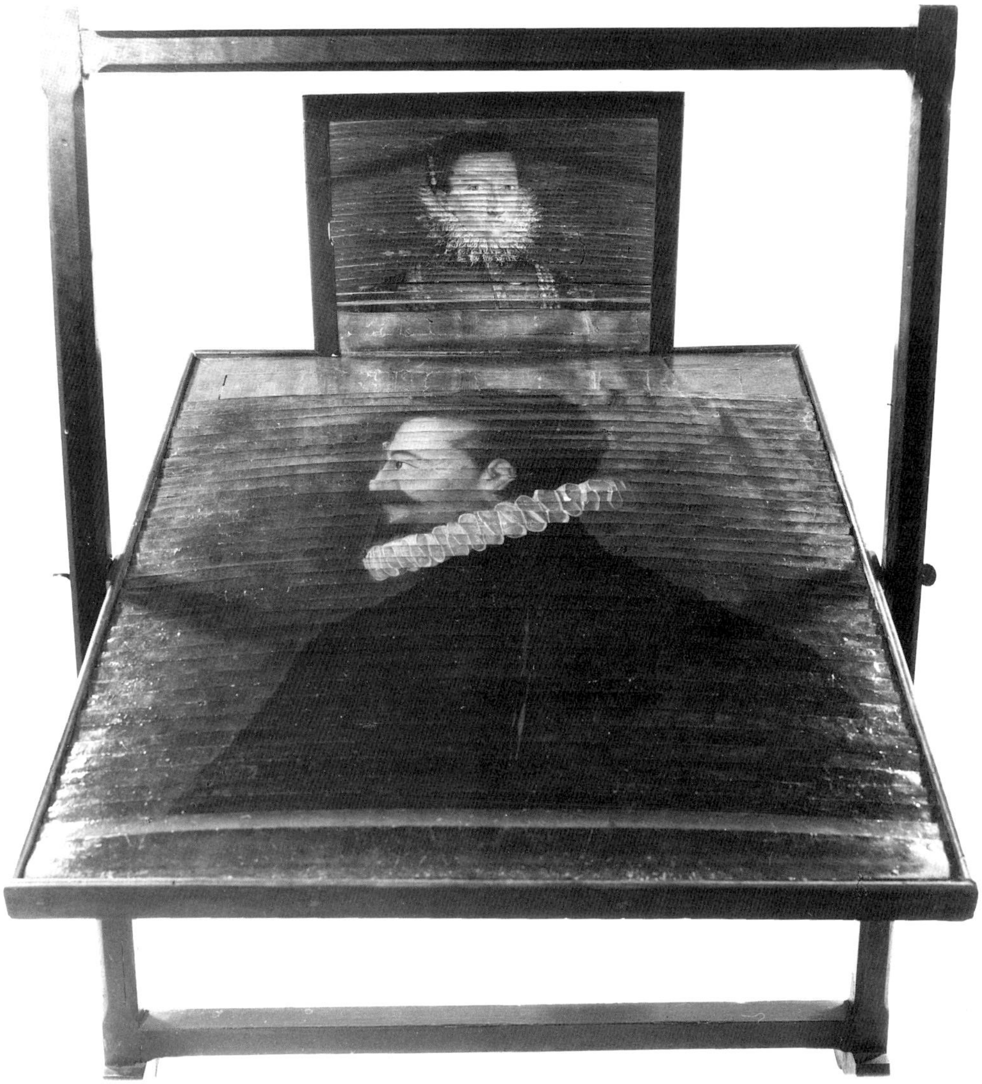

father the Duke of Lorraine. The first portrait is seen in a mirror attached to the frame of the second (plate 222).[73] Henry II of France gave a similar portrait of himself to Cardinal Caraffa.[74] In a book published in 1638, Nicéron explained how to make such objects and also how to manufacture pictures that, seen from different angles, represented two or three different things; 'and in truth these images, when they were novelties, had some success, although they are not difficult to make: but now they have become so common and trivial that they are seen everywhere'.[75] Satirical portraits were likewise produced to amuse the court, for instance Henry VIII of England's portrait of his rival Francis I of France (plate 224), which is described in his 1542 inventory as 'oone table with the pictures of the Frenche king, the Quene his wiff and the foole standing behing hym'.[76]

Portraits of the dwarfs and other freaks employed at the courts were also painted, and sometimes burlesqued the poses used in the grand state portraits of princes (plates 124, 166). Portraits of royal children, though not executed merely to amuse the court, often similarly burlesqued portraits of their elders: Sánchez Coello's *Infante Diego*, dated 1577, refers back to Titian's equestrian portrait of his grandfather the Emperor Charles V, and the humour of this would have been obvious to courtiers in Madrid, for the Titian was displayed in the palace there

223 (right) Alonso Sánchez Coello, *The Infante Don Diego*, canvas, 111 × 91 cm., Private Collection, United Kingdom.

Diego, born in July 1575, died in November 1582; his father was Philip II of Spain. The portrait once bore an inscription giving the subject's name; it is signed 'Alfonsus. sancius. F.' and dated 1577. The child wears several amulets.

See the exhibition catalogue London, 1981, p. 65 (21); here pp. 120, 206.

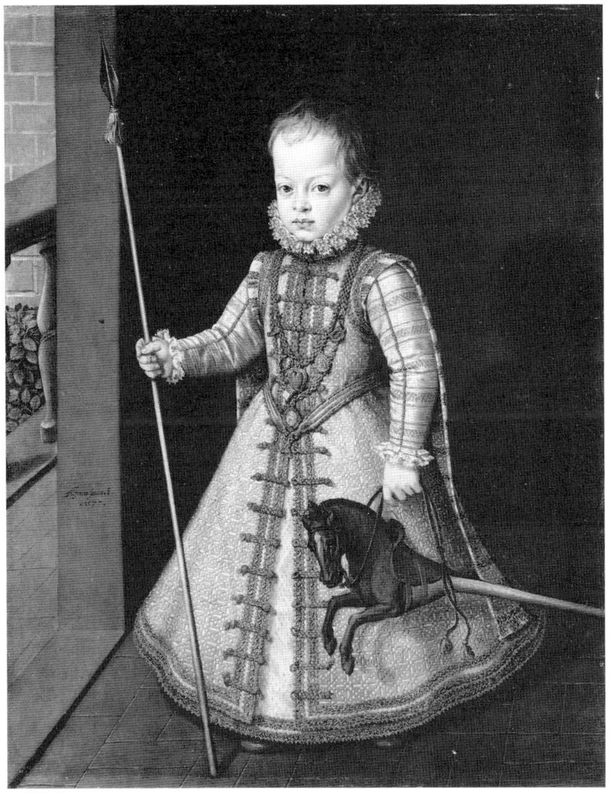

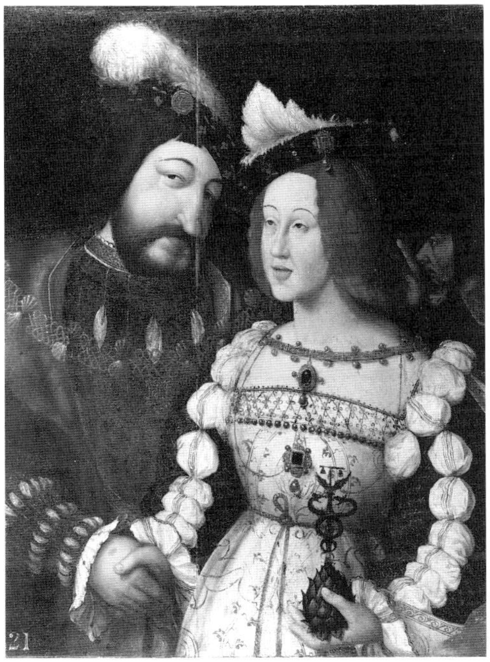

224 (above) English, c. 1535, *Francis I of France, Queen Eleonora and a Fool*, panel, 81 × 56 cm., Royal Collection, Hampton Court (321).

Francis I of France (1494–1547) married in 1530 as his second wife Eleonora of Austria (1498–1558), sister of the Emperor Charles V. Each wears a hat badge decorated with the initial of the other: L (for Leonor) and F. Eleonora holds an artichoke surmounted by a caduceus; the significance of this is uncertain. By 1542, the picture was in the collection of Francis's great rival Henry VIII of England, for whom it was probably painted. It resembles in composition those pictures of 'unequal lovers' which at that time were popular in Germany and the Low Countries: there are well-known examples by Quinten Metsys and by the elder Cranach. The intent of the portrait is clearly satirical and it was presumably painted for Henry's amusement by one of his court painters, who might have referred to paintings of Francis and Eleonora already in Henry's collection.

See p. 206.

225 (below) Alonso Sánchez Coello, *The Infantas Isabella and Catherine*, canvas, 133.5 × 145 cm., Royal Collection, Buckingham Palace, London.

Isabella (1566–1633) and Catherine (1567–97) were the daughters of Philip II of Spain by his third wife Elisabeth of Valois, who died in 1568. The painting reproduced, given to Charles I by the Earl of Ancrum, is dated 1571 and is attributed to Sánchez Coello on stylistic grounds. A better-known, similar portrait is in the Prado (1138): it is also attributed to Sánchez Coello and there the infantas are slightly older.

See Breuer, 1984, pp. 208–9; here p. 208.

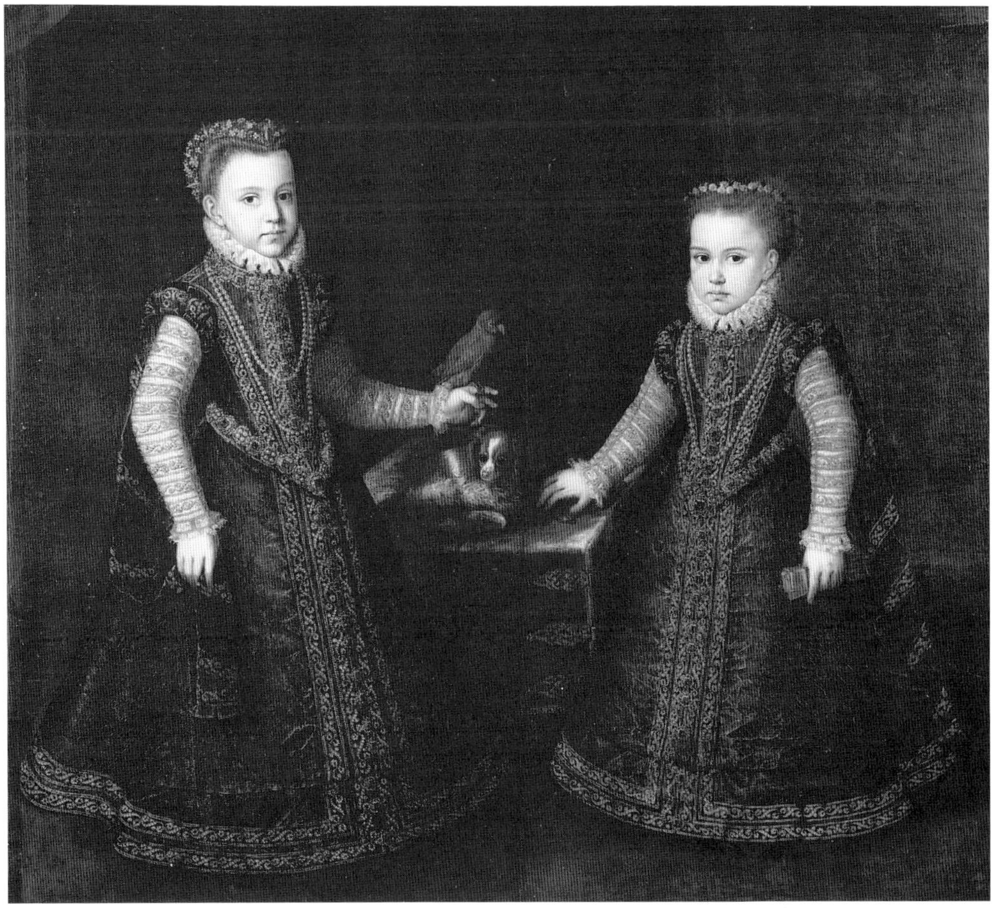

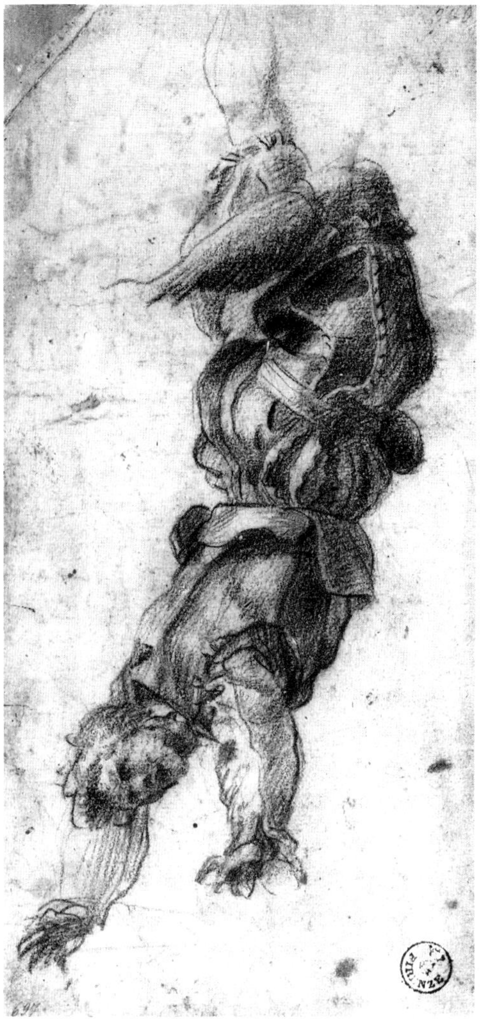

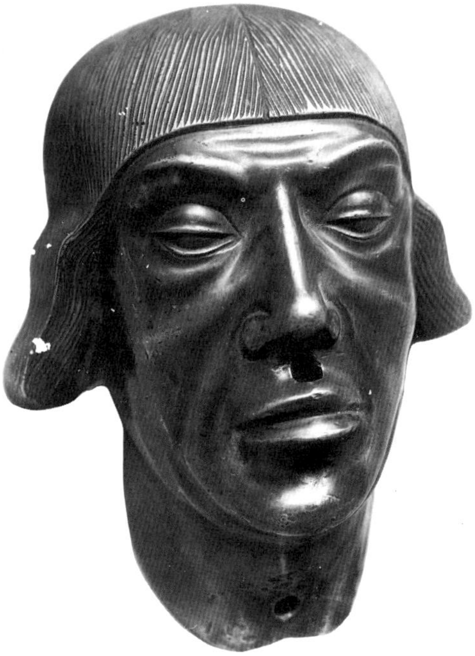

(plates 223, 258). In Sánchez Coello's portrait of Diego's half-sisters Isabella and Catherine, dated 1571, the infantas stand in slightly awkward imitations of the pose in which their dead mother, Elisabeth of Valois, had often been painted (plates 120, 225, 242). Partly, no doubt, because of the reference to portraits of Elisabeth, a similar painting of the infantas attracted malicious comment at the French court. As Brantôme recalled,

> I was once in a great company at court where we were looking at the portrait of two daughters of a very great queen. Everyone began to give his opinion on whom they resembled and all agreed that they inherited everything from their mother; but I . . . said that they inherited all their features from their father and that, if they had known and seen their father as I had done, they would allow that I was right . . . At this, the queen's sister thanked me . . . because there were certain persons who were saying this on purpose, as she was suspected of having taken lovers and of having, as they say, 'some dust in her flute'.[77]

At the courts, where portraits were of such importance in diplomacy and in diversion, it is hardly surprising that court portraitists became people of eminence and that princes behaved towards them with considerable familiarity. Their studios were treated almost as places of entertainment. The Dukes of Saxony often visited Cranach the Elder's workshop and praised his work;[78] Philip II of Spain lodged Sánchez Coello

> in a grand house beside the palace, and often used to arrive unexpectedly, in morning attire, by a secret passage – to which he alone had a key – surprising him at meal times with his family. When he wished to rise and show due reverence, the king would restrain him and go to entertain himself in the workshop. On other occasions, he would catch him seated painting and come up behind him putting his hands on his shoulders; seeing himself so favoured by His Majesty, he tried courteously to rise, but the king would make him sit and continue painting.[79]

The evidence for portraits of the less exalted and the uses to which they were put is a good deal more scattered and fragmentary than that for portraits of princes. It is, however, known that portraits were displayed to proclaim the disgrace of important criminals. In 1438, for example, there were exhibited on the four gates of Paris 'three very well painted canvases of very ugly subjects; for in each of them was painted one of the great English lords, hanging by his feet from a gibbet . . . on either side was a devil who chained him up and two ugly and hideous crows . . . seemed to pluck his eyes from his head'. Inscriptions stated that the three, the Earl of Suffolk, Lord Willoughby and Sir Thomas Blount, were guilty of oath-breaking.[80] In May 1470, Galeazzo Maria Sforza, Duke of Milan, ordered an official at Parma to commission and exhibit in various public places in the town images of the rebel lord Manfredo da Correggio and to take care 'to have him painted dressed in gold brocade and with white hair and as lifelike as possible so that everyone will understand that it is he'.[81] Manfredo was shown hanging by the feet. In the following September, Galeazzo Maria received at Parma Borso d'Este, Duke of Ferrara, who obtained a pardon for Manfredo. The next night, the paintings of Manfredo were obliterated.[82] During the siege of Florence in 1530, Andrea del Sarto was engaged to paint representations of certain criminals, fugitives and rebels, and some of his preliminary drawings have survived (plate 226).[83] In the Netherlands, it was common to condemn the miscreants themselves

226 (facing page, top) Andrea del Sarto, *One of the 'Capitani'*, red and white chalks on paper, 24.5 × 11.8 cm., Uffizi, Florence, Gabinetto dei Disegni (330 F).

The three 'Capitani' were Florentine soldiers who on 2 February 1530 absconded from the besieged city. Sarto painted on the façade of the Palazzo della Mercatanzia in the Piazza della Signoria frescoes which showed them hanged by one foot and for which his pupil Bernardo del Buda was paid on 4 April 1530. The frescoes have been destroyed but six of Sarto's preliminary drawings survive, one of which is here reproduced. According to Benedetto Varchi, the lost frescoes were 'so life-like and natural that whoever had seen them, if only on one occasion, instantly recognised them'.

See the exhibition catalogue Florence, 1986–7, p. 325 (100); here p. 208.

227 (facing page, bottom) Netherlandish, 1499, *Mask of Pieter de Beert*, bronze, 25 × 13 cm., Stadhuismuseum, Furnes (Veurne).

See p. 209.

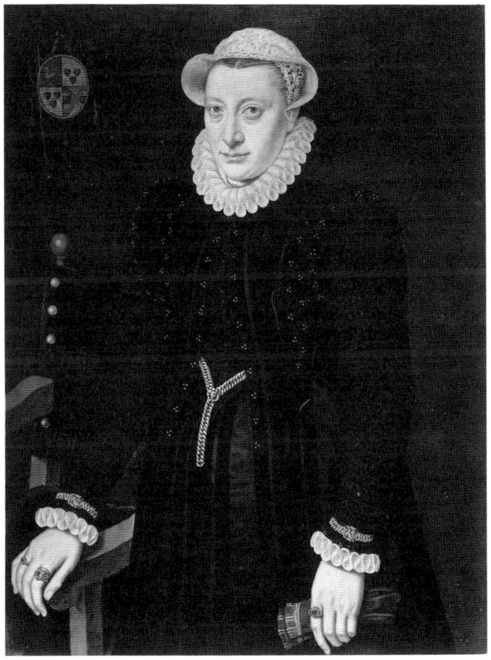

228 Cornelis de Zeeuw, *Maria Gameel, Wife of Jacob della Faille*, oak panel, 102.7 × 77 cm., Musées Royaux des Beaux-Arts de Belgique, Brussels (6278).

The sitter is identified by her coat of arms. The pendant portrait of her husband, also at Brussels (6277), is signed by Cornelis de Zeeuw and dated 1569. Jacob was a prominent Antwerp merchant who was particularly active in the textile trade with Venice and who owned several estates outside Antwerp (Brulez, 1959, pp. XXIV, 216, 229).

See p. 209.

to commission and exhibit images and placards that proclaimed their guilt, and at Furnes are preserved a bronze mask, presumably intended as a portrait (plate 227), and a tablet inscribed: 'Pieter de Beert is condemned . . . to exhibit this head because he has spoken against the magistrates, threatening to throw them out of the window. 1499.'[84]

Portraits of the victims, as well as the perpetrators,of crimes were on occasion publicly displayed. After the murder of the Earl of Moray at Donibristle in 1592, a representation of his naked corpse was painted in which his wounds were carefully depicted and which was inscribed 'GOD REVENGE MY CAVS'. The inscription suggests that the picture was exhibited in order to win public support for efforts to discover and apprehend the assassins;[85] and, indeed, it was recorded that the earl's mother 'caused draw her sonne's picture, as he was demained, and presented it to the king in a fyne lane cloath, with lamentatiouns, and earnest sute for justice'.[86] In 1595, David Forrester, bailie of Stirling, was murdered. Those who conveyed his body to Stirling for burial took with it 'the portraite of the dead with the wounds he had received in a white sheet, to move the beholders to a great detestation of the fact'.[87]

Many portraits commemorated events of private significance. The soldiers of the French army that invaded Italy in 1494 kept a book in which were painted the likenesses of many women whom they had raped in different towns: they were taking it home as a keepsake, but it fell into the hands of the Venetians during the Battle of Fornovo.[88] Metsys's *Pilgrim* holds a paper inscribed 'In 1509, in the 51st year of my age, I was in the Holy Land.'[89] Lotto's double portrait of 1523 obviously commemorates the marriage of the sitters (plate 229). The Augsburg businessman Matthäus Schwarz, who kept a book in which his clothes were depicted, had portraits painted in the same book to record his giving up alcohol on 14 May 1542 and his taking it up again exactly one year later (plate 230). When in 1586 Anthony Babington was plotting to kill Elizabeth I of England and enthrone Mary, Queen of Scots, in her stead, he commissioned portraits of himself and five of his fellow conspirators. On his own portrait he rather unwisely caused to be inscribed, in Latin: 'These men are my Companions, whom very Dangers draw.'[90] Taking considerable trouble over the paintings, he planned to send the painter to Wales to complete the series and said that he would keep them 'as a memorial of so worthy an act as attempting her majesty's person';[91] but the authorities, proceeding against the conspirators, secured the pictures and drafted a proclamation ordering that

> the portraiture of their faces, agreeable even to such large portraitures as both they themselves and other conspirators of their company . . . had caused to be made in the city of London, shall be in open places of the city of London published, and shall also be dispersed to sundry other places of the realm.[92]

Portraits might also be used for the purposes of social climbing. Imaginary portraits of ancestors, sometimes themselves imaginary, could do something to enhance the grandeur of a family,[93] and living persons might be painted in poses and clothes that made them seem more like their social superiors than they may in fact have been. In about 1569, Cornelis de Zeeuw painted Maria Gameel, the wife of an Antwerp merchant, in a pose and wearing an expression devised by Mor for his portraits of Habsburg princesses (plates 228, 266). In 1584, the Italian theorist Lomazzo complained that 'merchants and bankers who have never seen a drawn sword and who should properly appear with quill pens behind their ears, their

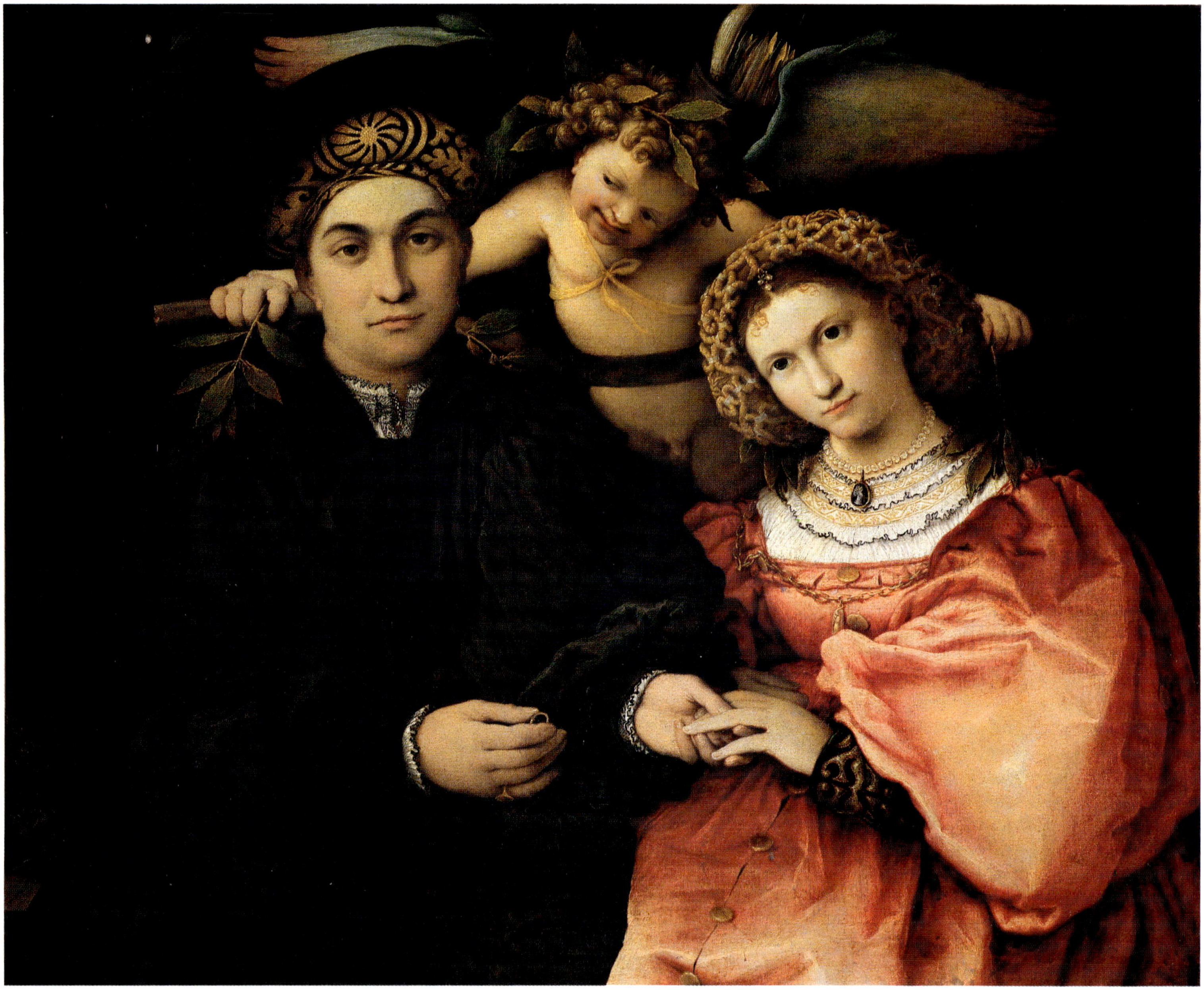

229 Lorenzo Lotto, *Messer Marsiglio and his Bride*, canvas, 71 × 84 cm., Museo del Prado, Madrid (240).

Signed and dated 'L. Lotus pictor 1523', the portrait was one of several pictures listed in an account sent by Lotto to Giovanni Casoto, a gentleman of Bergamo: the sitters were there described as 'misser Marsilio et la sposa sua' and a *Madonna* painted for the same Marsiglio's *Camera* was also mentioned (Zampetti, 1969, p. 260).

See Canova, 1974, p. 98 (71); here p. 209.

gowns about them and their day-books in front of them, have themselves painted in armour holding generals' batons . . .'.[94] A Florentine visiting Ferrara in 1589 observed:

> Absolutely all of them, mean and great, wear swords at their sides . . . they are always trying, in all the streets, to appear as knights, and to advance this impression they have themselves painted as such. I have seen many portraits of private persons of no great consequence which, if I had not been told the sitters' names, I would have believed to be images of Achilles or Hector, so heavily ornamented with gold are the armours painted by Dosso.[95]

The less exalted, as well as princes, commissioned portraits to give to friends and acquaintances. The best-known and best-documented examples are the portraits of Erasmus and Pieter Gillis which the sitters commissioned from Quinten

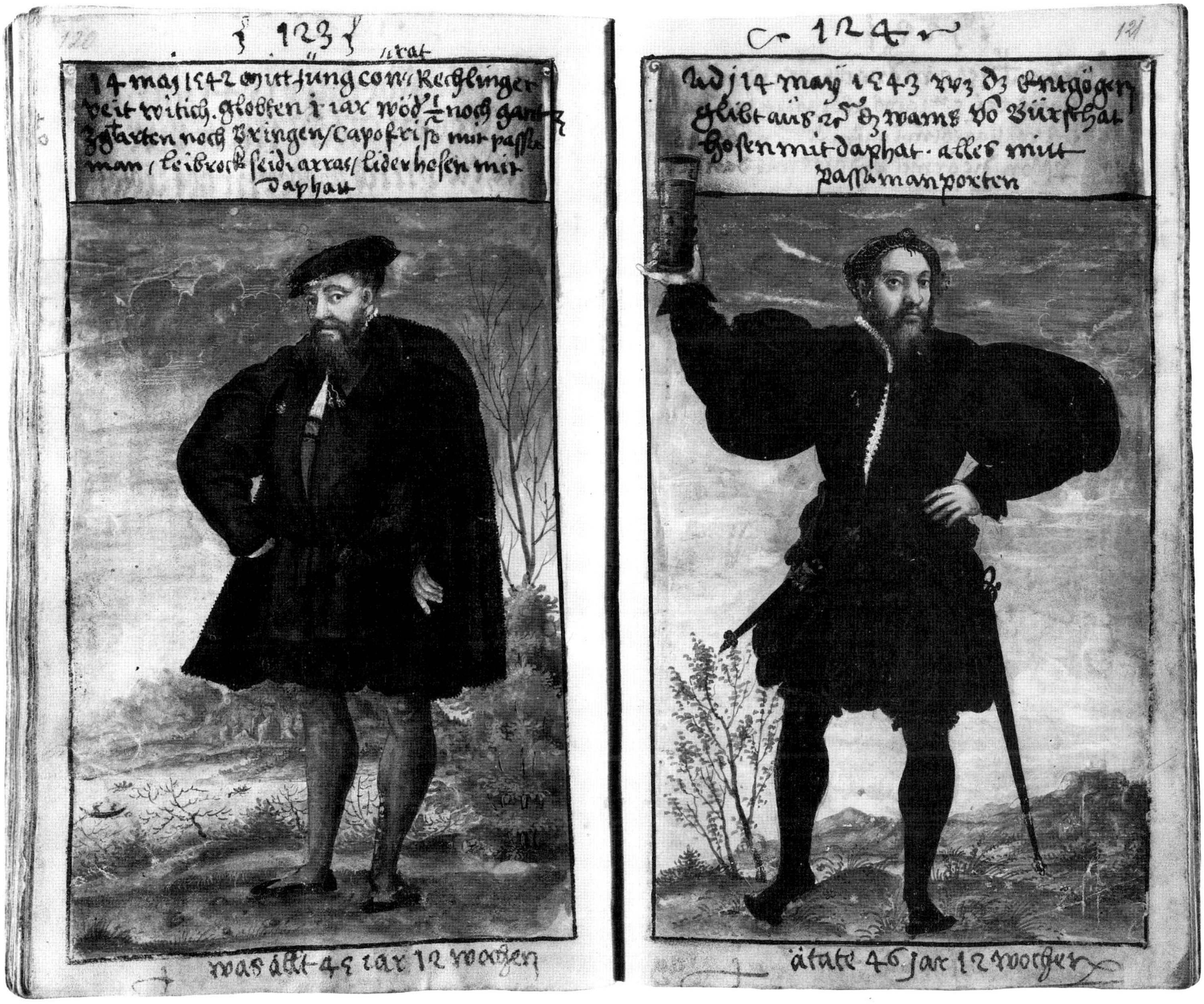

230 German (Augsburg), 1542–3, *Matthäus Schwarz on 14 May 1542 and on 14 May 1543*, parchment, each page 16 × 10 cm., from the '*Trachtenbuch* of Matthäus Schwarz', Herzog Anton Ulrich-Museum, Brunswick, H. 27, Nr. 67a, pp. 123–4.

On the *Trachtenbuch* see the note to plate 18. The inscription above the miniature on the left refers to a vow made by Schwarz and two friends on 14 May 1542 to moderate their drinking for a year; the inscription on the facing page relates that the year of abstinence expired on 14 May 1543.

See Fink, 1963, pp. 168–9; here p. 209.

Metsys in 1517 as a gift for Sir Thomas More (plates 178–9). The *album amicorum*, said to have evolved in Germany, might be either a glorified autograph book or a volume of miniature portraits.[96] People were of course flattered to be asked for their portraits but might be negligent about handing them over. Christopher, Count of Roggendorf, visiting the Netherlands in 1541, requested several noblemen to give him their portraits and then made them sign a paper certifying that they had promised them.[97]

Portraits of Barthélemy Alatruye and Marie de Pacy his wife, possibly of 1425 and in the style of the Master of Flémalle, are known from two independent pairs of sixteenth-century copies: paintings in Tournai (plates 231–2) and drawings in the 'Recueil d'Arras'.[98] The copies may be shown to have been made from originals traceable to two of the sitters' children: the Arras drawings are after portraits bequeathed by their son Philippe to the church of Berclau;[99] the Tournai paintings

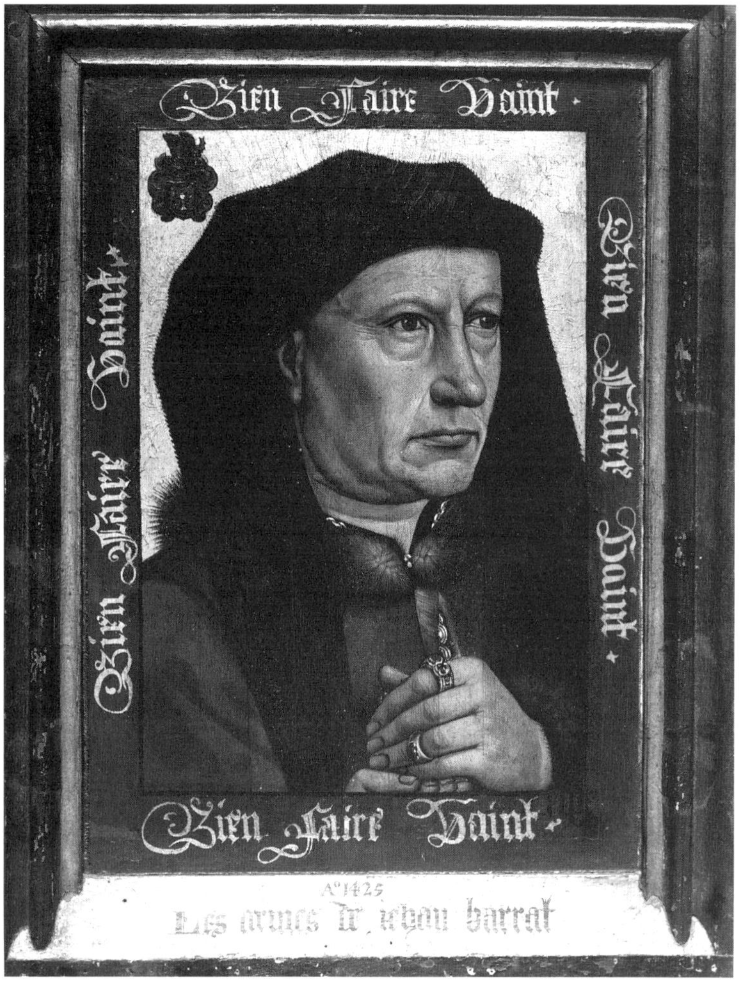

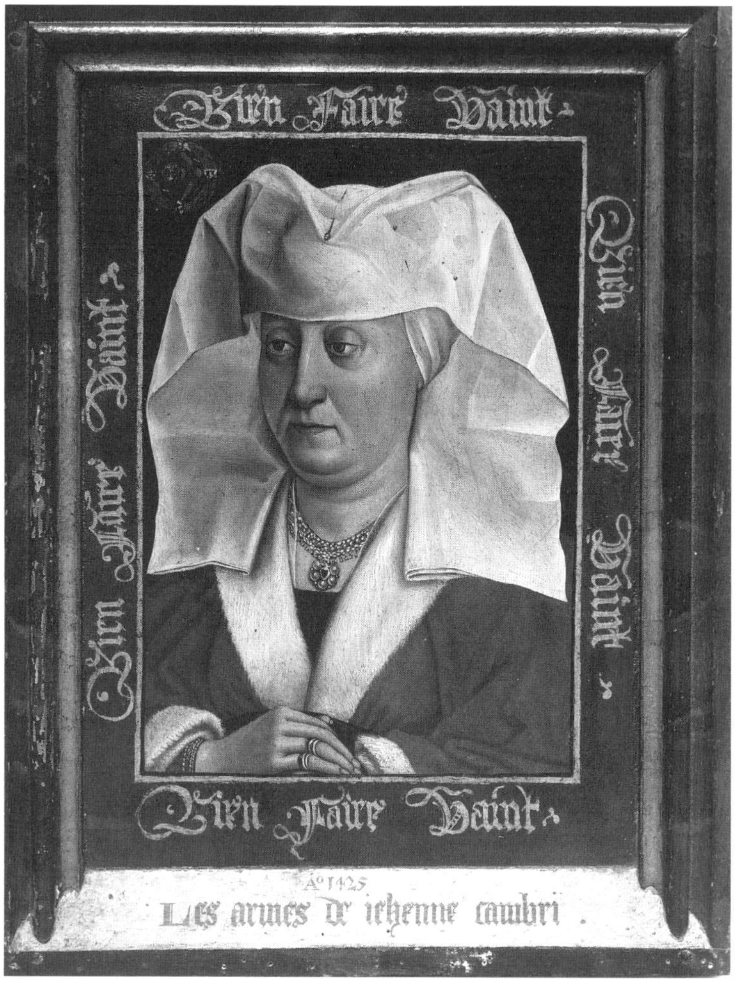

231 After the Master of Flémalle, *Barthélemy Alatruye*, oak panel, painted surface 44 × 31.5 cm., Musée des Beaux-Arts, Tournai (deposited from the Musées Royaux des Beaux-Arts de Belgique, Brussels, 406).

The pair to the portrait reproduced as plate 232.

232 After the Master of Flémalle, *Marie de Pacy, Wife of Barthélemy Alatruye*, oak panel, painted surface 44.5 × 31.5 cm., Musée des Beaux-Arts, Tournai (deposited from the Musées Royaux des Beaux-Arts de Belgique, Brussels, 407).

The pair to the portrait reproduced as plate 231. The sitters are identified by the coats of arms in the upper-left corners of the two portraits and by the inscription on the version of the *Barthélemy* in the 'Recueil d'Arras'. Barthélemy was one of the chief officials of the *Chambre des Comptes* at Lille, the centre from which the finances of the Burgundian dukes were administered; he died in 1446. In 1416–17 it was recorded that 'he has for a long time lodged in his mansion the Count of Charolais' (Philip the Good, afterwards Duke of Burgundy) and that 'he is still lodging there the Count of St Pol' (Philip of Burgundy, cousin to Philip the Good and afterwards Duke of Brabant: see Dehaisnes, 1881, p. 77). He was clearly a person of some consequence. His wife Marie de Pacy died in 1452. The words 'Bien Faire Saint', written four times around each portrait, are presumably Barthélemy's motto. On the original frames are the inscriptions 'A° 1425/ Les armes de iehan barrat' and 'A° 1425/Les armes de iehenne cambri'. Indeed, beneath the paint surfaces of the portraits and clearly visible in raking light, are representations of the coats of arms of Jean Barrat and Jeanne Cambry, who were married in 1529. Two of their daughters married, in 1562 and 1567, two great-great-grandsons of Barthélemy and Marie. The Tournai portraits are therefore copies, executed after 1562 on used panels, for descendants of the sitters. The dates 'A° 1425', which cannot refer to the coats of arms beneath the copies, may have been taken from the lost originals, which were in the style of the Master of Flémalle.

See pp. 72, 112, 211–13.

233 Antonis Mor, *Jan van Scorel*, oak panel, diameter 58.1 cm., Society of Antiquaries, London.

Beneath the modern inscription are a different Latin inscription and the signature 'Antonius Morus pingebat A° 1559'. Mor had been Scorel's pupil and after Scorel's death in 1562 the portrait was incorporated into the elaborate monument erected in his memory in the Mariakerk at Utrecht.

See the exhibition catalogue Amsterdam, 1986, pp. 334–5 (212); here pp. 61, 213.

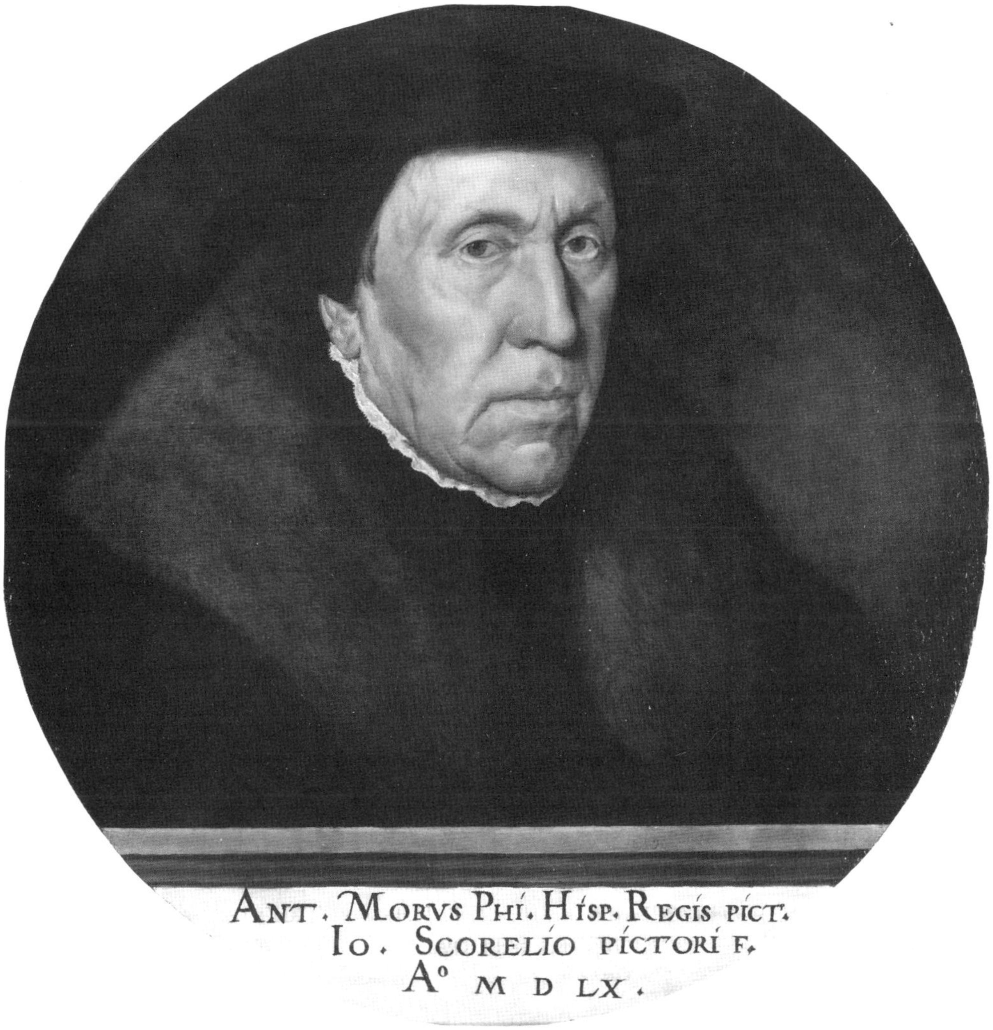

are from originals that descended through the family of their son Hugues.[100] The implication may be that the sitters commissioned identical pairs of portraits to bequeath to all their children; or that, after their deaths, one son inherited their portraits and had copies made for his brothers and sisters.[101] Such practices, though difficult to document, were evidently widespread. Other family portraits, for example the group by Otto van Veen of himself, his parents and their other descendants, were to pass like an entailed estate to the senior male heir.[102] Family portraits might apparently be put to very practical use, for, according to Paleotti, portraits might be produced in lawsuits to prove relationships by resemblance.[103]

Someone who was about to set forth on a dangerous venture might have his portrait painted so that, if he died, he would leave behind a painted memorial. Richard Madox, in 1582, commissioned a portrait from John Bettes before leaving England on an Atlantic voyage, and he did in fact die the next year in Brazil.[104]

Some portraits were intended to be placed on the sitters' tombs. In 1559, the Utrecht painter Jan van Scorel had his portrait painted by his former pupil Antonis Mor (plate 233). After Scorel's death in 1562, the portrait was placed on his tomb and it is quite possible that he had commissioned the portrait for that purpose. Other tomb portraits were evidently specially executed, posthumous likenesses, while others, for example Van Orley's *Marie Haneton*, were converted into tomb

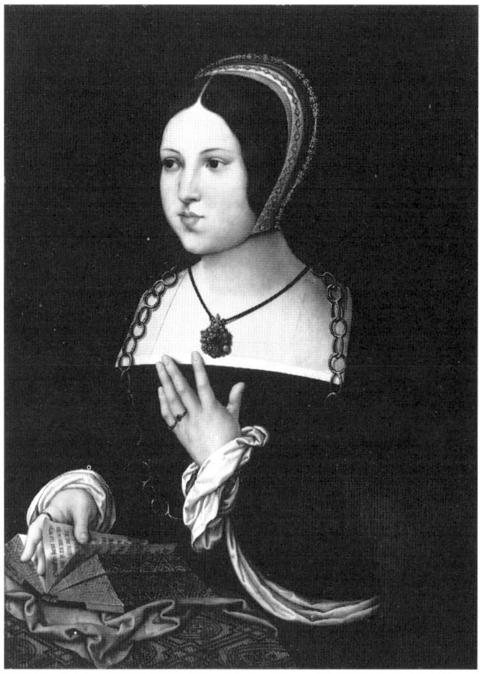

234 Bernard van Orley, *Marie Haneton*, panel, 72.4 × 54.6 cm., National Gallery of Scotland, Edinburgh (1895).

The text in the book that she holds is from Psalm 6, 'O Lord, rebuke me not in thine anger . . .', the first of the Penitential Psalms found in most Books of Hours. On the reverse of the panel are the coats of arms of the sitter's husband and the sitter herself and an inscription recording that she was Marie Haneton, wife of Lambert du Briaerd, and that she died on 22 August 1525 in her nineteenth year. It ends with a request for prayers for her soul. ('En ce tableau est la protraicture de damoiselle Marie haneton Jadis feme a maistre lãbert du briaerd Cõseillier et maistre des Req̃stes ordinaire de lhostel de Lẽper' ñre sire q̃ trespassa le xxii^{e} Jour daoust lã xv^{c} xxv Et de son eage le dix neufiesme. priez die[u] pour son ame'.) The panel, which was conceivably the right wing of a diptych or triptych, seems to have been adapted for display on the sitter's tomb. As she died in 1525 in her nineteenth year, the portrait cannot have been painted long before 1525. Marie reappears with her parents and siblings in Van Orley's 'Haneton Triptych' at Brussels (358): the head there is virtually identical to that in the Edinburgh portrait.

See Van den Bergen-Pantens, 1973, pp. 51–2; here pp. 74, 91, 213–14.

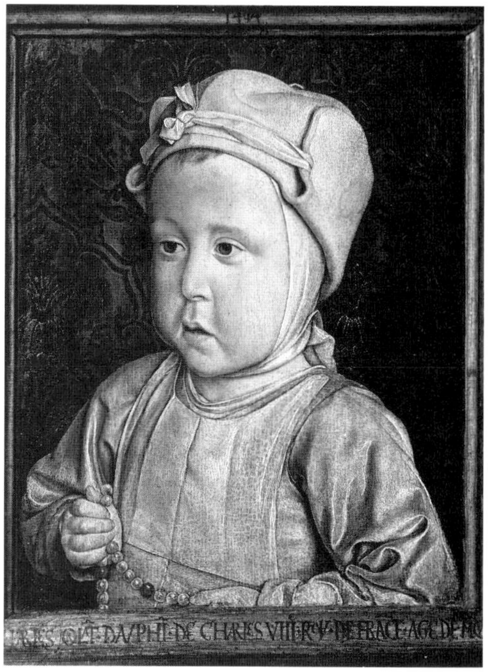

235 Master of Moulins, *Charles-Orlant, Dauphin of France*, oak panel, painted surface 28.5 × 23.5 cm., Louvre, Paris (R.F. 1942–28).

The frame (39.2 × 33.3 cm.) is original and bears the date 1494 and the inscription 'CHARLES ORLÃT. DAVPHĨ. DE CHARLES VIIIE ROY. DE FRÃCE. AGE DE XXVI MOYS'. The child was born on 10 October 1492 and died on 6 December 1495; the portrait would have been painted at the end of 1494 and was sent to his father, then campaigning in Italy. On grounds of style, it is attributed to the Master of Moulins.

See Sterling and Adhémar, 1965, pp. 12–13; here pp. 115, 214.

pictures. Marie died in 1525 in her nineteenth year, and her epitaph is lettered on the reverse of the portrait (plate 234).

Evidently the most natural reason for commissioning a portrait is the desire to have a record of the sitter's appearance at a given time. Many portraits are dated and inscribed with the sitters' ages. Portraits of children are interesting in this connection, for example the *Dauphin Charles-Orlant*, painted in 1494 and sent to his father Charles VIII of France, who was then campaigning in Italy (plate 235). He kept it, with his and his father's seals, in a silver chest, which was seized by Venetian soldiers during the Battle of Fornovo.[105] The English musician Thomas Whythorne, who had pretensions to gentility but who earned his own living, had himself painted at least four times. On the first occasion, in about 1549, he had his virginals decorated with his portrait, where he was shown playing the lute. A year later, he sat again to the same painter, after an attack of the ague, 'to see how I was changed'. In about 1562, he sat for a third time to the same painter:

> I being at this time nigh a dozen years older than I was when I made my last counterfeit, I determined to have it made new again. And for that I saw by my last counterfeit that I was much changed from that I was at that time, as by the long and fulness of my beard, the wrinkles on my face and the hollowness of mine eyes, and also that, as my face was altered, so were the delights of my mind changed, I caused to be written in the table . . .
>
> *As time doth alter every wight*
> *So every age hath his delight.*

An extant portrait of 1569 was not mentioned in Whythorne's autobiography, but a woodcut reproduction was made for a volume of songs that he published in 1571. He included it partly to stress his claim that he was a gentleman.[106]

According to Vasari, Andrea del Sarto said one day to his wife Lucrezia 'I want to paint you, so that it may be seen how well preserved you are for your age but yet so that it may be known how you have changed, as this will differ from your first portraits.' Understandably, perhaps, the lady refused to sit.[107]

Portraits came to be considered out of date after a year or two. Mary of Hungary, sending one of Titian's portraits of Philip II of Spain to Mary Tudor in 1553, apologised for it and admitted that it was three years old, but that it had been considered very like at the time.[108] Efforts were sometimes made to improve and update portraits, usually by modernising the costume. In 1512, Isabella d'Este wrote to a Ferrarese correspondent: 'we have a portrait of our late father, very like and good . . . we wish to have another copied from this, but with a hat and doublet like those that he wore at the time of his death . . .'.[109] In 1528, the same correspondent wrote to Isabella about a pair of portraits of her parents: 'I have had Dosso improve the two portraits . . .'.[110]

Some portraits were produced without being commissioned. The court painters, having to meet a steady demand for portraits of princes, appear to have kept stocks of portraits in readiness. The fact that a portrait of Christian II of Denmark, dated 1515, is painted over a portrait of the Emperor Charles V of a standard type, seems to indicate that the artist had the portrait of Charles in stock, but that it was an outdated likeness, no longer in demand: the panel was consequently re-used (plates 236–8). Such stocks of portraits might be exhibited for the benefit of visitors to the workshop. In 1546, the Leipzig painter Hans Krell, who had been asked to paint portraits of several princes and notables for the Duke of Prussia, wrote to remind the duke that he had seen his stock of princely portraits and enclosed a list of those acquired since the duke had visited him.[111] A Venetian, visiting Corneille de Lyon's workshop at Lyons in 1551, saw there 'the entire court of France, gentlemen and ladies, most naturalistically represented in many small pictures'.[112] Brantôme recalled that Catherine de' Medici had visited Corneille at Lyons, perhaps in 1564, and had inspected 'a large room' where there were paintings of all the lords and ladies of the French court. She discovered there a portrait of herself as a young woman, examined it carefully and confirmed that it was a good likeness.[113]

As we have already seen, many, perhaps most, portrait painters were in the habit of keeping reproductions of portraits that had left their studios. From these they were able, if the occasion arose, to paint replicas. Krell and Corneille de Lyon evidently exhibited their stocks of patterns, from which versions might be taken, and the practice may have been widespread. When Thomas Whythorne's mistress had her portrait painted, he was able subsequently to secure a version of her portrait, without her knowledge, from the same painter. On another occasion, he noticed in that painter's house 'many pictures, as well of those that were much elder than I, as of some such that were of my years, yea, and much younger than I was . . .'.[114]

In London, portraits were apparently sold on the streets. In 1582, the Painter-Stainers Company decreed that no one should 'go in and about the street to sell, or proffer to be sold, the King's or Queen's Majesty's pictures, or the counterfeit or portrait of any other . . .'. Pictures were to be sold only from the painters' shops.[115]

Other portraits were produced for the artists' own diversion and instruction: self-portraits, portraits of members of their families and portraits of friends and acquaintances, which the sitters would normally have wanted to look like commissioned paintings. Self-portraits would have been useful as samples, since the painter would be able to show to a prospective client both himself and his own portrait as an indication of his talent for getting a likeness. When Joris Hoefnagel met the Duke of Bavaria, the duke asked him whether he had any of his work with

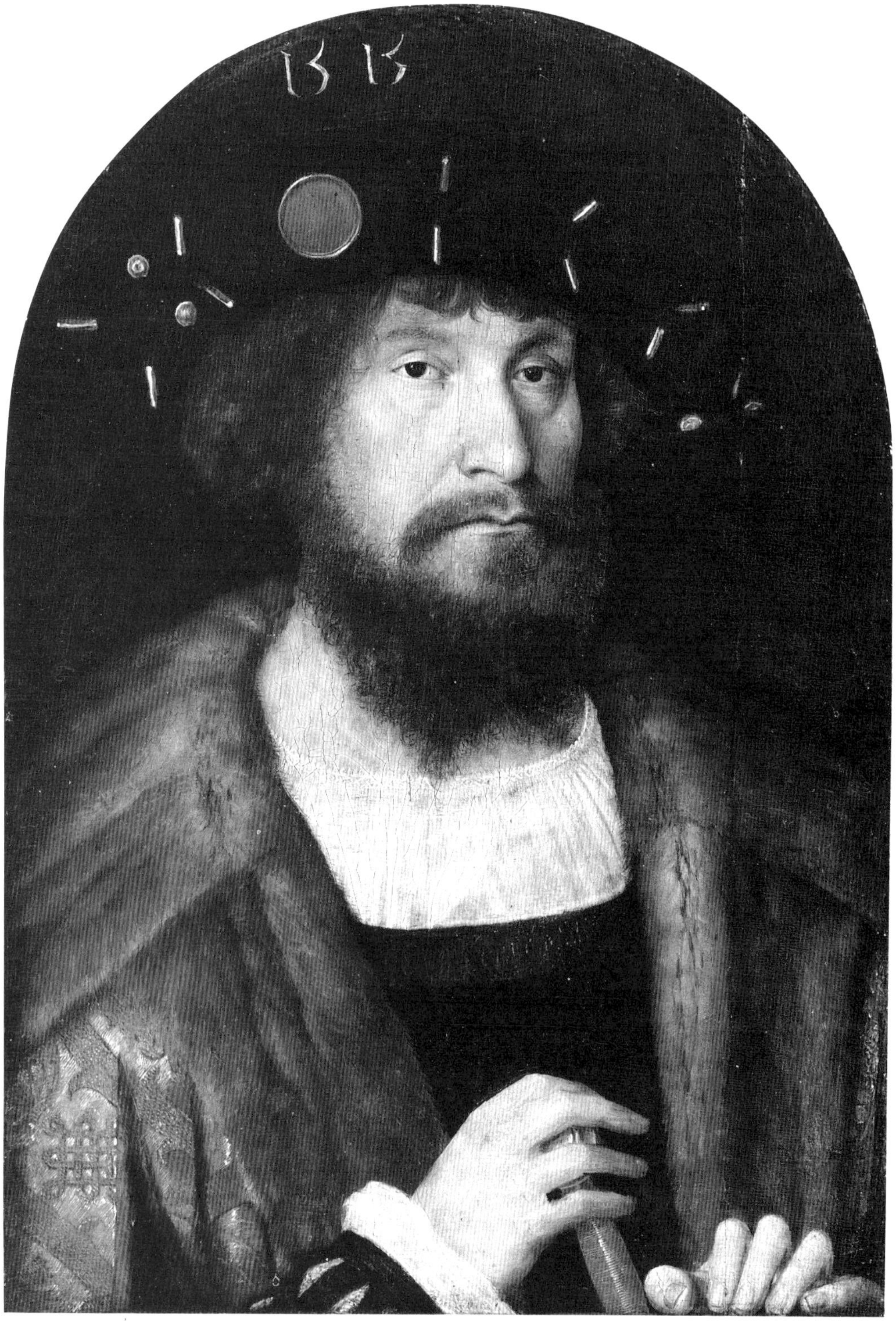

236 Attributed to Michel Sittow, *Christian II, King of Denmark*, oak panel, 31 × 22 cm., Statens Museum for Kunst, Copenhagen (Sp. 789).

The sitter (1481–1559) is identified from other portraits and the painting is in the style of the Esthonian artist Michel Sittow, who was trained in Bruges and who worked as court painter to Queen Isabella of Spain and to Philip the Handsome in the Netherlands. In 1514, he was sent from Elsinore to Christian II in Copenhagen; he probably painted his portrait, which would then have been sent to the Netherlands. Christian's future wife, Isabella of Austria, sister of the Emperor Charles V, was in possession of a portrait of Christian by 1515, before she left the Netherlands for Denmark. The portrait reproduced, like those illustrated in plates 66, 231 and 232, is on a re-used panel (see plate 237) and in quality it falls short of a portrait in Washington (1937.1.46) securely attributed to Sittow (Hand and Wolff, 1986, pp. 228–36). Dated 1515, it is perhaps a copy painted in the Netherlands of a portrait executed by Sittow in 1514 in Copenhagen.

See Trizna, 1976, pp. 45–9, 92 and references; here pp. 64, 215.

him: Hoefnagel showed him a portrait of himself and his first wife, which he was evidently carrying with him on his travels.[116] Some painters used self-portraits to make statements about their aspirations. Dürer, in 1498, showed himself as very much a gentleman (plate 26); Mor, in 1558, showing himself soberly and expensively dressed, was able to demonstrate his intellectual status by including, on a

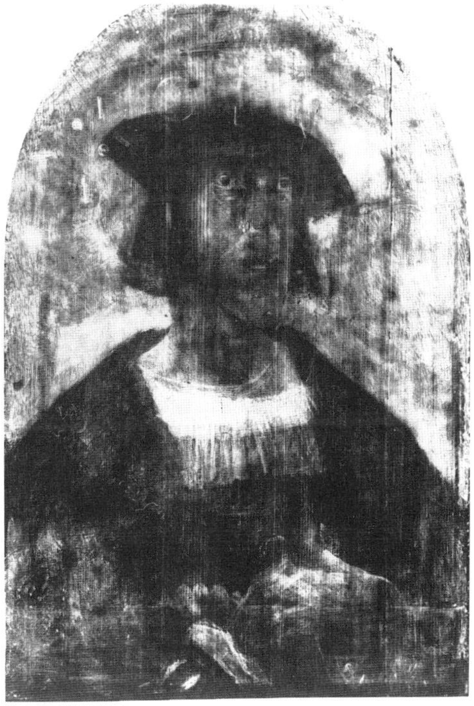

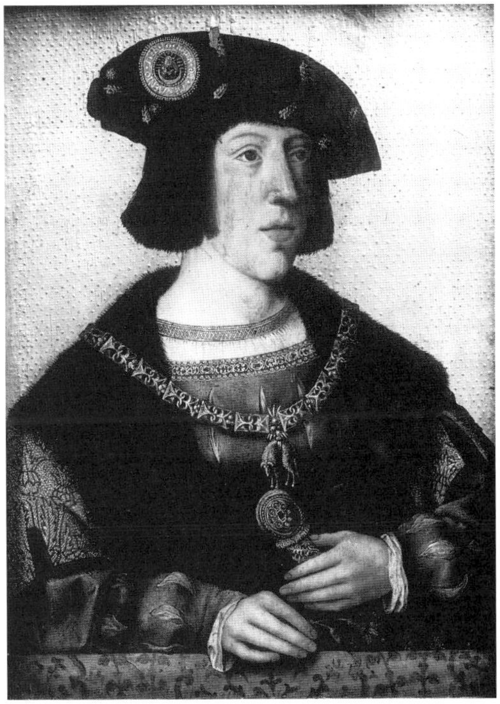

237 X-radiograph of the painting reproduced as plate 236.

Beneath the paint surface is an earlier painting, clearly legible in the X-radiograph and identifiable as a portrait of the Emperor Charles V (see plate 238).

238 Netherlandish, c. 1512–14, *The Emperor Charles V as a Youth*, panel, 41 × 30 cm., Sint-Salvatorshoofdkerk, Bruges, Museum.

The sitter (1500–58), identifiable from other portraits, is placed before a gilded background, holds a bluish flower in his right hand and wears a hat badge bearing a representation of the Virgin as the apocalyptic Woman Clothed with the Sun and the inscription 'O Mother of God, remember me'. Many versions of the portrait were produced in a workshop or workshops where stocks of portraits were kept, for there would have been a large demand for pictures of Charles. During his adolescence, Charles's appearance would have changed fairly rapidly, so that likenesses would quickly have become outdated. Unsold stocks of this outdated likeness clearly remained with the artist, or perhaps with a dealer, for one unwanted version was disposed of in order that its panel might be re-used for the portrait of Christian II of Denmark reproduced as plate 236. Since the portrait of Christian is dated 1515, the image of Charles, obsolete by 1515, was probably being circulated in about 1512–14.

See pp. 112, 215.

paper pinned to the unpainted panel on his easel, a poem written in Greek by Lampsonius, praising Mor and placing him above Apelles and Zeuxis (plate 171). Artists on occasion gave self-portraits to other artists, or to important patrons,[117] and a few were hung in palaces. In Philip II's 'Royal Room of Portraits' in his palace at El Pardo, self-portraits by Mor and Titian were placed next to their portraits of members of Philip's family. Titian's painting showed him holding a portrait of Philip.[118]

During his visit to the Netherlands in 1520–1, Dürer frequently made portrait drawings of people whom he met and often gave them to the sitters. They generally gave him something in return, but, in 1520, he noted in his diary: 'Six of the people whose portraits I drew at Brussels have given me nothing.'[119] In 1521, Ridolfo Ghirlandaio was at Colle di Val d'Elsa to paint an altarpiece and a fresco for Mario Beltramini. Mario's son recorded that 'One holiday the whim took him to paint on tile a very naturalistic portrait of my father', and the portrait hung in Mario's house until his death.[120]

Any portrait might command a market value. On the death of the painter Philippe Truffin at Tournai in 1506, his executors sold his effects, including several pictures. Some of them were portraits, and the sitters, not named in the record of the sale, may have been unknown. This did not prevent certain of the portraits from fetching higher prices than many of the religious paintings, which might have been presumed to have been more readily saleable.[121] The numbers of portraits of unidentified sitters listed in inventories are slightly surprising. Margaret of Austria, for example, apparently owned the Master of Frankfurt's *Self-Portrait with his Wife*, dated 1496 (plate 61). It seems to be described in the 1516 inventory of her collection: 'Another picture of a man and a woman, which is done by a good hand and which is very old; the man holds a cup and the woman a flower.'[122] Perhaps Margaret had acquired the painting for its aesthetic merits or its iconographic interest. In either case, there would have been an incentive for

239 Israhel van Meckenem, *The Artist and his Wife Ida*, engraving, 12.9 × 17.4 cm., British Museum, London, Department of Prints and Drawings (E.1–94).

The print, which exists in two states, is signed with the artist's monogram and is inscribed 'figuration of the faces of Israhel and Ida his wife'. Israhel died in 1503; the engraving may have been produced in about 1490.

See the exhibition catalogue Washington, 1967–8, No. 244; here pp. 115, 218.

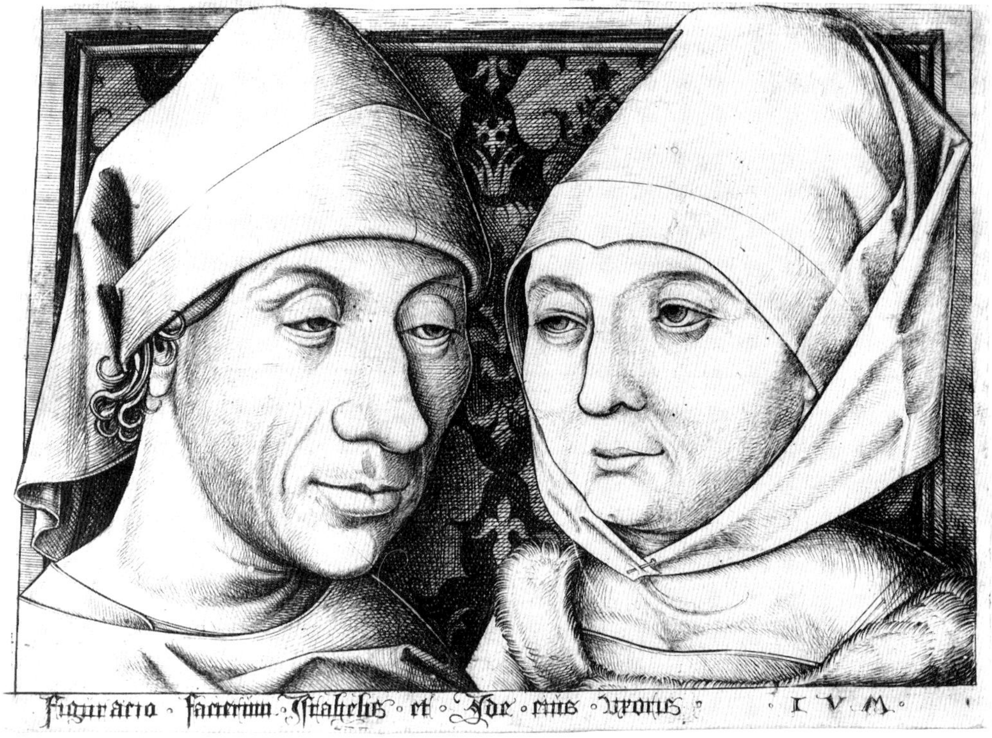

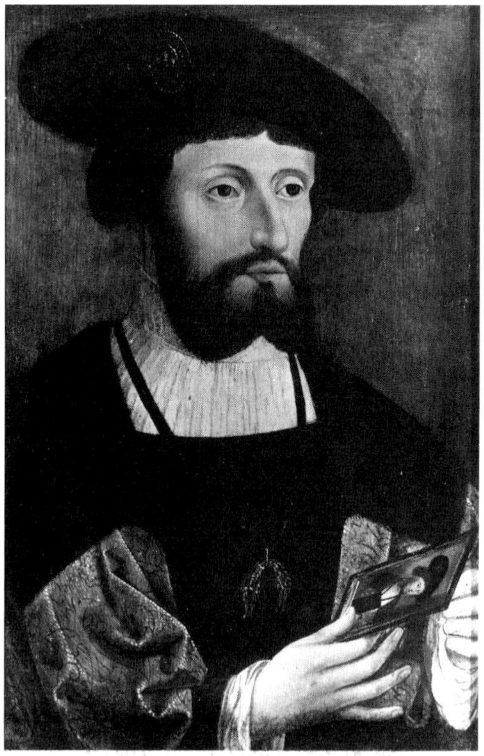

240 Attributed to the Master of the Legend of the Magdalen, *Christian II, King of Denmark*, panel, 31 × 22 cm., Nationalhistoriske Museum paa Frederiksborg, Hillerød (A 4371).

The sitter (1481–1559) is identified by comparison with other portraits and holds a small picture which is a version of the whole composition. Christian was frequently in the Low Countries and sat to many different artists there. The Master of the Magdalen Legend, however, seems to have copied royal portraits by other painters (Campbell, 1985, p. 35); the painting reproduced is probably such a copy, perhaps of about 1520 and conceivably after Van Orley.

See Friedländer, 1967–76, XII, p. 93 (28); here p. 218.

painters to produce portraits for the open market. Even so, it is difficult to understand who the people were who bought prints of Israhel van Meckenem's portrait of himself with his wife Ida, an engraving that exists in two states and that may have been executed in about 1490 (plate 239).

Some independent portraits were painted for churches, and others, not originally intended for ecclesiastical settings, were later given to churches.[123] Certain of them were displayed on tombs.[124] Not all portraits designed for secular settings were necessarily hung on walls. Some were set upright on tables, while others were designed to be held in the hand (plate 240).[125] Though it seems likely that some small fifteenth-century portraits were supposed to be worn,[126] the earliest extant representations of people wearing portrait miniatures seem to be of about 1560: portraits of Francesco de' Medici holding a miniature of his sister Lucrezia (plate 241) and of Elisabeth of Valois holding a miniature of her husband Philip II of Spain (plate 242).[127]

Very little information is available on the conditions under which people looked at portraits. In 1499, an unnamed, probably French, painter sent from Milan to the Marquis of Mantua a portrait of a little girl, with a letter in which he indicated 'that he wants it to be shown in a subdued light so that it will be seen at its best'.[128] Mary of Hungary advised Mary Tudor, Queen of England, to examine a portrait by Titian from a distance, as none of Titian's paintings was recognisable at close range.[129]

Portrait galleries of a kind existed at the beginning of the fifteenth century, notably that of John, Duke of Berry, at his castle of Bicêtre, destroyed during riots in 1411.[130] In February 1473, Galeazzo Maria Sforza was commissioning portraits of the beautiful and eligible young ladies of his duchy. On 17 February, he was advised: 'Giovanni Avogadro has a most beautiful daughter of twelve or thirteen, big for her age, and I therefore ask your Lordship if you would intimate whether

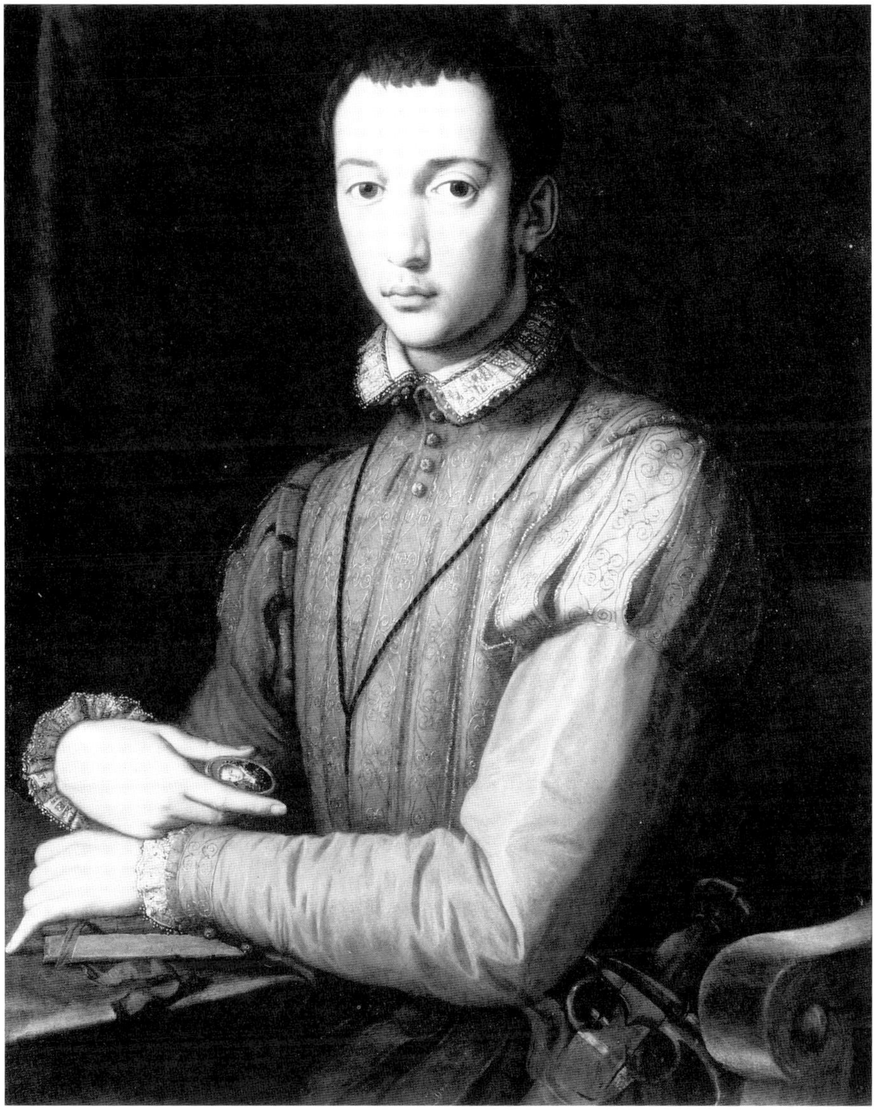

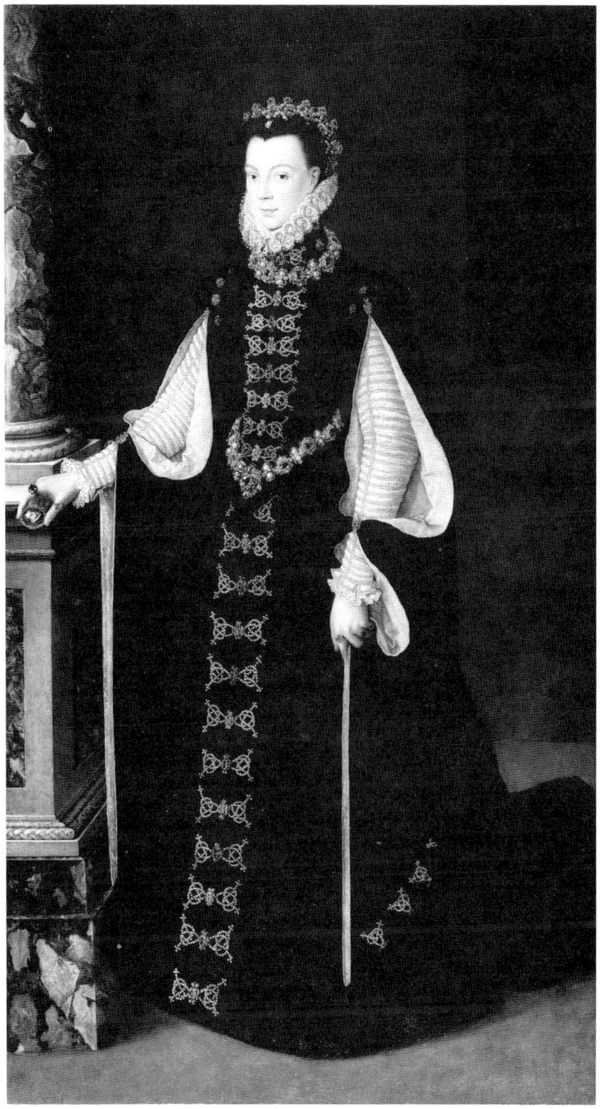

241 Attributed to Alessandro Allori, *Francesco I de' Medici, Grand Duke of Tuscany*, panel, 82.7 × 65 cm., sold at Christie's, New York, 12 January 1978 (86).

The sitter (1541–87), who succeeded his father Cosimo I as Grand Duke in 1574, is easily identifiable from other portraits and holds a miniature of a lady identifiable, again from other portraits, as his sister Lucrezia (1545–62). It is thought that the picture was painted in 1560, when Francesco went with Lucrezia to Ferrara, where she was to take up residence with her husband Alfonso II d'Este. It has been attributed to Bronzino but is more probably by his pupil Allori.

See Langedijk, 1981–3, II, pp. 855–6; here p. 218.

242 Attributed to Sofonisba Anguissola, *Elisabeth of Valois, Queen of Spain*, canvas, 205 × 123 cm., Museo del Prado, Madrid (1031).

The subject (1545–68), identified by comparison with other portraits, is dressed in black, white and gold and holds a miniature of her husband Philip II of Spain. Though catalogued as a copy by Pantoja after Sánchez Coello, the portrait bears little resemblance to Sánchez Coello's work (compare plate 120). In its more forthright presentation of the subject, it is closer in style to pictures by Sofonisba (compare her signed portrait at Vienna, reproduced by Klauner, 1961, p. 145). Sofonisba, who was Elisabeth's lady-in-waiting and drawing-teacher, painted the queen on several occasions: one of her portraits was sent in 1561 to the pope; another was painted in 1564 in collaboration with Sánchez Coello. Whatever the correct attribution, this portrait may be dated around 1565.

See Breuer, 1984, p. 170; here pp. 208, 218.

you wish to have her portrait done, like the others . . .'.[131] It is possible that Galeazzo Maria was planning a 'gallery of beauties'. Galleries of a rather specialised kind came to be formed. In 1604, the Duke of Mantua had two parallel projects: the first for a chapel with copies of miraculous images of the Virgin; the second for a room of portraits of the most beautiful women in the world.[132]

Acknowledging their superstitions more readily then than now, people used portraits quite openly to act as substitutes for the sitters. Donor portraits, and other portrait images placed in churches, evidently had a talismanic function.[133] At a more mundane level, portraits became proxies for absent sitters in a variety of ways.

Borso d'Este, Duke of Ferrara, died in May 1471. In September, Galeazzo Maria Sforza wrote to Ercole, Borso's brother and successor:

> We understand that your lordship has in the castle a recent portrait of the late Duke Borso . . . by the hand of master Baldassare and we would be glad and grateful to have it, and so we beg your lordship to be pleased to send the said picture by boat to Pavia and to instruct your messenger who will bring it to take care that it is not harmed by rain or water and to deliver it into the hands of our castellan of Pavia.[134]

Ercole sent the portrait, which was delivered by its painter Baldassare d'Este,[135] and in November 1471 Galeazzo Maria wrote to thank Ercole:

> The picture of the late most illustrious lord Duke Borso, which you have sent on our request with master Baldassare, is more dear and agreeable than anything that could have befallen us: and this because we have always desired to have a representation of that lord, whom we loved like a father, and we have always striven to imitate his attire as most praiseworthy and truly befitting for a prince: and the picture is all the more dear to us because it has been done in a most distinguished manner, so that, when we look at him thus painted, we seem to see the living man, as if nothing but his soul were missing . . . we will keep this painting continually near us, to remind us of the said lord and of your lordship who sent it . . . master Baldassare deserves the highest commendation.[136]

In 1495, five years after Isabella d'Este had married and left Ferrara for Mantua, a Ferrarese friend wrote to tell her that 'when I dine, I have your portrait placed on a chair opposite me, so that, seeing it there, I imagine that I am at table with your ladyship'.[137] Leonardo wrote that 'the painter . . . can place the true image of the beloved before the lover, who often kisses it and speaks to it'.[138] Baldassare Castiglione, in a poem on his portrait by Raphael (plate 243), imagined his wife writing to him during his absence:

> When alone, the portrait by Raphael's hand
> Recalls your face and relieves my cares,
> I play with it and laugh with it and joke,
> I speak to it and, as though it could reply,
> It often seems to me to nod and motion,
> To want to say something and speak your words.
> Your boy knows and greets his father, babbling.
> Herewith I am consoled and beguile the long days.[139]

A courtier wrote to the Duchess of Urbino in 1538:

> I was already on horseback and about to leave Pesaro when Giovanantonio, the

243 Raphael, *Baldassare Castiglione*, canvas, 82 × 67 cm., Louvre, Paris (INV. 611).

The portrait was probably painted in 1514–15 when the sitter (1478–1529) was in Rome as the Duke of Urbino's ambassador.

See the exhibition catalogue Paris, 1983–4, pp. 84–7 (7); Béguin, 1984, pp. 36–8; here pp. 30, 115, 220, plate 244.

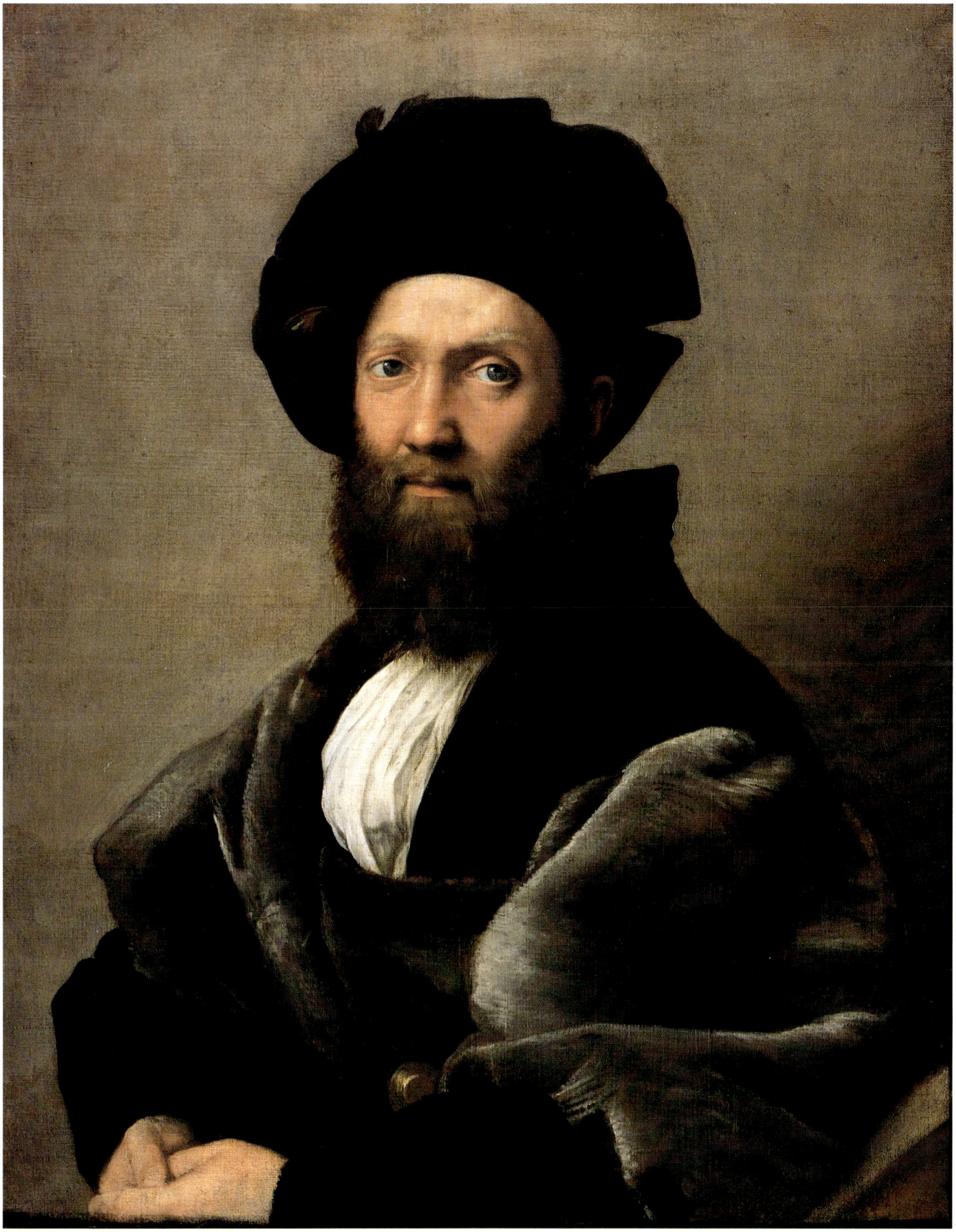

keeper of the Wardrobe, told me that the new portraits of your ladyship and our most illustrious lord had arrived; and so I dismounted and stayed a good while considering the marvellous likenesses, and I could scarcely refrain from kissing your hand, so lifelike did it appear to me; and I said more than once, 'My dear lady, you are indeed she'; and, wishing to speak to the picture, I went close to it, but saw that it did not attend to what I said; and suddenly I recalled that great wrong which you have done me, for so many times you have promised me your portrait but you have never given me one . . .[140]

The two portraits were by Titian (plates 45, 198).

In 1527, Francis I of France, seeing a portrait of Henry VIII or England, took off his bonnet, said that he knew Henry's face well and remarked, 'I pray to God that He will give him a good and long life'.[141] It was reported in 1551 that a portrait of Edward VI of England, presented to a possible consort, the five-year-old Elisabeth of Valois, had been placed in her bedchamber. She had said to her mother Catherine de' Medici, Queen of France: '"I have wished good day to the King of England, my lord". This is what she is taught and trained to do.'[142] On 7 January 1605, it was noted that the three-year-old Dauphin of France had looked at, and made his reverence to, portraits of the king and queen his parents: this was apparently a ritual that he performed daily.[143] In Webster's play *The White Devil*, first printed in 1612, Isabella, the wife of the faithless Brachiano, goes nightly to 'visit' his portrait: 'she kneels down as to prayers, then draws the curtain of the picture, does three reverences to it, and kisses it thrice'; and so she feeds

her eyes and lips
On the dead shadow; Doctor Julio,
Observing this, infects it with an oil
And other poisoned stuff . . .

so that she is murdered by kissing the poisoned lips of the portrait.[144]

In her youth, Elizabeth I of England wrote a touching letter to her younger brother Edward VI, to whom she was sending her portrait:

For the face, I graunt, I might wel blusche to offer, but the mynde I shal neuer be asshamed to present. For thogth from the grace of the pictur the coulers may fade by time, may giue by wether, may be spotted by chance, yet the other nor time with her swift winges shal ouertake, nor the mistie cloudes with ther loweringes may darken, nor chance with her slipery fote may ouerthrow . . . I shal most humbly beseche your Majestie that whan you shal loke on my pictur you wil witsafe to thinke that as you haue but the outwarde shadow of the body afore you, so my inward minde wischeth that the body it selfe wer oftner in your presence . . .[145]

Elizabeth's subjects, however, did not make such subtle distinctions between portrait and sitter. In 1586, the Irish rebel Sir Brian O'Rourke insulted an image of Elizabeth. Sir William Fitzwilliam, the Lord Deputy of Ireland, related that O'Rourke 'fell with such spiteful and traitorous speeches to rail at it, and otherwise so filthily to use it, as I protest . . . I abhor to remember, and can by no means frame my pen to write'. The 'image' was in fact a wooden statue, but some believed that it was a painted portrait.[146] Also in 1586, the Scots-Irish rebel Sorley Buidhe MacDonald came to Dublin to make his submission to the Lord Deputy; seeing in his chamber a portrait of Elizabeth, he threw aside his sword, repeatedly cast himself at her feet and protested his devotion to her.[147] William Hacket,

244 Raphael, *Baldassare Castiglione*, detail (see plate 243).

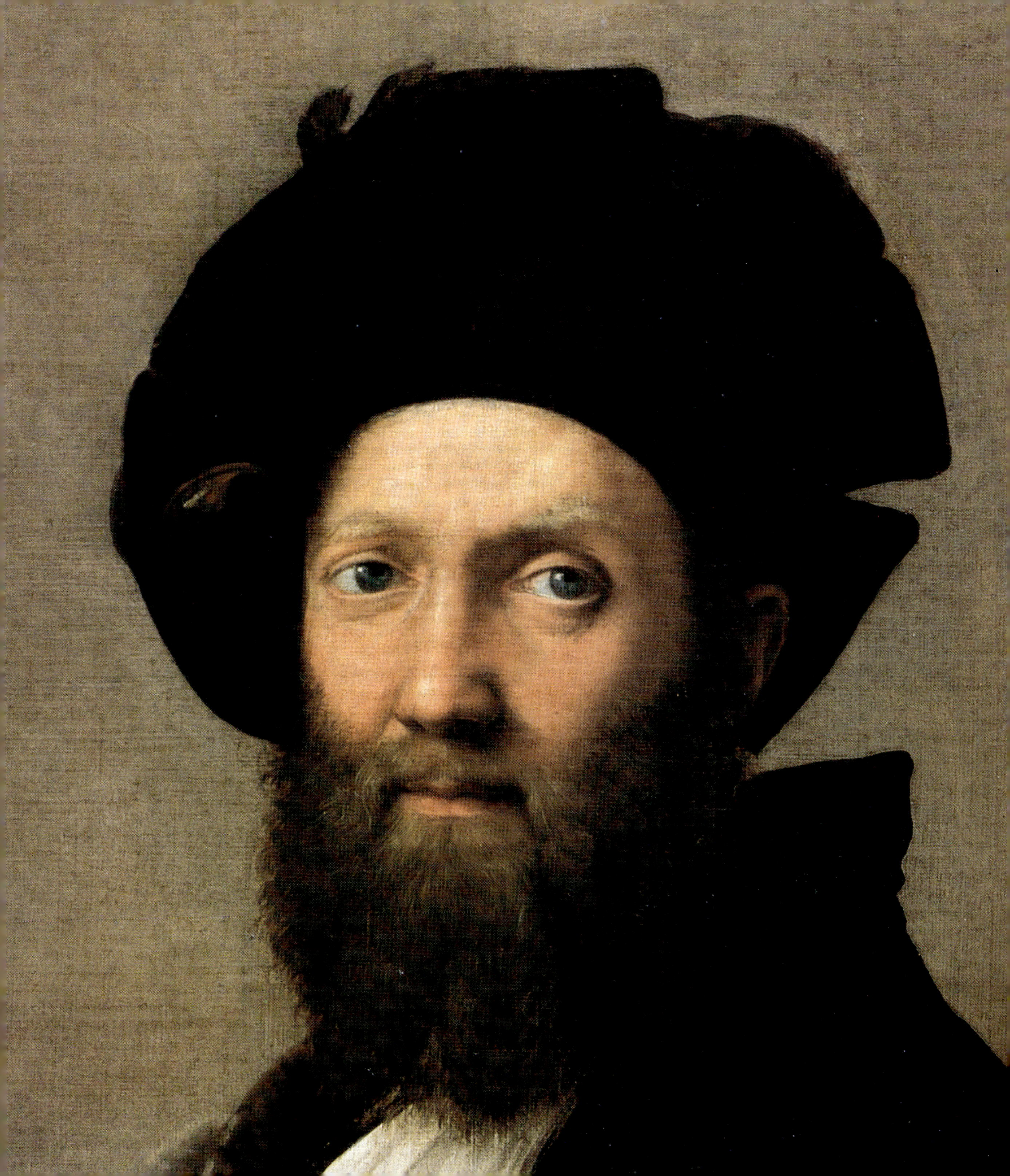

245 Hermann tom Ring, *Johannes Münstermann*, oak panel, 67 × 47 cm., Westfälisches Landesmuseum für Kunst und Kulturgeschichte, Münster (688 LM).

On the bases of the coats of arms on the shields behind him and the coat of arms and initials MJ on the signet ring which he wears on the index finger of his left hand, the sitter has been identified as Johannes Münstermann, apparently a younger son of Dietrich Münstermann (died 1551), Burgomaster of Münster. Very little is known about Johannes. The ring on the wedding finger of his left hand is set with a cameo of Alexander the Great; on the table are a flute and the four parts of a printed score of Italian madrigals by Philippe Verdelot. The sitter points at a madrigal addressed by a frustrated lover to his cruel mistress. The portrait is dated 1547 and is attributed on stylistic grounds to Hermann tom Ring.

See Westhoff-Krummacher, 1967, and references; here pp. 99, 128, 225.

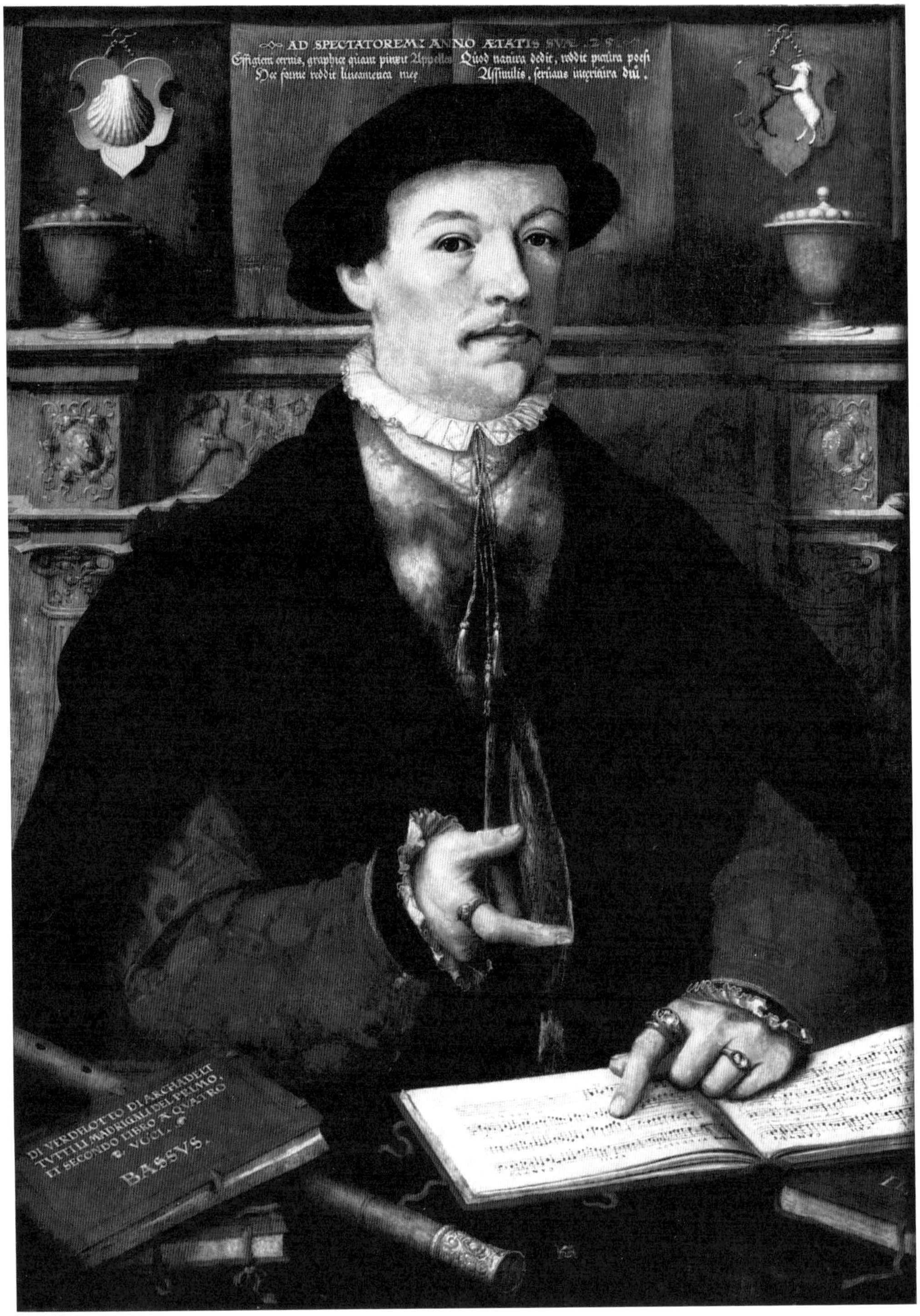

executed for treason in 1592, was accused of having defaced a portrait of Elizabeth that he had found in his landlord's house in London. It was alleged that he had 'maliciously and traiterously put in and thrust an yron Instrument into that part of the sayde picture, that did represent the Brest and Hart of the Q. Maiestie'. Though Hacket denied the charge, he admitted having abused a representation of the queen's coat of arms 'and that hee was mooued therunto inwardly by the spirit, to take away her whole power of her authoritie . . .'.[148]

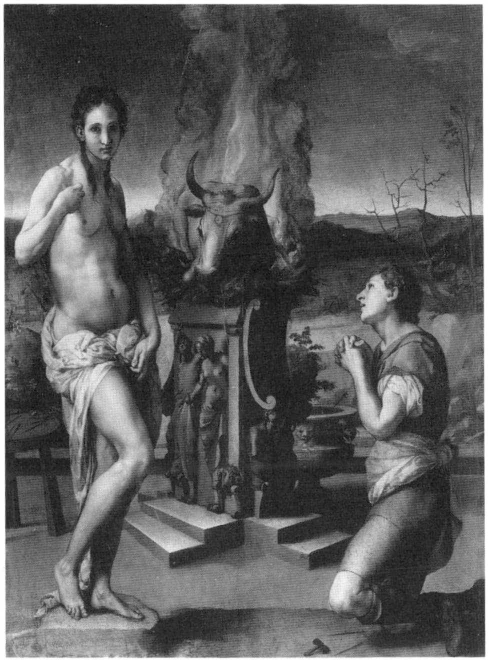

246 Bronzino, *Pygmalion and Galatea*, panel, 81 × 64 cm., Palazzo Vecchio, Florence, Opere d'arte recuperate (36).

The picture is described by Vasari, who states that it was painted by Bronzino as the cover for a portrait by Pontormo of Francesco Guardi dressed as a soldier. Pontormo's portrait, executed in 1529–30, is lost (Vasari-Milanesi, 1878–85, VI, p. 275).

See Bacchcschi, 1973, p. 87; here pp. 67, 225.

In 1601, when James VI of Scotland heard that an Edinburgh sheriff officer had heedlessly sold at the gallows' foot portraits of himself and his queen, the confiscated property of a debtor, he was so incensed that he insisted on the execution of the officer.[149] When James went to England as king in 1603, the Venetian ambassador reported that the English courtiers were hiding their portraits of Queen Elizabeth and were quickly acquiring portraits, of James's mother, Mary, Queen of Scots, to hang in their stead.[150] They had perhaps heard of James's sensitivity about the uses of portraits.

Mary Tudor, Queen of England, hearing that her husband Philip II of Spain would not return to her for a long time, was enraged and had his picture removed from her Privy Chamber; some said that she kicked it from the room.[151] In another fit of jealousy, she was reported to have scratched at the portraits of Philip that were in her chamber.[152] Charles IX of France, lying in 1574 on his death-bed, sent for a portrait of his brother Henry, then absent in Poland, and apologised to it: 'Would that you were here, dear brother; would that I had never sent you from my side.'[153]

The conventional way of praising a portrait was to say that it was so like that it lacked only speech. Portraits, however, could be made to speak if inscriptions in which the sitters addressed the viewer were added. Heemskerck, having painted his father's portrait in 1532 (plate 162), lettered upon it the inscription: 'My son has counterfeited me here when I had lived for seventy five-years, so they say.'[154] The Münster painter Hermann tom Ring inscribed his portrait of Johannes Münstermann (plate 245) with the words: 'TO THE SPECTATOR: . . . You see an image that Apelles has artistically painted. He reproduces my features in this form. What Nature has given is given again by Painting which, like Poetry, serves the creation of God.'[155]

It was possible to go further. The humanist Lampsonius wrote a Latin epigram on his portrait by Antonis Mor and had it lettered on the frame of the picture, now lost. He stated that Mor had wished to confer life and a soul upon his image and imagined Nature, seeing the portrait and addressing Mor, refusing his request but asking, 'Allow me, pupil, this praise: is it nothing to have created the sitter?'[156] Bronzino, making a protective cover for a lost portrait by Pontormo, chose, or was instructed, to paint upon it a representation of Pygmalion and Galatea (plate 246). The artist Pygmalion, having fallen in love with the statue that he has created, prays to Venus to bring it to life. The owner of Pontormo's lost picture, opening the cover to see the portrait, may have had similar thoughts and desires, even if Venus was not there to grant his wishes.

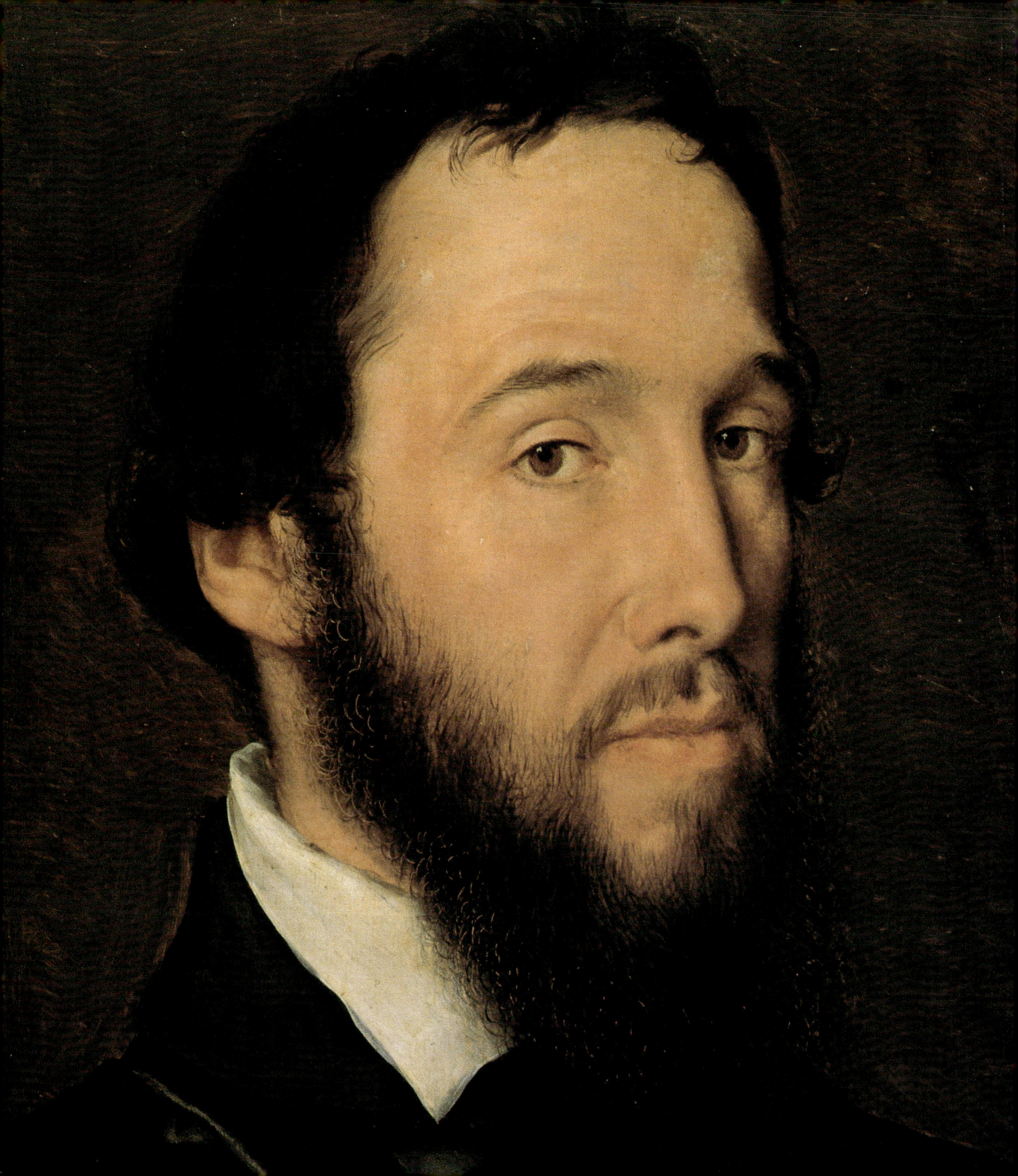

9 Italy and 'the North'

We are conditioned to look at Renaissance works of art with the eyes of a sixteenth-century Florentine. The ideals and values of Vasari and his contemporaries have been accepted with surprising alacrity by succeeding generations. Many of their assumptions, which, as they themselves might have admitted, were often based on an incomplete and prejudiced grasp of the facts, continue to be echoed by modern writers on Renaissance art. The concepts of 'the Renaissance' and 'the North' were evolved in Italy. Few sixteenth-century Italians knew or cared much about the lands beyond the Alps, unless armies crossed the mountains and invaded and occupied areas of the peninsula. Referring to the other peoples of Europe as 'ultramontanes', the Italians were so entranced by the glories of the Roman past that they were inclined to view the ultramontanes as barbarians, just as the ancient Romans had regarded the tribes of Gaul and Germania. Since they made few distinctions among the ultramontane states but were inevitably aware of the disparities among the states of Italy, they could conceive of non-Italian Europe as an entity as homogeneous as Italy itself. Most modern historians of Renaissance art are content to refer to Europe outside Italy as 'the North', though it is clearly difficult to generalise about an area so vast as that which stretches from the Hebrides to the Urals and from Scandinavia to Granada.

Since the sixteenth century, one generalisation has been consistently applied to the art of 'the North' by Italians and ultramontanes alike and has had a most damaging effect on the evaluation and appreciation of northern art. It is that northern artists were more concerned than Italian artists with the faithful imitation of reality. The Fleming Van Mander wrote in 1604 that the antique marbles and bronzes rediscovered in Rome

> have given to our art of painting a great light and have opened the eyes of its practitioners to the differences, in life or in nature, between the ugly and the beautiful, between the beautiful and the supremely beautiful, as regards the forms of men and beasts. So that the Italians, thus enlightened, discovered earlier the right and sound way of making images, while our Netherlanders . . . with incomplete knowledge, contented themselves with following vulgar life and remained . . . in relative darkness . . . until Jan van Scorel brought to them from Italy the knowledge of the best kinds or forms of our art and placed them before their eyes.[1]

The concept of 'northern realism' has become entrenched and, as it is obvious that most northern artists studied and reproduced detail with greater attention and skill than most Italian artists, it may seem unnecessary to question the validity of the concept. The 'realism', however, in such paintings as Van der Weyden's *Descent from the Cross*, or the *Crucifixion* of Grünewald's Isenheim altarpiece, is only superficial. The immense emotional and aesthetic impact of these pictures is created not merely by their painters' capacity to observe and record the surfaces of reality, but by their power to command and distort reality. They deliberately flouted laws of anatomy, relative scale and spatial recession to produce images of

247 Antonis Mor, *Antoine Perrenot de Granvelle*, detail (see plate 259).

248 (facing page) Andrea del Castagno, *Man*, panel, 54 × 40.5 cm., National Gallery of Art, Washington (1937.1.17, Andrew W. Mellon Collection).

The sitter has not been identified. On grounds of style and costume, the portrait is attributed to Castagno and dated around 1450.

See Shapley, 1979, pp. 127–9; Sterling, 1988, pp. 24–6; here pp. 86, 120, 232.

249 (p. 230) Andrea Mantegna, *Cardinal Ludovico Trevisan*, poplar panel, 44 × 33 cm., Staatliche Museen Preussischer Kulturbesitz, Berlin (West), Gemäldegalerie (9).

The sitter (1401–65), who became a cardinal in 1440, is identified from an inscription on the reverse of a version and by comparison with a portrait medal. The picture is attributed to Mantegna on stylistic grounds and was probably painted at Mantua in 1459–60, when Trevisan attended the Congress there.

See Lightbown, 1986, pp. 408–10; here pp. 86, 232.

startling and disturbing force which readily bear comparison with Picasso's *Guernica*.[2] The Italians were in this respect encumbered by an artistic theory that was based on classical texts and that exalted both naturalism and idealisation as the supremely desirable qualities. It was hardly astonishing that they treated foreign art, about which they knew relatively little, with suspicion and with a degree of contempt, that their appreciation of it should have been very superficial and that they failed to understand its subtleties and its power. Since the Italians were more ready to write about works of art and since their Latinate vocabulary allowed them to be more articulate in their discussions of art, they put forward their views eloquently. Not unnaturally, they created a historical pattern in which the development of northern art cannot easily find its place. Italian Renaissance preconceptions are still maintained, to the detriment of an understanding of northern art.

As we have seen, Italian Renaissance theorists were led, by their infatuation with the pursuit of ideal beauty, to take a patronising attitude to portraiture and to make some strange and even ludicrous statements about portrait-painting.[3] It was conceded that northern artists, because they were supposedly content to copy with care what they saw in front of them, were good portraitists. In their portraits as in their religious paintings, however, their fidelity to nature might not go much beyond the surfaces of things. It has been shown that even Jan van Eyck and Holbein, seemingly the most objective and meticulous of the northern portraitists, consciously distorted natural appearances for aesthetic and expressive effect;[4] whereas most Italian portrait-painters, though less inclined to lavish attention on detail, limited themselves to depicting people as they actually were. To this extent, it is the Italian and not the northern portraits that are superficial and 'photographic'. The historian of Renaissance portrait-painting must be continuously alert to the prejudices against portraiture and against non-Italian and non-Florentine art which have gained widespread acceptance. While it may be seductively easy to adopt the sixteenth-century Florentine views persuasively expressed by Vasari, it is surely advisable to question them.

Because portraits were frequently sent across Europe and could be transported about the continent without much trouble, it may be assumed that artists in different areas would have had greater opportunities to acquaint themselves with foreign portraits than with foreign pictures of religious or secular subjects. It is not difficult to discover instances of Italian artists borrowing ideas from northern portraits and of northern painters responding to Italian portraits. Though ideas were constantly being exchanged, the fundamental difference between northern and Italian attitudes to reality remained largely unaffected.

It seems possible that, in the mid- and late fourteenth century, there was in France and the Low Countries a passing vogue for profile portraits and that this fashion was stimulated by Italian example.[5] As the visual and documentary evidence for the early period is sadly limited, it is not feasible to arrive at more definite conclusions.

In the fifteenth century, many Italians clearly took an intense interest in northern art, and French and Netherlandish portraits were reaching Italy in fair numbers. Fouquet's portrait of Pope Eugenius IV with two of his familiars, painted in Rome in the 1440s, was perhaps a full length and was placed in the sacristy of Santa Maria sopra Minerva, where it was much admired as an extremely life-like image (see plate 208).[6] A Neapolitan merchant imported from the Netherlands a portrait of the Duke of Burgundy which evidently caused such a sensation in Naples that the painter Colantonio made a copy of it, stated to have been indistinguishable from

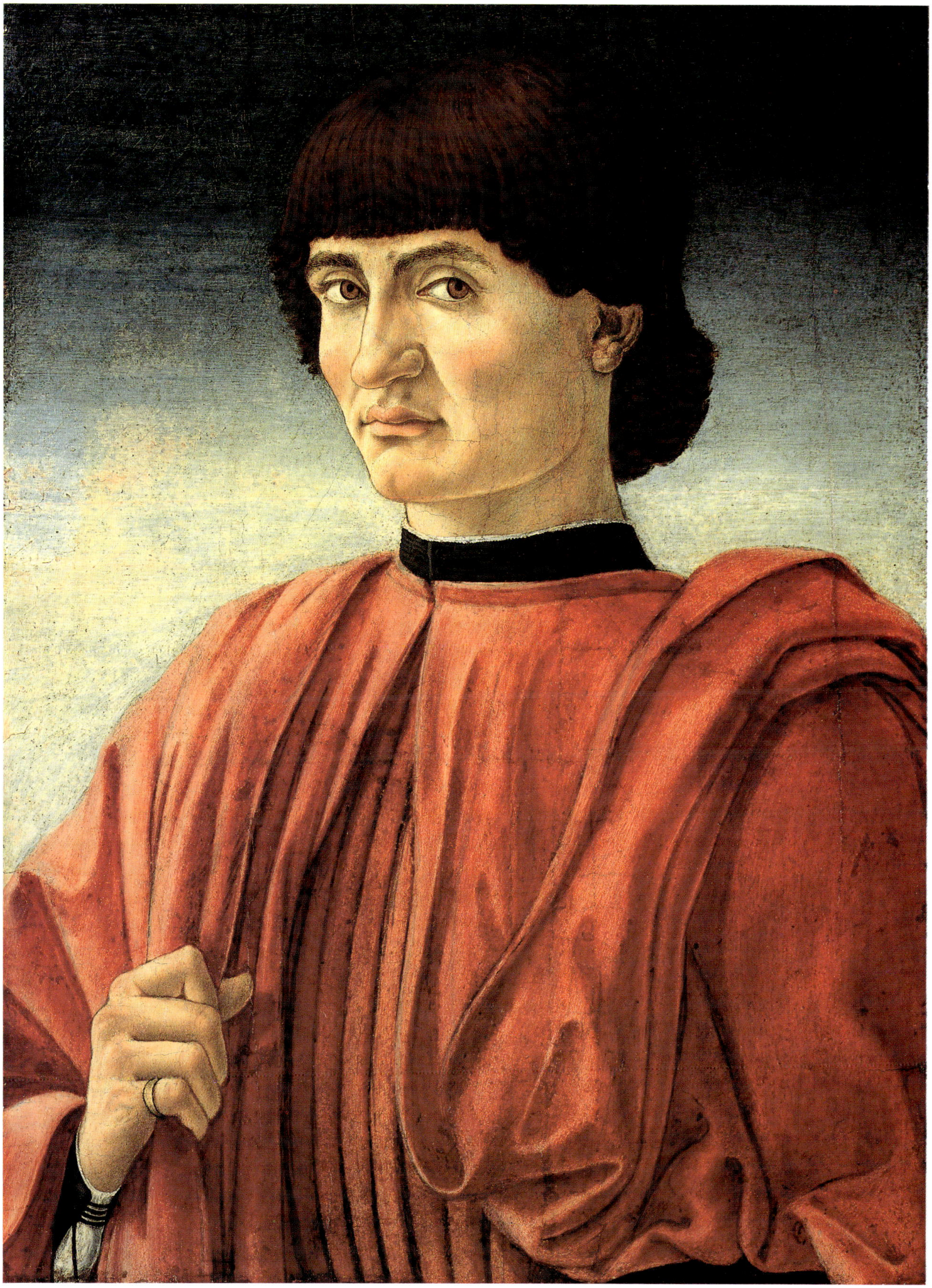

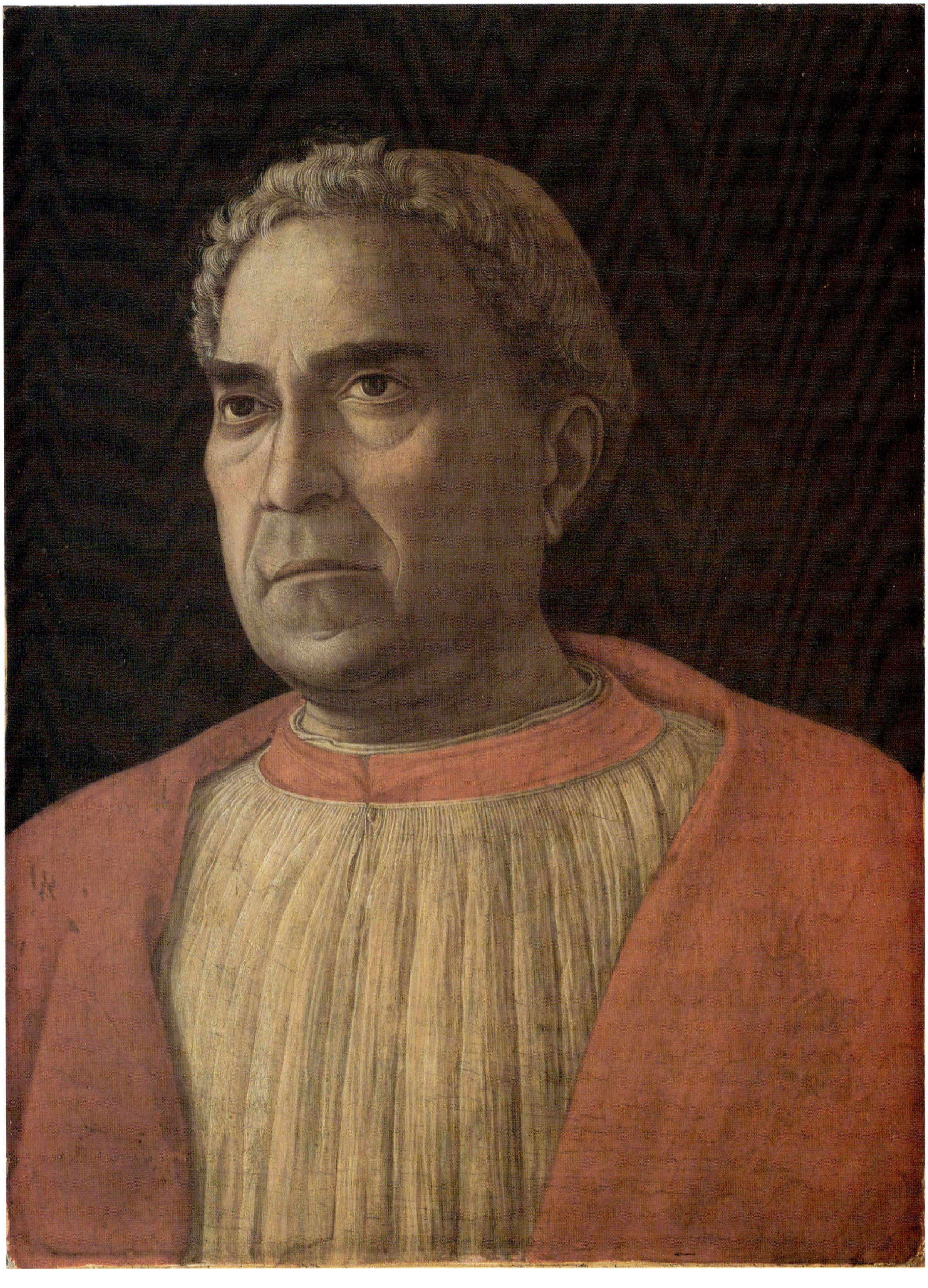

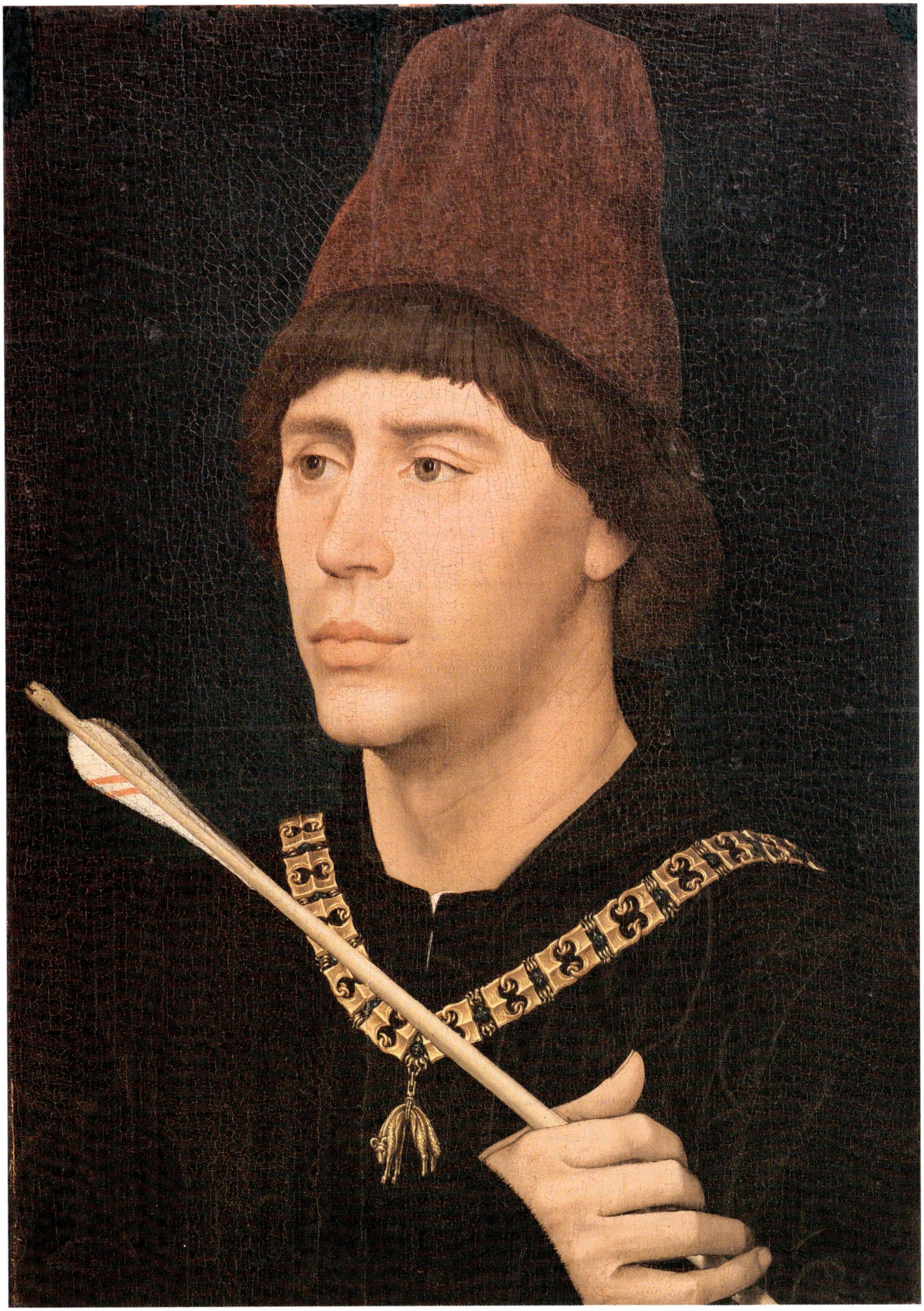

250 (prev. page) Rogier van der Weyden, *Antoine, the 'Grand Bâtard' of Burgundy*, oak panel, 39 × 28.5 cm., Musées Royaux des Beaux-Arts de Belgique, Brussels (1449).

The sitter (c. 1430–1504), one of the numerous illegitimate children of Philip the Good, Duke of Burgundy, is identified from an early version which has on its reverse the emblem and motto of Antoine. The portrait is attributed on stylistic grounds to Van der Weyden, who died in 1464. The sitter wears the Order of the Golden Fleece, which he received in 1456, and the picture may therefore be dated between 1456 and 1464. The arrow, which he clasps against his heart, is of unexplained emblematic significance.

See Campbell, 1972, *passim*; here pp. 16, 37, 61, 86, 128, 232.

251 (facing page, left) Perugino, *Self-Portrait*, panel, 51 × 37 cm., Uffizi, Florence (1482).

The sitter is identified by comparison with the fresco self-portrait that Perugino painted in about 1500 in the Collegio del Cambio in Perugia. Though the picture has been attributed to Lorenzo di Credi and to Raphael, it is apparently by Perugino himself and may have been painted shortly before 1500. Its composition is closely based on a portrait by Memlinc.

See Berti, 1979, p. 343; here p. 233.

the original.[7] In the 1470s, Federico da Montefeltro employed at Urbino the Netherlander Justus of Ghent, who painted there portraits and a series of famous men, including the reigning Pope Sixtus IV (plates 52, 68). At least one portrait by Memlinc can be shown to have been in Florence by the 1470s.[8] During the same decade Antonello da Messina, who evidently knew a good deal about Netherlandish portraiture as well as about Netherlandish techniques of oil-painting, was in Venice and his presence there must have helped to familiarise Venetian painters with styles of portraiture current in the Low Countries (plate 100). In many parts of Italy, Netherlandish pictures of religious subjects in which donor portraits were included were available to local artists. Van der Weyden's lost triptych of the *Descent from the Cross* with 'a certain prince as suppliant' was at Ferrara by 1449.[9] In the 1450s, a triptych by Jan van Eyck of the *Annunciation* was at Naples:

> On the outer side of the same picture is painted Battista Lomellini, whose picture it was – you would judge he lacked only a voice – and the woman whom he loved, of outstanding beauty; and she too is portrayed exactly as she was. Between them, as though through a chink in the wall, falls a ray of sun that you would take to be real sun-light.[10]

The *Portinari Triptych* by Van der Goes arrived in Florence in 1483 (plates 30, 32, 192).

It has been claimed that it was Netherlandish influence that led certain fifteenth-century Italian artists to abandon the profile convention and also to introduce landscape backgrounds into their portraits. This may be broadly true, though it would be an oversimplification to suggest that, throughout the century, every Italian three-quarters-view portrait and every Italian portrait with a landscape background depended directly upon Netherlandish originals. Two of the earliest surviving Italian portraits in which the sitters are seen in three-quarters view are Castagno's *Portrait of a Man* of about 1450 and Mantegna's *Cardinal Ludovico Trevisan* of about 1460 (plates 248, 249). Both Castagno and Mantegna would appear to have studied antique portrait busts, but as both, in their treatment of detail and light, owe something to Netherlandish art, it is probable that they had seen Netherlandish portraits similar to Van der Weyden's *Antoine, the 'Grand Bâtard' of Burgundy* (plate 250) and that such pictures may have caused them to look anew at Roman portrait sculpture and to produce classicising adaptations of a Netherlandish portrait type. In Castagno's and Mantegna's portraits, the details of the sitters' eyebrows, eyelids and hair are painted with great precision, though the lines that render individual hairs are so thick and insistent that they suggest wire or fibres coarser than human hairs. The lighting in both portraits is extremely sharp, so that the tonal contrasts in the flesh are exaggerated, and much reliance is placed on line to define the contours of the features. This would appear to be a result of attempting the impossible task of emulating in tempera the effects obtained with different media by the Netherlanders. The subtleties of Van der Weyden's rendering of textures, particularly those of the skin, where there are endless slight modulations of colour, were beyond the capabilities of the Italians. Even Antonello, better acquainted with Netherlandish techniques, tended to produce flashy imitations of Netherlandish paintings by using very sharp lighting and by concentrating detail in and around the eyes (plate 100). Individual hairs are painted but are again too coarse in texture. It is as if Antonello were obtrusively indicating that his virtuosity should be noticed and admired. Other areas of his portrait heads, most noticeably the ears, are rather negligently simplified or indeed omitted.

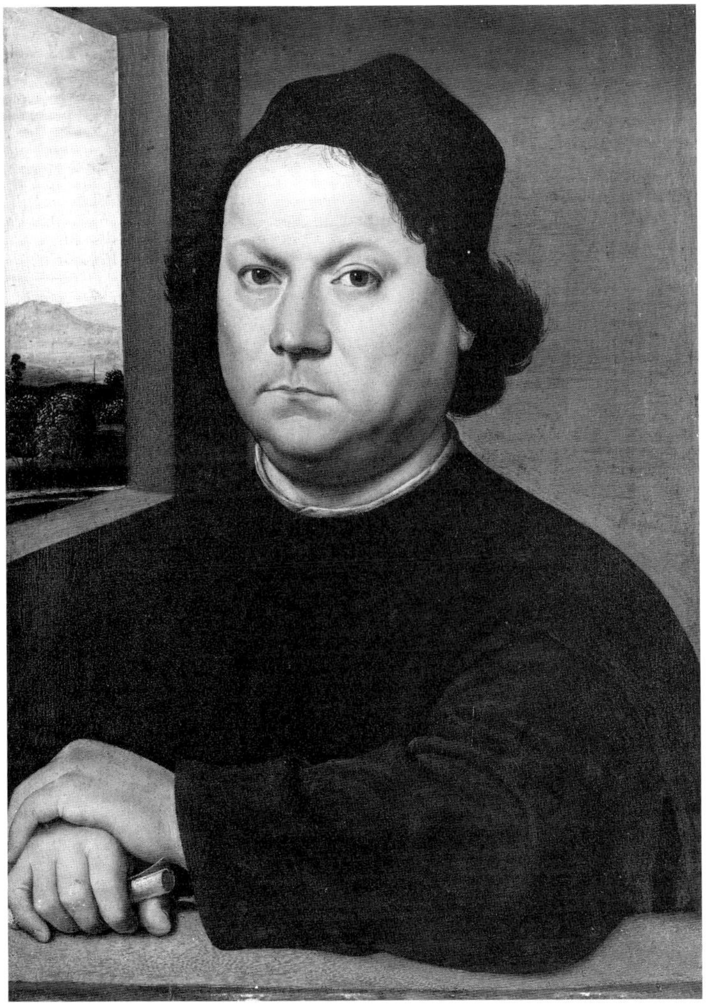

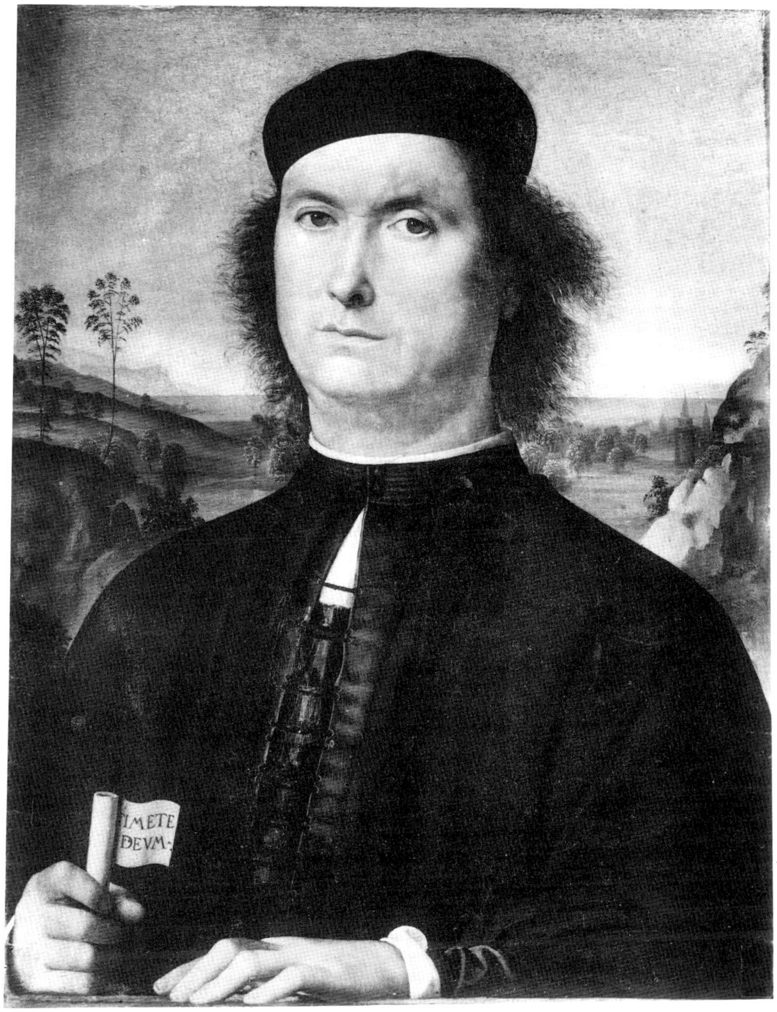

252 (above right) Perugino, *Francesco delle Opere*, panel, 52 × 44 cm., Uffizi, Florence (1700).

An old inscription on the reverse reads: '1494 di Luglio/Pietro Perugino pinse Franc°. de Lopre Peynaga [?]', 'In July 1494 Pietro Perugino painted Francesco delle Opere . . . ', the last word being incomprehensible. The inscription on the obverse is 'TIMETE DEVM', 'Fear God', perhaps the motto of the sitter, who was married in 1488 and who died in Venice in 1516. His brother Giovanni 'delle Corniole' was a gem-engraver and in 1505 worked in association with Perugino (Milanesi, in Vasari-Milanesi, 1878–85, v, pp. 368–9, note).

See Berti, 1979, p. 406; here pp. 74, 121, 233.

By the end of the century, it can be demonstrated that some Italian painters were imitating specific Netherlandish portraits. Perugino's *Self-Portrait* is based on a Memlinc portrait that he probably saw in Florence (plate 251);[11] the composition and landscape of his *Francesco delle Opere* are so close to Memlinc that it may be safely assumed that, there too, Perugino was following quite faithfully another portrait by Memlinc (plates 127, 252). Though Perugino was better able than his predecessors to emulate Netherlandish techniques, his tonal contrasts are rather sharp and his effects of detail can be obtrusive. The pale-blue highlights reflected from the sky in the hair of Francesco delle Opere and the individual hairs straying across his forehead in his *Self-Portrait* are impressively painted; but, if Memlinc's portraits are compared, a want of subtlety becomes apparent in the details of figures and landscapes.

In Raphael's early portraits, borrowings from Netherlandish art may frequently be found.[12] Later in his career he continued to turn for inspiration to northern art: in his portrait of Pope Julius II he adapted the composition of the *Pope Sixtus IV* by Justus of Ghent, which he would have seen at Urbino (plates 68, 69); his portrait of Pope Leo X with two cardinals clearly follows in the tradition of Fouquet's lost portrait of Pope Eugenius IV with two of his familiars, which he would have seen in Rome (plates 141, 208).[13]

It is more difficult to establish that northern artists of the fifteenth and early

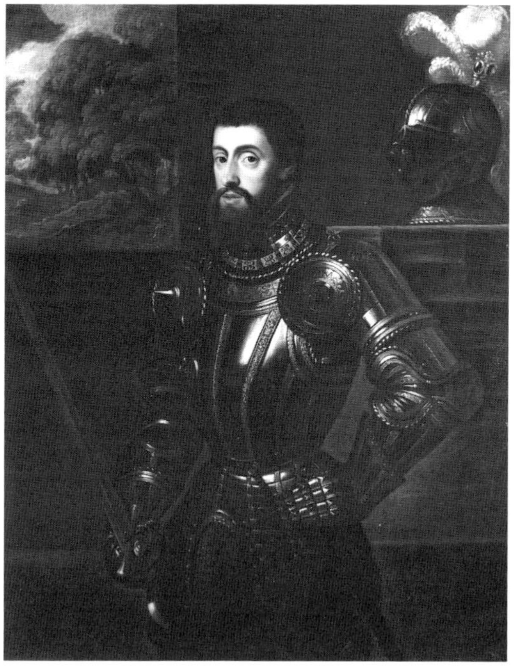

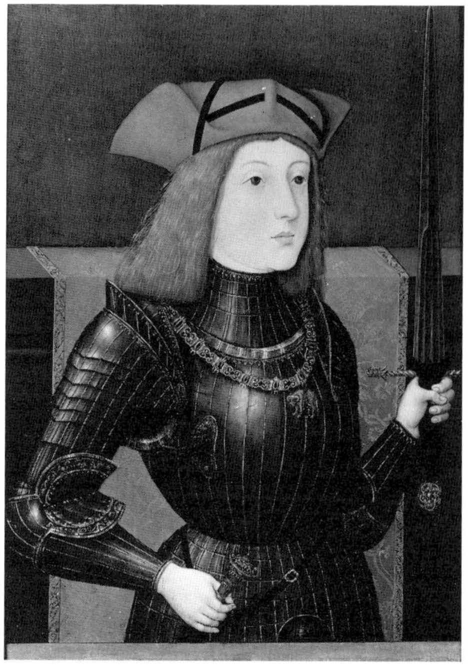

253 After Titian, *The Emperor Charles V holding a drawn Sword*, canvas, 126.5 × 101.1 cm., Orlando Montagu Collection, London.

There are additions above and below, both about 3 cm. high. Titian's original, painted at Bologna in 1532–3, and all the versions that Titian himself made of it are lost. Various copies are known, not all of which include landscapes, but the landscape here seems to be in the style of Titian and cannot be the invention of the copyist.

See Wethey, 1971, pp. 191–3; Hope, 1980, pp. 76–8; here p. 234.

254 German, c. 1515, *The Emperor Charles V as a Boy holding a drawn Sword*, panel, 60 × 42.5 cm., Kunsthistorisches Museum, Vienna, Gemäldegalerie (5618: exhibited at Schloss Ambras, Innsbruck).

The sitter (1500–58) is identified from other portraits; his armour is thought to be one of the suits ordered for him in Augsburg in 1512–14 by his grandfather Maximilian I. The unidentified German painter probably copied the face from a portrait executed in the Low Countries, where Charles was brought up.

See Heinz and Schütz, 1976, pp. 62–3; here p. 234.

sixteenth centuries benefited much from studying Italian portraiture. Italian portraits reached the courts and towns of northern Europe and northern artists visited Italy;[14] but Dürer, for example, did not significantly change his approach to portrait-painting during his visit to Venice in 1505–7.[15] The presence of Leonardo and Andrea del Sarto at the French court did not radically affect the development of French portraiture. Raphael's *Joanna of Aragon*, sent to France immediately after it was painted, exerted a powerful influence on Italian portraiture, for the cartoon remained in Italy and was much admired; but the picture itself had no impact on the fashionable French painters of formal portraits (plate 71).[16]

The situation apparently changed during the 1530s and 1540s when Titian was working for the Habsburgs and when large numbers of his portraits, commissioned by them and their courtiers, could be seen at the courts of the Netherlands, the Empire and Spain. It is, however, arguable that the influence of Titian upon northern portraiture has been overstressed and that his debt to northern precedents has been seriously underestimated.

Titian first painted the Emperor Charles V at Bologna in 1532–3. Though he is supposed to have executed five versions of the portrait, it is now known only from copies (plate 253). Though Charles was later to tell Francisco de Holanda, in the presence of three dukes, that Francisco's father Antonio had painted him more successfully at Toledo than had Titian at Bologna,[17] he was evidently pleased with Titian's picture, rewarded the artist well and soon afterwards created him a Count Palatine and a Knight of the Golden Spur. In the patent of nobility, he compared Titian with Apelles and referred to the story that Alexander the Great allowed himself to be painted only by Apelles.[18] In so doing, he may have been recalling his grandfather the Emperor Maximilian I. An inscription relating to Strigel's portrait of Maximilian and his family states that, by edict, Strigel alone could paint Maximilian, as once Apelles had had a monopoly of Alexander's portraits.[19]

In showing Charles in armour and holding a drawn sword, Titian was following northern precedents and was doubtless instructed to do so. Charles himself had been painted in that way when he was a boy, in about 1515 (plate 254);

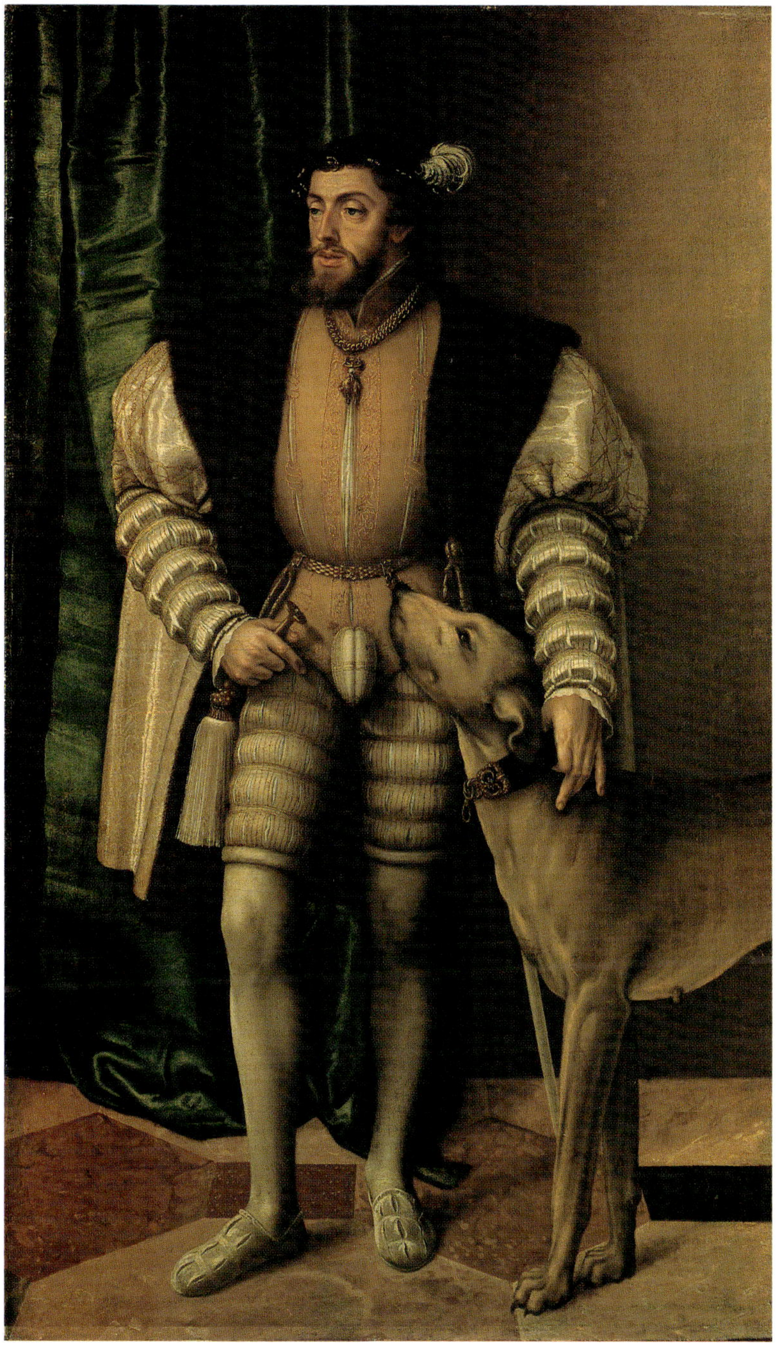

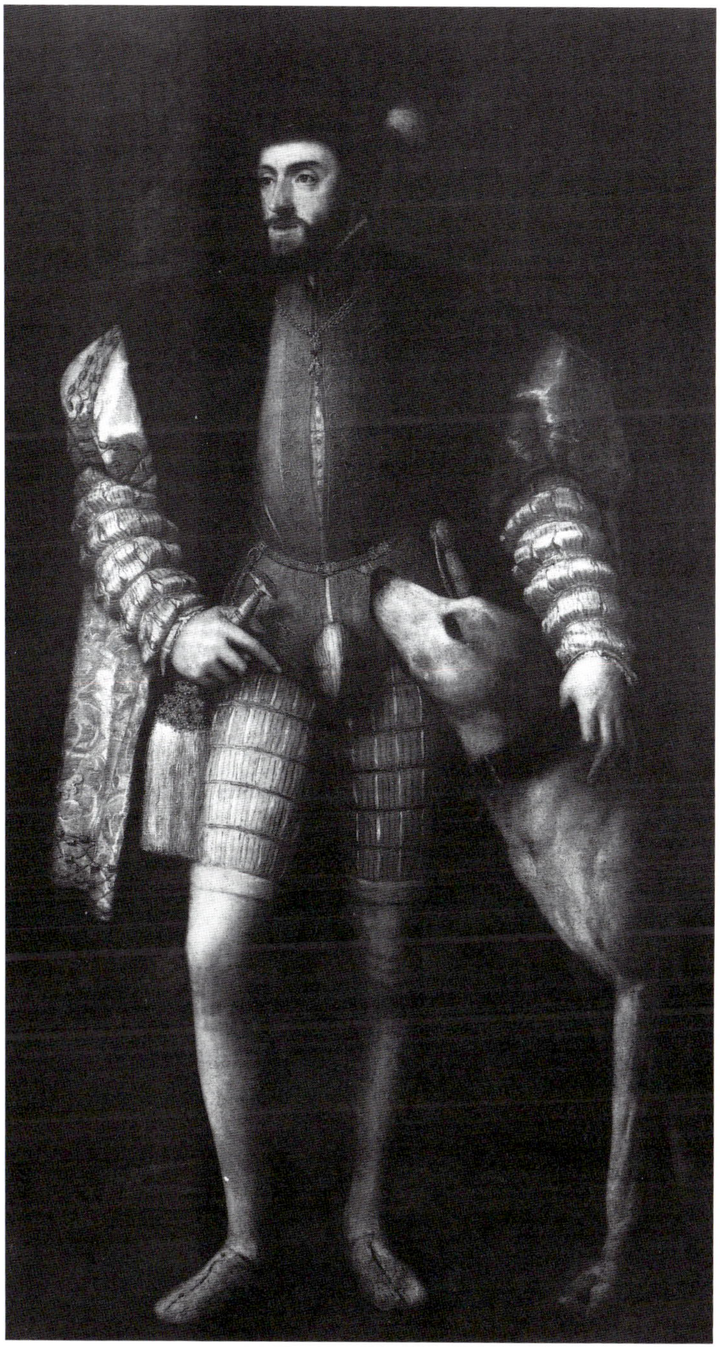

255 Jakob Seisenegger, *The Emperor Charles V with a Dog*, canvas, 205 × 123 cm., Kunsthistorisches Museum, Vienna, Gemäldegalerie (A 114).

The painting, signed with the artist's monogram and dated 1532, is described in great detail in a bill presented by Seisenegger in 1535 to his employer, Charles's brother Ferdinand I. Evidently writing from notes made during sittings, Seisenegger mentions that he painted the portrait from life at Bologna, lists the clothes that Charles is wearing and identifies the materials from which they are made, calls the dog an 'English water dog' and asks for 50 Rhenish florins for his work (Kreyczi, 1887, p. CXVII).

See the exhibition catalogue Brussels, 1987, pp. 64–5 (8); here pp. 56, 99, 104, 120, 236.

256 Titian, *The Emperor Charles V with a Dog*, canvas, 192 × 111 cm., Museo del Prado, Madrid (409).

Titian's copy of Seisenegger's portrait (plate 255) is so damaged and its surface is so obscured by dirt and discoloured varnishes that it can be discussed only in the most general compositional terms. Apparently working from drawings made at Bologna and not directly from Seisenegger's original, Titian has greatly increased the height and width of Charles's body and has altered the angles of his sword and the dog's neck to accord with the greater breadth of the figure and the differing shape of the support.

See Wethey, 1971, pp. 85–7; Hope, 1980, p. 78; here pp. 104, 236.

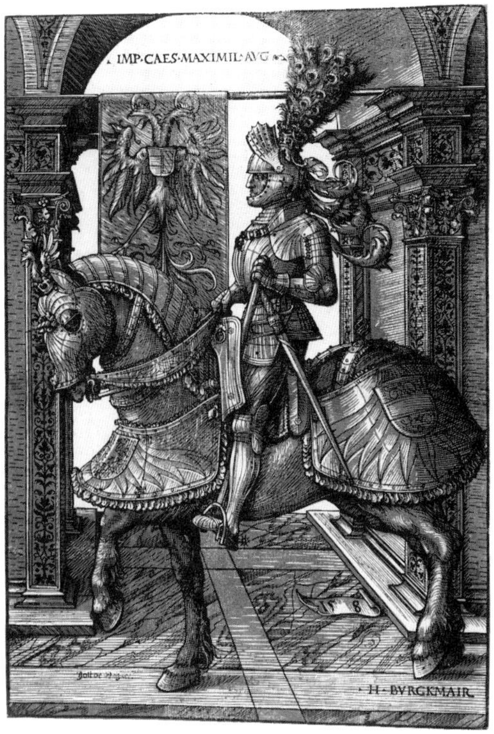

257 Hans Burgkmair, *The Emperor Maximilian I on Horseback*, chiaroscuro woodcut, 32.4 × 22.7 cm., British Museum, London, Department of Prints and Drawings (1895–1–22–377).

Signed and dated 1508, the woodcut is printed in two colours from two blocks. Burgkmair had some knowledge of classical and contemporary Italian art and architecture and this he has used in designing the arch in the background.

See the exhibition catalogue Stuttgart, 1973, No. 22; here pp. 56, 103, 120, 236.

258 Titian, *The Emperor Charles V on Horseback*, canvas, 332 × 279 cm., Museo del Prado, Madrid (410).

Titian painted this portrait at Augsburg in 1548, when he was reported to have spent a great deal of time with Charles and to have had many opportunities to converse with him. The picture was damaged while the paint was drying and was repaired by the Augsburg artist Amberger.

See Wethey, 1971, pp. 87–90; Hope, 1980, pp. 110–13; here pp. 56, 124, 206, 236.

Maximilian had appeared in portraits of about 1500 wearing the imperial crown and gilded armour and holding both a sceptre and a sword;[20] his son, Charles's father Philip the Handsome, was shown similarly posed in a Netherlandish portrait of about 1505 (plate 121); Dürer, in his imaginary portrait of Charlemagne painted in about 1512, chose to represent him carrying a drawn sword.[21] Titian in the Bologna portrait was conforming closely to a northern tradition of imperial portraiture.

The Austrian court painter Seisenegger was at Bologna in Charles's suite and there painted his life-size, full-length portrait of Charles, which is dated 1532 (plate 255). Seisenegger was also richly rewarded by Charles, and other princes, cardinals and the pope himself are supposed to have competed to employ him. He was later to be ennobled and exempted from taxation.[22] Seisenegger's portrait of Charles belongs to a Germanic tradition of which Cranach and Holbein are the best-known representatives (plates 1, 145–6). Titian was evidently so impressed by it that he copied it (plate 256). His copy, now sadly damaged, is thought to have been made not at Bologna but after Titian's return to Venice, from drawings made at Bologna. He may have presented it to Charles when they next met at Asti in 1536.[23] As Charles did not own Seisenegger's original, which belonged to his brother Ferdinand, he was probably very pleased to have Titian's version.

At Augsburg in 1548, Titian painted his great equestrian portrait of Charles, there wearing the armour in which he had won his victory over the Protestant princes at Mühlberg in 1547 (plate 258). Once again, Titian's painting can be related to a northern tradition of equestrian portraiture; it may be compared with Burgkmair's chiaroscuro woodcut of 1508 showing Charles's grandfather Maximilian I (plate 257).

If Titian's Habsburg portraits seem less innovative when they are considered in a northern context, that is not to deny his crucial importance in the history of court portraiture. After his second visit to Augsburg in 1550–1, Titian virtually stopped painting portraits of the Habsburgs. There appear to have been two main reasons: the first was that he never again went to court – though the Habsburgs could have sent him portraits by other artists which, as he had done before, he could have copied in Venice;[24] the second was that they were now employing a portrait-painter whom they may have preferred, the Netherlandish artist Antonis Mor. When Philip II of Spain complained in 1551 to his aunt Mary of Hungary that he was dissatisfied with Titian's portrait of him in armour and that, if there had been time, he would have made him go over it again,[25] and when Mary of Hungary wrote in 1553 that Titian's portraits were unrecognisable at close range,[26] they were making criticisms that could not have been levelled against Mor.

Mor became a master of the Antwerp guild in 1547, but by 1549 was in the service of Cardinal Granvelle in Brussels and was working for various members of the Habsburg family. Several of these people had been painted by Titian at Augsburg in 1548 and Mor was profoundly influenced by the Titian portraits he would have seen in Brussels. His portrait of his patron Granvelle is dated 1549 and is clearly rather different from his earliest known work, a double portrait painted at Utrecht in 1544.[27] It may be compared with Titian's portrait of Granvelle, painted at Augsburg, the composition of which Mor has adapted (plates 259–60), and it shows the precision in the description of form and texture that Philip II and Mary of Hungary evidently missed in Titian's work.

Paradoxically, Mor's portrait is in many ways less factual than Titian's. The compositions are similar, though the pose in Mor's portrait is very much less

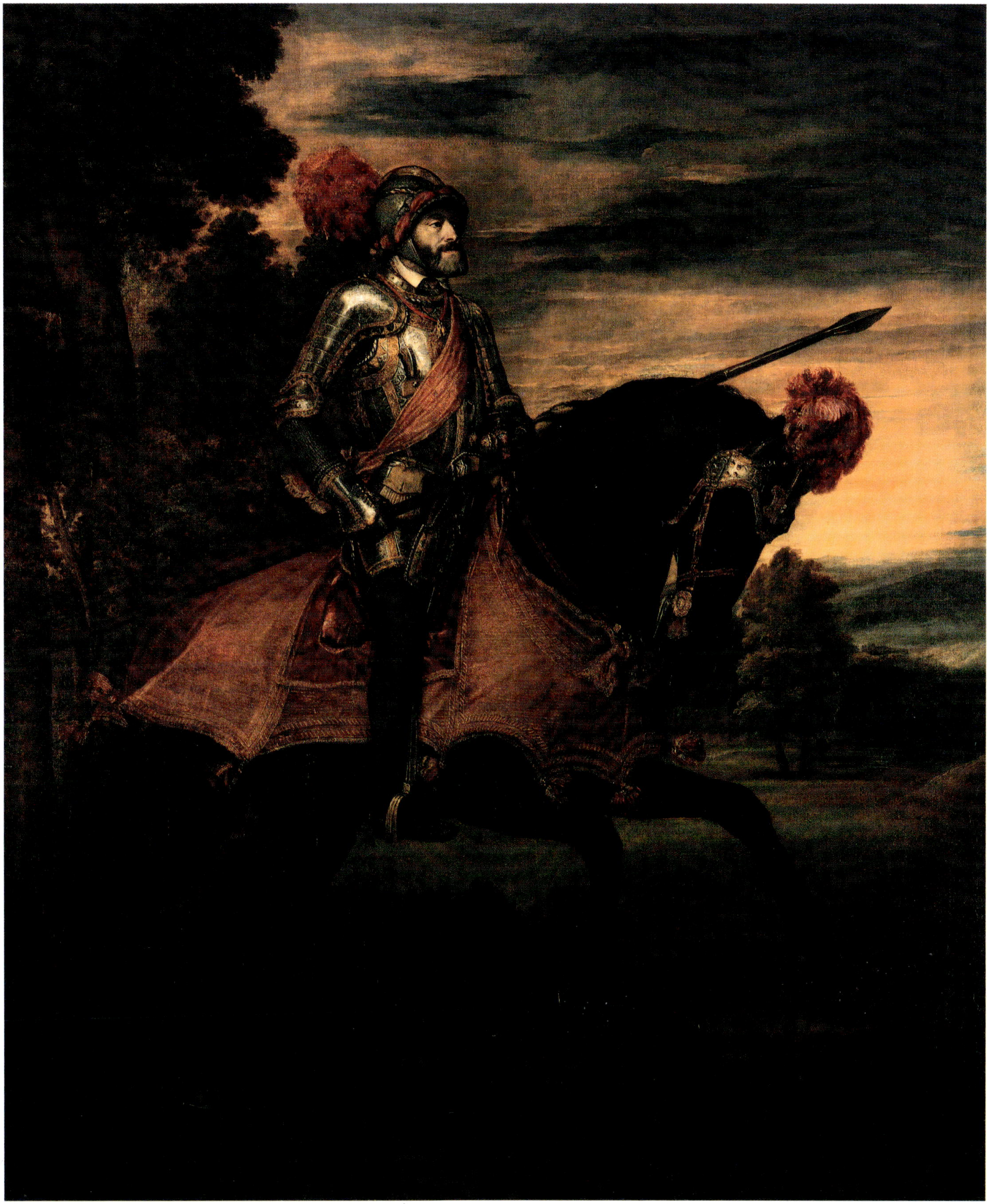

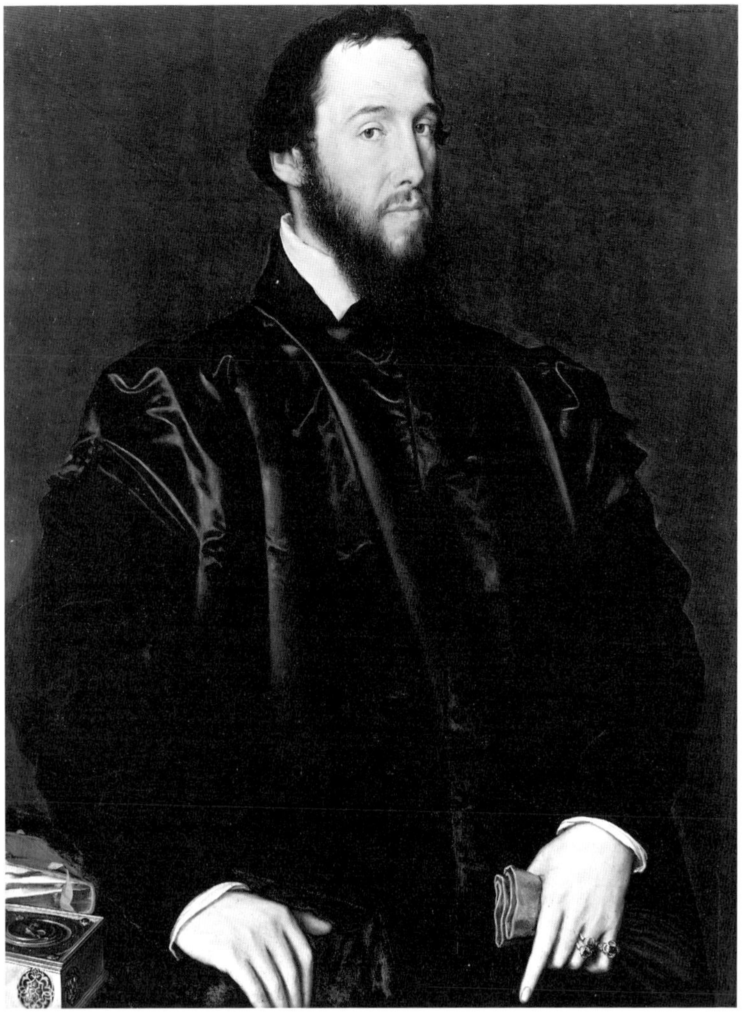

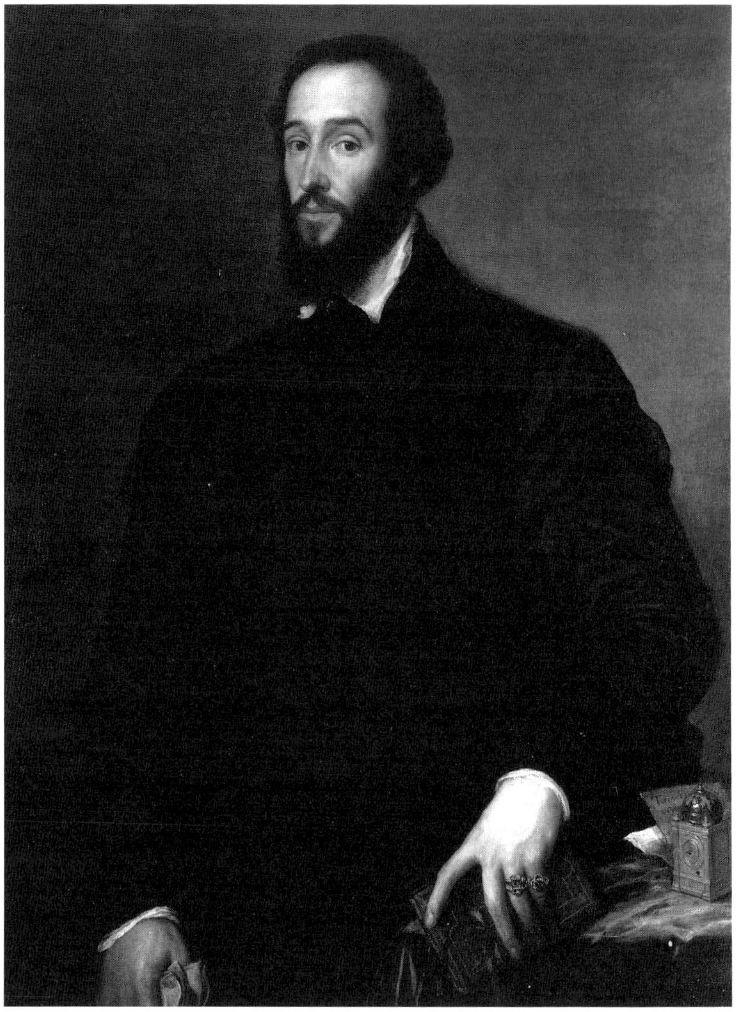

259 (above left) Antonis Mor, *Antoine Perrenot de Granvelle*, oak panel, 107 × 82 cm., Kunsthistorisches Museum, Vienna, Gemäldegalerie (1035).

The portrait has been slightly cut on all four sides; it is signed and dated in the upper-right corner: 'Antonius mor faciebat 1549'. The sitter (1517–86), identified from other portraits, became a cardinal in 1562 and was an important and discerning patron of the arts. In 1549, Mor was in his service and was accommodated in his Brussels residence.

See Demus, 1972, pp. 64–5; here pp. 86, 99–100, 124, 183, 236–9, plate 247.

relaxed and the sitter is imprisoned into a tighter geometrical pattern. His near eye is exactly at the centre of the panel's width; the table occupies half the breadth of the picture and so ends directly below the eye. As Mor has not bothered much about the perspective of the table or of the objects upon it, it is impossible to work out exactly where the painter's eye-level should be. It seems to be in the region of the shoulders, and we are certainly looking down on the table and the hands. We therefore imagine that we look up at the sitter's head and indeed quite a large amount of nostril is visible; yet wide areas of the linings of the lower eyelids are exposed, which implies that we are looking down on the eyes. The shifting viewpoint and the exactness and clarity with which the beard and black satin robes are rendered imply a close, indeed a dangerously close, proximity.

As is usual with Mor, the lighting is from the left and slightly from above. The shadows in the flesh are curiously sharp and narrow, so that the nose is clearly silhouetted, the junction between the nose and the far cheek is lost in shadow and the shadow between the nose and the near cheek is well defined and linear. It implies an incipient sneer, as does the slightly flared nostril (plate 247). To counter-balance the sneer, the far corner of the mouth is foreshortened out of the horizontal. The distance between eyelids and eyebrows and the lines of the forehead show that the eyebrows are raised. The pupil and iris of the near eye, dominant by virtue of its central position, float clear of the lower lid, the width of which is

260 (left) Titian, *Antoine Perrenot de Granvelle*, canvas, 113 × 87.5 cm., Nelson-Atkins Museum of Art, Kansas City, Missouri (30–15).

On the paper beside the clock in the lower-right corner is the signature 'Titianus/D Cador[e]'. The sitter is identified from other portraits and the painting is believed to have been executed at Augsburg in 1548.

See Wethey, 1971, p. 126; Hope, 1980, p. 113; here pp. 124, 236, 239.

exaggerated and which is further stressed by a highlight so that the impression of the floating pupil is enhanced. This suggests that Granvelle is looking through us or above us. In such ways, Mor gives Granvelle an expression of subtle and aristocratic disdain which he was later to apply to most of his sitters.

In Mor's portrait, Granvelle gives us a distinct impression that he has deigned to look at us but will not trouble to turn his head. The lack of balance in the head painted by Mor, particularly disturbing in the rigidly controlled composition, is due to the discrepancies between the eyes and the corners of the mouth. As we have seen, such asymmetries were used by portraitists to give some mobility to their sitters' features, so that facial expressions change according to the areas of the faces on which attention is focussed.[28] Mor's head consequently has an enigmatic quality of expression less apparent in Titian's portrait.

Mor's first surviving full-length portrait, the *Emperor Maximilian II*, dated 1550, was apparently inspired by Titian's *Philip II of Spain in Armour* (plates 261, 263). Mor has constricted the space around his sitter and has flattened him into a stricter geometric pattern. A stiffness is particularly noticeable in the sitter's hanging left hand and, though the curious, low-waisted costume makes it less than obvious, the figure is slightly elongated. The pendant portrait of Maximilian's wife, Philip II's sister Maria, is dated 1551 (plate 262); there Mor makes a further reference to Titian's *Philip II* in the column base. Columns were of course Habsburg emblems and Maria's dress is decorated with clasps in the form of her father Charles V's device of double columns. The perspective of the column base and of the table, once again occupying half the width of the picture and terminating directly under the sitter's near eye, allows the eye-level of the painter to be determined with precision: it is in the region of the sitter's chest. She looks down on him as she looks down on us: yet we see the thicknesses of her lower eyelids. The iris of her near eye, though not the iris of her far eye, floats clear of the lower lid and the expressions of both hooded eyes completely negate the suggestion of a smile on her lips, or at least at the far corner of her mouth. As the sitter here faces left, and is therefore turned towards rather than away from the light, Mor's tendency to twist the foreshortened side of the mouth away from the horizontal takes on a different effect in the different lighting. Maria's curious jaw formation contributes to the impression. Her crucifix bears no perspectival relation to her body and is not distorted by foreshortening. Her left hand hangs very stiffly, the fingers straight and held apart; her right hand is elegantly contorted around her glove. The figure is again elongated, for she is almost seven heads high, whereas Philip II in Titian's portrait is just over six heads high.

After the battle of Saint Quentin in 1557, Mor painted a full-length portrait of Philip II in the armour that he wore as he watched the fighting (plate 219). Once again, Mor has made reference to Titian's *Philip II in Armour*; once again, he shows himself more ready than Titian to distort natural appearances for artistic effect. While Titian had found it convenient, in order to accommodate the table and helmet on which Philip rests his right hand, to twist his right arm out of drawing and out of perspective, Mor has radically adjusted the anatomy of Philip's body and head to suit his aesthetic requirements. The king's figure has been slightly elongated and arranged into a system of isosceles triangles around the uncompromising horizontal of the baton, which is set in false perspective so that it is parallel to the frame. The ribbon of the Order of the Golden Fleece, the commander's sashes tied round both arms and the narrow stripes above his cuffs are red: they and their reflections in the polished armour, providing the only

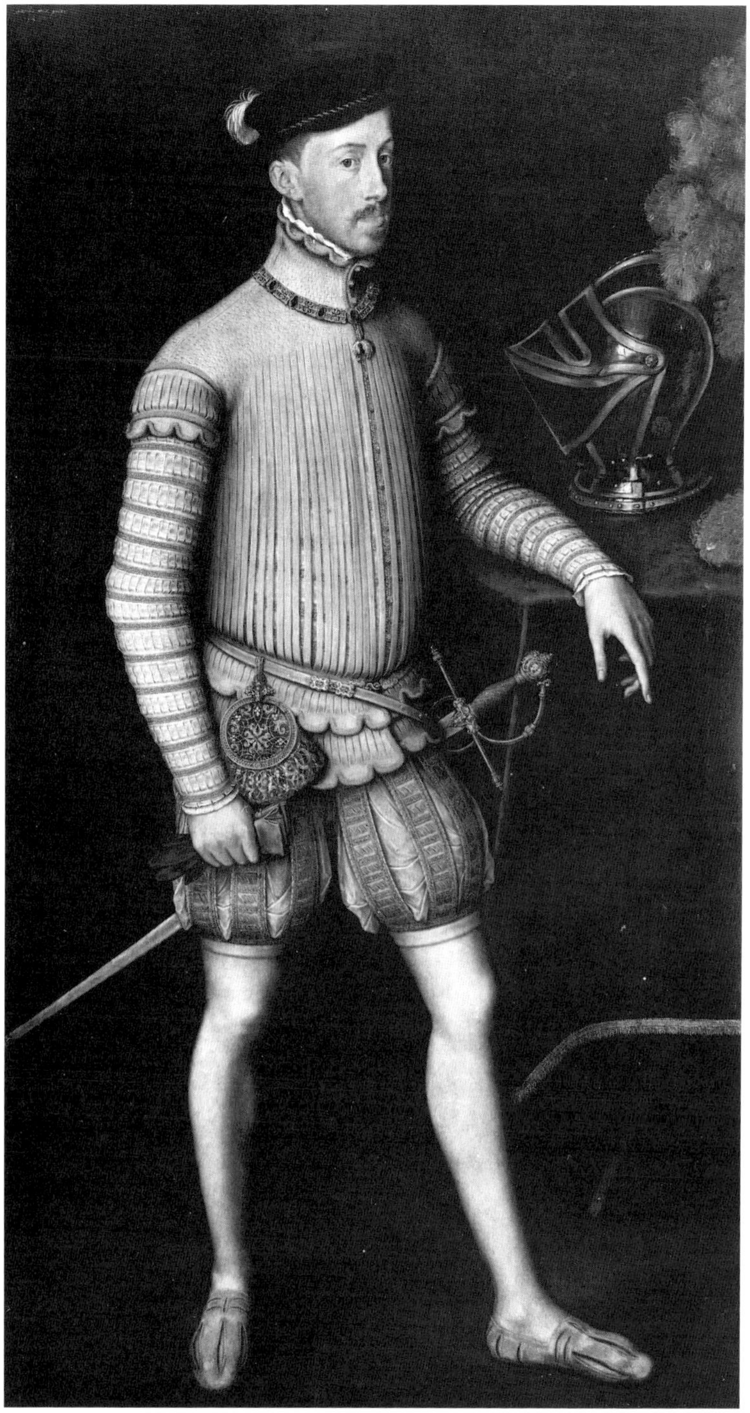

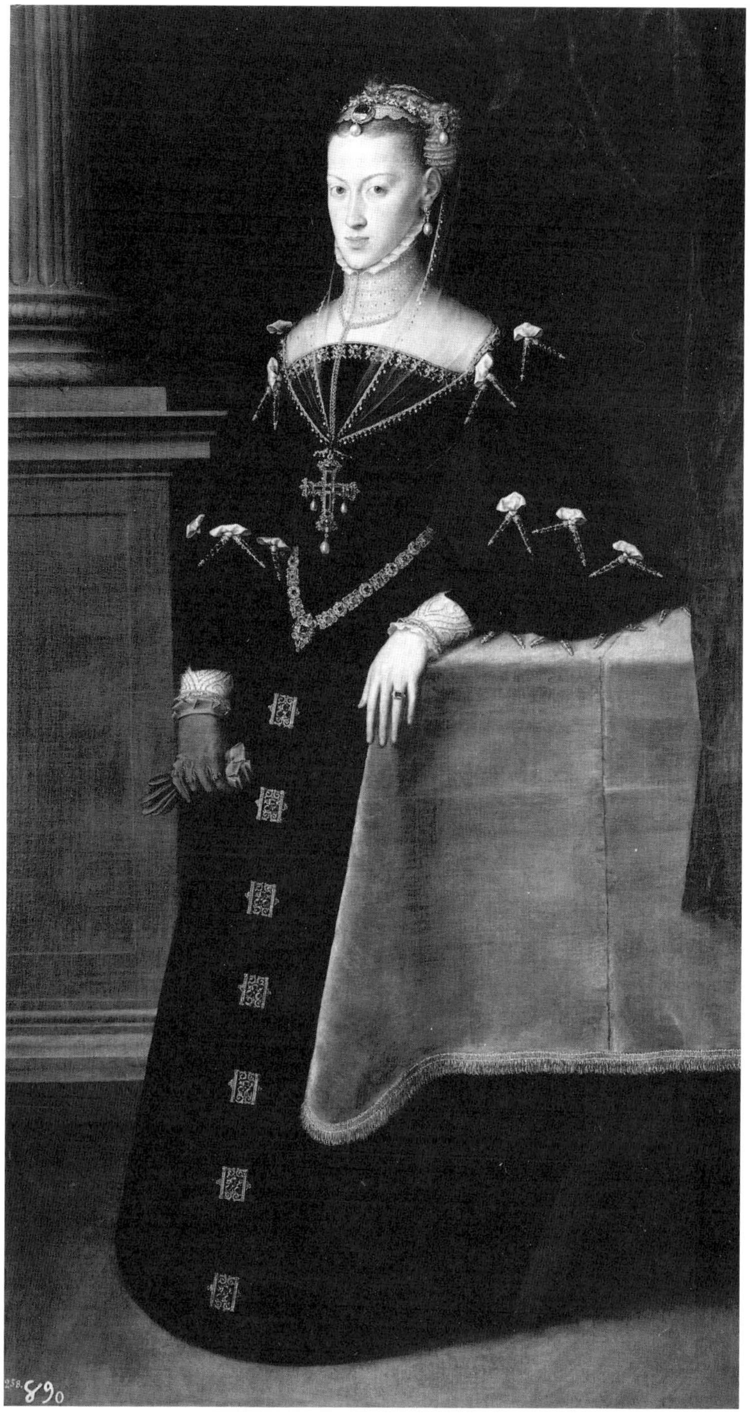

262 (above right) Antonis Mor, *Maria of Austria, Wife of the Emperor Maximilian II*, canvas, 181 × 90 cm., Museo del Prado, Madrid (2110).

The subject (1528–1603) was the elder daughter of the Emperor Charles V and married her cousin Maximilian in 1548. She is identified from other portraits and from descriptions of this picture in early inventories of the Spanish royal collections. Signed and dated: 'Antonius Mor pinx. Año 1551.', it is clearly the pair to the portrait of Maximilian reproduced as plate 261 and with which it was listed in an inventory of 1600 (Sánchez Cantón, 1956–9, XI, p. 230). It is not clear why the two pendant portraits should differ in size and should bear different dates, but both would have been painted in Spain, where the sitters were regents. Maximilian left Spain in November 1550 but Maria remained there for most of 1551.

See pp. 99, 107, 120, 124, 128, 239.

261 (far left) Antonis Mor, *The Emperor Maximilian II*, canvas, 184 × 100 cm., Museo del Prado, Madrid (2111).

The subject (1527–76) is identified from other portraits and from descriptions of this picture in early inventories of the Spanish royal collections. The painting is signed and dated: 'Antonius Mor pinxit 1550' and would have been painted in Spain, where Maximilian was regent between 1548 and 1550.

See pp. 99, 124, 239.

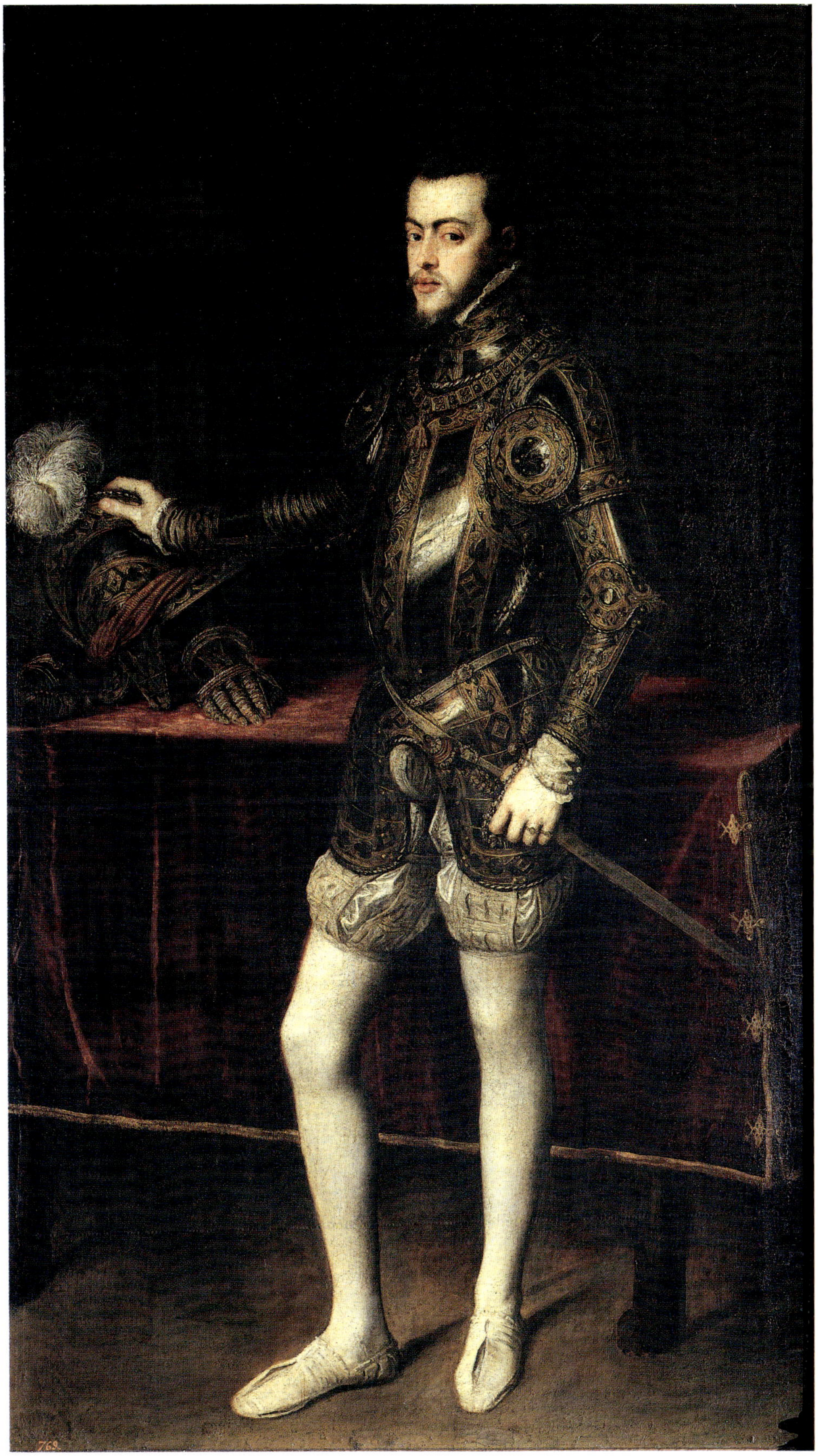

263 Titian, *Philip II of Spain in Armour*, canvas, 193 × 111 cm., Museo del Prado, Madrid (411).

Philip (1527–98) encountered Titian at Milan in 1548–9 and at Augsburg in 1550–1. On both occasions Titian painted portraits of Philip but it is extremely difficult to make sense of the scattered documentary references to the pictures and to relate them to surviving portraits of Philip by and after Titian. In the winter of 1548–9 Philip summoned Titian to Milan, where he painted Philip's portrait. In the summer of 1549, this picture was sent to Philip in the Low Countries; Titian was then working on two versions, one for Cardinal Granvelle and the other for Mary of Hungary. Granvelle's version seems to have reached him in the spring of 1550 but Titian may have delayed completing Mary's version. In 1551, Philip wrote to Mary from Augsburg that he was sending her a portrait by Titian of himself in armour. Mary's portrait of Philip in armour, described in the 1556 inventory of the pictures that she took to Spain from the Netherlands, was similar to the painting now in the Prado and reproduced here. Many believe that it is in fact Mary's picture, that Titian painted it at Augsburg in 1551 and that the portrait of Philip begun at Milan in 1548–9, and the two recorded versions, have been lost. It is, however, possible that the picture sent from Augsburg in 1551 was not painted there but that it was the long-promised version of the Milan portrait. There are two principal reasons for believing that the Prado picture is the Milan portrait or one of its versions: Philip here looks markedly younger than in versions of a portrait certainly painted at Augsburg in 1551; and Mor had evidently seen a version of the Prado composition before he left the Netherlands in 1550 for Portugal and Spain (see plates 261, 262). It seems impossible to tell whether the Prado picture is the portrait begun at Milan in 1548–9 or the version executed for Mary of Hungary.

See Wethey, 1971, pp. 126–8; Hope, 1980, p. 117; here pp. 99, 120, 124, 142, 239.

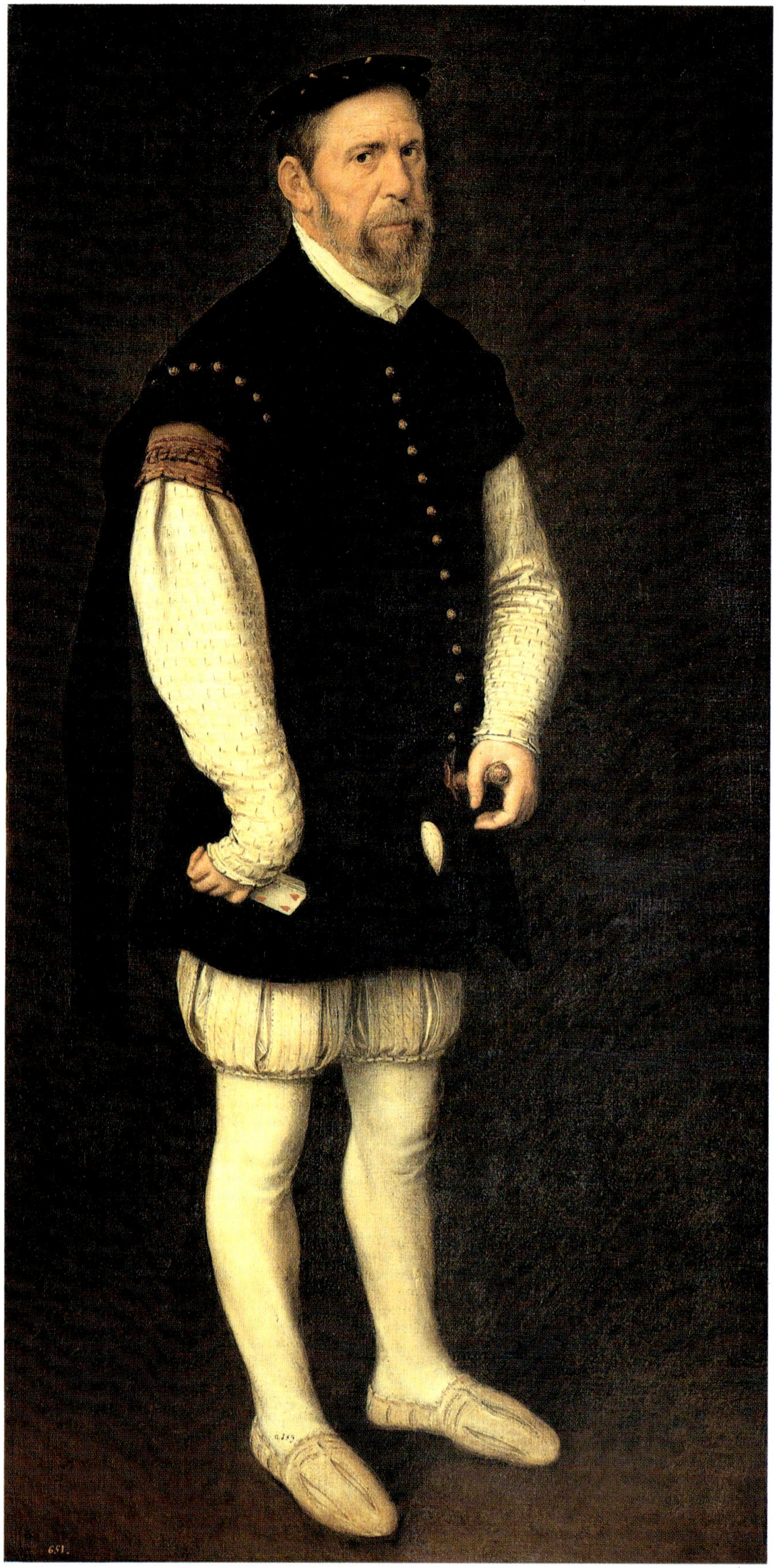

264 Antonis Mor, *The Jester Pejerón*, canvas, 181 × 92 cm., Museo del Prado, Madrid (2107).

In the inventory of the Spanish royal collections taken in 1600, the portrait is described as 'Pejerón, the Count of Benavente's fool, with white stockings and doublet and a pack of cards in his right hand'. It was then hanging next to a full length of a female jester who had served Mary of Hungary and who was dressed in the 'German' fashion (Sánchez Cantón, 1956–9, XI, p. 248). The Count of Benavente was probably Antonio Alfonso Pimentel (1514–75); Pejerón may have passed from his employ into that of Philip II, for a 'Pereson, royal jester' was at Brussels in December 1557. The Prado portrait, attributed to Mor on stylistic grounds, would have been painted in Brussels in the late 1550s or in Spain in about 1560.

See the exhibition catalogue Madrid, 1986, pp. 58–9 (14); here pp. 120, 243, 246.

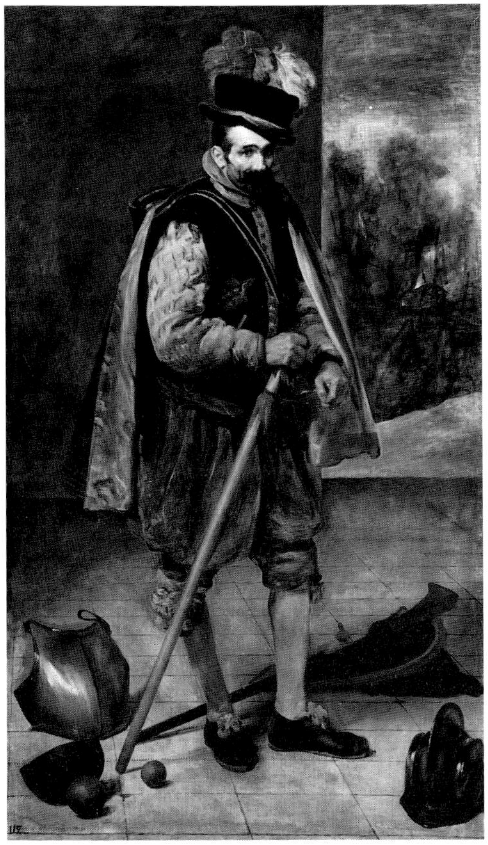

265 Velázquez, *The Jester 'Don John of Austria'*, canvas, 210 × 123 cm., Museo del Prado, Madrid (1200).

The subject, whose real name has not been discovered, was called after Philip II's illegitimate brother, the victor of Lepanto, to which the burning ships in the background allude. He was employed at the Spanish court between 1624 and 1654 and the clothes he wears are believed to be those described in an account dated 1632.

See the exhibition catalogue Madrid, 1986, pp. 84–5 (21); here p. 246.

strong accents of colour, are used with a skill worthy of Mor's contemporary Bruegel to punctuate the composition and stress the triangles around which it is designed. As often occurs in Mor's work, the ear is not foreshortened, so that its forms are fully revealed, and it is deliberately misplaced, so that its outer contour continues the line of the bearded chin to assert a diagonal.

Philip's head is lit and distorted according to the same method, and with the same shifting viewpoints, which are applied in Mor's *Granvelle*. The hooded, baleful near eye is at the centre of the width of the canvas; the pupil floats clear of the lower lid, the thickness of which is exaggerated and which is stressed by a highlight to increase the gap of high tone beneath the iris. The sharp diagonal lighting accents the line rising in an elegant curve from the near cheek to the lobe of the nose, the downward turn of the moustache and the shadowing of the twisted mouth, and all this suggests a slight sneer, contradicted by the differing expressions of the two eyes.

Mor's portrait of Philip's nephew Alessandro Farnese was painted in 1557, when the sitter was twelve (plate 140). A first impression of aristocratic self-confidence results from the pose, the careless way in which the expensive jacket is slung from the shoulders and Mor's usual adjustments to the features. It is belied by the angled neck, the sunken chest and the spindly, splayed legs of an adolescent not yet assured of his importance. The inward turning of his right foot and the placing of the line marking the junction between walls and floor, which is drawn through the thickest parts of both the subject's calves to make his legs look still thinner, increase the effect of gangling awkwardness. Mor has here produced a sympathetic parody of his portraits of adult princes. The painting may be compared with Titian's portrait of Alessandro's uncle Ranuccio Farnese, painted in 1542 when Ranuccio was also twelve (plate 194). Titian's is a much more direct representation of a twelve-year-old youth, conceived in a way totally different from Mor's. The contrasts between Mor's work and Titian's indicate not only that Mor approached his sitters less directly and with considerably more forethought and artifice than Titian, but also that Mor's compositional borrowings from Titian, evidently an artist of rather alien tastes and interests, may have been forced upon him by sitters who would have seen Titian's portraits of the 1540s as marking the height of international fashion in portraiture.

Mor parodied or burlesqued his own portrait types not only in his portrait of the youthful Alessandro Farnese but also in his painting of the jester Pejerón who, in his expression and pose, fails to achieve the easy and disdainful aloofness with which Mor endowed his aristocratic sitters (plate 264). Pejerón's eyebrows are not raised, his upper eyelids are not exposed to hood his eyes, his irises do not clear his lower eyelids and the lines of his forehead and cheeks imply anxiety rather than superiority. His near eye is not at the centre of the width of the canvas, so that he does not dominate the picture space, and the pattern made by his figure is neither a complex geometric construction nor in very strict accord with the lines of the frame. His right arm and apparently deformed hand are positioned with distressing awkwardness; his stockings are twisted and wrinkled; and his right foot is uncomfortably turned on its outside edge. As Mor has here decided against making many of the small adjustments and distortions by which he gave to a noble sitter an air of authority, in this less abstracted and more direct portrait he comes closer in spirit, though hardly in style, to Titian.

Because Mor, from choice or from compulsion to follow fashion, borrowed certain Titian poses, and because his work, from the exactness of the surface detail,

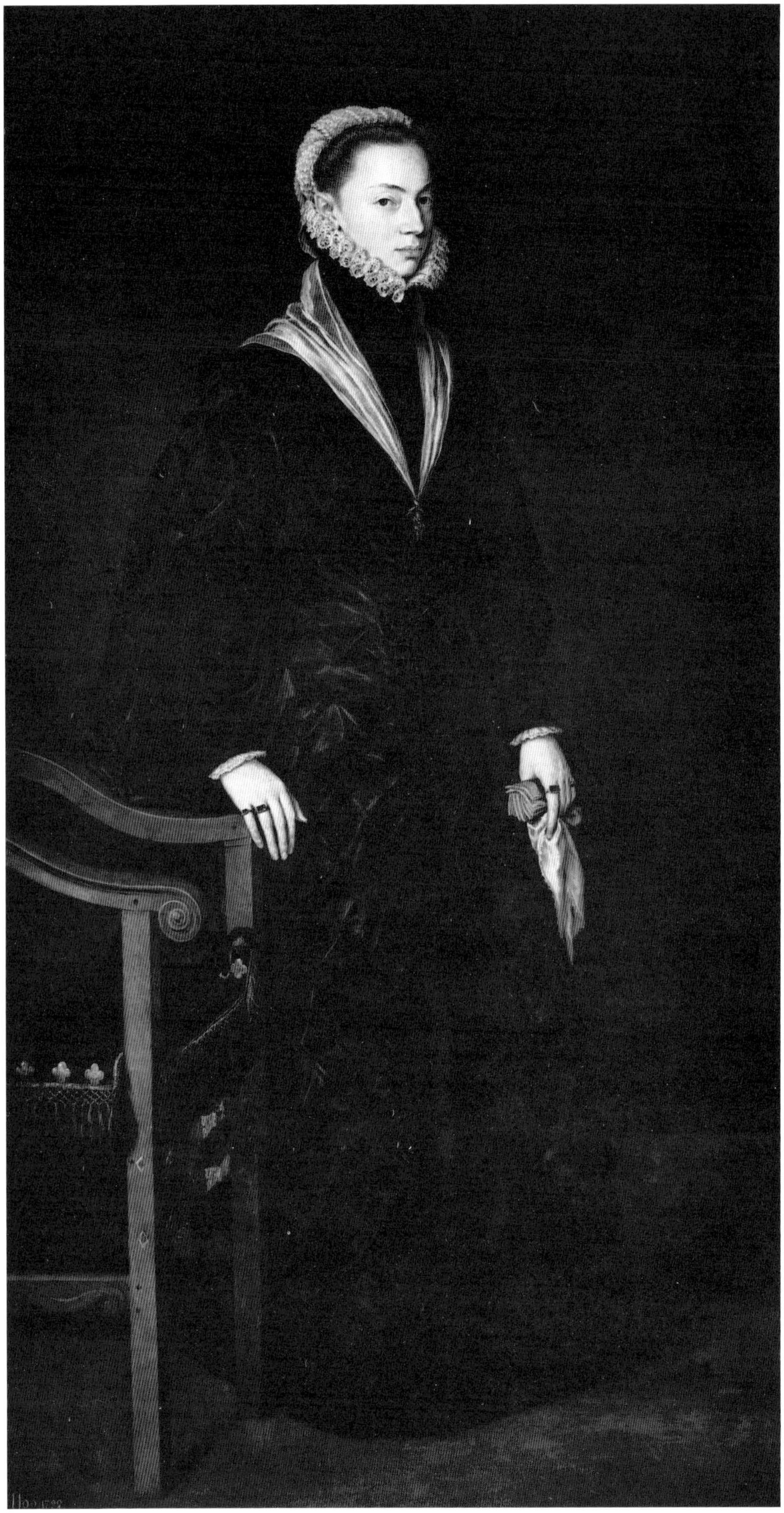

266 Antonis Mor, *Joanna of Austria*, canvas, 195 × 104 cm., Museo del Prado, Madrid (2112).

The subject (1537–73) was the younger daughter of the Emperor Charles V and the sister of Philip II of Spain. On the death of her husband, John, Prince of Portugal, in January 1554, she returned to Spain, where she ruled as regent until 1559. The portrait reproduced, painted by Mor in Spain in about 1560, remained in her possession and was listed in the inventories taken after her death as 'Another full-length portrait, painted on canvas, of the Most Serene Princess, our lady, who places her right hand on a chair, done by Antonis Mor . . . ' (Pérez Pastor, 1914, p. 365). It afterwards passed to her brother Philip II and was listed in the inventory of the Spanish royal collections taken in 1600 (Sánchez Cantón, 1956–9, XI, p. 229).

See pp. 107, 124, 209, 246.

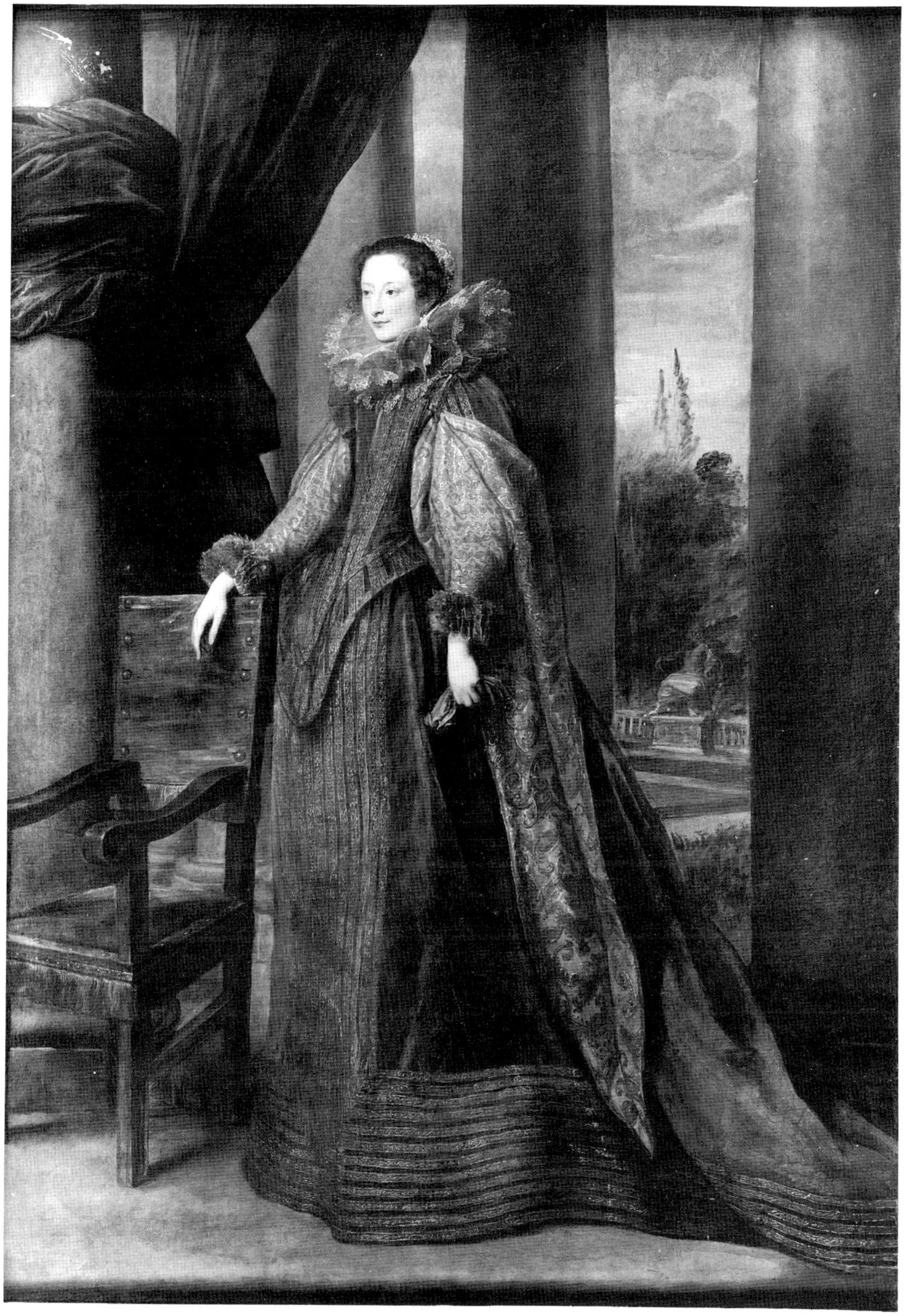

267 Van Dyck, *A Genoese Noblewoman*, canvas, 239 × 170 cm., Louvre, Paris (R.F. 1949–36).

The subject's costume identifies her as a noblewoman of Genoa; the portrait was painted during one of Van Dyck's stays in Genoa between 1621 and 1627.

See pp. 120, 246.

appears 'realistic', he has been dismissed by art historians as a superficial and provincial imitator of Titian and as one who, in the northern tradition, was content to be nothing other than a slavish copyist of nature. The fact that Titian himself took many of his portrait compositions from northern pictures is ignored or dismissed as irrelevant. Such are the ironies of an art history where sixteenth-century Florentine values are maintained. It has been demonstrated that Mor was, in most respects, a less faithful imitator of reality than Titian. He was also a colourist of outstanding subtlety and his technical skill is admirably apparent in his head of Hubert Goltzius, painted in an hour (plate 181). His importance in the history of Spanish portraiture has been admitted, though he is often seen merely as one link in the chain of development that connects Titian with Velázquez. A cursory glance at Mor's portrait of Pejerón and at Velázquez's portrait of the jester nicknamed 'Don John of Austria' will, however, indicate something of the extent of Velázquez's debt to Mor (plates 264–5). A comparison between Mor's portrait of Philip II's sister Joanna and Van Dyck's portrait of a Genoese noblewoman will demonstrate how profound was his influence, direct or indirect, upon Van Dyck (plates 266–7).

Though Mor occupies a pivotal position in the history of portraiture, he has been unjustly overshadowed by Titian. When the notion of 'northern realism' is dismissed and forgotten, and when it is recognised how northern artists reconciled forceful distortion with an apparent fidelity to nature and also with a superb command of colour and design, it will be easier to perceive the importance of Mor and his northern predecessors in the history of European portraiture.

Notes

Chapter 1 Introduction

1. Vasari-Milanesi, 1878–85, v, p. 229.
2. Antonio Salimbene to Gianfrancesco Gonzaga, Marquis of Mantua, Venice, 23 December 1493: 'il retracto de S.^{to} Marcho, cum tutta la piaza et pallazo de Venetia' (A. Luzio, 'Disegni topografici e pitture dei Bellini', *Archivio storico dell'arte*, I (1888), pp. 276–8 (p. 277)).
3. Memorial by Teodoro Sangiorgio on paintings to be executed by Tintoretto: 'Non trovandosi in Vinegia il ritratto di Parma, Milano e Pavia, che vanno rapresentate in questi quadri, si manderanno da qui' (Luzio, 1890, p. 398).
4. Titian to Philip II, Venice, 11 October 1552: Ferrarino, 1975, p. 31. The painting in question is thought to be the *St Margaret* now in the Escorial (Hope, 1980, p. 123; reproduced in H. E. Wethey, *The Paintings of Titian*, I: *The Religious Paintings*, London, 1969, pl. 175).
5. Argote de Molina wrote in 1582 that he had seen at the palace of El Pardo 'un lienço al temple del retrato de Fonte-Nebleu, casa de plazer de los Reyes de Francia' (Roblot-Delondre, 1910, p. 55).
6. In 1555, Vermeyen was paid 'pour avoir faict ung pourtraict d'ung Dieu de pitié semblable à autre faict de la main de Tysian' and 'pour avoir faicx en pourtraict premièrement à charbon une bourdure avecq les cincq escuz asmoïez des armes de Sadite Majesté en hault, la royne de France, la royne de Hongrie, le prince d'Espaigne et du légat embas, et au milieu les escriptures de la consécration de la chappelle de la court à Bruxelles, laquelle pourtraicture il a délivré au fourrier Hannart . . .' (Pinchart, 1856, p. 138 n. 1). In 1560, the French painter Eloy Le Mannier was paid for making for the royal stables 'plusieurs pourtraicts en pappier aux devises du dict s^{r} pour faire marques pour marquer les grands chevaulx de la grande escuirie du dict s^{r} . . .' (Moreau-Nélaton, 1901, pp. 30–1).
7. The Emperor Ferdinand I, in a letter dated Vienna, 19 July 1548, asked for 'ein klains musster vnd conterfech' to indicate how portraits of the monarchs of Bohemia were to be hung in the restored hall of Prague castle (Birk, 1864, p. 84).
8. Isabella d'Este to the Countess of Acerra, 3 April 1493: 'sapendo cum quanta difficultà se ritrovano pictori che perfectamente contrafaciano el vulto naturale . . .' (Luzio, 1913, p. 188). Compare the letter from the same to the same, 20 April 1493: 'havemo mandato per uno forestere, qual ha fama de contrafare bene el naturale' (*ibid.*, p. 189).
9. Memoirs of Sophia, Electress of Hanover; 'Les beaux pourtraits de Van Dyck m'avoient donné une si belle idée de toutes les dames d'Angleterre que j'estois surprise de voir que la reine, que je m'avois veue si belle en peinture, estoit une petite femme montée sur du siége, les bras longs et secs, les épaules dissemblables et des dens comme des défences qui luy sortoient de la bouche' (A. Köcher, ed., *Memoiren der Herzogin Sophie nachmals Kurfürstin von Hannover* (*Publicationen aus den K. Preussischen Staatsarchiven*, IV, 1), Leipzig, 1879, p. 38).
10. Niccolò Martelli to 'Rugasso, servitor del S. Oratio da Farnese', Florence, 28 July 1544: 'Michel'agnolo . . . non tolse dal Duca Lorenzo, ne dal Sig. Giuliano il modello apunto come la natura gli hauea effigiati e composti, ma diede loro una grandezza una proportione un decoro una gratia uno splendore qual gli parea che piu lodi loro arrecassero, dicendo che di qui à mille anni nessuno non ne potea dar cognitione che fossero altrimenti . . .' (*Il primo libro delle lettere di Niccolò Martelli*, Florence, 1546, f. 49).
11. Gertrude Stein, *The Autobiography of Alice B. Toklas* (1933), Penguin edn, Harmondsworth, 1966, p. 16.
12. The drawing is inscribed 'Der man was alt 93 jor und noch gesunt und vermuglich zw antorff' and is probably to be linked with a note made early in 1521 in Dürer's Netherlandish journal: 'Jtem hab 3 stüber den mann geben, den ich conterfet hab' ('I gave 3 stuivers to the man whose portrait I drew': Rupprich, 1956–69, I, p. 164; Conway, 1889, p. 112). Dürer gave the painting away in March 1521.
13. Vasari-Milanesi, 1878–85, II, p. 620; III, p. 292. In his identification of Pollaiuolo's model, Vasari was repeating a theory advanced by earlier writers (Davies, 1961, pp. 444–5).
14. Savonarola's sermon on Amos 5: 21, delivered in Lent 1496: 'voi fate dipingere le figure nelle chiese alla similitudine di quella donna o di quell'altra, il che è molto male fatto e in grande dispregio delle cose di Dio' (Girolamo Savonarola, *Prediche sopra Amos e Zaccaria*, II, ed. P. Ghiglieri, Rome, 1971, p. 25; translated in Gilbert, 1980, p. 157); Paleotti in 1582: 'Ma in nessun modo mai siano ritratti con faccie de particolari e di persone mondane e dagli altri conosciute' (Barocchi, 1971–7, III, p. 2735).
15. Deliberations of the hospital authorities, 15 May 1606: 'un quadro de la uirtud de la charidad . . . en el qual Puso el dho Pintor dos figuras y Rostros de personas señaladas y conocidas de la dha ciudad de Toledo con unas lechuguillas grandes abiertas con mucha yndecencia Para el lugar en que esta . . .' (Cossío, 1908, p. 690). For the altarpiece, see the exhibition catalogue Madrid, Washington, Toledo and Dallas, 1982–3, pp. 168–9.
16. Vasari-Milanesi, 1878–85, III, p. 654; v, p. 294.
17. 'Dì 16 novembre 1538, in Ancona. Die dar monsignor Joan Maria Pizone prothonotario/per un retratto suo fatto con ogni mio sapere e diligentia . . .'; 'Adì . . . dicembre del 42, die dar el sopradito misser Bortolamio Carpan per una testa colorita/a olio de un retratto del prothonotario misser Joan Maria Pizoni quale m'é remasta per deferentia tra noi . . . et dita testa/la aconciai e redussi in foza de san Bartolomio Apostolo . . .' (Zampetti, 1969, pp. 88–9, 20).
18. '1551 in Ancona/adì . . . agosto, die dar misser Alexandro dito el Robaza per un quadro de retratto suo/in forma de santo Alexandro armato' (*ibid.*, p. 14). See further p. 137.
19. Vasari-Milanesi, 1878–85, IV, pp. 337, 347–8.
20. Exhibition catalogue Paris, 1973–4, pp. 203–7 (86).
21. Vandenbroeck, 1985, pp. 153–8 and references.
22. A. M. Cetto, 'Der Berner Traian- und Herkinbald-Teppich', *Jahrbuch des Bernischen Historischen Museums*, XLIII/XLIV (1963–4), pp. 5–230, pp. 102–4.
23. Pope-Hennessy, 1966, pp. 4–28.
24. W. H. J. Weale and M. W. Brockwell, *The Van Eycks and their Art*, London, New York and Toronto, 1912, pp. 230–1; Dhanens, 1980, pp. 16–17.
25. C. Hope, 'Historical Portraits in the "Lives" and in the Frescoes of Giorgio Vasari', in G. C. Garfagnini, ed., *Giorgio Vasari, Tra decorazione ambientale e storiografia artistica, Convegno di studi (Arezzo, 8–10 ottobre 1981)*, publication of the Istituto Nazionale di studi sul rinascimento (Arezzo), Florence, 1985, pp. 321–38.
26. Hoff and Davies, 1971, pp. 1–28.
27. For example in the *Venus of Urbino* (Uffizi) and the *Girl with a Fur* (Vienna, 89): Wethey, 1971, pp. 23, 82, 106, pl. 73; Hope, 1980, p. 82, pl. XVI. Beneath the surface of the *Girl with a Fur* is a painted version of *La*

Bella (J. Wilde, *Venetian Art from Bellini to Titian*, Oxford, 1974, p. 248).

28. Francesco Maria della Rovere, Duke of Urbino, to Gian Giacomo Leonardi, Padua, 2 May 1536: 'Direte al Titiano . . . che quel retratto di quella Donna che ha la ueste azurra, desideriamo che la finisca . . .' (Gronau, 1936, p. 92). Holbein's *Laïs of Corinth*, dated 1526, and his *Venus and Cupid* (Basle, 322, 323) were described in 1586 as 'Zwei täfelin doruf eine Offenburgin conterfehet ist vf eim geschriben Lais Corinthiaca, die ander hat ein kindlin bÿ sich. H. Holb. beide, mit ölfarben vnd in ghüsern'. The model was recognised as one of the Offenburgs, a patrician family of Basle, but the paintings do not seem to have been conceived as portraits (Rowlands, 1985, p. 131, pls 51, 48).
29. Lightbown, 1978, II, pp. 116–19.
30. See further Hirst, 1981, pp. 93–7.
31. 'Alfonso di Tommaso Cambi, giovinetto allora bellissimo, letterato, virtuoso, e molto cortese e gentile, si fece ritrarre ignudo e tutto intero in persona d'uno Endimione, cacciatore amato dalla Luna . . .' (Vasari-Milanesi, 1878–85, VII, p. 690).
32. Dürer's pen-and-brush drawing of himself naked is in the Schlossmuseum at Weimar (White, 1971, pp. 90–1); Pontormo's drawing of himself naked is in the British Museum (1936–10–10–10 recto: J. Cox Rearick, *The Drawings of Pontormo*, 2 vols, Cambridge (Mass.), 1964, p. 247 (253), pl. 241).
33. Uffizi (911), attributed to Cavazzola: Berti, 1979, p. 213.
34. Shearman, 1983, pp. 253–6 (271).
35. Inventory of the property of Riccardo Romolo Riccardi, taken in Florence after his death on 26 January 1612: 'Un ritratto della stessa grandezza si crede di mano di d.° Jac.° dell'Ecc.^mo Duca Cosimo quand'era giovanetto, con calze rosse, e berretta rossa, et una picca in mano con arme a' canto, e giubbone bianco, e collana al' collo con ornam.^to dorato bellissimo' (H. Keutner, 'Zu einigen Bildnissen des frühen Florentiner Manierismus', *Mitteilungen des Kunsthistorischen Institutes in Florenz*, VIII (1957–9), pp. 139–54, p. 152).
36. For example, by Langedijk, 1981–3, I, pp. 431–3, and by Simon, 1982, pp. 170–87, 338–41.
37. Compare, for example, the attendant on the left of his *Visitation* at Carmignano (L. Berti, *L'opera completa del Pontormo*, Milan, 1973, pl. LVI).
38. 'con facilità grandissima faceva i suoi ritratti similissimi al naturale, ancorchè in altro non avesse molto disegno: ed io ho veduto alcune teste di sua mano ritratte dal vivo, che ancor che abbiano verbigrazia il naso torto, un labro piccolo ed un grande, ed altre sì fatte disformità, somigliano nondimeno il naturale . . .' (Vasari-Milanesi, 1878–85, IV, pp. 462–3).
39. See p. 160.
40. 'si son grandes, hagámoslos un poco más grandes, y si fuesen pequeños queden algún tanto más pequeños' (Sánchez Cantón, 1921, p. 265).
41. Leonardo: 'spesso le figure somigliano il maestro . . .' (Richter, 1970, I, p. 343); Dürer: 'Doraws kumt, das vill moler machen, daz jnen geleich ist' (Rupprich, 1956–69, II, p. 121; Conway, 1889, p. 180).
42. Jean Bellegambe, for example, made very little distinction between the heads of donors and the heads of the saints in his religious paintings: see R. Genaille, 'L'oeuvre de Jean Bellegambe', *Gazette des beaux-arts*, 6e pér., LXXXVII (1976), pp. 7–28.
43. See the comparison between the two portraits by J. Desneux, 'Nicolas Rolin, authentique donateur de la "Vierge d'Autun"', *Revue des arts*, IV (1954), pp. 195–200.
44. 'Ritrasse Michelagnolo messer Tommaso in un cartone, grande di naturale, che nè prima nè poi di nessuno fece il ritratto, perchè aboriva il fare somigliare il vivo, se non era d'infinita bellezza' (Vasari-Milanesi, 1878–85, VII, pp. 271–2). The drawing is lost.
45. 'i ritratti, i quali son fatti per mano degli eccellenti, si trovano essere con miglior maniera e con più perfezzion dipinti che non son gli altri, ma le più volte men somiglianti' (G. B. Armenini, *De' veri precetti della pittura*, Ravenna, 1587; the relevant passage is reprinted in Barocchi, 1971–7, III, p. 2750).
46. Bronzino to Pier Francesco Riccio, Pisa, 27 January 1551: 'tanta Donna piena di bontade . . .', '[il] più perfettissimo S.^re che mai fusse . . .', 'mi pare, quando io gli veggo, vedere tanti angeli et udendoli sentire tanti Spiriti del cielo' (Heikamp, 1953–6, pp. 137–8).
47. A still clearer example of a sitter winged with draperies is Pantoja's portrait of the Archduke Albert, dated 1600, at Munich (898: Kusche, 1964, pl. 9).
48. 'Ea autem est certa quedam obseruatio, Qua ex iis que corpori insunt signis, animorum etiam qualitates denotamus' (Pomponius Gauricus, *De sculptura (1504)*, ed. and trans. A. Chastel, R. Klein et al. (*Centre de recherches d'histoire et de philologie de la IVe section de l'Ecole pratique des hautes études*, V, Hautes études médiévales et modernes, 5), Geneva, 1969, p. 128).
49. Francisco de Holanda, for example, gives it some attention in his dialogues on portraiture (Sánchez Cantón, 1921).
50. The quotations are from Robert Copland, *The Secrete of Secretes of Arystotle* (1528), reprinted in *Secretum Secretorum, Nine English Versions*, ed. M. A. Manzaloui (Early English Text Society publication, no. 276), Oxford, 1977, pp. 378–9.
51. *The Statutes of the Realm*, IV, London, 1819, p. 899.
52. Shakespeare, *Macbeth*, I. iv.
53. 'se quella [poetry] descrive l'operationi della mente, che considera quella [painting], se la mente opera nei movimenti' (Richter, 1970, I, p. 58).
54. On Burgundian court etiquette, see Aliénor de Poitiers, *Les honneurs de la cour*, written between 1484 and 1491, printed in La Curne de Sainte Palaye, 1759, pp. 184–267. On rhetoric, see Quintilian, 1921–2 edn, particularly IV, pp. 242–349; Jodocus Willich, *Liber de pronunciatione rhetorica*, Basle, 1540 (extracts reprinted in Herrmann, 1914).
55. Huic ego delicias facio, arrideoque iocorque,
    Alloquor, et tanquam reddere verba queat
    Assensu nutuque, mihi saepe illa videtur
    Dicere velle aliquid, et tua verba loqui
    (reprinted in Golzio, 1971, p. 43).
56. Jsta refert vultus, qua cernis Jmago Georgi
    Sic oculos viuos, sic habet ille Genas
    Anno aetatis suae xxxiiij
    Anno dom̃. 1532.
57. Nulla sine merore voluptas/.G. Gisze.
58. I have not had the opportunity to examine the *Portrait of a Man*. The panel of the *Portrait of a Lady* retains its unpainted edge only at the lower margin; the other three sides have been cut and on the left a vertical strip 1 cm. wide has been sawn off and then joined again to the picture. This might indicate that a double portrait has been cut in two and that, at the first attempt, it was sawn through in the wrong place.
59. Campbell, 1979, p. 10.
60. 'Orations for and against the Queen's Marriage', printed in J. Strype, *The Life of the Learned Sir Thomas Smith*, new edn, Oxford, 1820, p. 242.
61. Henry de Mesmes to the Président Fauchet, Angers, 7 February 1570: 'La Royne en a faict le jugement qui n'a garde de trouver bonne aucune portraiture de luy. Car, à ce que nous avons et voyons à toute hure, nul paintre peult suffire pour le représenter à nostre contentement . . .' (Laborde, 1850–5, II, p. 586).
62. 'MEMOIRE d'vne personne de condition, et des premieres de la Cour de France, donné au sieur de Walsingham, touchant Monsieur le Duc d'Aniou . . .': 'Il a ce malheur, que toutes les peintures luy font tort, & que Ianet luy mesme ne luy a iamais donné cet admirable ie ne sçay quoy qu'il a receu de la Nature. Ses yeux, cet agrément qu'il a autour de la bouche quand il parle, cette douceur auec laquelle il surprend ceux qui ont l'honneur de le voir en particulier ne peuuent estre bien representez ny par la plume, ny par le pinceau' (printed in M. Le Roy de Gomberville, *Les memoires de Monsievr le dvc de Nevers prince de Mantovë, pair de France*, Paris, 1665, p. 543. Certain other

letters and reports printed there have been shown to be forgeries: see G. de Bremond d'Ars, 'Une question de critique historique. Pièces fausses des Mémoires de Nevers', *Revue des questions historiques*, XXXV (1884), pp. 226–35).

63. Sur son pourtraict à I. DE-COVR, peintre du Roy.

TV t'abuses, DECOVR, pensant representer
Du CHASTEAVNEVF d'Amour la Deesse immortelle:
Le Ciel peintre sçauant l'a pourtraitte si belle,
Que son diuin tableau ne se peut imiter

(*Les premieres oevvres de Philippes des Portes*, revised edn, Paris, 1583, f. 280v; Moreau-Nélaton, 1924, I, p. 129).

64. *Epigrams*, Book X, XXXII:

ars utinam mores animusque effingere posset!
pulchrior in terris nulla tabella foret

(W. C. A. Ker, *Martial. Epigrams with an English Translation* (The Loeb Classical Library), 2 vols, London and New York, 1920, II, pp. 176–9). The Ghirlandaio portrait is in the Thyssen-Bornemisza collection (150) and is reproduced, for example, by Pope-Hennessy, 1966, p. 27, pl. 25.

65. 'se col pennello si potesse così rappresentare agli occhi di Vostra Beatitudine le bellezze dell'animo di questa serenissima reina, non potria veder cosa più maravigliosa. Ma in quelle parti, le quali con l'arte si sono potute figurare, non ho mancato di usare tutta quella diligenza che ho saputo maggiore, per rappresentare alla Santità Vostra il vero' (Vasari-Milanesi, 1878–85, VI, p. 500).

66. 'mi è stata mostra la vostra effigie da voi medesima dipinta, et di tal sorte, che in un medesimo tempo ho scorto in voi la gratia del vostro volto, la vivezza del vostro spirito, et l'eccellenza di quell'arte, de la quale io fo professione' (undated letter to an unnamed lady, printed in G. Vasari, *Vite de' più eccellenti pittori, scultori e architetti*, ed. G. della Valle, X, Siena, 1793, p. 354 note. The lady was perhaps Levina Teerlinc: see J. Schlosser, 'Two Portrait Miniatures from Castle Ambras', *Burlington Magazine*, XLI (1922), pp. 194–8).

67. Sonnet included in a letter dated Venice, 7 November 1537, to Veronica Gambara:

L'unione dei colori, che lo stile
Di Tiziano ha distesi, esprime fora
La concordia, che regge in Lionora
Le ministre del spirito gentile.
Seco siede modestia in atto umile,
Onestà nel suo abito dimora,
Vergogna il petto e il crin le vela e onora,
Le affigge Amore il guardo signorile.
Pudicizia e beltà, nimiche eterne,
Le spazian nel sembiante, e fra le ciglia
Il trono de le Grazie si discerne

(Camesasca, 1957–60, I, p. 78). Similarly extravagant protestations are found in other contexts, for example a letter written in 1566 by Emmanuel Philibert, Duke of Savoy, to his ambassador in Germany: 'essendocj stata gratissima la larga relatione che ci fate di quanto hauete passato in Sassonia col rapprescntarcj sì propriamente ciascuna particolarità, che a punto ci è parso hauer veduto et udito l'animo et la uoce del signor Duca Elettore nostro parente et godute le amoreuolissime accoglienze fatte in persona vostra reputando ueramente il tutto fatto ne la nostra propria' (L. Cibrario, *Lettere inedite di santi, papi, principi illustri, guerrieri e letterati*, Turin, 1861, pp. 203–4).

68. Shakespeare, *Timon of Athens*, I. i.

Chapter 2 Portrait Types

1. A. Vandenpeereboom, *Ypriana*, II, *La chambre des échevins*, Bruges, 1879, p. 87.
2. *Ibid.*, pp. 90, 271–7, etc.; K. G. van Acker, 'Iconografische beschouwingen in verband met de 16e eeuwse gegraveerde portretten der graven van Vlaanderen', *Oud Holland*, LXXXIII (1968), pp. 95–116 (pp. 105–6 (figs 38, 40, 42, 44)).
3. F. vande Putte, 'La chapelle des Comtes de Flandre à Courtrai', *Annales de la Société d'Emulation [de Bruges]*, 3e sér., x (1875), pp. 189–282; J. de Cuyper, 'De gravenkapel van Kortrijk', *Verslagen en mededelingen van De Leiegouw*, IV (1962), pp. 4–54; L. Devliegher, *De Onze-Lieve-Vrouwekerk te Kortrijk* (Kunstpatrimonium van West-Vlaanderen, 6), Lannoo, Tielt and Utrecht, 1973, pp. 72–5, pls 198–215.
4. Vandenpeereboom, *op. cit.*, p. 272.
5. De Cuyper, *op. cit.*, p. 21 n. 42.
6. E. de Busscher, 'Recherches sur les anciens peintres gantois', *Messager des sciences historiques*, 1859, pp. 105–271 (pp. 145–6).
7. R. van Luttervelt, 'Bijdragen tot de iconographie van de graven van Holland', *Oud Holland*, LXXII (1957), pp. 73–91.
8. J. C. Overvoorde, 'De portretten der Hollandsche graven in het stadhuis te Leiden' in *Feest-bundel Dr. Abraham Bredius*, I, Amsterdam, 1915, pp. 221–9.
9. A. de Schryver and C. van de Velde, *Stad Gent, Oudheidkundig Museum, Abdij van de Bijloke, Catalogus van de schilderijen*, Ghent, 1972, pp. 186–8.
10. A. H. J. Couvez, *Histoire de Bruges*, Bruges, 1850, p. vii.
11. Vande Putte, *op. cit.*, p. 219.
12. J. Neuwirth, *Der Bilderzyklus des Luxemburger Stammbaumes aus Karlstein*, Prague, 1897; V. Dvořáková et al., *Gothic Mural Painting in Bohemia and Moravia 1300–1378*, London, 1964, pp. 53–6, 83–6, 134, pls 62–70.
13. For example, the series in the Banca Popolare Agricola, Crema; the Cassa di Risparmio, Palazzo Fondi, Cremona; the Museo Poldi-Pezzoli, Milan; and the Museo Civico, Turin (see W. Terni di Gregory, *Pittura artigiana lombarda del rinascimento*, Milan, 1958, *passim*).
14. Sala capitolare, former convent of St Nicholas, now the Seminary, Treviso (exhibition catalogue *Tomaso da Modena*, S. Caterina, Capitolo dei Domenicani, Treviso, 1979, pp. 115–29).
15. J. Shearman, 'The Chapel of Sixtus IV' in M. Giacometti, ed., *The Sistine Chapel*, London, 1986, pp. 22–91, pp. 78–85.
16. Vasari-Milanesi, 1878–85, VI, p. 383.
17. H. Michelant, 'Un grand monastère au XVIe siècle', *Annales archéologiques*, III (1845), pp. 223–39 (p. 233).
18. See the extract of 13 September 1460 from the records of the Faculty of Theology printed in A. Lhotsky, *Die Geschichte der Sammlungen (Festschrift des Kunsthistorischen Museums zur Feier des Fünfzigjährigen Bestandes*, II), 2 vols, Vienna, 1941–5, I, p. 35 n. 88.
19. P. d'Ancona, 'Gli affreschi del castello di Manta nel Saluzzese', *L'Arte*, VIII (1905), pp. 94–106, 183–98; H. Schroeder, *Der Topos der 'Nine Worthies' in Literatur und bildender Kunst*, Göttingen, 1971, p. 94, pls 3,4, etc.
20. Vasari-Milanesi, 1878–85, I, pp. 390–1.
21. Rovelli, 1928, pp. 135–42; M. Gianoncelli, *L'antico museo di Paolo Giovio in Borgovicò*, Como, 1977; exhibition catalogue *Paolo Giovio: collezioni Giovio, le immagini e la storia*, Musei civici, Como, 1983.
22. 'Facies eciam et effigies corporales Clementis pape defuncti, cardinalium sibi assistencium, dum vivebat, regum eciam Francorum et principum, nec non et imperatorum Romanorum et Grecie representabant, nec eruditissimorum pictorum judicio tam sumptuosum nec tam acceptissimum opus in regno poterat repperiri' (Bellaguet, 1839–52, IV, pp. 522–3).
23. Accounts of the town of Leyden, 1464: 'Idem dezelven Willem Engel gegeven voir zijn loen van een tavereel te maken, dairinne dat hertoich Aelbrecht mit zynen kinderen ende mit grave Willem, zijn broeder, staen sullen...' (Overvoorde, *op. cit.* (n. 8 above), p. 228).
24. See the payment authorised on 2 January 1399 to Colart d'Auxy 'pour avoir osté d'un des grans tappis où sont les XII pers de France l'ymaige de feu Mgr. le comte de Flandres...et y mettre en lieu d'icellui un autre semblable plus richement ouvré' (David, 1947, p. 165). An engraving of a tapestry of *Charles VI and the Twelve Peers of France*, then in the chapel of the palace of Brussels, was published by B. de Montfaucon, *Les monumens de la monarchie françoise*, III, Paris, 1731, pl. XIX.

25. 'Neuf grans tapiz et deux mendres de haulte-lice, ouvrez à or, de volerie de plouviers et perdriz, èsquelz sont les personnages de feux monseigneur le duc Jehan et madame la duchesse, sa femme, tant à pié comme à cheval' (Pinchart, 1878–85, p. 24).
26. A copy dated 1463 was formerly in the Figdor collection in Vienna (G. Glück, 'Rubens' Liebesgarten', *Jahrbuch der Kunsthistorischen Sammlungen in Wien*, XXXV (1920–1), pp. 49–98 (p. 52)); another, dated 1454, is at Amsterdam (A 4212: *All the Paintings of the Rijksmuseum in Amsterdam*, Amsterdam, 1976, p. 639).
27. Described in the *De triumphis religionis* written in 1497 by Giovanni Sabadino degli Arienti: 'Se li vede effigiata la illustre memoria del prelibato principe Alberto Estense con molti gentilhomini e dame a cavallo, ad venatione con pardi e veltri a lepore, a caprioli, a cervi et ad ursi . . . Finita la venatione se vedeno poi, posti in uno fiorito prato, le mense parate . . . existendo da uno canto in sedia il principe Alberto vestito di brocato d'oro, havendo in capo una purpurea bireta lunga sino al dorso, ala fogia de quel tempo. Mangiato che hano si vedeno ad uno limpido fonte reducti et alcuni pelegrini gioveni e dame danzare al suono de cythare e tibie et al suono de una arpa sonata da una dama, et altre donne e donzelle che tesseno girlande de fiori et de herbette per ornarse le bianche trezze' (Gundersheimer, 1972, p. 68 and compare pp. 22–3).
28. 'Ordine secundo el quale el nostro Illmo Signore vole se depinza et repinza li infrascripti lochi del Castello di Pavia . . . Item in caduno dessi lochi sia el nostro Illmo Sig.[re] et la Illma Madona retracti al naturale in diversi acti a pede, salvo in quello ove è ritracto Petro da Birago et Falconeri, che li vole essere a cavallo col Girifalco in pugno, et in laltro ove sarà Carlo da Cremona, chel ferisca levemente el Cervo con la Stambechina, et gli siano quelli che portano la spada, et la capa, et li staferi . . .
   'Item la Camera rossa dal razo sia tutta repinta excepto la fazata deverso la torre, ove se pinza el Sig.[re] con li Ambaxatori a sedere et li fratelli et D. Cicho in pede in acto de consultare et expedire fazende . . .
   'Item in la Camera de la Torre el Signore ad tavola solo cum Hieronymo de Becharia che li daghi bevere, lo Sescalco, et quello porta el piatello, et se faci che sua Signoria mangia in oro et che li siano Cortesani et Zentilhomini intorno . . .
   'La Salla prima dopoy la rossa sia hystoriata dal primo sposamento facto dell'Illma Madonna Duchessa per mezo del Mag.[co] Domino Tristano in presentia de la M.[ta] del Re et Regina de Franza, continuando el camino como la monta in mare, descende ad Zenua, et lo Signore gli andò incontra, el zonzere ad Milano, la solemnità se fece denanzi al Domo la presentatione de li feudatarij, la venuta ad Pavia, et mutatione del habito francese in Lombardo con le donzelle date da lo Illmo Sig.[e] et li altri de Casa etc.[a]
   'La secunda Salleta ove manzano le donne la Illma Madonna, la Ill.[e] M.[a] Isabeta che zoghi al ballone, o ala pomma cum le sue donzelle ad triumphi al pelluco, et gli sia Vergilio, D. Biaso et Zohanne Antonio Buffono . . .' (Rosmini, 1820, pp. 147–8).
29. 'Lista de le cose vole il nostro Ill.[o] S.[e] se depingano in Castello . . . La sala de sopra grande se depinga tutta a boschi cum cervi . . . E chel nostro Illmo S.[re] sia depincto con la stambuchina. Il. S.[re] D. Filippo: Il duca de Barri: . . . E tutti questi stagano in acti da caciatori differenti. Item che Alexio sia depincto che uno cervio labia butato da cavallo, e lui alci le gambe suso al cello in più bello acto sia possibile.
   'Item chel prefato Sig.[re] sia depincto ad cavallo suso el Gallesse con una spata in mano per ferire uno cervio . . .' (Beltrami, 1894, pp. 280–1).
30. '1474. Ordine de la pictura che se ha ad fare nel muro Castellano dela Salla de Milano. p.[o] se depenza tutta la fazada del Castello de Milano, con la torre de li burchioni che guardino ne la piaza . . . donde payra essere ussito il nostro Ill.[mo] Sig.[re] armato suso el Galeso bardato . . . Lo Ill.[o] Marchese de Monferrato con le soe foze armato e sopraveste. Lo Ill.[o] Marchese de Mantova armato ut supra . . . Tutti li suprascripti . . . siano tracti dal naturale et gli sia descripto el nome loro ad mordente in lettere doro, et similiter li nomi deli cavalli megliori che habiano, neli loci più convenienti . . . como parerà ad sua signoria . . .' (*ibid.*, pp. 365–7).
31. 'ad uno lato gli è la triumphale e regale venuta ad marito dela serena memoria de Madama Elionora tua chara et pudicissima moglie. E dal'altro uno bellissimo torniamento d'arme et il danzare che se facea in la grande sala sopra il tribunale per la matrimoniale festa . . .'; 'Se li vede ancora seriosamente quando la tua Excellentia exitte fuori dela cità di Ferrara per andare in Hyspagna . . . con splendidissima compagnia . . .'; etc. (Gundersheimer, 1972, pp. 71, 69).
32. 'De quindi passiamo in la iocundissima camera, in cui anchora vidi la tua Excellentia a cavallo triumphalmente, che pare l'anima havere adcompagnata dali gentili signori Sigismondo et Alberto tuoi amantissimi fratelli . . . e di Carri Lodovico tuo physico . . . Poi in una altra camera passiamo, dove anchora con dolce piacere vidi la tua illustrissima Signoria naturalmente depincta, torqueata d'oro . . . con una picola cintura de geme ala sinistra gamba . . . dela quale fusti munificato dal Serenissimo Re de Anglia . . . Quivi lì sono anchora in tua compagnia effigiati, torqueati d'oro, alcuni altri curiali' (Gundersheimer, 1972, pp. 61–2).
33. R. Signorini, *Opvs hoc tenve, La camera dipinta di Andrea Mantegna*, Mantua, 1985; Lightbown, 1986, pp. 99–117.
34. '1473. per m[o] Baldissera Credito . . . Lo Illu.mo et E.mo S.re nostro de dare ducati 200 doro per una tella grande. suso la quale e retracto dal naturale il quondam Duca Borso Lo Illustrissimo Messer Alberto, Conte Lorenzo et messer Theophilo a cavallo la quale me fece fare il prefato quondam Duca Borso' (Venturi, 1885[2], p. 721 n. 1). The same picture was mentioned on 30 December 1473 (*ibid.*, p. 722 n. 1).
35. Sterling, 1988, pp. 22–3 and references.
36. The copy, made for Gaignières, is in the Bibliothèque Nationale, Estampes, Oa 11, f. 85–88; see Sterling, 1987, pp. 140–4.
37. 'La quale sagrazione dipinse poi Lorenzo . . . nella facciata di quella chiesa, ritraendovi di naturale quel papa ed alcuni cardinali: la quale opera, come cosa nuova e bella, fu allora molto lodata' (Vasari-Milanesi, 1878–85, II, p. 55). The fresco is reproduced by Pope-Hennessy, 1966, p. 5.
38. 'di verde terra dipinse di chiaro e scuro . . . tutta la sagra come ella fu . . .' (Vasari-Milanesi, 1878–85, II, p. 295); see also Pope-Hennessy, 1966, p. 5.
39. E. Carli, *Il Pintoricchio*, Siena, 1960, pls 122–42.
40. P. Junquera, 'Las batallas navales en los tapices', *Reales Sitios*, V, 17 (1968), pp. 40–55. The Tunis tapestries are unusual in the prominence accorded to the full-length self-portrait that Vermeyen included in the first of the series.
41. Will of Isabelle Moriel, 1410: 'Je donne à Alart des Noettes ung drap point de la trairie de Tournai' (E. Soil, *Les tapisseries de Tournai* (*Mémoires de la Société historique et littéraire de Tournai*, XXII), Tournai, 1891, p. 350).
42. Antwerp (529): Vandenbroeck, 1985, pp. 97–103b.
43. See n. 22 above.
44. Fazio's life of Gentile: 'Eiusdem est altera tabula in qua martinus pontifex maximus. et cardinales decem ita expressi ut naturam ipsam aequare et nulla re uiuentibus dissimiles uideantur' (Baxandall, 1964, p. 101).
45. Louvre (INV. 1911): Michel, 1953, pp. 264–6.
46. 'conosciuto da don Martino, ambasciadore del re di Portogallo, andò a star seco; e gli fece una tela con forse venti ritratti di naturale, tutti suoi familiari ed amici, e lui in mezzo di loro a ragionare' (Vasari-Milanesi, 1878–85, VI, p. 27). For D. Mar-

tinho, see S. Deswarte-Rosa, 'Domenico Guintalodi, peintre de D. Martinho de Portugal à Rome', *Revue de l'art*, LXXX (1988), pp. 52–60.

47. A diptych of the six children of Philip the Handsome, King of Castile, is now in the Museo de Santa Cruz at Toledo (119, deposited from the Prado) and would have been painted in about 1510 (*Catalogue des tableaux anciens ... composant la collection de feu M. Edouard Fétis*, sale Brussels (Le Roy), 8–12 November 1909, p. 30 (47)). Holbein's portrait of his wife and children (Basle 325) is dated 152[9?] (Rowlands, 1985, pl. 63). Notable Italian examples are by Licinio, dated 1524, at Hampton Court (152: Shearman, 1983, pp. 138–9 (137)) and by Lotto, probably of 1547, in the National Gallery (1047: Gould, 1975, pp. 134–5).

48. On the portraits of pilgrims by Jan van Scorel at Haarlem and Utrecht, see Friedländer, 1967–76, XII, pls 184–5; exhibition catalogue Amsterdam, 1986, pp. 185–7 (65) and references.

49. A version, said to be signed by John Bettes, was in the Chester-Master collection (*Country Life*, CXIV (1953), p. 494); another belonged to the Earl of Derby (G. Scharf, 'Observations on an Elizabethan Picture ...', *Archaeologia*, LI (1888), pp. 347–50, reproduced facing p. 348; exhibition catalogue *Works of Art from Private Collections in the North West of England and North Wales*, City Art Gallery, Manchester, 1960, pp. 58–9 (236)).

50. National Portrait Gallery, London (710): Strong, 1969[1], pp. 315–19.

51. Longnon, 1895–9, II, pp. 316–18, etc.; Sterling, 1983, p. 181.

52. For example the Bavarian votive picture of Andreas von Ettling, of 1586 (Wallfahrtskirche Mariä Himmelfahrt, Tuntenhausen), discussed and reproduced in the exhibition catalogue Munich, 1980, II, pp. 69–70 (104).

53. 'Ung grant tappis de haulte-lice, à Moutons, où sont pourtraiz Madame d'Artois et Monseigneur de Flandres' (Pinchart, 1878–85, p. 16).

54. Longnon, 1895–9, II, pp. 336–7.

55. 'Respond qu'elle vit a Arras une panicture en la main d'un Escot; et y avoit la semblance d'elle toute armee, et presentoit unes lectres a son roy et estoit agenoullee d'un genoul' (P. Tisset, ed., *Procès de condamnation de Jeanne d'Arc* (Société de l'histoire de France), 3 vols, Paris, 1960–71, I, pp. 98–9).

56. Valerius Maximus, *Faits et dits mémorables*, Staatsbibliothek Preussischer Kulturbesitz, Berlin (West), MS Dep. Breslau 2, II, f. 6v, reproduced in O. Smital, *Le livre d'heures noir du duc Galeazzo Maria Sforza*, 2 vols, Vienna, 1930, text vol., pl. XV, fig. 24.

57. 'een raemkin zes voeten hoghe ende V voeten breet ziinde, daer up de figuren ende ymagen of personagen van den Roemschen coninc ende ziinen zone ghemaect ende ghestelt ziin in schilderien ...' (W. H. J. Weale, 'Le Palais du Franc à Bruges', *Le Beffroi*, IV (1872–6), pp. 46–92, 216–37 (p. 81)).

58. '1473. per m^{o} Baldissera Credito ... Et per una altra tella suso la quale e el Duca Galeazo et la dona retracta dal naturale, la quale have il prefato Duca Borso in schivenoio ... duc. 100' (Venturi, 1885[2], p. 721 n. 1).

59. Galleria Nazionale delle Marche, Urbino (702): reproduced in Pope-Hennessy, 1966, p. 163.

60. Buchner, 1953, pp. 170–3. The picture at Lauenburg an der Elbe, not mentioned by Buchner, is discussed and reproduced in the exhibition catalogue Nuremberg, 1983, p. 47 (43). The banderole next to the young man is inscribed 'To lust der werlt wil wy vns geue[n]. Wy mogen vp erde[n] lange leuen'; on the reverse, the cadaver on the left holds a banderole inscribed 'Der werlde lust hadde wy vt gekoren vnd hebbe[n] dat ewige leuent verloren'.

61. Buchner, 1953, pp. 170–83, pls 195, 199–205, 207. A half-length double portrait of a man and a woman attributed to Fra Filippo Lippi is at New York (89.15.19: Pope-Hennessy, 1966, p. 42); in the 'Recueil d'Arras' is a copy of a double portrait of Philip the Good, Duke of Burgundy, and his son Charles the Bold (f. 161). The original would have been painted in about 1460 by an artist from the circle of Van der Weyden (Campbell, 1977[1], pl. 24b).

62. For example, those of the Countess of Barcelhos, from the monastery of Sigena (Huesca) and now in the Museo provincial de bellas artes, Saragossa, and of Beatriz Cornel, prioress from 1427 to 1451, still at Sigena: reproduced in J. Camón Aznar, *Pintura medieval española* (*Summa artis, Historia general del arte*, XXII), Madrid, 1966, p. 542.

63. Hilliard, *Henry Percy, Earl of Northumberland* (Amsterdam); Oliver, *Edward Herbert, Baron Herbert of Cherbury* (Powis Castle): reproduced in R. Strong, *The English Renaissance Miniature*, London, 1983, pp. 109, 181.

64. R. W. Kennedy, *Alesso Baldovinetti*, New Haven, 1938, pp. 133–5 and references.

65. '1473. per m^{o} Baldissera Credito ... Et per una figura Intiera. Cioe suso uno quadro grande dal naturale, la quale statua il nostro duca presente mando a donar al Ill.mo duca galeazo ... duc. 080' (Venturi, 1885[2], p. 721 n. 1). See also p. 220 below.

66. 'Lo retracto del Ill. S. Alex. tucto jntiero' (Vernarecci, 1886, p. 522).

67. ' cominciò Tiziano quello che è poi venuto in uso, cioè fare alcuni ritratti interi' (Vasari-Milanesi, 1878–85, VII, p. 445).

68. See n. 12 above.

69. M. Mallory and G. Moran, 'New Evidence concerning "Guidoriccio"' and A. Martindale, 'The Problem of "Guidoriccio"', *Burlington Magazine*, CXXVIII (1986), pp. 250–9, 259–73.

70. The frescoes are in the cathedral of Florence: see E. Borsook, *The Mural Painters of Tuscany*, 2nd edn, Oxford, 1980, pp. 74–9, pl. 91; M. Horster, *Andrea del Castagno*, Oxford, 1980, pp. 182–3, pls 113–17.

71. 'Ioannes Carrapha strenuus Decurio Neapolitanus, cum in arce, quae dicitur Capuana, imaginem regis armati, equoque insidentis, pingendam curasset, et circum eam quatuor virtutes ...' (L. Valla, *In Bartolomaeum Facium Ligurem Invectivae seu recriminationes*, reprinted in M. Baxandall, *Giotto and the Orators*, Oxford, 1971, pp. 112, 174).

72. Galeazzo Maria Sforza, Duke of Milan, to the castellan of Pavia, Milan, 27 October 1469: 'Volimo che subito ne mandate una certa tela grande che e in la libraria dove e dipinto lo Illmo q.^{m} nostro patre et Signore ad cavallo, havendo advertentia ad mandarla per messo fidato ligata in un altra tela a cio che non se guasti' (Malaguzzi Valeri, 1902, p. 143). Ludovico, Duke of Milan, to his brother Ascanio, 27 January 1491: 'la salla grande de la balla è stata preparata ... havemo per questa festa facto mettere tutte le victorie et gesti memorabili de lo Illmo S. nostro avo, cum la effigie sua de un capo contro la porta, a cavallo sotto un arco triumphale ...' (Beltrami, 1894, p. 455). Beatrice d'Este, wife of Ludovico, to her sister Isabella, 29 December 1493, describing a triumphal arch erected in Milan cathedral for the marriage on 30 November 1493 of Bianca Maria Sforza to the Emperor Maximilian I: 'era tutto depincto et haveva nel fronte la effigie de lo Illmo S.^{re} quondam Duca Francesco, a cavallo ...' (Luzio and Renier, 1890, p. 384).

73. For the tapestry equestrian portrait of Jean de Daillon (Montacute House), apparently part of a gift of tapestries made in 1483 to Jean's heirs by the city of Tournai, see the exhibition catalogue Paris, 1973–4, pp. 122–4 (44). An equestrian portrait of Ludwig Klingkhamer, probably painted at Innsbruck in 1487, commemorates his escape from death in battle in that year (Prämonstratenserstift Wilten, Innsbruck: discussed and reproduced in the exhibition catalogue *Der Herzog und sein Taler: Erzherzog Sigmund der Münzreiche*, Burg Hasegg, Hall in Tirol and Ferdinandeum, Innsbruck, 1986, p. 124 (I.65)).

74. The tapestries, once in the castle of Le

Verger, were copied for Gaignières: Bibliothèque Nationale, Estampes, Oa 15, ff. 97–101.

75. At Bruges in 1477, the court painter Pierre Coustain was paid 'van ghemaect thebbene van schilderijen een figure van eene scoone maecht te paerde, heerlike ghestoffeert; voord van den scilden metter wapene van alden landen van onzer voors. gheduchter joncvrauwe . . .'. This was clearly an equestrian portrait of Mary, made for her entry into Bruges in April 1477 (L. Gilliodts-Van Severen, *Inventaire des archives de la ville de Bruges*, Section première, VI, Bruges, 1876, p. 159). Her daughter Margaret of Austria owned in 1530 'Une chasse de bois de chasne, bien ouvrée au cler, dehors et dedens la representacion de madame Marie de Bourgogne, que dieu pardoint, mere de Madame, estant sus ung cheval, et l'oyseau sus le point, et au frontal du dit cheval a ung grant plumal, et plusieurs chiens la suyvent' (Zimerman, 1885, no. 156). This would have been similar to the miniature in the *Hours of Maximilian and Mary of Burgundy* at Berlin, Kupferstichkabinett, 78 B 12, f. 220v (reproduced in the exhibition catalogue *Zimelien*, Staatliche Museen Preussischer Kulturbesitz, Berlin (West), 1975–6, p. 244).
76. Further Netherlandish or French examples are the *John the Fearless, Duke of Burgundy*, perhaps of 1404, known from an early copy in the Louvre (M.I. 831: H. Adhémar, 'La date d'un portrait de Jean sans Peur', *Revue du Louvre*, X (1961), pp. 265–8); the similar *John, Duke of Berry*, of about 1410, known from a copy made for Gaignières (Bibliothèque Nationale, Estampes, Oa 13, f. 15: Meiss, 1967, pl. 490); and the *Colart d'Oignies* of about 1410(?), known from a copy in the 'Recueil d'Arras', f. 223. For German portraits, see Buchner, 1953, pp. 17–18.
77. See below, p. 72.
78. Louvre (INV. 779): Pope-Hennessy, 1966, pp. 106–7.
79. Item iordonne a saincte auoye
    Et non ailleurs ma sepulture
    Et affin que chascun me voye
    Non pas en chair mais en paincture
    Que lon tire mon estature
    Dancre sil ne coustoit trop cher
    De tumbel rien ie nen ay cure
    Car il greueroit le plancher

    (F. Villon, *Le grant testament villon et le petit, Son codicille, Le iargon & les balades*, Paris, 1489, not paginated).
80. 'Item, unes tablettes de boys à huit fueilletz, où sont les pourtraitures tirées de plompt du roy de Sicille, de la royne, de feu mons[r] de Calabre et autres seigneurs' (A. Lecoy de la Marche, *Extraits des comptes et mémoriaux du roi René* (*Documents historiques publiés par la Société de l'Ecole des Chartes*, 1), Paris, 1873, p. 262).
81. Ludovico Gonzaga, Marquis of Mantua, to Zaccaria Saggi, his ambassador in Milan, 30 November 1475: 'quando Andrea Mantegna altra volta lo ritrette, non parse gli satisfacesse et intendessemo ch'el haveva facto brusare quelli fogli, parendoge non lo havesse facto bene' (Signorini, 1974, p. 232; translated in Gilbert, 1980, p. 131).
82. Mantegna to Ludovico Gonzaga, 6 July 1477: 'aviso la Ex[cia] vostra chome volendo far queli ritrati, non intendo, volendolj la S. vostra si presto, in che modo habia a fare, o solamente disegnati o coloriti in tavola o in tela e de che statura' (Kristeller, 1902, p. 534; translated in Gilbert, 1980, p. 12).
83. Mantegna to Francesco Gonzaga, 15 June 1489: 'Como io el ueda subito lo mando dessignato alla Ex[cia] V.' (Kristeller, 1902, p. 547; translated in Gilbert, 1980, p. 13).
84. Marchesino Stanga to Ludovico il Moro, Milan, 1 September 1492: 'Questa quadrigesima passata venne in questa Cità uno Todesco ed ebbe noticia che era venuto solum per vedere la Ill.ma M.a Biancha, et per havere la effigie sua retracta: . . . da Io. Ambrosio Preda cavò uno dissegno de Carbone et se partite . . . Hora è ritornato un altra volta . . . voria . . . uno retracto colorito de la effigie de la prefata Madonna . . .' (F. Malaguzzi, 'Ambrogio Preda e un ritratto di Bianca Maria Sforza', *Rassegna d'arte*, II (1902), pp. 93–4).
85. Beatrice d'Este to her mother the Duchess of Ferrara, 16 April 1493: 'sperava che el depintore me portase el retrato dercule el qualle el .S.[re] et io lo mandamo ala .S.V. . . .' (Venturi, 1885[1], p. 227); the duchess to Isabella d'Este, 1 July 1493: 'Qui incluso gli serà uno designo che ne è mandato da Milano circa el bene stare de quello ill.[mo] figliolino nostro . . .' (Luzio and Renier, 1890, p. 368).
86. Baldassarre Pusterla and Giason del Maino to Ludovico il Moro, 29 December 1493: 'Et poy fece portar duy designi qual gli haveva mandato la Maestà dil Re da Fiandra, l'uno hera di la Regina, trato d'uno altro retrato, et l'altro dil duca di Borgogna suo fiolo. Et vedendo quisti Johanne Ambrosio Preda disse che l'hera dreto uno designo di la Signoria Vostra che l'haveva facto luy qual hera molto bello, et como l'hebbe enteso fu necessario farglilo portar . . . et como fu gionta dal Duca gli disse d'haver visto il retrato di la Signoria Vostra, et subito mandò messer Georgio da Predapiana . . . per farsi portare questo retrato . . .' (Seidlitz, 1906–7, p. 17; Malaguzzi Valeri, 1917, pp. 7–8; translated in Gilbert, 1980, pp. 139–40). In a letter to Ludovico dated 28 December 1493, Bianca Maria herself gave a less detailed account of these events: 'havendone facto domandare la imagine de la Excellentia Vostra, gle l'havemo mandato per videre, quale n'è stato referto haverla vista tanto voluntiera quanto dire se possa' (F. Calvi, *Bianca Maria Sforza-Visconti*, Milan, 1888, pp. 48–50).
87. Isabella d'Este to Taddeo de Lardi, 30 September 1495: 'habiamo recevuto . . . lo retratto del R.[mo] Mons. nostro fratello, qual n'è stato grato, ma molto più ne serà se ne mandareti l'altro colorito che cossì vi pregamo' (Luzio, 1913, p. 191).
88. Lorenzo da Pavia to Isabella d'Este, 13 March 1500: 'Le a Venecia Lionardo Vinci el quale ma mostrato uno retracto de la Signoria Vostra . . .' (A. Baschet, *Aldo Manuzio, lettres et documents 1495–1515*, Venice, 1867, p. 72); Isabella d'Este to Fra Pietro da Nuvolara, 27 March 1501: 'Apresso lo pregarà ad volerne mandare uno altro schizo del retracto nostro, perochè lo Ill. S. nostro consorte ha donato via quello che'l ce lassò quà, che 'l tutto haveremo . . .' (Luzio, 1887, p. 33).
89. Isabella d'Este to Leonardo, 14 May 1504: 'quando fusti in questa terra et che ne retrasti de carbono, ne promettesti farni ogni mo' una volta di colore' (Luzio, 1887, p. 34).
90. See below, pp. 183–5.
91. The best known is perhaps the 'Recueil d'Arras', on which see Campbell, 1977[1].
92. Holbein's portrits of Jakob Meyer and his wife (Basle, 312) and the preliminary drawings (Basle, 1823.137, 137a) all descended in the sitters' family, as did the three surviving preliminary drawings (Basle, 1823. 140–142) for the donor portraits of Jakob, his wife and his daughter in Holbein's *Virgin with Jakob Meyer and his Family*, now in the Schloss-museum, Darmstadt (exhibition catalogue Basle, 1988, pp. 10, 34–9, 191–8). It would appear that Jakob Meyer acquired the drawings with the paintings – unless, of course, he or one of his heirs purchased the drawings when the contents of Holbein's studio at Basle were dispersed.
93. The portrait drawings that Holbein executed in England probably passed to Henry VIII on the artist's death in 1543 (Foister, 1983, p. 12); François Clouet's drawings appear to have been acquired on his death in 1572 by Catherine de'Medici (R. de Broglie, 'Catalogue des Clouet de Chantilly', *Gazette des beaux-arts*, 6e pér., LXXVII (1971), pp. 269–336).
94. For example, the 'Visierungbuch' of Philip II of Pomerania, formerly at Szczecin (H. Bethe, *Die Kunst am Hofe der pommerschen Herzöge*, Berlin, 1937, p. 90).
95. 'Item, 1 tableau de bois a ymaige de me dame, pendant a une chainette d'argent'

(C. Dehaisnes, *Documents et extraits divers concernant l'histoire de l'art dans la Flandre, l'Artois et le Hainaut avant le XVe siècle*, Lille, 1886, p. 913).

96. Undated inventory of objects found by Margaret of Austria 'au petit cabinet de deçus l'oratoyre': 'ung petit tableau d'yvoyre, donné à Madame par Monseigneur de Chièvres, auquel tableau est le visage du duc Philippe au vif' (Finot, 1895, p. 208); 1523–4 inventory of Margaret of Austria's collection: 'Item, ung petit tableau d'ivoire, à ung vieux personnaige pourtant la Thoison d'or, les quatre coins dudit tableau d'argent doré et sur ung chascun ung fusil pendant à une petites chaine d'argent' (Michelant, 1871, p. 93); inventory of goods belonging to the deceased Mary of Hungary and brought from Turnhout to Brussels, 1560: 'Ung petit tableau d'ivoire, à ung vieu personnaige, portant la thoison d'or à son col, les quatre coings dudit tableau d'argent doré et sur chacun coing y a ung fusil, pendant ledit tableau à une chainette, lequel tableau l'on dict que c'est l'effigie du bon duc Philippe de Bourgoingne' (H. Michelant, 'Inventaire de joyaux . . .', *Compte-rendu des séances de la Commission royale d'histoire, ou Recueil de ses Bulletins*, 3e sér., XIII (1872), pp. 199–368, p. 366).

97. 1516 inventory of Margaret of Austria's collection: 'ung autre tableaul d'anluminure où est le chief de Madame qui est ung peu gasté; ung autre de Madame de Hornes fait aussi d'illuminure' (Finot, 1895, p. 210).

98. Inventory of the goods of deceased Philip of Cleves, Lord of Ravenstein, at the castle of Enghien, 1 April 1528: 'unze petis tableaux esquelz sont pourtraiz sur parchemin plusieurs princes, princesses et grans seigneurs, encassez en or estans en ung petit coffret d'argent doré' (Finot, 1895, p. 431).

99. Melville, 1827, p. 122.

100. For example, Jean Bandol of Bruges, who in 1371 painted and signed the presentation miniature of the *Bible historiale* given by Jean de Vaudetar to Charles V of France (Museum Meermanno-Westreenianum, The Hague, MS 10 B 23, ff. lv-2: Panofsky, 1953, pl. 23). The presentation miniature of the first volume of the *Chroniques de Hainaut* (Bibliothèque Royale, Brussels, MS 9242, f. 1) is surrounded by a gilded border resembling a picture frame, is unlike in style and in technique any of the other miniatures in this or related manuscripts and may well have been painted in the Van der Weyden workshop (P. Cockshaw in the exhibition catalogue Brussels, 1979, pp. 172–3 (36)).

101. Bibliothèque Nationale, Paris, MS fr. 13429: Mellen, 1971, pls 3, 5, 7, 9, 11, 16, 56.

102. For miniature group portraits, see the descriptions of various miniatures given by Levina Teerlinc to Elizabeth I of England in 1562–5, 1568 and 1575 (Campbell, 1985, pp. xxviii-xxix), the *Elizabethan Maundy* of about 1565, in the collection of the Countess Beauchamp, and Isaac Oliver's *The Three Brothers Browne* of 1598 at Burghley House (exhibition catalogue London, 1983, pp. 19 pl. x, 55 (42), 164 (272)). For full length miniature portraits attributed to Hilliard and Oliver, see the same catalogue pp. 156–8 (263–5), 161 (268), 166 (276). For a miniature double portrait of 1525 attributed to Hans Leu the Younger, see G. C. Williamson, 'Two Important Miniatures', *Connoisseur*, LXIV (1922), pp. 40–5, p. 42.

103. A round portrait of a man, once in the Sachs collection at Santa Barbara (Cal.), is reproduced in P. Wescher, *Jean Fouquet and his Time*, Basle, 1947, pl. 43.

104. Rüstkammer, Schloss Ambras, Innsbruck: see L. Luchner, *Denkmal eines Renaissancefürsten, Versuch einer Rekonstruktion des Ambraser Museums von 1583*, Vienna, 1958, pl. 52.

105. The method of construction is explained in M. S. Tucker, 'Discoveries made during the Treatment of Bronzino's "Cosimo I de'Medici as Orpheus"', *Philadelphia Museum of Art Bulletin*, LXXXI (348, fall 1985), pp. 28–32.

106. For half-length portraits Mor ordinarily used panels measuring approximately 110 × 85 cm. (plates 216, 259).

107. The reverses of portraits might be decorated with coats of arms, other devices or inscriptions (see plates 74, 113, 154, 234). Sometimes another picture occupied the other face of the panel. On the reverse of the *Lady* by a follower of Van der Weyden in the National Gallery (1433) is a *Christ crowned with Thorns* (Davies, 1972, pp. 221–2, pls 108–9). On the reverse of a *Virgin and Child* by a follower of Dirk Bouts is an unfinished portrait of a man (private collection, U.K., unpublished, but described in P. Remy, *Catalogue raisonné des tableaux . . . de M. de Julienne*, Paris, 1767, p. 37 (86); the *Virgin* is a version of the *Virgin and Child* at Berlin (545 C) reproduced in Friedländer, 1967–76, III, pl. 97 (93)). In 1501 in the chapel of the Hôtel-Dieu at Beaune was a painting 'où est Nostre-Dame et saint Bernard d'un costé et de l'autre costé la portraicture de feu Monseigneur le duc Philippe' (J.-B.-C. Boudrot, 'Inventaire de l'Hôtel-Dieu de Beaune (1501)', *Société d'histoire, d'archéologie et de littérature de l'arrondissement de Beaune, Mémoires*, 1874, pp. 117–204, p. 123). Mythological, allegorical and moralising subjects also occur: the *Triumphs* on the reverses of Piero della Francesca's portraits of the Duke and Duchess of Urbino (Uffizi, 1615: Pope-Hennessy, 1966, pp. 160, 211); the *Memento Mori* painted upside down on the reverse of Previtali's *Man* in the Museo Poldi-Pezzoli, Milan (1598: Berenson, 1957, II, pl. 744); the *Nude Lovers* on the reverse of Jacopo de'Barbari's *Man* at Berlin (1664: *ibid.*, I, pls 309–10); the *Pyramus and Thisbe* on the reverse of a Nuremberg portrait of a man of about 1505 at Colmar (P 52); the *Vanitas* on the reverse of Dürer's portrait of a young man, dated 1507, at Vienna (849: Anzelewsky, 1980, pp. 130–1). Two portraits painted on the obverse and reverse of the same panel are mentioned in a Ferrarese document of 1449: this concerns a 'quadro lungo' purchased for Lionello d'Este 'per farse retrare del naturale a M.° Andrea da padoa dipintore da uno lato dal altro lato folco de Villafora . . .' (Campori, 1885, p. 537; the painter was probably Mantegna).

108. Mantegna to Ludovico Gonzaga, 6 July 1477: 'Se la S. vostra li volesse mandare lontano se possono farli suso tela sotile per poterli avoltare suso un bastonzelo' (Kristeller, 1902, p. 534; translated in Gilbert, 1980, p. 12).

109. Roll of New Year's gifts, 1552: 'the phismanye of the duke of . . . [decayed] steyned upon cloth of silver, in a frame of woode' (J. G. Nichols, 'Notices of the Contemporaries and Successors of Holbein', *Archaeologia*, XXXIX (1863), pp. 19–46, p. 36).

110. Uffizi 1711, *Young Man* and 1485, *Old Man*, both attributed to Filippino Lippi, and 1694, Andrea del Sarto's self-portrait, on which see Vasari-Milanesi, 1878–85, V, p. 48 (Berti, 1979, pp. 918, 331, 789).

111. 'un nuovo modo di colorire in pietra, ciò piaceva molto a' popoli, parendo che in quel modo le pitture diventassero eterne, e che nè il fuoco nè i tarli potessero lor nuocere' (Vasari-Milanesi, 1878–85, V, p. 579). See Hirst, 1981, pp. 124–6.

112. Holbein's portrait of his wife and children is on paper mounted on panel (Basle, 325: Rowlands, 1985, pl. 63).

113. 'Ich hab 6 stübers fürs täffelein geben und des Portugalers diener mit den kohln darauff conterfet. Das alles hab ich zum Neuen Jahr geschenckt . . .' (Rupprich, 1956–69, I, p. 164; translated in Conway, 1889, p. 112).

114. Small mosaic portraits of Charles V and Ferdinand I, both after Titian, are in the Kunstkammer at Schloss Ambras (P 3055, P 3054: Scheicher, 1977, pp. 131–2, pls 30–1). Small tapestry portraits of Maximilian and Christina of Bavaria, woven in 1576 after designs by Friedrich Sustris and mounted in an ivory case, are in the Bayerisches Nationalmuseum, Munich (R1554). The faces are partially painted (exhibition catalogue Munich, 1980, II, p. 97 (140) and

col. pl. 4).

115. See above, note 38.

116. Seen by Marcantonio Michiel in 1530 in the collection of Gabriel Vendramin: 'El retratto de Francesco Zancho brauo, de chiaro et scuro dacquarella negra, fo de man de Jacometto' (Frimmel, 1896, p. 108).

117. Undated inventory: 'ung visage de l'Empereur fait de blanc et de noyr' (Finot, 1895, p. 208); 1516 inventory: 'ung petit tableau du chief d'ung portugalois, fait sans couleur par maistre Jacques Barbaris' (*ibid.*, p. 210.

118. See below, p. 218.

119. This observation is based on an examination of the original frames of a random selection of early Netherlandish portraits: the matter should be more carefully investigated.

120. David, 1947, p. 132.

121. Covers were supplied, at an extra charge, by the painters: Van Orley, delivering portraits in 1532 to the Countess of Nassau, entered in his bill, 'Item a déboursé ledict maistre Bernart pour XIII layetes ou custodes pour garder et preserver lesdits tableaux, chacune desdites layetes a cincq patars' (Steppe, 1969, p. 481). In the 1516 inventory of Margaret of Austria's collection, it is noted when portraits lacked covers or shutters: for example, 'ung moien tableau de la face d'une portugalaise que Madame a eu de don Diego, fait de la main de Johannès et est fait sans huille et sur toille sans couverte ni feuillet' (Finot, 1895, p. 210). Most of the portraits in Henry VIII's collection were protected by curtains of sarsenet (see the 1542 inventory published by Shaw, 1937). Queen Isabella of Castile appears to have kept many of her portraits in cases or boxes: for example, 'mas otra caxa Redonda en que esta una pyntura de una muger forastera con una Ropa colorada' (Sánchez Cantón, 1950, p. 168). The diptych of René of Anjou and his wife, attributed to Nicolas Froment and painted in about 1475, was kept in a red velvet bag, which is still preserved (Louvre, R.F. 665: Sterling and Adhémar, 1965, pp. 14–15).

122. Berlin (557 E): W. H. Köhler in H. Bock et al., *The Gemäldegalerie, Berlin*, London, 1986, pp. 68–9.

123. Dürer's portrait already cited has a cover decorated with the sitter's coat of arms. Margaret of Austria owned 'ung aultre petit double tableau où il y a une jeusne fille habillée à la mode d'Espaigne, ayant ung bonnet rouge sur sa teste, l'aultre cousté plain d'escripture' (1523–4 inventory: Michelant, 1871, p. 85). Isabella of Castile owned 'mas otra pyntura puesta en dos tablas en la una la duquesa de bretaña y en la otra su tierra' (Sánchez Cantón, 1950, p. 168).

124. Jacometto Veneziano's *Portrait of Alvise Contarini* seems originally to have had as its cover Jacometto's *Nun of San Secondo* (Robert Lehman Collection, Metropolitan Museum of Art, New York, 1975.1. 85–86). See the description by Marcantonio Michiel, written when the pictures were in the collection of Michele Contarini (Frimmel, 1896, p. 112; Pope-Hennessy, 1966, pp. 211–13, 321–2). Margaret of Austria owned 'ung tableaul de bonne paincture d'une belle fille exclave, sur la couverte duquel sont Charles Overssin, contrerolleur de Madame, et son père, et aussi le chien de Madame qui s'appelle Bonté' (1516 inventory: Finot, 1895, p. 211).

125. The cover for Lotto's portrait of Bernardo de' Rossi, Bishop of Treviso (Naples, Q 57) is his *Allegory*, now in Washington (1939.1.156); an inscription once on the reverse of the *Allegory* gave the names of sitter and painter, the sitter's age and the date 1 July 1505 (Pope-Hennessy, 1966, pp. 214–16; Shapley, 1979, pp. 277–80). A panel in Florence (Deposito della Soprintendenza, Inv. 1890/6042) is thought to be a Florentine portrait cover of about 1510: it represents a mask, with the inscription '.SVA.CVIQVE.PERSONA', 'To every man his mask' (exhibition catalogue Florence, 1980, pp. 257–8 (480)).

126. 'In Ancona, adì junio 1552, die haver mastro Domenico Salimbene mastro de lignami per un quadretino con l'ornamenti de noce et suo coperto a uso de specchio, quale fu fato per lo inanti per misser Donato de Nobili, mercante fiorentino, quale fu per farli un retratino che non passò effetto et il quadretto mi rimase . . .' (Zampetti, 1969, p. 45).

127. 'un fort beau et riche mirouer où estoit sa peinture'. The lady, asked to return the prince's gifts, 'prit une plume et de l'ancre, et luy ficha dedans de grandes cornes au beau mitan du front . . .' (Brantôme, 1864–82, IX, p. 510).

Chapter 3 Poses

1. 'Non expectes igitur a me singulorum hominum et locorum nomina, nec historiam ipsam omnibus suis partibus absolutam, sed tanquam hominis simulacrum, cui aliqua membra desunt, et tamen hominem plane designat spectator' (C. A. J. Armstrong, ed., *The Usurpation of Richard the Third. Dominicus Mancinus ad Angelum Catonem De Occupatione regni Anglie per Riccardum Tercium libellus*, 2nd edn, Oxford, 1969, pp. 56–7). Compare Van Mander, 1604, f. 17 (*Grondt*, c. 5 s. 24), translated in Stechow, 1966, p. 59.

2. For example, the *Portrait of a Man* attributed to Baldassare d'Este in the Museo Correr, Venice (I. 35: G. Mariacher, *Il Museo Correr di Venezia, Dipinti dal XIV al XVI secolo*, Venice, 1957, pp. 21–2) or the *Sacrati Family* attributed to the same painter at Munich (8709: reproduced in Berenson, 1968, II, pl. 745). In a portrait of a man by Moretto, thought to have been painted in 1535–40, the sitter is seen through a stone window (Brescia, 151: exhibition catalogue *Alessandro Bonvicino, Il Moretto*, Monastero di S. Giulia, Brescia, 1988, pp. 117–18, 213–14 (51)).

3. For example, in Veronese's *Man in a Fur-Trimmed Robe*, Pitti (216), reproduced – without the parapet – by Pope-Hennessy, 1966, p. 286.

4. Other examples are the *Youth* attributed to Giorgione at Berlin (12 A), the Giorgionesque *Two Young Men* in the Palazzo Venezia, Rome, and the Venetian(?) *'Teofilo Folengo'* in the Uffizi (791): reproduced in Pope-Hennessy, 1966, pp. 135, 137, and in Berti, 1979, p. 511.

5. And similarly in Raphael's *Gravida*, Pitti (229); exhibition catalogue Florence, 1984, pp. 99–104 (7), 249–51.

6. Few of the original frames of Memlinc's portraits have survived, but it is possible that once the hands overlapped onto the frames of others, for example, the *Man with an Arrow* at Washington (1937.1.42: Hand and Wolff, 1986, pp. 188–93). Compare also the *Engelbert, Count of Nassau*, dated 1487, at Amsterdam (A 3140), attributed to the Master of the Portraits of Princes (Friedländer, 1967–76, IV, pl. 104 B).

7. 'La testa del Ill. S. Constantio Sfortia de ma del perusino in duy occhij . . . La testa del Duca de Borgogna de man de Ruzieri da Burges in duy ochij . . . La testa del Ill. S. Alex. in duy ochij de man de Rugieri . . .' (Vernarecci, 1886, p. 522).

8. See below, p. 160.

9. In Titian's *Pesaro Altarpiece*, for example, the principal donors are in profile (Pope-Hennessy, 1966, p. 278). See also Moroni's *Gentleman in Adoration before the Madonna* of c. 1560 (Washington, 1939.1.114: Shapley, 1979, pp. 337–8, pl. 245).

10. Pontormo's *Cosimo il Vecchio de'Medici* in the Uffizi (3574: Pope-Hennessy, 1966, p. 180) and Titian's *Francis I of France* in the Louvre (INV. 753: Wethey, 1971, pl. 79) are based on medals; Bronzino's *Laura Battiferri* in the Palazzo Vecchio in Florence (Loeser bequest: Pope-Hennessy, 1966, p. 234) is probably intended to be reminiscent of portraits of Dante, so that a parallel is being made between poetess and poet (Plazzotta, 1988, pp. 37–8).

11. Apart from the *John II of France*, the only surviving painted profiles are the damaged *Lady*, perhaps of about 1415, at Washington (1937.1.23: Hand and Wolff, 1986, pp.

90–7), the *Wenceslas of Luxemburg, Duke of Brabant*, thought to be an early fifteenth-century copy after an original of about 1371 (Thyssen-Bornemisza Collection, 101: J. Duverger, 'Jan van Woluwe en de portretten van Wenceslas van Bohemen', *Jaarboek van het Koninklijk Museum voor Schone Kunsten, Antwerpen*, 1972, pp. 7–18), and the *Louis II of Anjou* in the Bibliothèque Nationale, which is on paper and which is a mid-fifteenth-century copy after an original possibly of about 1410 (J. A. and F. G., 'Encore le portrait de Louis II d'Anjou . . .', *Gazette des beaux-arts*, 6ᵉ pér., XCII (1978), pp. 66–8). Those known from later copies include portraits of Louis of Male, Count of Flanders, Margaret of Cleves, Countess of Hainault and Holland, Froissart, 'Wenceslas of Luxemburg', John, Duke of Touraine, and John the Pitiless of Bavaria-Holland, all known from drawings in the 'Recueil d'Arras' (ff. 54, 29, 278, 173, 35, 30); two portraits of Philip the Bold, Duke of Burgundy, one known from painted versions at Schloss Ambras and elsewhere (KHM 4442: Heinz and Schütz, 1976, pl. 14), the other from versions at Versailles (4001) and elsewhere (Meiss, 1967, pl. 508); a portrait of John the Fearless, Duke of Burgundy, known from an early painted copy in the Louvre (M.I. 831: Meiss, 1967, pl. 506); and a portrait of John, Duke of Berry, known from a drawn copy made for Gaignières (Biliothèque Nationale, Estampes, Oa 13, f. 15: Meiss, 1967, pl. 490).

12. Notably in Holbein's *Simon George* (Frankfurt, 1065: Rowlands, 1985, pl. 101), which is a roundel, and in his *Erasmus* in the Louvre (INV. 1345: Foucart-Walter, 1985, pp. 9–26, 72–3), which is similar to the medal of 1519 by Quinten Metsys (Friedländer, 1967–76, VII, pl. 133).
13. 'el rostro frontero es casi sin gracia . . .' (Sánchez Cantón, 1921, p. 263).
14. 'soo gheheel levendigh/dat een yeder wie 't siet verschrickt' (Van Mander, 1604, f. 222).
15. 'Sacar un rostro trazado es: en un cierto medio y moderación, que ni queda el rostro con la poca gracia de frontero del todo, ni con el grande rigor de medio rostro, sinó mostrándose medio frontero y medio entero hace una proporción y igualdad que satisface y contenta mucho . . . el rostro frontero es casi sin gracia y llano y no muestra nada del perfil y facíon del medio rostro, ni de los lados del rostro: el medio es muy austero y grave . . . el trazado muestra lo bueno de entrambos estos modos, y poco de lo malo, y por esto es el mejor; porque muestra parte de la frente y parte del perfil . . . el rostro trazado . . . es el más seguro y peor de hacer . . .' (Sánchez Cantón, 1921, pp. 262–3).
16. See below, p. 232.
17. For example, Botticelli's *Youth with a Medal of Cosimo il Vecchio de'Medici* in the Uffizi (1488) and Leonardo's *Ginevra de'Benci* in Washington (1967.6.1): reproduced in Pope-Hennessy, 1966, pp. 30, 103.
18. 'teniendo el rostro levantado como que mira hacia el cielo, con los ojos altos y las faciones vistas por abajo, pareciendo las ventanas de las narices y la boca y toda la barba y toda la garganta: y este modo es muy dificultoso y noble' (Sánchez Cantón, 1921, p. 263).
19. For example Jacopo da Strada in Titian's portrait at Vienna (81: Hope, 1980, p. 159). Titian disliked his sitter (see below, Chapter 5 n. 8). Compare also the strange *Portrait of a Man* attributed to Niccolo dell'Abate in the Uffizi (1377: Berti, 1979, p. 242).
20. Ladies of doubtful virtue were sometimes represented with downcast eyes, presumably to give them an air of false modesty: see the drawings in the 'Recueil d'Arras' of Eustache de Cornehuse, mistress of Louis of Male, Count of Flanders (f. 57) and Catherine Thieffries, mistress of Philip the Good, Duke of Burgundy (f. 101).
21. Hilliard, 1981 edn, p. 76.
22. 'De superciliis . . . si deducta, tristitiam [notant] . . .' (J. Willich, *Liber de pronunciatione rhetorica*, Basle, 1540, reprinted in Herrmann, 1914, p. 263).
23. A. Smith, *The National Gallery Schools of Painting, Early Netherlandish and German Paintings*, London, 1985, p. 30.
24. 'De superciliis . . . si inaequalia, videlicet cum unum fuerit sublatum et alterum compositum, crudelitatem portendunt' (Herrmann, 1914, p. 263).
25. Leon Battista Alberti, *Opere volgari*, III, ed. C. Grayson, Bari, 1973, pp. 72–3.
26. R. Latham and W. Matthews, eds, *The Diary of Samuel Pepys*, VII: *1666*, London, 1972, pp. 74–5.
27. 'Vitiosa est immodica pedum divaricatio' (Herrmann, 1914, p. 265).
28. For example, the portrait at Hampton Court (1246) attributed to Guillaume Scrots: Millar, 1963, p. 66, pl. 33.
29. 'cada mano es de nuevo otro rostro . . .' (Sánchez Cantón, 1921, p. 275).
30. Munich (537): reproduced in Pope-Hennessy, 1966, p. 130.
31. See below, p. 134.
32. Quintilian, 1921–2 edn, IV, p. 295.
33. *Ibid.*
34. *Ibid.*, p. 297.
35. 'Monseigneur, vostre venue par deçà m'est une grant joye en coeur, je loue Dieu et vous de l'honneur et de la bonne aventure que j'ay aujourduy à vostre cause, et aussi bien soiez-vous venu comme fut l'angle Gabriel à la Vierge Marie, car si grant joye ne reçus onques, ne tant d'honneur . . .' (reported in Chastellain's *Chronique*, IV, xliii: Kervyn de Lettenhove, ed., *Oeuvres de Georges Chastellain*, 8 vols, Brussels, 1863–6, III, p. 209).
36. G. T. Langosco da Stroppiana to Granvelle, London, 25 November 1554: 'both shed tears and the Queen felt her child move, so it may well be said: exultavit infans in utero pius' (R. Tyler, ed., *Letters, Despatches, and State Papers, relating to the Negotiations between England and Spain*, XIII, London, 1954, pp. 104–5. Compare Luke 1: 41: 'exultavit infans in utero ejus et repleta est spiritu sancto Elisabeth').
37. R. B. Simon, 'Bronzino's "Cosimo I de' Medici as Orpheus"', *Philadelphia Museum of Art Bulletin*, LXXXI (348, fall 1985), pp. 17–27.
38. For Lucas van Leyden's paintings, see Friedländer, 1967–76, X, pls 108–11. Hemessen's portrait, formerly in the collection of the Earl of Crawfurd, was sold at Christie's, 6 July 1984 (106); Paris Bordone's painting is at Berlin (169: exhibition catalogue *Paris Bordone*, Palazzo dei Trecento, Treviso, 1984, pp. 92–3 (25)); Sofonisba's is at Poznań (Berenson, 1968, III, pl. 1968); for the English portrait, see above, Chapter 2 n. 49.
39. Friedländer, 1967–76, VII, pls 91–2, 94; see H. Eger in the catalogue *Ausstellung Friedrich III*, Kaiserresidenz, Wiener Neustadt, 1966.
40. 10 May 1606: 'Maître Martin, son peintre, vient pour le peindre, le peint armé de son corselet . . . Il se fait donner des couleurs et un pinceau, imite le peintre mêlant ses couleurs, regarde parfois la besogne de son peintre. Il tenoit sa chienne Isabelle, la caressoit, la baisoit . . . il disoit à son peintre qu'il peignit sa chienne auprès de lui. Mˡˡᵉ Menier lui dit: "Monsieur, il ne faut pas que ceux qui sont armés aient des chiens avec eux;" il répond soudain: Mais ce sera pour prendre les ennemis pas les jambes' (Héroard, 1868 edn, I, p. 187). In Bronzino's portrait of Guidobaldo della Rovere, however, painted in 1532 (Pitti), the sitter wears armour and is accompanied by a large dog (Baccheschi, 1973, pl. VII).
41. Shearman, 1965, I, pp. 112–30.
42. See the portraits by or attributed to Franciabigio reproduced in Berenson, 1963, II, pls 1365–8.
43. . . . mi alma . . .

    entre tu mano, y la de Dios, perpleja,
    qual es el cuerpo en que ha de viuir duda

    ('Al mismo Griego en un retrato que hizo del Autor': reprinted in Cossío, 1908, p. 660).
44. S. Ringbom, *Icon to Narrative*, Åbo, 1965, p. 44. See, for example, Vermeyen's *Tournament at Toledo in 1539* (Drayton House: reproduced in G. Glück, 'Bildnisse aus dem Hause Habsburg, I. Kaiserin Isabella', *Jahrbuch der Kunsthistorischen Sammlungen in Wien*, N. F., VII (1933), pp. 183–210, p.

200); Siesenegger's *Sermon of the Papal Nuncio at Vienna in 1560*, dated 1561 (Harrach Collection: reproduced in Löcher, 1962, pl. 50); or the Netherlandish *Archduke Ferdinand's Journey to Brussels in 1555* (Schloss Ambras, KHM 5682: Scheicher, 1977, pl. 34).

45. Compare the *St Luke painting the Virgin* of 1487 by the Master of the Augustinian Altarpiece, Germanisches Nationalmuseum, Nuremberg (Gm 144, lent from the Bayerische Staatsgemäldesammlungen: *Germanisches Nationalmuseum, Führer durch die Sammlungen*, revised edn, Munich, 1985, p. 69).

46. 'Era vestito di nigro positivamente, con una beretta che chiamano gorra, con la spada et cappa. Quando entrassimo, Sua Maiestà era a sedere in una sedia di velluto negro, et subbito che Monsignore fu in camera, levòssi im piedi, appogiato ad un tavolino coperto di velluto parimente nero, sotto il baldacchino' ('Diario in relatione del viaggio di monsig^{r} Camillo Borghese auditore della Rev. Camera da Roma in Spagna mandatovi nuntio alla corte . . .', printed in A. Morel-Fatio, *L'Espagne au XVIe et au XVIIe siècle, Documents historiques et littéraires*, Paris and Madrid, 1878, pp. 161–93, p. 175).

Chapter 4 Settings, Clothes and Attributes

1. For example, in the *Portrait of a Lady* by a follower of Van der Weyden in the National Gallery, London (1433: Davies, 1972, pl. 108); in the 'Matheron' diptych of René of Anjou and his wife, attributed to Nicolas Froment, in the Louvre (R.F. 665: Sterling and Adhémar, 1965, pl. 106); or in the portraits of Philip the Handsome and Joanna the Mad attributed to Juan de Flandes at Vienna (3872, 3873: Demus, Klauner and Schütz, 1981, pp. 177–9).
2. Compare, for example the miniatures of Philip the Good enthroned in a manuscript of Martin Le Franc's *Champion des Dames* written at Arras in 1451 (Bibliothèque Nationale, MS fr. 12476, f. lv) and of Philip IV of France in the *Privileges of Ghent and Flanders* illuminated shortly after 1453 for Philip the Good (Österreichische Nationalbibliothek, cod. 2583, f. 174: reproduced in Pächt, Jenni and Thoss, 1983, fig. 44, pl. 34); and the drawing after a lost painting by a follower of the Master of Flémalle (Jacques Daret?) of the *Virgin and Child with Saints and Donors* (Louvre, Dessins, 20.669: exhibition catalogue Brussels, 1979, pp. 161–2 (25)).
3. Compare also the wing panels of *Philip VI(?) of France presented by St Hippolytus* and *Blanche of Navarre, Queen of France, and her daughter Jeanne presented by St Louis*, painted in about 1370 and once at St Denis, known from copies made for Gaignières (Bibliothèque Nationale, Estampes, Oa 11, ff. 90, 91: Sterling, 1987, pp. 204–5); or the miniature of *Philip the Good at Mass* in the *Traité sur l'oraison dominicale* (Bibliothèque Royale, Brussels, MS 9092, f. 9: L. M. J. Delaissé, *Miniatures médiévales de la librairie de Bourgogne*, Geneva, 1959, p. 173).
4. Berlin (West), Kupferstichkabinett, 75 D 5, description of the entry of Joanna the Mad into Brussels in 1496 (many of the miniatures reproduced in Herrmann, 1914, pls 60–76).
5. See also the late fifteenth-century Brussels(?) portrait of a man holding a book: exhibition catalogue *The Northern Renaissance*, Colnaghi, New York, 1983 (12), colour reproduction on the cover.
6. Compare the Netherlandish *Portrait of a Man* of c. 1450/60 in the National Gallery, London (2602: Davies, 1968, p. 146); the Spanish *Lady with the Pansies* of c. 1500 in the Louvre (INV. 9925: Sterling and Adhémar, 1965, pl. 146); or the *Francis I of France* attributed to Jean Clouet, also in the Louvre (INV. 3256: *ibid.*, pl. 171).
7. See the donor portrait in the *Diptych of Guillaume Sculteti*, apparently painted in 1482 for the church of St Nicholas in Brussels (Berlin, B84, B85: Bock, 1986, pl. 402); the Ferrarese *Sacrati Family* at Munich (see above, Chapter 3 n. 2); Bartolommeo Veneto's *Gentleman* of c. 1520 in the Galleria Nazionale, Rome (F.N. 610: A. L. Mayer, 'Zur Bildniskunst des Bartolommeo Veneto', *Pantheon*, II (1928), pp. 571–81, p. 577).
8. Panofsky, 1953, I, fig. 58.
9. Exhibition catalogue London, 1983, p. 16.
10. Compare the German portrait reproduced by Buchner, 1953, pl. 15, and Jan van Eyck's *Virgin of the Fountain*, dated 1439, at Antwerp (411: Vandenbroeck, 1985, pp. 174–6).
11. See above, p. 25.
12. Compare the *Virgin of the Firescreen* by a follower of the Master of Flémalle, the *Magdalen Reading* by Van der Weyden and the *St Ivo* from the workshop of Van der Weyden, all in the National Gallery, London (2609, 654, 6394: Davies, 1972, pls 160, 18, 75).
13. See also the *Smeralda Bandinelli* in the Victoria and Albert Museum, London (CAI.100: Lightbown, 1978, I, pl. 16).
14. Berlin, 338 A: Pope-Hennessy, 1966, p. 236.
15. See the portrait of a man attributed to Francesco Napoletano at Kansas City (61–63: F. R. Shapley, *Paintings from the Samuel H. Kress Collection, Italian Schools, XV – XVI Century*, London and New York, 1968, fig. 318).
16. See, for example, Dürer's *Oswolt Krel*, dated 1499, at Munich (WAF 230: Anzelewsky, 1980, p. 89); the portraits of Giovanni II Bentivoglio and his wife attributed to Ercole de'Roberti at Washington (1939.1. 219–220: Shapley, 1979, pls 288–9); or Bartolommeo Veneto's *Gentleman* also at Washington (1939.1.257: *ibid.*, pl. 17).
17. See the portraits of men sometimes attributed to the young Raphael at Munich (1059) and in the Getty Museum (78.PA. 364), reproduced in K. Oberhuber, *Raffaello*, Milan, 1982, p. 201.
18. Compare Cranach the Younger's portraits of Augustus, Elector of Saxony, and his wife (versions in the Historisches Museum, Dresden, and at Schloss Ambras, KHM 3252, 3141: Heinz and Schütz, 1976, pls 88–9).
19. M. Gregori, 'Giovan Battista Moroni' in G. A. dell'Acqua, ed., *I pittori bergamaschi dal XIII al XIX secolo, Il Cinquecento*, III, Bergamo, 1979, pp. 95–377, pp. 153, 162, 165, 328. One of these portraits, the full length of an unidentified man dated 1554 in the Ambrosiana, Milan (44), is inscribed 'IMPAVIDVM/FERIENT/RVINAE', from Horace, *Odes*, III, iii, 7: this may be roughly translated as 'The ruins leave him fearless' and the ruins are therefore contrasted with the endurance of the sitter (see also the exhibition catalogue by A. Braham, *Giovanni Battista Moroni*, National Gallery, London, 1978, p. 13).
20. Compare the portrait of Johann von Melem by a Frankfurt painter of c. 1495, where a convex mirror reflects the sitter's profile (Munich, WAF 718: Buchner, 1953, pl. 20). For Savoldo's so-called *'Gaston de Foix'* in the Louvre (INV. 659) see P. Hecht, 'The *paragone* debate: Ten Illustrations and a Comment', *Simiolus*, XIV (1984), pp. 125–36, p. 126.
21. For example, the *Jourdain de Blaye* tapestry in the Museo Civico at Padua (exhibition catalogue Paris, 1973–4, pp. 43–6 (5)) or the *'Don du Coeur'* in the Musée de Cluny, Paris (R.-A. d'Hulst, *Flemish Tapestries from the Fifteenth to the Eighteenth Century*, Brussels, 1967, pp. 25–32).
22. A Netherlandish example is the *John the Fearless, Duke of Burgundy*, a posthumous portrait perhaps of c. 1460, at Antwerp (540: Vandenbroeck, 1985, pp. 28–32).
23. Louvre, R.F. 2063: Davies, 1972, pls 49–53.
24. Piero della Francesca's portraits of Federico da Montefeltro, Duke of Urbino, and his wife were probably painted shortly before 1466 and are now in the Uffizi (1615: Pope-Hennessy, 1966, p. 160). For a portrait of a man attributed to the Master of the Life of the Virgin (Staatliche Kunsthalle, Karlsruhe, 139), see Buchner, 1953, pl. 9.
25. Compare the Florentine portrait of a lady inscribed NOLI ME TANGERE at Berlin (80: Berenson, 1963, II, pl. 945) and Leonardo's *Mona Lisa* in the Louvre (INV. 779: Pope-

Hennessy, 1966, p. 106), etc.

26. See the *Francis I of France* attributed to Jean Clouet in the Uffizi (987: Pope-Hennessy, 1966, p. 191) and the *Henry II of France* attributed to François Clouet at New York (45.128.12: Strong, 1969^{2}, p. 24).
27. Compare Lorenzo di Credi's *Venus* (Uffizi, 3094: Berti, 1979, p. 343), Cranach's *Venus and Cupid* of 1509 (Leningrad) and his *Venus* of 1532 (Frankfurt, 1125), who stands on a rocky globe (Schade, 1980, pls. 48, 149).
28. According to Francisco de Holanda: see Sánchez Cantón, 1921, pp. 277–8.
29. Victoria and Albert Museum, London, P 43–1921, P 144–1931, P 10–1978, all three attributed to Netherlandish artists and all three portraits of unidentified ladies. The talc overlays show an Eastern European, a Turkish and a nun's costume.
30. 'Talvolta anco si facevano ignudi per accennare che l'imperatore deve esser libero e mostrare apertamente quello che è a' popoli, e così che debbe essere riverito per la bontà sua e temuto per la giustizia che ministra' (G. P. Lomazzo, *Trattato dell'arte della pittura, scoltura et architettura*, Milan, 1584, reprinted in Barocchi, 1971–7, III, p. 2740).
31. Similar hammers are held by Philip the Good in the presentation miniature of the *Chroniques de Hainaut* (see above, Chapter 2 n. 100) and by Eustace, Count of Boulogne, in the miniature reproduced as pl. 206. For the limited information available on Francesco's life, see E. Kantorowicz, 'The Este Portrait by Roger van der Weyden', *Journal of the Warburg and Courtauld Institutes*, III (1939–40), pp. 165–80.
32. Presumably the vanity of the pursuits of gaming and hunting is being indicated: dice and hares are placed in close proximity in certain representations of Hell by Bosch, for example in the right wing of his triptych of the *Garden of Earthly Delights* in the Prado (2823).
33. The letter has often been printed, for example in Barocchi, 1971–7, III, pp. 2709–11, and by M. Campbell, 'Il ritratto del duca Alessandro de' Medici di Giorgio Vasari' in G. C. Garfagnini, ed., *Giorgio Vasari: Tra decorazione ambientale e storiografia artistica. Convegno di studi (Arezzo, 8–10 ottobre 1981)*, Istituto nazionale di studi sul rinascimento (Arezzo), Florence, 1985, pp. 339–61, pp. 360–1. The passages translated here are as follows: '... Sua Eccellenza ... mi diede il campo libero ch'io facessi una invenzione secondo il mio capriccio ... Ora eccovi qui sotto il significato del quadro: L'armi indosso bianche, lustranti sono quel medesimo che lo specchio del principe dovrebbe essere, tale che i suoi popoli potessino specchiarsi in lui nelle azzioni della vita ... E perché molti per l'oscurità della cosa non l'intenderebbono, uno amico mio e servitore loro ha stretto in questi pochi versi quel ch'io vi ho detto ...'
34. Barocchi, 1971–7, III, pp. 2707–9; the portrait is exhibited in the Uffizi (1578: Langedijk, 1981–3, II, pp. 1144–6).
35. Exhibition catalogue New York, 1985, pp. 241–2 (153) and references.
36. On carnation symbolism, see I. Bergström, *Den symboliska Nejlikan*, Malmö, 1958.
37. See the anonymous treatise printed with Sicily herald's *Le blason des Couleurs en Armes/Liurees et Deuises*, Paris, 1507, e.g., f. xli, on 'lhabit moral' for a man: 'Le chapeau doibt estre de couleur p[er]se q̃ demonstre sciẽce: en signe q̃ sciẽce viẽt de dieu q̃ est au ciel'.
38. The relevant passage from Angelo Decembrio, *De Politia Litteraria*, is reprinted in W. L. Gundersheimer, *Ferrara: The Style of a Renaissance Despotism*, Princeton, 1973, pp. 106–7.
39. Castiglione-Hoby, 1928 edn, p. 67.
40. 'cirotecatus enim incessit diutius, ut manus soli subtractus emolliret ad diuitis usum' (John of Salisbury, *Policraticus*, ed. C. C. I. Webb, 2 vols, Oxford, 1909, I, p. 505).
41. *Horloge de Sapience*, Bibliothèque Royale, Brussels, MS IV 111, 'Declaration des hystoires', f. 5v: 'Oyseuse est jouvencelle qui ne veult que jouer et perdre son temps et ce demonstre elle qui tient sa main en son sain et de l'autre se joue a son gan' (P. R. Monks, 'Reading Fifteenth Century Miniatures: The Experience of the "Horloge de Sapience"', *Scriptorium*, XL (1986), pp. 242–8, pp. 246–7).
42. Aliénor de Poitiers, *Les honneurs de la cour*: 'en grand deuil, comme de marit ou de pere, on ne soloit porter ny verge [bague] ny gants ez mains' (La Curne de Sainte-Palaye, 1759, p. 255).
43. Nichols, 1850, pp. 78–9.
44. Several versions are known: that at Dresden (221) is reproduced in Berenson, 1957, II, pl. 695.
45. Flies appear, for example, on the backgrounds of versions of Van der Weyden's *Philip the Good without Headgear* (e.g., Palacio Real, Madrid: Friedländer, 1967–76, II, pl. 127); in Petrus Christus's *Carthusian Monk* at New York (49.7.19: *ibid.*, I, pl. 74); in Sebastiano's *Cardinal Bandinelli Saulli with Three Companions* in Washington (1961.9.37: Pope-Hennessy, 1966, p. 124); and in Sánchez Coello's *Joanna of Austria* at Schloss Ambras (KHM 3127: Heinz and Schütz, 1976, pl. 114). On flies and decay, see Bergström, 1960; S. Ringbom, 'Nuptial Symbolism in some Fifteenth-Century Reflections of Roman Sepulchral Portraiture', *Temenos*, II (1966), pp. 68 ff. For Vasari's anecdote of Giotto, who is said to have painted a fly on the nose of a head by Cimabue, see Vasari-Milanesi, 1878–85, I, p. 408.
46. 'on voit un excellent peintre qui, après avoir faict le portraict d'une fort belle et agréable dame, luy appose auprès d'elle, ou quelque vieille, ou quelque esclave more, ou quelque nain très laid, afin que leur laideur et noirceur donne plus de lustre et de candeur à ceste grand beauté et blancheur' (Brantôme, 1864–82 edn, II, p. 414).
47. Panofsky, 1934, *passim*; Panofsky, 1953, pp. 201–3; Dhanens, 1980, pp. 193–205.
48. For the texts of the relevant documents, see M. Davies, *Les primitifs flamands, I: Corpus ..., 3, The National Gallery, London*, 2 vols, Antwerp, 1953–4, II, pp. 125–7.
49. Dresden, 799: *Virgin and Child with Saints Michael and Catherine and a Donor* (Dhanens, 1980, pp. 247, 249).
50. See for example the miniature of Charles VI of France and Pierre Salmon by the Boucicaut Master (Bibliothèque publique et universitaire, Geneva, MS fr. 165, f. 4: Panofsky, 1953, pl. 32) or the miniature of Jean Miélot presenting his book to Philip the Good of Burgundy in his *Traité sur l'oraison dominicale* (Bibliothèque Royale, Brussels, MS 9092, f. 1: exhibition catalogue *La miniature flamande*, Palais des beaux-arts, Brussels, 1959, pl. 37).
51. L. Bril and E. Lejour, 'Les oranges dans nos provinces au XIVe et au XVe siècles', *Archives, bibliothèques et musées de Belgique*, XXVI (1955), pp. 56–9.
52. Panofsky, 1934, p. 124.
53. '*Mabuse* heeft onder ander oock gheschildert een Mary-beeldt/terwijlen hy was in dienst van den *Marquijs* van der Veren/wesende de tronie ghedaen nae de Huysvrouw van den *Marquijs*, en t' kindeken quam nae haer kindt ...' (Van Mander, 1604, f. 225v). For five of the known versions of the picture, see Friedländer, 1967–76, VIII, pl. 37. The child was probably their third and youngest son Hendrik, born on 26 September 1519 (J. Ermerins, *Eenige Zeeuwsche oudheden*, III, ii, Middelburg, 1786, p. 39).
54. Langedijk, 1981–3, I, pp. 675–6; V. Branca, ed., *Tutte le opere di Giovanni Boccaccio*, X: *De mulieribus claris*, ed. V. Zaccaria, Milan, 1967, pp. 326–31.
55. Thümmel, 1980, *passim*. The two panels are at Vienna (832, 6411) and in a private collection.
56. Munich, 3511: reproduced and discussed in the exhibition catalogue Munich, 1980, II, pp. 96–7 (138) and col. pl. III.
57. Schloss Ambras, KHM 2516: Heinz and Schütz, 1976, pl. 124.

Chapter 5 The Sitters

1. The most striking example is perhaps Philip the Good, Duke of Burgundy, who had a magnificent wardrobe but who appears in his two most copied portraits relatively simply dressed in black and without much jewellery (Friedländer, 1967–76, II, pl. 127).

2. When in 1666 Samuel Pepys sat to John Hayls, he hired 'an Indian gown' (R. Latham and W. Matthews, eds, *The Diary of Samuel Pepys*, VII: *1666*, London, 1972, p. 85).
3. In November 1639, the Countess of Sussex wrote: 'Put Sr Vandyke in remembrance to do my pictuer wel. I have sene sables with the clasp of them set with dimons – if thos that i am pictuerde in wher don so i think it would look very will in the pictuer'. In January 1640, she noted that Van Dyck's portrait was 'to rich in ihuels i am suer, but it tis no great mater for another age to thinke me richer then i was' (F. P. and M. M. Verney, *Memoirs of the Verney Family during the Seventeenth Century*, 2nd edn, 2 vols, London, 1907, I, p. 155).
4. Héroard, 1868 edn, I, pp. 18, 19, 21, 30, 44, 64, 71, 79, 89–90, 91, 119, 120, 187, 206, 235–6, 262.
5. Schade, 1980, p. 449.
6. Osborn, 1961, pp. 305–6.
7. Van Mander, 1604, ff. 244v–245.
8. Titian's portrait is now in Vienna (81: Wethey, 1971, pp. 141–2, pls 206–7). For Titian's opinion of Strada, given when the portrait was being painted, see Niccolo Stoppio's letter of 29 February 1568 to Johann Jacob Fugger: '"Il Strada è uno delli solenni ignoranti que si possa trovare; lui non sa niente ma bisogna haver ventura et sapersi accomodare alle nature delle persone, come ha fatto il Strada in Alemagna, dove caccia tante carotte a quelli Todeschi quanto si può imaginare et loro, come reali di natura, non conoscono la dopiezza di questo galanthuomo." Queste furono le parole di messer Titiano . . .' (Zimmermann, 1901, p. 850; translated in Hope, 1980, p. 160).
9. Dumq; diem, & uarios alternat inepta paratus,
   Quod cupit, in longas protrahit usq; moras

   (*Strozii poetae pater et filius*, Venice, 1513, Eroticon, f. 55; translated in Gilbert, 1980, pp. 187–8).
10. Isabella to Leonardo, Mantua, 14 May 1504: 'quando fusti in questa terra et che ne retrasti de carbono, ne promettesti farni ogni mo' una volta di colore. Ma perchè questo seria quasi impossibile non havendo vui comodità di transferirvi in quà vi pregamo che . . . voliati convertire el retratto nostro in un' altra figura . . .' (Luzio, 1887, p. 34).
11. Luzio, 1913, pp. 210–13, 222–3; see also below, pp. 185–90.
12. Castiglione-Hoby, 1928 edn, p. 66.
13. *Ibid.*, p. 39.
14. 'no sé cuál es la razón porque quiriendo ellas perecer hermosas van a arrancar y sacar de sí aquella parte en que consiste la mayor parte de su hermosura y gracia' (Sánchez Cantón, 1921, p. 267).
15. On 3 June 1419, the Ghent authorities contracted with Willem van Axpoele and Jan Martins who were to complete and restore a series of portraits of the Counts of Flanders (see above, Chapter 2 pp. 41–2 and n. 6). Monique Kornell has kindly sent me a transcript of a document that she discovered in Florence (Archivio di Stato, Notarile Antecosimiano A 224, 1550–1553, f. 330v) and that records that on 18 August 1553 the painter Carlo Portelli received from Francesco Buoninsegni the sum of 4 *scudi*, being the residue of 15 *scudi* owed to him in payment for a portrait of Faustina Baglioni, wife of the late Carlo Orsini. This had been commissioned in May 1552, was painted on canvas, measured $2\frac{1}{4} \times 1\frac{1}{2}$ *braccia*, showed the sitter to the knees and had in the background 'ornaments and supports' ('Quam imaginem seu effigiem tenus genibus prefatus Franciscus de Boninsegnis effingi et fieri fecit a dicto Carolo pictore pro se ipso Francisco de Mense Maii MDLII, ea ad huc vivente, et ipsam fecit pingi in tela longitudinis brachiorum circiter duorum et $\frac{1}{4}$, et latitudinis brachii unius cum dimidio, cum suis ornamentis et fulcimentis in spacio et [ut] vulgariter dicitur nel campo ipsius picture'). It is possible that the original contract is here being paraphrased.
16. 'Ha dipinto quasi di tutte le sorti pitture a fresco, a olio, ritratti di naturale, e ad ogni pregio . . .' (Vasari-Milanesi, 1878–85, VI, p. 588).
17. Pourbus to the Duke of Mantua, Paris, 20 January 1610: 'per un retratto senza mani ne ho 20 pistole, et da piccolini 10 senza che io ne faccia il prezzo, ma solo per la differenza che fanno di mia mano a quelle di tutti gli altri pittori di Francia . . .' (Baschet, 1868, p. 454 n.).
18. Innes, 1855, p. 440.
19. See particularly his account of 1535, Kreyczi, 1887, pp. CXV–CXVII.
20. Letter of 10 August 1580 to Catherine of Küstrin, afterwards Electress of Brandenburg (J. C. W. Moehsen, *Beiträge zur Geschichte der Wissenschaften in der Mark Brandenburg*, Berlin and Leipzig, 1783, p. 112).
21. The drawings are in the Bayerisches Hauptstaatsarchiv: exhibition catalogue Munich, 1980, II, pp. 98–9 (142).
22. 'In Treviso./Adì . . . zenar del 45, die dar el signor Tomaso Costanzo per un suo retrato grande quanto/el natural armato a tute arme et su una tavolo el saio d'armar et l'elmeto senza/altro de sotto la guarda de l'arnese in suso, et il mercato disse suo signoria darmi scuti/10; et perché jo dissi che eran pochi denarj, pur jo lo volevo servir con speranza/che ultra li scuti 10 alfine me usasse cortesia.

    In Venetia./Adì . . . otobre del 48. Noto jo Lorenzo Lotto como in questi dì io scrissi al signor Thomaso che/sua signoria già tanto tempo aspetato che 'l me satisfacesse la mercede mia ut supra, et/che 'l levase el suo quadro quale era in Treviso . . . /qual signor Thomaso sempre mi dete bone parole . . . li scrissi per venir a capo . . . disse . . . che el mi respondea resoluto che al quadro/lui mi renonciava et insema quelli denari che jo havea havuto da suo signoria . . . perché el quadro non se li somigliava né se conosea per sua efige,/et la sua letera tengo apresso a mi per tal discortesia . . . tal opera non è vendarescha, pacienza ne le mano del Signor Dio . . .' (Zampetti, 1969, pp. 174–6, 230–1).
23. Undated letter, George Frederick to Cranach: 'Was dan die vbrigen drej kleinen Stucklein anlangt, di weill dieselben vnserer f Gemahlin nicht fast ehnlich oder gleich sehen, thun Wir Sie Dir hineben wieder hin senden, do du aber dieselben nochmals dermaszen verbessern würdest, das sie Ihrer fstl. Gn. gleich sehen, wollen wir solche stucklein alsdan auch behalten vnd zahlen . . .' (C. von Bardeleben, 'Zwei bisher unbekannte Briefe von Lucas Cranach dem Jüngeren aus dem Jahre 1579', *Repertorium für Kunstwissenschaft*, XXXII (1909), pp. 260–5, p. 265). For Cranach's bill, see *ibid.*, p. 263.
24. 'Eens had hy gheconterfeyt eenen Enghels Capiteyn/*Pieter Andries*, een groot brageerder/die t' conterfeytsel hẽ liet houden sonder betalen: waerom *Iaques* uyt onverdult maeckte met Water-verwe voor de tronie een tralie/dat het scheen dat den Capiteyn sat in vangnis/en steldet ten tooon. Dẽ Capiteyn dit verhoorende/quam vragẽ wat hy voor een stuck rabbauts was/sulcx te doen. Hy antwoorde/dat hy dus most ghevangen sitten/tot dat hy betalen soude. Den Capiteyn heeft t' gelt gegheven/en woudet sien uytdoen. Den anderen nam een spongie/en wischtet uyt' (Van Mander, 1604, f. 228v). Pieter Andries or Peter Andrews was apparently the captain of a company of English sappers serving in the Low Countries during the 1550s (R. Tyler, *Letters, Despatches and State Papers, relating to the Negotiations between England and Spain . . .*, XIII, London, 1954, pp. 378, 395). See also J. G. van Gelder, 'Nieuw werk van Jacob de Punder (Jacques de Poindre)', *Oud Holland*, LIX (1942), pp. 129–33.
25. Catherine to M. d'Humières, 4 May 1547: 'Je vous prye . . . de me faire paindre tous mes enffans; mais que ce soit d'un autre cousté que le painctre n'a accoustumé de les paindre et portraire . . .' (Moreau-Nélaton, 1901, pp. 14–15).
26. Philip II to Mary of Hungary, Augsburg, 16 May 1551: 'Con ésta van los retratos de Ticiano . . . Al mio armado se le parece bien la priesa con que le ha hecho y si hubiera mas tiempo yo se le hiciera tornar hazer' (Ferrarino, 1975, p. 29).
27. Hilliard, 1981 edn, p. 86.

28. Pagni to Riccio, Pisa, 21 October 1549: 'Queste Ecc.e si contentano per commodità del Bronzino, et per più celere speditione de' ritratti che desidera di loro Mons. R.mo d'Aras, che il vestimento della Duchessa non si facci di broccato riccio, ma di qualche altro drappo ornato che facci bella mostra' (G. Pieraccini, *La stirpe de' Medici di Cafaggiolo*, 3 vols, Florence, 1924–5, II, p. 56).
29. Paolo Mario to Gian Giacomo Leonardi, Fossombrone, 8 February 1547: 'si manda a V.S. una sottana di la S.ra Duchessa, accio che per sua parte la dia a Titiano, al quale potrà dire, che si saria data una di più importanza, se egli non hauesse adimandata una di ueluto cremesi o di rosato, de' quali non hauendo S.E. ha pensato, che questa di damasco del medesimo colore sia segondo il suo intento' (Gronau, 1936, p. 98).
30. Sánchez Cantón, 1921, pp. 261–2, 257–9; see also pp. 178, 180.
31. Account of 4 May 1532: 'Supplie ledict maistre Bernart a madame que de sa grace il luy plaise pardessus ladicte somme donner et octroyer a icelluy maistre Bernart une gracieuse recompense et gratuité, pour ses peines et labeurs, d'avoir allé, venu et retourné plusieurs journées a court et devers elle, pour au vray prendre les vrayes semblances desdictes figures. En quoy il a emploié grant temps, lequel il eust peu employer en sa maison, en plusieurs autres ouvraiges, dont il eust peu avoir grant prouffit et avantaige. Et quant a ce, il s'en remect en la bonne grace de Madame dessusdite' (Steppe, 1969, pp. 480–1).
32. Innes, 1855, p. 440.
33. Vasari-Milanesi, 1878–85, VII, p. 601.
34. On Gonsalvus, his family and their portraits, see M. Bartels, 'Ueber abnorme Behaarung beim Menschen (Zweiter Aufsatz)', *Zeitschrift für Ethnologie, Organ der Berliner Gesellschaft für Anthropologie, Ethnologie und Urgeschichte*, XI (1879), pp. 145–94, pp. 150–77, 193, pls VI–VII; Kenner, 1894, pp. 250–3. Archduke Charles to his father-in-law William V of Bavaria, 11 March 1583: 'ich bedanck mich gegen E.G. zum höchsten von wegen des eben stuckten tafelein mit des rauhen mann sambt weib und kinden abcontrafehung' (Vignau-Wilberg, 1985, p. 143 n. 194).
35. 'hîc Basileae vidi, Anno 1583, & depingendos curavi' (F. Platerus, *Observationum libri tres*, Basle, 1680, p. 573).

Chapter 6 The Painters

1. Galeazzo Maria Sforza to Leonardo Botta, 9 March 1476: 'Essendo morto magistro Zannetto nostro pictore, quale retraseva dal naturale in singulare perfectione, havemo pure volunta de havere uno altro che in simile artificio ne satisfaxa. Et pero havendone portato lo Ill.° Duca de Bari nostro fratello una figura cavata dal naturale per uno pictore ceciliano, quale stanzia in quella città, quale molto ne è piaciuto, volemo che ... li persuaderete ... che voglia venire da noi con tucte sue cose ...' (L. Beltrami, 'Antonello da Messina', *Archivio storico dell' arte*, VII (1894), pp. 56–7).
2. Isabella d'Este to the Countess of Acerra, 3 April 1493: 'sapendo cum quanta difficulta se ritrovano pictori che perfectamente contrafaciano el vulto naturale ...' (Luzio, 1913, p. 188).
3. Antoinette, Duchess of Guise, to Mary of Guise, Queen of Scots, 10 June 1539: 'Je suis apres pour le vous faire tirer de sa grandeur en toile mais je ne trouves point bien ouvrier a mon gre ...' (Wood, 1923, p. 27).
4. Antonio Maria Salviati to Tolomeo Galli, Paris, 15 February 1573: 'Che siano totalmente naturali, sarà difficile, perché in Francia si sa tanto poco del ritrarre del naturale, che non ci si vede quasi mai ritratto che habbia garbo ...' (Hurtubise, 1975, I, p. 414).
5. Schade, 1980, p. 451.
6. Malaguzzi Valeri, 1902, p. 126.
7. Bianca Maria, Duchess of Milan, to Philip the Good, Duke of Burgundy, 26 December 1460: 'Habemus ibi adolescentem nomine Zanetum et hic quidem presentium est ad dominationem Vestram exhibitor, singularis Ingenij circa depingendi artem in qua summe prevalet et adeo eidem arti deditus est, ut audita fama Magistri Gulielmi [*recte* Rogerii] ... qui artis illius pre ceteris optimam cognitionem habere predicatur obtenta a nobis licentia instituerit illum adire dediscendi aliquid ab eo gratia ...' (*ibid.*, pp. 126–7).
8. Prospero da Camogli to Cicco Simonetta, Brussels, March 1461: 'Magistro Johanetto hé corso a grande fatica cum Magistro Rogero, pictore nobilissimo, et hé stato necessaria la intercession de Monsignor lo Dalphino. Tamen per uno anno se gli hé promisso ducati L.ta per lo viver suo et non debe bever vino questo anno, et cossì ha promisso Magistro Iohannetto' (P. M. Kendall and V. Ilardi, eds, *Dispatches with Related Documents of Milanese Ambassadors in France and Burgundy, 1450–1483*, II, Athens (Ohio), 1971, p. 201).
9. Malaguzzi Valeri, 1902, p. 127.
10. *Ibid.*, pp. 128–36.
11. See above, note 1.
12. Niccolo Roberti to Paulo Antonio Troto, 27 July 1477: 'Quello de la Illustrissima .M.a Anna hancora non e fornito e questa e sta per Manchamento del Magistro che e Franzoso che si e sdignato e ricussava volerlo liverarlo ... pur epso e reconceliato e va dreto liverandolo ...' (Venturi, 1885[1], p. 227).
13. 'Intanto, essendo portata da un Fiamingo in Milano una testa d'un giovane ritratta di naturale e dipinta a olio, la quale era da ognuno in quella città ammirata, nel vederla Giovan Francesco se ne rise ... ritrasse un gentiluomo vecchio e raso con un sparviere in mano; ma ancora che molto somigliasse, fu giudicata migliore la testa del Fiamingo' (Vasari-Milanesi, 1878–85, V, p. 282). On the competition and on Caroto as a portraitist, see S. Béguin, *Andrea Solario en France* (*Les dossiers du Département des Peintures*, 31), Paris, 1985, pp. 39–42.
14. Beck, 1974; for the identification of Luigi Fiammingo as Louis van Oort, see Simon, 1982, p. 58 n. 1; for Van Oort's career in Antwerp, see P. Rombouts and T. van Lerius, *Les Liggeren et autres archives historiques de la gilde anversoise de Saint Luc*, I, Antwerp and The Hague, 1864–76, pp. 171, 178, 188.
15. On Bahuet, see V. Pagani, 'Notes on a Flemish Portraitist at the Court of Vincenzo Gonzaga: Giannino Bahuet (c. 1552–1597)', *Burlington Magazine*, CXXIX (1987), pp. 110–15; for Pourbus at Mantua, see Baschet, 1868; Luzio, 1913, pp. 275–8. Jan Kraeck, from Haarlem, worked at the Savoyard court from 1568 until 1607 and was known there as Giovanni Carracha (exhibition catalogue Turin, 1963, II, Pittura, pp. 45–7).
16. O. de la Marche, 'L'estat de la maison du duc Charles de Bourgoingne ... : Le duc a bien quarante varletz de chambre ... Les paintres font les cottes d'armes, banieres et estandars ...' (H. Beaune and J. d'Arbaumont, eds, *Mémories d'Olivier de la Marche*, IV (Société de l'histoire de France), Paris, 1888, p. 18).
17. Philip the Good to the officials of the Chambre des Comptes at Lille, Dijon, 12 March 1435 (W. H. J. Weale, *Hubert and John van Eyck*, London, 1908, pp. xlii–xliii).
18. L. Campbell, 'L'art du portrait dans l'oeuvre de Van der Weyden' in the exhibition catalogue Brussels, 1979, pp. 56–67, p. 63.
19. On Van Orley, see A. Wauters, *Bernard van Orley*, Paris, s.d.; on Vermeyen, see Pinchart, 1856, pp. 135–8; Houdoy, 1872, pp. 516–18.
20. Ludovico, Marquis of Mantua, to Zaccaria Saggi, 30 November 1475: 'Et è vero che Andrea è bon maestro in le altre cose, ma nel retrare porìa havere più gratia et non fa cussì bene ...' (Signorini, 1974, p. 232).
21. Isabella d'Este to Jacopo d'Atri, January 1493: 'Per satisfare a la ill.ma M.na Contessa de la Cerra ... havemo ordinato de esser retrata in tavola per mane de Andrea Mantinea ...'; Isabella to the Countess of Acerra, 20 April 1493: 'Dolne summamente che non gli potiamo mandare al presente el nostro retracto, perchè el Pictore ne ha tanto mal facta che non ha alcuna de le nostre simiglie: havemo mandato per un forestere, qual ha

fama de contrafare bene el naturale' (Luzio, 1913, pp. 188–9).

22. 'nè prima nè poi di nessuno fece il ritratto, perchè aboriva il fare somigliare il vivo, se non era d'infinita bellezza' (Vasari-Milanesi, 1878–85, VII, p. 272).
23. 'Nè de' ritratti fatti da me, che pur sono assai, farò menzione alcuna, chè sarebbe cosa tediosa; e per dire il vero, me ne sono difeso, quanto ho potuto, di farne' (*ibid.*, VII, p. 688).
24. 'essendo stato in fin dalla sua giovanezza molto inclinato a ritrarre di naturale, ha voluto che questa sia stata sua principale professione . . . Costui, da giovanetto, disegnava tanto bene, che diede speranza, se avesse seguitato, di farsi eccellentissimo, e saria stato veramente; ma, come ho detto, si voltò a quello a che si sentiva da natura inclinato: nondimeno non si possono le cose sue se non lodare' (*ibid.*, VII, p. 576).
25. 'Girolamo da Ferrara era più atto a' ritratti ed a cose appartate, che a storie terribili, dove bisognasse la forza dell'arte e del disegno' (*ibid.*, V, p. 118).
26. 'soo dat den meesten deel/door het aensoeten des ghewins/oft om hun mede t'onderhouden/desen sijd-wegh der Consten (te weten/het conterfeyten nae t'leven) veel al instaen/en henẽ reysen/sonder tijt oft lust te hebbẽ/den History en beelde-wegh/ter hooghster volcomenheyt leydende/te soecken/oft na te spooren: waer door menigen fraeyen edelen geest gelijck vruchtloos/en uytgeblust/tot een jammer der Consten/ moet blijven' (Van Mander, 1604, f. 281; translated in Stechow, 1966, p. 56).
27. M. de Limoges to Catherine de' Medici, 9 February 1560: 'Je l'ai trouvée passant le temps en ung brouillas de portrait qu'elle a faict devant moi aussi promptement qu'elle a bon esprit. Estant incroyable comme, ayant quelque peu apprins d'une de ses dames italiennes que le roy luy a donnée, elle a proufité en la paincture . . . M'ayant commandé de vous suplier par le premier lui adresser des crayons de toutes couleurs et bien faicts, qu'elle sçayt que Jannet sçaura luy préparer dextrement' (Amezua y Mayo, 1949, I, p. 261 n. 108).
28. Girolamo Negri to 'Duke William', Toledo, 18 February 1561: 'ella ha cominciato a depingere, e dice la Sofonisba Cremonense, che è quella che le insegna, . . . que ritra con un carbone in maniera che si conosce subito la persone che ha ritratta' (*ibid.*, I, p. 262).
29. Elisabeth to the Cardinal, Toledo, March 1561: 'Je vous envoie la peinture d'une dame de se païs: je ne say si vous la connoitrés' (*ibid.*, III, p. 24).
30. Madame de Vineux to Catherine de' Medici, Toledo, 30 September 1561: 'elle pasoit son temps la plus part a paindre, a quoi elle prand grand plaisir, de sorte que ie panse devant que soit un an quelle en sera si bonne mestresse que celle mesme qui laprant, qui est des meilleures du monde' (*ibid.*, III, pp. 168–9).
31. 9 January 1609: 'il copie en huile le portrait du Roi qui étoit devant lui; il étoit fort reconnoissable' (Héroard, 1868 edn, I, pp. 377–8).
32. Longnon, 1895–9, II, pp. 320–67; Sterling, 1983, p. 181.
33. R. Tyler, ed., *Letters, Despatches and State Papers, relating to the Negotiations between England and Spain*, X, London, 1914, p. 171 (Simon Renard to Charles V, Poissy, 1 September 1550).
34. M. Soenen, 'Chartreuse de Scheut, à Anderlecht' in *Monasticon belge*, IV: *Province de Brabant*, 6 vols, Liège, 1964–72, VI, pp. 1385–1427, p. 1407.
35. 'In 't Iaer 1599. quam hem in den sin eenẽ lust/te schilderen sonder Pinceelen metter handt . . . Het eerste dat hy dede/was zijn eyghen Conterfeytsel . . . Nu dat noch vreemder is/A.° 1600. werdt hem voor te comen te schilderen sonder handen/met zijn voeten . . .' (Van Mander, 1604, f. 278).
36. Mantuan chancery to Manerbio, Mantuan ambassador at the imperial court, 16 May 1602: 'Intanto V.S. iscuserà la tardanza perchè questo pittore di S.A. è assai humorista et non se ne può cavar construtto se non quando gli piace di lavorare, fingendo hora d'essere amalato, hora qualch'altro impedimento, il che tutto gli viene sopportato per l'eccellenza del suo valore' (Luzio, 1913, p. 275).
37. 'sa maniere de vivre et de parler y attiroit plus de gens que ses ouvrages . . . prenant Pamphile par les espaules, il le jetta dehors en l'appellant *bourguemestre de Sodome*, et luy osta son livre' (Tallemant des Rieux, 1862 ed., III, pp. 139, 143).
38. Galeazzo Maria Sforza to Borso d'Este, 5 June 1469: ' . . . havendo nuy caro esso Baldesarre si per essere luy acconza persona et da bene, si anche perchè vale molto nel mestiere suo, nel che in molte cose nha satisfacto benissimo et hanne riportato commendatione assay' (Motta, 1889, p. 405).
39. Same to same, 7 October 1469: 'Ne congratulamo con la Ex.^{tia} V.^{ra} de la fraternità tandem retrovata con M.^{ro} Baldesaro da Regio, la quale como prudentemente V.S. ne scrive gli pò meritamente piacere per essere persona virtuosa et de bono ingegno et arte dotata . . .' (*ibid.*, p. 406).
40. Baldassare to the duke, 3 November 1493: 'El vostro Servjtore Baldassare da Est schiavo deli vostri schiavi' (Campori, 1885, p. 597; Venturi, 1889, p. 382). In a document of 1489, he was described as 'Baldassare estensi filio condam Illustrissimi d. domini Nicolai estensis Marchionis ut asseruit' (A. Venturi, 'Di chi fosse figlio il pittore Baldassare d'Este?', *Archivio storico dell'arte*, I (1888), pp. 42–3). On his parentage, see also V. Nironi, 'Contributo alla biografia del pittore Baldassarre da Reggio', *Nuove lettere emiliane*, III (1963), pp. 33–6.
41. '. . . è di gentilissimi costumi e molto amato . . .' (Vasari-Milanesi, 1878–85, VII, p. 586).
42. See the letter cited above, Chapter I n. 46.
43. Giovanni della Casa to Cardinal Alessandro Farnese, 10 November 1548: 'Ms. Titiano è stato lungo tempo con S.M. Ces. per ritrarla, et mostra di haver hauto tanto gran commodità di ragionar dipingendo etc. Et referisce in somma, che S.M. sta bene della persona ma pensoso e melanconico fuor di modo . . .' (Campana, 1908, p. 387).
44. Leone Leoni to Ferrante Gonzaga, 29 June 1549: '. . . soventi volte Sua M.^{tà} sta due hore et tre ragionando con meco et con pompeo mio . . .' (Campori, 1855, pp. 286–7).
45. G. Parker, *Philip II*, London, 1979, p. 7.
46. '. . . en soo vry werdt/dat den Coningh eens hem met de handt op de schouderen clopte/ en *Moro* hem uyt voerde weder den maelstock op de schouder leyde/t'welck een sorghlijck doen was: want het schricklijck is den Leeuwen aen te roeren' (Van Mander, 1604, f. 231).
47. Galeazzo Maria Sforza to Bianca Maria Visconti, 6 March 1468: '. . . in questo giorno e retornato dicto maestro Zannecto el quale habiandomi portata la figura de la predicta che me pare non solo bella ma bellissima . . .' (M. Caffi, 'Creditori della duchessa Bianca Maria Sforza', *Archivio storico lombardo*, III (1876), pp. 534–42, p. 538; Malaguzzi Valeri, 1902, p. 128); Bianca Maria to Galeazzo Maria, 8 March 1468: 'Havemo ricevuto la vostra lettera, qualle ne ha portato maestro Zaneto, concernendo el retrato de la illustrissima madona Bona vostra mogliere' (Caffi, *op. cit.*, p. 538).
48. Guido de Paratis to Galeazzo Maria, Genoa, 28 June 1468: 'Della pinctura de Magistro Zanneto vostra signoria ne po fare un presente, perchè non attinge a questa viva e mostra più tempo assai cha questa' (C. Magenta, *I Visconti e gli Sforza nel Castello di Pavia*, 2 vols, Milan, 1883, II, p. 315).
49. 'Fué su casa frecuentada de los mayores personajes de su tiempo . . . de tal manera, que muchos dias, los caballos, literas, coches y sillas, ocuparon dos grandes patios de su casa . . .' (Pacheco, 1866 edn, I, pp. 126–7; translated in Mulcahy, 1984, p. 775).
50. 'König Christian von Dänemark ist kommen gegen Wittenbergk bei Maler mit dem Namen Lucas Cranach zew hawsz gewest' (extract from a chronicle published in M. B. Lindau, *Lucas Cranach*, Leipzig, 1883, p. 158 n. 1).
51. Hilliard, 1981 edn, pp. 74, 72.
52. 'Hans unam ex tribus imaginibus complevit; et propter temporis frigiditatem et intemperiem, propter quas colores excutari, seu

affimari, non potuerunt, citius eandem explere non potuit; licet ad id exactam diligentiam adhibuerit. Hic incipit expedire alias duas, quas auxiliante Domino brevius et citius expedierit; cumque frigus cessavit et omnia necessaria opportunius habebuntur . . .' (G. Williams, ed., *Official Correspondence of Thomas Bekynton* (*Rerum Britannicarum Medii Aevi Scriptores*), 2 vols, London, 1872, II, p. 243); translated in Nicolas, 1828, p. 94.

53. Letter written at Cornogiovine: 'Recevute queste andaraij ad Pavia et porterai con te le cosse necessarie ad ritrare persone del naturale et expecterai la nostra venuta . . .' (Malaguzzi Valeri, 1902, p. 130).
54. Francesco Vettori to Goro Gheri, undated: 'Io quando andai in alvernia harei volentieri menato uno di questi discepoli di Lionardo da Vinci che e qui ma domandono le centinaia di ducati et io conosco la Ex.tia del Duca havere tanto spese in questo mariaggio che non liono' vorrei aggiungere davantaggio pure si troverro chi vi voglia andare per prezzo conveniente . . . et quando Madama sara in corte sara facile a farla ritrarre bene et mandarla a Madama Ill.ma' (Langedijk, 1981–3, II, p. 1215).
55. 'cuando mi padre en Toledo sacaba al natural a César, el Emperador Carlos V, estando la mesa un poco baja y queriéndola mi padre más alta, dijo el Emperador a mi padre, por no llamar a alguno que los inquietase, que tuviese él las tablas de la mesa y que él alzaría más los bancos y acortaría las correas. Y ansí, su Majestad por sus manos alzó los bancos de la mesa, y con su mesma daga hizo los agujeros en las correas' (Sánchez Cantón, 1921, p. 257).
56. Hilliard, 1981 edn, p. 86.
57. *Ibid.*, p. 72.
58. Baldassare to the duke, 29 April 1502: 'me vergogno a domandare questa Elemosina' (Campori, 1885, p. 599; Venturi, 1889, p. 387 n. 1).
59. Ulisse Aleotti, 'Pro insigni certamine', published by Campori, 1885, p. 591; M. Baxandall, 'A Dialogue on Art from the Court of Leonello d'Este', *Journal of the Warburg and Courtauld Institutes*, XXVI (1963), pp. 304–26, pp. 314–15.
60. He was described on his tombstone as 'pictor celerrimus'.
61. 'wir haben dir vngeferlich vor dreyen Jaren befolen, vns . . . vnsere freundliche liebe Gemahel abzucontrafeiten, welche Contrafactur wir bisher noch nit gesehen adder bekommen. Begeren derhalben, dasz du vns solch gemalt Contrafeit Bilde (woe es anders nit albereidt gemolet) dweile du die Besoldung albereidt empfangen. Nochmale verfertigest vnd vns forderlich tegen Freibergk zu schicken . . .' (Lindau, *op. cit.*, pp. 232–3).
62. 'Hieri cominciai il retratto della Regina in presentia sua con grandissima satisfattione di S. Maestà et applauso d'altre principesse, et questa sera debbo andare a San Germano per fare il retratto del Dolfino, et io credo di fare anche quello del Re, il tutto per portarlo a V.A.S. . . .' (Baschet, 1868, p. 297).
63. *Ibid.*, p. 298; Héroard, 1868 edn, I, p. 206.
64. Ferdinando Gonzaga to his brother Francesco, 7 January 1607: 'Il assure qu'il n'a que deux mains, il parle en vérité assez mal, piusqu'il a des élèves des mains desquels il peut disposer pour les joindre aux siennes. Je ne fais pas exclusivement appel à ses mains, une copie me suffirait pourvu qu'elle fût bonne' (Baschet, 1868, p. 439: the original Italian is not given). Pourbus to Francesco, 15 January 1607: 'non potendo giovani lavorarvi atorno senza havere un retratto finito inanzi . . .' (*ibid.*, p. 439).
65. Pietro da Nuvolara to Isabella d'Este, Florence, 3 April 1501: 'Altro non ha facto, se non che dui suoi garzoni fano retrati et lui a le volte in alcuno mette mano' (Luzio, 1887, pp. 32–3).
66. 'Ricordo come io ho rifatto una testa al detto Messer Raffaello di Messer Luchino suo figliuolo a un quadro che haueua fatto Alessandro Pieroni mio giovane di valuta di L. ventotto' (Supino, 1908, p. 28).
67. 'Dit is het leven van Conraet Schot, hoe ende in wat manieren dat hy geleeft van jonge kinsgedage . . .', published, with a French translation, by Hymans, 1910, pp. 37–42. Only a few extracts can be given here: 'den prince van Spaegnien selve is aengesproken heeft menichmael; ende alle syn baggen, ketenen ende juweelen ende veel costelycke cleederen denselven Conraet bewaert heeft, die denselve meester Anthoni geconterfeyt den prins van Spaegnien ende die cleederen oick die hy droech . . . in menich groot huys van heeren daer Conraet dagelyx frequenteerde . . . Denselven meester Anthoni Conraet begeerde in Spaegnen met hem te vueren . . .'. Deposition of Jan Schot (*ibid.*, pp. 36–7): 'hy hem vorts bestaedde by eenen van den principaelen werckgeselle van den voorschreven meester Anthonis, genaempt Jan Maes . . .'
68. Breuer, 1984, pp. 16–27 and references.
69. For a portrait of John, Prince of Portugal, probably produced by Mor's assistants in Portugal in 1552, see Campbell, 1985, pp. 96–9.
70. 'hy wrocht hier en daer oock in daghhuyzen/als by *Antonis Moro*, om conterfeytsel cleeren te maken/en voor anderen . . .' (Van Mander, 1604, f. 238v).
71. Payment of October 1564 'por lo que pintó en otro de S.M. de que hizo el rostro de Sofonisua' (Amezua y Mayo, 1949, I, p. 264 n. 114).
72. 'seis retratos de su Alteza todos de una manera y sacados de uno que hizo Sosonistra, dama de su magestad' (P. Beroqui, *Tiziano en el Museo del Prado*, Madrid, 1927, p. 106).
73. 'Il S.mo G. D. di Toschana de' dare alli 3 di Lullio 1603 per fatura di dua abiti dal mezo in su con le mane, fati a e ritratti dele Ill.me principesse, che le teste erono fate dal S. Gostantino de' Servi . . .' (Langedijk, 1981–3, I, p. 679).
74. Pinchart, 1856, p. 136 n. 2 ('pour l'achat de son cheval sur lequel . . . puis naguères il est allé devers le roy d'Hongrie et de Bohesme, en Allemaigne . . .').
75. Bill of 1535: 'hat mich di kgl. maj. . . . von Prag aus gen Prun in Merhern zu khomen ervordert mit anzaigung, das ich ehe geld aufbringen und ain ross khaufen und unverzogenlich aufsein und zu seiner maj. ziehen soll, das ich also gethan und umb ross, satl und anders ausgeben 12½ gulden rheinisch' (Kreyczi, 1887, p. CXV).
76. Bill of 1535: 'hab ich . . . andere maister und gesellen aufgenomen, di die tafln leimgetrenkht, grundt und farbn und anders geriben und zugericht, di nachmals vorgeund und an die stat zu dem gemel verfertigt . . .'; 'ich von furdrung der arbait hab di besten zwen maister, so in Teutschen landen, darzu brauchen und ob mir halten muessen . . .' (*ibid.*, pp. CXV, CXVI).

Chapter 7 Portrait Method

1. 'Estimo facto per Magistro Bonifacio Bembo . . . Per retrare al naturale homini cavalli et cani . . . 500' (Rosmini, 1820, p. 150).
2. 'Item uno retracto del cane giamato bareta' (Malaguzzi Valeri, 1902, p. 134).
3. 'Avendo il Gran Turco per un suo uomo mandato a presentare al marchese un bellissimo cane, un arco ed un turcasso, il marchese fece ritrarre nel detto palazzo di Gonzaga il cane, il turco che l'aveva condotto, e l'altre cose: e ciò fatto, volendo vedere se il cane dipinto veramente somigliava, fece condurre uno de' suoi cani di corte, nimicissimo al cane turco, là dove era il dipinto sopra un basamento finto di pietra. Quivi dunque giunto il vivo, tosto che vide il dipinto, non altrimenti che se vivo stato fusse e quello stesso che odiava a morte, si lanciò con tanto impeto, sforzando chi lo teneva, per addentarlo, che, percosso il capo nel muro, tutto se lo ruppe' (Vasari-Milanesi, 1878–85, V, pp. 303–4; compare Richter, 1970, I, p. 56 and n.)
4. 'ung tableaul de bonne paincture d'une belle fille exclave, sur la couverte duquel sont Charles Overssin, contrerolleur de Madame, et son père, et aussi le chien de Madame qui s'appelle Bonté' (Finot, 1895, p. 211).
5. 'e nelle facciate sono ritratti di naturale tutti i cavalli più belli e più favoriti della razza del marchese, ed insieme con essi i

cani, di quello stesso mantello o macchie che sono i cavalli, co' nomi loro, che tutti furono disegnati da Giulio, e coloriti sopra la calcina a fresco da Benedetto Pagni e da Rinaldo Mantovano, pittori e suoi creati . . .' (Vasari-Milanesi, 1878–85, v, p. 537; for the frescoes, see F. Hartt, *Giulio Romano*, 2 vols, New Haven, 1958, i, pp. 112–15; ii, pls 181–6).

6. *Instructions given by King Henry the Seventh to his Embassadors, When he intended to marry The young Queen of Naples: together with the Answers of the Embassadors*, London, 1761, pp. 10, 14, 17–18 (see also J. Gairdner, *Memorials of King Henry the Seventh* (*Rerum britannicarum medii aevi scriptores*), London, 1858, pp. 229, 233, 236–7).
7. '1473. per m^{o} Baldissera Credito. – Lavoreri fatti al quondam D. Borso . . . Et per aconzare 36 teste de Schivenoio del duca Borso et parte de busti e per altre teste de comission del duca Borso . . . duc. 036' (Venturi, 1885^{2}, p. 721 n. 1).
8. C. Thompson and L. Campbell, *Hugo van der Goes and the Trinity Panels in Edinburgh*, Edinburgh, 1974, pp. 20–1, 32–3, pls 13, 14, 39.
9. Charles V to Diego Hurtado de Mendoza, Ghent, 30 October 1545: 'Sola una cosa nos paresce que se devrá aderezar un poco, es en la nariz . . . quando passaremos por Italia, él mismo lo adereze' (Ferrarino, 1975, p. 24).
10. Catherine to La Mothe-Fénélon, 3 July 1571: 'Il [Janet] n'eust le loisir que de faire, comme vous verrez, le visage qui est fort bien et parfaitement faict, après le vray naturel' (H. de la Ferrière and Baguenault de Puchesse, eds, *Lettres de Catherine de Médicis*, 11 vols, Paris, 1880–1943, iv, p. 52).
11. La Mothe-Fénélon to Catherine, 20 July 1571: 'elle m'a dict qu'encor que ce ne soit que le créon, et que son teint n'y soit que quasi tout chafouré de charbon, si ne layssoit ce visaige de monstrer beaucoup de beaulté . . .' (C. P. Cooper, ed., *Correspondance diplomatique de Bertrand de Salignac de la Mothe-Fénélon, ambassadeur de France en Angleterre de 1568 à 1575*, iv, Paris and London, 1840, p. 186); Catherine to La Mothe-Fénélon, 3 July 1571: 'l'aultre peinture . . . servira seullement pour la taille, qui est aussi la vraye semblance de mondict fils; mais il ne s'est pas, en ceste peinture, amusé à faire parfaictement le visage, pour ce que l'aultre estoit faict et que je voulois faire partir en dilligence ce porteur' (La Ferrière and Baguenault, *op. cit.*, iv, p. 52).
12. Unsigned letter to the duke, Paris, 20 February 1577: 'il n'y a rien qui touche guères le coeur des simples personnes que les effigies de leurs princes et seigneurs, lesquelles estans recogneues par ceux qui sont présentement en vie, ilz en laissent de main en main la memoire à leur postérité, si d'aventure ilz les veoient bien faittes et les honorent et les benissent, là où, si elles ne ressemblent point ou si elles sont faittes de quelque mauvaise main, ilz les resnient et desdaignent' (H. Bouchot, 'La préparation et la publication d'un livre illustré au XVIe siècle', *Bibliothèque de l'Ecole des Chartes*, LIII (1892), pp. 612–23 (p. 616)).
13. E. Sellers, ed., *The Elder Pliny's Chapters on the History of Art*, London, 1896, pp. 84–5, 151–2.
14. A. Dürer, *Vnderweysung der Messung*, Nuremberg, 1525, ff. Q i v-Q ii v ('Solichs ist gut all dennen die yemand wollen ab Conterfeten/vnd die jrer sach nit gewisz sind . . .').
15. See the discussion in K. T. Parker, *The Drawings of Hans Holbein . . . at Windsor Castle*, Oxford and London, 1945, pp. 30–3; Foister, 1983, pp. 14–15.
16. Cennino Cennini, *Il libro dell'arte o trattato della pittura*, ed. G. and C. Milanesi, Florence, 1859, pp. 135–9: 'Ora ti voglio toccare d'un'altra, la quale è molto utile (e al disegno fatti grande onore) in ritrarre e simigliare cose di naturale; la quale si chiama improntare' (translated in Cennini, *The Craftsman's Handbook*, tr. D. V. Thompson, New Haven, 1933, pp. 123–7).
17. Letter of 16 April 1495: 'de ora in ora sperava che el depintore me portase el retrato dercule el qualle el .S.^{re} et io lo mandamo ala.S.V. e la zertifichamo che le molto più groso che none questo retrato per che le più de octo di che le sta retrato la mesura de la lungeza non se manda ala.S.V. perche diseno che le male a piare la mesura per respeto del cresere altramente se li seria mandato . . .' (Venturi, 1885^{1}, pp. 227 8; translated in J. Cartwright, *Beatrice d'Este*, London, 1903, p. 172).
18. 'DO ICH WAS ZWAYR IAR ALT/DO HET ICH DISE LENG UND GESTALT'. The portrait is in the Liechtenstein collection (950): R. Baumstark, *Trésors du Liechtenstein, Chefs-d'oeuvre des collections de peintures du prince de Liechtenstein*, Paris, 1980, p. 278, pl. 126.
19. 'Item, pour la fachon de la pourtraicture et figure au vif de la ducesse de Milan, faict sur toille, de la grandeur qu'elle est, laquelle il a livré en mars xv^{c}xxxiij: xxx livres' (Pinchart, 1856, p. 142 n. 2).
20. M. Campbell, review of Langedijk, 1981–3, *Burlington Magazine*, cxxvii (1985), pp. 386–8, p. 387.
21. Leoni to Ferrante Gonzaga, 29 June 1549: 'hogli Illmo Principe fatta la sua testa grande dal naturale et tutta compasato che un capelo non c'è de diferentia, stano tutti stupiti in questa corte et non tanto della detta testa la quale non ha una linea di mancho o di più che s'abbia quella de la M.^{tà} Sua' (Campori, 1855, pp. 286–7).
22. Leoni to Granvelle, Milan, 20 December 1549: 'Vi prego caldamente che mi facciate gratia, se uoi foste partito da Brusele (ch'io non credo) di comandar al padre Uiuone che uoglia andare nella fonderia, et con una listetta di legno, ouero una asta sotille, et pigliare la misura giustamente de Sua M^{tà}, come sapete che in detto luogo stà lineata. Quest'errore et questa fatica nascie che, cadendo il mio seruitor giu da cauallo, ruppe l'asta che haueua segnata la detta misura, et tutti i pezzi non si poterno cosi ben core, a tal che io ne hauero bisogno'. On the reverse of the letter, Granvelle's secretary wrote: 'Dimanda una misura del Imperatore, per che la sua si ruppe per il camino'. Compare the letters from the same to the same, 3 January, 12 January, 17 January and 23 March 1550 (Plon, 1887, pp. 355–8).
23. *Ibid.*, p. 283.
24. Mme de Clermont's account of Elisabeth's life in Spain, 17 May 1560: 'Ils disnèrent ensemble, et après veyrent le pourtraict du feu Roy que vous madame auiez envoyé, duquel le Roy s'enquist fort s'il estoyt bien faict et de mesme grandeur' (Amezua y Mayo, 1949, iii, p. 115).
25. Hieronimo Lippomano to the Signoria, Paris, 21 November 1578: R. Brown and G. Cavendish-Bentinck, *State Papers and Manuscripts relating to English Affairs, existing in the Archives and Collections of Venice* . . . , vii, London, 1890, p. 587.
26. Mantegna to Ludovico Gonzaga, 6 July 1477: 'non si può far bene dal naturale chi nona comodita di vedere' (Kristeller, 1902, p. 534).
27. For the drawing (Louvre), see White, 1971, pp. 178–9.
28. Francesco to Angelo da Viterbio, Milan, 12 August 1462: 'Intendendo nuy che li in Viterbo, et maxime appresso un certo speciale se trova la imagine del Illmo quondam sig.^{r} Sforza nostro patre tracta dal naturale, ve confortiamo, et carichiamo che usati ogni vostro studio et dilgentia per trovarla, et trovandola fatela retrare de novo suso una tavoleta, o suso uno folio in quella medesima forma et al naturale, come la trovareti, et mandatecela per le poste . . .' (Malaguzzi Valeri, 1902, p. 144).
29. 'pour la fachon de la pourtraicture et figure au vif du feu roy Loys d'Hongrie faict sur toille, de la grandeur qu'il estoit en son vivant: xxxviij livres' (Pinchart, 1856, p. 142 n. 2).
30. 'A maistre Jehan Vermay, la somme de lxxv livres vj solz que deue luy estoit pour, le xxve de may xv^{c} trente, estre party de la ville de Malines et . . . allé à Ausbourg, en Allemaigne, devers l'empereur et le roy d'Hongrie et la royne d'Hongrie, vers lesquelz madicte dame l'envoyoit pour tirer et pourtraire leur philozomie au plus

près du vif que possible luy seroit, ensemble les enffans dudict sieur roy . . .' (Pinchart, 1856, p. 136 n. 4).

31. Minute by Teodoro Sangiorgio: 'In questo quadro hanno da essere ritratti al naturale il suddetto Imperatore Sigismondo et il Marchese Gio. Francesco' (Luzio, 1890, p. 399). The picture is at Munich (7303).

32. 'Mestre Colin d'Amiens, il faut que vous faciez la pourtraiture du Roy nostre sire: c'est assavoir qui soit à genoux sur ung carreaul comme icy dessoubs . . . le plus beau visaige que pourrés fere et jeune et plain, le netz longuet et ung petit hault, comme savez et ne le fectes point chauve . . . Le netz aquillon, Les cheveux plus longs derriere . . .' (Laborde, 1850–5, I, p. 59 n. 2).

33. 'Francesco, andando talora a vederlo mangiare, fece senza ritrarlo l'imagine di esso Cesare a olio in un quadro grandissimo; ed in quello dipinse la Fama che lo coronava di lauro, ed un fanciullo in forma d'un Ercole piccolino che gli porgeva il mondo, quasi dandogliene il dominio: la quale opera finita che fu, la fece vedere a papa Clemente, al quale piacque tanto, che mandò quella e Francesco insieme . . . all'imperadore . . . Francesco . . . dicendo che non era finita, non la volle lasciare: e così Sua Maestà non l'ebbe, ed egli non fu, come sarebbe stato senza dubbio, premiato . . .' (Vasari-Milanesi, 1878–85, V, p. 229).

34. Records of the Cour des monnoyes, 9 December 1569: '. . . Claude de Hery tailleur général . . . a dict que le dict S. estant dernierrement, au moys de juillet, en l'abbaye Sainct Germain des Prés, après l'avoir veu par diverses foys, il en auroit faict le porteraict au myeulx qui lui auroit esté posible et faict et gravé ung nouveau poinçon de son efigye, lequel de Hery a montré à la dicte court et icelluy veu par icelle et faict voir à Me François, Clouet dict Janet, paintre et varlet de chambre du roy, pour ce mandé au bureau, qui auroit rapporté ledict poinçon estre fort aprochant de l'efigye du roy, en la aige qu'il est à présent . . .' (Laborde, 1850–5, II, p. 584).

35. Charles IX to the officials of the Mint, Angers, 5 February 1570: 'd'autant que la dicte effigie ne représente aucunement nostre aaige, ne pareillement nostre visaige, ne la taille dont nous sommes à présent et que nous estimons que cella vient à cause qu'il y a longtemps que vous ne nous avez veu, nous voullons que vous atendiez à faire nouveaulx coings des dictes monnoyes jusques à tant que nous soyons à Paris et lors il sera plus aisé de les bien faire et représenter plus au naturel nostre personne . . .' (*ibid.*, II, p. 587).

36. Baldassare Pusterla and Giason del Maino to Ludovico il Moro, 29 December 1493: 'fece dire a la Regina che la intendeva che la Maestà sua la faceva ritrar da Johanne Ambrosio Preda per mandarla a la duchessa di Barrhi et che la non voleva esser mandata a volta che la non fusse ben ritrata; et fu domandato Johanne Ambrosio qual vienne lì a ritrarla et ebbe patientia di star forsa per due hore fin che fu retrata . . .' (see above, Chapter 2 n. 86).

37. Erasmus to More, Antwerp, 30 May 1517: 'Petrus Aegidius et ego pingimur in eadem tabula: eam tibi dono breui mittemus. Verum incidit incommode quod reuersus Petrum offenderim nescio quo morbo laborantem grauiter, nec citra periculum; vnde nec adhuc satis reualuit. Nos belle valebamus, sed nescio quomodo medico venit in mentem vt purgandae bili iuberet me pilulas aliquot sumere, et quod ille stulte suasit, ego stultius feci. Iam pingi coeperam; verum a pharmaco sumpto cum ad pictorem redirem, negauit eundem esse vultum. Dilata est igitur pictura in dies aliquot, donec fiam paulo alacrior . . . Scribam fusius intra mensem, cum mittam tabellam . . .' (Allen and Garrod, 1906–47, II, pp. 576–7). See Campbell, 1985, pp. 86–9 and references.

38. 'An unser Frawen heimsuchung, do ich gleich weg von Antorff wohlt, do schicket der könig von Dennenmarck zu mir, dasz ich eylend zu ihm kem und in conterfeyet. Das thet ich mit dem kohln. Und ich conterfeyet auch sein dinner Anthony. Und ich must mit dem könig essen, [er] erzeuget sich gnädiglich gegen mir . . . Um am andern tag fuhren wir geng Prüssel, auff des königes von Denenmarck geschefft . . . Jtem herr Anthonij hat mir geben 12 hornisch gulden. Davon hab ich geben 2 hornisch gulden dem mahler, fürs täffelein zu conterfetten und das er mir färblein hat lassen reiben . . . Jch hab 12 stüber vors königes futrall geben. Und ich hab dem könig von öhlfarben conterfett, der hat mir 30 gulden geschenckt' (Rupprich, 1956–69, I, pp. 176–7; translated in Conway, 1889, pp. 124–5).

39. 'Credo dimane partirmi da Roma et andar insino a Fondi a retrarre una signora, et credo starò 15 zorni' (Hirst, 1981, p. 115).

40. 'ed egli in termine d'un mese fece quel ritratto, il quale venendo dalle celesti bellezze di quella signora e da così dotta mano, riuscì una pittura divina' (Vasari-Milanesi, 1878–85, V, p. 578; Hirst, 1981, p. 115).

41. Moritz Ferber, Bishop of Ermland, to Johannes Dantiscus, 21 October 1535: 'Der Hofmaler HA.'s hat sich drei Tage bei mir aufgehalten, und angeblich auf Euern Befehl, mir porträtiert. Er hat das Bild mit sich geführt und mir ein zweites Exemplar (eandem meam figuram etiam confectam) versprochen' (Ehrenberg, 1899, p. 157).

42. Hutton to Cromwell, 14 March 1538: 'Mr Haunce . . . havyng but thre owers space hathe shoid hym self to be a master of that siens, for it is very perffight . . .' (*State Papers during the Reign of Henry the Eighth*, VIII, London, 1852, p. 19).

43. Francesco Marcolini to Aretino, Venice, 15 September 1551: 'Ma doue si lascia il Ritratto stupendo trenta volte non che vna, che il Celebrato Pittor Cesareo (del prefato Titiano s'intende) fece a richiesta mia in tre giorni; che chi conobbe voi in quella età, vede uoi in Carne & in spirito al presente mirando lui; talmente par egli viuo & naturale' (*Lettere scritte al signor Pietro Aretino da molti signori*, Venice, 1551, II, p. 437).

44. 'Hy hadde *Antonio Moro* geschoncken een zijn Medaglie-boeck/seer schoon ghebonden/welcken hem seyde/niet te willen beloonen dan met zijn Const/en dede hem een oft twee reysen aen den morghen comen om te sitten/hy soude hem conterfeyten/en liet hem wel ontbeten hebbende weder t' huys gaen/tot de derde reys/doe dede hy nae hem een conterfeytsel in een ure oft weynigh tijts/dat wonder wel ghedaen was/en ghelijck . . .' (Van Mander, 1604, f. 248v).

45. Salviati to Galli, Paris, 15 February 1573: 'usando questi principi dar loro tanto poco tempo quando vogliono un ritratto, che è impossibile che faccino cosa che buona sia' (Hurtubise, 1975, I, p. 414).

46. 'Dipinse la Serenissima sposa di Ferdinando Medici a sua requisizione, che non volle esser ritratta se non da un francese; e così accomodato a fare il suo ritratto, dove vi era il Duca Gondi, al quale disse che facessi stare allegra la Granduchessa e la facessi ridere. E lo fece detto ritratto in mezza ora, dove la Serenissima restò maravigliata che sì presto l'avesse fatto tal ritratto, e sì bello e presto, perché li Franzesi la tenevano 3 ovvero 4 ore a disagio' ('Notizie inviate a Filippo Baldinucci', published in P. Barocchi, ed., *Notizie dei professori del disegno . . . di Filippo Baldinucci, Appendice*, VII, Florence, 1975, p. 21).

47. Pantoja's account, work done for the queen, 1600–7: 'Más, en nueue de marҫo de 1603 y en doҫe de mayo del dicho año tres retratos de la Serenísima Ynfanta Doña María, muerta, en su ataud . . .' (Kusche, 1964, p. 237). Pantoja supplied three further versions of this portrait, on 1 and 23 September 1603 and 7 April 1607 (*ibid.*, pp. 237, 241).

48. Same account: 'Más, en 20 de febrero de 1607 vn retrato original de la Reyna . . . estube en E1 Escorial vn mes para este rretrato . . . E1 mismo dia dos rretratos enteros de Sus Alteҫas Prínҫipe e Ynfanta Doña Ana . . . originales, que fui a San

Lorenço açer las cabeças . . .' (*ibid.*, pp. 239–40).

49. British Library, MS Harl. 6000, 'An exact & Compendious Discours concerning the Art of Miniatura or Limning', ff. 6–8v.
50. 'Den appel vanden ouge/alre naest den swarten . . . /bruyngeelachtich Jnd omtrent/alre naest den witten blauachtich/ . . . Dat . . . geelachtich/Dat witte ouch geelachtich/Die nase bruynsanguinachtich/gelijc den kinbac of den/wangen Die lippen zere witachtich/purper Die stoppelen vanden barde/wal grijsachtich/Die kinne roedachtich' (A. L. Dierick, *Van Eyck*, Ghent, 1970, note to pl. 1).
51. Foister, 1983, pp. 24–5; M. W. Ainsworth and M. Faries, 'Northern Renaissance Paintings: The Discovery of Invention', *Bulletin of the Saint Louis Art Museum*, n.s., XVIII, 1 (summer 1986), pp. 25–7; exhibition catalogue Houston, 1987, pp. 24, 70, 104, 110.
52. Marijnissen and Van de Voorde, 1983, *passim*; summarised in *Burlington Magazine*, CXXVI (1984), p. 304.
53. Shapley, 1979, pp. 483–5.
54. Hilliard, 1981 edn, p. 114.
55. 'vos tendréis aviso y tiento de hacerla despierta con alguna palabra hasta que dé aquella postura y manera en que ella más a la contina suele parecer . . . que le mandase afirmar los ojos y mirar a una cierta parte o a una señal o punto, y que de allí no se mueva sin licencia' (Sánchez Cantón, 1921, p. 261).
56. Hilliard, 1981 edn, p. 80.
57. *Ibid.*, p. 114.
58. *Ibid.*
59. British Library, MS Harl. 6000, f. 8v.
60. 'E pochi mesi prima, il 21 dicembre 1494, suo fratello card. Ippolito faceva dire ad Isabella da Taddeo di Lardi che per amor di lei si sarebbe sottoposto alla noia di *posare*, cosa che "non avea voluto far per nisuno de soi fratelli . . ."' (Luzio, 1913, pp. 186–7).
61. 'Ma le venne "tanto in fastidio la patientia di star ferme et immote" che dichiarava di non volerne più sapere di questo supplizio' (*ibid.*, p. 209).
62. Isabella to d'Atri, ambassador in France, 28 February 1516: 'Quanto sia per mandarvi il ritracto nostro, questo non potemo nè volemo fare, si perchè non ni havemo alcuno nè volemo più quella [noia] di star paciente a farni ritrare, si anche perchè seria prosumptione la nostra a mandarlo in Franza' (*ibid.*, p. 216).
63. 'teneva, mentre che la ritraeva, chi sonasse o cantasse, e di continuo buffoni che la facessino stare allegra, per levar via quel malinconico che suol dar spesso la pittura a' ritratti che si fanno . . .' (Vasari-Milanesi, 1878–85, IV, pp. 39–40).
64. Silvestro Calandra to Isabella, 14 March 1494: 'ogi maistro Francisco depintore la ha comenzà ad retrare, ma non la posete finire, che ella se adormensete et ello ha diferito a dimane' (Luzio, 1913, p. 191 n. 1).
65. Two accounts of this conversation are known, the first written by Cranach's pupil Matthias Gunderam in 1556 (J. Heller, *Lucas Cranach's Leben und Werke*, 2nd edn, Nuremberg, 1854, pp. 279–82), the second written in 1609 by Valentin Sternenboke, who had married one of Cranach's grand-daughters and who was then in his seventy-third year (F. Warnecke, *Lucas Cranach der Aeltere*, Görlitz, 1879, pp. 11–13). According to Gunderam, Charles asked 'quomodo tunc in ista aetate fuerim compositus, interea dum me depingeres. Vestra, ait Lucas, Majestas erat nata annos octo . . . habebatis praeceptorem, qui tunc se vestrum ingenium nosse ajebat affirmans vos mirifice delectari inspectione ferri ac Malibis. Mox ergo deprompturn ferreum faculum in pariete sic collocabat, ut spiculam vestris oculis obverteret. In hanc postea Majestas tua tantisper oculos directos tenebat, donec a me pictura esset absoluta' (Heller, *op. cit.*, p. 281). According to Sternenboke, Charles had the portrait with him. 'Do der kaiser gefraget, wie er in den so gemalet als wan er aufwarts nach der wandt sehe, und shiekete, hat Lucas Maler gesaget, Seine Maiestadt were ein iunges herlein gewesen, vnd nicht stille sitzen wollen. Der praeceptor aber hatte einen pfeil geholet, und in die wandt gestecket, darnach der Kaiser gesehen, und also stille gesessen, dan er lust zu solchen sehen gehabt' (Warnecke, *op. cit.*, pp. 11–12).
66. Hieronymus von Sprinzenstein to Sabino Calandra, Innsbruck, 28 October 1548: 'et perchè lo signor Ticiano archipentore l'ha ritratto naturale quanto sia possibile, una sol cosa è alquanto meno del naturale, cioè che nella pictura ha il volto alquanto più severo di quello è il naturale. Et questo non è per colpa del maestro, ma quando Sua Serenita stava a sedere alla longa tediata parea stesse pensosa, donde è reuscito quel volto meno alegro, suave et dolce di quello è in se. Del resto è tanto naturale che non li manca altro che 'l spirito vivo' (Archivio di Stato, Mantua, AG b. 545; translated in Hope, 1980, p. 116. I am most grateful to Dr Hope for the transcript of the Italian text and for permission to use his translation).
67. Bronzino to Pier Francesco Riccio, Pisa, 27 January 1551: 'Trovomi a dipignere dove imparano le lettere latine et le greche et mi piglio grandissimo piacere a vedere che queste tenere piante et così ben nate, siano così bene et purgate et custodite et così perfettamente corrette et indiritte a ottimo segno . . .' (Heikamp, 1953–6, p. 137).
68. Héroard, 1868 edn, I, pp. 64 (21 March 1604, 'Il s'amuse à ses échecs d'argent, pendant que le jeune Du Monstier tire son crayon'), 79 (6 August 1604, 'il mange assis, ayant devant lui ses petites besognes d'armes, pendant que le sieur Decourt . . . en tire le crayon'), 91 (27 September 1604, 'Il s'amuse à ses échecs d'argent pendant que Mallery en tire le crayon'; 30 September 1604, 'il est peint en crayon pour le deuxième jour par Mallery, à patience, s'amuse à crayonner sur du papier . . .'), 143 (5 August 1605, 'Il va en la chambre de Madame, où étoit son peintre, maître Martin, qui la peignoit; il se fait donner un pinceau . . .'), 187 (10 May 1606, 'Maître Martin, son peintre, vient pour le peindre . . . Il se fait donner des couleurs et un pinceau, imite le peintre mêlant ses couleurs, regarde parfois la besogne de son peintre'). Louis was born on 27 September 1601.
69. See above, p. 178.
70. 'Quand il peignoit les gens, il leur laissoit faire tout ce qu'ils vouloient; quelquefois seulement il leur disoit: "Tournez-vous."' (Tallemant des Rieux, 1862 edn, III, p. 141).
71. 'no me aconteciese a mí esto, estando sacando al Rey nro. señor al natural . . . estando delante el conde de Castañeda hablando, en la obra que yo hacía, con el Rey, comencé yo a no poder hacer nada y, preguntándome el Rey por qué no hacía, dije yo: "Hágame V. Alteza tanta merced, que mande al Conde que se aparte hacia una parte; porque, estando él delante, no puedo hacer lo que deseo quietamente, ni lo que pertenece a la perfección de la obra." Luego se apartó el Conde como discreto, y se puso a una parte do no podía estorbar, desculpándome la Reina, que allí estaba, para con él' (Sánchez Cantón, 1921, p. 258).
72. Hilliard, 1981 edn, p. 74.
73. 'adũque. tu. pittore avrai una corte accommodata coi mvri tĩti in nero cõ alquãto sporto di tetto sopra esso mvro, e sia larga di braccia 10 e lũga 20 e alta 10, e quãdo è sole conviene coprire cõ tẽda, opur ritrare una opera sul fare della sera. quãdo è nvuolo o nebbia e questo è perfecta aria' (Richter, 1970, I, pp. 316–17).
74. 'se debe de asentar en una silla de frente del príncipe o persona ilustre que hubiere de retratar; y con su mesa o tabla en medio, y la luz de la ventana templada y música, y la vista en su lugar (con la casa desembarazada de gente) . . .' (Sánchez Cantón, 1921, p. 257).
75. Hilliard, 1981 edn, pp. 72–4.
76. Some striking examples, taken at random, are: his drawings of Conrad Merkel, dated 1508, and of a man, dated 1516, both in the British Museum (5218–27, 5218–44: W

429, 564); his woodcut of Ulrich Varnbüler, dated 1522; his engravings of Cardinal Albrecht of Brandenburg, dated 1519, of Frederick the Wise of Saxony, dated 1524, and of Willibald Pirckheimer, also dated 1524; and his painting of Hieronymus Holzschuher, dated 1526, at Berlin (557 E: Anzelewsky, 1980, pp. 226, 196, 227, 228, 229). Similar reflections are in the eyes of Jean Carondelet in the diptych by Gossaert in the Louvre, dated 1517 (INV. 1442–1443: Friedländer, 1967–76, VIII, pl. 10) and of John Frederick of Saxony in his engraved portrait of 1543 by Pencz (Bartsch 126).

77. 'Jch hab maister Conrad zu Prüssel beym licht in der nacht conterfet, der meiner herren wirth ist gewesen. Auch hab ich Doctor Lamparters sohn zu der selben zeit mit dem kohln conterfet und die wirthin' (Rupprich, 1956–69, I, p. 155; translated in Conway, 1889, p. 101).

78. Bill presented by Vermeyen to Margaret's executors in 1533: 'Le dit Jehan Vermay a fait et pourtraict au vif la figure d'ung nommé Jehan Denis, lequel feue madame a prins et retenu devers elle et la fait mettre en son cabinet . . .' (Houdoy, 1872, p. 517); inventory of Margaret's collection, 1524–30: 'Ung tableau de la portrecture Jehan Denyr, fait au lustre de la chandoille' (Zimerman, 1885, No. 955).

79. Frans Halsmuseum, Haarlem (150): Friedländer, 1967–76, XIII, pl. 92.

80. '¿ por qué acostumbran los pintores italianos servirse en los retratos que sacan con luz de candela? Hácenlo para más determinación de las sombras y para más claridad de lo claro, y más fuerza de lo escuro y también lo hacen para más declaración de los sentidos o sentimientos' (Sánchez Cantón, 1921, p. 283).

81. 'Ritrasse il cardinal Caraffa nel suo ritorno di Germania, e lo rubò a lume di torchi, mentre che nel vescovado di Verona cenava' (Vasari-Milanesi, 1878–85, V, p. 298).

82. Hymans, 1910, pp. 40–1; see above, p. 156.

83. 'Ricordo questo dì 14 di novembre [1580] come io ho consegnato a . . . guardaroba della Granduchessa e fratello di Piero suo guardaroba più veste di drappo che havevo . . . per commessione della Granduchessa . . .'; 'Ricordo questo dì detto [28 January 1581] come io ho consegnato una ghirlanda o acconciatura di perle della Gran Duchessa, la quale S.A.S. mi haveva data con sue mani per ritralla per il ritratto suo per mandare a Venetia: e detta acconciatura consegnai a Monna Lena presente la Signora Portia Pietra, nella quale era dieci rosette con dieci diamanti' (Supino, 1908, p. 24).

84. Francesco Maria, Duke of Urbino, to Gian Giacomo Leonardi, Brescia, 17 July 1536: 'et quanto alle arme che ha in mano il Thitiano ch'elle ne sono sommamente care e per bene assai, non uorressimo che se guastassino . . .' (Gronau, 1936, p. 92).

85. *Ibid.*, p. 98; see above, p. 145.

86. See the drawings of the head and body of René de Laval, Seigneur de Bois-Dauphin, attributed to François Clouet, in the British Museum (1910-2-12-65, 1910-2-12-53: Moreau-Nélaton, 1924, I, figs 31, 34); and J. R. Judson, 'A New Insight into Cornelis Ketel's Method of Portraiture', *Master Drawings*, I, 4 (1963), pp. 38–41 (who puts forward a different interpretation of two drawings by Ketel).

87. 'i^{c} ix gulden xiiij gl. Lucas malhern Inhalt seiner quitantz lx par teffelein daruff gemalt sein die bede churfursten selige und lobliche gedechtnus, sonnabents nach Jubilate Jndus. iij gl. vor ein schrein dartzu' (C. Schuchardt, *Lucas Cranach des Aeltern Leben und Werke*, 3 vols, Leipzig, 1851–71, I, p. 88).

88. Antonio Patanella to Granvelle, 12 February 1550: 'Messer Leone Aretino mi ha detto che V.S. Illma et R^{ma} ha molti ritratti suoi, fatti per mano de pittori eccellenti . . . io la pregarei a farmene gratia d'uno . . .'; same to same, 23 February 1550; 'Prego V.S. mi faccia gratia d'un suo ritratto, fatto per mani del suo ex^{mo} pintor, da posserlo tener per mia contemplatione, et ornamento del palazzotto che ho fatto qui, in la nostra sala' (Plon, 1887, p. 358).

89. Bembo to Bianca Capello, Siena, 13 October 1585: 'et se n' andremo à gran giornati verso Roma, dove il primo sara parlar à gran pittore che invero ha fatto miracoli in quel ritratto . . . Desidero in estremo haverne un simile . . .'; same to same, Venice, 20 April 1586: 'il ritratto di V.A. è stato veduto questi festi et il di Sta. Apollonia da più di trecento . . . il Palma, et il Tintoretto stetero da me due hore . . . il med.o ha fatto M. Aless.ro Vittoria . . . La portai à Casa Capello la settimana passata, e vi steti un pezzo; fu veduto volentieri da tutti, et fù dalla giovani basciata . . . Il Tentoretto ne fà due o tre copie; per il Sig.r Pio, per la contessa, et per Cà Capello. Il Sig.r Giac.o Contarini ne vuole uno, ma di man' del Bassano et sarà fatto anco dal Palma, et da Paulo Veronese' (Langedijk, 1981–3, I, p. 321, with extracts from many other letters about the portrait and the copy).

90. 'vi si trovò dentro solamente disegni, ritratti in carta, ed un libretto che insegnava a far le pietre del musaico' (Vasari-Milanesi, 1878–85, II, p. 598).

91. 'in Mantoa ne sono ancora molti . . . de' quali si serbò copia Francesco in carte di chiaroscuro, le quali sono oggi in Mantoa appresso gli eredi suoi' (*ibid.*, V, pp. 300–1).

92. 'un peintre, qui s'appelloit Corneille, . . . avoit peint en une grand' chambre tous les grands seigneurs . . . et grandes reynes, princesses, dames, filles de la court de France' (Brantôme, 1864–82 edn, VII, p. 343). See below, p. 215.

93. Granvelle to Titian, 28 April 1549: 'Io desiderarei aver un ritratto del Prencipe N.S., che faceste a Milano . . . se ne avete ritenuto alcuno disegno, fatemene aver un estratto della perfezione ch'io lo spero dalla eccellente vostra mano' (L. Ferrarino, *Lettere di artisti italiani ad Antonio Perrenot di Granvelle* (*Documenti e ricerche*, VII), Madrid, 1977, p. 28).

94. Vasari-Milanesi, 1878–85, VI, pp. 499–500; see above, p. 39.

95. Madame de Vineux to Catherine, 30 September 1561: 'Elle a faict la paincture de la Royne, que le Nonse qui est ici a anvoié au Pape, qui li resamble mieus que pas une que iaye encore veue. Je panse, madame, que lon vous en fera fere une por vous envoyer, ce que ie desire bien fort por le contantement que en porés recevoir' (Amezua y Mayo, 1949, III, pp. 168–9).

96. Inventory of Pantoja's house and workshop, 3 November 1608: 'Mas treinta y cinco retratos bosquexados de diferentes personas' (Kusche, 1964, p. 262).

97. Jamesone to Sir Colin Campbell of Glenorchy, 23 June 1636, printed in Innes, 1855, p. 440; for the date, see D. Thomson, *The Life and Art of George Jamesone*, Oxford, 1974, p. 136.

98. For the relevant documents, see Luzio, 1913, pp. 209–16, 222–3. Some extracts follow: Lucrezia to Isabella, 13 July 1511: 'Lo Francia pictore al qual ho dato lo retratto suo mi ha dicto che manderà il carthono facto de sua mano presto presto ad V. Ex. . . .'; same to same, 31 July 1511: 'quando serà portato al judicio mio, per havere in lo animo scolpita la imagine viva de V. Ex., credo se non me ingano gli saprò demostrare tuti gli suoi veraci lineamenti . . .'; same to same, 26 September 1511: 'non più exhorterò il Francia pictore che venga a Mantoa a dessignare il suo natural retracto per le cause ad me allegate'; Isabella to Francia, 25 November 1511: 'Havemo recevuto il retratto che ni haveti mandato . . . avendoni vui cum l'arte vostra facta assai più bella che non ni ha facto natura, ringratiamovine quanto più potemo'; Lucrezia to Isabella, 9 December 1511: 'Perciò essendo a commutar gli occhij de nigri in bianchi lo evento dubio, per non guastare quel che sta appresso de bene et per non perdere lo certo per lo incerto, malvolenteri se metteria a tal periglio . . .'; Gian Francesco Zaninello to Isabella, Ferrara, 30 May 1512: 'mi è stata presentato la delicata efige de lo ex.^{te} S.^{r}

Federico suo figliolo . . . V.S. . . . ha ornato et favorito insieme con lo ritracto suo il mio basso tugurio, benchè hora se po' dire alto, et già assaissime persone vi concoreno, ove . . . ne restano amirative et forse con qualche invidia per havere ne la stantia mia et Venere et Cupidine'; Battista Stabellino to Isabella, Ferrara, 3 March 1534: 'V. Ex. mi scrisse una sua lettera per la quale mi comettea ch'io dimandassi il ritratto di quella al Zaninello, fratello de Joan Francesco Zaninello di b. m. e ge lo mandassi a Mantova con promissione di rimetterlo in qua fra il termine di un mese . . . Ma il retratto non è più mai ritornato in qua'; Isabella to the Mantuan ambassador in Venice, 6 March 1534: 'Perchè coloro che ci prestarono il ritratto di noi el qual ebbe Mess. Titiano per cavarne di lui uno simile ci fanno instantia grandissima che glielo restituiamo, volemo che voi ve lo facciate rendere . . .'; the ambassador Agnello to Isabella, 5 May 1536: 'lei medesima gli [Titian] potrà parlar del ritratto di Zaninelli et ordinarli glielo mandi subito sarà giunto qui'; Isabella to Agnello, 29 May 1536: 'Il ritratto nostro di man di Titiano ne piace di sorte che dubitiamo di non esser stata in quell' etade ch'egli rappresenta di quella beltà che in sè contiene . . . habbiamo deliberato di voler prima il ritratto de Zanninelli, il che gli farete intendere sollecitando che lo restituisca, acciò che homai sia renduto a quei gentilhomini che con desiderio l' aspettano et ben hanno ragione' (Luzio, 1913, pp. 210, 211, 212, 213, 214–15, 222, 223).

99. Giovanni della Casa to Cardinal Alessandro Farnese, 20 September 1545: 'Ms. Titiano mi ha donato un ritratto di N.S. di sua mano . . . E apparecchiato a ritrar l'Ill.ma Casa di V.S.R.ma in solidum tutti fino alle gatte, et se D. Iulio gli manda lo schizzo della cognata della Signora Camilla, lo farà grande et somigliaralla certo' (Campana, 1908, pp. 382–3). Titian's portrait of Francis I of France (Louvre, INV. 753) was done from a medal by Cellini (Wethey, 1971, p. 102, pl. 79).

100. Aretino to Giulia Varano, October 1545: 'Tiziano ha compreso il vostro esempio ne le parole del duca, né più né meno vivo e vero, che vero e vivo in voi stessa si sia . . . non altrimenti naturale vi ha ritratta che se gli foste stata senza far motto in presenza' (Camesasca, 1957–60, II, p. 92).

101. 'Altri si trovano, che alla sola relazione narratale della faccia, colore, aria, fatezze et altre proprietà della persona che non hanno mai veduta, apprendono con la felicità dell' ingegno talmente il tutto, e con l'arte così mirabilmente l'esprimono, come se l'avessero avuto longamente presente' (Paleotti, 1582; reprinted in Barocchi, 1971–7, III, p. 2722).

102. The drawing is in Stockholm (1/1863): Pope-Hennessy, 1966, p. 56.

103. 'gli fece un di loro . . . fare il ritratto di quel sceleratissimo capitano . . . o che gliele facesse vedere così morto, o in altro modo che glie lo mostrasse con disegni o con parole' (Vasari-Milanesi, 1878–85, IV, p. 601).

104. 'Dopo, si cominciò al tempo suo a formare le teste di coloro che morivano, con poca spesa; onde si vede in ogni casa di Firenze, sopra i cammini, usci, finestre e cornicioni, infiniti di detti ritratti, tanto ben fatti e naturali, che paiono vivi' (Vasari's life of Verrocchio: *ibid.*, III, p. 373).

105. Testimony of Jean Bourdichon, Tours, 19 July 1513: 'Joannes Bourdichon testis i deponit, quod ipse post obitum d. fr. Francisci accessit ad d. Conventum minimorum, & vidit corpus defuncti exanime, &, ut similitudinem vultus ejus secundum veram figuram depingeret, molavit & impressit . . . Et fuit presens praedictus testis, quando ipsum corpus à d. terra fuit elevatum . . . viditque vultum d. defuncti, illis jam decem aut duodecim diebus elapsis, ita sanum, ita integrum & sine corruptione, sicut erat eo tempore quo prius fuerat inhumatum . . . Deponit insuper quod iterum molavit seu impressit vultum d. defuncti, ut certius & melius ipsum pingeret' (G. Henschenius and D. Papebrochius, *Acta Sanctorum, Aprilis, I*, Antwerp, 1675, pp. 148, 159, 160: D. Macgibbon, *Jean Bourdichon*, Glasgow, 1933, pp. 52–3, etc.).

106. Vasari-Milanesi, 1878–85, V, p. 547; VII, p. 445; Langedijk, 1981–3, I, pp. 110–11; II, p. 1028, 1034. The portrait sent to Cosimo, Uffizi 934, is by Gianpaolo Pace (Langedijk, 1981–3, II, p. 1029).

107. 'Ricordo questo dì 29 di luglio detto [1583] come io ho consegnato a M.[a] Lucretia Capponi de' Torrigiani un ritratto di Messer Raffaello suo marito fatto dopo suo morte, alto br. 2 e largo a corrispondenza, con molto tempo sì di uestito come nella testa, che non ho hauuto altro un poco di forma di terra che lo feci poi dopo suo morte parechi mesi, e detto ritratto è suo prezzo rispetto alle dette fatiche e tempo scudi trenta d'oro' (Supino, 1908, p. 30).

108. Albrecht, Duke of Prussia, to the widow of Veit Dietrich, 1 July 1549: 'Ferner verstehen wir, dasz die Moler zu Nuremberg Euers seligen Herrn Biltnus in ein Gybs gossen und Ir geneigt, uns ein Stück davon zuzusenden; weil es uf die Zeit allerding nicht fertig gewesen, seint wir desselben in Gnaden noch gewertig' (Ehrenberg, 1899, p. 183); same to same, 22 June 1550: 'Und seintemal Ir Euch gegen uns Euers lieben Herrn Contrafect halben, ob wir die vielleicht auf einem Tuch oder sonsten haben wollten, erbieten thut, so begeren wir gnediglich, wo Ir solche Contrafect in Gestalt eines Brustbildes auf ein Tafel zu Weg bringen und verfertigen lassen kontet, Ir wollet dasselbe zu bestellen unbeschwert sein' (*ibid.*, p. 184); the widow to the duke, 8 December 1550: 'hab mich darauf, weil Jorg Pentz, seliger, von hinen verreifet war, neben Ueberschickung der abgossnen Bildnisz bei Meister Lucas Cronacher zu Wittenberg um solche Contrafaktur beworben, welcher vor wenig Tagen mir eine zugeschickt, doch solcher Unform, dasz sie weiter zu schicken nit würdig' (*ibid.*, p. 186).

109. See *ibid.*, pp. 154, 160, 170–1, 172–3, 182, 192–4, etc.

110. Albrecht to Sigismund Augustus, King of Poland, 18 January 1546: 'Quod s.r.v. majestas novis edibus ornandis illustrium virorum et mulierum hierarchiae Germanicae cum eorum progenie effigies veras et aetates, nomina et cognomina habere exoptat, dabo operam quam potero maximam, ut mediantibus meis literis a praestantissimis artis pictoriae magistris s.r.v. majestas voti compos reddatur et quidquid eiusmodi ad me missum fuerit, conabor, ne quid in eo transmittendo s.r.v. majestas de promptu et officiosa mea diligentia desiderare videatur' (*ibid.*, p. 171).

111. Giovio to Equicola, 28 August 1521, expressing his desire to adorn rooms with 'verissimis clarorum in litteris virorum imaginibus ut boni mortales eorum exemplo ad virtutes aemulatione gloriae accenderentur' (P. Giovio, *Lettere*, ed. G. G. Ferrero, I, Rome, 1956, p. 92).

112. Rovelli, 1928, pp. 139–41.

113. Vasari-Milanesi, 1878–85, VII, pp. 608–9; W. Prinz, 'La serie Gioviana' in Berti, 1979, p. 603.

114. L. Lalanne, 'Inventaire des tableaux et des autres curiosités qui se trouvaient au Louvre en 1603', *Archives de l'art français*, V (1853–5), pp. 49–60, pp. 55–60; Dimier, 1924–7, I, p. 142.

115. See above, p. 44.

116. Schade, 1980, pp. 448–9.

117. 'perchè non aveva i ritratti naturali, fece il Mattaccio il più delle teste a caso, ed in alcune ritrasse de' frati vecchi che allora erano in quel monastero' (Vasari-Milanesi, 1878–85, VI, p. 383).

118. J. Leeuwenberg, 'De tien bronzen "plorannen" in het Rijksmuseum te Amsterdam, hun herkomst en de voorbeelden waarvan zij zijn ontleend', *Gentse bijdragen tot de kunstgeschiedenis*, XIII (1951), pp. 13–59; Comblen-Sonkes and Van den Bergen-Pantens, 1977, I, pp. 166–9.

Chapter 8 The Functions and Uses of Portraits

1. 'Dan dy kunst des molens würt geprawcht jm dinst der kirchen vnd dordurch angetzeigt daz leiden Christi, behelt awch dy gestalt der menschen noch jrem absterben' (Rupprich, 1956–69, II, p. 113; translated in Conway, 1889, p. 117). Compare the wing panels painted at Arras but now at Douai (INV. 24) where on the interior faces are donor portraits of Nicaise Ladam (d. 1547) and his wife and on the outside faces are a representation of Death and the epitaph of Nicaise, which begins:

   Precogitant que lhomme est serf a pourriture
   En ce tableau est mis du corps la pourtraicture

   (exhibition catalogue *Les successeurs de Jean Bellegambe*, Musée de la Chartreuse, Douai, 1981–2, pp. 32–3 (23)).
2. The drawing is mentioned in Dürer's journal of his visit to the Netherlands: 'Jch hab den Erasmum Roterodam[um] noch einmal conterfet' (Rupprich, 1956–69, I, p. 156; translated in Conway, 1889, p. 102) and by Erasmus in a letter of 14 March 1525 to Pirckheimer: 'A Durerio, tanto nimirum artifice, pingi non recusem; sed qui possit, non video. Nam olim me Bruxellae deliniauit tantum, at coeptum opus interruperunt aulici salutatores' (Allen and Garrod, 1906–47, VI, p. 46). Erasmus expressed his opinion of the engraving in a another letter to Pirckheimer dated 30 July 1526: 'Si minus respondet effigies, mirum non est. Non enim sum is qui fui ante annos quinque' (*ibid.*, VI, pp. 371–2).
3. 'Un giorno festivo per capriccio ritrasse Mario mio padre in una tegola molto naturalmente, la qual ritenuta sopra l'uscio di una camera in sala, fu levata dopo la morte, acciocché non rinfrescasse di continuo la morte di persona tanto amata da tutta la famiglia; et per trascuraggine fu rotta, con infinito mio dispiacere, essend'io ancor forse in fasce; la quale, se fosse possibile, ricomperrei quantunque grandissimo prezzo' (note in a copy of the 1568 edition of Vasari's lives, published by Milanesi in Vasari-Milanesi, 1878–85, VI, p. 546). See further A. Brown, 'A Contract for Ridolfo Ghirlandaio's "Pietà"', *Burlington Magazine*, CXXX (1988), pp. 692–3.
4. 'con questa si risuerua le bellezze, le quali il tempo e la natura fa fugitive'; 'quante pitture hanno conservato il simulacro d'una divina bellezza, ch'el tempo o' morte in breve ha distrutto il suo naturale esempio, et è restata più degna l'opera del pittore che della natura sua maestra!' (Richter, 1970, I, pp. 77–8).
5. *Ibid.*, I, p. 77 n.
6. Christopher Hales to Heinrich Bullinger, London, 10 December 1550: 'Idirco enim cupiebam habere, ut et bibliothecae ornamento essent; et vestrae imagines effigies in tabella quasi in speculo conspicerentur iis, qui loci intercapedine prohiberentur, quo minus vos coram cernere possent. Non hoc agitur, vir praeclare, ut ex vobis idola faciamus: iis quas dixi de causis, non honoris aut cultus gratia, desiderantur' (*Epistolae Tigurinae*, Parker Society publication, Cambridge, 1848, p. 126; translated in H. Robinson, *Original Letters relative to the English Reformation*, I, Parker Society publication, Cambridge, 1846, pp. 190–1).
7. 'ich fühlte so viel Süssigkeit beim Anblick dieses so sehnsüchtig und inbrünstig erwarteten Bildes, dass ich nicht mehr wusste, in welcher Welt ich mich befand. Bei der Bewunderung und beim immer wiederholten Anblick der schönen Figur glaubte ich mich angesungen und verlor dabei die Erinnerung an alles andere in der Welt ... So fliesst mir nun die Zeit der Abwesenheit mit weit geringerer Pein dahin als anfangs, da ich mich nun an dieser Ansicht erfreuen werde bis zu Eurer Heimkunft' (L. Welti, *Graf Jakob Hannibal I. von Hohenems, 1530–1587, Ein Leben im Dienste des Katholischen Abenlandes*, Innsbruck, 1954, p. 234).
8. 'quando il padre, la madre, la moglie, o altre persone strette di lecita benevolenza chiedessero altrui in grazia il suo ritratto, per potere con questo mezzo dell presenza della pittura ristorare i danni dell'assenza di lui' (Paleotti, 1582; reprinted in Barocchi, 1971–7, III, pp. 2720–1).
9. 'introdusse usanza in quella città, che chi era in qualche grado si faceva o da lui o da altri ritrarre; onde in tutte le case di Vinezia sono molti ritratti, e in molte de' gentiluomini si veggiono gli avi e padri loro insino in quarta generazione, ed in alcune più nobili molto più oltre: usanza, certo, che è stata sempre lodevolissima, eziandio appresso gli antichi. E chi non sente infinito piacere e contento, oltre l'orrevolezza ed ornamento che fanno, in vedere l'imagini de' suoi maggiori; e massimamente se per i governi delle repubbliche, per opere egregie fatte in guerra ed in pace, e per lettere, o per altra notabile e segnalata virtù, sono stati chiari ed illustri?' (Vasari-Milanesi, 1878–85, III, pp. 168–9).
10. 'Dicesi, che essendogli stato occiso in Cortona un figliuolo che egli amava molto, bellissimo di volto e di persona, che Luca così addolorato lo fece spogliare ignudo, e con grandissima constanza d'animo, senza piangere o gettar lacrima, lo ritrasse, per vedere sempre che volesse, mediante l'opera delle sue mani, quello che la natura gli aveva dato e tolto la nimica fortuna' (Vasari-Milanesi, 1878–85, III, p. 691).
11. Funeral expenses of Ferdinand I, 1565: 'Johann Poyancz, gewester maller, hat khaiser Ferdinanden hochlöblichister und seliger gedächtnus toter abgemallet und dieselb conterfectur der herzogin von Mantua geschikht worden...' (Kreyczi, 1887, p. CIV (4391)).
12. Inventory dated 23 July 1593: 'Khaiser Maximilian des Ersten contrafactur, wie er auf die gejaider zogen mit einem armbrost an der hand; Khaiser Maximilian des Andern contrafactur, wie ir maj. seligist schon gestorben gewesen' (H. von Voltelini, 'Urkunden und Regesten', *Jahrbuch der kunsthistorischen Sammlungen des allerhöchsten Kaiserhauses*, XV (1894), pp. XLIX–CLXXIX (p. CXVII (12154/104–5))). A version of the deathbed portrait of Maximilian II is in the 'Portrait Book' of Hieronymus Beck: G. Heinz, 'Das Porträtbuch des Hieronymus Beck', *Jahrbuch der kunsthistorischen Sammlungen in Wien*, LXXI (1975), pp. 165–310 (p. 209, fig. 244).
13. 'Zu Eisleben/ehe diese Kirchen Ceremonien alle gebraucht/haben zweu Maler also das todte angesicht abconterfeit/einer von Eisleben/dieweil er noch im stüblin auff dem bett gelegen/Der ander/Meister Lucas Fortennagel von Hall/da er schon eine nacht im Sarck gelegen' (J. Jonas and M. Celius, *Vom Christlichen abschied aus diesem tödlichen leben des Ehrwirdigen Herrn D. Martini Lutheri, bericht*, Nuremberg, 1546, f. C iii v). The Eisleben painter's portrait is thought to have been used as the basis for various paintings produced in the Cranach workshop (Hanover and elsewhere); Furtenagel's drawing is at Berlin (KdZ 4545): see the exhibition catalogue Nuremberg, 1983, pp. 436–8 (603, 604). Girolamo Marchesi is said to have made a representation of the corpse of Gaston of Foix, killed at Ravenna in 1512 (Vasari-Milanesi, 1878–85, V, p. 183). A portrait of Alessandro Farnese, Duke of Parma, who died in 1592, 'morto vestito da Cappucino' was in the Palazzo Farnese in Rome in 1653 (Bertini, 1987, p. 207 (5)). Among surviving deathbed portraits may be noted those of Tanneken Balsoen, a nun of the Hospital of the Magdalen at Bruges, who died in 1534 (Hospital of St John, Bruges, PEN. XIX); an unidentified man and a woman who, according to the inscription on the frame, died in 1568 (attributed to Barthel Bruyn the Younger; Brussels, 7618–7619); Roger de Jonghe, confessor to the Black Nuns of St Augustine at Bruges, who died in 1579 (Bruges, 0.1616); and the unidentified lady who died in 1621 and who was depicted by a Netherlandish painter of great ability 'two hours after her death' (Rouen, 36–6: O. Popovitch, *Catalogue des peintures du*

Musée des beaux-arts de Rouen, Rouen, 1978, p. 49).

14. Aretino to Francesco Cusano, January 1544: 'Io nel mondo, che ciascun vede, appaio sculto non pure in piombo, in bronzo, in ariento e in oro, ma dipinto in tele, in tavole, in carte e in mura'; Aretino to Iunio Petreo, May 1545: 'le medaglie di conio, di getto in oro, in ariento, in rame, in piombo e in istucco io tengo il naturale de la effigie ne le facciate dei palazzi, io l'ho improntata ne le casse dei pettini, negli ornamenti degli specchi, nei piatti di maiolica al par d'Alessandro, di Cesare e di Scipio' (Camesasca, 1957–60, II, pp. 14, 73–4).
15. Isabella d'Este to Ludovico Sforza, Duke of Milan, 13 March 1499: 'Dubito venire in fastidio non solum a la S.V. ma ad tuta Italia cum mandare questi mei retracti in volta . . .' (Luzio and Renier, 1890, p. 665).
16. J. H. Lupton, ed., *The Utopia of Sir Thomas More*, Oxford, 1895, p. 233; E. Surtz and J. H. Hexter, eds, *The Complete Works of St Thomas More*, IV, New Haven and London, 1965, pp. 192–3.
17. 'non dovriano porsi in ritratto se non le persone le quali o con bontà morale o con santità cristiana potessero essere incitamento alle virtù'; 'quando vediamo ch'uno ha fatto ritrarre sé stesso, pare che in conseguenza venghi a dare un tacito giudicio di sé medesmo, di essere persona onorata, virtuosa o bella, il che . . . gli sminuisce il credito, parendo sciochezza ridicola che uno presuma tanto di sé stesso, che si reputi degno . . . di stare in prospettiva degli altri per essere veduto et ammirato'; 'non debbono procurarsi i ritratti di persone viziose o infami . . .'; 'si dovria curare ancora che la faccia o altra parte del corpo non fosse fatta o più bella o più grave o punto alterata da quella che la natura in quella età gli ha conceduto . . .'; 'nei ritratti di persone di grado e dignità dovriano i patroni procurare che fossero espressi con la gravità e decoro che conviene alla condizione loro, e non con cagnuoli o fiori o ventarole in mano, non con uceletti o papagalli o bertuccie appresso, non con abiti poco lodevoli . . .'; 'a' tempi nostri uno già valente e molto pio pittore bolognese, non si potendo difendere da simili ritratti per la importunità di persone di condizione, . . . si mosse, a conseglio de un religioso, quando era richiesto di tali ritratti, di dipingerli in iscambio una molto divota imagine di Cristo flagellato, o della Madonna, o d'altro santo o santa; la quale poi presentando al giovine lascivo, egli e gli altri, sì tosto che ciò vedevano, restavano stupefatti del santo inganno e sodisfattissimi del cambio . . .' (Paleotti, 1582, reprinted in Barocchi, 1971–7, III, pp. 2722, 2716, 2725, 2723, 2727).
18. 'el tratar de la Pintura es cosa dignísima, y el sacar al natural aquello que sólo Dios hizo por tan investigable sabiduría como Él sabe, quererlo un hombre de tierra imitar, debe de ser cosa muy grande y la mayor que los hombres pueden hacer . . . Digo . . . que solamente los claros Príncipes y Reyes o Emperadores merecen ser pintados y que queden sus imágines y figuras en su buena memoria a los futuros tiempos y edades . . . una illustre y clara Princesa o Reina que por su virtud y saber es dina de ser conocida de los venideros. Y también tiene entre éstos lugar cualquier hombre famoso en armas, o en debujo, o en letras, o en singular liberalidad, o virtud y no algún otro cualquier hombre; y ansimesmo es cosa lícita que tengan los hijos la memoria de su padre y madre y agüelos sacados al natural, para tenerlos siempre presentes para el acrescentamiento de su virtud y para su consolación y de los suyos, imitando cuanto pudieren a sus antecesores en la bondad y con ellos augmentando su pasada genealogía; y si alguno supiere amar muy fiel y castamente, dino es de tener al natural pintado el vulto que ama, ansí para las ausencias de la vida, como para la recordación después de la muerte' (Sánchez Cantón, 1921, pp. 253–4, 255).
19. Isabella d'Este to the Countess of Acerra, 13 January 1494: 'Per satisfare al desiderio de V.S., non perchè la effigie mia sia de tal beleza che la meriti andare in volta depincta, gli mando . . . el retracto in tavola facto per mano de Zohan de Sancte pictor de la Illma Duchessa di Urbino . . .' (Luzio, 1913, p. 189).
20. Tolomei to Sebastiano, Rome, 20 August 1543: 'Ecco io parlarò con uoi per lettere di quelle cose; di cui non hauerei mai ardimento parlarui in presenza . . . non so bene, s'ella è ambitione, o uanità, o l'una e l'altra mescolata insieme. Voi sapete quante uolte da uoi stesso . . . m'hauete detto, che in ogni modo mi uolete ritrarre . . . quando da uoi mi uegan gratia (come spero) alhora mi parerà hauer guadagnato uno specchio, il quale io sempre chimarò specchio diuino, percioche in quello uedrò uoi, e me stesso insieme. Voi, uedendo ne l'imagin mia la uostra singolar uirtu, e'l uostro marauiglioso artificio. Me, uedendo nell'arte uostra espressa uiuamente la mia imagine, laquale mi sarà continuo stimolo a purgare l'anima di molti suoi mancamenti . . . mi s'accenderà l'anima a bel desiderio d'honore e di gloria' (*Delle lettere di M. Claudio Tolomei libri sette*, Venice, 1581, ff. 97–98v).
21. Osborn, 1961, p. 133.
22. National Gallery, London (1036: Davies, 1968, pp. 137–8).
23. B. Capilupo, her secretary, to Isabella d'Este, then away from Mantua, 24 November 1514: 'questa nocte [il marchese Francesco] mandò a tore il suo retracto qual era ne la camera de le arme et quello de V.S. che era nel camerino et li manda al p.to Re. Credo che andando in così alto loco non spiacerà a V.S. chel ne habbi compiaciuto questo ambassadore [de Inghilterra] qual li ha richiesti' (Luzio, 1913, p. 208 n. 3).
24. Mulcahy, 1984, pp. 775–7.
25. 'nos portraits que je vous envoie afin de vous en rafraîchir la mémoire' (L. Battifol, 'Marie de Médicis et les arts', *Gazette des beaux-arts*, 3e pér., XXXV (1906), pp. 221–43, p. 223).
26. Undated letter: 'Con vuestra pintura, hija, he holgado mucho, pues no puedo ver la natural, plega à Dios pueda ser alguna hora, con vuestra contentamiento, que serà el mio, y os guarde como deseo. Vuestra madre Leonor' (M. Pacheco, *Vida de la Serenissima Infanta Doña Maria*, Lisbon, 1675, f. 24).
27. Undated letter: 'Madame grant mamen me envoyra a la Roynne Madame, mais que je soy pinct en une toille et sy grant que moy et suis tant jolly que je suis tondu comme mes oncles' (Wood, 1923, pp. 81–2).
28. Catherine to M. d'Humières, 17 June 1548: 'J'ai receu les painctures de mes enffans que vous m'avez faict faire, lesquelles j'ay trouvées fort belles et fort bien faictes; et me semble advis par là que mesdicts enffans sont bien amendez depuis que je ne les ay veuz . . .' (Moreau-Nélaton, 1901, p. 15).
29. Catherine to Madame d'Humières, 1 June 1552: 'Ne fauldrez de faire paindre au vif par le painctre que vous avez par delà tous mes dicts enfans, tant fils que filles, avec la roine d'Escosse, ainsi qu'ils sont, sans rien oublier de leurs visaiges; mais il suffist que ce soit au créon pour avoir plus tost faict, et me les envoiez le plus tost que vous pourrez . . .'; same to same, 16 June 1552: 'sitost qu'ils seront paincts, je vous prie ne faillir de m'en envoyer les portraicts . . . je vous prie de m'envoyer lesditz portraicts par la poste' (*ibid.*, pp. 21–2).
30. Francesco I, Grand Duke of Tuscany, to Vincenzo I, Duke of Mantua, 24 May 1586: 'Metta all'Alt.^{za} V. in consideratione, se . . . ueggendo dal Ritratto, et sentendo da ognuno, che il Puttino, che Dio lo benedica, è così grasso, et grosso, et rigoglioso, fusse a' proposito in capo al Mese incenderlo . . . io ho inceso sempre tutti i miei Figliuoli . . . non hauessino Cerusio pratico di questo affare, ne manderei uno di quà . . .' (Archivio di Stato, Mantua, AG b. 1089: I am grateful to Dr David Chambers for sending me a photocopy of this letter). The child, later Francesco IV of Mantua,

was born on 7 May 1586.

31. The paintings are now in the Pitti: Langedijk, 1981–3, II, pp. 781–2.
32. Nicolas, 1828, p. 10.
33. 'Tam elegantis formae et praestantissimae facetiae fuit haec domina . . . quòd Christianissimus rex Franciae, auditâ ipsius famâ, misit secreto modo pictorem subtilem ad portrahendam effigiem virginei sui vultûs, proponens eam sibi assumere in uxorem: sed antequam pictor ad Scotiam pervenit, ab alio suo amatore . . . praeventa fuit et eidem matrimonialiter copulata' (W. Goodall, ed., *Joannis de Fordun Scotichronicon, cum Supplementis et Continuatione Walteri Bower*, 2 vols, Edinburgh, 1759, II, p. 403).
34. 'ad regiones memoratas pictorem peritissimum mittentes, qui trium insignium puellarum graciosas facies tabulis effigiaret. Quas cum regi obtulissent, dominam Ysabellam de Bavaria, quartum decimum annum agentem, preelegit, et longe ante alias specie et pulchritudine insignem judicavit' (Bellaguet, 1839–52, I, p. 358).
35. 'per Duo Teste designate e colorite in tella de man de Cosome depinctore una de lo Illmo D.S. n. laltra de M.ª Lucretia fiola de Sua Ex.ª le qualli teste forno mandate a Napoli ala Illma Duchessa M.ª Elionora Consorte del prefato n.s.' (account of extraordinary expenditure, 1472: Venturi, 1888, p. 355 n. 1).
36. Payment of 13 October 1477 'a Goseme depinctore . . . per soa mercede de havere depincto tre Imazine naturale de lo Illu. don Alfonso primozenito de prefacto n.S.' (*ibid.*, p. 361 n. 2).
37. Nicolò Roberti to Paolo Antonio Troto, Milan, 27 July 1477: 'Poi. chel retracto del nostro Illustrissimo don Alfonso e sta dato ali Anbasatori de questa Madonna che ritornano *sit cum dei nomine* me piaze. Quello de la Illustrissima. M.ª Anna hancora non e fornito e questo e sta per Manchamento del Magistro che e Franzoso che si e sdignato e ricussava volerlo liverarlo . . .' (Venturi, 1885^{1}, p. 227).
38. Adam von Zwetkowich to the Emperor Maximilian II, London, 4 June 1565: V. von Klarwill, *Queen Elizabeth and Some Foreigners*, London, 1928, p. 218.
39. Dispatch of Adam von Dietrichstein, Madrid, 29 June 1564: 'Von angesicht ist er zimblich wol gestalt, hat kheine bose Faction . . . der ain axl hoher ain wenig alls die andere . . . den linkhen fuess auch vmb ain gutz lenger dan den rechten, vnd braucht die ganz recht seiten ybler dan die linkhe . . .' (M. Koch, *Quellen zur Geschichte des Kaisers Maximilian II.*, 2 vols, Leipzig, 1857–61, I, p. 127; Zimmermann, 1909–10, p. 165 n. 5).
40. Dispatch of Dietrichstein, Madrid, 4 July 1564: 'allain das angesiht ist nit so vol und er blacher dan er in gemäl, die augen nit so offen und aufgethan, der munt stats offen, der linkh fues ain guetz lenger dan der reht und dekht der rokh auch vill, wie den euher majestet aus meinen schreiben vernumen' (*ibid.*, p. 166 n. 3).
41. Dispatch of Dietrichstein, Madrid, 10 October 1567: 'Er hat meinen weib gester abents ain diemantes khreiz geschikht, ist iwer tausent dukhaten wert, vonwegen meiner genadigisten frauen der prinzesa Ana abconterfehung, welche er stats bei sich tregt' (*ibid.*, p. 165 n. 2).
42. M. de Noailles to Mary of Guise, 1 September 1559: 'ladicte Dame me monstra vostre pourtraict qu'elle a dans sa gallerie de Hamptoncourt, non sans me tenir plusieurs propos de vostre bonté, honnesteté et vertu, me chargeant pour la fin de vous présenter ses très affectueuses recommandations' (A. Teulet, *Papiers d'état . . . relatifs à l'histoire de l'Ecosse*, I, Paris, 1851, p. 338).
43. L. de Burbure, *De Antwerpsche ommegangen in de XIVe en XVe eeuw* (Maatschappij der Antwerpsche bibliophilen, Uitgave N^{r} 2), Antwerp, 1878, pp. 1–5.
44. '*Item*, devant le Chastellet de Paris, avoit ung grant escharfault devant lequel avoit ung pavillon de couleur jaune et violete; et au milieu dudit pavillon avoit un lis ou estoient figurez et emprains IX pourtraictures de roys . . .' (Louis himself and his ancestors back to St Louis: printed description republished in B. Guenée and F. Lehoux, *Les entrées royales françaises de 1328 à 1515* (Sources d'histoire médiévale publiées par l'Institut de recherche et d'histoire des textes, 5), Paris, 1968, p. 132).
45. Nichols, 1850, pp. 78–9; see above, p. 134.
46. M. van der Vennet, 'Le peintre bruxellois Antoine Sallaert', *Bulletin des Musées royaux des beaux-arts de Belgique*, XXIII/XXIV (1974–80), pp. 171–98, pp. 171–2.
47. 'wer ime in seinem leben kain gedachtnus macht, der hat nach seinem tod kain gedächtnus und desselben menschen wird mit dem glockendon vergessen, und darumb so wird das gelt, so ich auf die gedechtnus ausgib, nit verloren . . .' (A. Schultz, 'Der Weisskunig', *Jahrbuch der kunsthistorischen Sammlungen des allerhöchsten Kaiserhauses*, VI (1888), p. 66).
48. Anzelewsky, 1980, pp. 168–72, pl. 160.
49. Schultz, *op. cit.*
50. Alfonsina Orsini (Lorenzo's mother) to Giovanni Lepucci, 7 September 1518: 'Hovvi a dire ch' la Pictura di N.S. et monsignor reverendissimo de' Medici et Rossi, el Duca la fece mectere sopra alla tavola, dove mangiava la Duchessa et li altri signori, che veramente rallegrava ogni cosa' (Langedijk, 1981–3, I, p. 42).
51. 'Un retrato entero del Rey Don Phelippe nuestro señor armado, con mangas de malla y corselete, con vn bastón en la mano, y banda roja, con botas y espuelas y calças blancas, de pinzel sobre lienzo, de mano de Antonio Moro, puesto en su marco de madera, dorado y pintado de azul; que tiene dos baras y dos tercias de alto y bara y media de ancho; es retrato de la manera que andaua quando la guerra de Sant Quintin' (J. Zarco Cuevas, *Inventario de las alhajas . . .*, Madrid, 1930, p. 131).
52. Stafford to Walsingham, Paris, 17 November 1583 (Public Record Office, London, SP 78/10/79; see also Strong, 1963, p. 32). For a satirical picture 'fait à Milan lors de la guerre de Sauoye' which in 1603 hung in the king's cabinet in the Louvre, see L. Lalanne, 'Inventaire des tableaux et des autres curiosités qui se trouvaient au Louvre en 1603', *Archives de l'art français*, V (1853–5), pp. 49–60, pp. 52–4.
53. J. Kaulek, *Inventaire analytique des Archives du Ministère des affaires étrangères. Correspondance politique de MM. de Castillon et de Marillac, ambassadeurs de France en Angleterre (1537–1542)*, Paris, 1885, p. 350.
54. P. L. Hughes and J. F. Larkin, eds, *Tudor Royal Proclamations*, II: *The Later Tudors (1553–1587)*, New Haven and London, 1969, pp. 240–1.
55. J. R. Dasent, ed., *Acts of the Privy Council of England*, n.s., XXVI, London, 1902, p. 69.
56. D. Digges, *The Compleat Ambassador*, London, 1655, p. 30.
57. M. de Noailles to Henry II of France, 7 September 1553: '& me semble, sire, qu'il seroit aussy bien à propoz que la royne luy envoyast quelques presens . . . luy envoyant aussy par mesme moyen sa paincture, & luy demandant la sienne que je sçay desja avoir faict faire, & qu'elle desire bientost faire apparoistre' (Abbé de Vertot, ed., *Ambassades de Messieurs de Noailles en Angleterre*, II, Leyden, 1763, pp. 145–6).
58. Schade, 1980, p. 451.
59. See the gaming board dated 1537 and signed by Hans Kels the Elder at Vienna (3419: *Katalog der Sammlung für Plastik und Kunstgewerbe*, II: *Renaissance* (*Führer durch das Kunsthistorische Museum*, 11), Vienna, 1966, pp. 62–4, pls 48–9). Mary I of England received as a New Year's gift in 1557 from Sir Henry Neville 'a lute in a case couerid with blake silke and golde/ with two litell rounde blak tables thone of the Phisnamy of the Emperour and the kings Maiestie thother of the king of Boheme and his wif' (Roll of gifts, British Library MS Add. 62525: published by J. Nichols, *Illustrations of the Manners and Expences of Antient Times*, London, 1797, p. 7).
60. Letter of 26 April 1498: 'Essendone hogi

accaduto vedere certi belli retracti de man de Zoanne Bellino siamo venute in ragionamento de le opere de Leonardo cum desiderio de vederle al parangone di queste havemo, et ricordandone che'l v'ha retracta voi dal naturale vi pregamo che per il presente cavallaro quale mandiamo a posta per questo ne vogliati mandare esso vostro retracto, perchè ultra che 'l ne satisfarà al parangone vederemo anche voluntieri il vostro volto et subito facta la comparatione vi lo remetteremo' (Luzio, 1887, p. 32). For Cecilia's reply, dated 29 April, see A. Luzio, 'Ancora Leonardo da Vinci e Isabella d'Este', *Archivio storico dell'arte*, I (1888), pp. 181–4, p. 181.

61. Luzio, 1913, p. 184 (Girolamo da Sestola to Isabella, 24 January 1532).
62. Isabella to Girolamo, 31 January 1532: 'Mando per contento della Illma S. Duchessa il retratto mio che ho pensato esser quello del qual voi mi scrivete per esser fatto in tempo ch'io era in età di circa tre anni . . . Ho fatto dare al Pittore un altro mio retratto che si fece dopo ch'io venni a marito per farlo rinfrescare. Come el sii in ordine ve lo mandarò' (Luzio, 1913, p. 184).
63. Girolamo to Isabella, 8 February 1532: 'O' abuto li retrati e subito li portai a la S.^{ra} Duchessa e tanto li son piaciuti che non lo poteria dire, e subito andasimo da la putina. S.^{ra} mia, il retrato putina li suomia certissimamente, dal naso in zoso è tuta de V.S.' (*ibid.*, p. 185).
64. *Ibid.*
65. Letter of 18 April 1507: 'Et quant la chançon sera faicte par Fenyn et voz visaiges pourtraitz par Jehan de Paris, ferez bien de les m'envoyer pour monstrer aux dames de par deça, car il n'en y a point de pareilz' (R. de Maulde, 'Jean Perréal et Pierre de Fénin, A propos d'une lettre de Louis XII (1507)', *Nouvelles archives de l'art français*, 3e sér., II (1886), pp. 1–9, p. 9).
66. Francis, Earl of Bedford, to Sir Nicholas Throckmorton, Berwick, 14 February 1566: Historical Manuscripts Commission, *Report on the Pepys Manuscripts preserved at Magdalene College, Cambridge*, London, 1911, p. 77.
67. Letter of 5 July 1567: Kervyn de Lettenhove and L. Gilliodts-Van Severen, eds, *Relations politiques des Pays-Bas et de l'Angleterre sous le règne de Philippe II*, 11 vols (Commission royale d'histoire), Brussels, 1882–1900, IV, p. 470.
68. *Ibid.*, IX, p. 336.
69. Henry Cobham to Walsingham, Paris, 22 January 1581–2 (Public Record Office, London, SP 78/7/12; see also Strong, 1963, pp. 20–1).
70. Dimier, 1924–7, III, pp. 5–14; Moreau-Nélaton, 1924, II, pp. 157–62.
71. 'elle fut si ravie et entra en tel extase d'amour et d'ardent désir à l'imitation de ces lascives peintures, qu'elle ne peut voir qu'au quatriesme feuillet, et au cinquiesme elle tomba esvanouie' (Brantôme, 1864–82 edn, IX, pp. 516–17).
72. It would appear that Seisenegger at Augsburg in 1530 had to execute two portraits of this kind of the Emperor Ferdinand I. In his bill of 1535, he complained at some length of the difficulties of painting such 'perspectifische angesicht' (Kreyczi, 1887, p. CXV).
73. Langedijk, 1981–3, I, pp. 657–8.
74. Vasari-Milanesi, 1878–85, VII, pp. 131–3. Henry's widow Catherine de' Medici appears to have owned a similar portrait: 'Ung portraict du feu roy Henry représenté en perspective dans ung miroir au haut de ladicte cheminée' (Bonnaffé, 1874, p. 162).
75. '& à la verité ces images dans la nouueauté ont eu assez de cours, encore qu'il n'y ait pas grand artifice à les dresser: mais maintenant elles se sont rendües si communes et triuiales, qu'on en veoit par tout . . .' (J. F. Nicéron, *La perspective curieuse*, Paris, 1638, pp. 78–80, 50–1).
76. Shaw, 1937, p. 37.
77. 'Je me suis trouvé une fois en une grande compagnie de cour où l'on advisoit le pourtrait de deux filles d'une très-grande reine. Chacun se mit à dire son advis à qui elles ressembloyent, de sorte que tous et toutes dirent qu'elles tenoyent du tout de la mère; mais moy . . . je pris l'affirmative, et dis qu'elles tenoyent du tout du père, et que si l'on eust cogneu et veu le père comme moy, l'on me condescendroit. Sur quoy la soeur de cette mère m'en remercia . . . d'autant qu'il y avoit aucunes personnes qui le disoyent à dessein, pour ce qu'on la soupçonnait de faire l'amour, et qu'il y avoit quelque poussière dans sa fleute, comme l'on dit' (Brantôme, 1864–82 edn, IX, p. 155).
78. 'sepe in officinā tuam venditant . . . ingenii tui monumenta cū summo stupore admirantes/et cum summa animi voluptate exemplaria tua collaudantes . . .' ('Ad Lucam Chronū . . . Doctoris Schewrli Epistola' in C. Scheurl, *Oratio doctoris Scheurli attingens litteratū prestantiam/necnon laudem Ecclesie Collegiate Vittenburgensis*, Leipzig, 1509, f. A iij).
79. 'Aposentólo en unas casas principales junto á palacio, donde, teniendo él solo la llave, por un tránsito secreto, con ropa de levantar, solia muchas veces entrar en su casa á deshora y asaltarlo comiendo con su familia, y queriendo levantarse á hacerle la debida reverencia como á su rey, le mandaba que se estuviese quedo, y se entraba á entretener en su obrador. Otras veces le cogia sentado pintando, y llegando por las espaldas le ponia las manos sobre los hombros, y viéndose Alonso Sanchez tan favorecido de Su Majestad, y procurando con justo comedimiento ponerse en pié, le hacia sentar y proseguir su pintura' (Pacheco, 1866 edn, I, p. 126; translated in Mulcahy, 1984, p. 775).
80. 'Item, la premiere sepmaine de may audit an mil IIII^{c} XXXVIII, à chascune des IIII portes de Paris, deux à la porte et une dessus les barrieres encontre le mur, on attacha III pieces de toile tres bien peintes de tres laides histoires; car en chascune avoit painct ung chevalier des grans signeurs d'Angleterre, icelluy chevallier estoit pendu par les piez à un gibet, les esperons chaussés; tout armé senon la teste, et à chascun costé un diable qui l'enchaînoit et II corbeaux laidz et hideux qui estoient en bas en son visage, qui luy arrachoient les yeux de la teste par semblant' (A. Tuety, ed., *Journal d'un Bourgeois de Paris 1405–1449* (Société de l'histoire de Paris), Paris, 1881, p. 340).
81. Galeazzo Maria Sforza to Giorgio de Annono, Pavia, 1 May 1470: 'Volimo et cosi vi commettiamo che subito faciati depingere li suso la piazza et suso la torre del horologlio et in li altri loghi publici messer Manfredo da Corezo per ribelle nostro, havendo advertentia de farlo depingere vestito de brochato doro et con li capelli canuti, et più naturale sij possibile acciò che ogniuno intenda che e' (Malaguzzi Valeri, 1902, p. 140).
82. 'la nocte seguente fu rascado Messer Manfredo predicto zoxo dove era depinto con li pedi in suso per traditore del Duca di Milano' ('Diario ferrarese dall'anno 1409. sino al 1502. Di autori incerti' in L. A. Muratori, *Rerum Italicarum Scriptores*, XXIV, Milan, 1738, cols 173–408 (col. 227)).
83. Shearman, 1965, II, pp. 320–1, 324, 340–1. See also S. Y. Edgerton, *Pictures and Punishment: Art and Criminal Prosecution during the Florentine Renaissance*, Ithaca and London, 1985.
84. 'Pieter de Beert es ghecōdēpneert bij vōnesse vā der wet slants van Veurenambocht te stellene dit hoofd ōme dat hij gheseijt heift eeneghe woorden inhoudende dreeghement vā der wet tvorseits slās ter veīstere uut te worpene 1499' (exhibition catalogue *Flanders in the Fifteenth Century*, Detroit Institute of Arts, 1960, pp. 285–6 (124)). See also J. B. Canaert, *Bydragen tot de kennis van het oude strafrecht in Vlaenderen*, 3rd edn, Ghent, 1835.
85. Exhibition catalogue *Painting in Scotland 1570–1650*, Scottish National Portrait Gallery, Edinburgh, 1975, p. 34 (25) and pl. facing p. 38.
86. D. Calderwood, *The History of the Kirk of Scotland*, ed. T. Thomson, V, Edinburgh, 1844, p. 145.

87. J. Spotswood, *The History of the Church of Scotland*, London, 1655, p. 411; compare *The Historie and Life of King James the Sext* (Bannatyne Club publication), Edinburgh, 1825, p. 347.
88. 'ui fu trouato uno libro nel quale sotto diuersi habiti & etate: al naturale erano depicte molti femine per loro uiolate in molte citate: e seco il portauano per memoria' (B. Corio, *Historia . . . di Milano . . .*, Milan, 1503, f. V iii v); 'In quella preda uidi io un libro, nel quale erano dipinte uarie imagini di meretrici sotto diuerso habito, & età, ritratte al naturale: secondo che la lasciuia, & l'amore l'haueua tratto in ciascuna città: queste portaua egli seco dipinte per ricordarsene poi' (A. Benedetti, *Il fatto d'arme del Tarro*, Venice, 1549, f. 31).
89. Sammlung Oskar Reinhart 'Am Römerholz', Winterthur. The inscription is 'Etas mea 51 dum scriberetur 1.5.0.9. fui in terra sancta' (Friedländer, 1967–76, VII, pl. 43).
90. 'Hi mihi sunt Comites, quos ipsa Pericula ducunt' (W. Camden, *The History of the Most Renowned and Victorious Princess Elizabeth, Late Queen of England*, 4th edn, London, 1688, p. 340). Babington was later advised to change the second clause to 'quorsum hec alio properantibus' (T. B. Howell, *A Complete Collection of State Trials*, I, London, 1816, p. 1138; W. K. Boyd, *Calendar of State Papers relating to Scotland and Mary, Queen of Scots*, VIII, London, 1914, p. 687).
91. Boyd, *op. cit.*, pp. 689, 687.
92. *Ibid.*, pp. 581–2.
93. For example, the series at Lumley Castle of the ancestors of John, Lord Lumley (1533–1609): Strong, 1969[2], pp. 45–6.
94. 'i mercanti e banchieri che non mai videro spada ignuda, a quali propriamente si aspetta la penna nell'orecchia con la gonella intorno et il giornale davanti, si ritraggono armati con bastoni in mano da generali . . .' (G. P. Lomazzo, *Trattato dell'arte della pittura, scoltura e architettura*, Milan, 1584; reprinted in Barocchi, 1971–7, III, p. 2743).
95. Orazio della Rena to Ferdinando I, Grand Duke of Tuscany, Ferrara, 13 May 1589: 'Universalmente tutti, piccoli e grandi portan la spada a canto . . . cercan sempre tutte le strade di parer cavalieri, a che s'aiutano ancora col farsi dipinger tali, che ho osservato in molte imagini di private et mediocri persone aver visto dal ritratto, che se non mi fosse stato detto il nome harei pensato esser l'imagine di un Achille o di un Hettore così fregiate d'oro son le dipinte armature del Dosso' (G. Agnelli, 'Relazione dello stato di Ferrara di Orazio della Rena (1589)', *Atti della Deputazione ferrarese di storia patria*, VIII (1896), pp. 245–322, p. 269).
96. See, for example, the album that belonged to Johan Franck, who appears to have taught law at the University of Douai and who between 1575 and 1578 collected in this book portraits of his pupils: sold at Sotheby's, 22 June 1982 (51).
97. 'Les seigneurs qu'ilz m'ont promis me donner leur paintures ou pourtretures se sont ichy soubzsinés, 1541' (Pinchart, 1860–81, II, pp. 91–2).
98. The drawing of Barthélemy is on f. 282 of the Recueil; the drawing of Marie has been removed but has left an impression on the verso of f. 282. On f. 282 is the note: 'Ce portrait et celuy de sa femme se trouvoient al eglise de berclau en 1725'.
99. 'Cernitur etiamnum effigies suae gentis numerosae, desuper tabellam summi judicii, in templo Berclavensi appensa cum gentilitiis' (Chanoine van Drival, *Nécrologe de l'abbaye de St-Vaast*, Arras, 1878, p. 70).
100. E. Renders and F. Lyna, 'Le Maître de Flémalle, Robert Campin et la prétendue école de Tournai', *Gazette des beaux-arts*, 6e pér., VI (1931), pp. 298–97. On the Alatruye family, see P. Denis du Péage, 'Recueil de généalogies lilloises, III', *Mémoires de la Société d'études de la province de Cambrai*, XIV (1908), pp. 899–918.
101. By her will of 13 July 1654, Baertjen Martens, widow of Herman Doomer, left their portraits by Rembrandt to their son Lambert on condition that he should have copies made, at his own expense, for each of his siblings (W. L. Strauss and M. van der Meulen, *The Rembrandt Documents*, New York, 1979, p. 318).
102. Louvre, INV. 1911, inscribed: 'D. MEMORIAE SACR. HANC TABVLAM SIBI SVISQ. PINXIT AC DEDICAVIT OTHO VENIVS ANNO M D XXCIV HAC LEGE VT SI IPSVM NVLLIS VIRILIS SEXVS LIBERIS SVPERSTITIBVS MORI CONTINGAT, IN FAMILIA NATV MAXIMI FRATRIS SIT QVADIV IBI MASCVLA PROLES FVERIT, QVA DEFICIENTE CEDAT SEMPER FRATRI AETATE ILLI PROXIMO EJVSQ FAMILIAE QVAMDIV ET ILLI MASCVLA PROLES SVPER FVERIT' (Michel, 1953, p. 265).
103. 'altro sarà quando, per occasione de liti in parte lontana, bisognasse provare la somiglianza tra padre e figliuoli o fratelli o altri' (Paleotti, 1582; reprinted in Barocchi, 1971–7, III, p. 2721).
104. E. S. Donno, *An Elizabethan in 1582. The Diary of Richard Madox, Fellow of All Souls* (Hakluyt Society publication, 2nd ser., 147), London, 1976, pp. 89–90. It is often claimed that Johann, Count of Solms-Lich, had his portrait painted in 1483 by Erhard Reuwich before setting out on a pilgrimage to the Holy Land, but the evidence is inconclusive (F. Uhlhorn, 'Zur Geschichte der Breidenbachschen Pilgerfahrt', *Gutenberg-Jahrbuch*, 1934, pp. 107–11).
105. Described as 'un retratto de so fio de età de tre anni' ('Annali veneti dall'anno 1457 al 1500 del senatore Domenico Malipiero', *Archivio storico italiano*, VII (1843–4), p. 371). By 1532 it was in the collection of Andrea Odoni, where it was seen by Marcantonio Michiel. He stated that it had been 'acquistato da soldati nostri nel fatto d'arme dal Taro tralla preda regia' (Frimmel, 1896, p. 86).
106. Osborn, 1961, pp. 20, 49, 133, frontispiece and pl. facing p. 211.
107. 'io ti voglio ritrarre, acciò si veggia in questa tua età, come ti sei ben conservata, e si conosca nondimeno quanto hai mutato effigie, e sia per esser questo diverso dai primi ritratti' (Vasari-Milanesi, 1878–85, V, p. 48).
108. Mary of Hungary to the ambassador Renard, Brussels, 19 November 1553: 'Et vous lui direz dadvantaige qu'ayant entendu . . . le désir qu'elle avoit de veoir la pourtraicture dudict sieur prince, que nous vous en envoyons, avec ceste, une faicte de la main de Titiano il y a trois ans, jugée par tous, selon qu'il estoit lors, fort naturelle . . . Et si pourra, de ce qu'estoit lors, conjecturer le progrez qu'il aura faict par l'adjonction de trois ans davantaige d'eage . . .' (Weiss, 1843, p. 150).
109. Isabella d'Este to Hieronymo Ziliolo, Mantua, 28 April 1512: 'havemo uno retracto di la fe. me. delo Ill.o S. nostro patre, molto simile et bono, ma cum una beretta et zupone antiqui de quelli che se solevano usare. Voressimo farne cavare un altro da questo cum una beretta et zupone de quelli chel portava al tempo chel moritte' (Luzio, 1913, p. 187 n. 1).
110. Ziliolo to Isabella, 9 April 1528: 'ho fatto acconciare da M.ro Dosso li doi retratti de l'ill.mi S. Duca Hercole et Madama Eleonora di bo. me.' (*ibid.*)
111. Letter of 22 February 1546: 'kann ich auf dis Mal nicht mer König oder Fürsten Conterfekt schicken. E.F.G. haben vor gesehen, was ich noch gehabt hab. Was E.F.G. nicht gesehen hat, die seind hier aufgezeichent in ein Registerlein . . .' (Ehrenberg, 1899, p. 172).
112. Journal of a nephew of Giovanni Capello, Venetian ambassador to France: 'Et andassemo a veder in detto tempo un pittor eccellentissimo qual oltrà le sue belle pitture che ne mostro, vedessemo tutta la corte de Franza si de gentilhuomini come di damiselle in molti quadretti naturalissimamente espressa' (A. Baschet, 'Un peintre et curieux à Lyon, en 1551', *L'Intermédiaire des chercheurs et curieux*, V (1869), cols 277–8).
113. 'il me souvient qu'elle estant ung jour allée voir à Lyon un peintre, qui s'appelloit Corneille, qui avoit peint en une grand' chambre tous les grand seigneurs . . . et . . .

dames . . . de la court de France, estant donc en ladicte chambre de ces paintures, nous y vismes cette reyne parestre painte très-bien en sa beauté et en sa perfection . . . A quoy elle prist fort grand plaisir à telle veue . . . si bien qu'elle n'en peust retirer ses yeux de dessus . . .' (Brantôme, 1864–82 edn, VII, pp. 343–4).

114. Osborn, 1961, pp. 48, 133.

115. W. A. D. Englefield, *The History of the Painter-Stainers Company of London*, London, 1923, p. 68.

116. 'Desen liet den Hertogh sien/zijn en zijns eerstẽ Huysvrouwen Conterfeytsel . . .' (Van Mander, 1604, f. 262v). For Hoefnagel's activity at the Bavarian court, see Vignau-Wilberg, 1985, *passim*.

117. Dürer gave to Raphael a self-portrait painted on linen (Vasari-Milanesi, 1878–85, IV, p. 354); a female painter, possibly Levina Teerlinc, gave to Giulio Clovio a self-portrait, and Clovio certainly owned at the time of his death 'Un scattolino tondo con il ritratto di Livinia meniatrice della Regina d'Inghilterra' (A. Bertolotti, 'Don Giulio Clovio, principe dei miniatori', *Atti e memorie delle RR. Deputazioni di storia patria per le provincie dell'Emilia*, n.s., VII, ii (1882), pp. 259–79, p. 274; see also above, Chapter 1 n. 66). The humanist Lampsonius, who was also an amateur painter, offered in 1564 to send a small self-portrait to Vasari (Vasari-Milanesi, 1878–85, VII, p. 591). Sofonisba Anguissola gave a self-portrait to Pope Julius III (*ibid.*, VII, p. 133).

118. 'Antonio Moro, Natural de Utrec civdad en Olanda, Pintor famosissimo, retratado de su propria mano'; 'Ticiano Pintor, el mas excelente de su tiempo, natural de Venecia, cuyo retrato se ve, teniendo en sus manos otro con la Ymagen del Rey don Phelippe nuestro señor' (Roblot-Delondre, 1910, pp. 58–9).

119. 'Item 6 persohn haben mir nichts geben, die jch zu Prüssel hab conterfet' (Rupprich, 1956–69, I, p. 156; translated in Conway, 1889, p. 102).

120. See above n. 3.

121. Executors' accounts: 'ung personnage poinct au vif, 14 s. 2 d./ un autre, 55 s. 2 d./ un autre, 21 s. 2 d./ ung personnage point au vif, 57 s. 2 d./ ung tableau de Ste Barbe, 20 s./ ung tableau de S. Anthonne, 24 s. 2 d.' (A. de la Grange and L. Cloquet, *Etudes sur l'art à Tournai et sur les anciens artistes de cette ville* (*Mémoires de la Société historique et littéraire de Tournai*, XX, XXI), Tournai, 1887–8, XXI, p. 263).

122. 'ung autre tableaul d'ung homme et une femme qui est fait d'une bonne main et est bien vieulx, l'homme tient une tasse et la femme une fleur' (Finot, 1895, p. 210).

123. On portraits bequeathed in 1486 to the church of Berclau, see note 99 above. Those who became members of the order of St Anthony at Barbefosse were evidently expected to give portraits to the chapel of St Anthony at Barbefosse (L. Devillers, 'La chevalerie et le prieuré de Saint-Antoine-en-Barbefosse', *Annales de l'Académie d'archéologie de Belgique*, 2e sér., I (1865), pp. 561–73). In 1417–18, 'Piettre, le poindeur' was paid for 'j tavlet ouquel est pourtraite le ymage de Madamme [Margaret of Burgundy, Countess of Hainault and Holland] et l'escut de ses armes, ledit tavlet mis en le capelle de Saint-Anthonne, à Barbefosse' (Pinchart, 1860–81, II, p. 158). In 1423, John IV, Duke of Brabant, paid the widow of Piérart Henne, painter at Mons, for 'ung tableau de nostre personnage et armoyé de noz armes, mis en ladicte église de Saint-Anthoine' (A. Pinchart, 'Archives des arts', *Messager des sciences historiques*, 1868, pp. 308–55, p. 312).

124. A portrait of a lady, inscribed 'Obyt AN° DNI 1479.' and thought to have been painted by Memlinc, once ornamented a tomb in the church of St Donatian in Bruges (C. J. Nieuwenhuys, *Description de la galerie des tableaux de S.M. le Roi des Pays-Bas*, Brussels, 1843, no. 13; Friedländer, 1967–76, VIa, pl. 126).

125. Further examples of pictures of people holding portraits are: the *Lady holding a Portrait of a Man* attributed to Licinio in the Castello Sforzesco, Milan (28: Berenson, 1957, II, pl. 853); the *Man holding a Profile Portrait of a Lady* attributed to Cariani (sold at Sotheby's, 9 April 1986 (84)); and the *Lady holding a Portrait of a Man*, sold as 'A Lady of Saluzzo and her Love' by Moroni (Savoy sale, American Art Association, New York, 16–18 February 1922 (386)).

126. See above, p. 64.

127. A group portrait of Catherine de' Medici and her children, in which Catherine held a miniature of her husband Henry II of France and in which her daughter Elisabeth held a miniature of Don Carlos would also have been painted in about 1560 and was described in the inventory of the Spanish royal collection taken in 1600 (Sánchez Cantón, 1956–9, XI, pp. 243–4).

128. Giovanni d'Atri to the Marquis, 15 November 1499: 'Mando alla S.V. lo retracto de la putta loquale fo finito heri, per mezo de Jo. Jacobo mio, insieme cum l'alligata lettere del depinctore, dicendo chel vole essere monstrati al picolo lume, perche fara meglior vedere. E se vole che gli facia il retracto de la testo del Re V.S. gli scriva una lettera' (L. Pélissier, 'La politique du Marquis de Mantoue pendant la lutte de Louis XII et de Ludovic Sforza (1498–1500)', *Annales de la Faculté des Lettres de Bordeaux*, 1892, pp. 35–120, p. 85 n. 3).

129. Mary of Hungary to Renard, Brussels, 19 November 1553: 'elle verra assez par icelle sa ressemblance, la voyant à son jour et de loing, comme sont toutes poinctures dudict Titian que de près ne se recognoissent' (Weiss, 1843, p. 150).

130. See above, p. 44.

131. Filippo da Borsano to the duke, Milan, 17 February 1473: 'ho inteso como Jouane Ahogadro ha una belissima fiola de ani xij o xiij et e granda per el tempo chala per la quale chosa suplico a V.S. se digne de farme intendere se la vole che la faza retrare como ho facto de altre et parendo che la faza aretrare si digna de scrivere al dito Johanne che la voia lasare aredrare' (Malaguzzi Valeri, 1902, p. 141). See also the other letters on beautiful girls, *ibid.*, pp. 140–2.

132. Vincenzo I, Duke of Mantua, to Carlo Rossi, 11 February 1604: 'Al presente faccio fare una capella nella quale desidero d'havere li ritratti più simili che sia possibile delle imagini di Nostra Signora che fanno o hanno fatto miracoli in diverse parti del mondo . . . Di più faccio fare una camera nella quale penso di raccogliere li ritratti di tutte le più belle dame del mondo così principesse come dame private . . .' (Baschet, 1868, pp. 441–2).

133. R. Margonari and A. Zanca, *Il Santuario della Madonna delle Grazie presso Mantova*, Mantua, 1973.

134. Letter of 19 September 1471: 'Nuy intendemo che la S.V. ha in castello novo retracto al naturale per mano de maistro Baldassare la bona memoria dell'Illmo quondam signore duca Borso, haveriamo caro et grato haverla, et cossì pregamo la S.V. li piaza mandarne dicta pictura sopra duna barca fino ad Pavia ordinando ad lo suo messo che la farà condure, che l'ordine in modo che per piogia nè per lumido de laqua se possa guastare: et che la consegni in mano del nostro Castellano de Pavia' (Motta, 1889, p. 407).

135. '1473. per m° Baldissera Credito. – Lavoreri fatti al quondam D. Borso . . . Et per una figura Intiera. Cioe suso uno quadro grande dal naturale, la quale statua il nostro duca presente mando a donar al Ill.mo duca galeazo . . . duc. 080' (Venturi, 1885^2, p. 721 n. 1). 'M° Baldessera da rezo depintore deve dari adi x de otobre [1471] fiorini dodexe contanti a lui per una andata a milano a portare una Imagine del quondam duca Borso cioè per montare in nave con due compagni e per viatico' (*ibid.*).

136. Letter of 5 November 1471: 'La imagine del Illmo quond. Sig. Duca Borso quale ne havete mandata, rechiesta da nuy, insieme con Magistro Baldasar, la havemo havuta tanto grata et accepta quanto cosa alcuna che ne fusse potuta accadere: et questo perchè havimo sempre desiderato havere qualche representatione de quel Signore,

el quale continuamente amassimo come patre, et si siamo sforzati imitare li suoi vestigij et costumi como laudatissimi et veramente degni de principe: et tanto più ne è stata essa imagine cara quanto ne è stata fatta degnissimamente perchè quando el guardassemo così depincto ne pare vederlo vivo quasi non li manchi altro che l'animo . . . Nuy adoncha tenerimo essa depentura continuamente presso de nuy, et per la memoria de dicto Signore et per recordarse de la V. Signoria, la quale ne la mandata: . . . mag. Baldesar merita in ciò summa mendatione . . .' (Motta, 1889, p. 408).

137. Beatrice de' Contrari to Isabella d'Este, 10 April 1495: 'come vado a tavola lo fazio ponere suso una cadrega per scontro a me, che vedendolo me pare pur essere a tavola cum V.S.' (Luzio, 1913, p. 186).

138. 'mette inanzi all'amante la propria effigie della cosa amata, il quale spesso fa con quella bacciandola e parlandole con quella quello . . .' (Richter, 1970, I, p. 64).

139. 'Balthassaris Castilionis elegia qua fingit Hippolyten suam ad se ipsum scribentem . . .

Sola suos vultus referens Raphaelis imago
Picta manu, cura allevat usque meas.
Huic ego delicias facio, arrideoque iocorque,
Alloquor, et tanquam reddere verba queat
Assensu nutuque, mihi saepe illa videtur
Dicere velle aliquid, et tua verba loqui.
Agnoscit, balboque patrem puer ore salutat,
Hoc solor, longosque decipioque dies.'

(reprinted by Golzio, 1971, p. 43; translated in Richter, 1970, I, p. 56 n.).

140. Giovanmaria della Porta to Eleonora, Duchess of Urbino, Parma, 14 April 1538: 'Al partir mio da Pesaro ero già a cauallo, quando Giouanantonio guardaroba mi disse hauer gli noui ritratti di V.S. e del S.r Ill.mo, e cosi smontato e stato buon poco a considerar la merauigliosa naturale loro similitudine, a fatica mi contenni di basciarle la mano, tanto mi parue uiua, e dissi più d'una uolta, padrona mia cara, uoi sete pur essa, e uolendo raggionar seco m'accorsi essa pictura, uedendo ch'ella non curaua cosa ch'io mi dicessi, e subito mi uene a memoria il torto grande fattomi da lei, d'hauermi tante uolte promesso il ritratto suo e non me l'hauer uoluto mai dare . . .' (Gronau, 1936, pp. 93–4).

141. John Clerk, Bishop of Bath and Wells, et al., to Henry VIII, Paris, 10 June 1527: J. S. Brewer, ed., *Letters and Papers, Foreign and Domestic, Henry VIII*, IV, ii, London, 1872, no. 3169.

142. Simon Renard to Charles V, Blois, 21 March 1551: R. Tyler, ed., *Letters, Despatches, and State Papers, relating to the Negotiations between England and Spain*, X, London, 1914, pp. 249–50.

143. 'Puis regardant et faisant la révérence aux portraits du Roi et de la Reine, il dit: Papa n'a point de chapeau. Je lui demande pourquoi? – Pource que c'est une peinture' (Héroard, 1868 edn, I, p. 114).

144. Webster, *The White Devil*, II. iii.

145. British Library, MS Cotton Vespasian F III, f. 48, dated Hatfield, 15 May [1551?]; printed by J. Nichols, *The Progresses and Public Processions of Queen Elizabeth*, 3 vols, London, 1823, I, p. *28.

146. H. C. Hamilton, ed., *Calendar of State Papers relating to Ireland, Henry VIII, Edward VI, Mary and Elizabeth*, IV, London, 1885, pp. 142–3 (Fitzwilliam to Lord Burghley, 9 April 1589), 273, 336.

147. 'in Proregis Cameram admissus vbi primùm Elizabethae Reginae effigiem in tabula depictam vidit, semel atque iterum gladio abiecto ad pedes se aduoluit, eiusque Maiestati se deuouit' (W. Camden, *Britannia*, revised edn, London, 1607, p. 769). Compare J. S. Brewer and W. Bullen, eds, *Calendar of Carew Papers in the Lambeth Library*, II, London, 1868, p. 427.

148. R. Cosin, *Conspiracie, for Pretended Reformation: viz. Presbyteriall Discipline*, London, 1592, pp. 67, 61.

149. R. Pitcairn, *Ancient Criminal Trials in Scotland*, II, Edinburgh, 1833, pp. 349–51; M. Wood and R. K. Hannay, *Extracts from the Records of the Burgh of Edinburgh, A.D. 1589 to 1603*, Edinburgh, 1927, pp. 284–5.

150. H. F. Brown, ed., *State Papers and Manuscripts relating to English Affairs existing in the Archives and Collections of Venice*, X, London, 1900, p. 10.

151. Public Record Office, London, SP 11/7, ff.71, 122; R. Lemon, ed., *Calendar of State Papers, Domestic. Edward VI, Mary, Elizabeth and James I*, I, London, 1856, pp. 77–8.

152. Gilles de Noailles to the Constable of France (Anne de Montmorency), London, 30 June 1556: 'j'entens, par aulcuns de ses plus privez, qu'elle a esté depuis agitée de tel dépit et colère, que l'on l'a veue esgratigner les pourtraicts du Roy d'Espagne son mary qu'elle tient en sa Chambre' (Public Record Office, London, Baschet transcripts, PRO 31/3/22, ff. 129–129v).

153. 'Aliquot diebus ante mortem, Curtius Pictor imaginem Henrici fratris ad Carolum tulit scientissimè depictam; quam ego apud Curtium antè videram. Mandato Regis venerat, igitur contemplatus absentis faciem, ô boni fratris imaginem, inquit, quem utinam à me nunquam dimisissem' (P. Masson, 'Historia vitae Caroli Valesii . . . conscripta 1575' printed in J. Le Laboureur, ed., *Les Memoires de Messire Michel de Castelnau*, 3 vols, Brussels, 1731, III, p. 20).

154. 'mīj. soē. mij. hier. gheconterfeit ~ doē. ic. gheleeft. had. lxxv. iarē. somē. seijt./ 1532 MH'.

155. 'AD SPECTATOREM:ANNO AETATIS SVAE .25./ Effigiem cernis, graphice quam pinxit Appelles/Hec forme reddit lineamenta mee/Quod natura dedit, reddit pictura poesi/Assimilis, seruans intexitura dñi'.

156. Lampsoni in tabula vivos simulantia vultus
Morus Apellea pinxerat ora manu.
Nec satis hoc illi: pictae (quis crederet?) umbrae
Visus erat motum, atque indere velle animam.
Noluit, ut iuxta adstabat Natura, laborem
Discipuli spectans daedala Diva sui;
Atque ait: hanc certe mihi cedes, aemule, laudem.
An nihil est, una parte fuisse parem?

(Puraye, 1949, p. 179 and references).

Chapter 9 Italy and 'the North'

1. 'hebben onse Schilder-const een groot licht ghegheven/en den Oeffenaers van deser den oogen gheopent/om t'onderscheyden/wat leelijck/en schoon/en t'alderschoonste in 't leven oft in der natueren was/aengaende de ghestaltnissen der Menschen lichamen en der Dieren litmaten. So dat d'Italianen dus verlicht wesende/hebben vroegher ghetroffen den rechten aerdt en welstandt der beelden/als wel ons Nederlanders/die soo op een seker aenghewende wijse van wercken/met onvolcomen kennis/tot beter en beter doen stadigh en vlijtigh hebben ghetracht/hun selven veel met t' gemeen leven te volghen vernoegende/saten (ghelijck of men segghen soude) ghenoech doncker/oft met weynigh lichts/tot dat *Ioan* van *Schoorel*, hun uyt Italien het wesen van de beste wijse oft ghestalt onser Consten bracht/en voor ooghen stelde' (Van Mander, 1604, f. 234).

2. See the discussion of Rogier's Prado *Descent* in Campbell, 1979, pp. 6–8.

3. See above, pp. 22–4, 150.

4. See above, pp. 12–14, 30–4.

5. See above, p. 81.

6. 'grachetto francoso . . . fe a roma papa Eugenio & due altri de suoi appresso di lui che ueramente pareuono uiui . . .' (J. R. Spencer, *Filarete's Treatise on Architecture*, 2 vols, New Haven and London, 1965, II, Book IX, f. 69); Francesco Florio to 'Jacobus Tarlatus', c. 1477: 'in sacrario nostro in Minerva poteris de hujus viri arte aliquid praegustare, si ibi in tela pictum Eugenium pontificem advertere curaveris . . . potens est hic Fochetus vivos penicilo effingere vultus ac ipsum pene Prometheum imitari' (A. Salmon, 'Description de la ville de Tours sous le règne de Louis XI. Par F. Florio', *Mémoires de la Société archéologique de*

Touraine, VII (1855), pp. 82–108, p. 105).

7. Summonte to Marcantonio Michiel, Naples, 20 March 1524: 'Venne ad tempo suo da Fiandra la testa del duca di Burgugna Carlo, ritracta dal naturale. Colantonio fé opera che li fosse prestata dal mercante che la tenea; e, facta un'altra simile, tanto che non si potea discernere l'una dall'altra, rendìo al patrone la nova che ipso avea facta di man sua, la quale lo mercante tenne per la sua propria, finché Colantonio li scoverse lo bello inganno' (F. Nicolini, *L'arte napoletana del Rinascimento*, Naples, 1925, pp. 161–2).
8. Metropolitan Museum of Art, New York, Robert Lehman Collection (1975.1.112): see L. Campbell, 'Memlinc and the Followers of Verrocchio', *Burlington Magazine*, CXXV (1983), pp. 675–6.
9. Fazio, 'De viris illustribus': ' Eius est altera tabula in penetralibus principis Ferrariae . . . In alteris regulus quisdam supplex . . .' (Baxandall, 1964, p. 105). Lionello d'Este had shown the same triptych to Cyriacus of Ancona in 1449 (G. Colucci, *Delle antichità picene*, XV, Fermo, 1792, p. CXLIII).
10. Fazio's description: 'In eiusdem tabulae exteriori parte pictus est baptista lomelinus cuius fuit ipsa tabula. cui solam uocem deesse iudices. et mulier quam amabat praestanti forma. et ipsa qualis erat ad unguem expressa. Inter quos solis radius ueluti per rimam illabebatur. quem uerum solem putes.' (Baxandall, 1964, p. 103).
11. For the Memlinc portrait, see above, note 8.
12. See the '*Muta*', plate 82; the '*Gravida*' mentioned above, Chapter 3 n. 5; the portraits of young men at Malibu and Munich mentioned above, Chapter 4 n. 17; and the *Self-Portrait* at Hampton Court (278: Shearman, 1983, pp. 208–11 (217)).
13. Reynaud, 1981, p. 11; see also above, p. 52.
14. In 1468, Louis XI of France bought from Zanetto Bugatto a double portrait of Francesco Sforza and Galeazzo Maria Sforza (Laborde, 1850–5, I, p. 65 n. 1). Portraits by Bonsignori of members of the Gonzaga family are said to have been sent as gifts to different princes in France and Germany (Vasari-Milanesi, 1878–85, V, p. 300). For the collection of portraits brought from Milan to France by Louis XII, see J. Adhémar, 'Une galerie de portraits italiens à Amboise en 1500', *Gazette des beaux-arts*, 6ᵉ pér., LXXXVI (1975), pp. 99–104.
15. It has been suggested that his *Portrait of a Lady* (Berlin, 557 G) is heavily influenced by Venetian art (see, for example, E. Panofsky, *The Life and Art of Albrecht Dürer*, 4th edn, Princeton, 1955, p. 116). The 'Giorgionesque' qualities of this portrait are, however, due largely to its damaged condition. In the last century, it was attributed to Giovanni Bellini (exhibited as by Bellini at the British Institution, 1858 (109): see Sir George Scharf's sketchbooks, National Portrait Gallery, SSB 52, p. 46) and a nineteenth-century restorer may have done much to enhance its Venetian appearance.
16. In François Clouet's *Lady in her Bath* (plate 15), however, and in related paintings (e.g., plate 16), the backgrounds seem dependent on that of the *Joanna of Aragon*.
17. 'El más famoso pintor de retratos que yo estimo haber en cristianos . . . es Ticiano veneciano, puesto que a mí me dijo el Emperador Don Carlos en Barcelona delante del nuestro Duque de Aveyro y delante del Duque de Albuquerque y del Duque de Alba: "que mejor le había sacado al natural Antonio de Holanda en Toledo de iluminación, que Ticiano en Bolonia."' (Sánchez Cantón, 1921, p. 282). Antonio de Holanda painted Charles V at Toledo in 1528–9 (Bury, 1986, p. 16).
18. For the Latin text, see the incomplete and misdated transcription in C. Ridolfi, *Le maraviglie dell'arte*, ed. D. von Hadeln, 2 vols, Berlin, 1914–24, I, pp. 180–2; an Italian translation of the whole document is in F. Beltrame, *Cenni illustrativi sul monumento a Tiziano Vecellio*, Venice, 1852, pp. 99–103.
19. The inscription, which is on the reverse of the pendant portrait of Johannes Cuspinian and his family (Private Collection), reads: '. . . BERNARDINVS STRIGIL PICTOR CIVIS MEMINGEN[SIS] NOBILIS, QVI SOLV[S] EDICTO CAESARE[M] MAXIMILIANV[M] VT OLIM APELLES ALEXANDRVM PINGERE IVSSVS, HAS IMAGINES MANV SINISTRA PER SPECVLA FERME SEXAGENARIVS VIENNAE PINGEBAT' (Thümmel, 1980, pp. 99, pl. 104b, 100). The exact meaning of 'manu sinistra per specula' is far from clear.
20. G. Otto, *Bernhard Strigel* (*Kunstwissenschaftliche Studien*, XXXIII), Munich and Berlin, 1964, pls 124–5; Heinz and Schütz, 1976, pp. 53–6, pls 1, 19, 21, 23.
21. Germanisches Nationalmuseum, Nuremberg (Gm 167/68): Anzelewsky, 1980, p. 149.
22. Seisenegger's petition of 1549 to the Emperor Ferdinand I and his letter of February 1553 to the same (Kreyczi, 1887, pp. LIV-LV, LXI). For the patent of nobility (16 October 1558) and the exemption from taxation (16 March 1559), see Birk, 1864, pp. 87–90.
23. Hope, 1980, p. 78.
24. Titian had already copied portraits of the Empress (Hope, 1980, pp. 86–8). In the mid-1570s, Titian included in his *Allegory of the Battle of Lepanto* (Prado, 431) a portrait of Philip II copied from an original by Sánchez Coello (Wethey, 1971, pp. 132–3, pl. 183; Hope, 1980, pp. 151–2).
25. See above, Chapter 5 n. 26.
26. See above Chapter 8 n. 129.
27. *Canons Cornelis van Horn and Anthonis Taets van Amerongen as Jerusalem Pilgrims*, Berlin (585 A: Friedländer, 1967–76, XIII, pl. 169).
28. See above, pp. 30–4.

References

Books and articles

Affò, I., *Memorie degli scrittori e letterati parmigiani*, III, Parma, 1791.

Allen, P. S. and H. M., and Garrod, H. W., eds, *Opvs epistolarvm Des. Erasmi Roterodami*, 11 vols, Oxford, 1906–47.

Amezua y Mayo, A. G. de, *Isabel de Valois, reina de España (1546–1568)*, 3 vols, Madrid, 1949.

Anzelewsky, F., 'Erzherzog Maximilians schwerer Rossharnisch von 1480', *Waffen- und Kostümkunde*, V (1963), pp. 77–88.

Anzelewsky, F., *Dürer, His Art and Life*, Fribourg, 1980.

Baccheschi, E., *L'opera completa del Bronzino*, Milan, 1973.

Barocchi, P., ed., *Scritti d'arte del Cinquecento*, 3 vols, Milan and Naples, 1971–7.

Baschet, A., 'François Porbus, peintre de portraits à la cour de Mantoue', *Gazette des beaux-arts*, XXV (1868), pp. 277–98, 438–56.

Baxandall, M., 'Bartholomaeus Facius on Painting', *Journal of the Warburg and Courtauld Institutes*, XXVII (1964), pp. 90–107.

Beck, J. H., 'The Medici Inventory of 1560', *Antichità viva*, XIII (1974), no. 3, pp. 64–6, no. 4, pp. 61–3.

Béguin, S., *Les peintures de Raphaël au Louvre*, Paris, 1984.

Béguin, S. and de Groër, A., 'A propos d'un nouveau Corneille: le portrait de Pierre Aymeric', *Revue du Louvre*, XXVIII (1978), pp. 28–42.

Bellaguet, L., ed., *Chronique du réligieux de Saint-Denis, contenant le règne de Charles VI, de 1380 à 1422*, 6 vols, Paris, 1839–52.

Beltrami, L., *Il Castello di Milano sotto il dominio dei Visconti e degli Sforza*, Milan, 1894.

Berenson, B., *Italian Pictures of the Renaissance, Venetian School*, 2 vols, London, 1957.

Berenson, B., *Italian Pictures of the Renaissance, Florentine School*, 2 vols, London, 1963.

Berenson, B., *Italian Pictures of the Renaissance, Central Italian and North Italian Schools*, 3 vols, London, 1968.

Bergström, I., 'On Religious Symbols in European Portraiture in the XVth and XVIth Centuries' in E. Castelli, ed., *Umanesimo e esoterismo, Atti del V convegno internazionale di studi umanistici, Oberhofen, 16–17 settembre 1960* (Centro internazionale di studi umanistici, Rome), Padua, 1960, pp. 335–43.

Bernardi, M., *La Galleria Sabauda di Torino*, Turin, 1968.

Berti, L., et al., *Gli Uffizi, Catalogo generale*, Florence, 1979.

Bertini, G., *La galleria del duca di Parma, Storia di una collezione*, Parma, 1987.

Biedermann, G., *Katalog, Alte Galerie am Landesmuseum Joanneum, Mittelalterliche Kunst*, Graz, 1982.

Birk, E., 'Jakob Seisenegger, Kaiser Ferdinand I. Hofmaler', *Mittheilungen der k.k. Central-Commission zur Erforschung und Erhaltung der Baudenkmale*, IX (1864), pp. 70–94.

Bock, H., et al., *Gemäldegalerie Berlin, Gesamtverzeichnis der Gemälde*, Berlin, 1986.

Bonnaffé, E., *Inventaire des meubles de Catherine de Médicis en 1589*, Paris, 1874.

Brantôme, P. de Bourdeille, seigneur de, *Oeuvres complètes*, ed. L. Lalanne, 11 vols (Société de l'histoire de la France), Paris, 1864–82.

Breuer, S., *Alonso Sánchez Coello*, doctoral dissertation, Munich, 1984.

Brulez, W., *De firma della Faille en de internationale handel van Vlaamse firma's in de 16e eeuw* (Verhandelingen van de Koninklijke Vlaamse Academie voor wetenschappen, letteren en schone kunsten van België, Klasse der letteren, 35), Brussels, 1959.

Buchner, E., *Das deutsche Bildnis der Spätgotik und der frühen Dürerzeit*, Berlin, 1953.

Bury, J., 'Francisco de Holanda and his Illustrations of the Creation', *Portuguese Studies*, II (1986), pp. 15–48.

Camesasca, E., ed., *Lettere sull'arte di Pietro Aretino*, 3 vols, Milan, 1957–60.

Campana, L., 'Monsignor Giovanni della Casa e i suoi tempi: vita privata', *Studi storici*, XVII (1908), pp. 381–606.

Campbell, L., 'Rogier van der Weyden's "Portrait of a Knight of the Golden Fleece"', *Bulletin des Musées royaux des beaux-arts de Belgique*, XXI (1972), pp. 7–16.

Campbell, L., 'Robert Campin, the Master of Flémalle and the Master of Mérode', *Burlington Magazine*, CXVI (1974), pp. 634–46.

Campbell, L., 'The Authorship of the "Recueil d'Arras"', *Journal of the Warburg and Courtauld Institutes*, XL (1977), pp. 301–13.

Campbell, L., 'A Double Portrait by Memlinc', *Connoisseur*, CXCIV (1977), pp. 187–9.

Campbell, L., *Van der Weyden*, London, 1979.

Campbell, L., *The Early Flemish Pictures in the Collection of Her Majesty The Queen*, Cambridge, 1985.

Campori, G., *Gli artisti italiani e stranieri negli stati Estensi, Catalogo storico*, Modena, 1855.

Campori, G., 'I pittori degli Estensi nel secolo XV', *Atti e memorie delle RR. Deputazioni di storia patria per le provincie modenesi e parmensi*, 3ª ser., III (1885), pp. 526–604.

Canova, G. M., *L'opera completa del Lotto*, Milan, 1974.

Castiglione, B., *The Book of the Courtier*, trans. Sir Thomas Hoby, ed. W. H. D. Rouse and D. Henderson, London and New York, 1928.

Chamberlain, A. B., *Hans Holbein the Younger*, 2 vols, London, 1913.

Comblen-Sonkes, M. and Van den Bergen-Pantens, C., *Les primitifs flamands*, III: *Contributions. . .*, 7, *Les Mémoriaux d'Antoine de Succa*, 2 vols, Brussels, 1977.

Conway, W. M., *Literary Remains of Albrecht Dürer*, Cambridge, 1889.

Coor, G., *Neroccio de' Landi*, Princeton, 1961.

Cossío, M. B., *El Greco*, Madrid, 1908.

David, H., *Philippe le Hardi, Le train somptuaire d'un grand Valois*, Dijon, 1947.

Davies, M., *National Gallery Catalogues, The Earlier Italian Schools*, 2nd edn, London, 1961.

Davies, M., *National Gallery Catalogues, Early Netherlandish School*, 3rd edn, London, 1968.

Davies, M., *Rogier van der Weyden*, London, 1972.

Dehaisnes, C., *Inventaire sommaire des archives départementales antérieres à 1790, Nord, Archives civiles – Série B*, IV, Lille, 1881.

Demus, K., *Katalog der Gemäldegalerie, Hollandische Meister des 15., 16. und 17. Jahrhunderts* (*Führer durch das Kunsthistorische Museum*, 17), Vienna, 1972.

Demus, K., Klauner, F. and Schütz, K., *Katalog der Gemäldegalerie, Flämische Malerei von Jan van Eyck bis Pieter Bruegel d. Ä.* (*Führer durch das Kunsthistorische Museum*, 31), Vienna, 1981.

Dhanens, E., *Hubert and Jan van Eyck*, Antwerp, 1980.

Dimier, L., *Histoire de la peinture de portrait en France au XVI*ᵉ *siècle*, 3 vols, Paris and Brussels, 1924–7.

Dubois, A. and Huyghebaert, N., 'Abbaye des Dunes, à Koksijde et à Bruges' in *Monasticon belge*, III: *Province de la Flandre Occidentale*, II, Liège, 1966, pp. 353–445.

Ehrenberg, H., *Die Kunst am Hofe der Herzöge von Preussen*, Leipzig and Berlin, 1899.

Ferrarino, L., *Tiziano e la corte di Spagna nei documenti dell'Archivio generale di Simancas* (*Collana "Documenti e ricerche"*, II), Madrid, 1975.

Fink, A., *Die Schwarzischen Trachtenbücher* (Deutscher Verein für Kunstwissenschaft), Berlin, 1963.

Finot, J., *Inventaire sommaire des archives départementales antérieures à 1790, Nord, Archives civiles – Série B*, VIII, Lille, 1895.

Foister, S., *Drawings by Holbein from the Royal Library, Windsor Castle*, 2 vols, New York, 1983.

Foucart-Walter, E., *Les peintures de Hans Holbein le jeune au Louvre* (*Les dossiers du Département des Peintures*, 29), Paris, 1985.

Friedländer, M. J., *Early Netherlandish Painting*, trans. H. Norden, 14 vols, Leyden and Brussels, 1967–76.

Frimmel, T., ed., *Der Anonimo Morelliano* (*Quellenschriften für Kunstgeschichte und Kunsttechnik*, N.F., I), Vienna, 1896.

Gardner, J., 'Saint Louis of Toulouse, Robert of Anjou and Simone Martini', *Zeitschrift für Kunstgeschichte*, XXXIX (1976), pp. 12–33.

Gilbert, C. E., *Italian Art 1400–1500, Sources and Documents*, Englewood Cliffs (N.J.), 1980.

Goethals, F.-V., *Dictionnaire généalogique et héraldique des familles nobles du royaume de Belgique*, 4 vols, Brussels, 1849–52.

Golzio, V., *Raffaello nei documenti nelle testimonianze dei contemporanei e nella letteratura del suo secolo*, 2nd edn, London, 1971.

Gould, C., *National Gallery Catalogues, The Sixteenth-Century Italian Schools*, London, 1975.

Gronau, G., *Documenti artistici urbinati*, Florence, 1936.

Groos, G. W., *The Diary of Baron Waldstein, a Traveller in Elizabethan England*, London, 1981.

Gundersheimer, W. L., *Art and Life at the Court of Ercole I d'Este: The 'De triumphis religionis' of Giovanni Sabadino degli Arienti* (*Travaux d'humanisme et Renaissance*, CXXVII), Geneva, 1972.

Hand, J. O. and Wolff, M., *The Collections of the National Gallery of Art, Systematic Catalogue, Early Netherlandish Painting*, Washington, 1986.

Heikamp, D., 'Agnolo Bronzinos Kinderbildnisse aus dem Jahre 1551', *Mitteilungen des Kunsthistorischen Institutes in Florenz*, VII (1953–6), pp. 133–8.

Heinz, G. and Schütz, K., *Katalog der Gemäldegalerie, Porträtgalerie zur Geschichte Österreichs von 1400 bis 1800* (*Führer durch das Kunsthistorische Museum*, 22), Vienna, 1976.

Hendy, P., *European and American Paintings in the Isabella Stewart Gardner Museum*, Boston, 1974.

Hepburn, F., *Portraits of the Later Plantagenets*, Woodbridge, 1986.

Héroard, J., *Journal de Jean Héroard sur l'enfance et la jeunesse de Louis XIII (1601–1628)*, ed. E. Soulié and E. de Barthélemy, 2 vols, Paris, 1868.

Herrmann, M., *Forschungen zur deutschen Theatergeschichte des Mittelalters und der Renaissance*, Berlin, 1914.

Hill, G. F., *Pisanello*, London and New York, 1905.

Hilliard, N., *A Treatise concerning the Arte of Limning*, ed. R. K. R. Thornton and T. G. S. Cain, Ashington and Manchester, 1981.

Hirst, M., *Sebastiano del Piombo*, Oxford, 1981.

Hoff, U., *National Gallery of Victoria, European Painting and Sculpture before 1800*, 3rd edn, Melbourne, 1973.

Hoff, U. and Davies, M., *Les primitifs flamands*, I: *Corpus* . . ., 12, *The National Gallery of Victoria, Melbourne*, Brussels, 1971.

Hope, C., *Titian*, London, 1980.

Horne, H. P., *Botticelli*, London, 1908.

Houdoy, J., 'Marguerite d'Autriche, l'église de Brou et les artistes de la Renaissance en Flandre', *Gazette des beaux-arts*, 2e pér., V (1872), pp. 515–18.

Hulin de Loo, G., *Bruges 1902, Exposition de tableaux flamands des XIVe, XVe et XVIe siècles, Catalogue critique*, Ghent, 1902.

Hurtubise, P., ed., *Correspondance du nonce en France Antonio Maria Salviati* (*1572–1578*), 2 vols (*Acta Nuntiaturae Gallicae*, 12–13), Rome, 1975.

Hymans, H., *Antonio Moro, son oeuvre et son temps*, Brussels, 1910.

Innes, C., *The Black Book of Taymouth with Other Papers from the Breadalbane Charter Room* (Bannatyne Club publication), Edinburgh, 1855.

Janssens de Bisthoven, A., *De Vlaamse primitieven*, I: *Corpus* . . ., 1, *Stedelijk Museum voor Schone Kunsten* (*Groeningemuseum*), *Brugge*, I, Brussels, 1981.

Kenner, F., 'Die Porträtsammlung des Erzherzogs Ferdinand von Tirol', *Jahrbuch der kunsthistorischen Sammlungen des allerhöchsten Kaiserhauses*, XIV (1893), pp. 35–186, XV

(1894), pp. 147–259, XVII (1896), pp. 101–274, XVIII (1897), pp. 135–261, XIX (1898), pp. 6–146.

Klauner, F., 'Spanische Portraits des 16. Jahrhunderts', *Jahrbuch der kunsthistorischen Sammlungen in Wien*, LVII (1961), pp. 123–58.

Klauner, F. and Heinz, G., *Katalog der Gemäldegalerie*, II: *Vlamen, Holländer, Deutsche, Franzosen* (*Führer durch das Kunsthistorische Museum*, 7), 2nd edn, Vienna, 1963.

Klauner, F. and Heinz, G., *Katalog der Gemäldegalerie*, I: *Italianer, Spanier, Franzosen, Engländer* (*Führer durch das Kunsthistorische Museum*, 3), 2nd edn, Vienna, 1965.

Koepplin, D., *Cranachs Ehebildnis des Johannes Cuspinian von 1502, Seine christlich-humanistische Bedeutung*, Basle, 1973.

Kreyczi, F., 'Urkunden und Regesten aus dem k. u. k. Reichs-Finanz-Archiv (Forsetzung)', *Jahrbuch der kunsthistorischen Sammlungen des allerhöchsten Kaiserhauses*, V (1887), ii, pp. XXV-CXIX.

Kristeller, P., *Andrea Mantegna*, Berlin and Leipzig, 1902.

Künstler, G., 'Das Bildnis Rudolfs des Stifters, Herzogs von Österreich, und seine Funktion', *Mitteilungen der Österreichischen Galerie*, XVI (1972), pp. 5–15.

Kusche, M., *Juan Pantoja de la Cruz*, Madrid, 1964.

Kwiatkowski, K., *'La Dame à l'hermine' de Leonardo da Vinci, Etude technologique*, Wrocław, 1955.

Laborde, Comte de, *La Renaissance des arts à la cour de France*, 2 vols, Paris, 1850–5.

La Curne de Sainte Palaye, M. de, *Mémoires sur l'ancienne chevalerie*, II, Paris, 1759.

Langedijk, K., *The Portraits of the Medici, 15th–18th Centuries*, 2 vols, Florence, 1981–3.

Lavalleye, J., *Les primitifs flamands*, I: *Corpus . . .*, 7, *Le palais ducal d'Urbin*, Brussels, 1964.

Leeuwenberg, J. and Halsema-Kubes, W., *Beeldhouwkunst in het Rijksmuseum, Catalogus*, Amsterdam, 1973.

Levey, M., *National Gallery Catalogues, The German School*, London, 1959.

Lightbown, R., *Sandro Botticelli*, 2 vols, London, 1978.

Lightbown, R., *Mantegna*, Oxford, 1986.

Lobelle-Caluwe, H., *Musée Memling, Bruges*, Fribourg, 1985.

Löcher, K., *Jakob Seisenegger, Hofmaler Kaiser Ferdinands I.* (*Kunstwissenschaftliche Studien*, XXXI), Munich and Berlin, 1962.

Longnon, A., ed., *Méliador par Jean Froissart* (Société des anciens textes français), 3 vols, Paris, 1895–9.

Luzio, A., *I precettori d'Isabella d'Este, Appunti e documenti*, Ancona, 1887.

Luzio, A., 'Fasti Gonzagheschi dipinti dal Tintoretto', *Archivio storico dell'arte*, III (1890), pp. 397–400.

Luzio, A., *La galleria dei Gonzaga venduta all'Inghilterra nel 1627–8*, Milan, 1913.

Luzio, A. and Renier, R., 'Delle relazioni di Isabella d'Este Gonzaga con Ludovico e Beatrice Sforza', *Archivio storico lombardo*, XVII (2ª ser., VII, 1890), pp. 74–119, 346–99, 619–74.

Malaguzzi Valeri, F., *Pittori lombardi del Quattrocento, Ricerche*, Milan, 1902.

Malaguzzi Valeri, F., *La corte di Ludovico il Moro*, III, Milan, 1917.

Marijnissen, R. H. and Van de Voorde, G., 'Een onverklaarde werkwijze van de Vlaamse primitieven', *Mededelingen van de Koninklijke Academie voor wetenschappen, letteren en schone kunsten van België, Klasse der schone kunsten*, XLIV (1983), pp. 43–51.

Marini, R., *L'opera completa del Veronese*, Milan, 1968.

Martindale, A., *Simone Martini*, Oxford, 1988.

Matthioli, A., *Il magno palazzo del Cardinale di Trento*, Venice, 1539.

Meiss, M., *French Painting in the Time of Jean de Berry, The Late XIV Century and the Patronage of the Duke*, 2 vols, London and New York, 1967.

Mellen, P., *Jean Clouet*, London, 1971.

Melville, Sir James, of Halhill, *Memoirs of his own Life M.D.XLIX – M.D.XCIII* (Bannatyne Club publication), Edinburgh, 1827.

Michel, E., *Musée National du Louvre, Catalogue raisonné des peintures . . . Peintures flamandes du XVe et du XVIe siècle*, 2 vols, Paris, 1953.

Michelant, H., 'Inventaire . . . de Marguerite d'Autriche . . .', *Compte rendu des séances de la Commission royale d'histoire, ou Recueil de ses Bulletins*, 3ᵉ sér., XII (1871), pp. 5–78, 83–136.

Millar, O., *The Tudor, Stuart and Early Georgian Pictures in the Collection of Her Majesty The Queen*, 2 vols, London, 1963.

Molajoli, R., *L'opera completa di Cosmè Tura e i grandi pittori ferraresi del suo tempo*, Milan, 1974.

Monballieu, A., 'De schilderscarrière van Hubertus Goltzius', *Jaarboek van het Koninklijk Museum voor Schone Kunsten, Antwerpen*, 1984, pp. 203–18.

Moreau-Nélaton, E., *Les Le Mannier, peintres officiels de la cour des Valois au XVIᵉ siècle*, Paris, 1901.

Moreau-Nélaton, E., *Les Clouet et leurs émules*, 3 vols, Paris, 1924.

Motta, E., 'Il pittore Baldassare da Reggio (1461–1471)', *Archivio storico lombardo*, XVI (2ª ser., VI, 1889), pp. 403–9.

Mulcahy, R., 'Two Letters by Alonso Sánchez Coello', *Burlington Magazine*, CXXVI (1984), pp. 775–7.

Nichols, J. G., ed., *The Chronicle of Queen Jane and Two Years of Queen Mary* (Camden Society publications, XLVIII), London, 1850.

Nicolas, N. H., *A Journal by One of the Suite of Thomas Beckington . . . during an Embassy to negotiate a Marriage between Henry VI. and a Daughter of the Count of Armagnac. A.D. MCCCCXLII*, London, 1828.

Osborn, J. M., ed., *The Autobiography of Thomas Whythorne*, Oxford, 1961.

Pacheco, F., *Arte de la pintura, su antigüedad y grandezas*, ed. D. G. Cruzada Vilaamil, 2nd edn, 2 vols, Madrid, 1866.

Pächt, O., Jenni, U. and Thoss, D., *Die illuminierten Handschriften und Inkunabeln der Österreichischen Nationalbibliothek, Flämische Schule*, I, 2 vols, Vienna, 1983.

Panofsky, E., 'Jan van Eyck's Arnolfini Portrait', *Burlington Magazine*, LXIV (1934), pp. 117–27.

Panofsky, E., *Early Netherlandish Painting, Its Origins and Character*, 2 vols, Cambridge (Mass.), 1953.

Passerini, L., *Genealogia e storia della famiglia Panciatichi*, Florence, 1858.

Pérez Pastor, C., *Noticias y documentos relativos a la historia y literatura españolas*, II (*Memorias de la Real Academia Española*, XI), Madrid, 1914.

Pinchart, A., 'Tableaux et sculptures de Marie d'Autriche, reine douairière de Hongrie (1558)', *Revue universelle des arts*, III (1856), pp. 127–46.

Pinchart, A., *Archives des arts, sciences et lettres, Première série*, 3 vols, Ghent, 1860–81.

Pinchart, A., *Histoire de la tapisserie dans les Flandres* (*Histoire générale de la tapisserie*, III), Paris, 1878–85.

Plazzotta, C., '*Il Pennel Dotto*', *The Presentation of Women in Three Portraits by Bronzino*, M.A. dissertation, Courtauld Institute of Art, London, 1988.

Plon, E., *Leone Leoni sculpteur de Charles-Quint et Pompeo Leoni sculpteur de Philippe II*, Paris, 1887.

Pope-Hennessy, J., *The Portrait in the Renaissance*, London and New York, 1966.

Popham, A. E., *Catalogue of the Drawings of Parmigianino*, 3 vols, New Haven and London, 1971.

Puraye, J., 'Antonio Moro et Dominique Lampson', *Oud Holland*, LXIV (1949), pp. 175–83.

Quintilian, *The Institutio Oratoria of Quintilian with an English Translation* by H. E. Butler (The Loeb Classical Library), 4 vols, London and New York, 1921–2.

Reynaud, N., *Jean Fouquet* (*Les dossiers du Département des Peintures*, 22), Paris, 1981.

Reynaud, N., 'La radiographie du *Portrait de Charles VII* par Fouquet', *Revue du Louvre*, XXXIII (1983), pp. 97–9.

Richter, J. P., *The Literary Works of Leonardo da Vinci*, 3rd edn, 2 vols, London, 1970.

Roblot-Delondre, L., 'Argote de Molina et les tableaux du Pardo', *Revue archéologique*, 4ᵉ sér., XVI (1910), pp. 52–70.

Rosmini, C. de', *Dell'Istoria di Milano*, IV, Milan, 1820.

Rovelli, L., *L'opera storica ed artistica di Paolo Giovio comasco vescovo di Nocera*, Como, 1928.

Rowlands, J., *Holbein, The Paintings of Hans Holbein the Younger, Complete Edition*, Oxford, 1985.

Rupprich, H., ed., *Dürer, Schriftlicher Nachlass*, 3 vols, Deutscher Verein für Kunstwissenschaft, Berlin, 1956–69.

Sánchez Cantón, F. J., ed., *De la pintura antigua por Francisco de Holanda (1548), Versión castellana de Manuel Denis (1563)*, Madrid, 1921.

Sánchez Cantón, F. J., *Libros, tapices y cuadros que coleccionó Isabel la Católica*, Madrid, 1950.

Sánchez Cantón, F. J., 'Inventarios reales: Bienes muebles que pertenecieron a Felipe II', *Archivo documental español*, x, xi (1956–9).

Schade, W., *Cranach, A Family of Master Painters*, New York, 1980.

Scharf, G., 'Observations on the Portrait of Edward Grimston', *Archaeologia*, xl (1866), pp. 471–82.

Scheicher, E., *Sammlungen Schloss Ambras, Die Kunstkammer* (*Führer durch das Kunsthistorische Museum*, 24), Innsbruck, 1977.

Scott, M., *Late Gothic Europe, 1400–1500* (*The History of Dress Series*), London, 1980.

Seidlitz, W. von, 'Ambrogio Preda und Leonardo da Vinci', *Jahrbuch der kunsthistorischen Sammlungen des allerhöchsten Kaiserhauses*, xxvi (1906–7), pp. 1–48.

Shapley, F. R., *National Gallery of Art, Washington, Catalogue of the Italian Paintings*, 2 vols, Washington, 1979.

Shaw, W., *Three Inventories of the Years 1542, 1547 and 1549–50 of Pictures in the Collections of Henry VIII & Edward VI*, London, 1937.

Shearman, J., *Andrea del Sarto*, 2 vols, Oxford, 1965.

Shearman, J., *The Early Italian Pictures in the Collection of Her Majesty The Queen*, Cambridge, 1985.

Signorini, R., 'Federico III e Christiano I nella Camera degli Sposi del Mantegna', *Mitteilungen des Kunsthistorischen Institutes in Florenz*, xviii (1974), pp. 227–50.

Simon, R. B., *Bronzino's Portraits of Cosimo I de' Medici*, doctoral dissertation, Columbia, 1982.

Solerti, A., *Ferrara e la corte Estense nella seconda metà del secolo decimosesto*, Città di Castello, 1891.

Stechow, W., *Northern Renaissance Art 1400–1600, Sources and Documents*, Englewood Cliffs (N.J.), 1966.

Stechow, W., et al., *The Cleveland Museum of Art, Catalogue of Paintings*, i: *European Paintings before 1500*, Cleveland, 1974.

Stechow, W., et al., *The Cleveland Museum of Art, Catalogue of Paintings*, iii: *European Paintings of the 16th, 17th and 18th Centuries*, Cleveland, 1982.

Steppe, J. K., 'Mencía de Mendoza et ses relations avec Erasme, Gilles de Busleyden et Jean-Louis Vivès' in J. Coppens, ed., *Scrinium Erasmianum*, 2 vols, Leyden, 1969, ii, pp. 447–506.

Sterling, C., *Enguerrand Quarton*, Paris, 1983.

Sterling, C., *La peinture médiévale à Paris 1300–1500*, i, Paris, 1987.

Sterling, C., 'Fouquet en Italie', *L'Œil*, no. 392 (March 1987), pp. 22–31.

Sterling, C. and Adhémar, H., *Musée National du Louvre, Peintures, Ecole française, XIVe, XVe et XVIe siècles*, Paris, 1965.

Strehlke, C. B., 'Pontormo, Alessandro de' Medici and the Palazzo Pazzi', *Philadelphia Museum of Art Bulletin*, lxxxi, no. 348 (fall 1985), pp. 3–15.

Strong, R. C., *Portraits of Queen Elizabeth I*, Oxford, 1963.

Strong, R. C., *National Portrait Gallery, Tudor & Jacobean Portraits*, 2 vols, London, 1969.

Strong, R. C., *The English Icon*, London and New York, 1969.

Supino, I. B., *I Ricordi di Alessandro Allori*, Florence, 1908.

Tallemant des Rieux, G., *Les historiettes*, ed. de Monmerqué and Paulin Paris, 6 vols, Paris, 1862.

Thorpe, J., *Book of Hours, Illuminations by Simon Marmion*, San Marino (Cal.), 1977.

Thümmel, H. G., 'Bernhard Strigels Diptychon für Cuspinian', *Jahrbuch der kunsthistoris-*

chen Sammlungen in Wien, LXXVI (1980), pp. 97–110.

Trizna, J., *Les primitifs flamands*, III: *Contributions* . . ., 6, *Michel Sittow, peintre revalais de l'école brugeoise (1468–1525/1526)*, Brussels, 1976.

Van Buren-Hagopian, A., 'Un jardin d'amour de Philippe le Bon au parc de Hesdin', *Revue du Louvre*, XXXV (1985), pp. 185–92.

Van den Bergen-Pantens, C., 'Le "Triptyque Micault" de J. C. Vermeyen', *Bulletin des Musées royaux des beaux-arts de Belgique*, XXII (1973), pp. 33–57.

Vandenbroeck, P., *Koninklijk Museum voor Schone Kunsten, Antwerpen, Catalogus schilderijen 14e en 15e eeuw*, Antwerp, 1985.

Van de Velde, C., *Frans Floris (1519/20–1570), Leven en werk* (Verhandelingen van de Koninklijke Academie voor wetenschappen, letteren en schone kunsten van België, Klasse der schone kunsten, XXXVII Nr. 30), 2 vols, Brussels, 1976.

Van de Velde, C., 'Nieuwe gegevens en inzichten over het werk van Frans Pourbus de Oudere', *Gentse bijdragen tot de kunstgeschiedenis*, XXV (1979–80), pp. 124–57.

Van Mander, C., *Het Schilder-Boeck*, Haarlem, 1604.

Vasari, G., *Le vite de' più eccellenti pittori scultori ed architettori*, ed. G. Milanesi, 9 vols, Florence, 1878–85.

Veldman, I. M., *Maarten van Heemskerck and Dutch Humanism in the Sixteenth Century*, Maarssen, 1977.

Venturi, A., 'Relazioni artistiche tra le corti di Milano e Ferrara nel secolo XV', *Archivio storico lombardo*, XII (2a ser., II, 1885), pp. 225–80.

Venturi, A., 'L'arte a Ferrara nel periodo di Borso d'Este', *Rivista storica italiana*, II (1885), pp. 689–749.

Venturi, A., 'L'arte ferrarese nel periodo d'Ercole I d'Este', *Atti e memorie della R. Deputazione di storia patria per le provincie di Romagna*, 3a ser., VI (1888), pp. 91–119, 350–422, VII (1889), pp. 368–412.

Vernarecci, A., 'La libreria di Giovanni Sforza signore di Pesaro', *Archivio storico per le Marche e per l'Umbria*, III (1886), pp. 501–23.

Veronée-Verhaegen, N., *Les primitifs flamands*, I: *Corpus* . . ., 13, *L'Hôtel-Dieu de Beaune*, Brussels, 1973.

Vignau-Wilberg, T., 'Joris Hoefnagels Tätigkeit in München', *Jahrbuch der kunsthistorischen Sammlungen in Wien*, LXXXI (1985), pp. 103–67.

Vignau-Wilberg, T., '"Qualche deseigni d'importanza". Joris Hoefnagel als Zeichnungssammler', *Münchner Jahrbuch der bildenden Kunst*, 3. F., XXXVIII (1987), pp. 185–214.

Wehle, H. B. and Salinger, M., *The Metropolitan Museum of Art, A Catalogue of Early Flemish, Dutch and German Paintings*, New York, 1947.

Weiss, C., *Papiers d'état du Cardinal de Granvelle*, IV, Paris, 1843.

Westhoff-Krummacher, H., 'Ein Brautwerbungsporträt von Hermann tom Ring', *Westfalen*, XLV (1967), pp. 250–5.

Wethey, H. E., *The Paintings of Titian, Complete Edition*, II: *The Portraits*, London, 1971.

White, C., *Dürer, The Artist and his Drawings*, London, 1971.

Wood, M., ed., *Foreign Correspondence with Marie de Lorraine Queen of Scotland from the Originals in the Balcarres Papers 1537–1548* (Scottish History Society publications, 3rd ser., IV), Edinburgh, 1923.

Zampetti, P., ed., *Lorenzo Lotto: Il "Libro di spese diverse" con aggiunta di lettere e d'altri documenti* (*Civiltà veneziana, Fonti e testi*, Serie prima, 6), Venice and Rome, 1969.

Zimerman, H., 'Inventar des gesammten Besitzes der Erzherzogin Margarethe', *Jahrbuch der kunsthistorischen Sammlungen des allerhöchsten Kaiserhauses*, III (1885), ii, pp. XCIII–CXXIII.

Zimmermann, H., 'Zur richtigen Datierung eines Portraits von Tizian', *Mittheilungen des Instituts für oesterreichische Geschichtsforschung*, VI. Ergänzungsband (1901), pp. 830–57.

Zimmermann, H., 'Zur Ikonographie des Hauses Habsburg, II. Angebliche und wirkliche Bildnisse des Don Carlos', *Jahrbuch der kunsthistorischen Sammlungen des allerhöchsten Kaiserhauses*, XXVIII (1909–10), pp. 153–69.

Exhibition catalogues (in alphabetical order of place)

Amsterdam, 1958	*Middeleeuwse kunst der noordelijke Nederlanden*, Rijksmuseum, Amsterdam, 1958.
Amsterdam, 1986	*Kunst voor de beeldenstorm*, Rijksmuseum, Amsterdam, 1986.
Basle, 1974	*Lukas Cranach, Gemälde, Zeichnungen, Druckgraphik*, Kunstmuseum, Basle, 1974.
Basle, 1988	*Hans Holbein d. J., Zeichnungen aus dem Kupferstichkabinett der Öffentlichen Kunstsammlung Basel*, Kunstmuseum, Basle, 1988.
Bologna, 1986	*Nell'età di Correggio e dei Carracci*, Pinacoteca Nazionale and Museo Civico Archeologico, Bologna, 1986.
Bruges, 1969	*Primitifs flamands anonymes*, Groeningemuseum, Bruges, 1969.
Brussels, 1979	*Rogier van der Weyden*, Musée communal, Brussels, 1979.
Brussels, 1987	*Trésors de la Toison d'Or*, Palais des Beaux-Arts, Brussels, 1987.
Dijon, 1988	*La Dame à sa Toilette, Exposition-Dossier N° 1*, Musée des Beaux-Arts, Dijon, 1988.
Florence, 1978–9	*Tiziano nelle Gallerie fiorentine*, Palazzo Pitti, Florence, 1978–9.
Florence, 1980	*Committenza e collezionismo medicei*, Palazzo Vecchio, Florence, 1980.
Florence, 1984	*Raffaello a Firenze, Dipinti e disegni delle collezioni fiorentine*, Palazzo Pitti, Florence, 1984.
Florence, 1986–7	*Andrea del Sarto 1486–1530, Dipinti e disegni a Firenze*, Palazzo Pitti, Florence, 1986–7.
Houston, 1987	*Drawings by Holbein from the Court of Henry VIII*, Museum of Fine Arts, Houston, 1987.
London, 1981	*El Greco to Goya*, National Gallery, London, 1981.
London, 1983	*Artists of the Tudor Court*, Victoria and Albert Museum, London, 1983.
London, 1983–4	*The Genius of Venice 1500–1600*, Royal Academy of Arts, London, 1983–4.
London, 1988–9	*Treasures from the Royal Collection*, The Queen's Gallery, London, 1988–9.
Madrid, Washington, Toledo and Dallas, 1983–4	*El Greco of Toledo*, Museo del Prado, Madrid, National Gallery of Art, Washington, Toledo Museum of Art, Toledo (Ohio) and Dallas Museum of Fine Arts, Dallas, 1982–3.
Madrid, 1986	*Monstruos, enanos y bufones en la corte de los Austrias*, Museo del Prado, Madrid, 1986.
Malibu, 1983–4	*Renaissance Painting in Manuscripts, Treasures from the British Library*, J. Paul Getty Museum, Malibu, 1983–4.
Messina, 1981–2	*Antonello da Messina*, Museo Regionale, Messina, 1981–2.
Munich, 1980	*Wittelsbach und Bayern, Um Glauben und Reich, Kurfürst Maximilian I*, Residenz, Munich, 1980.
New York, 1985	*Liechtenstein: The Princely Collections*, Metropolitan Museum of Art, New York, 1985.
Nuremberg, 1971	*Albrecht Dürer*, Germanisches Nationalmuseum, Nuremberg, 1971.
Nuremberg, 1983	*Martin Luther und die Reformation in Deutschland*, Germanisches Nationalmuseum, Nuremberg, 1983.
Paris, 1973–4	*Chefs-d'oeuvre de la tapisserie*, Grand Palais, Paris, 1973–4.
Paris, 1983–4	*Raphaël dans les collections françaises*, Grand Palais, Paris, 1983–4.
Rotterdam and Bruges, 1965	*Jean Gossaert dit Mabuse*, Museum Boymans-Van Beuningen, Rotterdam and Groeningemuseum, Bruges, 1965.

Stuttgart, 1973	*Hans Burgkmair, Das graphische Werk*, Staatsgalerie, Stuttgart, 1973.
Turin, 1963	*Mostra del barocco piemontese*, Palazzo Madama, Palazzo Reale and Palazzina di Stupinigi, Turin, 1963.
Washington, 1967–8	*Fifteenth Century Engravings of Northern Europe*, National Gallery of Art, Washington, 1967–8.
Washington and New York, 1986–7	*The Age of Bruegel*, National Gallery of Art, Washington and Pierpont Morgan Library, New York, 1986–7.

Index

Photographic Acknowledgements

Photographic material has been supplied by and reproduced courtesy of the owners, unless indicated otherwise below.

By Gracious Permission of Her Majesty The Queen: 19, 52, 110, 115, 128, 139, 173, 178, 183, 189, 224, 225
MAS, Barcelona: 219
Museumsfoto B. P. Keiser, Brunswick: 18, 230
Copyright A.C.L., Brussels: 10, 28, 47, 54, 55, 61, 65, 81, 83, 108, 121, 159, 212, 227, 228, 231, 232, 238
Copyright Bibliothèque Royale Albert Ier, Brussels: 204, 205
Scala, Istituto Fotografico Editoriale, S.p.A.: 30, 37, 49, 51, 165
Soprintendenza per i beni artistici e storici, Florence: 12, 30, 32, 45, 82, 94, 99, 109, 137, 141, 142, 155, 165, 167, 168, 171, 175, 192, 197, 198, 199, 208, 226, 246, 251, 252
Gerhard Reinhold, Leipzig-Mölkau: 145, 146
Trustees of the British Museum, London: 174, 210, 239, 257
Conway Library, Courtauld Institute of Art, London: 34, 36
Trustees of the National Gallery, London: 13, 14, 22, 69, 78, 79, 101, 133, 135, 200, 223
Royal Academy of Arts, London: 72, 179, 182
Courtesy of the Society of Antiquaries, London: 233
Courtesy of the Dean and Chapter of Westminster, London: 34
Patrimonio Nacional, Madrid: 180
National Gallery of Victoria, Melbourne: 11, 91
Soprintendenza per i beni artistici e storici, Milan: 8
Westfälisches Landesmuseum für Kunst und Kulturgeschichte, Münster: 245
Soprintendenza per i beni artistici e storici, Naples: 60, 90, 196
The Frick Collection, New York: 20, 127
Phot. Bibl. Nat., Paris: 176
Giraudon, Paris: 184, 214
Cliché des Musées Nationaux, Paris: 16, 27, 50, 59, 66, 73, 96, 100, 112, 116, 131, 152, 158, 160, 235, 267
Soprintendenza per i beni artistici e storici, Parma e Piacenza: 107, 130, 140, 153
Provincia Autonoma di Trento: 132
Soprintendenza per i beni artistici e storici del Piemonte, Turin: 119, 218
Photo Chomon, Turin: 38
Bild-Archiv der Österreichischen Nationalbibliothek, Vienna: 206